THE GREAT AMERICAN SLOW COOKER BOOK

THE GREAT AMERICAN
SLOW
COOKER
BOOK

500
Easy Recipes for Every Day and Every Size Machine

BRUCE WEINSTEIN and **MARK SCARBROUGH**

PHOTOGRAPHS BY ERIC MEDSKER

Clarkson Potter/Publishers
New York

Library of Congress Cataloging-in-Publication Data
Weinstein, Bruce.
    The great American slow cooker book: 500 easy
recipes for every day and every size machine /
Bruce Weinstein and Mark Scarbrough; photographs
by Eric Medsker.—First edition.
    1. Electric cooking, Slow—United
States.   I. Scarbrough, Mark.   II. Title.
    TX827.W45 2014
    641.5'884—dc23   2013013505

ISBN 978-0-385-34466-1
Ebook ISBN 978-0-385-34467-8

Printed in the United States of America

Book design by Jan Derevjanik
Cover design by Jennifer K. Beal Davis for Ballast Design

10 9 8 7 6 5 4 3 2

First Edition

acknowledgments

A book is a complex ecosystem of talent. Ours thrived because of its sources.

Kudos to Pam Krauss for having the vision—and guts—to let us stake out a big plot in a crowded world. Second books together aren't always better or easier. This one was.

Much thanks, too, to Jessica Freeman-Slade for helping us tend and cull the book with the modern miracle of old-fashioned editing: line by line, methodical but forgiving. It was a pleasure to work alongside a pro.

We couldn't keep laying out new books without our agent of almost twenty years, Susan Ginsburg at Writers House. Agents who build long-term relationships, editors who edit, publishers who dream—have we fallen back in time? We hope so. Thanks, too, to Susan's assistant, Stacy Testa, for making sure that the demands of neurotic writers didn't flood the landscape.

The spade work of recipe-testing was effortless with a storehouse of slow cookers. We couldn't have done it without Cuisinart® and their PR firm, Rachel Litner Associates; KitchenAid®, via Kim Roman at Digitas; and All-Clad® Metalcrafters through Melanie Tennant.

Even after we had a flourishing manuscript, we still didn't have a book. It came into maturity because Mark McCauslin was an exacting copyeditor, Jan Derevjanik was a terrific designer, and Jane Treuhaft was a patient and precise art director.

We found ourselves a simpatico match in Eric Medsker, whose photography and eye made the book bloom. NPR and tattoos. Somehow it works. His assistant, Maddy Talias, was efficient, able, and professional, despite the rampant giddiness on the set.

Finally, we want to thank both our mothers. Neither had a slow cooker when we were growing up, so we were spared splintered chicken breasts glued together with cream of mushroom soup. The book's way better for it.

contents

introduction

If you've got a slow cooker, raise your hand. Yep, we thought so. Almost everyone. Over 80 percent of U.S. households own this appliance. To put that into perspective, more people in America own a slow cooker than own a coffee maker.

And it's not just households. We live in rural New England, near a small general store—the type that serves coffee and pastries all morning, and lunches until mid-afternoon—with loggers, retired bankers, plumbers, and trust-fund ne'er-do-wells sitting higgledy-piggledy around the room at wooden tables. There's always a slow cooker or two on the counter, stocked with some spiky chili or a warm, smooth vegetable soup.

If truth be told, the slow cooker is the best device for preparing a deep, complex stew; a hot-breakfast-is-ready-when-your-alarm-rings miracle; a dinner-is-ready-when-you-get-home wonder; a surprisingly successful cake or steamed pudding; and fare as diverse as a dried-fruit compote (perfect on ice cream or oatmeal) or a hot toddy punch that'll knock your lights out when you need them so knocked.

Even so, why did *we* decide to tackle a slow cooker book? We got tired of recipes that cut us out of the mix. For years, we had a 7-quart model. (Yes, for two people. Yes, we're big eaters. If you invite us over, double your recipe.) We'd look through books and articles to discover that, while some of the recipes were made for the bigger models, most were made for the 4-quart slow cookers—despite the fact that these smaller guys represent just one slice of the bigger pie. We couldn't very well make such puny fare in our ginormous machine. So we slimmed down and bought a 2½-quart model, mostly for oatmeal and hot cereals on cold mornings, but also to keep the servings more in the range of normal. Again, our slow cooker didn't fit most of the recipes out there. A standard braise swamped it. Slow cooker recipe yields didn't seem to be changing, despite the fact that so-called nuclear households were shrinking (just 2.48 members these days), while blended and extended families were steadily growing. That 4-quart, mid-range model is no longer a one-size-fits-all for the American scene.

So we decided to do something about it. We decided to write a book in which almost every recipe can be made by a range of models: small ones that are 2 to 3½ quarts; medium ones that are 4 to 5½ quarts; and large ones that are 6 to 8 quarts. We set aside a year, blew off our waistlines, and crafted a book that can be used by anyone, no matter what model is in the cabinet. And thus, almost anyone who has a slow cooker can use almost *all* of these recipes.

We're not leaving anyone out—or ignoring any situation. Maybe you, too, need a smaller model for those nights when the house has quieted down to just the two of you—and none of your old recipes work. Or maybe you need a gargantuan vat of a slow cooker meal because you've suddenly found yourself in a world of potluck dinners and church socials. We hear your pain. We've got your back.

If you're new to this game of cooking (welcome!), or if you've just received your first slow cooker as a wedding or graduation gift (congratulations!), you'll want to start simple: a classic Minestrone (page 76) or perhaps Garlic-Roasted Chicken Drumsticks (page 260), or Mushroom Sloppy Joes (page 398). If you're an old hand around the kitchen, someone who knows the difference between parsley and chervil, you'll want to head for the Oxtails Braised in Red Wine with Carrots and Prunes (page 166) or even the Pork Mole Rojo with Plantains (page 189). In any event, let's start cooking.

why you should use a slow cooker

It's true: you won't see many slow cookers on the top food shows. But you will see them in many professional kitchens around the country. Chefs love the way the appliance blends the flavors of a soup or sauce, then holds the concoction at a safe temperature for hours.

You need to get in on the game. There's no other appliance that retains as much natural moisture in dishes—not your oven, not your grill, not your smoker. No wonder, then, that slow cookers make the best braises, the creamiest soups, and the finest stews. Think of this appliance as an old-fashioned take on ultra-modern *sous-vide* cooking: hours at a low temperature under a tight lid. Chicken comes out moist and flavorful every time. Carrots stay plump and juicy. Pulled pork is outrageous.

That said, you don't need to try to do what a slow cooker can't. You won't find a roasted beef tenderloin here. Or fried fish. But you will find cakes—yep, a slow cooker holds that moisture so well that it can turn out some of the finest coffee cakes around. And it makes pudding in a flash, no stirring needed. If you really want to go over the top, wait until you try our recipe for Olive Oil–Poached Salmon (page 338). That alone might be a reason for this appliance.

There are no perfect solutions in this world, nor perfect appliances. But there are ways to get around the machine's sticking points. Here's how.

solving some problems

Times have changed since those first slow cookers came off the assembly line in the 1970s. More important, slow cookers have changed. For better meals in this post-disco world, we've got to make some adjustments.

By and large, twenty-first-century slow cookers run hotter. A friend of ours says that she can never get a low-bubble simmer in her new-model slow cooker. She's resurrected her vintage, harvest-gold one from the back cabinet and now spends her life scouring garage sales to find replacement parts. Despite such heroic efforts to stave off progress, she might as well face the facts and modify her expectations.

In reality, temperature's not the pressing concern; food safety is. Nobody should have a vat of chicken soup sitting below 140°F for hours: all sorts of bad bacteria will sprout to life. Since the cooking temperature of modern slow cookers was ratcheted up to address this problem, we need to make a bunch of modifications. Specifically, we need to

1. Up the liquid to compensate for a slightly more intense bubbling.

2. Completely forget about veal chops and other cuts of meat that dry out quickly.

3. Go for cheaper cuts like brisket and pork shoulder (which taste better anyway).

4. Set a more precise time marker on the recipe; the old days of the big swings in recipe timings ("cook on low for 9 to 12 hours") are, like bipartisan compromise, a fond memory.

Modern slow cookers come in multiple sizes. As this appliance began to fan out across the land in the 1980s and '90s, its size both grew *and* shrank to meet everyone's needs. So what happens if you have a 4-quart and the recipe calls for a 6-quart? We solved that problem by offering almost all of our recipes in three sizes: a chart of ingredients that states what you need for a small slow cooker, a medium slow cooker, and a large model.

By the way, it's not just math to convert a recipe to different size yields: some spices have an exponential affect. For example, you can't just double or triple the ground cumin

without annihilating other flavors. Likewise, doubling or tripling the oil can lead to a greasy mess. Two cups of broth may be right for a small cooker; eight cups would swamp a large model.

In modern slow cookers, the flavors meld, but not always in a good way. Frankly, a slow cooker stew can be like melted crayons. You start out with pink, green, blue, and yellow; you end up with brown. That doesn't sound like a rousing endorsement (unless you like brown). But there's no use in not facing facts—flavors can lose their spiky or shallow notes. A few tablespoons of minced oregano leaves will brighten a pot of ragù on the stove; they'll dissolve into an herby haze in a modern slow cooker, little more than the notion of oregano. What's more, bold flavors, whether acidic or sweet (tomatoes or carrots, as well as maple syrup and lemon juice) can TKO the lithe subtleties of thyme or parsley. Cinnamon will knock out black pepper; brown sugar, blueberries. In other words, the ends of the flavor spectrum vanquish the middle. So we put velvet covers over certain flavor sledgehammers, like salt, vinegar, or ground cardamom. And we goose the shy flavors to get them to speak. (We're looking at you, thyme.) In fact, we goose more than we cover. Life's too short for pallid food.

OUR CHARTS HAVE WIGGLE ROOM

If you've got a 6-quart model and you need to feed four, with one serving of leftovers for lunch tomorrow, use the ingredient amounts for the medium slow cooker (4- to 5½-quart) in your model if (and it's an important *if*) you're making a soup, stew, or braise. However, you cannot swap sizes for gooey casseroles, baked goods, or puddings. Of those, you'll just have leftovers for the days ahead.

If there's one thing this book will do, it will help you build a better spice cabinet. You'll need a good range of choices to complete some of these recipes. We may have nixed lots of gourmet ingredients in this book—no Shaoxing, no foie gras—but we didn't stint on the dried herbs and spices. Slow cookers can wear them out; we beefed them up for battle.

TOP SEVEN TIPS FOR SLOW COOKERS

• **Lift the lid as little as possible.** Modern slow cookers restabilize the temperature more quickly than old models, but peeking is still discouraged unless you see a problem.

• **Stir only when the recipe asks you to.** The less action, the better.

• **Don't overfill the cooker.** Half to two-thirds full is best, although some soups can fill it up more without dinging their success.

• **Thaw frozen ingredients.** Use frozen or even partially thawed ingredients only when specifically requested by the recipe.

• **When in doubt, overseason but undersalt.** Slow cookers eat the flavors of herbs but amplify the taste of salt.

• **Treat the cooker gently.** To keep ceramic inserts from cracking because of abrupt temperature changes, place a kitchen towel under an insert before setting it on a cold, granite counter.

• **Clean the cooker thoroughly between uses.** Don't use steel wool. We fill ours with water, set it aside to soak, and then wipe it out before putting the canister in the dishwasher. Read the instructions for your model to see if it's dishwasher-safe.

our commitments to you

When we set out to develop the recipes for this book, we laid down some ground rules—which we came to see as the book's promises.

Only real food. Yes, slow cookers came on the scene in a time of canned this and cream of that. The appliance moved on, adding features and becoming energy efficient. Unfortunately, many recipes didn't. They still call for processed ingredients: dry soup mixes, taco flavorings, and other chemical miasma.

We shun most processed food. Yes, we occasionally call for canned broth, tomatoes, and even some frozen vegetables. But we've left out most convenience products and condiments that would up the fakery of these dishes. We've read the labels and decided on products that are no different in their convenience form than if we'd made them ourselves. So pickle relish and prepared horseradish are in; marinated chicken tenders and fat-free Italian dressing are out. We've gone real—or as real as we can without milling flour and canning tomatoes. There's no "cream of" anything here. But we've kept our rule in check. For example, a bottled Italian dried spice blend is no more than the sum of the dried spices themselves. It's in.

Only ingredients from your local supermarket. These recipes do not require a trip to a high-end grocery supermarket or a specialty grocery store. We don't call for ajwain seeds or goat shoulder. Sure, there are Asian-style braises here, even a massaman curry; but we only call for the Asian condiments found in the typical international aisle of a North American supermarket, like hoisin sauce, rice vinegar, coconut milk, and soy sauce. But that doesn't mean we can't produce a tongue-snapping, Sichuan-style dish.

We live in backwoods New England. The closest grocery store is a long drive down country roads. It's not a high-end store but also not a mom-and-pop joint; it's a large supermarket that caters to a rural population. We geared every recipe to that store. Yes, there may be a few things at our supermarket that aren't at yours. But we doubt it, unless you live in an even more rural spot than we do. (Do you, too, stake flapping plastic bags on tall poles to chase the moose away from your elderberry bushes?)

Modern American dishes. This is a book for a distinctly American appliance, but that doesn't mean we have to stick to hamburger casseroles. These days, we live among many cultures, each with its own tradition. And we can relish each other's food: Chinese braises, Indian curries, Southern stews, Yankee pot roast, Jewish brisket, Polish sausage. Our recipes run the gamut of American cultures, from the new to the old-fashioned. In that way, we can celebrate the new American century.

Only basic kitchen gadgetry. When slow cooker recipes step away from the cream-of-whatever, they can devolve into culinary esoterica. We're always amazed at recipes that require us to build some sort of aluminum-foil pyre inside a slow cooker. Frankly, we don't see the point. Yes, we might be able to lift a chicken out of its juices as it roasts. But if truth be told, we're not really worried about air circulation in a slow cooker. It's not worth the time to raise a bird up when it will not get crisp in the cooker the way it would in an oven. Some of the meat will sit down in those juices as it cooks. But is that a bad thing?

We wanted the slow cooker to be the appliance at hand. Yes, some recipes require a standard blender or an immersion blender. No more than a handful ask for a food processor.

And yes, a few baking recipes do call for one specific piece of equipment: a 1-quart, high-sided, soufflé or baking dish. But those items are available at our local supermarket among the cookware equipment. (Don't worry: in many of these baking recipes, we advocate pouring the batter right into the cooker itself.) Let's embrace convenience without compromising our principles.

your part in all this

Recipes, like a good party, are a group effort. We've all got to chip in.

Follow sensory cues, not timings. Since these recipes have been calibrated for more than one size of slow cooker, we considered giving no timings whatsoever, even for browning or searing or steaming ingredients. After all, if you're cooking a small batch of a stew, you might first need to soften 1 cup of onions on the stove—which might take you under 5 minutes; if you're working on a large batch, those onions might increase to 3 cups—and the task suddenly jumps to 10 minutes or more. But then we took a deep breath and realized we didn't need to rewrite the rules of the cookbook game. So we offer the timings as a range: "Cook until translucent, between 4 and 10 minutes." The real cue here is the visual one—*translucent.*

Experiment the second time, not the first. Will every recipe be to your liking? Of course not. But hold off on manipulating the ingredients until you've made the dish once. You'll have a better understanding of how it stands. We also hope you read and cook the recipes with a pen in hand, marking the book to remind you what you've done.

Read the ingredients carefully. Where possible, we have tried to list the things you'll need as they might appear on a shopping list: *1 tart medium green apple*. However, life doesn't always work out in round numbers and neat quantities, so we've also listed some ingredient amounts that are not whole items—like *3 tablespoons chopped tart green apple*. That's certainly less than even a small apple would yield, and so it has been stated as a *volume* amount, rather than its supermarket amount. In that vein, we've also given some ingredients in *weight*, not volume: for example, *2 pounds peaches, peeled and pitted*. Here, we've assumed you can use the scale at the supermarket to get the correct weight. When a little more or less of something would have no effect on the results, we've felt free to go with the market equivalent: *2 medium carrots, chopped*. But when we're trying to balance flavors carefully and accurately, we've been far more precise, asking you to chop and then measure what you've got: *½ cup chopped carrot*.

Don't confuse fresh and dried herbs. After twenty-one cookbooks (not counting those for celebs), we've come to think of fresh and dried herbs as separate ingredients. Yes, there's a longstanding cookbook tradition that says you can use half the amount of dried for fresh. But you can't. Dried tarragon is more like licorice than its fresh kin, which has grassy and lemony overtones; fresh sage is far more subtle than dried; and dried basil has a tealike taste that bears little resemblance to fresh, peppery basil leaves. We use dried thyme rather than fresh when we want a subtler, more sophisticated finish; we use fresh rosemary rather than dried when we want the more pungent, even savory, perfume of the former.

Brighten leftovers. Because the slow cooker shears off spiky notes from herbs, cools the heat of chiles, and mutes acids like lemon juice, reheating the leftovers can be particularly daunting. Storing a stew overnight

blunts its flavors even more; freezing it, further yet. For a successful day-after meal, you need to perk it back up. Stir in a bit more of the herbs used in the original. Add a little more chili powder, a little more spiky chili sauce. Or take the easiest way out: stir a little lemon juice into the leftovers before you reheat them.

If you've got a nonstick slow cooker, modify your tools. Some slow cookers have that special nonstick coating because the insert can be removed to set it on the stovetop and brown various ingredients. If yours is so made, you'll need to use a nonstick-safe whisk or spatula; otherwise, you can nick the coating. In fact, even ceramic canisters should be given the kid-glove treatment. You can certainly scratch them when you cut a cake into slices while it's still inside. Always err on the side of tools made to work with nonstick surfaces, even if you have a standard cooker.

HIGH-ALTITUDE ISSUES

It's all about the lower temperature at which liquids boil: the liquids will bubble sooner without being as hot. Here are three ways to compensate:

• Increase the cooking time, sometimes by as much as 50 percent, depending on where you live. At very high altitudes, dried beans can take almost double the stated time.

• For soups, stews, and braises, start cooking on high for the first hour, then switch to low heat for the remaining time if the recipe calls for it.

• Always use an instant-read meat thermometer for meat and poultry. Beef, pork, lamb, and veal cuts should be at least 145°F; any ground meat should reach at least 160°F, and any poultry, at least 165°F.

THIS IS A REDUCED-SALT ZONE

We always call for no-salt-added tomatoes and low-sodium broth. And the stated amounts of added salt are low, too. While we do know that excessive salt consumption poses a health risk, we're making a culinary claim. Since there's almost no browning inside a slow cooker, there are fewer complex flavors developed to balance the salt. Its flavor can then ride up over everything—and quickly. Standard cans of broth or tomatoes make stews and braises just too salty.

WATCH THE LOGIC

For all the ingredients, pay close attention to the wording. When you see *1 tablespoon chopped raisins*, you'll need 1 tablespoon *after* chopping. Likewise, *2 tablespoons minced oregano leaves* means you'll need to measure them *after* you've done your prep work with the knife. *Drained canned diced tomatoes* are measured *after* draining, not before. *Packed brown sugar* is measured *after* you've packed it into the measuring cup or spoon.

how to read the recipes

Almost every recipe in this book has a set of specific components. Here's what they mean.

THE OPENING BITS

Effort. We've divided these recipes into three categories, based on their difficulty: *Not much, A little,* and *A lot.* We arrived at these categories by taking into account (1) the work you do (the prepping involved as well as any out-of-the-cooker cooking) and (2) the payoff. Merely browning something at the stove often disqualifies a recipe from the *Not*

MINCING, DICING, AND CHOPPING

Because these recipes are sized for various slow cooker models, they often call for various volumes of standard ingredients—for example, *1¾ cups chopped yellow onion,* rather than *1 large yellow onion, chopped.* Because of that, your part may be a little more exacting when it comes to prepping ingredients. Here's what we mean when we say:

Roughly chopped	1- to 1½-inch pieces
Chopped	¾- to ½-inch, irregular pieces
Cubed	½-inch, fairly uniform cubes
Finely chopped	½- to ¼-inch irregular pieces
Diced	¼-inch, fairly uniform cubes
Minced	⅛-inch bits

much category, but not always; there are a few recipes where browning is so minimal compared to the supper payoff that the effort gets discounted. Making a spice rub for a brisket is not enough to kick the recipe into *A little*; opening a flank steak, stuffing it with vegetables, and rolling it closed is enough to bump the recipe into the *A lot* ranks. So look at the level of effort as a general guide and compare it to the following bit of information, the two in tandem. That is . . .

Prep time. This represents the time you'll spend doing anything *outside* the slow cooker. Prepping includes chopping, mincing, and rubbing, *as well as* browning, marinating, and even hauling stuff out of the pantry. It also includes post-slow-cooker activities: deboning, straining, pureeing, and reducing. (But it does not include clean-up. That's why you have children.)

Cook time. This is the time everything spends *inside* the appliance. Most recipes are exact: *8 hours on low*, for example. A few, however, have ranges: *5 to 6 hours on low*, mostly because of the way some cuts of chewy, tough meat get tender at their own rate. Some recipes offer two timings: *5 hours/8 hours*, for example. In this case, we offer a time frame for cooking on low and also one for cooking on high. Finally, a handful of recipes, particularly in the fish chapter, have a qualification on the timing: *2 hours 20 minutes on high at most*. In these cases, the fish will be done quickly once it's added to the hot sauce—so you'll need to stay in the kitchen and keep checking on the dish for the best dinner possible.

Keeps on warm. Most modern slow cookers have a *keep warm* setting that precludes the necessity of many of the old-fashioned time swings: 6 to 9 hours. If your model doesn't have a *keep warm* setting, you'll need to be a tad more exacting in the overall timing. We do not, for example, believe that dried whole wheat pasta can sit on low for 4 to 7 hours; at 4 hours, it's good to go, and at 7, it's mush. To that end, we've taken into account the various components of a dish—that pasta, as well as vegetables, go boggy and meatballs fall apart—to come up with some notion of how long the dish can sit before you get to it, once the appliance clicks to its *keep warm* setting.

TIMING IS NOT EVERYTHING

Various slow cookers have varying temperature calibrations based on their factory settings, their age, and their repeated use. The *keep warm* on your model may be hotter than that setting on any of ours; your *low* may be lower than ours. If you find the oatmeal crusting around the edges of the canister, or if you find your short ribs are not ever done in the stated time, you'll need to adjust accordingly.

Servings. Because we're working with a range of ingredient quantities, we also give the number of servings in a range: from 4 to 10, for example. We're two guys who can polish off a big bowl of short ribs each and still want a salad. Your appetite might be daintier—or heftier. Use our suggestion for the number of servings as just that: a suggestion.

THE RECIPE CHARTS

These are probably the single most innovative piece of this book—and subject to confusion, as innovations are. Here is an example of a recipe chart:

INGREDIENTS	2- TO 3½-QT	4- TO 5½-QT	6- TO 8-QT
Water	1¼ cups	2½ cups	3¾ cups
Coconut milk (regular or lite)	¾ cup	1½ cups	2¼ cups
Steel-cut oats	½ cup	1 cup	1½ cups
Ripe medium bananas, chopped	½	1	2
Chopped dried pineapple	2½ tblsp	⅓ cup	½ cup
Unsweetened shredded coconut	2½ tblsp	⅓ cup	½ cup
Packed light brown sugar	2½ tblsp	⅓ cup	½ cup
Vanilla extract	¼ tsp	½ tsp	¾ tsp
Salt	¼ tsp	½ tsp	¾ tsp
Grated nutmeg	Pinch	¼ tsp	¼ tsp

The ingredients for a specific recipe are listed vertically on the left. Read all the way down that list to determine what you have on hand and what you need to buy. Then find the size of slow cooker you'll be using along the top row before reading down (or vertically) under that heading to determine the exact amounts.

We should make two notes about these charts.

- Be careful not to cross columns as you work. You can end up with too much or too little broth in a soup, for example.

- If you have a slow cooker that sits right on the column break—that is, it's a 4-quart or a 6-quart model—you can use the amounts for the smaller slow cooker in your model (the 2- to 3½-quart quantities for the 4-quart, the 4- to 5½-quart quantities for the 6-quart), provided you're working with a soup, stew, or braise. (Baking and casseroles are less forgiving.) What you *can't* do in almost all cases is go the other way—that is, put the larger quantities into smaller models.

THE FOLLOW-UPS

- **Testers' Notes.** These bits of information will help you complete the recipe to success. We offer tips on ingredient preparation, tricks of the trade when it comes to working with certain items, and even alternatives that can customize the dish to your taste. Check out these notes *before* you start cooking!

- **Serve It Up!** We offer a range of suggestions for what to do with the finished dish, from garnishes to ideas for salads, soups, and sides that will round out the meal.

- **Shortcuts.** If we know of a quick but still real-food way to spend less time in the kitchen, we give it; for example, frozen mixed vegetables, jarred minced ginger, presliced bell peppers on the supermarket's salad bar, or bottled spice blends.

- **Ingredients Explained.** Here's where we provide a glossary for some of the ingredients: kale, red curry paste, short ribs, and white balsamic vinegar, to name a few. Long-time cooks will find some of this redundant; novices will most likely appreciate its help. These entries are cross-referenced throughout the book, but you needn't look if you know.

- **All-American Know-How.** Here, we condensed our kitchen wisdom: how to cut up a chicken, how to clean leeks, how to store clams. Together, these will help this book become your cooking primer that focuses on America's favorite appliance.

So that's the story—all that's left are the recipes. You might start with Oat, Barley, and Apple Porridge (page 23) for a morning in the very near future. Or if you're more in the mood for a main course, Pork Butt with Whiskey and Sage (page 194). Or Sticky Chicken Thighs with Apricots (page 253). Or Shell-less Clams Casino (page 377). Or shoot, just Mac and Cheese (page 391). Really, we can't pick. You go ahead. Then write and let us know what happened. We're at www.bruceandmark.com. With this many recipes to try, you're about to hear a lot from us. We'd love to hear from you.

THE

GREAT AMERICAN

SLOW
COOKER
BOOK

breakfast

LET'S FACE IT: IF YOU'RE GOING TO SKIP A MEAL, IT'S BREAKFAST.
Before you really get a chance to think about it, you're out the door.

Head back inside. Missing the morning meal is not the best choice.
Your blood sugar levels are out of whack after your sleep-enforced fast.
A few hours later, when they've fallen even further, plunk will go your
energy—and your productivity. University studies the world over have
shown that children who go without breakfast seriously underperform
those who've had something to eat. What's more, we know that adults who
skip breakfast suffer memory deficiencies by mid-morning. Everyone
knows that guy who drags himself into work with an artificially sweetened coffeehouse frappawhatever in hand and can't even remember yes-
terday's bottom-line discussion until he bums an apple off of someone.

Of course, some of the more earnest among us go without breakfast in a misguided attempt to cut calories. But those who do tend to chow

down on 300 to 500 *more* calories a day. If you don't eat breakfast, you're famished by mid-morning, foraging in the break room or running to the convenience store, although lunch is fast approaching.

In truth, the fault lies with our ridiculously accelerated world. Back in the day—sadly, not forty years ago—nine o'clock was a decent time to roll in to work and five P.M. was quitting time. But everything moves more quickly over longer hours. Breakfast gets tossed out the window. Look out below.

Fortunately, there's a way to catch an extra hour of sleep and still eat breakfast: the slow cooker. You can have a hot breakfast without much fuss—and a healthy meal, too, stocked with whole grains, no processed and packaged this or that in the mix. As you'll see, the slow cooker was seemingly made for whole-grain porridges, a comforting breakfast any day of the year. But you needn't stop there. You can also use the slow cooker for egg casseroles and (yes!) decidedly more decadent fare, all without standing over a hot stove. There are also a few fruit compote and applesauce recipes that'll stand you in good stead for many mornings to come (or even for dessert some evening).

A slow cooker is perfect for breakfast. It blends flavors, muting bitter notes in whole grains, fruits, and vegetables, all the while foregrounding the natural sweetness of everything from oatmeal to bacon, apples to polenta. Those mellower tastes are a better fit for the morning.

A slow cooker is also the most convenient breakfast tool: you can set it up the night before and look forward to a hearty meal when the alarm goes off. Or you can set up a tasty brunch casserole and have it ready when your friends arrive.

With a slow cooker on the counter, give breakfast a try. Then begin to morph these recipes into your own signature breakfasts. Try one, then figure out how to adapt it. Don't like maple syrup? Try honey or agave nectar. Don't like chives? How about thyme? Just remember the basic rule: keep the liquid-to-dry ratio intact. (Granulated white and brown sugars are tough—they count on both sides of the ratio, measured as dry ingredients in a batter but acting as liquids as they melt. We recommend leaving their quantities intact; besides, we've tried to keep these recipes fairly low in sugar.) After that, you're free to create a breakfast that'll set you up right. And that's a win/win situation you can set your alarm for.

oatmeals and porridges

If there's a stellar example of how a slow cooker works, it's probably found among these hot cereals. Yes, the slow cooker can be a blunt instrument, smashing the subtle notes of individual flavors. But to soften steel-cut oats into a luxurious meal, morph the bitter accents in quinoa into a sweet porridge, and smooth the crags of cornmeal into a creamy breakfast polenta, these are the reasons you bought the appliance in the first place! Okay, maybe you weren't thinking of breakfast when you got yours. But almost all of these hot cereal recipes are overnight wonders.

Before we jump to these recipes, we should say a word here about whole grains. Within reason, we use them in this section so breakfast can be as nutritious as possible. But looks can be deceiving. Pearled barley is like white rice—a refined grain. Even standard polenta made from ground corn can lack some of the components of whole-grain goodness, although corn itself is the only whole grain we can digest completely, even in its raw form. If you're concerned about these issues, look at our "Testers' Notes" to find ways to add even more whole grains to the mix.

We also began developing these recipes with fat-free milk—and in truth, they were just about as creamy as the ones we later tried with whole or low-fat milk. We don't call for fat-free sour cream in baking or cooking because it can separate over prolonged heat, resulting in a watery mess rather than a satisfying meal. But we like to save fat and calories where we can (mostly so we can butter the toast).

So hop to. Stir everything together the night before and let the slow cooker do its work. Forget watching the pot of hot cereal, praying it doesn't boil over. Skip that irritating volcano of oatmeal in the microwave. Instead, wake up to some of the best (and most nutritious) comfort food around.

overnight oatmeal

EFFORT: **NOT MUCH** • PREP TIME: **10 MINUTES** • COOK TIME: **6 HOURS** • KEEPS ON WARM: **3 HOURS** • SERVES: **4 TO 10**

INGREDIENTS	2- TO 3½-QT	4- TO 5½-QT	6- TO 8-QT
Water	2 cups	4 cups	6 cups
Milk	2 cups	4 cups	6 cups
Steel-cut oats	1 cup	2 cups	3 cups
Maple syrup	¼ cup	½ cup	¾ cup
Salt	Pinch	¼ tsp	½ tsp

Stir all the ingredients in a slow cooker until the maple syrup is distributed evenly throughout. Cover and cook on low for 6 hours, or until the oats are tender and creamy.

TESTERS' NOTES

• If you've skipped steel-cut oats because (1) you didn't want to cook breakfast for an hour when you're barely conscious, or (2) you've tried preboiling them for a couple of minutes the night before and then finishing the next morning, only to end up with gummy glue, you're in for a treat. The slow cooker can turn steel-cut oats into a smooth and creamy breakfast cereal, no stirring or consciousness needed.

• For a treat for later in the week, butter or grease the inside of an 8- or 9-inch baking pan and spread the leftover oatmeal in it; cover and refrigerate overnight or up to 2 days. When you're ready, cut the block into wedges, and fry them in butter in a nonstick skillet set over medium heat under they are golden and brown, 2 to 3 minutes per side. Serve with more maple syrup on the side (of course).

INGREDIENTS EXPLAINED Steel-cut oats (often called "Irish oats" or "pinhead oats") are hulled oat groats sliced into smaller segments, loaded with fiber and all the essential nutrients in the whole grain. The more familiar rolled oats are actually processed, steamed, and flattened oats—in effect, precooked so they don't take so long at the stove. And in the United States, so-called Scottish oats are actually steamed, *ground* oat groats. Use only steel-cut oats in this recipe (as well as many of the ones to follow).

ALL-AMERICAN KNOW-HOW The longer a whole-grain cereal sits, the thicker it becomes. The cereal may also brown a bit at its edges. Some of us like this stiffer part; other late-sleepers may want to scoop the cereal right out of the cooker's center. In any event, if you let most hot cereals and porridges stay on warm for more than a couple of hours, be prepared to thin them out with more milk or water.

Serve It Up! Top bowls of oatmeal with chopped, pitted dates, sliced and cored apples, crumbled graham crackers, apple butter, any preserve or jam you like, dried fruit, sliced bananas, orange zest, or a pat of butter.

oatmeal with banana, pineapple, and coconut

EFFORT: **NOT MUCH** • PREP TIME: **15 MINUTES** • COOK TIME: **7 HOURS** • KEEPS ON WARM: **3 HOURS** • SERVES: **3 TO 8**

INGREDIENTS	2- TO 3½-QT	4- TO 5½-QT	6- TO 8-QT
Water	1¼ cups	2½ cups	3¾ cups
Coconut milk (regular or lite)	¾ cup	1½ cups	2¼ cups
Steel-cut oats (see page 21)	½ cup	1 cup	1½ cups
Ripe medium bananas, chopped	½	1	2
Chopped dried pineapple	2½ tblsp	⅓ cup	½ cup
Unsweetened shredded coconut	2½ tblsp	⅓ cup	½ cup
Packed light brown sugar	2½ tblsp	⅓ cup	½ cup
Vanilla extract	¼ tsp	½ tsp	¾ tsp
Salt	¼ tsp	½ tsp	¾ tsp
Grated nutmeg	Pinch	¼ tsp	¼ tsp

Stir all the ingredients in a slow cooker until the brown sugar has dissolved. Cover and cook on low for 7 hours, or until the oats are tender and the bananas have begun to melt into the sauce.

TESTERS' NOTES
• Make sure the bananas are as ripe as they can be, with plenty of dark spots mottled across their yellow skins, no green bits in sight.
• Use a fork to stir the coconut milk right in the can, thereby reincorporating the solids into the liquid.

• Cut the bananas and pineapple into very small bits, between ¼- and ½-inch pieces. That way, they'll almost melt into the porridge.
• It wouldn't hurt to stir 1 to 3 tablespoons rum into the mix with the other ingredients. Don't want the booze first thing in the morning? Try a drop or two of rum extract.

INGREDIENTS EXPLAINED Coconut milk is a favorite ingredient for vegans who want a creamy, buttery flavor. It's a thick, viscous liquid pressed out of chunks of coconut. So-called lite coconut milk is actually a second (or third or even further) pressing of the original coconut solids to create a less indulgent, less viscous, and (darn it) healthier ingredient.

Unsweetened shredded coconut—sometimes labeled as "desiccated coconut flakes"—is available in larger supermarkets, often not in the baking aisle but in either the international section or the health-food aisle. It's also available in almost all health-food stores. If the flakes are large, about the size of old-fashioned washing soap flakes from 1950s sitcoms, pulverize them in a cleaned spice grinder or a mini food processor until the bits are about the consistency of modern laundry detergent.

sweet potato oatmeal, coffee cake style

EFFORT: **A LITTLE** • PREP TIME: **15 MINUTES** • COOK TIME: **6 HOURS** • KEEPS ON WARM: **3 HOURS** • SERVES: **3 TO 8**

INGREDIENTS	2- TO 3½-QT	4- TO 5½-QT	6- TO 8-QT
Milk	1½ cups	3 cups	4½ cups
Steel-cut oats (see page 21)	½ cup	1 cup	1½ cups

Chopped canned yams in syrup, drained, liquid reserved	½ cup	1 cup	1½ cups
Canning liquid from yams	½ cup	1 cup	1½ cups
Salt	¼ tsp	½ tsp	¾ tsp
Packed light brown sugar	3 tblsp	6 tblsp	½ cup plus 1 tblsp
Chopped pecans	3 tblsp	6 tblsp	½ cup plus 1 tblsp
Ground cinnamon	½ tsp	1 tsp	1¼ tsp

1 Stir the milk, oats, sweet potato bits, syrup from the can, and salt in the slow cooker. Cover and cook on low for 6 hours, or until the oats are tender.

2 Combine the brown sugar, pecan pieces, and cinnamon in a bowl. Sprinkle on the oatmeal just before serving, either while it's still in the slow cooker or over individual bowlfuls.

TESTERS' NOTES
• This recipe mimics a very sweet Southern coffee cake by using canned yams (or sweet potatoes) and then adding a crunchy topping to the oatmeal the next morning.
• If the can of sweet potatoes doesn't have enough liquid to make the full amount needed, make up the difference with equal parts water and maple syrup.
• If you're prone to morning grogginess, mix the topping ingredients the night before; cover and set aside at room temperature.
• Consider adding a little minced peeled fresh ginger—no more than 2 teaspoons for the big batch. Or skip the ginger and try a pinch (or two) of grated nutmeg.
• For richer fare, stir 1 to 3 tablespoons melted unsalted butter into the topping ingredients. Believe it or not, the butter will actually cut the sweetness a bit.

INGREDIENTS EXPLAINED Canned yams in syrup (that is, canned sweet potatoes in a sweetened, thickened liquid) are a Southern tradition, often served at the holidays. They can be hard to track down in some parts of the country, or even at other times of the year, so stock up when you see them.

oat, barley, and apple porridge

EFFORT: **NOT MUCH** • PREP TIME: **10 MINUTES** • COOK TIME: **8 HOURS** • KEEPS ON WARM: **3 HOURS** • SERVES: **4 TO 12**

INGREDIENTS	2- TO 3½-QT	4- TO 5½-QT	6- TO 8-QT
Water	3 cups	6 cups	9 cups
Steel-cut oats (see page 21)	¾ cup	1½ cups	2¼ cups
Pearled barley	½ cup	1 cup	1½ cups
Sliced almonds	6 tblsp	¾ cup	1 cup plus 2 tblsp
Maple syrup	2 tblsp	¼ cup	6 tblsp
Large apples, preferably Gala, Fuji, or Jonagold, cored and chopped	1	2	3
Salt	¼ tsp	½ tsp	¾ tsp

Stir all the ingredients in a slow cooker until thoroughly mixed. Cover and cook on low for 8 hours, or until the oats and barley are tender and luscious.

TESTERS' NOTES
• Oats and barley are a great combo: creamy and chewy, smooth and toothsome, all at once in every bite.
• For more flavor, toast the sliced almonds until golden brown in a nonstick skillet set over medium heat, stirring often, 4 to 5 minutes.

(continued)

• Although tart apples are the standard in many recipes with other sweeteners in the mix, we feel this works best with a medium-sweet apple that will break down a bit and become part of the creamy "sauce" around the grains.

Serve It Up! For an over-the-top treat, warm some heavy or light cream in a small saucepan until bubbles fizz around the pan's interior. Ladle the warmed cream over the cereal in the bowls.

INGREDIENTS EXPLAINED Pearled barley (sometimes labeled *perlato barley*) is a refined grain. The hull and bran have been scored or even removed so the barley cooks quickly. Do not substitute quick-cooking barley, which is processed like instant oatmeal.

Stir all the ingredients in a slow cooker, then cover and cook on low for 7 hours, or until the rice is tender.

TESTERS' NOTES
• This sweet, autumnal breakfast porridge is well stocked and very aromatic. It would pair well with a cup of black tea instead of coffee.
• A white sweet potato would be the best, although a yellow or orange variety will do just as well. Cut the sweet potato into ½-inch cubes.

INGREDIENTS EXPLAINED Short-grain rice is sometimes called "sweet rice" or "sushi rice" in North America. It's often available in the Asian aisle of larger supermarkets packed by brands such as Kalrose. It's a sticky rice, short not necessarily in length but "short" of a certain dry starch that keeps long-grain rice fluffier.

sweet rice porridge

EFFORT: **NOT MUCH** • PREP TIME: **20 MINUTES** • COOK TIME: **7 HOURS** • KEEPS ON WARM: **4 HOURS** • SERVES: **3 TO 10**

INGREDIENTS	2- TO 3½-QT	4- TO 5½-QT	6- TO 8-QT
Water	2 cups	4 cups	6 cups
Peeled and diced sweet potato	1 cup	2 cups	3 cups
Short-grain rice (sweet rice or sushi rice)	½ cup	1 cup	1½ cups
Jarred roasted chestnuts	½ cup	1 cup	1½ cups
Packed light brown sugar	¼ cup	½ cup	¾ cup
Mirin (see page 250)	1 tblsp	2 tblsp	3 tblsp
Minced peeled fresh ginger	½ tsp	1 tsp	1½ tsp

sweet squash porridge

EFFORT: **NOT MUCH** • PREP TIME: **15 MINUTES** • COOK TIME: **8 HOURS** • KEEPS ON WARM: **4 HOURS** • SERVES: **4 TO 10**

INGREDIENTS	2- TO 3½-QT	4- TO 5½-QT	6- TO 8-QT
Water	3 cups	4 cups	6 cups
Peeled, seeded, and cubed pumpkin or kabocha squash	3 cups	4 cups	6 cups
Short-grain rice (sweet rice or sushi rice)	3 tblsp	⅓ cup	½ cup
Packed light brown sugar	2½ tblsp	¼ cup	6 tblsp
Minced peeled fresh ginger	1½ tsp	2 tsp	1 tblsp
Salt	Pinch	¼ tsp	¼ tsp

1 Combine all the ingredients in a slow cooker, stirring until the brown sugar has dissolved into the mix. Cover and cook on low for 8 hours, or until the pumpkin and rice are tender.

2 Use a potato masher or the back of a wooden spoon to mash the vegetable and rice into a creamy, thick, hot cereal.

TESTERS' NOTES
• Although excellent at breakfast, this porridge can also be served at dinner, particularly as the first course of a more formal dinner party. Or consider it a side dish at a holiday meal—perhaps a little bit of pumpkin sweetness before the turkey at Thanksgiving.

Serve It Up! For crunch in the bowls, sprinkle plain granola on top.

baked pear porridge

EFFORT: **NOT MUCH** • PREP TIME: **10 MINUTES** • COOK TIME: **7 HOURS** • KEEPS ON WARM: **1 HOUR** • SERVES: **3 TO 10**

INGREDIENTS	2- TO 3½-QT	4- TO 5½-QT	6- TO 8-QT
Ripe medium pears, peeled, cored, and chopped	2	3	5
Water	1¾ cups	2½ cups	5 cups
Milk	1½ cups	2 cups	4 cups
Medium-ground bulgur (or #2; see page 26)	¾ cup	1 cup	2 cups
Finely chopped walnuts	½ cup	⅔ cup	1⅓ cups
Packed dark brown sugar	3 tblsp	⅓ cup	⅔ cup
Ground cinnamon	½ tsp	½ tsp	1 tsp
Salt	¼ tsp	¼ tsp	½ tsp

Stir all the ingredients in a slow cooker. Cover and cook on low for 7 hours, or until the liquid has been absorbed and the porridge is thick.

TESTERS' NOTES
• Despite the brown sugar and the pears, it's amazing how savory bulgur keeps this breakfast cereal from tasting too sweet.
• Mince the walnut pieces into small bits so there are no chunks in the spoonfuls. Rock a large knife through the walnuts on a cutting board, gathering them together after they spread out and going at it several more times.
• Although milk adds a lovely sweetness, you can substitute almond milk, prized for its delicate flavor.
• Soft, mushy pears will dissolve into the porridge and lose much of their oomph. Choose firm but very sweet-smelling pears. That said, the pear's fragrance is key. Better a sweet-smelling, soft pear than a firm pear with no fragrance whatsoever.

ALL-AMERICAN KNOW-HOW
Use a melon baller to core a pear before you peel it. Start at the blossom end—opposite the stem—and slowly turn the melon baller into the pear, scooping out tiny bits at a time, moving slowly up into the fruit, and eventually taking out the seeds and their fibrous membranes inside. Then peel the pear and chop it into ½-inch bits.

peanut butter and banana porridge

EFFORT: **NOT MUCH** • PREP TIME: **15 MINUTES** • COOK TIME: **7 HOURS** • KEEPS ON WARM: **1 HOUR** • SERVES: **4 TO 12**

INGREDIENTS	2- TO 3½-QT	4- TO 5½-QT	6- TO 8-QT
Milk	2 cups	4 cups	6 cups
Water	1½ cups	3 cups	4½ cups
Honey	6 tblsp	¾ cup	1 cup
Creamy natural-style peanut butter	6 tblsp	¾ cup	1 cup
Ground cinnamon	½ tsp	1 tsp	1¼ tsp
Salt	¼ tsp	½ tsp	¾ tsp
Medium-ground bulgur (such as #2)	¾ cup	1½ cups	2¼ cups
Ripe medium banana, peeled and chopped	½	1	2

Whisk the milk, water, honey, peanut butter, cinnamon, and salt in the slow cooker until the mixture is creamy and smooth. Stir in the bulgur and banana bits. Cover and cook on low for 7 hours.

TESTERS' NOTES

• We prefer this classic-sandwich-made-into-a-breakfast-cereal with creamy "natural-style" peanut butter, rather than the traditional peanut butter with its added fat and sugar. However, the porridge can be made with either—and is richer with the latter.

• This cereal will get stiff as it sits; it may also singe at the sides of the cooker. If you sleep late and the cereal keeps warm for 2 hours, thin it out by stirring some milk into it; cover and cook on low for 20 minutes to warm the milk through.

INGREDIENTS EXPLAINED Most often made from durum wheat, bulgur is common in Middle Eastern dishes like tabbouleh, a parsley salad. Although sometimes confused with cracked wheat, bulgur is actually parboiled crushed grains. We prefer the whole-grain variety for its nuttiness. In any case, bulgur is available in four grinds in North America: fine, medium, coarse, and extra-coarse. For the best consistency, use a medium-ground bulgur here, sometimes labeled #2. The recipes in this book will always indicate the grind of the bulgur to be used.

savory rice porridge

EFFORT: **NOT MUCH** • PREP TIME: **10 MINUTES** • COOK TIME: **10 HOURS** • KEEPS ON WARM: **4 HOURS** • SERVES: **4 TO 12**

INGREDIENTS	2- TO 3½-QT	4- TO 5½-QT	6- TO 8-QT
Water	4 cups	8 cups	12 cups
Long-grain white rice	½ cup	1 cup	1½ cups
Soy sauce	1 tblsp	2 tblsp	3 tblsp
Minced peeled fresh ginger	2 tsp	4 tsp	5 tsp

Stir all the ingredients in a slow cooker, then cover and cook on low for 10 hours, or until the rice has partially dissolved into a thin gruel.

TESTERS' NOTES

• By swamping long-grain white rice with plenty of water and cooking the mixture for a very long time with low heat, you'll create a rich and starchy, if thin, rice porridge.

• This cereal is sometimes called "congee," eaten by Chinese immigrants on their way to work in North America. The recipe replicates a Cantonese version, fashioned here for the slow cooker.

Serve It Up! Although this rice porridge is a simple thing of beauty, it's also an excuse for the garnishes. For a traditional Chinese version, offer sliced scallions or chives as well as chopped, salted peanuts to sprinkle on the bowls. Beyond those, you might consider some cooked and chopped shrimp; cooked, skinned, boned, and chopped chicken meat (particularly if you snagged a rotisserie chicken for dinner the night before); or even some finely diced smoked tofu. If you want to spend a little time at the stove, fry slivered garlic in a little peanut oil in a medium skillet until crisp and brown.

quinoa vanilla bean porridge

EFFORT: **NOT MUCH** • PREP TIME: **5 MINUTES** • COOK TIME: **7 HOURS** • KEEPS ON WARM: **2 HOURS** • SERVES: **3 TO 8**

INGREDIENTS	2- TO 3½-QT	4- TO 5½-QT	6- TO 8-QT
Milk	3⅓ cups	5 cups	6¾ cups
Quinoa (white or red)	1 cup	1½ cups	2 cups
Sugar	⅓ cup	½ cup	⅔ cup
Instant tapioca	1½ tblsp	2 tblsp plus 1 tsp	3 tblsp
Vanilla bean, split lengthwise, the seeds scraped into the cooker and the pod added	½	½	1
Salt	¼ tsp	¼ tsp	½ tsp

Stir all the ingredients in a slow cooker until the sugar has dissolved. Cover and cook on low for 7 hours, or until the mixture is rich and thick. Discard the vanilla pod before serving.

TESTERS' NOTES
• Although cooked quinoa is sometimes dry, it becomes a moist cereal in a slow cooker. Its slightly bitter notes are offset in this recipe by a little sugar and lots of vanilla.
• Tapioca gives the porridge its body, since quinoa will not thicken it the way oats would. Use only instant tapioca, often available in the baking aisle and commonly used as a thickener in pie fillings. Don't substitute larger tapioca pearls.
• Feel free to add some chopped dried fruit to this porridge: golden raisins, stemmed dried figs, dried nectarines, or the like. However, keep the additions small, no more than ½ cup for a large slow cooker. You don't want that added fruit to mute the flavor of the quinoa.

INGREDIENTS EXPLAINED Quinoa is naturally coated in a bitter, defensive compound (saponin) to keep animals from eating it. Most quinoa sold today is washed to remove the rank taste, but check your package to make sure. If its directions say you should rinse the quinoa, do so in a fine-mesh sieve or a colander lined with paper towels (otherwise the grains will fall through the larger holes of a standard colander). Shake dry over the sink; then as a precaution, give the grains a second rinse under cool water.

ALL-AMERICAN KNOW-HOW To split open a vanilla bean, lay it on your cutting board and draw a paring knife down its length, opening it up. Use the blunt back of the knife tip to scrape the inside of the bean, scooping out the sticky mass of tiny seeds in each half. Add the pods to your mix for more flavor.

buckwheat porridge with figs and dates

EFFORT: **NOT MUCH** • PREP TIME: **10 MINUTES** • COOK TIME: **7 HOURS** • KEEPS ON WARM: **3 HOURS** • SERVES: **3 TO 8**

INGREDIENTS	2- TO 3½-QT	4- TO 5½-QT	6- TO 8-QT
Water	1⅓ cups	2 cups	3½ cups
Milk	1⅓ cups	2 cups	3½ cups
Buckwheat groats	⅔ cup	1 cup	1¾ cups
Diced pitted dates	3 tblsp	¼ cup	⅓ cup
Dried figs, stemmed and diced	1	2	4
Honey	2 tblsp	3 tblsp	¼ cup
Ground cinnamon	¼ tsp	½ tsp	½ tsp
Salt	Pinch	¼ tsp	¼ tsp

Stir all the ingredients in a slow cooker until the honey has dissolved. Cover and cook on low for 7 hours, or until the groats are tender, if still sticky.

TESTERS' NOTES
• Buckwheat groats are a tasty, rich source of fiber, always a great way to start the day. Look for the groats in the natural- or organic-food section of your supermarket.
• Buckwheat groats will get quite sticky over time; the longer this porridge sits, the pastier it becomes. It'll keep well for several hours; but serve it as soon as it's ready if you prefer a chewier, less gummy texture.
• Cut the dried fruit into tiny bits so that they're evenly distributed throughout the porridge.

INGREDIENTS EXPLAINED
All dates are not created equal! Try soft and luscious Medjool dates here, cut into tiny bits that almost melt into the cereal. Keep in mind the rule for dates, figs, and all dried fruit: they should be juicy and plump.

ALL-AMERICAN KNOW-HOW
Dicing dried fruit can be a difficult job; your knife has to be continuously washed to get rid of the sugary stickiness. To counter (but not stop) the problem, spray your knife with nonstick spray before you begin chopping.

---

trail mix porridge

EFFORT: **NOT MUCH** • PREP TIME: **15 MINUTES** • COOK TIME: **6 HOURS** • KEEPS ON WARM: **1 HOUR** • SERVES: **6 TO 12**

INGREDIENTS	2- TO 3½-QT	4- TO 5½-QT	6- TO 8-QT
Water	4 cups	6 cups	8 cups
Chopped fresh cranberries	1 cup	1½ cups	2 cups
Pearled barley (see page 24)	½ cup	¾ cup	1 cup
Packed light brown sugar	½ cup	¾ cup	1 cup
Walnut pieces, toasted and coarsely ground	⅓ cup	½ cup	⅔ cup
Medium-ground bulgur (or #2; see page 26)	¼ cup	6 tblsp	½ cup
Corn (or hominy) grits	¼ cup	6 tblsp	½ cup
Millet	¼ cup	6 tblsp	½ cup
Maple syrup	¼ cup	6 tblsp	½ cup
Ground cinnamon	½ tsp	½ tsp	1 tsp
Salt	¼ tsp	¼ tsp	½ tsp

Stir all the ingredients in a slow cooker until the maple syrup has dissolved and all the grains are moistened. Cover and cook on low for 6 hours, or until the porridge is creamy and the grains are tender.

TESTERS' NOTES
• For more whole-grain goodness, use whole-grain corn grits, a specialty item not always available in supermarkets but certainly offered by online suppliers. They'll give a much more intense, sweet, even earthy corn taste to the cereal.
• Fresh cranberries are not necessarily available year-round. When you see them in the supermarket around the holidays, buy a few extra bags and toss them into the freezer. There's no need to thaw the cranberries before using them in a cooking or baking recipe.

ALL-AMERICAN KNOW-HOW Grind walnuts in a food processor fitted with the chopping blade, pulsing repeatedly until the consistency is a little coarser than sand, but with no chunks in the mix. For more flavor, first toast the walnuts in a dry skillet over medium heat for about 4 minutes, then cool for 30 minutes before grinding. Save any leftover nuts in a zip-sealed plastic bag in the freezer to add to cookie and bread batters, or to coatings for pan-fried or oven-fried fish or chicken.

INGREDIENTS EXPLAINED Millet is the smallest grain available in the modern supermarket—tiny little yellow specks that can turn into a pain in the neck if you spill the bag. Unless otherwise specified, use whole millet, not finely ground millet grits. Because millet goes rancid quickly at room temperature, store it in a well-sealed bag in the freezer for up to 5 months. But always smell it first. It should smell grassy and sweet, not bitter or acrid.

pecan pie porridge

EFFORT: **NOT MUCH** • PREP TIME: **10 MINUTES** • COOK TIME: **8 HOURS** • KEEPS ON WARM: **2 HOURS** • SERVES: **3 TO 8**

INGREDIENTS	2- TO 3½-QT	4- TO 5½-QT	6- TO 8-QT
Milk	3 cups	4½ cups	6 cups
Wheatberries	⅔ cup	1 cup	1⅓ cups
Maple syrup	⅓ cup	½ cup	⅔ cup
Finely chopped pecans	⅓ cup	½ cup	⅔ cup
Farina, such as Cream of Wheat	3 tblsp	¼ cup	6 tblsp
Ground cinnamon	¼ tsp	½ tsp	¾ tsp
Salt	¼ tsp	¼ tsp	½ tsp

Stir all the ingredients in a slow cooker until the maple syrup is evenly distributed throughout. Cover and cook the mixture on low for 8 hours, or until the wheatberries are tender and the mixture has turned into a porridge.

TESTERS' NOTES
• There's not one kind of wheatberry but several, based on the wheat variety. For the creamiest texture befitting a breakfast porridge, look for soft spring white wheatberries. By contrast, hard red winter wheatberries will offer more far more chew.
• You can save any leftovers in a covered container in the fridge. Stir in plenty of milk the next morning to loosen up the cereal, then heat it slowly in a saucepan over medium-low heat, stirring frequently to prevent scorching.

(continued)

INGREDIENTS EXPLAINED Wheatberries are minimally processed grains of wheat, just minus their hulls and dried for storage. They're a nutritious whole grain, usually available near the quinoa and brown rice in your supermarket, or sometimes in the health-food aisle.

ALL-AMERICAN KNOW-HOW Ground cinnamon has a shelf life: about nine months if stored in a dark, cool place. After that, it loses much of its zip. Smell yours to make sure it's fresh and irresistible. Double its shelf life by storing it in the freezer, although the ambient humidity means you can never "thaw" it without its clumping. You'll have to forgo sprinkling it on cinnamon toast, but you can scoop it out frozen for most recipes.

creamy brown rice porridge

EFFORT: **A LITTLE** • PREP TIME: **15 MINUTES** • COOK TIME: **10 HOURS** • KEEPS ON WARM: **NO** • SERVES: **3 TO 8**

INGREDIENTS	2- TO 3½-QT	4- TO 5½-QT	6- TO 8-QT
Milk	2½ cups	5 cups	7½ cups
Long-grain brown rice (such as brown basmati or brown Texmati)	½ cup	1 cup	1½ cups
Chopped golden raisins	¼ cup	½ cup	¾ cup
Sugar	2½ tbls	⅓ cup	½ cup
Vanilla extract	½ tsp	1 tsp	1½ tsp
Salt	Pinch	¼ tsp	¼ tsp
Large egg yolks	2	3	4

1 Combine the milk, rice, raisins, sugar, vanilla, and salt in a slow cooker, stirring until the sugar has dissolved. Cover and cook on low for 10 hours, or until the rice is tender.

2 Whisk the egg yolks in a large bowl until creamy, then whisk 1 to 2 cups of the rice porridge into the egg yolks, beating fairly furiously to keep the egg yolks from curdling.

3 When the mixture is mostly smooth, whisk it back into the rest of the porridge in the slow cooker. Serve at once.

TESTERS' NOTES
• This is like a thicker, richer version of rice porridge, here made with brown rice (so it's a whole-grain breakfast). There are also eggs in the mix; they'll make the dish even heartier, sort of a creamy rice pudding.
• Use only long-grain brown rice here. Short- or medium-grain brown rice will clump.
• The eggs will have been warmed to a safe temperature by the time the whisked mixture is incorporated back into the slow cooker. If you're concerned, cover the cooker and cook for 5 minutes—but no more, as the egg yolks may "scramble" in the porridge.
• The golden raisins are really for aesthetics—to better complement the color of the brown rice. If you've got only black on hand, substitute at will!

southwestern hominy stew

EFFORT: **NOT MUCH** • PREP TIME: **15 MINUTES** • COOK TIME:
7 HOURS • KEEPS ON WARM: **2 HOURS** • SERVES: **4 TO 12**

INGREDIENTS	2- TO 3½-QT	4- TO 5½-QT	6- TO 8-QT
Canned reduced-sodium diced tomatoes, with juice	1¾ cups	3½ cups	5¼ cups
Canned hominy, drained and rinsed	1¾ cups	3½ cups	5¼ cups
Thinly sliced celery	¾ cup	1½ cups	2 cups
Chopped red onion	¾ cup	1½ cups	1¾ cups
Reduced-sodium fat-free chicken broth	⅓ cup	⅔ cup	1 cup
Canned chopped green chiles (hot, medium, or mild)	¼ cup	½ cup	¾ cup
Dried oregano	1 tsp	2 tsp	1 tblsp
Ground cumin	¾ tsp	1½ tsp	2 tsp
Ground black pepper	¼ tsp	½ tsp	¾ tsp
Ground cloves	Pinch	¼ tsp	¼ tsp
Turkey sausage meat, any casings removed	½ pound	1 pound	1½ pounds

1 Stir the tomatoes, hominy, celery, onion, broth, chiles, oregano, cumin, pepper, and cloves in the slow cooker. Crumble the sausage into quarter-size chunks over the stew; gently stir it in without breaking it up.

2 Cover and cook on low for 7 hours, or until the vegetables have softened and the flavors have blended.

TESTERS' NOTES
• Breakfast stews like this one are popular in small eateries across the American Southwest. It's a big taste in the morning, laced with chile and onion.
• A 14-ounce can of diced tomatoes with juice or of drained hominy yields about 1¾ cups; a 28-ounce can of either yields about 3½ cups.

Serve It Up! Offer warmed corn or flour tortillas on the side—and perhaps a poached or fried egg to "float" in the bowl.

INGREDIENTS EXPLAINED: Hominy is made from dried field corn that has been soaked in an alkali solution to loosen the hulls and tenderize the kernels. Even the oil and protein structure of the grain is changed. Hominy has been a staple of North American diets for centuries, a chewy, sweet way to relish the corn harvest all year long. It should definitely be a breakfast staple in your home.

cheddar and apple grits

EFFORT: **NOT MUCH** • PREP TIME: **10 MINUTES** • COOK TIME: **6 HOURS** • KEEPS ON WARM: **2 HOURS** • SERVES: **3 TO 8**

INGREDIENTS	2- TO 3½-QT	4- TO 5½-QT	6- TO 8-QT
Water	2 cups	4 cups	6 cups
Whole-grain corn grits	½ cup	1 cup	1½ cups
Chopped, peeled, and cored tart apple	½ cup	1 cup	1½ cups
Minced scallions (white and pale green parts only)	2 tblsp	¼ cup	6 tblsp
Cajun spice blend	½ tsp	1 tsp	1½ tsp
Red pepper flakes	¼ tsp	½ tsp	¾ tsp
Shredded Cheddar cheese	½ cup	1 cup	1½ cups

Stir all the ingredients in a slow cooker. Cover and cook on low for 6 hours, or until the grits are smooth and creamy.

TESTERS' NOTES
• Skip the instant grits and instead use whole-grain, yellow grits, made from dried field corn and available at larger supermarkets and most health-food stores.
• Although we've campaigned for sweeter, softer apples in some porridges, these grits benefit from tart, firm apples like Granny Smith or Empire.
• Look for Cajun spice blends that aren't simply doctored cayenne, but instead include a wide range of herbs and spices.
• Because the Cheddar has plenty of sodium, and also because Cajun spice blends often include salt in the mix, there's none added in this recipe.

Serve It Up! Most Southerners wouldn't consider this a breakfast on its own. It needs a fried egg (or two) to round out the meal.

polenta with apricot nectar and almonds

EFFORT: **NOT MUCH** • PREP TIME: **15 MINUTES** • COOK TIME: **8 HOURS** • KEEPS ON WARM: **2 HOURS** • SERVES: **4 TO 12**

INGREDIENTS	2- TO 3½-QT	4- TO 5½-QT	6- TO 8-QT
Water	3 cups	6 cups	9 cups
Pitted and sliced fresh apricots	2 cups	4 cups	6 cups
Polenta (see page 33)	¾ cup	1½ cups	2¼ cups
Apricot nectar	6 tblsp	¾ cup	1 cup plus 2 tblsp
Ground almonds	6 tblsp	¾ cup	1 cup plus 2 tblsp
Packed light brown sugar	6 tblsp	¾ cup	1 cup plus 2 tblsp
Salt	¼ tsp	½ tsp	½ tsp

Combine all the ingredients in a slow cooker, stirring until the polenta is thoroughly moistened. Cover and cook on low for 8 hours, until the polenta is thick and creamy.

TESTERS' NOTES
• Breakfast polentas have a delicate creamy texture, less hearty than the more familiar side dish.
• Although this is a sweet dish, you can add an elegant touch by stirring in 1 to 2 teaspoons stemmed fresh thyme leaves before cooking.

polenta with smoked ham and dried cherries

EFFORT: **NOT MUCH** • PREP TIME: **15 MINUTES** • COOK TIME: **7 TO 8 HOURS** • KEEPS ON WARM: **2 HOURS** • SERVES: **4 TO 8**

INGREDIENTS	2- TO 3½-QT	4- TO 5½-QT	6- TO 8-QT
Water	4 cups	6 cups	8 cups
Smoked ham, chopped	½ pound	¾ pound	1 pound
Polenta	1 cup	1½ cups	2 cups
Chopped dried cherries, minced	½ cup	¾ cup	1 cup
Thinly sliced scallions (white and pale green parts only)	¼ cup	6 tblsp	½ cup
Fresh thyme leaves, stripped from stems	1½ tsp	2 tsp	1 tblsp
Ground black pepper	½ tsp	¾ tsp	1 tsp
Grated Monterey Jack cheese	¾ cup	1 cup plus 2 tblsp	1½ cups

1 Mix the water, ham, polenta, cherries, scallions, thyme, and pepper in the slow cooker until the polenta is moistened. Cover and cook on low for 7 hours in a small cooker, 7½ hours in a medium cooker, or 8 hours in a large cooker, until the liquid has been absorbed and the cereal is almost velvety.

2 Stir in the cheese just before serving.

TESTERS' NOTES
• Chop the ham, cherries, and scallions so they are all about the same size; that way, they'll "balance" each other in every spoonful. Yes, you should further cut up the chopped dried cherries; otherwise, they end up as bloated bombs of searingly hot juice.
• Because there's so much sodium in the ham and cheese, we've not included any additional salt in this recipe.
• For more zip in your cheese topping, use pepper jack or even jalapeño jack.

INGREDIENTS EXPLAINED Although so-called instant polenta is a boon for quick cooks, it doesn't work too well in the slow cooker: the texture is compromised after long cooking. For this dish and all others that use polenta, search out the standard Italian variety, a slightly coarser grind of cornmeal that normally requires hours of stirring over a hot stove. Don't substitute regular cornmeal. Or look for whole-grain polenta from online suppliers like Anson Mills. Slightly coarser grinds of whole-grain polenta, often labeled "corn polenta or grits," work best.

pancakes, breakfast puddings, and coffee cakes

Now we come to the decadent breakfasts—most of them sweet, all of them potential family favorites, and every one a great use of the slow cooker. Yes, you can even "bake" in a slow cooker, although as you can tell from the quotes around the word, there are some caveats.

For one thing, nothing will brown. In baking, browning occurs because of (1) the caramelization of sugars; and (2) the breakdown of proteins found naturally in milk, butter, and even some flours. Both effects require dehydration, and the slow cooker is famous for keeping every drop of moisture under the lid; so you'll have to make some adjustments to keep up the browning, as we'll discuss. You just have to face facts and work around them—you know, as you do in the rest of life.

Although the lack of evaporation can be a problem, it can also be a bonus. Coffee cakes and breakfast puddings come out incredibly moist. Yes, we also need to balance the flavors carefully; subtle tastes get lost over a long cooking time. But once these problems are solved, you can use the slow cooker to make some pretty fine morning fare.

That said, no recipe in this section is an overnighter; most take just a few hours. You can't set up the cooker before bed—unless you've pulled an all-nighter and think you can power-nap your way into coherence while the coffee cake cooks. For the rest of us, we'll have to plan on a later breakfast, which isn't all that bad given that these recipes are perfect for weekend mornings. Head to the kitchen, toss together some simple ingredients, then go to your workout or the shower. By the time you're back, the feast will be in sight. Or better yet, make a coffee cake the night before, have the first piece for dessert, then save the rest in the fridge for breakfast the next morning (and maybe for a snack that afternoon, too). A coffee cake's not just for breakfast. Or what's a heaven for?

dutch apple pancake

EFFORT: **A LITTLE** • PREP TIME: **20 MINUTES** • COOK TIME: **2½ TO 3 HOURS** • KEEPS ON WARM: **NO** • SERVES: **4 TO 8**

INGREDIENTS	2- TO 3½-QT	4- TO 5½-QT	6- TO 8-QT
Unsalted butter, plus additional for buttering the inside of the slow cooker	4 tblsp (½ stick)	6 tblsp (¾ stick)	8 tblsp (1 stick)
Packed dark brown sugar	½ cup	¾ cup plus 1 tblsp	1 cup plus 2 tblsp
Apples, preferably Braeburn, Empire, Granny Smith, or Pippin, cored, peeled, and thinly sliced	3 medium	4 large	6 large
Ground cinnamon	1 tsp	1½ tsp	2 tsp
Milk	1 cup	1¾ cups	2½ cups
Large eggs	4	7	10
All-purpose flour	¾ cup	1 cup plus 2 tblsp	2 cups
Granulated sugar	⅓ cup	½ cup plus 1 tblsp	1 cup
Vanilla extract	1 tsp	1½ tsp	2½ tsp
Salt	¼ tsp	¼ tsp	½ tsp

1 Generously butter the inside of the slow cooker.

2 Melt the butter in a large skillet set over medium heat. Add the brown sugar; stir until bubbling, about 1 minute. Add the apples and cinnamon. Cook until the apples have softened a bit, stirring frequently, about 3 minutes. Pour and scrape the apples into the cooker.

3 In a large bowl, whisk the milk, eggs, flour, granulated sugar, vanilla, and salt together until there are no lumps or pockets of dry flour in the mix. Pour over the apples.

4 Cover and cook on low for 2½ hours to 3 hours, or until the cake has puffed and set, until it feels somewhat firm to the touch, and until a flatware knife inserted into the center comes out without any eggy liquid on it. (There may be some buttery, syrupy liquid on top of the cake, but the interior should be cooked.)

TESTERS' NOTES

• Here's a reinvention of the classic skillet breakfast using the slow cooker to keep the apples luscious. You won't be able to turn the cake out onto a plate, as with the traditional recipe. Instead, scoop out the servings with a large spoon; make sure you get all the way to the bottom for all the apples, cake, *and* sauce.

• The cake will be somewhat softer than the traditional "pancake," since the moisture is kept inside the cooker as the pancake bakes. It's no sweat really—just a more luxurious consistency. The apples will also rise to the top, with the custard-like cake on the bottom.

ALL-AMERICAN KNOW-HOW Buttering or greasing the inside of a slow cooker isn't much of a chore. Save the wrapper from a stick of butter, then use the butter-coated side to grease the insert. Take care to butter the angle where the side meets the bottom. If you don't have a butter wrapper, put a little softened butter on a paper towel or a piece of wax paper to rub around the inside of the cooker.

banana pecan coffee cake

EFFORT: **A LITTLE** • PREP TIME: **25 MINUTES** • COOK TIME: **2½ TO 4½ HOURS** • KEEPS ON WARM: **NO** • SERVES: **4 TO 12**

INGREDIENTS	2- TO 3½-QT	4- TO 5½-QT	6- TO 8-QT
FOR THE CAKE			
Granulated sugar	⅔ cup	1 cup	1⅔ cups
Canola oil	3½ tblsp	⅓ cup	½ cup plus 1 tblsp
Large eggs/white	1 whole plus 1 white	2 whole	4 whole
Mashed ripe bananas	⅔ cup (about 1½ medium)	1 cup (about 2¼ medium)	1⅔ cups (about 3½ medium)
Vanilla extract	½ tsp	1 tsp	1½ tsp
All-purpose flour	1 cup	1½ cups	2½ cups
Baking powder	½ tsp	½ tsp	1 tsp
Baking soda	¼ tsp	½ tsp	1 tsp
Salt	¼ tsp	½ tsp	1 tsp
FOR THE TOPPING			
Finely ground pecan pieces	4½ tblsp	½ cup	¾ cup
Packed light brown sugar	1½ tblsp	2 tblsp	¼ cup
All-purpose flour	2 tsp	1 tblsp	2 tblsp
Ground cinnamon	½ tsp	½ tsp	1 tsp

1 Spray the inside of a slow cooker with non-stick baking spray.

2 Beat the granulated sugar and oil in a large bowl with an electric mixer at medium speed until creamy and light, 3 to 5 minutes. Beat in the eggs, then the mashed bananas and vanilla. Scrape down the sides of the bowl.

3 Whisk the flour, baking powder, baking soda, and salt in a second bowl until the leaveners are evenly distributed throughout. Use a wooden spoon to stir the flour mixture into the beaten egg mixture just until well incorporated.

4 Mix the topping ingredients in a medium bowl: the pecans, brown sugar, flour, and cinnamon.

5 Pour half the banana batter into the slow cooker; sprinkle half the topping mixture on this first layer. Then pour the remaining batter into the cooker, smoothing it out into an even layer. Top with the remaining topping, taking care to cover the cake evenly and as thoroughly as possible.

6 Cover and cook on low for 2½ to 3 hours for a small cooker, 3 to 3½ hours for a medium cooker, or 4 to 4½ hours for a large cooker, or until the cake is set and firm to the touch.

TESTERS' NOTES
• The bananas will cause the batter to break. Don't worry; the problem will be fixed when you stir in the flour mixture.
• Pulse the pecan pieces in a small food processor or spice grinder until the consistency of standard cornmeal. For even more flavor, toast (and cool) the pecans before you grind them.
• Because of varying sizes among the slow cookers—oval or round, of course, but also varying volumes—we have to give a range of timings on many baking recipes, as in this one. Check the cake at the lowest time marker to see if a toothpick comes out with a few crumbs. If the batter is not yet set, continue baking, checking in 15-minute increments.

Serve It Up! Cut slices right out of the cooker, using a knife suitable for nonstick surfaces. If the insert to your cooker can be removed, cool the cake in the insert on a wire rack, uncovered, for 1 hour. Then set a cutting board over the cooker and turn the cake upside-down to release the cake. Remove the canister and set another cutting board on the cake; invert the whole kit and caboodle to stand the cake upright on the second cutting board.

sour cream chocolate chip coffee cake

EFFORT: **A LITTLE** • PREP TIME: **15 MINUTES** • COOK TIME: **3 TO 5 HOURS** • KEEPS ON WARM: **NO** • SERVES: **6 TO 16**

INGREDIENTS	2- TO 3½-QT	4- TO 5½-QT	6- TO 8-QT
All-purpose flour	1 cup	1½ cups	2½ cups
Semisweet or bittersweet chocolate chips	½ cup	¾ cup	1¼ cups
Baking powder	¾ tsp	1 tsp	2 tsp
Salt	¼ tsp	½ tsp	¾ tsp
Cold unsalted butter, cut into small pieces, plus additional for greasing the slow cooker	8 tblsp (1 stick)	12 tblsp (1½ sticks)	20 tblsp (2½ sticks)
Sugar	½ cup	¾ cup	1¼ cups
Large eggs/white, at room temperature	1 whole plus 1 white	2 whole	4 whole
Sour cream (regular or low-fat)	¼ cup	½ cup	⅔ cup
Vanilla extract	1 tsp	1¼ tsp	2½ tsp

1 Lightly butter the inside of a slow cooker.

2 Combine the flour, chocolate chips, baking powder, and salt in a large bowl until the chips are evenly distributed throughout.

3 Beat the butter and sugar in a second bowl with a mixer at medium-high speed until creamy and rich, almost fluffy, 6 to 10 minutes. Beat in the eggs one at a time. Scrape down the inside of the bowl and beat in the sour cream and vanilla until smooth.

4 Use a wooden spoon to stir in the flour ingredients until a fairly thick and moist batter forms. Pour the mixture into the cooker.

5 Create an even layer of paper towels over the opening of the cooker, with no gaps where moisture can escape. Set the lid in place and cook on low for 3 to 3½ hours for a small cooker, 3½ to 4 hours for a medium cooker, or 4 to 5 hours for a large cooker, or until the cake is set enough that a toothpick or cake tester inserted into its center comes out with no crumbs attached. (The cake will feel moist to the touch, but be done throughout.)

TESTERS' NOTES
• The layer of paper towels keeps any moisture from dripping back onto the cake from the slow cooker's lid, so there are no soggy bits across the top.
• Although the cake will taste great warm, it will be quite moist. It will continue to firm up, particularly if you remove it from the cooker and allow it to cool on a cutting board before slicing it into wedges. See the "Serve It Up" note for the previous recipe with exact instructions on how to do that maneuver.

cinnamon-raisin bread pudding

EFFORT: **A LITTLE** • PREP TIME: **15 MINUTES** • COOK TIME: **2½ TO 3 HOURS** • KEEPS ON WARM: **NO** • SERVES: **4 TO 8**

INGREDIENTS	2- TO 3½-QT	4- TO 5½-QT	6- TO 8-QT
Unsalted butter, softened, plus additional for greasing the slow cooker	4½ tblsp	6 tblsp (¾ stick)	10 tblsp (1 stick plus 2 tblsp)
½-inch-thick slices cinnamon-raisin bread	12	16	24
Chopped pecans	½ cup	⅔ cup	1 cup
Packed light brown sugar	¼ cup	⅓ cup	½ cup
Milk	4 cups	5⅓ cups	8 cups
Large eggs	3	4	6
Vanilla extract	1 tsp	1½ tsp	2 tsp
Salt	Pinch	¼ tsp	¼ tsp

1 Butter the inside of a slow cooker. Butter one side of each of the slices of the bread.

2 Layer the bread slices buttered side up in the slow cooker along with the pecans and brown sugar, making a layer of bread, then sprinkling it with pecans and brown sugar, before making another layer—and even more. The top layer should be only bread, buttered side up.

3 Whisk the milk, eggs, vanilla, and salt in a large bowl until smooth and creamy; pour over the layers in the cooker, pressing the bread down with the back of a wooden spoon to make sure the egg and milk mixture has soaked through the layers.

4 Cover and cook on low for 2½ to 3 hours, until the casserole is puffed up and a flatware knife inserted into the center of the pudding comes out clean.

TESTERS' NOTES
• Bread puddings for breakfast? You bet! This one cooks up into a fluffy, sweet, and moist cake.
• The best bread for this dish will in fact be slightly stale, certainly day-old—maybe even two-day-old. It'll add extra firmness to balance all that butter.
• Because of varying sizes and shapes among slow cookers, there's no way to predict the number of layers you'll make in Step 2. The count is actually less important than an even top layer.
• Whisk those eggs in the milk for a good while, until the whole thing is uniform, even foamy, with no bits of egg white floating in the mix.

ALL-AMERICAN KNOW-HOW Ingredient lists call for light or dark brown sugar to be "packed." That's because brown sugar has added moisture (molasses) that keeps the sugar grains separated a bit. A true, dry measure is then hard to come by. To pack brown sugar into a measuring cup, mound it, then press down gently—not firmly—with the back of a flatware tablespoon, pushing the grains together to be able to add a little more sugar to the measure and thereby end up with the right amount.

sausage bread pudding

EFFORT: **A LITTLE** • PREP TIME: **30 MINUTES** • COOK TIME: **2 TO 2½ HOURS** • KEEPS ON WARM: **30 MINUTES** • SERVES: **4 TO 8**

INGREDIENTS	2- TO 3½-QT	4- TO 5½-QT	6- TO 8-QT
Small cubes of French baguette	4 cups	6 cups	8 cups
Breakfast sausage links, cut into 1-inch pieces	12 ounces	1 pound	1½ pounds
Large eggs	2	3	4
Milk	1⅓ cups	2 cups	2⅔ cups
Maple syrup	⅓ cup	½ cup	⅔ cup
Vanilla extract	½ tsp	1 tsp	1½ tsp

1 Position the rack in the center of the oven and preheat the oven to 350°F. Spread the bread cubes in an even layer on one or two baking sheets, then toast (one sheet at a time if necessary) until light browned and crisp, about 15 minutes, tossing occasionally. Cool on the baking sheet for 15 minutes.

2 Meanwhile, heat a large nonstick skillet over medium heat. Add the sausage bits and brown completely, turning occasionally, about 5 minutes. Transfer the sausage pieces to a plate lined with paper towels, discarding any grease in the skillet.

3 Toss the bread cubes and sausage bits in the cooker. Whisk the eggs, milk, maple syrup, and vanilla in a large bowl until creamy, then pour over the contents of the slow cooker, pressing down to submerge the bread cubes as much as you can.

4 Cover and cook on low for 2 to 2½ hours, until the bread pudding has set and the liquid has been absorbed, with no excess liquid around the inside surfaces of the cooker.

TESTERS' NOTES
• This is certainly a hearty meal, rich and filling. You'll want some strong coffee on the side.
• Because of differences in the size of breakfast sausages—varying thickness of the links—it's important you buy them by weight and use the appropriate amount. Choose mild or hot breakfast sausage, as desired. Or use your favorite breakfast sausage, even ones with cheese or chiles in the mix.
• You can substitute honey for the maple syrup for a sweeter, brighter flavor.

SHORTCUTS If you don't want to make your own bread cubes, look for plain *fresh* croutons in your supermarket's bakery section. (The ingredient list on the package should say "bread cubes," period—no seasonings and no oil.)

INGREDIENTS EXPLAINED Maple syrup is sold in at least two grades in North American supermarkets: grade A (also labeled *grade 1*) and grade B (also labeled *grade 2*). Grade A is further divided into three categories: light, medium, and dark amber. Although we prefer the dark, rich, slightly bitter grade B for most baking, its punch can cancel out other flavors in a slow cooker, so we feel grade A (or 1) dark amber is the best choice.

Serve It Up! A poached egg on each serving would certainly be welcome. Or toast pecan halves in a skillet with melted butter and season them with a little brown sugar and a pinch of cayenne before spooning them over the servings.

corn muffin migas

EFFORT: **A LITTLE** • PREP TIME: **20 MINUTES** • COOK TIME: **3 HOURS** • KEEPS ON WARM: **1 HOUR** • SERVES: **4 TO 10**

INGREDIENTS	2- TO 3½-QT	4- TO 5½-QT	6- TO 8-QT
Dried Spanish chorizo, diced	2 ounces	4 ounces	6 ounces
Medium corn muffins (about 5 ounces each), quartered	4	8	12
Medium red bell peppers, stemmed, seeded, and diced	1	2	3
Canned chopped green chiles, hot or mild	½ cup	1 cup	1½ cups
Monterey jack, shredded	4 ounces (about 1 cup)	½ pound (about 2 cups)	¾ pound (about 3 cups)
Large eggs	2	4	6
Milk	2 cups	4 cups	6 cups

1 Lightly grease the inside of a slow cooker with unsalted butter.

2 Heat a nonstick skillet over medium heat. Add the chorizo and cook, stirring often, until browned, about 6 minutes. Use a slotted spoon to transfer the chorizo bits to the slow cooker.

3 Add the corn muffins, bell pepper, chiles, and cheese. Toss well.

4 Whisk the eggs and milk in a large bowl until smooth, no bits of white floating in the mix. Pour into the casserole, moistening the corn muffin quarters.

5 Cover and cook on low for 3 hours, until the custard has set.

TESTERS' NOTES
• Here's a Southwestern breakfast casserole that sort of takes on the flavors of migas, or scrambled eggs with peppers, chiles, and cheese, often served with corn tortillas (or here, corn muffins). Dice the chorizo and bell pepper into tiny bits so you can eat the casserole with a spoon, not a knife and fork.
• Buy corn muffins without any added sugar so that the casserole stays savory, rather than becomes too sweet.

INGREDIENTS EXPLAINED Spanish chorizo is a dried sausage, quite red from paprika and ready to eat right out of the package. It needs to be browned for more flavor here before it's added to this casserole. You can also use Mexican chorizo, a fresh (that is, raw) sausage that tastes much like a spicy bratwurst; however, it should be cut into thin rounds and fully cooked before adding it to the slow cooker.

biscuits and sausage gravy

EFFORT: **A LOT** • PREP TIME: **35 MINUTES** • COOK TIME: **2 TO 2½ HOURS** • KEEPS ON WARM: **1 HOUR** • SERVES: **3 TO 8**

INGREDIENTS	2- TO 3½-QT	4- TO 5½-QT	6- TO 8-QT
FOR THE GRAVY			
Mild or hot breakfast sausage, any casings removed	½ pound	1 pound	1½ pounds
Yellow onion, chopped	1 medium	1 large	2 large
All-purpose flour	3 tblsp	6 tblsp	½ cup plus 1 tblsp
Grated nutmeg	¼ tsp	½ tsp	¾ tsp
Evaporated milk (regular, low-fat, or fat-free)	1½ cups	3 cups	4½ cups
FOR THE BISCUITS			
All-purpose flour	1 cup plus 2 tblsp	2¼ cups	3 cups plus 6 tblsp
Baking powder	2 tsp	4 tsp	2 tblsp
Salt	¼ tsp	½ tsp	¾ tsp
Unsalted butter, melted and cooled	2½ tblsp	5 tblsp	8 tblsp (1 stick)
Milk	6 tblsp	¾ cup	1¼ cups

1 Make the gravy: Heat a nonstick skillet over medium heat, then crumble in the sausage. Cook, stirring often, until well browned, about 4 minutes. Stir in the onion; continue cooking until the onion softens, stirring often, about 3 minutes.

2 Sprinkle the flour and the nutmeg over the sausage mixture, then stir well just to incorporate, about 30 seconds. Pour in the evaporated milk, raise the heat to medium-high, and stir until the sauce bubbles and thickens slightly. Scrape and pour the contents of the skillet into a slow cooker.

3 Make the biscuits: Mix the flour with the baking powder and salt in a large bowl. Stir in the melted butter, then the milk, just until all the flour has been incorporated and a soft dough has formed.

4 Turn the dough out onto a floured work surface. Gently press out the dough until it's about ½ inch thick. Cut the dough into 3-inch circles; lay these on top of the sausage mixture in the cooker.

5 Cover and cook on low for 2 to 2½ hours, or until the biscuits have set and firmed up.

TESTERS' NOTES

• Although this is a fairly traditional casserole, keep in mind that the biscuits will not brown as they "bake" in a slow cooker. If you want pitch-perfect aesthetics, thin a little bit of Worcestershire sauce with an equal amount of water and brush the biscuits' tops just before baking.

• A large, round slow cooker will have less available surface area than an oval one, so you may have a little extra dough. If you're concerned, use the dough ingredient list sized for the slow cooker *below* the one you're actually working with and leave a few extra gaps in the biscuit topping.

eggs, breakfast casseroles, and hash

Consider these brunch items—or the dishes you'll make on the weekend when time is not so precious. Here, you'll find many strata (*STRAH-tah*, or egg casseroles layered with bread or tortillas). You may have a favorite recipe for one of these that you bake in the oven on a holiday morning. Using a slow cooker can make that morning less busy and more celebratory. In fact, if you grate and chop things in advance, strata are great dishes for the kids to make, layering the ingredients in the slow cooker before you pour in the beaten milk mixture.

But the world doesn't turn on egg casseroles. We've also got two hearty hash brown recipes. In these last, the potatoes won't brown, but they will turn luxuriously soft. Serve these alongside fried or scrambled eggs—or even on their own if it's a more substantial recipe.

Before we get started, let us offer one bit of advice. Most of the egg dishes here are not meant to be kept warm for very long. Eggs can *break* in the slow cooker; that is, they tighten up so much that their natural moisture slips out of the protein bonds and ends up as a watery mess. There's no way to fix that mess if you let the dish sit too long. So once these strata are done, dig in. Or if you need time before serving, turn off the slow cooker, keep it covered, and give yourself fifteen minutes—the final dish will not be as tender, but you'll have bought yourself a little time on a busy morning.

Most of these dishes are not overnight affairs. They're also not as forgiving as some of the other breakfast fare. But they take only a few hours to cook—and that's a good thing, too. Because these are the dishes that will keep your house guests and family contented for hours.

quiche lorraine strata

EFFORT: **A LITTLE** • PREP TIME: **15 MINUTES** • COOK TIME: **2 TO 2½ HOURS** • KEEPS ON WARM: **NO** • SERVES: **2 TO 8**

INGREDIENTS	2- TO 3½-QT	4- TO 5½-QT	6- TO 8-QT
Slices of thin-cut bacon	4	10	16
Swiss cheese, grated	3 ounces (about ¾ cup)	7 ounces (about 1¾ cups)	12 ounces (about 3 cups)
Whole scallions, thinly sliced	½	1	3
Fresh thyme leaves, stripped from stem	½ tsp	1 tsp	2 tsp
Ground black pepper	¼ tsp	½ tsp	¾ tsp
½-inch-thick slices white bread	4	8	14
Milk	¾ cup	2 cups	3¼ cups
Large eggs/yolks, at room temperature	1 whole plus 1 yolk	3 whole plus 1 yolk	4 whole plus 3 yolks

1 Slather the inside of the slow cooker with unsalted butter.

2 Heat a large nonstick skillet over medium heat. Fry the bacon in batches as necessary to avoid overcrowding, turning often, about 4 minutes per batch, until crisp. Transfer the bacon to a plate lined with paper towels; blot dry. Let cool for a few minutes.

3 Crumble the bacon into a big bowl; stir in the cheese, scallions, thyme, and pepper.

4 Lay a single layer of bread slices in the cooker, then spoon a thin, even layer of the bacon mixture over the bread. Soldier on, repeating this layering as you use up the ingredients, ending with a layer of the bacon mixture on top to protect the bread as it "bakes."

5 Whisk the milk, eggs, and egg yolks in a large bowl until smooth and velvety; pour evenly and gently over the ingredients in the cooker, pressing the bread down with the back of a wooden spoon so it's soaked in the liquid mixture.

6 Cover and cook on low for 2 to 2½ hours, until the eggs are set enough that a flatware knife inserted into the center comes out clean and almost no liquid remains around the casserole.

TESTERS' NOTES
• Traditional quiche Lorraine has no cheese, but many American versions do. We just couldn't resist.
• If possible, use nitrate-free bacon. Yes, it's brown, not pink; but you won't be ingesting the chemicals that keep bacon unnaturally pink.
• How long you cook the bacon is really a matter of preference. If you like extra-crunchy bits of bacon in the strata, then fry it until it breaks into shards on the plate when cooled. If you prefer a softer finish to the dish without crunchy bits in the mix, then fry until it's browned but still soft.

ALL-AMERICAN KNOW-HOW For any strata, the eggs should be at room temperature prior to cooking so they cook evenly. Either leave the eggs out on the counter for 20 minutes or submerge them (in their shells) in a bowl of warm—not hot!—tap water for 5 minutes.

cowboy strata
with sausage and beans

EFFORT: **A LITTLE** • PREP TIME: **20 MINUTES** • COOK TIME: **2 TO 2½ HOURS** • KEEPS ON WARM: **NO** • SERVES: **3 TO 10**

INGREDIENTS	2- TO 3½-QT	4- TO 5½-QT	6- TO 8-QT
Breakfast sausage, any casings removed	8 ounces	1 pound	1¾ pounds
Small cubes of fresh Italian bread	4 cups	8 cups	14 cups
Chopped sun-dried tomatoes	½ cup	1 cup	1½ cups
Drained and rinsed canned pinto beans	¾ cup	1½ cups	2¾ cups
Cheddar cheese, grated	3 ounces (about ¾ cup)	6 ounces (about 1½ cups)	11 ounces (about 2¾ cups)
Crumbled dried sage	½ tsp	1 tsp	1½ tsp
Milk	1½ cups	3 cups	5¼ cups
Large eggs/yolks, at room temperature	2 whole plus 1 yolk	4 whole plus 2 yolks	7 whole plus 3 yolks

1 Heat a large nonstick skillet over medium heat for a couple of minutes, then crumble in the sausage meat. Cook, stirring often, until browned and cooked through, about 8 minutes. Use a slotted spoon to transfer the sausage meat to a plate lined with paper towels to drain off the excess fat.

2 As the sausage cooks, preheat your broiler and position the oven rack about 5 inches away. Spread the bread cubes on a rimmed baking sheet. (If you're using a large slow cooker, you may need to toast the bread cubes in two batches.) Broil until the bread cubes are toasted on all sides, turning and stirring occasionally, about 5 minutes. Cool on the baking sheet for 5 minutes.

3 Mix the browned sausage, toasted bread cubes, tomatoes, pinto beans, cheese, and sage in the slow cooker.

4 Whisk the milk, eggs, and egg yolks in a large bowl until smooth and foamy. Pour the mixture over the ingredients in the cooker, pressing down gently with the back of a spoon to make sure the bread cubes are moistened throughout.

5 Cover and cook on low for 2 to 2½ hours, until the eggs are set or until a flatware knife inserted into the center of the strata comes out without any eggy milkiness.

TESTERS' NOTES

• Skip the sun-dried tomatoes packed in oil and look for dry-packed vibrant, pliable sun-dried tomatoes in a bin in the produce section of a larger supermarket or on the salad bar.

• Should you take the crust off the bread cubes? We say no because the crust adds more texture.

• Check after 2 hours and then continue cooking until the liquid has been absorbed and the strata sets in the cooker. In general, larger cookers will take longer for the eggs to set.

• Substitute grated Swiss or even Gruyère for the Cheddar cheese.

tortilla strata
with red peppers and sausage

EFFORT: **A LITTLE** • PREP TIME: **15 MINUTES** • COOK TIME: **4 HOURS**
• KEEPS ON WARM: **NO** • SERVES: **4 TO 12**

INGREDIENTS	2- TO 3½-QT	4- TO 5½-QT	6- TO 8-QT
Mild Italian or turkey breakfast sausage, any casings removed	1 pound	2 pounds	3 pounds
Milk	2 cups	4 cups	6 cups
Large eggs, at room temperature	4	8	12
8-inch flour tortillas	4	8	12
Pepper jack cheese, finely grated	8 ounces (2 cups)	1 pound (4 cups)	1½ pounds (6 cups)
Jarred roasted red peppers, chopped	2	4	6

1 Heat a large skillet over medium heat. Crumble in the sausage and cook, stirring often, until well browned, about 8 minutes. Transfer the cooked sausage to a plate lined with paper towels.

2 Grease the inside of the slow cooker well with unsalted butter. Whisk the milk and eggs in a large bowl until smooth.

3 Layer the tortillas, sausage, cheese, and red peppers in the cooker, starting with some of the tortillas and ending with a layer of cheese. Alternate the ingredients to create several layers, tearing the tortillas so they'll fit the contours of the slow cooker without creeping up the sides, then use the leftover bits of tortilla to plug holes in the next layer. Pour the

milk mixture over everything. Make sure the tortillas are completely moistened by pressing down with the back of a wooden spoon where necessary.

4 Cover and cook on low for 4 hours, or until the eggs are set and a flatware knife inserted into the center of the strata comes out clean (with the possible exception of a couple of cheese threads).

TESTERS' NOTES
• There's no heat from chiles here because the acids in some chiles can curdle the milk as it cooks. If you want more pop, pass pico de gallo on the side.

SHORTCUTS Rather than having to remove sausage casings, you can often find bulk sausage meat in the deli case of larger supermarkets. Or you can buy your favorite ground pork, meat, or chicken and season it as you prefer.

Serve It Up! If you turn the cooker off and keep it covered for 30 minutes, you can take this strata out whole—or in large chunks. Save leftover pieces wrapped in foil in the fridge, then reheating them, still wrapped, on a baking sheet in a preheated 350°F oven for about 20 minutes. (Or unwrap individual servings and microwave them on high for 2 minutes.)

manchego, chickpea, and red pepper strata

EFFORT: **A LITTLE** • PREP TIME: **15 MINUTES** • COOK TIME: **3 HOURS** • KEEPS ON WARM: **1 HOUR** • SERVES: **4 TO 12**

INGREDIENTS	2- TO 3½-QT	4- TO 5½-QT	6- TO 8-QT
½-inch-thick slices of oat bread	8	14	20
Jarred roasted red peppers, chopped	1	2	3
Drained and rinsed canned chickpeas	1½ cups	2½ cups	4 cups
Manchego cheese, grated	6 ounces (about 1½ cups)	11 ounces (about 2¾ cups)	1 pound (about 4 cups)
Milk	2⅓	4 cups	6¼ cups
Large eggs/yolks, at room temperature	4 whole plus 1 yolk	7 whole plus 2 yolks	10 whole plus 3 yolks
Mild smoked paprika	½ tsp	¾ tsp	1¼ tsp

1 Dab some olive oil on a paper towel and grease the inside of the slow cooker.

2 Layer the bread slices, red peppers, chickpeas, and cheese in the cooker, starting with the bread and ending with the cheese, but making two, three, or even more layers of ingredients depending on the size and shape of your cooker. You'll need to cut or tear the bread so that it fits.

3 Whisk the milk, eggs, egg yolks, and paprika in a large bowl until foamy but creamy. Gently pour this mixture over the ingredients in the cooker, taking care to pour it all over, not just in one spot. Press down with the back of a wooden spoon to make sure the bread is thoroughly moistened.

4 Cover and cook on low for 3 hours, until the egg mixture has set and is firm, and a flatware knife inserted into the center comes out with some moist bits on it but no eggy milkiness.

TESTERS' NOTES

• Because of the way the oat bread soaks up and holds the milk mixture, this strata can actually be kept warm for a bit—in case everyone's alarm clock didn't go off at the same time.

• This strata is modeled on the basic flavors of some typical Spanish egg dishes. The chickpeas—a bit of a surprise for some—add lots of body plus a creamy mellowness.

• There's no added salt here because the cheese, chickpeas, and jarred roasted red peppers add plenty of sodium. You can always pass some flakey salt or sea salt at the table.

INGREDIENTS EXPLAINED Manchego is a Spanish sheep's-milk cheese from the La Mancha region. It actually comes in three varieties: *fresco* (or fresh), *curado* (or cured), and *viejo* (or aged). Avoid the fresh Manchego here—it's difficult to find in North America—and go for either the creamy beige *curado* for a sweeter, richer casserole or the more expensive *viejo* for a refined, slightly bitter taste.

loaded
two-potato
hash browns

EFFORT: **A LITTLE** • PREP TIME: **20 MINUTES** • COOK TIME: **8 HOURS**
• KEEPS ON WARM: **2 HOURS** • SERVES: **3 TO 8**

INGREDIENTS	2- TO 3½-QT	4- TO 5½-QT	6- TO 8-QT
Fresh Italian sausage, turkey sausage, or Mexican chorizo, any casings removed	6 ounces	¾ pound	1 pound
Russet or other baking potatoes, peeled and cut into 1-inch cubes	6 ounces	¾ pound	1 pound
Sweet potatoes, peeled and cut into 1-inch cubes	6 ounces	¾ pound	1 pound
Seeded and thinly sliced Cubanelle peppers	1 cup	2¼ cups	3 cups
Chopped ripe tomatoes	⅓ cup	¾ cup	1 cup
Pitted and sliced black olives	¼ cup	⅓ cup	½ cup
Reduced-sodium chicken broth	⅓ cup	¾ cup	1 cup

1 Heat a nonstick skillet over medium heat. Crumble in the sausage meat and cook, stirring often, until browned and cooked through, about 5 minutes.

2 Use a slotted spoon to transfer the cooked sausage to the slow cooker, taking some or even all of the fat as well. Stir in the potatoes, sweet potatoes, peppers, tomatoes, and olives.

3 Continue tossing until everything is well mixed. Pour the broth over the top of the ingredients in the slow cooker.

4 Cover and cook on low for 8 hours, until the potatoes are fork-tender.

TESTERS' NOTES
• This is a main-course hash, stocked with lots of sausage and vegetables. You don't need much else—except maybe a bottle of hot pepper sauce at the table.
• There's no need to seed the tomatoes. The extra juice will just add more moisture to the hash as it cooks.

INGREDIENTS EXPLAINED Cubanelle peppers (also called *Italian frying peppers*) are long, thin, sweet peppers reminiscent of bell peppers, but with a thinner skin and a little more brightness in the flavor. When immature, they are green and a tad more sour. They can mature to a deep red with a mellower flavor. We prefer the green ones in slow cooker dishes, although either will do.

Serve It Up! Of course, you'll want fried eggs and crunchy, whole-grain toast to round out the plates. Together, they're a welcome meal even for dinner. Or skip the heartier fare and just offer applesauce on the side. Or even a green salad for a late-summer supper.

bacon and onion hash browns

EFFORT: **A LITTLE** • PREP TIME: **20 MINUTES** • COOK TIME: **8 HOURS**
• KEEPS ON WARM: **2 HOURS** • SERVES: **4 TO 8**

INGREDIENTS	2- TO 3½-QT	4- TO 5½-QT	6- TO 8-QT
Slices of thick-cut bacon	3	5	8
Roughly chopped yellow onion	¼ cup	½ cup	¾ cup
Waxy white potatoes, washed and cut into ½-inch pieces	1 pound	2 pounds	3 pounds
Thinly sliced scallion	2 tblsp	¼ cup	⅓ cup
Caraway seeds	¼ tsp	½ tsp	¾ tsp
Celery seeds	¼ tsp	½ tsp	½ tsp

1 Heat a skillet over medium heat. Add the bacon and cook until brown and crunchy, turning occasionally, 3 to 4 minutes. Transfer the slices to a cutting board, but do not drain the skillet.

2 Add the onion and cook, stirring often, just until barely softened, about 2 minutes. Scrape and pour the bacon fat and onion into the slow cooker; chop the bacon and add it to the cooker.

3 Stir in the potato cubes, scallion, and caraway and celery seeds. Toss well, ensuring all the potatoes are coated in the bacon grease.

4 Cover and cook on low for 8 hours, or until the potatoes are tender.

TESTERS' NOTES
• Hash browns don't brown in the slow cooker. But they do get incredibly creamy. If you'd like some crusty bits, spoon the hash browns out of the cooker and into a skillet, add a generous pour of olive oil, and cook over medium heat, stirring occasionally, for up to 10 minutes.
• If your supermarket doesn't offer thick-cut bacon, buy a chunk of slab bacon (or smoked pork belly) and cut it into ½-inch slices. Use 2 ounces for a small slow cooker, 3 ounces for a medium model, or 5 ounces for a large one.

Serve It Up! Since these hash browns are not a main course, you'll need some scrambled eggs or smoked salmon, cream cheese, and whole-grain toast to go with them.

INGREDIENTS EXPLAINED Don't use Idaho or other baking potatoes for this recipe. Rather, you want small white new potatoes, like Irish creamers or white fingerlings, sliced into ½-inch-thick disks.

tomatillo sauce for eggs

EFFORT: **A LITTLE** • PREP TIME: **20 MINUTES** • COOK TIME: **8 HOURS** • KEEPS ON WARM: **3 HOURS** • SERVES: **3 TO 8**

INGREDIENTS	2- TO 3½-QT	4- TO 5½-QT	6- TO 8-QT
Olive oil	1 tblsp	2 tblsp	3 tblsp
Medium yellow onions, chopped	2	3	4
Seeded and diced Cubanelle peppers (see page 47)	½ cup	1 cup	1¾ cups
Seeded and minced fresh jalapeño chile	Up to 1 tblsp	Up to 2 tblsp	Up to ¼ cup
Minced garlic	½ tblsp	1 tblsp	1½ tblsp
Tomatillos, husked and chopped	1½ pounds	3 pounds	4½ pounds
Low-sodium chicken broth	½ cup	1 cup	1½ cups
Cider vinegar	½ tblsp	1 tblsp	1½ tblsp
Dried oregano	½ tblsp	1 tblsp	1½ tblsp
Ground cumin	1½ tsp	2½ tsp	3½ tsp

1 Heat the oil in a large nonstick skillet over medium heat. Swirl in the oil, then add the onions. Reduce the heat to low and cook until the onions begin to soften, stirring often, about 3 minutes.

2 Reduce the heat further, cover, and continue cooking, stirring every once in a while, until the onions are very soft and luxurious, about 10 minutes.

3 Stir in the peppers, chile, and garlic. Raise the heat to medium; cook until the peppers begin to soften, about 2 minutes.

4 Scrape every last bit from the skillet into the slow cooker. Stir in the tomatillos, broth, vinegar, oregano, and cumin. Cover and cook on low for 8 hours, or until the tomatillos are tender and the mixture has morphed into a thick sauce.

TESTERS' NOTES
• This sauce is based on sofrito, a Spanish favorite sauce that now finds incarnations across the American Southwest, as well as in Portugal, Haiti, the Philippines, Greece, and even some Sephardic communities.
• Store any leftover sauce in a covered glass or plastic container for up to 1 week in the refrigerator or up to 4 months in the freezer.

Serve It Up! Poach, fry, or even hard-boil the eggs and then ladle this sauce over them when serving. Or bake the eggs right in the sauce—although not in the slow cooker. Ladle the sauce into a 9-inch square or 9 x 13-inch baking dish, then make wells in it with the back of a tablespoon. Crack eggs into each of these wells, then bake in a 375°F oven for about 15 minutes, until the eggs are set.

INGREDIENTS EXPLAINED Tomatillos are like small, firm green tomatoes, sometimes sold still covered in their papery hulls. They have a slightly sour but still sweet taste and a crisp texture that softens into a rich sauce. Look for firm, vibrantly colored fruit without any mushiness (although there may still be a little stickiness on the skin).

applesauce and compotes

Nothing beats applesauce that you make yourself. The fresh and tart apples are the perfect foil for the sweeteners and spices. The sauce also will be missing any unpronounceable chemicals! All these dishes pair well with plain yogurt for a morning starter. But don't stop there. The compotes can also morph into a sophisticated dessert at the end of the day.

There's only one rule for fruit dishes like these: pick the freshest fruits you can find. Despite all the pinching, shaking, or squeezing people do to the fruit in the grocery store or at a farmstand, there's really only one way to pick the best out of the bin—use your nose. The fruit should smell sweet and irresistible. Otherwise, it won't taste sweet and irresistible.

The same goes for dried fruit: it should still smell fresh and sweet, like its fresh kin. Okay, perhaps not exactly as sweet, but certainly within a small range. It should also be pliable and even sticky, with no signs of mold or brown rot anywhere in the package. If you find the dried fruit is subpar at your market, take your money and shop elsewhere. You deserve a store that offers you solid ingredients for your hard-earned cash.

With good fresh and dried fruit, the slow cooker can work its magic, slowly softening it into a luscious sauce or compote. There's no threat of scorching these sauces, a boon to busy cooks; but there's also no chance of its getting too thick, since every drop of tasty moisture will stay right in the cooker where it belongs.

slow cooker applesauce

EFFORT: **NOT MUCH** • PREP TIME: **15 MINUTES** • COOK TIME: **8 HOURS** • KEEPS ON WARM: **4 HOURS** • SERVES: **4 TO 12**

INGREDIENTS	2- TO 3½-QT	4- TO 5½-QT	6- TO 8-QT
Large apples, preferably Gala, Fuji, or Jonagold, peeled, cored, and chopped	4	8	12
Packed light brown sugar	¼ cup	½ cup	¾ cup
4-inch cinnamon stick	½	1	1½
Salt	⅛ tsp	¼ tsp	¼ tsp

1 Combine all the ingredients in a slow cooker, stirring until the brown sugar has completely coated the apple slices.

2 Cover and cook on low for 8 hours, until the apples are tender enough to mash.

3 Remove the cinnamon stick and mash the apples with a potato masher. Spoon into plastic or glass containers, seal, and refrigerate for up to 1 week or freeze for up to 4 months.

TESTERS' NOTES

• This thick sauce benefits from apples that break down a bit over the heat. Chop them into fairly small bits, about ½ inch each.

• No, you don't have to use a potato masher. Mash the apples with the back of a wooden spoon in the cooker, although the applesauce will not be as smooth and luscious. Or you can skip the mashing entirely for a chunkier sauce.

• You can also substitute honey for the brown sugar, but the sweetener's taste will be more pronounced. Consider using only one-half to two-thirds the amount of honey as a substitute for the sugar, depending on how sweet your apples are.

stone fruit compote

EFFORT: **NOT MUCH** • PREP TIME: **10 MINUTES** • COOK TIME: **6 HOURS** • KEEPS ON WARM: **4 HOURS** • SERVES: **3 TO 10**

INGREDIENTS	2- TO 3½-QT	4- TO 5½-QT	6- TO 8-QT
Medium nectarines or peaches, peeled, pitted, and sliced	3	6	8
Dried apricots, halved	⅔ cup	1½ cups	3½ cups
Orange juice	½ cup	1 cup	1½ cups
Dried cherries	⅓ cup	¾ cup	1¼ cups
Packed light brown sugar	⅓ cup	¾ cup	1¼ cups
Unsalted butter, cut into tiny bits	1 tblsp	2½ tblsp	4 tblsp (½ stick)
Vanilla extract	½ tsp	1 tsp	1½ tsp
Ground cinnamon	½ tsp	¾ tsp	1¼ tsp
Salt	⅛ tsp	¼ tsp	½ tsp

1 Combine all the ingredients in a slow cooker, stirring until the brown sugar coats the fruit completely.

2 Cover and cook on low for 6 hours, until all the fruit is soft and tender. Ladle into plastic or glass containers, seal closed, and store in the refrigerator for up to 4 days or in the freezer for up to 4 months.

TESTERS' NOTES

• You can use either California or Turkish apricots, depending on whether you prefer a tartness (the former) or a sweet mellowness (the latter).

• To keep the butter from melting and pooling on top of the compote, make sure the pieces are submerged in the mix before you set the lid on the cooker.

(continued)

Serve It Up! A compote like this is great when served on top of plain yogurt for breakfast, or save it for dessert and offer some crunchy gingersnap cookies on the side.

INGREDIENTS EXPLAINED Dried apricots come in two basic types: Turkish apricots, usually brown and quite sweet; and California, very orange (sometimes vibrantly so) and a little tarter. Either will do here. If a recipe is developed for a specific kind, it'll be so noted in the ingredient list.

fig compote

EFFORT: **NOT MUCH** • PREP TIME: **10 MINUTES** • COOK TIME: **8 HOURS** • KEEPS ON WARM: **4 HOURS** • SERVES: **4 TO 12**

INGREDIENTS	2- TO 3½-QT	4- TO 5½-QT	6- TO 8-QT
Water	2 cups	4 cups	6 cups
Sugar	6 tblsp	¾ cup	1 cup plus 2 tblsp
Sweet white wine, such as Riesling or Spätlese	¼ cup	½ cup	¾ cup
Salt	¼ tsp	½ tsp	¾ tsp
Dried Mission figs, stemmed and quartered	2 cups	4 cups	6 cups
Dried Turkish figs, stemmed and quartered	2 cups	4 cups	6 cups
Finely grated lemon zest	1 tblsp	1½ tblsp	2 tblsp

1 Whisk the water, sugar, wine, and salt in the slow cooker until the sugar dissolves, then stir in the remaining ingredients.

2 Cover and cook on low for 8 hours, or until the figs are tender, the syrup is thick, and much of it has been absorbed.

3 Spoon any leftovers into a plastic or glass container, seal, and store in the fridge for up to 4 days.

TESTERS' NOTES
• This one is probably for the adults. For one thing, the alcohol will not cook away. (It never does in any dish, by the way, but it's more concentrated here.) For another, the fig flavor is intense, like the best fig cookie filling ever. To that end, those dried figs should be luscious and soft, not dry or crumbly.
• Grate the lemon zest as fine as possible, preferably by using a microplane. You want the bits of zest to melt into the compote over time.

Serve It Up! Beyond breakfast, layer the cooled compote with vanilla custard in wine glasses; or with lady fingers, mandarin orange segments, and vanilla custard in a glass serving bowl; top with whipped cream and chill for a couple of hours to make an easy trifle. Or crush some vanilla meringues and mix a little compote with them and lots of whipped cream (otherwise known as an *Eton Mess*). Or make figgy short cakes by splitting open some biscuits and topping them with the compote and whipped cream.

INGREDIENTS EXPLAINED There are several varieties of dried figs available in supermarkets. Mission figs—sometimes called *Black Mission figs*—are dark blue or almost black, small and quite sweet, and prized for their ethereal aroma. Dried Turkish figs—sometimes called *dried Adriatic figs*—are brown and wrinkled, quite sticky as well, often used to make pastes and confections. If you can't find Turkish figs, substitute the more common dried Calimyrna fig, a greenish-beige fruit that's not so sweet as the Turkish figs but is a North American descendant of the Smyrna fig of the Middle East.

spice market
dried fruit compote

EFFORT: **A LITTLE** • PREP TIME: **10 MINUTES** • COOK TIME: **6 HOURS**
• KEEPS ON WARM: **4 HOURS** • SERVES: **4 TO 8**

INGREDIENTS	2- TO 3½-QT	4- TO 5½-QT	6- TO 8-QT
Roughly chopped pitted dried fruits, preferably apples, peaches, prunes, pears, and/or nectarines	3 cups	4½ cups	8 cups
4-inch cinnamon sticks	1	1½	2
Whole cloves	6	8	12
Green cardamom pods	2	3	5
Star anise	1	1	2
Water	2⅓ cups	3½ cups	6¼ cups
Sugar	1 cup	1½ cups	2⅓ cups
Salt	⅛ tsp	¼ tsp	½ tsp

1 Combine the fruit and spices in the slow cooker.

2 Whisk the water, sugar, and salt in a large bowl until the sugar dissolves. Pour over the fruit.

3 Cover and cook on low for 6 hours, or until the dried fruit is tender and luscious, the syrup is thick, and much of the liquid has been absorbed.

4 Remove the cinnamon sticks and star anise before ladling the compote into glass or plastic containers, sealing shut, and storing in the fridge for up to 5 days or in the freezer for up to 4 months.

TESTERS' NOTES
• This compote uses only dried fruit to make a very rich, sumptuous mélange. If possible, have at least three different kinds of fruit in the mix.
• Chunk the dried fruit into fairly large pieces, about 2 inches each. (Pitted prunes, for example, can be left whole.)
• We leave the cloves and cardamom pods in the compote because they continue to flavor it in storage—and we're quite partial to them. Remove them in Step 4 for a milder flavor—or before you dish up the compote if you want to avoid big hits of flavor in individual spoonfuls.

Serve It Up! For a great breakfast, ladle this compote into bowls, then add a splash of cream as well as some plain granola for crunch.

soups

CALL THIS CHAPTER YOUR OWN PRIVATE BONANZA—OR AT LEAST
the makings of it. You'll soon find yourself in the enviable position of happening upon a horde of delicious soups, all in your own freezer.

If there's ever a chapter in our slow cooker *oeuvre* that's made for the big-batch, large-capacity models, it's this one. Let's face it: a vat of soup makes a lovely meal for the evening; and the leftovers are a prize for the nights when you stumble home too tired to cook. Imagine pulling out a frozen quart of French Onion Soup (page 59), Lentil Soup (page 72), or Steak and Potato Soup (page 95), setting it to warm up while you get into more comfortable gear, anticipating a hot meal at the ready.

Better yet, these recipes are among the most forgiving in the book. What happens when we call for 1½ cups of diced peeled sweet potato and you have only 1 cup—or perhaps 2 cups? Not much—toss it all in. Sure, you may cross the line between a soup and a stew, but no one's looking.

That line is difficult to figure out, anyway; we tend to think of soups more as weighted toward the broth than the other ingredients. But then we think of a full bowl of vegetables, noodles, and chicken, all held together by a modest amount of broth, and we still call it Chicken Noodle Soup (page 85). In the end, we make the distinction on the dish's overall consistency at the end of cooking. A stew has a thickened broth, almost like a sauce; a soup has a thinner one, with room to spare between the ingredients.

Writing that brings us to the topic of broths. We've got plenty of warnings in this book about the dangers of canned broth. (Too much salt! Too much onion! Too much water!) Yes, there's a wide range of broths on the supermarket shelves. You should do a taste test, sipping each on a spoon. You'll soon discover which fits your fare. And if you really want to take a soup over the top, consider making your own stock. We end this chapter with six recipes

for stock (starting on page 108), and we encourage you to try one on some Sunday afternoon when you have a little time around the house. Making your own stock is a bit of a chore, but the slow cooker takes the edge off the work. Get it going and walk away; when you're done, strain the stock, throw some chopped quick-cooking vegetables in it for soup that night, and store the rest in the freezer.

And that brings us back to your own private bonanza. If you're going to get into soups, invest in a supply of those plastic 1-quart containers familiar from Chinese take-out soups. Ladle in what you've got, seal, label, and put away for a future date. It's better to store soup in discrete quantities rather than large batches. You never know when you're going to want a peaceful lunch by yourself: no crush of kids, no jangling phones, no harried schedule. The hope for those moments of peace may be the very best reason to make soup and have it ready in the freezer.

vegetable, bean, and grain soups

Yep, we started with these—not with chicken soup, not with shellfish bisque, and certainly not with stock. We started here because, if you're going to eat your vegetables, we bet you're going to eat them in a soup. We have a good friend, a real meat-and-potatoes guy, who pushes the green stuff to the edge of his plate at almost every meal. Yet he'll eat kale or Brussels sprouts when they've come to him in a bowl of warm soup. We've even watched him cross the beet barrier!

So here are soups that rely heavily on sweet potatoes, lentils, leeks, zucchini, mushrooms, or chard. Fear not: there's meat in this section, too. Who but the most committed vegetarians could resist a bean soup with a chunk of ham in it? That said, any meat used in these soups is more a flavoring agent. And yes, there's vegetarian fare here, too. In fact, quite a bit—even vegan choices. And of course, in those instances where we call for chicken broth, you can substitute vegetable broth, provided you understand you'll lose a little body in the final dish. Among the store-bought broths, none is more insipid than vegetable broth; most tastes like water steeped with a vegetable-colored crayon. You're best off if you make your own vegetable stock (page 110), or search for the brands with the best flavor.

One more thing before we get started. We steer clear of a lot of frozen vegetables, not because we want the freshest taste (we do) but mostly because we want the best texture. Yes, we use some canned tomatoes now and again; and yes, frozen vegetables can sometimes taste better than even their fresh kin. But fresh vegetables win big on the texture score: most remain firm and toothsome longer in the slow cooker than their frozen compatriots. And since soup is awash in liquid, a little texture counts for a lot. We hope it's enough to get the veggie-phobes in your life to dig in.

fresh tomato soup

EFFORT: **NOT MUCH** • PREP TIME: **15 MINUTES** • COOK TIME:
7 HOURS • KEEPS ON WARM: **4 HOURS** • SERVES: **3 TO 8**

INGREDIENTS	2- TO 3½-QT	4- TO 5½-QT	6- TO 8-QT
Chopped ripe tomatoes, preferably Roma or plum	4 cups (about 2 pounds)	7 cups (about 3½ pounds)	11 cups (about 5½ pounds)
Chopped red onion	⅔ cup	1 cup	1⅔ cups
Dried basil	3 tblsp	¼ cup	⅓ cup
Worcestershire sauce	1½ tblsp	2 tblsp	3 tblsp
Sugar	1½ tblsp	2 tblsp	3 tblsp
Olive oil	1½ tblsp	2 tblsp	3 tblsp
Minced garlic	½ tblsp	2 tsp	1 tblsp
Dried dill	½ tsp	1 tsp	½ tblsp
Salt	½ tsp	1 tsp	½ tblsp

1 Dump the tomatoes, onion, dried basil, Worcestershire sauce, sugar, olive oil, garlic, dill, and salt in the slow cooker and give it all a good stir.

2 Cover and cook on low for 7 hours, or until the tomatoes have broken down into a rich soup.

TESTERS' NOTES
• Make this soup in the summer when tomatoes are at their finest. Then save it in quart containers in the freezer until winter, when it will provide a surprising spark of sunshine on a gray day.
• Nope, there's no broth here. The tomatoes provide the liquid because the slow cooker forces it out of them.
• We prefer dried herbs to fresh because they offer a more mellow finish to the soup.

Serve It Up! Grate Parmigiano-Reggiano cheese over the bowlfuls.

creamy tomato soup

EFFORT: **A LITTLE** • PREP TIME: **15 MINUTES** • COOK TIME:
2½ HOURS/5 HOURS • KEEPS ON WARM: **2 HOURS** • SERVES: **3 TO 9**

INGREDIENTS	2- TO 3½-QT	4- TO 5½-QT	6- TO 8-QT
Low-sodium vegetable broth	3 cups	6 cups (1½ quarts)	9 cups (2 quarts plus 1 cup)
No-salt-added tomato paste	⅔ cup	1¼ cups	1¾ cups
Evaporated milk (regular or low-fat)	6 tblsp	¾ cup	1¼ cups
Heavy cream	¼ cup	½ cup	¾ cup
Honey	1 tblsp	2 tblsp	3 tblsp
Worcestershire sauce	½ tblsp	1 tblsp	1½ tblsp
Dried dill	¾ tsp	½ tblsp	2 tsp
Grated nutmeg	¼ tsp	½ tsp	¾ tsp
Unsalted butter, melted and cooled for 5 minutes	2 tblsp	4 tblsp (½ stick)	6 tblsp (¾ stick)
All-purpose flour	1½ tblsp	3 tblsp	⅓ cup

1 Stir the broth, tomato paste, evaporated milk, cream, honey, Worcestershire sauce, dill, and nutmeg in the slow cooker.

2 Cover and cook on high for 2½ hours or on low for 5 hours, or until the soup is thick, rich, and creamy.

(continued)

3 Stir the butter and flour in a small bowl to make a thick paste. Whisk it into the soup by the teaspoonful until smooth. Cover and cook on high for 1 hour, or until thickened.

TESTERS' NOTES

• A velvety soup that needs nothing more than some fresh grinds of black pepper, this rich meal is best in the winter, when tomatoes are not at their best. Tomato paste saves the day!

• For the best results, spend ten bucks on several brands of tomato paste and do a taste test. Some will taste flat and dull, others will be too sour, and a few will be just right.

corn chowder

EFFORT: **A LITTLE** • PREP TIME: **25 MINUTES** • COOK TIME: **3 HOURS 15 MINUTES/7 HOURS 15 MINUTES** • KEEPS ON WARM: **3 HOURS THROUGH STEP 2** • SERVES: **3 TO 8**

INGREDIENTS	2- TO 3½-QT	4- TO 5½-QT	6- TO 8-QT
Low-sodium chicken broth	2 cups	4 cups (1 quart)	6 cups (1½ quarts)
Corn kernels, fresh cut from the cob, or frozen, thawed	2 cups	4 cups	6 cups
Peeled and cubed Russet or other baking potatoes	¾ cup	1½ cups	2¼ cups
Chopped yellow onion	½ cup	¾ cup	1¼ cups
Stemmed, seeded, and chopped red bell pepper	¼ cup	½ cup	¾ cup
Medium celery ribs, chopped	1	2	3
Moderately sweet wine	¼ cup	½ cup	¾ cup
Dried thyme	½ tsp	1 tsp	½ tblsp
Ground cumin	½ tsp	1 tsp	½ tblsp
Dry mustard (see page 392)	½ tsp	1 tsp	½ tblsp
Minced garlic	½ tsp	1 tsp	½ tblsp
Salt	¼ tsp	½ tsp	¾ tsp
Ground black pepper	¼ tsp	½ tsp	¾ tsp
Heavy cream	¼ cup	½ cup	¾ cup

1 Stir the broth, corn, potatoes, onion, bell pepper, celery, wine, thyme, cumin, mustard, garlic, salt, and pepper together in the slow cooker.

2 Cover and cook on high for 3 hours or on low for 7 hours, or until the potatoes are very tender.

3 Use an immersion blender in the slow cooker, or ladle the soup into a large blender to puree it with the cream. Cover and cook on high for 15 minutes to warm through.

TESTERS' NOTES

• Do you have to blend the soup? Of course not—you can leave it chunky.

• To puree a soup in a blender, ladle about half into the canister, then stir in the cream. Take the center knob out of the lid, cover the canister, and set a clean kitchen towel over the lid. Blend until smooth, scraping down the inside of the canister once or twice. Pour the puree into a large bowl, then continue on, blending more. Finally, stir the blended mixture back into the soup. If your blender is too small to handle half the soup, particularly for the large batch in the large slow cooker, you'll then need to work in batches.

• A fairly sweet white wine like a Viognier would complement the corn.

• Some heat might be welcome here; consider adding up to 1 teaspoon red pepper flakes for the large batch (less for the smaller ones).

ALL-AMERICAN KNOW-HOW The top knob of the blender lid can be removed, specifically to help prevent blender explosions with hot ingredients. Pressure builds under the cap, creating a little vortex. Soon enough, you have filthy kitchen cupboards. That said, when you remove that top knob to alleviate some (but not all!) of the pressure, cover the lid with a clean kitchen towel to forestall a small mess.

french onion soup

EFFORT: **A LITTLE** • PREP TIME: **30 MINUTES** • COOK TIME: **8 HOURS** • KEEPS ON WARM: **5 HOURS THROUGH STEP 2** • SERVES: **4 TO 10**

INGREDIENTS	2- TO 3½-QT	4- TO 5½-QT	6- TO 8-QT
Unsalted butter	2 tblsp	3 tblsp	5 tblsp
Yellow onions, chopped	4 medium	4 large	7 large
Low-sodium beef broth	5 cups (1 quart plus 1 cup)	8 cups (2 quarts)	12 cups (3 quarts)
Brandy	2 tblsp	3 tblsp	⅓ cup
Fresh thyme leaves, stemmed	2 tsp	1 tblsp	1½ tblsp
Bay leaves	1	2	3
Salt	½ tsp	¾ tsp	½ tblsp
Ground black pepper	½ tsp	¾ tsp	½ tblsp
Slices of baguette, about 1 inch thick	4	6	10
Gruyère cheese, grated (see page 274)	4 ounces (about 1 cup)	6 ounces (about 1½ cups)	10 ounces (about 2½ cups)

1 Melt the butter in a large skillet set over medium-low heat. Add the onions, reduce the heat to low, and cook, stirring often, until they are soft and glistening, about 20 minutes. Raise the heat to medium-high and cook, stirring almost constantly, to brown the onions a bit, about 5 minutes.

2 Scrape the onions into the slow cooker. Stir in the broth, brandy, thyme, bay leaves, salt, and pepper. Cover and cook on low for 8 hours, or until sweet smelling and rich.

3 Before serving, position the oven rack 4 to 6 inches from the broiler and heat the broiler. Lay the baguette rounds on a large baking sheet; divide the cheese among them, about ¼ cup on each. Broil until melted and bubbling. Float one of these on top of each bowl of soup.

TESTERS' NOTES
• The slow cooker makes a simple job of this bistro favorite. The only hard part is getting those onions soft and sweet *before* they hit the slow cooker. That said, you don't need to cook them as long as you might if you were simmering the soup on the stovetop because those onions are going to go even longer in the cooker.
• Don't use frozen chopped onions for this dish. They'll be too soft and wet, and won't caramelize well.
• Originally, cognac would have been added to the soup, but brandy works just fine.

INGREDIENTS EXPLAINED There's not much good beef broth out there. The USDA sets the required formula at 1 ounce of beef (trimmings) for every gallon of water. Clearly, this ratio leads to a lack of flavor, which some brands fix with chemical additives including MSG (often labeled as "natural flavorings"). The best varieties are made with condensed beef stock, an ingredient on the label that ensures more beefy flavor in every spoonful.

vegetable "penicillin"

EFFORT: **NOT MUCH** • PREP TIME: **20 MINUTES** • COOK TIME:
4 HOURS/6 HOURS • KEEPS ON WARM: **2 HOURS** • SERVES: **3 TO 8**

INGREDIENTS	2- TO 3½-QT	4- TO 5½-QT	6- TO 8-QT
Low-sodium vegetable broth	3½ cups	6 cups (1½ quarts)	10 cups (2½ quarts)
Cauliflower florets	1 cup	2 cups	3 cups
Cored and shredded green cabbage	1 cup	2 cups	3 cups
Stemmed, seeded, and chopped red bell pepper	½ cup	⅔ cup	1 cup
Peeled and grated sweet potato	½ cup	⅔ cup	1 cup
Chopped ripe tomatoes	½ cup	⅔ cup	1 cup
Chopped yellow onion	¼ cup	½ cup	¾ cup
Minced peeled fresh ginger	Up to 1½ tblsp	Up to 2½ tblsp	Up to ¼ cup
Dried dill	1 tsp	2 tsp	1 tblsp
Minced garlic	½ tsp	1 tsp	1 tsp
Salt	½ tsp	¾ tsp	1 tsp
Ground black pepper	½ tsp	¾ tsp	1 tsp

1 Stir the broth, cauliflower, cabbage, bell pepper, sweet potato, tomato, onion, ginger, dill, garlic, salt, and pepper in the slow cooker.

2 Cover and cook on high for 4 hours or on low for 6 hours, or until the vegetables are tender.

TESTERS' NOTES

• Nothing will ease the chill or maybe even that seasonal cold like a bowl of this warm soup. It will also freeze well, sealed in containers, for up to 4 months, a boon for future sniffles.

• A 1-pound head of cauliflower will yield about 3 cups of florets.

• The amount of fresh ginger for this soup is up to you; the full amount will be a bit spicy. Or use less and the soup will be easier on the throat (if you've got a sore one).

SHORTCUTS Look for many of these vegetables already prepared in the produce section of your supermarket or even on the salad bar. Yes, they may cost a little more; but the convenience can outweigh the economics. Save the trouble of coring and chopping the cabbage by substituting bagged shredded cabbage.

ALL-AMERICAN KNOW-HOW To shred cabbage, cut the head in half through the center, then cut out the tough core in each half. Slice the halves as thinly as possible, then use your fingers to pull those slices into long threads. Or cut the cabbage into wedges, core these, and shred them in a food processor fitted with the shredding blade.

cheddar and beer soup

EFFORT: **NOT MUCH** • PREP TIME: **15 MINUTES** • COOK TIME:
6 HOURS 30 MINUTES • KEEPS ON WARM: **2 HOURS THROUGH STEP 2** • SERVES: **4 TO 10**

INGREDIENTS	2- TO 3½-QT	4- TO 5½-QT	6- TO 8-QT
Low-sodium chicken broth	3 cups	5 cups (1 quart plus 1 cup)	8 cups (2 quarts)
Beer, 12-ounce bottles (Pilsner, IPA, or Lager)	1	1½	2

White or yellow potatoes, peeled and finely chopped	5 ounces (about 1 cup)	9 ounces (about 1½ cups)	12 ounces (about 2½ cups)
Yellow onion, finely chopped	1 small	1 medium	3 small
Dried thyme	2 tsp	1 tblsp	1½ tblsp
Dry mustard (see page 392)	2 tsp	1 tblsp	1½ tblsp
Worcestershire sauce	2 tsp	1 tblsp	1½ tblsp
Minced garlic	2 tsp	1 tblsp	1½ tblsp
Sharp Cheddar cheese, shredded	11 ounces (about 2¾ cups)	1 pound 2 ounces (about 4½ cups)	1¾ pounds (about 7 cups)
Hot pepper sauce	½ tsp	¾ tsp	1 tsp

1 Stir the broth, beer, potatoes, onion, thyme, mustard, Worcestershire sauce, and garlic in the slow cooker.

2 Cover and cook on low for 6 hours, or until the potato pieces are tender.

3 Stir in the cheese and hot pepper sauce. Cover and continue cooking on low for 30 minutes, or until the cheese has melted.

TESTERS' NOTES
• This classic American tavern soup is best the day it's made, when the cheese is gooey and rich.
• We're all for cheese here, just not the fake stuff, sometimes labeled "cheese food product." If you're going, you might as well go all the way.

SHORTCUTS Substitute frozen grated hash browns for the potatoes. Make sure the hash browns are plain, not seasoned, though. Thaw them in the fridge overnight before adding them to the soup.

yellow bell pepper soup

EFFORT: **A LITTLE** • PREP TIME: **20 MINUTES** • COOK TIME: **3 HOURS/5 HOURS** • KEEPS ON WARM: **3 HOURS BEFORE STEP 2** • SERVES: **3 TO 10**

INGREDIENTS	2- TO 3½-QT	4- TO 5½-QT	6- TO 8-QT
Low-sodium chicken broth	3 cups	6 cups (1½ quarts)	10 cups (2½ quarts)
Medium yellow bell peppers, stemmed, seeded, and roughly chopped	4	8	14
Chopped yellow onion	½ cup	1 cup	1¾ cups
Chopped carrot	½ cup	1 cup	1¾ cups
Fresh thyme sprigs	2	4	6
Salt	½ tsp	1 tsp	½ tblsp
Ground black pepper	½ tsp	1 tsp	½ tblsp
Heavy cream	½ cup	1 cup	1½ cups

1 Stir the broth, bell peppers, onion, carrot, thyme, salt, and pepper in the slow cooker.

2 Cover and cook on high for 3 hours or on low for 5 hours, or until the vegetables are quite tender.

3 Use an immersion blender in the slow cooker, or ladle the soup in batches as necessary into a large blender; puree with the cream. Cover and cook on low for 15 minutes to heat through.

TESTERS' NOTES
• Yellow bell peppers offer a distinctly summery sweetness. Best of all, the soup freezes well, so stock up for the cold months.

(continued)

• Cook the soup until the vegetables are soft, even mushy. You're going to puree it, after all.

Serve It Up! Garnish with pomegranate seeds or dehydrated vegetables of any sort, like those green bean bits or bell pepper pieces found in most supermarkets. Or go really simple and decorate the top of each bowlful with a few drops of extra-virgin olive oil and two saffron threads.

ALL-AMERICAN KNOW-HOW To cut a bell pepper into strips, stand it stem up on your cutting board. Use a sharp knife to slice down the sides, taking the flesh off the core as you work around the pepper until you're left holding the stem with the chambers of seeds below. Discard this core, then slice the pieces of pepper into the requisite strips.

potato leek soup

EFFORT: **A LITTLE** • PREP TIME: **20 MINUTES** • COOK TIME: **4 HOURS 15 MINUTES/7 HOURS 15 MINUTES** • KEEPS ON WARM: **4 HOURS THROUGH STEP 1** • SERVES: **3 TO 8**

INGREDIENTS	2- TO 3½-QT	4- TO 5½-QT	6- TO 8-QT
Low-sodium chicken broth	3 cups	4½ cups	7 cups (1 quart plus 3 cups)
Leeks (white and pale green part only), halved lengthwise, washed to remove internal grit, then thinly sliced	1 pound	2 pounds	3 pounds
Russet or other baking potatoes, peeled and diced	6 ounces	10 ounces	1½ pounds
Unsalted butter, cut into small bits	1 tblsp	2 tblsp	3 tblsp
Salt	½ tsp	¾ tsp	1 tsp
Ground black pepper	½ tsp	¾ tsp	1 tsp
Heavy cream	¼ cup	½ cup	⅔ cup
Minced fresh chervil (optional)	2 tblsp	¼ cup	6 tblsp

1 Mix the broth, leeks, potatoes, butter, salt, and pepper in the slow cooker. Cover and cook on high for 4 hours or on low for 7 hours, or until the potatoes are very soft.

2 Stir in the cream. Use an immersion blender in the slow cooker, or ladle the soup in batches as necessary into a large blender to puree until smooth. Stir in the chervil (if using), cover, and cook on low for 15 minutes to heat through.

TESTERS' NOTES
• Exceptionally simple, this soup makes a straightforward, fuss-free meal. But to take it over the top, substitute chicken fat or even duck fat for the butter—and while you're at it, garnish the bowlfuls with fried chicken skin.
• Russet or other baking potatoes will have the right balance of starch, so that the soup tastes rich when pureed.

Serve It Up! Garnish the bowls with shredded Cheddar cheese, crumbled crisp bacon, slivered sun-dried tomatoes, diced radishes, or even diced firm pears. Each will take the soup in a different direction. Or offer them all at the table and let each person customize a bowlful.

ALL-AMERICAN KNOW-HOW Leeks are prone to sandy grit, particularly in the interior layers. To remove the grit, cut off and discard the tough upper leaves, then slice the white and pale green part in half lengthwise. Rinse under cool tap water, separating the inner layers to flush out the grit. Yep, you'll dope the vegetable with moisture; you can pull most of that out over the heat.

orzo soup with oregano, lemon, and dill

EFFORT: **NOT MUCH** • PREP TIME: **15 MINUTES** • COOK TIME: **5 HOURS** • KEEP ON WARM: **NO** • SERVES: **4 TO 10**

INGREDIENTS	2- TO 3½-QT	4- TO 5½-QT	6- TO 8-QT
Low-sodium chicken broth	4 cups (1 quart)	6 cups (1½ quarts)	10 cups (2½ quarts)
Dried orzo	¾ cup	1¼ cups	2 cups
Yellow onion, chopped	1 small	1 medium	1 large
Yellow bell pepper, stemmed, seeded, and chopped	⅔ cup	1 cup (about 1 medium)	1⅔ cups
Minced fresh oregano leaves	2 tsp	1 tblsp	1½ tblsp
Minced fresh dill fronds	2 tsp	1 tblsp	1½ tblsp
Drained and minced capers	2 tsp	1 tblsp	1½ tblsp
Minced garlic	½ tblsp	2 tsp	1 tblsp
Finely grated lemon zest	½ tsp	1 tsp	½ tblsp
Salt	¼ tsp	½ tsp	¾ tsp

1 Stir the broth, orzo, onion, bell pepper, oregano, dill, capers, garlic, lemon zest, and salt in the slow cooker.

2 Cover and cook on low for 5 hours, or until the pasta is tender.

TESTERS' NOTES
• If you like a thinner soup, double the broth in this herb-heavy recipe.
• Use whole wheat orzo for a firmer texture.

• For a treat, omit the salt and add minced anchovy fillets instead: up to 1 fillet for the small slow cooker, 2 for a medium one, and 3 for a large. The tiny bits will melt into the soup, giving it a salty, sophisticated taste.

INGREDIENTS EXPLAINED Orzo (*OR-zoh*, Italian for "barley") is a small pasta shaped like large rice grains.

butternut squash soup

EFFORT: **NOT MUCH** • PREP TIME: **20 MINUTES** • COOK TIME: **3 HOURS 15 MINUTES/7 HOURS 15 MINUTES** • KEEPS ON WARM: **4 HOURS THROUGH STEP 1** • SERVES: **4 TO 10**

INGREDIENTS	2- TO 3½-QT	4- TO 5½-QT	6- TO 8-QT
Low-sodium vegetable broth	4 cups (1 quart)	6 cups (1½ quarts)	9 cups (2 quarts plus 1 cup)
Peeled, seeded, and cubed butternut squash	2 cups	3 cups	4½ cups
Carrots, diced	2 ounces	¼ pound	½ pound
Medium celery ribs, diced	1	1½	2
Fresh lemon juice	1½ tblsp	2 tblsp	3 tblsp
Mild paprika	2 tsp	1 tblsp	½ tblsp
Salt	½ tsp	1 tsp	½ tblsp

1 Stir the broth, butternut squash, carrots, celery, lemon juice, paprika, and salt in the slow cooker. Cover and cook on high for 3 hours or on low for 7 hours, or until the vegetables are very soft.

(continued)

2 Puree the soup with an immersion blender right in the slow cooker; or ladle the soup into a large blender, working in batches as necessary, and puree it before returning it to the slow cooker. Cover and cook on low for 15 minutes to heat through. Serve with a pat of butter on each bowlful, if desired.

TESTERS' NOTES

• Although butternut squash is very sweet, it's a tad dull in the slow cooker. Carrots give the soup an earthiness; celery keeps the flavors fresher.

• For a slightly sweeter but also less earthy soup, add some chopped yellow onion with the other vegetables: ⅓ cup in a small slow cooker, ½ cup in a medium one, and up to ¾ cup in a large model.

sauerkraut soup

EFFORT: **NOT MUCH** • PREP TIME: **15 MINUTES** • COOK TIME: **5 HOURS 15 MINUTES** • KEEPS ON WARM: **4 HOURS** • SERVES: **3 TO 8**

INGREDIENTS	2- TO 3½-QT	4- TO 5½-QT	6- TO 8-QT
Packaged sauerkraut, drained and squeezed dry	1 pound	1½ pounds	2½ pounds
Low-sodium chicken broth	3 cups	4½ cups (1 quart plus ½ cup)	8 cups (2 quarts)
Cremini or brown button mushrooms, thinly sliced	4 ounces	8 ounces	11 ounces
Carrots, thinly sliced	4 ounces	7 ounces	11 ounces
Yellow potatoes (such as Yukon Gold), peeled and diced	3 ounces	5 ounces	8 ounces
Hard cider	¾ cup	1¼ cups	2 cups
Thyme sprigs	2	3	5
Minced fresh dill fronds	2 tblsp	3 tblsp	⅓ cup
Cider vinegar	2 tblsp	3 tblsp	⅓ cup
Sugar	1 tblsp	1½ tblsp	2½ tblsp
Ground black pepper	½ tsp	¾ tsp	1¼ tsp

1 Stir the sauerkraut, broth, mushrooms, carrot, potato, cider, and thyme sprigs in the slow cooker. Cover and cook on low for 5 hours.

2 Stir in the dill, vinegar, sugar, and pepper. Cover and continue cooking on low for 15 minutes to heat through. Discard the thyme sprigs before serving.

TESTERS' NOTES

• A preserved vegetable, sauerkraut makes a wonderful soup, slightly sour but also fragrantly sweet after hours of cooking. Don't use the sauerkraut in cans; instead, use the refrigerated kind found near the deli counter or the meat case.

• Squeezing the sauerkraut by handfuls will help get rid of its overly assertive edge and some of its sodium, as well as a lot of water that can bog down the soup.

• You can also add sliced smoked, ready-to-eat sausage (like smoked kielbasa) with the other ingredients in step 2: ½ pound for a small batch, 1 pound for a medium batch, or 1½ pounds for a large one. Cover and continue cooking about 30 minutes, until heated through.

INGREDIENTS EXPLAINED Hard cider is fermented apple cider, available at most liquor stores and some supermarkets. If you don't want the alcohol, substitute sparkling nonalcoholic apple cider.

cabbage and bacon soup

EFFORT: **A LITTLE** • PREP TIME: **20 MINUTES** • COOK TIME: **3 HOURS/6 HOURS** • KEEPS ON WARM: **3 HOURS THROUGH STEP 2** • SERVES: **3 TO 8**

INGREDIENTS	2- TO 3½-QT	4- TO 5½-QT	6- TO 8-QT
Unsalted butter	1 tblsp	2 tblsp	3 tblsp
Thin strips of bacon	6	8	12
Low-sodium chicken broth	4 cups (1 quart)	6 cups (1½ quarts)	10 cups (2½ quarts)
Cored and shredded white or green cabbage (see page 60)	4 cups	6 cups (about 1 pound)	10 cups
Drained and rinsed canned white beans	1¾ cups	2½ cups	4 cups
Dried thyme	¾ tsp	1¼ tsp	2 tsp
Caraway seeds	¾ tsp	1¼ tsp	2 tsp
Salt	½ tsp	¾ tsp	1¼ tsp
Ground black pepper	½ tsp	¾ tsp	1¼ tsp
Cider vinegar	1 tblsp	1½ tblsp	2½ tblsp

1 Melt the butter in a large skillet set over medium heat. Add the bacon and cook, stirring often, until crisp and crunchy, between 4 and 8 minutes. Scrape the contents of the skillet into the slow cooker.

2 Stir the broth, cabbage, beans, thyme, caraway seeds, salt, and pepper into the slow cooker. Cover and cook on high for 3 hours or on low for 6 hours, stirring once or twice, until the cabbage has wilted and turned tender.

3 Stir in the vinegar just before serving to brighten the flavors.

TESTERS' NOTES
• The slow cooker will be packed to the brim with this one, but don't worry; the cabbage will wilt and condense as it cooks.
• Fry the bacon until it is legitimately crisp. It needs to stand up to the long cooking.
• Add up to 1 teaspoon red pepper flakes for spicy notes in the soup.

garlic soup

EFFORT: **A LOT** • PREP TIME: **25 MINUTES** • COOK TIME: **7 HOURS 15 MINUTES** • KEEPS ON WARM: **3 HOURS THROUGH STEP 2** • SERVES: **3 TO 8**

INGREDIENTS	2- TO 3½-QT	4- TO 5½-QT	6- TO 8-QT
Unsalted butter	1 tblsp	2 tblsp	3 tblsp
Yellow onions, chopped	1 medium	2 small	2 medium
Thinly sliced garlic	6 tblsp	⅔ cup	1 cup
Low-sodium chicken broth	4 cups (1 quart)	6 cups (1½ quarts)	10 cups (2½ quarts)
Russet or other baking potatoes, peeled and diced	¾ pound (about 2½ cups)	1¼ pounds (about 4 cups)	1¾ pounds (about 6½ cups)
Chopped fresh sage leaves	2 tsp	1 tblsp	1½ tblsp
Mild paprika	2 tsp	1 tblsp	1½ tblsp
Salt	¼ tsp	½ tsp	¾ tsp
Heavy cream	½ cup	¾ cup	1¼ cups

1 Melt the butter in a large skillet over medium heat. Add the onions; cook, stirring often, until they soften and turn translucent, between 4 and 7 minutes. Add the garlic and

(continued)

continue cooking, stirring often, until it just begins to brown at the edges of the slivers.

2 Scrape the contents of the skillet into the slow cooker. Add the broth, potatoes, sage, paprika, and salt to the slow cooker. Cover and cook on low for 7 hours, or until the potatoes are ridiculously soft.

3 Puree the soup with the cream: use an immersion blender right in the slow cooker, or ladle the soup into a large blender, most likely in batches, cover, and blend until smooth before pouring it back into the slow cooker. Cover and cook on low for 15 minutes to heat through.

TESTERS' NOTES

• Garlic soup is a ridiculous indulgence, strangely sweet yet very aromatic. You might want to steer clear of human contact afterwards.
• For some smokiness in the soup, substitute smoked paprika for the mild sweet paprika.

Serve It Up! For a fancy presentation, omit the sage from the soup, then fry sage leaves in olive oil until crisp and float them on top of the servings.

beet soup

EFFORT: **A LITTLE** • PREP TIME: **15 MINUTES** • COOK TIME: **4 HOURS/8 HOURS** • KEEPS ON WARM: **4 HOURS THROUGH STEP 2** • SERVES: **3 TO 10**

INGREDIENTS	2- TO 3½-QT	4- TO 5½-QT	6- TO 8-QT
Low-sodium vegetable broth	2½ cups	5 cups	7½ cups
No-salt-added tomato paste	2½ tblsp	⅓ cup	½ cup
Red wine vinegar	1 tblsp	2 tblsp	3 tblsp
Dried dill	¾ tsp	1¼ tsp	2 tsp
Salt	¼ tsp	½ tsp	¾ tsp
Red beets, peeled and chopped	1 pound (about 3 cups)	2½ pounds (about 8 cups)	3½ pounds (about 11 cups)
Russet or other baking potatoes, peeled and chopped	10 ounces (about 1 cup)	1⅓ pounds (about 2 cups)	2 pounds (about 3 cups)
Red onion, chopped	1 small	1 medium	1 large

1 Stir the broth, tomato paste, vinegar, dill, and salt in the slow cooker until the tomato paste dissolves. Mix in the beets, potatoes, and onion. Cover and cook on high for 4 hours or on low for 8 hours, or until the vegetables are very tender.

2 Use an immersion blender right in the cooker to puree the soup, or work in batches as necessary and ladle it into a large blender, cover, and blend until smooth.

TESTERS' NOTES

• Beets are incredibly sweet, so a touch of vinegar in the mix mellows their assertiveness and curiously makes the earthy taste all the more present.
• Be careful of your counters and clothes. Beets will stain everything in sight. To avoid beet stains on your hands, wear rubber gloves when chopping the vegetable.

Serve It Up! There are two ways to eat this soup. For one traditional preparation, heat the puree in the slow cooker, covered, on low, for 15 minutes, then serve with a hot boiled potato in each bowl. Or for an alternative, chill the puree in a covered bowl in the fridge for up to 3 days and serve the cold soup with dollops of sour cream on top.

root vegetable bisque

EFFORT: **A LOT** • PREP TIME: **30 MINUTES** • COOK TIME: **4 HOURS 15 MINUTES/8 HOURS 15 MINUTES** • KEEPS ON WARM: **4 HOURS THROUGH STEP 2** • SERVES: **3 TO 8**

INGREDIENTS	2- TO 3½-QT	4- TO 5½-QT	6- TO 8-QT
Unsalted butter	½ tblsp	1 tblsp	2 tblsp
Yellow onion, chopped	1 small	1 medium	1 large
Low-sodium chicken broth	3 cups	5 cups	8 cups (2 quarts)
Medium celery ribs, thinly sliced	4	6	10
Peeled and thinly sliced parsnips	1 cup (about 5 ounces)	2 cups (about 10 ounces)	3 cups (about 1 pound)
Peeled and diced yellow potato	⅔ cup	1 cup	1¾ cups (about ½ pound)
Garlic cloves, peeled	1	2	3
Cayenne	Up to ⅛ tsp	Up to ¼ tsp	Up to ½ tsp
Salt	¼ tsp	½ tsp	¾ tsp
Heavy cream	⅔ cup	1 cup	1¾ cups
Finely grated orange zest	1 tblsp	2 tblsp	2½ tblsp

1 Melt the butter in a large skillet set over medium heat. Add the onion and cook, stirring often, until softened, between 4 and 6 minutes. Scrape the contents of the skillet into the slow cooker.

2 Stir the broth, celery, parsnips, potato, garlic, cayenne, and salt into the slow cooker. Cover and cook on high for 4 hours or on low for 8 hours, or until the vegetables are meltingly tender.

3 Puree the soup with the cream and orange zest by using an immersion blender right in the slow cooker, or by ladling the soup (in batches as needed) into a large blender and whirring it until smooth before pouring it back into the slow cooker. Cover and cook on low for 15 minutes to heat through.

TESTERS' NOTES
• Although a traditional bisque is thickened with a roux (a flour and butter mixture), there's none here because of the way the slow cooker works. But you won't miss it because of the layered flavors and textural nuance the root vegetables bring to the soup. Frankly, the longer you let it keep warm through step 2 (within reason), the deeper the flavor will become.
• If you'd like, give the soup a savory twist by adding a small amount of ground cumin: ¼ teaspoon for the small batch, ½ teaspoon for the medium, and ¾ teaspoon for the large.
• In storage, the orange zest can cause the cream to curdle. If you intend to make the soup and save back servings in the fridge or freezer, omit the zest from the soup and use it as a garnish in the bowls.

Serve It Up! Ladle the soup over homemade croutons in the bowls (see page 157). Also grate Manchego or Pecorino over each serving.

broccoli cheddar soup

EFFORT: **A LITTLE** • PREP TIME: **15 MINUTES** • COOK TIME:
3 HOURS/5 HOURS • KEEPS ON WARM: **2 HOURS THROUGH STEP 1**
• SERVES: **3 TO 8**

INGREDIENTS	2- TO 3½-QT	4- TO 5½-QT	6- TO 8-QT
Low-sodium chicken broth	2½ cups	4½ cups (1 quart plus ½ cup)	6 cups (1½ cups)
Broccoli florets	2½ cups (about 1¼ pounds)	4½ cups (about 2¼ pounds)	6 cups (about 3 pounds)
Milk	1 cup	1½ cups	2 cups
Chopped yellow onion	⅓ cup	½ cup	¾ cup
Dried thyme	¼ tsp	½ tsp	¾ tsp
Grated nutmeg	¼ tsp	½ tsp	¾ tsp
Salt	¼ tsp	½ tsp	¾ tsp
Ground black pepper	¼ tsp	½ tsp	¾ tsp
Cheddar cheese, mild or sharp, shredded	8 ounces (about 2 cups)	12 ounces (about 3 cups)	1 pound (about 4 cups)

1 Mix the broth, broccoli florets, milk, onion, thyme, nutmeg, salt, and pepper in the slow cooker. Cover and cook on high for 3 hours or on low for 5 hours, or until the broccoli is beyond tender, extremely soft.

2 Puree the soup with an immersion blender right in the slow cooker; or working in batches as necessary, ladle it into a large blender, blend until smooth, and return to the slow cooker. Stir in the cheese, then cover and cook on low for 30 minutes, until the cheese has melted and the soup is hot.

TESTERS' NOTES
• A family favorite, this soup can be spiked by using jalapeño Cheddar, or it can have a sweet, aromatic finish with port wine Cheddar. Although you don't need to use an aged Cheddar or an expensive white Cheddar, you should also avoid any Cheddar-like processed cheese.
• If you want to go more Wisconsin with this soup, cut the broth in half and use an amber beer or a lager to replace the missing liquid.

cream of white sweet potato soup

EFFORT: **A LITTLE** • PREP TIME: **20 MINUTES** • COOK TIME: **5 HOURS 15 MINUTES** • KEEPS ON WARM: **3 HOURS THROUGH STEP 1** • SERVES: **3 TO 8**

INGREDIENTS	2- TO 3½-QT	4- TO 5½-QT	6- TO 8-QT
White sweet potatoes, peeled and diced	1 pound (about 3 cups)	1 pound 10 ounces (about 5 cups)	2¼ pounds (about 8 cups)
Low-sodium chicken broth	2¾ cups	4 cups (1 quart)	6¾ cups (1 quart plus 2¾ cups)
Yellow potatoes (such as Yukon Gold), peeled and diced	¼ pound (about ⅔ cup)	6 ounces (about 1 cup)	10 ounces (about 1⅔ cups)
Packed light brown sugar	1½ tblsp	3 tblsp	⅓ cup
Dried thyme	¼ tsp	½ tsp	¾ tsp
Salt	¼ tsp	½ tsp	¾ tsp

Ground cloves	⅛ tsp	¼ tsp	½ tsp
Grated nutmeg	⅛ tsp	¼ tsp	½ tsp
4-inch cinnamon stick	½	1	2
Heavy cream	½ cup	¾ cup	1¼ cups

1 Stir the sweet potatoes, broth, potatoes, brown sugar, thyme, salt, cloves, nutmeg, and cinnamon stick together in the slow cooker until the brown sugar dissolves. Cover and cook on low for 5 hours, or until all the potatoes are beyond soft. Discard the cinnamon stick.

2 Stir the cream into the soup. Use an immersion blender to puree the soup right in the slow cooker; or working in batches, ladle the soup into a large blender, cover, and blend until smooth before pouring all of the soup back into the slow cooker. Cover and cook on low for 15 minutes to warm up.

TESTERS' NOTES
• Sweet and earthy, this soup would be the best when you're a tad under the weather. Better yet, make it when you're hale, then freeze some individual servings for when you need it.
• For even cooking results, dice both the sweet potatoes and the yellow potatoes into ¼-inch pieces.
• You can use regular sweet potatoes, although the soup will be garishly orange—sweeter, but not as earthy. You'll want to balance it by drizzling some bottled red pepper sauce over the servings.

INGREDIENTS EXPLAINED White sweet potatoes are popular in the American South—and elsewhere sometimes confused with the white sweet potatoes popular in Asia. The white varieties take longer to mature and develop fewer sugars, resulting in a subtly savory flavor.

ALL-AMERICAN KNOW-HOW Why put the soup back into the slow cooker after pureeing it with the cream? Because the puree has cooled off a bit and the cream needs a few moments of heat to get rid of its raw, unfinished taste.

cream of mushroom soup

EFFORT: **A LITTLE** • PREP TIME: **20 MINUTES** • COOK TIME: **3 HOURS 15 MINUTES/6 HOURS 15 MINUTES** • KEEPS ON WARM: **3 HOURS THROUGH STEP 1** • SERVES: **3 TO 8**

INGREDIENTS	2- TO 3½-QT	4- TO 5½-QT	6- TO 8-QT
White button mushrooms, thinly sliced	11 ounces (about 3½ cups)	1 pound 6 ounces (about 7 cups)	1 pound 14 ounces (about 10 cups)
Low-sodium vegetable broth	2 cups	4 cups (1 quart)	6 cups (1½ quarts)
Shallots, chopped	2 ounces	3 ounces	4 ounces
Minced fresh sage leaves	1 tsp	2 tsp	1 tblsp
Stemmed fresh thyme leaves	1 tsp	½ tblsp	2 tsp
Salt	½ tsp	¾ tsp	1 tsp
Ground black pepper	½ tsp	¾ tsp	1 tsp
Heavy cream	½ cup	1 cup	1½ cups

1 Mix the mushrooms, broth, chopped shallots, sage, thyme, salt, and pepper in the slow cooker. Cover and cook on high for 3 hours or on low for 6 hours, or until the mushrooms are quite soft.

2 Stir the cream into the soup. Puree it by using an immersion blender right in the slow cooker or by ladling it in batches as necessary into a large blender and blending until smooth before pouring it all back into the slow cooker. Cover and cook on low for 15 minutes to heat through. Serve by sprinkling chopped chives over bowlfuls, if desired.

(continued)

TESTERS' NOTES

• Although this is a fine soup for a winter evening, it's also wonderful to have a stash in the freezer, saved in 2- or 3-cup increments, for recipes that call for cream of mushroom soup.

• You can certainly use cremini or brown button mushrooms here, although the soup will be darker, not the traditional creamy white.

• Add up to 2 tablespoons brandy for a little kick.

ALL-AMERICAN KNOW-HOW For almost all of these creamy soups, you can substitute light cream or half-and-half for the heavy cream. However, never use fat-free half-and-half, as it's stocked with sweeteners and artificial thickeners.

cream of parsnip soup with bacon and dill

EFFORT: **A LOT** • PREP TIME: **30 MINUTES** • COOK TIME: **6½ HOURS**
• KEEPS ON WARM: **4 HOURS THROUGH STEP 3** • SERVES: **3 TO 8**

INGREDIENTS	2- TO 3½-QT	4- TO 5½-QT	6- TO 8-QT
Thin strips of bacon	5	8	10
Yellow onion, chopped	1 small	1 medium	1 small and 1 medium
Minced garlic	½ tblsp	2 tsp	1 tblsp
All-purpose flour	1½ tblsp	2 tblsp	2½ tblsp
Parsnips, peeled and thinly sliced	2 pounds	3 pounds	4 pounds
Low-sodium chicken broth	2¾ cups	4 cups (1 quart)	5½ cups
Dry white wine, such as Chardonnay, or dry vermouth	¾ cup	1 cup	1⅓ cups
Heavy cream	6 tblsp	½ cup	¾ cup
Minced fresh dill fronds	1 tblsp	1½ tblsp	2 tblsp

1 Put the bacon in a large high-sided skillet or sauté pan set over medium heat and fry, tossing occasionally, until crisp and brown, between 4 and 8 minutes. Transfer to a plate with a slotted spoon, leaving the grease behind. Chill the bacon in the fridge.

2 Add the onion to the skillet and cook, stirring often, until softened, between 3 and 6 minutes. Add the garlic, stir well, and sprinkle the flour over everything. Stir over the heat for 30 seconds, then whisk in the broth in a slow, steady stream. Continue cooking, stirring all the while, until thickened and bubbling.

3 Scrape the contents of the skillet into the slow cooker. Stir in the parsnips, broth, and wine. Cover and cook on low for 6 hours, until the parsnips are tender.

4 Use a slotted spoon to remove some of the cooked parsnips: about ½ cup from the small batch, 1 cup from the medium batch, or 1½ cups from the large. Stir the cream into the remainder of the soup, then puree it, either by using an immersion blender in the slow cooker or by ladling it into a large blender in batches; cover and blend until smooth before pouring it back into the slow cooker.

5 Stir in the chilled bacon and the dill as well as the reserved parsnips. Cover and cook on high for 30 minutes to heat through.

• Parsnips cook up into an appealing soup; their earthy flavors carry distinctly bright notes. When those flavors are combined with cream and bacon, they make a great meal, particularly with a glass of beer on the side.
• Unless you have a gigantic skillet, you will need to fry the bacon in batches.
• We don't advocate using frozen chopped onions here. The onions need as much flavor as possible to stand up to all that richness.

INGREDIENTS EXPLAINED Dry vermouth is a white wine delicately flavored with herbs and aromatics. It's also fortified, sometimes with a little brandy or other distillate. It should be a pantry staple; it can be stored for up to a year, maybe more. White wine, by contrast, will start to turn—that is, oxidize—within an hour of opening, even if you stopper it and refrigerate the bottle. In all but the fussiest recipes, vermouth can be substituted for dry white wine. It's a bit more savory, but it does exceptionally well in slow-cooker recipes where sweeter flavors tend to be amplified by the cooking method.

smoky bacon lentil soup

EFFORT: **A LITTLE** • PREP TIME: **20 MINUTES** • COOK TIME: **3 HOURS/7 HOURS** • KEEPS ON WARM: **2 HOURS** • SERVES: **3 TO 8**

INGREDIENTS	2- TO 3½-QT	4- TO 5½-QT	6- TO 8-QT
Slab bacon, diced	8 ounces	12 ounces	1¼ pounds
Yellow onions, chopped	1 medium	2 small	2 medium
Chopped carrots	½ cup	¾ cup	1½ cups

	4 cups (1 quart)	6 cups (1½ quarts)	10 cups (2½ quarts)
Low-sodium chicken broth			
Brown lentils (see page 119)	¾ cup	1¼ cups	2 cups
Drained no-salt-added canned diced tomatoes	½ cup	⅔ cup	1¼ cups
No-salt-added tomato paste	1 tblsp	1½ tblsp	3 tblsp
Mild smoked paprika	1 tblsp	1½ tblsp	2½ tblsp
Ground black pepper	½ tsp	¾ tsp	½ tblsp

1 Fry the bacon bits in a large skillet over medium heat until brown and crisp, stirring occasionally, between 6 and 10 minutes. Use a slotted spoon to transfer the pieces to the slow cooker.

2 Add the onions and carrots to the bacon fat in the skillet; cook, stirring often, until the onions are translucent, between 3 and 5 minutes. Scrape the contents of the skillet into the slow cooker. Stir in the broth, lentils, tomatoes, tomato paste, smoked paprika, and pepper.

3 Cover and cook on high for 3 hours or on low for 7 hours, or until the lentils are tender.

TESTERS' NOTES
• Although there's a little to do at the stove here, it's hard to imagine a simpler soup, one you'll be glad to find when you come home from the day. The smoky bacon bits pair gorgeously with the earthy, slightly musky lentils.
• Swap other vegetables for the carrot: diced peeled butternut squash, chopped fennel, chopped parsnips, or diced peeled sweet potatoes. In the case of the squash and the sweet potatoes, the pieces must be diced: ¼-inch cubes.

Serve It Up! Poach eggs in warm water until the yolks are barely set. Use a slotted spoon to transfer the eggs to bowls, then ladle the soup over them.

lentil soup

EFFORT: NOT MUCH • PREP TIME: **10 MINUTES** • COOK TIME: **4 HOURS/8 HOURS** • KEEPS ON WARM: **2 HOURS** • SERVES: **3 TO 8**

INGREDIENTS	2- TO 3½-QT	4- TO 5½-QT	6- TO 8-QT
Low-sodium vegetable broth	4½ cups (1 quart plus ½ cup)	8 cups (2 quarts)	12 cups (3 quarts)
Yellow onions, chopped	1 medium	2 medium	2 large
Brown lentils (see page 449)	¾ cup	1⅔ cups	2½ cups
Thinly sliced carrots	½ cup	1½ cups	2⅓ cups
Dried thyme	1 tsp	½ tblsp	1 tblsp
Dried sage	½ tsp	¾ tsp	½ tblsp
Salt	½ tsp	¾ tsp	1 tsp
Ground black pepper	½ tsp	¾ tsp	1 tsp

1 Stir the broth, onions, lentils, carrots, thyme, sage, salt, and pepper in the slow cooker.

2 Cover and cook on high for 4 hours or on low for 8 hours, or until the lentils are soft and luxurious.

TESTERS' NOTES

• Lentil soup is hearty and filling, a very earthy soup that's best for a chilly evening. Add up to 2 teaspoons red pepper flakes for some culinary heat.

• Add more vegetables if you like: for the largest slow cooker, up to ½ cup thinly sliced celery, 1 cup trimmed and chopped fennel, and/or 1 cup peeled, thinly sliced parsnips. (You won't have as much room for more in the smallest slow cooker.) If you do add more veggies, increase the broth as well, up to 50 percent more for the largest addition of all three.

Serve It Up! Make an easy **Frisée Salad:** Tear feathery bits of frisée lettuce from the root. Dress with a simple vinaigrette made from four parts walnut oil and one part cider vinegar, whisking in a dab of Dijon mustard and Worcestershire sauce before pouring it over the frisée.

southwestern split pea soup

EFFORT: NOT MUCH • PREP TIME: **15 MINUTES** • COOK TIME: **9 HOURS** • KEEPS ON WARM: **1 HOUR** • SERVES: **3 TO 9**

INGREDIENTS	2- TO 3½-QT	4- TO 5½-QT	6- TO 8-QT
Green split peas	1 cup (about 8 ounces)	2 cups (about 1 pound)	3 cups (about 1½ pounds)
Low-sodium vegetable broth	4 cups (1 quart)	8 cups (2 quarts)	12 cups (3 quarts)
Yellow onion, chopped	1 small	1 medium	2 medium
Minced canned mild green chiles	3 tblsp	⅓ cup	½ cup
Minced fresh cilantro leaves	3 tblsp	⅓ cup	½ cup
Unsalted butter	1 tblsp	2 tblsp	3 tblsp
Minced garlic	1 tsp	2 tsp	1 tblsp
Ground cumin	¾ tsp	1¼ tsp	2 tsp
Ground cinnamon	½ tsp	1 tsp	½ tblsp
Ground cloves	⅛ tsp	¼ tsp	½ tsp
Bay leaves	1	2	3

1 Rinse the split peas in a colander set in the sink.

2 Pour them into the slow cooker along with the broth, onion, chiles, cilantro, butter, garlic, cumin, cinnamon, cloves, and bay leaves. Cover and cook on low for 9 hours, or until the split peas are meltingly tender. Discard the bay leaf or leaves before serving.

TESTERS' NOTES
• Sort of a salsa verde version of split pea soup, this recipe shows our deep love for the foods of the American Southwest.
• For a spicier finish, don't use canned green chiles. Instead, add some red pepper flakes, up to 1 tablespoon in the large batch, or sprinkle some ancho chile powder into the mix—up to 1 tablespoon in the large batch.

chestnut and yellow split pea soup

EFFORT: **A LITTLE** • PREP TIME: **15 MINUTES** • COOK TIME: **7 HOURS 15 MINUTES** • KEEPS ON WARM: **1 HOUR THROUGH STEP 1** • SERVES: **3 TO 8**

INGREDIENTS	2- TO 3½-QT	4- TO 5½-QT	6- TO 8-QT
Low-sodium chicken broth	3 cups	4 cups (1 quart)	7 cups
Jarred steamed or roasted chestnuts	1 cup	1½ cups	2¾ cups
Yellow split peas	¾ cup	1 cup	1¾ cups
Chopped yellow onion	¼ cup	⅓ cup	½ cup
Stemmed fresh thyme leaves	2 tsp	1 tblsp	1½ tblsp
Grated nutmeg	¼ tsp	½ tsp	¾ tsp
Salt	¼ tsp	½ tsp	¾ tsp
Ground black pepper	¼ tsp	½ tsp	¾ tsp
Heavy cream	3 tblsp	¼ cup	⅓ cup

1 Stir the broth, chestnuts, split peas, onion, thyme, nutmeg, salt, and pepper in the slow cooker. Cover and cook on low for 7 hours, or until the soup is quite thick.

2 Stir in the cream. Use an immersion blender to puree the soup in the slow cooker; or working in batches, puree the soup in a large blender by ladling some in, covering, and blending until smooth, all before pouring it back into the slow cooker. Cover and cook on low for 15 minutes.

TESTERS' NOTES
• Yellow split peas give this soup most of its body. It's warm and mild, great for a late fall or early spring evening.
• For a bit more decadence, add up to 2 tablespoons unsalted butter with the broth and other ingredients.
• Black pepper will indeed leave dark dots in the soup. Use ground white pepper, if you prefer.

INGREDIENTS EXPLAINED Yellow split peas are simply the yellow version of the more familiar green split peas. Look for yellow split peas near the other dried beans or in the aisle with Latin American foods. Don't confuse yellow split peas with East Indian chana dal.

black bean soup

EFFORT: **A LITTLE** • PREP TIME: **12 HOURS 20 MINUTES (INCLUDES SOAKING THE BEANS)** • COOK TIME: **10 HOURS 15 MINUTES** • KEEPS ON WARM: **4 HOURS THROUGH STEP 2** • SERVES: **3 TO 8**

INGREDIENTS	2- TO 3½-QT	4- TO 5½-QT	6- TO 8-QT
Dried black beans	1 cup (about ½ pound)	1½ cups (about 12 ounces)	2½ cups (about 1¼ pounds)
Low-sodium beef broth	2 cups	3 cups	5 cups (1 quart plus 1 cup)
Low-sodium chicken broth	2 cups	3 cups	5 cups
Yellow onion, chopped	1 small	1 medium	1 large
Stemmed, seeded, and chopped green bell pepper	⅔ cup	1 cup	1½ cups
Minced fresh cilantro leaves	2 tblsp	3 tblsp	¼ cup
Minced fresh oregano leaves	1 tblsp	1½ tblsp	2 tblsp
Finely grated orange zest	½ tblsp	2 tsp	1 tblsp
Minced garlic	1 tsp	½ tblsp	2 tsp
Ground black pepper	¼ tsp	½ tsp	1 tsp
Bay leaves	1	2	3
4-inch cinnamon stick	½	1	1½
Frozen orange juice concentrate, thawed	1 tblsp	1½ tblsp	2 tblsp
Salt	¼ tsp	½ tsp	1 tsp

1 Pour the beans into a big bowl, fill the bowl about two-thirds full with cool tap water, and set aside to soak for 12 hours or up to 16 hours (that is, overnight).

2 Drain the beans in a colander set in the sink and pour them into the slow cooker. Stir in both broths, the onion, bell pepper, cilantro, oregano, orange zest, garlic, pepper, bay leaves, and cinnamon stick. Cover and cook on low for 10 hours, or until the beans are tender. Find and discard the bay leaves and the cinnamon stick.

3 Stir in the orange juice concentrate and salt. Cover and cook on low for 15 minutes to heat through.

TESTERS' NOTES
• Since salt can toughen black beans as they cook, add it at the end for creamier texture.
• If you want a sour pop, substitute sherry vinegar for the orange juice concentrate.
• Rather than adding heat to the soup itself, pass bottled hot pepper sauce at the table.
• We like a chunky black bean soup. However, you can puree it once the bay leaves and cinnamon stick have been removed. In fact, you don't have to puree the whole batch—you can puree a portion, stirring this back in to thicken the remaining soup.
• Throw a smoked ham hock into the soup as it begins to cook. Afterwards, take out the hock, shred the meat off the bone, and stir that meat into the soup before serving.

pasta and bean soup

EFFORT: **NOT MUCH** • PREP TIME: **20 MINUTES** • COOK TIME: **5 HOURS/7 HOURS** • KEEPS ON WARM: **NO** • SERVES: **2 TO 8**

INGREDIENTS	2- TO 3½-QT	4- TO 5½-QT	6- TO 8-QT
Low-sodium vegetable broth	2½ cups	5 cups (1 quart plus 1 cup)	8 cups (2 quarts)
No-salt-added canned diced tomatoes	1¾ cups	3½ cups	6 cups

Drained and rinsed canned kidney beans	1 cup	1¾ cups	3 cups
Chopped carrots	½ cup	1 cup	1⅔ cups
Chopped yellow onion	⅓ cup	¾ cup	1¼ cups
Medium celery ribs, chopped	1	2	3
No-salt-added tomato paste	2½ tblsp	¼ cup	⅓ cup
Dried basil	2 tsp	1 tblsp	1½ tblsp
Dried rosemary	½ tblsp	2 tsp	1 tblsp
Salt	½ tsp	1 tsp	½ tblsp
Ground black pepper	¼ tsp	½ tsp	¾ tsp
Dried small elbow macaroni	4 ounces (about 1 cup)	6 ounces (about 1½ cups)	10 ounces (about 2½ cups)

1 Stir the broth, tomatoes, beans, carrots, onion, celery, tomato paste, basil, rosemary, salt, and pepper in the slow cooker until the tomato paste dissolves. Cover and cook on high for 4 hours or on low for 6 hours, or until the vegetables are tender and the aromas are irresistible.

2 Stir in the macaroni. Cover and continue cooking on low for 1 hour, or until the pasta is tender.

TESTERS' NOTES
• To brighten the flavors, add up to 2 teaspoons finely grated lemon zest to the soup along with the herbs.
• Although we usually prefer whole wheat pasta, the traditional macaroni in this recipe has less tooth and more creaminess in every bite.

lima bean and kale soup

EFFORT: **A LOT** • PREP TIME: **12 HOURS 30 MINUTES (INCLUDES SOAKING THE BEANS)** • COOK TIME: **10 HOURS** • KEEPS ON WARM: **2 HOURS** • SERVES: **3 TO 8**

INGREDIENTS	2- TO 3½-QT	4- TO 5½-QT	6- TO 8-QT
Dried lima beans	1 cup (about ½ pound)	1½ cups (about ¾ pound)	2½ cups (about 1¼ pounds)
Olive oil	1 tblsp	1½ tblsp	2 tblsp
Sweet or spicy Italian sausage, cut into 1-inch pieces	8 ounces	12 ounces	1¼ pounds
Low-sodium beef broth	4 cups (1 quart)	6 cups (1½ quarts)	10 cups (2½ quarts)
Yellow onion, chopped	1 small	1 medium	2 medium
Minced fresh oregano leaves	1 tsp	2 tsp	1 tblsp
Red pepper flakes	⅛ tsp	¼ tsp	½ tsp
Kale, stemmed, washed, and chopped	3 cups	5 cups	8 cups
Red wine vinegar	1 tblsp	1½ tblsp	2 tblsp
Salt	½ tsp	1 tsp	½ tblsp

1 Pour the lima beans into a big bowl, fill it about two-thirds with water, and set aside to soak for 12 hours or up to 16 hours (that is, overnight).

2 The next day, heat a large skillet over medium heat for a few minutes, then pour in the olive oil. Add the sausage and brown well, turning occasionally, for 5 to 10 minutes, depending on the batch size. Use tongs or a

(continued)

fork to transfer the sausage pieces to the slow cooker.

3 Drain the lima beans in a colander set in the sink; transfer them to the slow cooker. Stir in the broth, onion, oregano, and red pepper flakes. Cover and cook on low for 6 hours.

4 Stir in the kale. Cover and continue cooking on low for 4 hours, or until the lima beans and kale are tender. Stir in the vinegar and salt before serving.

TESTERS' NOTES
• Since acid and salt can toughen the lima beans as they cook, we add both at the end. As a bonus, their flavors remain brighter against all the intensely dusky savoriness in the stew.
• For a somewhat lighter, less robust soup, substitute chicken broth for the beef broth.

minestrone

EFFORT: **A LITTLE** • PREP TIME: **12 HOURS 20 MINUTES (INCLUDES SOAKING THE BEANS)** • COOK TIME: **10 HOURS** • KEEPS ON WARM: **4 HOURS THROUGH STEP 2** • SERVES: **3 TO 8**

INGREDIENTS	2- TO 3½-QT	4- TO 5½-QT	6- TO 8-QT
Dried white beans	1 cup (about 8 ounces)	1½ cups (about ¾ pound)	2½ cups (about 1¼ pounds)
Low-sodium chicken broth	2 cups	5 cups	7 cups
No-salt-added canned diced tomatoes	1¾ cups	2¾ cups	3½ cups
Peeled and diced yellow potatoes (such as Yukon Gold)	1 cup	2 cups	3 cups (about 1 pound)
Chopped yellow onion	½ cup	1 cup	1½ cups
Chopped celery	¼ cup	½ cup	¾ cup
Thinly sliced carrot	¼ cup	⅓ cup	½ cup
Minced fresh oregano leaves	1 tsp	2 tsp	1 tblsp
Minced fresh rosemary leaves	1 tsp	2 tsp	1 tblsp
Minced garlic	1 tsp	½ tblsp	2 tsp
Bay leaves	1	2	3
White balsamic vinegar	1 tblsp	1½ tblsp	2 tblsp
Salt	½ tsp	1 tsp	½ tblsp

1 Pour the beans in a large bowl, then douse them with water until the bowl is about two-thirds full. Set aside to soak overnight.

2 Drain the beans in a colander set in the sink and pour them into the slow cooker. Stir in the broth, tomatoes, potatoes, onion, celery, carrot, oregano, rosemary, garlic, and bay leaves. Cover and cook on low for 10 hours, or until the beans are quite tender.

3 Remove and discard the bay leaves. Stir in the vinegar and salt before serving.

TESTERS' NOTES
• There's a great divide in various interpretations of this classic, including whether it has pasta or not. You can see which side we're on.
• For a more luxurious soup, save the rind from a hunk of Parmigiano-Reggiano, especially if it has a little cheese left on it. Add it with the beans: a 2-inch piece for the small batch, a 3-inch piece for the medium one, and a 4-inch piece (or two 2-inch pieces) for the large one. Scrape any soft cheese off the rind and discard the remainder before serving.

Serve It Up! Drizzle heady, aromatic extra-virgin olive oil over each bowlful. And don't forget the bread—lots of crunchy bread, preferably rubbed with a peeled garlic clove and then toasted.

INGREDIENTS EXPLAINED White balsamic vinegar is made from white wine vinegar and the *must* (the pressings of the skins and pulp) from white grapes. It's milder than dark balsamic vinegar, and even sweeter than standard bottlings of the dark stuff (although not nearly as sweet as the syrupy aged balsamics). Look for it among the other vinegars at the supermarket; it's a sweeter substitution in most salad dressings that call for white wine vinegar.

mushroom, barley, and lentil soup

EFFORT: **A LITTLE** • PREP TIME: **20 MINUTES** • COOK TIME: **4 HOURS/9 HOURS** • KEEPS ON WARM: **2 HOURS** • SERVES: **3 TO 8**

INGREDIENTS	2- TO 3½-QT	4- TO 5½-QT	6- TO 8-QT
Olive oil	1 tblsp	2 tblsp	3 tblsp
Yellow onion, chopped	1 small	1 medium	2 medium
Cremini or brown button mushrooms, thinly sliced	10 ounces (about 3 cups)	1 pound (about 5 cups)	1½ pounds (about 7½ cups)
Low-sodium vegetable broth	3 cups	5 cups (1 quart plus 1 cup)	8 cups (2 quarts)
No-salt-added canned diced tomatoes	1¼ cups	2 cups	3½ cups
Chopped carrots	⅓ cup	⅔ cup	1 cup
Pearled barley (see page 24)	¼ cup	⅓ cup	½ cup plus 2 tblsp
Brown or green lentils (see page 449)	¼ cup	⅓ cup	½ cup
Medium celery ribs, chopped	1	1½	2
Minced fresh rosemary leaves	1 tblsp	1½ tblsp	2 tblsp
Stemmed fresh thyme leaves	1 tsp	2 tsp	1 tblsp
Salt	½ tsp	¾ tsp	1 tsp
Ground black pepper	⅛ tsp	¼ tsp	½ tsp
Bay leaves	1	2	3

1 Heat a large skillet over medium heat, then swirl in the oil. Add the onion and cook, stirring often, until translucent, between 4 and 8 minutes. Add the mushrooms and continue cooking, stirring occasionally, until they give off their liquid and then it boils down to almost nothing, between 5 and 10 minutes.

2 Scrape the contents of the skillet into the slow cooker. Stir in the broth, tomatoes, carrots, barley, lentils, celery, rosemary, thyme, salt, pepper, and bay leaves.

3 Cover and cook on high for 4 hours or on low for 9 hours, or until the lentils and barley are tender. Remove the bay leaf or leaves before serving.

TESTERS' NOTES
• Everybody knows about beef barley soup, but here's a vegetarian version with lots of savory notes, thanks to all those lentils.
• You must cook the mushrooms first; otherwise they'll water down the soup. If you're working with the quantity

(*continued*)

for a large batch, you'll need a very big skillet to hold them all. Or work in two batches, half the oil, onion, and mushrooms in each.

• Our preference here is for the green French lentils (*lentils de Puy*). They hold up a bit better in the long run.

white bean and escarole soup

EFFORT: **A LITTLE** • PREP TIME: **20 MINUTES** • COOK TIME: **6 HOURS** • KEEPS ON WARM: **NO** • SERVES: **3 TO 8**

INGREDIENTS	2- TO 3½-QT	4- TO 5½-QT	6- TO 8-QT
Olive oil	1½ tblsp	2 tblsp	3 tblsp
Pancetta, chopped (see page 354)	4 ounces	6 ounces	9 ounces
Slivered peeled garlic	1½ tblsp	2 tblsp	3 tblsp
Low-sodium chicken broth	4 cups (1 quart)	6 cups (1½ quarts)	9 cups (2 quarts plus 1 cup)
Drained and rinsed canned white beans	1¾ cups	3 cups	4½ cups
Chopped yellow onion	⅓ cup	½ cup	¾ cup
Minced fresh sage leaves	2 tsp	1 tblsp	1½ tblsp
Head of escarole, cored, washed, and chopped	1 medium (about 6 cups)	1 large (about 8 cups)	2 medium (about 12 cups)
Finely grated Parmigiano-Reggiano cheese	⅓ cup	½ cup	¾ cup
Ground black pepper	¾ tsp	1 tsp	½ tblsp

1 Place a large skillet over medium heat for a few minutes, then swirl in the oil. Add the pancetta; cook, stirring often, until browned and even a bit crisp, between 3 and 6 minutes. Stir in the garlic and cook for about 15 seconds, stirring constantly.

2 Scrape the contents of the skillet into the slow cooker. Stir in the broth, beans, onion, and sage. Cover and cook on low for 4 hours.

3 Stir in the escarole. Cover and continue cooking on low for 2 hours, or until the escarole is tender. Stir in the cheese and pepper before serving.

TESTERS' NOTES

• An Italian favorite, this soup won't keep well because the escarole starts to turn mushy.

• As we developed these recipes, we wanted many bean soups that didn't involve soaking the beans. We usually prefer the texture of dried beans softened in the slow cooker, but convenience counts for a lot, too.

• For some heat, add up to 1 teaspoon red pepper flakes with the sage.

Serve It Up! A poached egg would be wonderful in each bowl, the soup ladled on top. If you're going to eat the whole batch, you can poach the eggs right in the cooker. Break as many as you need into individual custard cups and slip them into the soup, tilting the cup's lip into the soup so the egg just slips into the liquid. Cover and cook on low for 10 to 15 minutes, until the whites are set but the yolks are soft. Gather the eggs one at a time with a large spoon, transfer them to individual serving bowls, and ladle the soup on top.

INGREDIENTS EXPLAINED Escarole is a broad-leaf green, like a head of lettuce, sometimes called *broad leaf endive* (it is indeed related to Belgian endive). Look for compact heads without any dark green bits. Remove the tough core, then wash the leaves carefully—they're often coated with grit down by the core. Cut out any tough, large, white veins in the center of the leaves, then chop the remainder.

porky navy bean soup

EFFORT: **A LOT** • PREP TIME: **12 HOURS 40 MINUTES (INCLUDES SOAKING THE BEANS)** • COOK TIME: **10 HOURS 25 MINUTES** • KEEPS ON WARM: **4 HOURS THROUGH STEP 3** • SERVES: **3 TO 8**

INGREDIENTS	2- TO 3½-QT	4- TO 5½-QT	6- TO 8-QT
Dried navy beans	⅔ cup (about 5 ounces)	1⅓ cups (about 11 ounces)	2 cups (about 1 pound)
Water	4 cups (1 quart)	7 cups (1 quart plus 3 cups)	10 cups (2½ cups)
Russet or other baking potatoes, peeled and chopped into 1-inch cubes	½ pound	¾ pound	1¼ pounds
Chopped yellow onion	⅓ cup	⅔ cup	1 cup (1 medium)
Chopped celery	⅓ cup	⅔ cup	1 cup
Ground black pepper	¼ tsp	½ tsp	1 tsp
Bay leaves	1	2	3
Smoked ham hock	1 small	1 medium	2 small
Chopped fresh parsley leaves	¼ cup	⅓ cup	½ cup
Fresh lemon juice	2 tsp	1½ tblsp	2 tblsp
Salt (optional)	¼ tsp	½ tsp	¾ tsp

1 Dump the beans in a large bowl and fill it about two-thirds full with cool tap water. Set aside to soak for 12 hours or up to 16 hours.

2 Drain the beans in a colander set in the sink, then pour them into the slow cooker. Stir in the water, potatoes, onion, celery, pepper, bay leaves, and ham hock.

3 Cover and cook on low for 10 hours, or until the beans are tender.

4 Take the hock out of the cooker; keep the cooker covered and on low. Cool the hock for 10 minutes, then remove the meat from the bones and shred it. Stir this meat back into the slow cooker along with the parsley, lemon juice, and salt (if using).

5 Cover and cook on low for 15 minutes to heat through.

TESTERS' NOTES
• There's really no need for extra salt in this substantial soup; the hock will supply so much to the broth. That said, if you like saltier fare, add the optional amount.
• Because this soup cooks for so long and because the beans are so rich, there's also no need for broth here. Water will do the trick.

bean, beef, and carrot soup

EFFORT: **A LOT** • PREP TIME: **12 HOURS 35 MINUTES** • COOK TIME: **10 HOURS 15 MINUTES** • KEEPS ON WARM: **4 HOURS THROUGH STEP 4** • SERVES: **2 TO 6**

INGREDIENTS	2- TO 3½-QT	4- TO 5½-QT	6- TO 8-QT
Dried pinto beans	⅔ cup	1⅓ cups	2 cups
Meaty beef ribs	½ pound	1 pound	1½ pounds
Low-sodium beef broth	3 cups	6 cups (1½ quarts)	9 cups (2 quarts plus 1 cup)
Carrots, thinly sliced	5 ounces	10 ounces	1 pound
Yellow onion, chopped	1 small	1 medium	1 large
Chopped fresh sage leaves	2 tsp	1½ tblsp	2 tblsp
Stemmed fresh thyme leaves	1 tsp	2 tsp	1 tblsp
Celery seeds	⅛ tsp	¼ tsp	½ tsp
Bay leaf	1	1	2
Salt	¼ tsp	½ tsp	¾ tsp
Ground black pepper	⅛ tsp	¼ tsp	½ tsp

1 Pour the beans into a large bowl and souse them by filling the bowl at least two-thirds full of cool tap water. Set aside to soak overnight—that is, 12 hours, or up to 16 hours.

2 Position the rack in the center of the oven and heat the oven to 400°F. Lay the beef ribs on a large baking sheet and brown them, turning occasionally with tongs, about 20 minutes. Lay them in the slow cooker.

3 Drain the beans in a colander set in the sink; pour them into the slow cooker. Stir in the broth, carrots, onion, sage, thyme, celery seeds, and bay leaf.

4 Cover and cook on low for 10 hours, or until the beans are tender and any meat is falling off the rib bones.

5 Transfer the bones to a large cutting board, cool a few minutes, then shred the meat from those bones. Discard the bay leaf, then stir this meat back into the soup along with the salt and pepper. Cover and cook on low for 15 minutes to heat through.

TESTERS' NOTES
• Browning the ribs on a large baking sheet under the broiler will give them extra flavor in the soup.
• Make sure the beef ribs are cut into individual bones or ask the butcher to do so for you.

wheatberry and root vegetable soup

EFFORT: **A LITTLE** • PREP TIME: **25 MINUTES** • COOK TIME: **8 HOURS** • KEEPS ON WARM: **2 HOURS THROUGH STEP 2** • SERVES: **3 TO 10**

INGREDIENTS	2- TO 3½-QT	4- TO 5½-QT	6- TO 8-QT
Low-sodium vegetable broth	4 cups (1 quart)	8 cups (2 quarts)	12 cups (3 quarts)
Peeled and thinly sliced parsnips	⅔ cup	1⅓ cups	2 cups

Thinly sliced carrots	2/3 cup	1⅓ cups	2 cups
Peeled and diced celery root	2/3 cup	1⅓ cups (about ½ pound)	2 cups
Thinly sliced leek (white and pale green part only), washed for internal grit	1/3 cup	2/3 cup	1 cup
Wheatberries (see page 30)	1/3 cup	2/3 cup	1 cup
Peeled and shredded sweet potato	1/3 cup	2/3 cup	1 cup
Salt	½ tsp	¾ tsp	1 tsp
Ground black pepper	¼ tsp	½ tsp	¾ tsp
Ground allspice	⅛ tsp	¼ tsp	½ tsp
Grated nutmeg	⅛ tsp	¼ tsp	½ tsp
4-inch cinnamon stick	½	1	1½
Chopped fresh parsley leaves	2 tblsp	¼ cup	½ cup
Fresh lemon juice	1 tsp	2 tsp	1 tblsp

1 Stir the broth, parsnips, carrots, celery root, leek, wheatberries, sweet potato, salt, pepper, allspice, nutmeg, and cinnamon stick in the slow cooker.

2 Cover and cook on low for 8 hours, or until the wheatberries are tender.

3 Find and discard the cinnamon stick. Stir in the parsley and lemon juice just before serving.

TESTERS' NOTES

• Although there's not much to making this soup, we did list its effort level at "a little" because of all that chopping and slicing of the root vegetables, many of which you cannot find already prepped in the supermarket's produce section.

• Rather than stirring red pepper flakes into the soup, dot bowlfuls with bottled hot pepper sauce or even sambal oelek (see page 404), if you want more heat.

ALL-AMERICAN KNOW-HOW To peel a hairy, gnarly celery root (or celeriac, a plant that's a kissing cousin to celery), skip the vegetable peeler and work with a sharp paring knife, shearing off small bits of the tough peel as you work your way around the root. Carve down into the cracks to get out those spindly hairs. Cut out more troublesome spots completely. Once you've got that done, slice the root into 1-inch circles, then cut these into chunks.

quinoa and squash soup

EFFORT: **A LITTLE** • PREP TIME: **25 MINUTES** • COOK TIME: **6 HOURS 15 MINUTES** • KEEPS ON WARM: **2 HOURS THROUGH STEP 1** • SERVES: **3 TO 8**

INGREDIENTS	2- TO 3½-QT	4- TO 5½-QT	6- TO 8-QT
Low-sodium chicken broth	3 cups	5 cups (1 quart plus 1 cup)	8 cups (2 quarts)
Peeled, seeded, and chopped butternut squash	2½ cups (12 ounces)	4 cups (1¼ pounds)	6½ cups (2 pounds)
Coconut milk (regular or light)	1 cup	1⅔ cups	2⅔ cups
Yellow onion, chopped	1 small	1 medium	1 large
White quinoa, rinsed (see page 27)	½ cup	¾ cup	1⅓ cups
Curry powder (see page 395)	½ tblsp	2½ tsp	4 tsp
Salt	½ tsp	¾ tsp	1 tsp
Cayenne	Up to ¼ tsp	Up to ½ tsp	Up to ¾ tsp

(continued)

1 Mix the broth, squash, coconut milk, onion, quinoa, curry powder, salt, and cayenne in the slow cooker. Cover and cook on low for 6 hours, or until the squash and quinoa are very tender.

2 Puree the soup: use an immersion blender in the slow cooker, or ladle the soup in batches into a large blender, cover, and blend until smooth before pouring it back into the slow cooker. Cover and cook on low for 15 minutes to heat through.

TESTERS' NOTES

• By pureeing the quinoa, you end up with a mellow, sophisticated flavor to pair with the creamy, sweet butternut squash.
• Of course, you needn't just use yellow curry powder. Search out interesting blends, particularly those with plenty of warm spices like cinnamon and cardamom.

Serve It Up! Garnish the bowls with dollops of plain yogurt and minced chives.

beefy quinoa soup

EFFORT: **NOT MUCH** • PREP TIME: **20 MINUTES** • COOK TIME: **8 HOURS** • KEEPS ON WARM: **2 HOURS THROUGH STEP 2** • SERVES: **3 TO 8**

INGREDIENTS	2- TO 3½-QT	4- TO 5½-QT	6- TO 8-QT
Low-sodium chicken broth	3 cups	5 cups (1 quart plus 1 cup)	8 cups (2 quarts)
Yellow potatoes (such as Yukon Gold), peeled and diced	8 ounces (about 1½ cups)	11 ounces (about 2 cups)	1 pound (about 3 cups)
Beef chuck, finely chopped into ½-inch pieces	6 ounces	10 ounces	1 pound
White or red quinoa (see page 27)	⅓ cup	½ cup	¾ cup
Frozen fava beans, thawed	¼ cup	⅓ cup	½ cup
Thinly sliced leek (white and pale green part only), washed for internal grit	¼ cup	⅓ cup	½ cup
Salt	¼ tsp	½ tsp	¾ tsp
Ground black pepper	¼ tsp	½ tsp	¾ tsp
Chopped fresh parsley leaves	2 tblsp	3 tblsp	¼ cup
Chopped fresh cilantro leaves	2 tblsp	3 tblsp	¼ cup
Sherry vinegar	1 tblsp	1½ tblsp	2 tblsp

1 Mix the broth, potatoes, beef, quinoa, fava beans, leek, salt, and pepper in the slow cooker.

2 Cover and cook on low for 8 hours, or until the potatoes, quinoa, and beef are tender.

3 Stir in the parsley, cilantro, and vinegar before serving.

TESTERS' NOTES

• Here's an honest meat-and-potatoes meal that uses less beef than you might expect, thanks to the quinoa in the mix.
• Frozen fava beans are better than canned because they retain more of their texture during all this cooking. That said, if you can't find frozen, the canned ones will work fine so long as you add them *after* 5 hours of cooking.

meat and seafood soups

We didn't want you to get worried, what with all those vegetable and grain soups. We still had chicken, beef, pork, red snapper, shrimp, and scallops in our (apparently messy) back pockets. And it's not surprising we did, given what a slow cooker does for protein of all sorts.

Yes, slow cooker recipes often skip the browning, that essential method for complex flavors. And yes, the two of us think it's sometimes best to compensate by skillet-browning a cut before it gets tossed into the appliance. But even without that preliminary step, slow cookers still work their magic on the natural sugars in meat and fish of all sorts, breaking them down, if not into quite the wide range of flavors browning affords, nonetheless into cleaner, elemental flavors that sweeten a soup without the need for additional sugar. Strange to say but slow cooker soups end up brighter and even lighter than their stovetop kin, partly because the lack of browning lets less assertive, more floral notes come to the forefront. Think of it like this: slow cooker soups are more like woodwind quartets than stadium rock bands.

These recipes run the gamut from some done in a few hours to others that take a good long while. That's because we're working with the largest range of protein in this section, from quick-cooking shrimp to long-cooking beef bottom round. And since this is our first chapter focusing on animal protein, we need to caution you: do *not* put frozen or even partially thawed meat, poultry, fish, or shellfish in the slow cooker. Although it's great to stock up on these things at the supermarket when you see sales, you need to make sure that all these proteins are thoroughly thawed before you use them. If not, their lower temperatures will slow the cooking time dramatically—long enough, in fact, that food safety will become a concern. Even if bad bugs are killed off when the cooker finally hits its higher temperatures, their residue will lurk, a real-time nightmare soon enough.

To thaw protein of all sorts, unwrap it and set it in a bowl in the fridge for at least 24 hours, maybe 48 hours, depending on its size. Easy enough, but let's dispel one cooking myth straight off: if you've thawed any cut of meat or poultry (but not fish or shellfish) and you decide, on the spur of the moment, that it really doesn't suit your fancy, you can indeed refreeze it—*so long as* it has not left your fridge, your fridge has been set at 40°F or colder, and the protein has not been fully thawed for more than 24 hours. Drain off the liquid in the bowl, seal the meat or poultry in a plastic bag, and toss it back into the freezer. It may not be good for grilling or sautéing (it will have lost quite a bit of moisture), but it'll be perfect for the slow cooker on another day when you're more in the mood for soup.

chicken noodle soup

EFFORT: **NOT MUCH** • PREP TIME: **15 MINUTES** • COOK TIME: **9 HOURS** • KEEPS ON WARM: **4 HOURS THROUGH STEP 1** • SERVES: **3 TO 10**

INGREDIENTS	2- TO 3½-QT	4- TO 5½-QT	6- TO 8-QT
Low-sodium chicken broth	5 cups (1 quart plus 1 cup)	8 cups (2 quarts)	12 cups (3 quarts)
Boneless skinless chicken thighs	¾ pound	1¼ pounds	2 pounds
Thinly sliced carrots	¾ cup	1¼ cups	1¾ cups
Chopped yellow onion	½ cup	¾ cup	1¼ cups
Medium celery ribs, thinly sliced	1	1½	2
Dried dill	½ tblsp	2 tsp	1½ tblsp
Dried thyme	1 tsp	½ tblsp	2½ tsp
Finely grated lemon zest	½ tsp	¾ tsp	1 tsp
Salt	½ tsp	¾ tsp	1 tsp
Ground black pepper	½ tsp	¾ tsp	1 tsp
Dried egg noodles, preferably narrow ones	6 ounces	10 ounces	1 pound

1 Mix the broth, chicken, carrots, onion, celery, dill, thyme, lemon zest, salt, and pepper in the slow cooker. Cover and cook on low for 8 hours, or until the meat is very tender.

2 Use a wooden spoon to break the chicken thighs into smaller pieces right in the soup. Stir in the noodles; cover and continue cooking on low for 1 additional hour, or until the pasta is tender.

TESTERS' NOTES
• Nothing could be easier than this favorite, especially since you can use boneless skinless thighs. Skip the chicken skin; the vegetables offer most of the body.
• You can make the soup through step 1, then seal and freeze it in 1-quart containers for up to 4 months. Add the noodles when you reheat servings on the stovetop, simmering them in the soup for about 10 minutes. Break up the chicken pieces before serving.

lemon chicken and rice soup

EFFORT: **A LOT** • PREP TIME: **25 MINUTES** • COOK TIME: **3 HOURS 15 MINUTES/6 HOURS 15 MINUTES** • KEEPS ON WARM: **NO** • SERVES: **3 TO 8**

INGREDIENTS	2- TO 3½-QT	4- TO 5½-QT	6- TO 8-QT
Boneless skinless chicken breasts	½ pound	¾ pound	1¼ pounds
Medium carrots, peeled	2	4	6
Small yellow onions, halved and peeled	1	2	3
Bay leaves	1	2	3
Uncooked long-grain white rice	⅔ cup	1 cup	1⅔ cups
Low-sodium chicken broth	4 cups (1 quart)	6 cups (1½ quarts)	10 cups (2½ quarts)
Large eggs/yolk	1 whole plus 1 yolk	2 whole	3 whole plus 1 yolk
Fresh lemon juice	3 tblsp	¼ cup	7 tblsp
Cornstarch	2 tsp	1 tblsp	1½ tblsp
Chopped fresh parsley leaves	3 tblsp	¼ cup	½ cup

(continued)

1 Lay the chicken, carrots, onions, and bay leaves in the slow cooker; sprinkle the rice on top. Pour in the broth, making sure the grains of rice are fully submerged.

2 Cover and cook on high for 3 hours or on low for 6 hours, or until the rice is tender. Discard the onions, carrots, and bay leaves.

3 Transfer the chicken to a cutting board; cool for 5 minutes. Keep the slow cooker covered and on low.

4 Whisk the eggs, lemon juice, and cornstarch in a big bowl until frothy. Whisk at least a third of the hot soup into this egg mixture until smooth.

5 Whisk this egg-and-lemon mixture back into the remaining soup in the slow cooker. Chop the chicken and stir it in with the parsley. Cover and cook on high for 15 minutes or until hot.

TESTERS' NOTES

- This flavorful soup is based on a traditional Greek one, enriched with egg yolks and lemon juice. It's sour and bright, great on a spring evening.
- Use tongs or a slotted spoon to fish out the vegetables in step 2. Toss any rice grains back into the soup.
- When whisking the soup into the egg yolk mixture, pour in a slow, steady stream, whisking all the while, so the eggs don't scramble as they meet the hot liquid.

chicken goulash soup

EFFORT: **NOT MUCH** • PREP TIME: **15 MINUTES** • COOK TIME: **3 HOURS/5 HOURS** • KEEPS ON WARM: **4 HOURS** • SERVES: **3 TO 8**

INGREDIENTS	2- TO 3½-QT	4- TO 5½-QT	6- TO 8-QT
Low-sodium chicken broth	3 cups	5 cups (1 quart plus 1 cup)	8 cups (2 quarts)
Boneless skinless chicken breast, chopped	1 pound	1¾ pounds	2¾ pounds
No-salt-added canned diced tomatoes	1¾ cups	3 cups	4¾ cups
Peeled and diced Russet or other baking potatoes	1½ cups (about ½ pound)	2½ cups (about 14 ounces)	4 cups (about 1¼ pounds)
Green bell peppers, stemmed, seeded, and chopped	1 medium	2 medium	2 large
Yellow onion, chopped	1 small	1 medium	1 large
Mild paprika	2 tblsp	3 tblsp	5 tblsp
Minced garlic	½ tblsp	2½ tsp	1½ tblsp
Caraway seeds	1 tsp	½ tblsp	1 tblsp
Salt	½ tsp	¾ tsp	1 tsp

1 Mix the broth, chicken, tomatoes, potatoes, bell pepper, onion, paprika, garlic, caraway seeds, and salt in the slow cooker.

2 Cover and cook on high for 3 hours or on low for 5 hours, or until the vegetables are tender.

TESTERS' NOTES

• A bit of whimsy, this Old-World-braise-morphed-into-a-soup skips the traditional sour cream since it might break in the cooker over the long haul. Dollop it onto servings as a garnish.

• Even if you're a fan of chicken thighs, don't swap them for boneless skinless chicken breasts. The thighs will not get tender in the time stated.

• Replace your paprika every 18 months or so, after which it becomes nothing but a red food-coloring agent.

• For more heat, cut the amount of mild paprika by one-fourth and add enough hot paprika to make up the difference.

• For more heft, ladle the soup over serving bowls of cooked and drained egg noodles.

creamy corn and chicken soup

EFFORT: **A LITTLE** • PREP TIME: **25 MINUTES** • COOK TIME: **2 HOURS 45 MINUTES/5 HOURS 15 MINUTES** • KEEPS ON WARM: **2 HOURS THROUGH STEP 2** • SERVES: **3 TO 8**

INGREDIENTS	2- TO 3½-QT	4- TO 5½-QT	6- TO 8-QT
Boneless skinless chicken breasts	10 ounces	1 pound	1½ pounds
Low-sodium chicken broth	2½ cups	4 cups (1 quart)	6 cups (1½ quarts)
Corn kernels, freshly cut off the cob, or frozen, thawed	2½ cups	4 cups	6 cups
Thinly sliced leeks (white and pale green part only), washed to remove interior grit, thinly sliced	⅔ cup (about 5 ounces)	1 cup (about ½ pound)	1½ cups (about ¾ pound)
Peeled and diced Russet or other baking potato	⅔ cup	1 cup	1½ cups (about ½ pound)
Dry white wine, such as Pinot Grigio, or dry vermouth	⅓ cup	½ cup	¾ cup
Medium celery ribs, chopped	½	1	1½
Worcestershire sauce	1½ tblsp	2 tblsp	3 tblsp
Dried thyme	¼ tsp	½ tsp	¾ tsp
Heavy cream	½ cup	¾ cup	1¼ cups

1 Lay the chicken breasts in the slow cooker. Add the broth, corn, leeks, potato, white wine, celery, Worcestershire sauce, and thyme. Stir well.

2 Cover and cook on high for 2½ hours or on low for 5 hours, or until the meat is cooked through and the potato is tender.

3 Transfer the chicken breasts to a cutting board. Puree the remaining soup: use an immersion blender right in the cooker; or ladle the soup in batches into a large blender, cover, and blend until smooth, pouring the soup back into the slow cooker. Keep the slow cooker set on low or turn to low heat.

4 Chop the chicken into bite-size bits; stir these into the soup along with the cream. Cover and cook on low for 15 minutes to blend the flavors.

TESTERS' NOTES

• A salve for a rainy day, this creamy soup may be even better as leftovers, after the flavors have melded. (So make it the day before the storm blows in.) Save leftovers in sealed containers in the fridge for up to 4 days.

• Although chicken thighs are certainly sturdier and can cook longer, we like the more delicate taste of chicken breasts in this soup.

smoked turkey and wild rice soup

EFFORT: **A LITTLE** • PREP TIME: **20 MINUTES** • COOK TIME: **7 HOURS**
• KEEPS ON WARM: **2 HOURS THROUGH STEP 1** • SERVES: **4 TO 10**

INGREDIENTS	2- TO 3½-QT	4- TO 5½-QT	6- TO 8-QT
Low-sodium chicken broth	4 cups (1 quart)	7 cups (1 quart plus 3 cups)	11 cups (2 quarts plus 3 cups)
Smoked turkey, skinned and deboned if necessary, then chopped	¾ pound	1¼ pounds	2 pounds
Wild rice	¾ cup	1 cup plus 2 tblsp	2 cups
Chopped carrot	½ cup	¾ cup	1¼ cups
Whole medium scallions, thinly sliced	1	2	2½
Minced fresh rosemary leaves	2 tsp	1 tblsp	1½ tblsp
Ground black pepper	½ tsp	¾ tsp	1 tsp
Evaporated milk (regular or low-fat)	½ cup	¾ cup	1¼ cups
All-purpose flour	¼ cup	6 tblsp	⅔ cup
Dry vermouth	2 tblsp	3 tblsp	⅓ cup

1 Stir the broth, smoked turkey, wild rice, carrot, scallions, rosemary, and pepper together in the slow cooker. Cover and cook on low for 6 hours, or until the wild rice is tender.

2 Whisk the evaporated milk, flour, and vermouth in a bowl until smooth, every speck of the flour dissolved. Stir the flour mixture into the soup until well combined. Cover and cook on high for 1 hour, or until slightly thickened.

TESTERS' NOTES
• Look for smoked turkey at the deli counter, but avoid the processed, extruded turkey hunks that look something like footballs. If possible, buy a large chunk of breast meat, then chop it at home into ½-inch pieces.
• The intense nuttiness of wild rice balances the smokiness in the turkey more effectively than brown (or certainly white) rice.

Serve It Up! Offer this soup alongside thick-sliced challah bread, toasted and spread with chunky whole-fruit cranberry sauce or cranberry chutney.

INGREDIENTS EXPLAINED You can find wild rice in two varieties: the dark black grains that are grown on commercial farms (particularly in California) or the pale brown grains that are hand-harvested from lakes (particularly in the Upper Midwest). Either will do here—although the hand-harvested varieties often take longer to cook (and are quite a bit more costly).

turkey soup with apples and coconut

EFFORT: **NOT MUCH** • PREP TIME: **15 MINUTES** • COOK TIME:
6 HOURS • KEEPS ON WARM: **NO** • SERVES: **3 TO 8**

INGREDIENTS	2- TO 3½-QT	4- TO 5½-QT	6- TO 8-QT
Boneless skinless turkey breast, diced	¾ pound	1¼ pounds	2 pounds
Low-sodium chicken broth	4 cups (1 quart)	6 cups (1½ quarts)	10 cups (2½ quarts)

Ingredient	1 large (about 1¼ cups)	2 medium (about 2 cups)	1 large and 2 medium (about 3¼ cups)
Green apples (Granny Smith are best), cored, peeled, and diced	1 large (about 1¼ cups)	2 medium (about 2 cups)	1 large and 2 medium (about 3¼ cups)
Coconut milk (regular or low-fat)	½ cup	¾ cup	1¼ cups
Chopped yellow onion	½ cup	¾ cup	1¼ cups
Chopped carrot	½ cup	¾ cup	1¼ cups
Uncooked long-grain white rice	¼ cup	6 tblsp	⅔ cup
Curry powder	1 tsp	½ tblsp	1 tblsp
Ground cinnamon	⅛ tsp	¼ tsp	½ tsp
Ground cloves	⅛ tsp	¼ tsp	½ tsp
Ground mace	⅛ tsp	¼ tsp	½ tsp
Salt	⅛ tsp	¼ tsp	½ tsp
Cayenne	Pinch	⅛ tsp	¼ tsp

1 Mix the turkey, broth, apple, coconut milk, onion, carrot, rice, curry powder, cinnamon, cloves, mace, salt, and cayenne in the slow cooker.

2 Cover and cook on low for 6 hours, or until the turkey is cooked through, the rice is tender, and the soup is thickened a bit.

TESTERS' NOTES

• A simplified take on mulligatawny, this soup is even better the next day, after the flavors have mellowed.

• Double the cayenne at will.

• Although standard yellow curry powder will do the trick for a quick weeknight meal, you can up your game by searching out the astounding array of curry powders at East Indian markets. Or make your own—see page 395.

turkey soup
with fennel and spinach

EFFORT: **NOT MUCH** • PREP TIME: **15 MINUTES** • COOK TIME: **3 HOURS/5½ HOURS** • KEEPS ON WARM: **3 HOURS THROUGH STEP 1** • SERVES: **3 TO 9**

INGREDIENTS	2- TO 3½-QT	4- TO 5½-QT	6- TO 8-QT
Boneless skinless turkey breast, such as turkey London broil or turkey breast cutlets, diced	¾ pound	1½ pounds	2¼ pounds
Low-sodium chicken broth	3 cups	6 cups (1½ quarts)	9 cups (2 quarts plus 1 cup)
No-salt-added canned diced tomatoes	1¾ cups	3½ cups	5¼ cups
Fennel bulb, trimmed and chopped (see page 211)	6 ounces	10 ounces	1 pound
Herbes de Provence	2 tsp	1½ tblsp	2 tblsp
Salt	¼ tsp	½ tsp	¾ tsp
Red pepper flakes	¼ tsp	½ tsp	¾ tsp
Baby spinach leaves, chopped	3 ounces (about 2 cups)	6 ounces (about 4 cups)	9 ounces (about 6 cups)

1 Mix the turkey, broth, tomatoes, fennel, herbes de Provence, salt, and red pepper flakes in the slow cooker. Cover and cook on high for 2½ hours or on low for 5 hours.

2 Stir in the spinach. Cover and cook on high for 30 more minutes.

(continued)

• Cook this simple but rewarding soup during the day, then stir in the spinach when you get home. Dinner will be ready by the time you've changed into something more comfortable.

• If you have the small end of any of the slow cookers, you may think that the cooker is so full that the spinach will never fit. Drop the spinach leaves on top of the soup, perhaps even just a handful of them, stir gently, wait a minute, then add some more. After they wilt to almost no volume, you'll get them to fit and have a well-stocked soup.

INGREDIENTS EXPLAINED Herbes de Provence are a blend of dried seasonings that usually includes savory, fennel seeds, basil, thyme, and lavender leaves. Check the label to see if there's salt in the mix; if so, omit the additional salt from this recipe.

creamy turkey mushroom soup

EFFORT: **A LITTLE** • PREP TIME: **25 MINUTES** • COOK TIME: **3 HOURS/5 HOURS** • KEEPS ON WARM: **2 HOURS THROUGH STEP 3** • SERVES: **3 TO 10**

INGREDIENTS	2- TO 3½-QT	4- TO 5½-QT	6- TO 8-QT
Unsalted butter	2 tblsp	4 tblsp (½ stick)	6 tblsp (¾ stick)
Yellow onions, chopped	1 medium	2 medium	2 large
Cremini or brown button mushrooms, thinly sliced	5 ounces (about 1½ cups)	9 ounces (about 3 cups)	13 ounces (about 4½ cups)
Minced garlic	1 tsp	2 tsp	1 tblsp
Dry white wine, such as Chardonnay	¼ cup	½ cup	¾ cup
Low-sodium chicken broth	3 cups	5 cups (1 quart plus 1 cup)	8 cups (2 quarts)
Boneless skinless turkey breast, chopped	¾ pound	1¾ pounds	2½ pounds
Minced fresh sage leaves	1 tblsp	2 tblsp	3 tblsp
Salt	¼ tsp	½ tsp	¾ tsp
Ground black pepper	¼ tsp	½ tsp	¾ tsp
Heavy cream	1 cup	2 cups	3 cups

1 Melt the butter in a large skillet set over medium heat. Add the onion and cook, stirring often, until translucent, between 4 and 8 minutes.

2 Stir in the mushrooms and continue cooking, stirring often, until they give off their liquid and the mixture reduces to a thick glaze, between 5 and 10 minutes. Stir in the garlic; cook for a few seconds.

3 Pour the wine into the skillet; as the liquid comes to a boil, scrape up any browned bits in the bottom of the skillet. Scrape the contents of the skillet into the slow cooker. Stir the broth, turkey, sage, salt, and pepper into the slow cooker as well.

4 Cover and cook on high for 3 hours or on low for 5 hours, or until the flavors have blended and the turkey is cooked through.

5 Stir in the heavy cream just before serving.

TESTERS' NOTES

• Buy a turkey cutlet, sometimes called a turkey London broil, for this hearty, well-stocked soup. The meat should be sliced into small bits, the same size as the onion.

- Hold the cream until you're ready to serve; it may break down with the wine in the mix. If you're worried about the cream cooling the soup, warm the cream in a small saucepan over medium heat just until a few puffs of steam come off its surface.
- Substitute light cream for the heavy cream, but avoid half-and-half, which will make the soup watery.

turkey sausage, kale, and rice soup

EFFORT: **A LITTLE** • PREP TIME: **20 MINUTES** • COOK TIME: **4 HOURS/7 HOURS** • KEEPS ON WARM: **NO** • SERVES: **3 TO 10**

INGREDIENTS	2- TO 3½-QT	4- TO 5½-QT	6- TO 8-QT
Olive oil	1 tblsp	1½ tblsp	2 tblsp
Mild Italian turkey sausage, casings removed	8 ounces	12 ounces	1½ pounds
Yellow onion, chopped	1 small	1 medium	2 medium
Low-sodium chicken broth	4 cups (1 quart)	6 cups (1½ quarts)	11 cups (2 quarts plus 3 cups)
Red bell peppers, seeded, stemmed, and chopped	1 medium	2 medium	2 large
Uncooked long-grain brown rice	⅓ cup	½ cup	1 cup
Fennel seeds	1 tsp	½ tblsp	2½ tsp
Salt	½ tsp	¾ tsp	½ tblsp
Ground black pepper	½ tsp	¾ tsp	½ tblsp
Kale, stemmed, washed, and chopped	6 ounces (about 2¼ cups)	¾ pound (about 4½ cups)	1 pound (about 7 cups)

1 Set a large skillet over medium heat for a few minutes, then swirl in the oil. Crumble in the sausage and brown well, stirring occasionally, between 4 and 8 minutes. Use a slotted spoon to transfer the sausage meat to the slow cooker.

2 Dump the onion into the skillet, still set over the heat. Cook, stirring often, until translucent, between 4 and 7 minutes. Scrape the contents of the skillet into the slow cooker.

3 Stir in the broth, bell peppers, rice, fennel seeds, salt, and pepper. Cover and cook on high for 3 hours or on low for 6 hours, or until the rice is tender.

4 Stir in the kale. Cover and cook on high for 1 hour, or until the kale is tender.

TESTERS' NOTES
- Because of the rice, the soup will not keep well on warm. Refrigerate any leftovers promptly, or freeze them in small-serving containers for up to 4 months.
- Choose a fairly plain sausage here—no cheese or dried fruit in the mix. We prefer mild, although you can use spicy.

SHORTCUTS Some supermarkets now sell prewashed and chopped kale, available with the bagged salad greens.

INGREDIENTS EXPLAINED Dark green and tasty, kale comes in several varieties, any of which will work here. It's always a good idea to rinse the leaves under cool water to get rid of any sandy grit. Also, be sure to remove the tough, fibrous, central vein before chopping the leafy bits into 1- to 2-inch pieces.

duck soup
with ginger and scallions

EFFORT: **A LITTLE** • PREP TIME: **15 MINUTES** • COOK TIME:
4½ HOURS/7½ HOURS • KEEPS ON WARM: **4 HOURS THROUGH**
STEP 3 • SERVES: **3 TO 8**

INGREDIENTS	2- TO 3½-QT	4- TO 5½-QT	6- TO 8-QT
Skinless duck leg-and-thigh quarters	2	4	6
Low-sodium chicken broth	4 cups (1 quart)	8 cups (2 quarts)	12 cups (3 quarts)
Yellow onions, thinly sliced	2 medium	3 large	4 large
½-inch-thick round slices of peeled fresh ginger	3	6	9
Whole scallions, roots trimmed	3	6	9
Fish sauce (see page 96)	½ tblsp	1 tblsp	1½ tblsp
Packed dark brown sugar	½ tblsp	1 tblsp	1½ tblsp
Cored and shredded napa cabbage (optional)	1½ cups	3 cups	4½ cups
Shredded carrots (optional)	1 cup	2 cups	3 cups
Thinly sliced fresh shiitake mushroom caps (optional)	½ cup	1 cup	1½ cups
Rice vermicelli (optional)	2 ounces	4 ounces	6 ounces

1 Peel the skin off the duck leg quarters. Remove the thick layers of fat over the meat. Place the quarters in the slow cooker and top with the broth, onions, ginger, scallions, fish sauce, and brown sugar. Stir a bit to dissolve the sugar.

2 Cover and cook on high for 4 hours or on low for 7 hours, or until the duck meat is falling-off-the-bone tender.

3 Use a wide spatula *and* a slotted spoon to transfer the quarters to a cutting board; cool for 10 minutes. Meanwhile, use the slotted spoon to remove and discard all the solids from the cooker. Cover the cooker and keep it on high.

4 Shred the meat off the bones and stir it back into the cooker. Stir any, all, or none of the optional ingredients into the soup. Cover and cook on high for 30 minutes to warm through.

TESTERS' NOTES
• Nothing is so rich as duck soup. In this Asian-inspired version, the vegetables and aromatics are discarded so you have a fairly clear soup with some chopped meat (and perhaps some vegetables) in each bowl.
• The optional ingredients here are particularly necessary if you're making a meal from the soup the day you make it. If not, store the clear soup with the meat in sealed, small-serving containers in the fridge for up to 3 days or in the freezer for up to 4 months. Stir one or more of these optional ingredients into the soup as you reheat it on the stovetop.
• For a real treat, render the duck fat into a liquid by heating the skin and fat in a skillet over low heat. Strain out the solids, then save the fat in a covered jar in the fridge for up to 2 weeks or the freezer for 4 months. Your roasted potatoes won't know what hit them.

INGREDIENTS EXPLAINED Rice vermicelli are thin noodles made from rice flour and water, like translucent angel hair pasta. (They should not be confused with cellophane noodles.) Rice vermicelli are exceptionally adept at picking up and even amplifying other flavors, particularly hot, sour, and bitter notes.

new mexican meatball soup

EFFORT: **A LITTLE** • PREP TIME: **30 MINUTES** • COOK TIME: **6 HOURS**
• KEEPS ON WARM: **NO** • SERVES: **3 TO 10**

INGREDIENTS	2- TO 3½-QT	4- TO 5½-QT	6- TO 8-QT
Olive oil	1 tblsp	1½ tblsp	3 tblsp
Chopped yellow onion	½ cup	¾ cup	1½ cups (about 1 large)
Stemmed, seeded, and chopped red and/or yellow bell pepper	½ cup	¾ cup	1½ cups (about 1 large)
Low-sodium beef broth	4 cups (1 quart)	7 cups (1 quart plus 3 cups)	12 cups (3 quarts)
No-salt-added canned diced tomatoes	1 cup	1¾ cups	3½ cups
Stemmed and minced jalapeño chile	2 tsp	1½ tblsp	2 tblsp
Minced garlic	1 tsp	2 tsp	1 tblsp
Ground coriander	¾ tsp	1 tsp	2 tsp
Ground cumin	¾ tsp	1 tsp	2 tsp
Salt	½ tsp	¾ tsp	1¼ tsp
Lean ground beef (at least 93% lean)	8 ounces	1 pound	1½ pounds
Uncooked long-grain white rice	2 tblsp	3 tblsp	⅓ cup
Large egg yolks	1	2	3
Dried oregano	1 tsp	2 tsp	1 tblsp
Ground black pepper	½ tsp	1 tsp	½ tblsp

1 Put a large skillet over medium heat for a few minutes, then swirl in the oil. Add the onion and bell pepper. Cook, stirring often, until softened a bit, between 8 and 12 minutes, depending on the size of the batch.

2 Scrape the contents of the skillet into the slow cooker. Stir in the broth, tomatoes, jalapeño, garlic, coriander, cumin, and salt.

3 Mix the ground beef, rice, egg yolks, oregano, and pepper in a large bowl until the eggs and oregano are evenly distributed in the meat and rice. With your clean, dry hands, form the mixture into meatballs, using 2 to 3 tablespoons per meatball. Drop them into the soup.

4 Cover and cook on low for 6 hours, or until the meatballs are cooked through and the flavors have blended.

TESTERS' NOTES

• Although we cut down on the stove work by not browning the meatballs in this recipe, we prefer the onion and bell pepper softened over the heat so they have a leg up on their way to getting sweet.

• That said, you certainly could brown those meatballs in the skillet over medium heat with a little additional olive oil—if you're feeling energetic. You'll have a better-tasting dinner as the payoff.

• To brighten the flavors, stir in up to 1 tablespoon red currant jelly just before serving.

sloppy joe soup

EFFORT: **A LITTLE** • PREP TIME: **20 MINUTES** • COOK TIME:
3 HOURS/5 HOURS • KEEPS ON WARM: **4 HOURS THROUGH STEP 2**
• SERVES: **3 TO 8**

INGREDIENTS	2- TO 3½-QT	4- TO 5½-QT	6- TO 8-QT
Olive oil	1 tblsp	2 tblsp	3 tblsp
Lean ground beef (at least 93% lean)	¾ pound	1¼ pounds	2 pounds
Low-sodium beef broth	3 cups	5 cups	8 cups (2 quarts)
No-salt-added canned crushed tomatoes	1¾ cups	2¾ cups	3½ cups
Yellow onion, chopped	1 small	1 medium	2 medium
Packed dark brown sugar	2 tblsp	¼ cup	6 tblsp
Worcestershire sauce	1 tblsp	2 tblsp	3 tblsp
Chili powder	1 tblsp	2 tblsp	3 tblsp
Ground allspice	½ tsp	¾ tsp	1¼ tsp
Ground cloves	½ tsp	¾ tsp	1¼ tsp
Cider vinegar	2 tblsp	3 tblsp	⅓ cup

1 Heat a large skillet over medium heat for a few minutes, then swirl in the oil. Crumble in the ground beef and cook, stirring often, until the meat loses all its raw pink color and has truly browned (not just grayed) in places, between 4 and 6 minutes.

2 Use a slotted spoon to transfer the ground beef to the slow cooker, leaving any fat behind. Stir in the broth, tomatoes, onion, brown sugar, Worcestershire sauce, chili powder, allspice, and cloves. Cover and cook on high for 3 hours or on low for 5 hours, or until the flavors have blended.

3 Stir in the vinegar just before serving.

TESTERS' NOTES

• If you pass around some crunchy bread or even slices of whole wheat toast, you can have the whole Sloppy Joe experience as the meal. (A soup doesn't work very well in a hamburger bun!)

• We leave the beef drippings behind, rather than using them in the soup, because they add nothing except a sticky slick. We're not fans of draining ground beef on paper towels, since the heat can loosen dyes and chemicals in the material; a slotted spoon seems a better choice.

Serve It Up! To make this a five-napkin soup, top bowlfuls with pickled jalapeño rings, dollops of chow-chow or pickle relish, and grated Cheddar cheese.

beef vegetable soup

EFFORT: **NOT MUCH** • PREP TIME: **20 MINUTES** • COOK TIME:
4 HOURS/8 HOURS • KEEPS ON WARM: **4 HOURS** • SERVES: **3 TO 8**

INGREDIENTS	2- TO 3½-QT	4- TO 5½-QT	6- TO 8-QT
Beef chuck roast, trimmed and diced	¾ pound	1½ pounds	2 pounds
Low-sodium beef broth	3 cups	6 cups (1½ quarts)	10 cups (2 quarts plus 2 cups)
Brown ale or porter	1½ cups (12 ounces)	2¼ cups (18 ounces)	3 cups (24 ounces)
Carrots, thinly sliced	2 medium	3 medium	5 medium
Turnips, peeled and diced	½ pound	1 pound	1¼ pounds

Medium celery ribs, thinly sliced	1	1½	2
Chopped ripe tomato	½ cup	¾ cup	1 cup (about ½ pound)
Worcestershire sauce	1 tblsp	1½ tblsp	2 tblsp
Minced garlic	½ tsp	¾ tsp	1 tsp
Dried oregano	½ tsp	¾ tsp	1 tsp
Ground allspice	½ tsp	¾ tsp	1 tsp
Salt	½ tsp	¾ tsp	1 tsp
Ground black pepper	½ tsp	¾ tsp	1 tsp
No-salt-added tomato paste	1½ tblsp	2½ tblsp	3 tblsp
Red wine vinegar	2 tsp	1 tblsp	1½ tblsp

1 Stir the beef, broth, ale, carrots, turnips, celery, tomatoes, Worcestershire sauce, garlic, oregano, allspice, salt, and pepper in the slow cooker.

2 Cover and cook on high for 4 hours or on low for 8 hours, or until the meat is tender.

3 Stir in the tomato paste and vinegar just before serving.

TESTERS' NOTES

- Rich and well stocked, this beef soup will work best if you truly dice the chuck into tiny bits, no more than ¼ inch each. Also, cut off most of the large pieces of surface fat as you dice the meat.
- Dice the veggies into small pieces of equivalent size. You want lots of different things on the spoon with every slurp.
- A brown ale gives the stew a little bitter taste, which is up our alley but maybe not everyone's. The porter offers a sweeter finish.

steak and potato soup

EFFORT: **A LITTLE** • PREP TIME: **25 MINUTES** • COOK TIME: **6 HOURS** • KEEPS ON WARM: **2 HOURS** • SERVES: **3 TO 8**

INGREDIENTS	2- TO 3½-QT	4- TO 5½-QT	6- TO 8-QT
Low-sodium beef broth	4 cups (1 quart)	6 cups (1½ quarts)	10 cups (2½ quarts)
No-salt-added tomato paste	2 tblsp	3 tblsp	⅓ cup
Olive oil	2 tsp	1 tblsp	1½ tblsp
Beef top round, cut into 1-inch cubes	½ pound	1 pound	1½ pounds
Yellow potatoes (such as Yukon Gold), peeled and diced	½ pound	¾ pound	1¼ pounds
Worcestershire sauce	1 tblsp	1½ tblsp	3 tblsp
Dried oregano	½ tblsp	2½ tsp	1½ tblsp
Dried basil	1 tsp	½ tblsp	1 tblsp
Minced garlic	1 tsp	½ tblsp	1 tblsp
Ground black pepper	½ tsp	¾ tsp	1¼ tsp
Bay leaves	1	2	3

1 Whisk the broth and tomato paste in the cooker until smooth.

2 Set a large skillet over the medium heat for a few minutes. Swirl in the oil, then add some of the beef pieces, just enough to keep about ½-inch space between them. Brown on all sides, turning occasionally, 8 to 10 minutes per batch. Transfer to the slow cooker and continue browning more as necessary.

3 Add the potatoes, Worcestershire sauce, oregano, basil, garlic, pepper, and bay leaves

(continued)

to the cooker. Stir well, then cover and cook on low for 6 hours, or until the meat and potatoes are tender. Discard the bay leaves before serving.

TESTERS' NOTES

• For more intense flavor, pour about ½ cup red wine into the skillet when you're done browning the beef, crank the heat up to high, and boil the wine down to a thick glaze, scraping everything brown off the bottom of the pan. Stir the sauce into the cooker with the other ingredients.

• Flavors can dull during cooking. If desired, stir up to 1 tablespoon red wine vinegar into the stew before serving.

asian beef noodle soup

EFFORT: **A LITTLE** • PREP TIME: **20 MINUTES** • COOK TIME: **5 HOURS/7 HOURS** • KEEPS ON WARM: **3 HOURS THROUGH STEP 1** • SERVES: **3 TO 8**

INGREDIENTS	2- TO 3½-QT	4- TO 5½-QT	6- TO 8-QT
Low-sodium chicken broth	5 cups	8 cups (2 quarts)	12 cups (3 quarts)
Beef bottom round, cut into 1-inch cubes	10 ounces	1 pound	1½ pounds
Shallots, thinly sliced	2 ounces	3 ounces	4 ounces
Julienned peeled fresh ginger	3 tblsp	¼ cup	6 tblsp
Fish sauce	1½ tblsp	2 tblsp	3 tblsp
Packed dark brown sugar	1½ tblsp	2 tblsp	3 tblsp
4-inch cinnamon stick	1	1	2
Star anise	1	2	3
Wide rice noodles	8 ounces	12 ounces	1 pound
Chopped fresh cilantro leaves	⅓ cup	½ cup	¾ cup

1 Stir the broth, beef, shallots, ginger, fish sauce, brown sugar, cinnamon stick, and star anise in the slow cooker until the brown sugar dissolves. Cover and cook on high for 4½ hours or on low for 6½ hours, or until the beef is tender.

2 About 30 minutes before the soup is ready, bring a pot of water to a boil over high heat. Set the noodles in a big bowl and cover with boiling water. Set aside to soak for 20 minutes. Drain in a colander set in the sink.

3 Stir the soaked noodles and cilantro into the soup. Cover and continue cooking on low for 30 minutes to heat through. Discard the cinnamon stick and star anise before serving.

TESTERS' NOTES

• A fairly light soup, it's a great Asian-inspired meal from your local grocery store.

• We used chicken broth (rather than beef broth) for its cleaner, more straightforward flavor.

• If the noodles sit in the colander too long, they'll glom into a ball.

Serve It Up! Garnish the bowls with bean sprouts.

INGREDIENTS EXPLAINED Fish sauce, a pungent condiment from Southeast Asia, is made from fermented fish parts and salt (and in better bottlings, a host of aromatics). Known as *nam pla* in Thai, *nuoc mam* in Vietnamese, *teuk trei* in Cambodian, and *patis* in Filipino, it mellows beautifully when heated. If you have shellfish allergies or religious concerns, check the label since some bottlings include shellfish.

beef short rib and red cabbage soup

EFFORT: **NOT MUCH** • PREP TIME: **20 MINUTES** • COOK TIME: **9 HOURS** • KEEPS ON WARM: **4 HOURS** • SERVES: **3 TO 8**

INGREDIENTS	2- TO 3½-QT	4- TO 5½-QT	6- TO 8-QT
Flanken-style beef short ribs (see page 149)	½ pound	1 pound	1½ pounds
Low-sodium beef broth	3 cups	5 cups	8 cups (2 quarts)
Cored and chopped red cabbage	1½ cups	2½ cups	4 cups (about a 1-pound head)
Peeled and diced red beets	1½ cups	2½ cups (about 1 pound)	4 cups
Peeled and diced Russet or other baking potato	⅔ cup	1⅓ cups	2 cups (about 10 ounces)
Chopped red onion	⅓ cup	⅔ cup	1 cup (about 1 medium)
Thinly sliced carrot	⅓ cup	⅔ cup	1 cup (about 3 medium)
Red wine vinegar	3 tblsp	⅓ cup	½ cup
Minced fresh dill fronds	3 tblsp	⅓ cup	½ cup
Sugar	2 tsp	1½ tblsp	2 tblsp
Ground cloves	½ tsp	1 tsp	½ tblsp
Salt	¼ tsp	½ tsp	¾ tsp
Ground black pepper	¼ tsp	½ tsp	¾ tsp

1 Mix the short ribs, broth, cabbage, beets, potato, onion, carrot, vinegar, dill, sugar, cloves, salt, and pepper in the slow cooker.

2 Cover and cook on low for 9 hours, or until the beef is fork-tender. The bones will have fallen apart as the soup cooks; fish out the bare or almost-bare ones before serving, taking care to shred any straggling meat off them before discarding them.

TESTERS' NOTES
• All those bones add up to lots of flavor in this old-fashioned deli soup!
• If you can't find flanken-style or cross-cut short ribs, you can use the more common English-cut short ribs. The meat will be in larger chunks and may need up to 2 additional hours on low to get tender.

pork soup with red peppers and hominy

EFFORT: **NOT MUCH** • PREP TIME: **20 MINUTES** • COOK TIME: **3½ HOURS/8 HOURS** • KEEPS ON WARM: **3 HOURS** • SERVES: **3 TO 8**

INGREDIENTS	2- TO 3½-QT	4- TO 5½-QT	6- TO 8-QT
Low-sodium beef broth	4 cups (1 quart)	6 cups (1½ quarts)	10 cups (2½ quarts)
Boneless pork loin, diced	½ pound	¾ pound	1¼ pounds
Drained and chopped jarred roasted red peppers (pimientos)	1½ cups	2½ cups	4 cups
Drained and rinsed canned hominy	1 cup	1½ cups	2½ cups
Chopped yellow onion	¾ cup	1 cup	1½ cups
Minced fresh cilantro leaves	¼ cup	6 tblsp	⅔ cup
Fresh lime juice	2 tblsp	3 tblsp	⅓ cup
Minced fresh oregano leaves	1 tblsp	1½ tblsp	2½ tblsp
Ground black pepper	1 tsp	½ tblsp	2½ tsp
Salt	½ tsp	¾ tsp	1 tsp

1 Mix the broth, pork loin, roasted red peppers, hominy, onion, cilantro, lime juice, oregano, pepper, and salt in the slow cooker.

2 Cover and cook on high for 3½ hours or on low for 8 hours, or until the pork is tender.

TESTERS' NOTES

• Sort of like southwestern posole, a pork-and-hominy stew, this recipe offers gigantic flavors without much work. And it freezes well, sealed in containers for up to 4 months. (After thawing and reheating, squeeze a little lime juice over each serving to refresh the flavors.)

• The soup needs fresh herbs, not dried, to give it a lighter flavor.

Serve It Up! Top each bowl with diced avocado.

pork soup with cinnamon and potatoes

EFFORT: **A LITTLE** • PREP TIME: **20 MINUTES** • COOK TIME: **7 HOURS 15 MINUTES** • KEEPS ON WARM: **2 HOURS THROUGH STEP 2** • SERVES: **3 TO 8**

INGREDIENTS	2- TO 3½-QT	4- TO 5½-QT	6- TO 8-QT
Toasted sesame oil	1 tblsp	2 tblsp	2½ tblsp
Bone-in country-style pork ribs (see page 197)	1 pound	1½ pounds	2¾ pounds
Low-sodium chicken broth	4 cups (1 quart)	6 cups (1½ quarts)	10 cups (2½ quarts)
Medium red-skinned potatoes, peeled and quartered	½ pound	¾ pound	1½ pounds
Soy sauce	⅓ cup	½ cup	1 cup
Dry sherry	⅓ cup	½ cup	1 cup
Packed light brown sugar	¼ cup	6 tblsp	⅔ cup
Slivered peeled garlic	1 tblsp	1½ tblsp	2½ tblsp
Cinnamon sticks	1	2	3
Star anise	1	2	3

1 Set a large skillet over medium heat for a few minutes, then swirl in the oil (or part of the oil if you need to brown in batches). Add 2 or 3 country-style ribs, just to make sure there's no crowding in the skillet. Brown on all sides, turning occasionally, about 8 minutes per batch. Transfer them to the slow cooker and continue browning more ribs as necessary, using more oil as needed.

2 Stir in the broth, potatoes, soy sauce, sherry, brown sugar, and garlic in the slow cooker until the brown sugar dissolves. Tuck the cinnamon sticks and star anise into the soup. Cover and cook on low for 7 hours, or until the meat is very tender.

3 Discard the cinnamon sticks and star anise. Transfer the ribs to a cutting board and cool for a few minutes. (Keep the soup covered and cooking on low.) Shred the meat off the bones; discard the bones and any pieces of fat or cartilage. Stir the meat back into the soup. Cover and cook on low for 15 minutes to heat through.

TESTERS' NOTES
• Modeled on a fairly traditional Chinese braise, this soup has quite a heavy dose of aromatics.
• If you want to get more authentic, substitute Shaoxing (Chinese rice wine) for the dry sherry. Look for it at larger supermarkets, in all Asian grocery stores, and from suppliers online.

Serve It Up! Sprinkle rice vinegar over the soup in the bowls.

hot and sour soup

EFFORT: **A LITTLE** • PREP TIME: **15 MINUTES** • COOK TIME: **5½ HOURS** • KEEPS ON WARM: **3 HOURS THROUGH STEP 1** • SERVES: **3 TO 8**

INGREDIENTS	2- TO 3½-QT	4- TO 5½-QT	6- TO 8-QT
Low-sodium chicken broth	4 cups (1 quart)	6 cups (1 quart plus 2 cups)	10 cups (2½ quarts)
Boneless pork loin, cut into thin matchsticks	½ pound	¾ pound	1¼ pounds
Medium carrots, thinly sliced	2	3	5
Thinly sliced fresh shiitake mushroom caps	½ cup	¾ cup	1¼ cups
Rice vinegar	3 tblsp	⅓ cup	½ cup
Soy sauce	3 tblsp	⅓ cup	½ cup
Sambal oelek (see page 404)	1 tblsp	1½ tblsp	2½ tblsp
Sugar	1 tblsp	1½ tblsp	2½ tblsp
Cornstarch	2 tblsp	3 tblsp	⅓ cup
Cold water	2 tblsp	3 tblsp	⅓ cup
Whole medium scallions, thinly sliced	1	1½	2

1 Stir the broth, pork, carrots, mushrooms, vinegar, soy sauce, sambal oelek, and sugar in the slow cooker. Cover and cook on low for 5 hours, or until the pork is tender.

2 Whisk the cornstarch and cold water in a small bowl until smooth; stir into the soup. Add the scallions, stir one more time, cover, and continue cooking on high until hot and thickened, about 30 minutes.

(continued)

• You don't need to rely on take-out for this favorite. Although not exactly authentic (no lily buds, no tofu, no complicated selection of mushrooms), the flavors are close enough to satisfy the needs of a weeknight meal.
• If you want to make it ahead and save it either in the fridge or freezer, prepare the soup through step 1. Add the cornstarch slurry and scallions only when reheating on the stovetop; cover and simmer slowly for about 15 minutes, until thickened and hot.

ALL-AMERICAN KNOW-HOW To cut a pork loin into matchsticks, first slice it into ¼-inch rounds. Lay each round on your work surface and cut each circle into thin strips. Cut any long strips in half.

lamb and barley soup

EFFORT: **NOT MUCH** • PREP TIME: **15 MINUTES** • COOK TIME: **8 HOURS** • KEEPS ON WARM: **2 HOURS THROUGH STEP 2** • SERVES: **3 TO 8**

INGREDIENTS	2- TO 3½-QT	4- TO 5½-QT	6- TO 8-QT
Low-sodium chicken broth	4 cups (1 quart)	6 cups (1½ quarts)	10 cups (2½ quarts)
Boneless lamb shoulder, trimmed of any fat chunks and cut into ½-inch cubes; or lamb stew meat, diced	10 ounces	1 pound	1¾ pounds
Thinly sliced leeks (white and pale green part only), washed to remove interior grit	⅔ cup	1 cup (about ½ pound)	1⅔ cups
Chopped carrots	⅔ cup	1 cup (2 medium)	1⅔ cups
Pearled barley (see page 24)	½ cup	⅔ cup	1¼ cups
Salt	½ tsp	¾ tsp	1¼ tsp
Ground black pepper	¼ tsp	½ tsp	¾ tsp
Chopped fresh parsley leaves	¼ cup	⅓ cup	⅔ cup

1 Stir the broth, lamb, leeks, carrots, barley, salt, and pepper in the slow cooker.

2 Cover and cook on low for 8 hours, or until the lamb is tender.

3 Stir in the parsley just before serving.

TESTERS' NOTES
• You can't beat this kind of meal, sometimes called Scotch broth—simple but comforting.
• We used lamb shoulder because it's often milder than leg of lamb and certainly easier to chop.
• Chicken broth remains a favorite for soups like this because it has a lighter finish and is milder than beef broth, and thus better pairing to the lamb.
• If you happen to be at a farmers' market and find goat shoulder, give it a whirl in place of the lamb.

Serve It Up! Boil or steam peeled, medium, white potatoes until tender. Set one potato in each bowl and ladle the soup around it.

lamb and potato soup with beer and cilantro

EFFORT: **A LITTLE** • PREP TIME: **20 MINUTES** • COOK TIME: **7 HOURS**
• KEEPS ON WARM: **3 HOURS** • SERVES: **3 TO 9**

INGREDIENTS	2- TO 3½-QT	4- TO 5½-QT	6- TO 8-QT
Packed fresh cilantro leaves	½ cup	1 cup	1½ cups
Cider vinegar	2 tblsp	3½ tblsp	⅓ cup
Ground cumin	1 tsp	2 tsp	1 tblsp
Whole garlic cloves, peeled	1	2	3
Jalapeño chiles, stemmed; also seeded if you want less heat	Up to 1	Up to 2	Up to 3
Low-sodium chicken broth	3 cups	6 cups (1½ quarts)	9 cups (2 quarts plus 1 cup)
Dark beer, 12-ounce bottles, such as porter or stout	1	2	3
Chopped red onion	⅓ cup	½ cup	1 cup (about 1 medium)
Salt	½ tsp	¾ tsp	1¼ tsp
Boneless leg of lamb, trimmed and cut into ½-inch pieces, or lamb stew meat, diced	12 ounces	1½ pounds	2½ pounds
Medium yellow potatoes (such as Yukon Gold), peeled and halved	3	6	9

1 Place the cilantro, vinegar, cumin, garlic, and jalapeños in a large blender. Cover, whir a few seconds, scrape down the inside of the canister, and continue blending, adding just enough of the broth so that the mixture can become a smooth puree. Pour and scrape it into the slow cooker.

2 Stir in the remainder of the broth plus the beer, onion, and salt until fairly smooth (except for the onion and herb bits). Stir in the lamb and potatoes.

3 Cover and cook on low for 7 hours, or until the lamb and potatoes are tender.

TESTERS' NOTES

• The amount of heat in this soup is a matter of personal taste. Just remember that a slow cooker digests the spice in chiles; you may be able to stand more than you think. That said, err on the side of caution the first time you prepare this dish: you can always pass pickled jalapeño rings at the table for garnish.
• The porter will be a sweeter beer, better to balance the chiles and cilantro. A thick stout gives the soup a lot of body and a more sophisticated flavor. (Just don't use a flavored stout.)

Serve It Up! Serve this soup in a **Bread Bowl:** Buy small boules or round Tuscan loaves. Cut off the tops and use your fingers to pull out the doughy insides, leaving a 1-inch shell all around the bowl. Fill the bread with the soup but serve it in a bowl, just in case there's structural failure.

manhattan clam chowder

EFFORT: **A LITTLE** • PREP TIME: **20 MINUTES** • COOK TIME: **6 HOURS** • KEEPS ON WARM: **2 HOURS BEFORE STEP 3** • SERVES: **3 TO 8**

INGREDIENTS	2- TO 3½-QT	4- TO 5½-QT	6- TO 8-QT
Slab bacon, diced	4 ounces	6 ounces	10 ounces
Yellow onions, chopped	1 large	2 medium	2 large
Medium celery ribs, chopped	3	4	6
Bottled clam juice	1 cup	1½ cups	2½ cups
Low-sodium chicken broth	2 cups	3 cups	5 cups (1 quart plus 1 cup)
No-salt-added canned diced tomatoes	1¾ cups	2½ cups	4½ cups
Red-skinned potatoes, diced	¼ pound	½ pound	¾ pound
Dried thyme	1 tsp	½ tblsp	2½ tsp
Dried oregano	1 tsp	½ tblsp	2½ tsp
Ground black pepper	½ tsp	¾ tsp	1 tsp
Minced shucked, raw clams	2 cups	3 cups	5 cups

1 Fry the bacon bits in a medium skillet set over medium heat until brown and crisp, stirring often, from 4 to 8 minutes, depending on the size of the batch. Use a slotted spoon to transfer the bacon to the slow cooker.

2 Fry the onions and celery in the bacon fat in the skillet, still set over medium heat, stirring often, until the onions are translucent, between 5 and 9 minutes. Scrape the contents of the skillet into the slow cooker.

3 Stir in the clam juice, broth, tomatoes, potatoes, thyme, oregano, and pepper. Cover and cook on low for 5 hours.

4 Stir in the clams. Cover and continue cooking on low for 1 hour, or until the clams and potatoes are tender.

TESTERS' NOTES
• Manhattan clam chowder is tomato-based.
• We peeled the potatoes in the New England Clam Chowder (below) because we wanted the soup to be creamy white. Since there are already tomatoes in this mix, we don't have to go to the trouble.

SHORTCUTS Look for shucked (sometimes chopped) clams in the refrigerator section of the fish counter, or look for tubs of it in the freezer case.

new england clam chowder

EFFORT: **A LOT** • PREP TIME: **35 MINUTES** • COOK TIME: **4 HOURS/ 8 HOURS** • KEEPS ON WARM: **2 HOURS THROUGH STEP 4** • SERVES: **2 TO 6**

INGREDIENTS	2- TO 3½-QT	4- TO 5½-QT	6- TO 8-QT
Thin strips of bacon	4	6	10
Yellow onion, chopped	1 small	1 medium	1 large
Medium celery ribs, chopped	½	1	1½
Red-skinned potatoes, peeled and diced	10 ounces	1 pound	1½ pounds
Low-sodium chicken broth	2 cups	3 cups	5 cups (1 quart plus 1 cup)

Bottled clam juice	⅔ cup	1 cup	1¾ cups
Evaporated milk (regular or low-fat)	1⅓ cups	2 cups	2½ cups
All-purpose flour	3 tblsp	¼ cup	½ cup
Dried thyme	½ tsp	¾ tsp	1¼ tsp
Red pepper flakes (optional)	Up to ¼ tsp	Up to ½ tsp	Up to ¾ tsp
Minced shucked, raw clams	1⅓ cups	2 cups	2½ cups

1 Fry the bacon in a very large skillet set over medium heat, turning occasionally, until very crisp, between 4 and 8 minutes. Transfer the strips to a paper-towel–lined plate.

2 Fry the onion and celery in the bacon fat, stirring often, until the onion is translucent, between 3 and 7 minutes. Scrape the contents of the skillet into the slow cooker.

3 Blot the bacon dry with paper towels, then crumble it into the cooker. Stir in the potatoes, broth, and clam juice.

4 Whisk the evaporated milk and flour in a large bowl until the flour is completely dissolved; stir into the slow cooker. Stir in the thyme and red pepper flakes (if using).

5 Cover and cook on high for 3 hours or on low for 7 hours, or until the potatoes are tender. Add the clams and continue cooking on low for 1 hour, or until the flavors have blended and the clams are tender.

TESTERS' NOTES
• Creamy and rich, here's the celebrated coastal soup, a summertime favorite from Connecticut to Maine. By using evaporated milk and less flour, we guard against any chance that it might become wallpaper paste.
• New England clam chowder is traditionally not spicy. That said, we're not New Englanders (we just happen to live there), so we add red pepper flakes for pop.

• Oh, for good shellfish stock! You can make your own (see page 113), you can search out shellfish *demi-glace* at higher-end markets, or you can use clam juice, the bottles often shelved near the canned tuna or the chili sauce and other spicy condiments in supermarkets.

shrimp bisque

EFFORT: **A LOT** • PREP TIME: **40 MINUTES** • COOK TIME: **4 HOURS 20 MINUTES/7 HOURS 20 MINUTES** • KEEPS ON WARM: **4 HOURS THROUGH STEP 2** • SERVES: **3 TO 8**

INGREDIENTS	2- TO 3½-QT	4- TO 5½-QT	6- TO 8-QT
Medium shrimp (about 30 per pound), peeled and deveined, shells reserved	1 pound	1½ pounds	2½ pounds
Leeks (white and pale green part only), washed to remove grit, thinly sliced	¾ pound	1¼ pounds	2 pounds
Medium carrots, cut into 1-inch chunks	2	3	6
Medium celery ribs, cut into 2-inch pieces	2	3	6
Finely grated orange zest	1 tblsp	1½ tblsp	2½ tblsp
Fresh thyme sprigs	3	5	8
Fresh tarragon sprigs	1	2	3
Bay leaves	1	2	3
Brandy	¼ cup	⅓ cup	⅔ cup
No-salt-added tomato paste	2 tblsp	3 tblsp	⅓ cup
Water	4 cups (1 quart)	6 cups (1½ quarts)	10 cups (2½ quarts)
Heavy cream	⅓ cup	½ cup	1 cup
All-purpose flour	2 tblsp	3 tblsp	6 tblsp

(continued)

1 Set the shrimp in a large bowl, cover, and refrigerate. Place the shells in the slow cooker along with the leeks, carrots, celery, orange zest, thyme, tarragon, and bay leaves. Whisk the brandy and tomato paste in a small bowl until smooth, then stir into the other ingredients until everything's well coated. Pour in enough water to cover everything.

2 Cover and cook on high for 4 hours or on low for 7 hours, or until the soup is very fragrant.

3 Strain the soup into a large bowl through a fine-mesh sieve or a colander lined with cheesecloth. Pour the soup back in the cooker; discard all the solids. Cover and set the cooker on high heat.

4 Whisk the cream and flour in a bowl until all the flour has dissolved. Whisk this mixture into the soup. Stir in the shrimp; cover and continue cooking on high for 20 minutes, or until the soup is thickened and the shrimp are pink and firm.

TESTERS' NOTES

• We have a lot of recipes in this book that won't win the authenticity awards. But not this one! It's a rich, creamy bisque, a New Orleans favorite.

• There is no substitute for using the shrimp shells, which are essential for a flavorful and aromatic soup.

• If you use a large piece of cheesecloth to line a colander, you'll need to hold it in place while you strain the soup. Ladle the soup into it in small batches for better control.

ALL-AMERICAN KNOW-HOW A fine-mesh sieve comes in handy in the kitchen; after all, many of these vegetable bits would slip through a standard colander. If you don't have such a sieve, line a colander with a single layer of sturdy paper towels. A conical sieve is called a *chinoise* (*sheen-WAHZ*), originally named in less PC times because of its resemblance to a Chinese hat.

lobster bisque

EFFORT: **A LOT** • PREP TIME: **30 MINUTES** • COOK TIME: **4 HOURS 20 MINUTES/8 HOURS 20 MINUTES** • KEEPS ON WARM: **3 HOURS THROUGH STEP 2** • SERVES: **3 TO 8**

INGREDIENTS	2- TO 3½-QT	4- TO 5½-QT	6- TO 8-QT
Shell-on frozen lobster tails, thawed	2	3	5
Low-sodium chicken broth	2 cups	1¾ cups	2¾ cups
No-salt-added canned diced tomatoes	1 cup	1¾ cups	2¾ cups
Bottled clam juice	⅔ cup	1 cup	1⅔ cups
Thinly sliced leeks (white part only), washed to remove interior sand	⅔ cup	1 cup (about ¾ pound)	1⅔ cups
Dried sage	1 tsp	½ tblsp	2½ tsp
Dried thyme	¾ tsp	1 tsp	1¾ tsp
Grated nutmeg	⅛ tsp	¼ tsp	½ tsp
Ground allspice	⅛ tsp	¼ tsp	½ tsp
Cayenne	Up to ⅛ tsp	Up to ¼ tsp	Up to ½ tsp
Heavy cream	⅔ cup	1 cup	1⅔ cups

1 Remove the lobster tails from their shells. Chop the meat, set it in a bowl, cover, and refrigerate until needed.

2 Set the shells in the slow cooker. Add the broth, tomatoes, clam juice, leeks, sage, thyme, nutmeg, allspice, and cayenne. Cover and cook on high for 4 hours or on low for 8 hours.

3 Turn the cooker to high heat. Use tongs to remove the lobster shells from the soup; discard them. Stir in the cream. Puree the soup either by using an immersion blender right in the slow cooker or by ladling the soup in batches into a large blender, covering, and blending until smooth, all before pouring it back into the slow cooker.

4 Stir in the lobster meat. Cover and cook on high for 20 minutes, or until the lobster is cooked through.

TESTERS' NOTES
• Here, we don't need a thickener since all the vegetables add their heft to the soup. The results aren't as creamy smooth as Shrimp Bisque (page 103) but certainly brighter.
• In many recipes, you can use the pale green parts of the leek as well as the white bits. However, those green leaves will turn the bisque a lurid color once it's pureed. If wasting parts of the leek bothers you, substitute a diced sweet onion, such as a Vidalia, for a less complex flavor.

fish and rice soup with tarragon and lemon

EFFORT: **A LOT** • PREP TIME: **30 MINUTES** • COOK TIME: **4½ HOURS (AT MOST)** • KEEPS ON WARM: **NO** • SERVES: **3 TO 8**

INGREDIENTS	2- TO 3½-QT	4- TO 5½-QT	6- TO 8-QT
Low-sodium chicken broth	3 cups	4½ cups	6 cups (1½ quarts)
Bottled clam juice	1 cup	1½ cups	2 cups
Ripe tomatoes, chopped	½ pound	¾ pound	1 pound
Medium carrots, thinly sliced	1½	2½	4
Yellow onion, chopped	1 small	1 medium	1 large
Uncooked long-grain white rice, such as basmati	½ cup	¾ cup	1¼ cups
Finely grated lemon zest	2 tsp	1 tblsp	1½ tblsp
Fresh tarragon sprigs	2	3	4
Thick white-fleshed fish fillets (such as halibut, cod, scrod, haddock, or pollock), any skin removed	1 pound	1½ pounds	2 pounds

1 Combine the broth, clam juice, tomatoes, carrots, onion, rice, lemon zest, and tarragon in the slow cooker. Cover and cook on high for 4 hours, or until the rice and vegetables are very soft.

2 Discard the tarragon sprigs; maintain the cooker's heat. Puree the soup: use an immersion blender in the slow cooker; or ladle the soup into a large blender, in batches as necessary, cover, and blend until smooth before pouring it back into the slow cooker.

3 Chunk the fish fillets into serving-size pieces and set them in the soup. Cover and cook on high for 20 to 30 minutes, until the fish flakes when scraped with a fork.

TESTERS' NOTES
• The rice thickens the puree, creating a creamy soup with no dairy in sight.
• This soup does not freeze well—or even store well in the refrigerator. Plan on having a crowd for dinner if you're working with a large slow cooker.

shrimp and lime soup

EFFORT: **A LITTLE** • PREP TIME: **15 MINUTES** • COOK TIME: **4 HOURS 20 MINUTES** • KEEPS ON WARM: **3 HOURS THROUGH STEP 1** • SERVES: **3 TO 8**

INGREDIENTS	2- TO 3½-QT	4- TO 5½-QT	6- TO 8-QT
Low-sodium chicken broth	5 cups (1 quart plus 1 cup)	10 cups (2½ quarts)	14 cups (3½ quarts)
Medium yellow onions, peeled and quartered	2	3	4
Whole garlic cloves, peeled and smashed	8	12	16
Fresh cilantro sprigs	10	15	20
Jalapeño chiles, stemmed, halved, and seeded (or not, to increase the heat)	2	3	5
Whole cloves	2 tsp	1 tblsp	1½ tblsp
Medium shrimp (about 30 per pound), peeled and deveined	1 pound	2½ pounds	3½ pounds
Fresh, strained lime juice	¼ cup	7 tblsp	⅔ cup
Salt	⅛ tsp	¼ tsp	½ tsp

1 Stir the broth, onions, garlic, cilantro, jalapeños, and cloves in the slow cooker. Cover and cook on low for 4 hours.

2 Use a slotted spoon to remove and discard all the solids in the soup. Stir in the shrimp, lime juice, and salt. Cover and continue cooking on low for 20 minutes, or until the shrimp are pink and firm.

TESTERS' NOTES
• Based on a rather well-known soup from the Yucatán peninsula, this sour bowlful is a bright spark on a chilly evening.

• For even more shrimpy flavor, cook the shells in the soup for the first 4 hours. Strain these out as well.

red snapper chowder with zucchini and black olives

EFFORT: **NOT MUCH** • PREP TIME: **15 MINUTES** • COOK TIME: **3½ HOURS/6½ HOURS** • KEEPS ON WARM: **2 HOURS THROUGH STEP 1** • SERVES: **4 TO 10**

INGREDIENTS	2- TO 3½-QT	4- TO 5½-QT	6- TO 8-QT
Low-sodium chicken broth	4 cups (1 quart)	6 cups (1½ quarts)	10 cups (2½ quarts)
No-salt-added canned diced tomatoes	1 cup	1¾ cups	3 cups
Zucchini, diced	1 pound	1 pound 6 ounces	1¾ pounds
Green bell pepper, stemmed, seeded, and diced	1 small	1 medium	2 medium
Thinly sliced pitted black olives	⅓ cup	½ cup	¾ cup
Shallot, finely chopped	2 ounces	3 ounces	4 ounces
Red (sweet) vermouth (see page 258)	3 tblsp	¼ cup	½ cup
Dried basil	2 tsp	1 tblsp	1½ tblsp
Dried rosemary	¾ tsp	1 tsp	2 tsp
Salt	¼ tsp	½ tsp	¾ tsp
Ground black pepper	¼ tsp	½ tsp	¾ tsp

Skinless red snapper fillets, cut into 1-inch pieces	1 pound	1½ pounds	2½ pounds

1 Stir the broth, tomatoes, zucchini, bell pepper, olives, shallot, vermouth, basil, rosemary, salt, and pepper in the slow cooker. Cover and cook on high for 3 hours or on low for 6 hours.

2 Stir in the fish. Cover and continue cooking on low for 30 minutes, until the fish is cooked through.

TESTERS' NOTES
• Like an Italian fish stew, this well-stocked soup will stand up well on a chilly evening, provided you've also got some crunchy bread on hand—or at least crackers.
• The snapper must be skinless; otherwise, the pieces will curl as they cook. That said, the meat will still fall apart as it cooks, so don't stir it much and ladle it carefully into bowls.
• If you can't find skinless red snapper fillets, ask the fishmonger at your supermarket to skin the fish for you.

the ultimate seafood soup

EFFORT: **NOT MUCH** • PREP TIME: **20 MINUTES** • COOK TIME: **3 HOURS/5½ HOURS** • KEEPS ON WARM: **3 HOURS THROUGH STEP 1** • SERVES: **3 TO 8**

INGREDIENTS	2- TO 3½-QT	4- TO 5½-QT	6- TO 8-QT
Low-sodium chicken broth	2½ cups	5 cups (1 quart plus 1 cup)	8 cups (2 quarts)
No-salt-added canned diced tomatoes	1¾ cups	3½ cups	5¼ cups
Fennel bulb, trimmed and chopped (see page 211)	1 small	1 medium	1 large
Dry white wine, such as Pinot Grigio	1 cup	2 cups	3 cups
Bottled clam juice	½ cup	1 cup	1½ cups
Shallots, chopped	6 ounces	12 ounces	1¼ pounds
No-salt-added tomato paste	2 tblsp	¼ cup	6 tblsp
Minced garlic	1 tsp	2 tsp	1 tblsp
Fennel seeds	½ tsp	1 tsp	½ tblsp
Red pepper flakes	¼ tsp	½ tsp	¾ tsp
Bay leaves	1	2	3
Skinless halibut or snapper fillets, cut into 1-inch pieces	½ pound	1 pound	1½ pounds
Medium shrimp (about 30 per pound), peeled and deveined	½ pound	1 pound	1½ pounds

1 Stir the broth, tomatoes, fennel, wine, clam juice, shallots, tomato paste, garlic, fennel seeds, red pepper flakes, and bay leaves in the slow cooker until the tomato paste dissolves. Cover and cook on high for 2½ hours or on low for 5 hours.

2 Stir in the halibut or snapper and the shrimp. Cover and continue cooking on high for 30 more minutes, or until the fish is cooked through and the shrimp are pink and firm. Discard the bay leaves before serving.

TESTERS' NOTES
• Considering what you get for your effort, this soup is pretty amazing—tomato-laced, herbaceous, and well stocked. There's not much else you need.
• Substitute quartered sea scallops, chopped lobster tail, or lump crab meat for the fish.

Serve It Up! Serve alongside grilled bread slices spread smeared with pesto.

stocks

If you want to pump up your foodie creds without wasting money on crazy ingredients you'll never use again, you've come to the right place. Making your own stock is the hallmark of a careful cook; using it is a testament to how much you love your friends and family. You'll be surprised at how easy the slow cooker makes this very cheffy task.

Many of these recipes call for various trimmings: turkey necks, fish heads, shrimp shells. Here's your chance to get to know the people behind the meat or fish counter at your supermarket. Tell them you're making stock; you'll rack up big points (a real help when you later ask for short ribs cut the long way on a special order). Befriend your butcher and you'll be sure to get the freshest bits available for this very culinary extravagance.

If you're hankering for vegetable stock, start saving vegetable trimmings in sealed plastic bags in the freezer; collect extraneous bits of carrots, potato peels, even chopped onion. There's no need to thaw these before they hit the cooker; simply add an additional 2 hours to the cooking time.

Many of these stocks also ask you to brown some items first, because if you're going to the trouble of making stock, you might as well make the best you can. That said, you don't *need* to brown ahead; you can just toss the trimmings into the cooker. The results will be less intense, a bit more like soup than stock.

To strain the stock, you'll also need a fine-mesh sieve—a specialty tool available at all cookware stores or online outlets. A colander can let bits of herbs, grains of black pepper, and even protein or vegetable matter slip through its holes and cloud the stock. However, you needn't buy specialty equipment. You can indeed line a large colander with cheesecloth (look for it in the baking aisle or near the aluminum foil) or a very large coffee filter before straining the stock; unfortunately, these latter options require you to hold the filter in place so it doesn't slip around. In any case, underneath that fine-mesh sieve or jerry-rigged colander, you'll need a big bowl—a really big bowl. Think of how much stock you've got in the slow cooker. You may have to use two big bowls for large batches.

Don't pour the soup directly into the sieve or lined colander; use a big ladle. There'll be less splashing (and so less waste) and you'll be less likely to force bits of dissolved matter down into the broth under the waterfall whoosh of a gallon of stock. To avoid messy counters, set a bowl in the sink, haul the cooker to it, and put the sieve or colander over the bowl—*then* start ladling. It'll be easier to clean up the inevitable slips and spills.

Finally, store stock in sealed containers in the freezer. Smaller quantities are preferred; after all, substituting just a small portion of a homemade stock for a canned broth in a recipe will make a marked difference. If a recipe calls for 4 cups chicken broth, use 1 cup homemade stock and 3 cups canned broth. You'll be astounded at what happens— as well you should, since you went to the trouble to make the stock in the first place.

vegetable stock

EFFORT: **A LOT** • PREP TIME: **40 MINUTES** • COOK TIME: **8 HOURS** • KEEPS ON WARM: **6 HOURS** • MAKES: **1 TO 3 CUPS**

INGREDIENTS	2- TO 3½-QT	4- TO 5½-QT	6- TO 8-QT
Yellow onions, roughly chopped	1 medium	1 large	2 large
Medium carrots, roughly chopped	2	3	5
Medium parsnips, peeled and roughly chopped	2	3	4
Olive oil	1 tblsp	1½ tblsp	2 tblsp
Medium celery ribs, halved	2	4	6
Potato peels	1 cup	2 cups	3 cups
Salt	1 tsp	½ tblsp	2 tsp
Ground black pepper	1 tsp	½ tblsp	2 tsp
Fresh thyme sprigs	2	4	6
Whole garlic cloves, peeled	2	3	4
Bay leaves	1	2	3
Water	Around 4 cups	Around 7 cups	Around 11 cups

1 Position the rack in the center of the oven; heat the oven to 400°F.

2 Toss the onion, carrots, and parsnips with the olive oil in a large roasting pan or on a large, rimmed baking sheet. Roast for 30 minutes, stirring occasionally, until a bit browned. Use tongs to transfer the vegetable pieces to the slow cooker.

3 Stir in the celery, potato peels, salt, pepper, thyme, garlic, and bay leaves. Pour in enough water just to submerge the vegetables.

4 Cover and cook on low for 8 hours, or until the vegetables are soft and tender. Set

a fine-mesh sieve or a colander lined with cheesecloth over a large bowl; ladle in the stock and strain into the bowl below. Discard the solids; store the stock in sealed containers in the fridge for up to 3 days or in the freezer for up to 3 months.

chicken stock

EFFORT: **A LOT** • PREP TIME: **30 MINUTES** • COOK TIME: **10 HOURS** • KEEPS ON WARM: **6 HOURS** • MAKES: **1 TO 3 QUARTS**

INGREDIENTS	2- TO 3½-QT	4- TO 5½-QT	6- TO 8-QT
Chicken wings, backs, necks, and/or feet	1½ pounds	3 pounds	4½ pounds
Small yellow onions, quartered	2	3	5
Medium carrots, halved	2	3	5
Medium parsnips, peeled and halved	1	2	3
Fresh parsley (leaves and stems)	½ cup	1 cup	1½ cups
Salt	½ tsp	1 tsp	½ tblsp
Ground black pepper	½ tsp	1 tsp	½ tblsp
Ground allspice	¼ tsp	½ tsp	¾ tsp
Water	Around 3½ cups	Around 8 cups	Around 12 cups

1 Position the rack in the center of the oven; heat the oven to 425°F.

2 Set the chicken parts in a roasting pan, a broiler pan, or on a large, rimmed baking sheet. Roast for 20 minutes, until lightly browned. Use tongs to transfer the chicken pieces to the slow cooker.

3 Add the onions, carrots, parsnips, parsley, salt, pepper, and allspice. Pour in enough water to submerge everything and stir well.

4 Cover and cook on low for 10 hours. Strain through a fine-mesh sieve or a colander lined with cheesecloth and into a big bowl—or maybe two bowls for the large slow cooker. Seal and refrigerate for up to 4 days or freeze for up to 6 months.

turkey stock

EFFORT: **A LITTLE** • PREP TIME: **15 MINUTES** • COOK TIME: **10 HOURS** • KEEPS ON WARM: **4 HOURS** • MAKES: **1 TO 3 QUARTS**

INGREDIENTS	2- TO 3½-QT	4- TO 5½-QT	6- TO 8-QT
Turkey wings and/or necks; or an equivalent amount of leftover turkey carcass, chopped to fit the cooker	1½ pounds	3 pounds	4½ pounds
Medium carrots, halved	2	3	6
Medium celery ribs, halved	2	3	6
Small yellow onions, quartered	1	2	4
Whole garlic cloves, peeled	1	2	4
Salt	½ tsp	¾ tsp	1 tsp
Black peppercorns	1 tsp	2 tsp	1 tblsp
Bay leaves	1	2	4
Water	Around 3½ cups	Around 8 cups	Around 12 cups

1 Place the turkey pieces, carrots, celery, onions, garlic, salt, peppercorns, and bay leaves

in the slow cooker. Pour in enough water that the items are submerged; stir well.

2 Cover and cook on low for 10 hours. Strain the stock into a large bowl—or two—through a fine-mesh sieve or a cheesecloth-lined colander. Seal and store in the fridge for up to 4 days or in the freezer for up to 6 months.

beef stock

EFFORT: **A LOT** • PREP TIME: **45 MINUTES** • COOK TIME: **16 HOURS** • KEEPS ON WARM: **4 HOURS** • MAKES: **1 TO 3 QUARTS**

INGREDIENTS	2- TO 3½-QT	4- TO 5½-QT	6- TO 8-QT
Beef bones with meat still attached (such as shank bones, oxtails, short ribs, or bone trimmings)	1½ pounds	3 pounds	5 pounds
Medium yellow onions, quartered	1	2	3
Medium carrots, halved	2	3	4
Medium celery ribs, halved	2	3	4
Dry white wine, such as Chardonnay or Pinot Grigio	¼ cup	½ cup	⅔ cup
Fresh parsley (stems and leaves)	⅓ cup	⅔ cup	1 cup
Whole garlic cloves, peeled	4	8	12
Fresh sage leaves	6	8	10
Fresh thyme sprigs	3	5	8
Black peppercorns	1 tsp	2 tsp	1 tblsp
Salt	½ tsp	1 tsp	½ tblsp
Water	Around 4 cups	Around 8 cups	Around 12 cups

(continued)

1 Position the rack in the center of the oven; heat the oven to 400°F.

2 Lay the bones in a roasting pan or on a rimmed baking sheet. Bake until browned, about 30 minutes.

3 Transfer the bones to the slow cooker. Add the onions, carrots, celery, wine, parsley, garlic, sage, thyme, peppercorns, and salt. Pour in enough water so that everything's submerged; stir well.

4 Cover and cook on low for 16 hours. Strain through a fine-mesh sieve or a cheesecloth-lined colander into a big bowl (or two). Discard the solids; store the stock in sealed containers in the fridge for up to 4 days or in the freezer for up to 6 months.

Serve It Up! Although stock can be the basis for great soups, stews, and braises, it can also be quite a meal on its own—or even a course in a larger meal. Serve this hearty stock in small bowls at a holiday dinner for a very rich starter. Or put sliced scallions, canned sliced water chestnuts, and minced fresh ginger in bowls, then ladle the beef stock on top for a satisfying meal for a sick family member.

fish stock

EFFORT: **A LITTLE** • PREP TIME: **15 MINUTES** • COOK TIME: **8 HOURS** • KEEPS ON WARM: **3 HOURS** • MAKES: **1½ TO 3½ QUARTS**

INGREDIENTS	2- TO 3½-QT	4- TO 5½-QT	6- TO 8-QT
Fish heads, tails, backbones, and other trimmings (no innards)	1¼ pounds	2½ pounds	4 pounds
Chopped yellow onion	⅓ cup	¾ cup	1¼ cups
Thinly sliced carrot	⅓ cup	¾ cup	1¼ cups
Thinly sliced celery	⅓ cup	¾ cup	1¼ cups
Fresh parsley (stems and leaves)	¼ cup	½ cup	¾ cup
Black peppercorns	1 tsp	2 tsp	1 tblsp
Bay leaves	1	2	3
Water	Around 4 cups	Around 8 cups	Around 12 cups
Medium-dry white wine, such as Viognier	⅓ cup	⅔ cup	1 cup
Fresh lemon juice	½ tblsp	1 tblsp	1½ tblsp

1 Toss the fish bits, onion, carrot, celery, parsley, peppercorns, and bay leaves in the slow cooker. Pour in enough water so that everything is submerged, then stir in the wine and lemon juice.

2 Cover and cook on low for 8 hours. Strain into a large bowl—or two, for big batches— through a fine-mesh sieve or a colander lined with cheesecloth or a large paper towel. Discard the solids, seal the stock in individual containers, and store in the fridge for up to 3 days or in the freezer for up to 3 months.

shellfish stock

EFFORT: **A LITTLE** • PREP TIME: **20 MINUTES** • COOK TIME: **8 HOURS**
• KEEPS ON WARM: **3 HOURS** • MAKES: **1 TO 3 QUARTS**

INGREDIENTS	2- TO 3½-QT	4- TO 5½-QT	6- TO 8-QT
Shrimp, crab, or lobster shells	3 cups	5 cups	8 cups
Small yellow onions, halved	1	2	3
Medium carrots, halved	1	2	3
Fresh parsley (stems and leaves)	¼ cup	⅓ cup	⅔ cup
Whole garlic cloves, peeled	3	6	9
Fresh thyme sprigs	3	6	9
Black peppercorns	½ tsp	1 tsp	½ tblsp
Bay leaves	1	2	3
Medium-dry white wine, such as Pinot Blanc or Grüner Veltliner	¼ cup	½ cup	¾ cup
No-salt-added tomato paste	2 tblsp	¼ cup	¾ cup
Water	Around 4 cups	Around 8 cups	Around 12 cups

1 Mix the shells, onions, carrots, parsley, garlic, thyme, peppercorns, and bay leaves in the slow cooker.

2 Whisk the wine and tomato paste in a bowl until smooth; pour over the other ingredients and toss well. Add enough water that everything is submerged.

3 Cover and cook on low for 8 hours. Strain into a large bowl (or bowls) through a fine-mesh sieve or a cheesecloth-lined colander. Discard the solids; save the stock in sealed containers for up to 2 days in the fridge or up to 3 months in the freezer.

Serve It Up! Fish stock and shellfish stock are both exceptionally rich. Until you get the hang of cooking with their assertive flavors, use them for only half the required broth in fish or shellfish recipes, filling out the rest with vegetable broth.

meat

are you didn't get a slow cooker to make whole-grain porridges and chicken noodle soup. You bought it because of a promise: that you could put a cut of beef or pork in there, set the lid on tight, cook it all day on low, and morph that hunk of meat into dinner.

There's no doubt about it: a slow cooker can render pork ribs perfect, chuck roasts splendid, and lasagna easy. To that end, you'll find dozens of recipes for every cut that's fit for the appliance: brisket, pot roast, pork loin, pork shoulder, plus lots more. And that's not to mention what the machine can do for lamb, mellowing its more aggressive flavor considerably during the long cooking. There's little to worry about in most of these recipes: just make sure the lid fits tightly and walk away.

That's not to say that there's nothing to do. While this chapter is full of easy recipes for every night of the week, as well as plenty that are worthy of your next dinner party, it also reveals a fundamental problem when it comes to cooking meat in a slow cooker: the distinct lack of browning. Short ribs cooked over eight hours on low heat will end up gray—not all fifty shades of it, but close enough to be unappetizing.

Browned meat tastes better. Searing a cut snaps apart the relatively tasteless long-chain proteins into more delectable bits, caramelizing the meat's natural sugars and giving the cut more flavor and aroma—and offering us an all-around better dinner.

That said, browning is not just about adding good taste to meat; it also solves a culinary problem for our favorite appliance. Unbrowned *ground* meat can clump, morphing into blobs and chunks in the slow cooker. While that's all well and good when it comes to meatballs and some casseroles, it's nobody's idea of a good pasta sauce. So ground beef often has to be browned to improve not only its taste but also its texture.

Some people resist the very notion of cranking up the stove at 7:30 in the morning before they head out the door for work or school, but almost no one regrets it at 7:30

that evening, when dinner is far tastier and finished with minimal effort. The slow cooker is not some sort of magic DIY hard hat into which you dump everything only to pull out dinner by the ears eight hours later. Yes, the slow cooker braises—and as you'll see, even roasts—very well. But we have to compensate for its deficits. So have a go at the stove before you dump everything into the cooker, even if you do this task in your PJs. (Never brown naked, for obvious reasons.)

This chapter starts off with lots of beef recipes, arranged mostly by cuts: ground beef, then various round steaks, followed by briskets, pot roasts, and short ribs. Next, there's a section on pork, again arranged by cuts, starting with pork chops and the pork loin, then working through various cuts to end up at ground pork. We follow all that up with lamb recipes, and then a section on veal and rabbit.

Our best advice is to stock up on all sorts of meat when you see it on sale at the supermarket. A full freezer means easier meals in the weeks ahead. And better ones, too, with just a little work at the stove once in a while.

beef

There's a great and sure divide in cuts of beef. The line runs between the quick-cookers (for example, the tenderloin and most steaks fit for the grill) and the long-cookers (brisket, arm roasts, and beef ribs, to name a few). As the modern world has set in with a vengeance and recipes have required less and less time to complete, the first category has become more popular—and more expensive, to boot. A stack of New York strip steaks will take another chunk out of your IRA account.

Meanwhile, the long-cookers sit in the meat case, often at deep discounts if you catch the sales right (look right after holidays). And sure, briskets may make an appearance at summer holidays, when they're headed for the smoker, or at fall dinners, when they become a long-braised pot roast. But most of these cuts don't fit our modern lifestyles. We love steaks—and since the bulk of the cow isn't steak, the rest of the beast is divided into cuts your grandmother knew well, the cuts stocked with connective tissue and collagen. But this is the good stuff, arguably more flavorful than any strip steak around. Still, these cuts need moist heat and several hours to become luscious. Who has the time?

You do. The slow cooker is the perfect remedy. It tenderizes the toughness over a long cooking time. Why fight the machine's success? Especially when you can have a tasty (and economical) meal on an average Tuesday night.

So you won't find any rib-eyes or hanger steaks among these offerings. A well-done filet mignon from a slow cooker? What a waste. Rather, you'll find lots of ground beef recipes, as well as plenty more for short ribs and chuck roasts, plus even more ideas for the whole range of what the cow provides, from round steaks to beef ribs, arm roast to oxtail.

That being said, these cuts have a few weaknesses. After cooking meat over open flame for millennia, we humans have lost our ability to taste raw proteins. When it comes to steak tartare or beef carpaccio, we have to gussy them up with chopped onion, mustard, and other condiments. But once we subject beef to the heat, even for a few moments, we experience the meat as tastier. And that's good news, since there are few possibilities for rare meat when there's a slow cooker at work. After all, you're going to put the pot roast or brisket or short ribs in for many hours—and although the slow cooker may indeed keep the color pink, the meat will nonetheless be cooked through, taken at least to 160°F, maybe higher, and well beyond any understanding of rare or medium-rare.

Not wanting to kick against such obvious goads, our section on beef from the slow cooker is full up with stews and braises, comfort food galore. And despite caveats about browning that meat or the impossibility of a rare steak from a slow cooker, this may be the best news we have. You can make a deep braise without much fuss. There's an old rule in some culinary circles: people crave what they can't have—barbecue in the winter and stews in the summer. The slow cooker just might render that rule irrelevant. You can braise in any season without heating up your kitchen. And if the dish is made with a chuck roast or short ribs, it won't break your budget. What's to stop beef from being dinner tonight on your table?

"real food" sloppy joes

EFFORT: **NOT MUCH** • PREP TIME: **15 MINUTES** • COOK TIME: **6 HOURS** • KEEPS ON WARM: **4 HOURS** • SERVES: **4 TO 16**

INGREDIENTS	2- TO 3½-QT	4- TO 5½-QT	6- TO 8-QT
Olive oil	1 tblsp	1½ tblsp	2 tblsp
Lean ground beef, preferably 93% lean or ground round	1 pound	2½ pounds	4 pounds
Yellow onions, minced	1 small	2 medium	2 large
Green bell peppers, stemmed, seeded, and minced	1 small	2 medium	3 medium
Medium celery ribs, minced	2	3	5
No-salt-added tomato paste	¼ cup	⅔ cup	1 cup
Red wine vinegar	2 tblsp	⅓ cup	½ cup
Molasses, preferably unsulfured	2 tblsp	⅓ cup	½ cup
Mild paprika	1 tblsp	2½ tblsp	¼ cup
Worcestershire sauce	1 tblsp	2½ tblsp	¼ cup
Minced garlic	1 tsp	2 tsp	1 tblsp plus 1 tsp
Dry mustard (see page 392)	1 tsp	2½ tsp	1 tblsp plus 1 tsp
Ground black pepper	1 tsp	2½ tsp	1 tblsp plus 1 tsp
Toasted hamburger buns, grilled Kaiser rolls, or warmed pita pockets	4	6 to 8	At least 12

1 Warm a large skillet over medium heat for a few minutes, then pour in the oil and swirl it around to coat the hot surface. Crumble the ground beef into the skillet; cook, stirring often, until well browned, between 4 and 8 minutes, depending on how much ground beef you're using. Use a slotted spoon to get the ground beef into the slow cooker.

2 Stir in the onions, bell peppers, celery, tomato paste, vinegar, molasses, paprika, Worcestershire sauce, garlic, mustard, and pepper until the tomato paste has dissolved.

3 Cover and cook on low for 6 hours, or until the vegetables have almost melted into the thickened sauce. Serve by spooning the spiced beef mixture into the buns, rolls, or pockets.

TESTERS' NOTES
• This version of the American classic has no cheating: there's no bottled barbecue sauce or ketchup that can tip the flavors into a sweet, sticky mess. Instead, the sauce is a blend of sweet and savory because of the way the vegetables naturally balance the molasses and vinegar.
• If you're working with 4 pounds of ground beef, you'll probably need to divide the oil and meat, then work in batches to get it browned, even in a very large skillet. To invest in equipment for large-batch cooking, seek out a 14-inch cast-iron or heavy metal skillet with 2-inch sides.
• It's crucial that the vegetables are minced, not just chopped or diced, so they can dissolve into the sauce. Figure on bits of vegetable no wider than the "threads" of ground beef.

Serve It Up! Have lots of pickle relish, thinly sliced tomatoes, and chopped iceberg lettuce for topping the sandwiches.

ALL-AMERICAN KNOW-HOW To mince celery, set the ribs on your cutting board and slice each one lengthwise into three or four spears. Gather the spears from one rib together, then slice crosswise into very small bits.

beefy mac and mushroom casserole

EFFORT: **A LITTLE** • PREP TIME: **25 MINUTES** • COOK TIME: **4 HOURS** • KEEPS ON WARM: **2 HOURS** • SERVES: **4 TO 10**

INGREDIENTS	2- TO 3½-QT	4- TO 5½-QT	6- TO 8-QT
Unsalted butter	1½ tblsp	2 tblsp	4 tblsp (½ stick)
Lean ground beef, preferably ground round	12 ounces	1 pound	1¾ pounds
Minced garlic	1 tsp	½ tblsp	2 tsp
Dried oregano	¾ tsp	1 tsp	2 tsp
Ground cinnamon	½ tsp	1 tsp	2 tsp
Grated nutmeg	¼ tsp	½ tsp	¾ tsp
Ground black pepper	¼ tsp	½ tsp	1 tsp
White button mushrooms, thinly sliced	12 ounces (about 3¼ cups)	1 pound (about 5 cups)	1¾ pounds (about 8 cups)
Dry white wine or dry vermouth	6 tblsp	½ cup	¾ cup plus 2 tblsp
Worcestershire sauce	2 tsp	1 tblsp	1½ tblsp
Dried macaroni, preferably whole wheat elbow	6 ounces	8 ounces	14 ounces
Milk	1⅓ cups	2 cups	3½ cups
Reduced-sodium beef broth	1⅓ cups	2 cups	3½ cups
Parmigiano-Reggiano cheese, finely grated	1½ ounces (about ⅓ cup)	2 ounces (about ½ cup)	3½ ounces (about ¾ cup plus 2 tblsp)

1 Melt half the butter in a large skillet set over medium heat. Crumble in the ground beef; cook, stirring occasionally to break it up into even smaller bits, until well browned, between 4 and 8 minutes.

2 Stir in the garlic, oregano, cinnamon, nutmeg, and black pepper. Cook for 1 minute, stirring often, until aromatic. Scrape the contents of the skillet into the slow cooker.

3 Set the skillet back over medium heat; melt the rest of the butter in it. Drop in the mushrooms; cook, stirring occasionally, until they release their moisture and it evaporates to a glaze, between 6 and 12 minutes. (If you're using the amount for a large slow cooker, you'll have to stir far more often to make sure all the mushrooms are exposed to the heat.)

4 Pour in the wine and Worcestershire sauce; crank the heat up to medium-high, and bring to a full boil. Scrape the contents of the skillet into the slow cooker.

5 Stir in the macaroni, milk, broth, and cheese. Cover and cook on low for 4 hours, or until the casserole has absorbed most of the liquid and the macaroni is tender.

TESTERS' NOTES

• You can make this comfort-food casserole in advance, storing small portions in sealed containers in the refrigerator or freezer until you're ready to reheat them. To do so, thaw in the fridge if frozen, then dump what you've got into a saucepan, add a little beef or chicken broth, cover, and bring to a simmer over medium heat, stirring occasionally.
• There's no cheese on top of the casserole, just what's stirred inside. You can always add some extra to the top, particularly thinly sliced fresh mozzarella or finely grated aged Asiago.
• For a creamier casserole, substitute crumbled fresh goat cheese (chèvre) for the grated Parmigiano-Reggiano.

(continued)

ALL-AMERICAN KNOW-HOW The quality of the purchased broth used in any recipe will directly affect its success. If you want to take your cooking to new heights, you can make your own stocks (see pages 108–113), saving them in the freezer. Or go simpler and pump up your creds by buying a range of canned broths, then tasting them at room temperature and heated in the microwave. You'll soon know which you prefer.

INGREDIENTS EXPLAINED Parmigiano-Reggiano, sometimes called Parmesan cheese, is a part-skim cheese with a musky but sweet taste and a slightly sour aroma. Authentic Parmigiano-Reggiano is stamped with its Italian name on the rind and should be bought in chunks to be grated with a microplane or through the fine holes of a box grater. Seal a chunk of Parmigiano-Reggiano tightly in plastic wrap and store in the cheese drawer of your refrigerator for up to 3 months. Cut off any white, flour-like mold with ¼-inch margins all around before using the cheese.

double-decker cheeseburger casserole

EFFORT: **NOT MUCH** • PREP TIME: **10 MINUTES** • COOK TIME: **5 HOURS** • KEEPS ON WARM: **3 HOURS** • SERVES: **4 TO 10**

INGREDIENTS	2- TO 3½-QT	4- TO 5½-QT	6- TO 8-QT
Lean ground beef, preferably 93% lean	1¼ pounds	2 pounds	3¼ pounds
Yellow onion, finely chopped	1 small	1 medium	2 medium
Worcestershire sauce	2 tblsp	3½ tblsp	5 tblsp
Italian-seasoned tomato paste	2 tblsp	3½ tblsp	5 tblsp
Cheddar cheese, grated	6 ounces (about 1½ cups)	10 ounces (about 2½ cups)	1 pound (about 4 cups)
Uncooked dried whole wheat ziti	¾ cup	1¼ cups	2 cups
Jarred pickle relish	2 tblsp	3 tblsp	⅓ cup
Ketchup	2 tblsp	3 tblsp	⅓ cup

1 Stir the ground beef, onion, Worcestershire sauce, and tomato paste in a large bowl until the meat and onion are slathered in the sauce and tomato paste.

2 Make even, full layers of the ingredients in the slow cooker in this order: half the meat mixture, half the cheese, all of the pasta, all of the pickle relish, all of the ketchup, the remainder of the meat mixture, and the remainder of the cheese.

3 Cover and cook on low for 5 hours, or until the cheese has melted and even has browned a bit at the edges, and until the casserole is fairly firm to the touch.

TESTERS' NOTES
• Here's a family favorite that's, well, beefed up to mimic the flavors of a cheeseburger, right down to the whole wheat pasta standing in for the bun. The only thing missing is a big green salad on the side.
• There's no need to boil and drain the pasta; the ziti will soften and cook in the casserole.
• Swap out other cheeses for the Cheddar: Swiss, pepper jack, or even fancier Gruyère. And while you're at it, swap out the pickle relish for chow-chow or even salsa.

INGREDIENTS EXPLAINED Tomato paste—and indeed, most canned tomato products—are available plain or "seasoned," sometimes with Italian seasonings like basil and oregano or sometimes with Southwestern ones like chiles. You'll need to read the ingredient list carefully to determine if you have the right one.

ALL-AMERICAN KNOW-HOW Ground beef is a favorite in the slow cooker, although it has a maddening tendency to clump. In casseroles like this one, it doesn't matter much, as you're going for the texture of a hamburger patty anyway. We call for very lean meat: 93% lean, and occasionally we even call for ground round or sirloin. Because there's little evaporation and thus little condensation, all the fat stays right in the cooker. When you use higher-fat ground beef, all that fat can make the meal too oily, even gooey. Leaner ground beef gives you better results—and a healthier dinner!

american chop suey

EFFORT: **NOT MUCH** • PREP TIME: **20 MINUTES** • COOK TIME: **4 HOURS** • KEEPS ON WARM: **2 HOURS** • SERVES: **4 TO 10**

INGREDIENTS	2- TO 3½-QT	4- TO 5½-QT	6- TO 8-QT
Olive oil	1 tblsp	2 tblsp	3 tblsp
Lean ground beef, preferably 93% lean or ground round	¾ pound	1¼ pounds	2 pounds
Dried whole wheat farfalle (bow-tie pasta)	5 ounces	8 ounces	12 ounces
No-salt-added canned crushed tomatoes	1 cup plus 2 tblsp	1¾ cups	3¼ cups
Stemmed, seeded, and thinly sliced green bell peppers	¾ cup	1¼ cups	2 cups (about 2 medium)
Okra, trimmed and thinly sliced	6 ounces (about ¾ cup)	12 ounces (about 1½ cups)	1 pound (about 2 cups)
Reduced-sodium vegetable broth	¾ cup	1¼ cups	2 cups
Dry white wine or dry vermouth	¾ cup	1¼ cups	2 cups
No-salt-added tomato paste	3 tblsp	⅓ cup	½ cup
Dried basil	1 tblsp	1½ tblsp	2 tblsp
Dried oregano	¼ tsp	½ tsp	1 tsp
Onion powder	¼ tsp	½ tsp	1 tsp
Garlic powder	⅛ tsp	¼ tsp	½ tsp
Red pepper flakes	⅛ tsp	¼ tsp	½ tsp
Salt	⅛ tsp	¼ tsp	½ tsp

1 Set a large skillet over medium heat for a couple of minutes, then add the oil, swirling it around the hot surface. Crumble in the ground beef and cook, stirring occasionally, until browned, between 4 and 8 minutes. Transfer the browned beef into the slow cooker with a slotted spoon.

2 Stir in the pasta, tomatoes, bell pepper, okra, broth, wine, tomato paste, basil, oregano, onion powder, garlic powder, red pepper flakes, and salt. Keep stirring until the tomato paste has dissolved into the mix.

3 Cover and cook on low, stirring once or twice, for 4 hours, or until the pasta is tender and the flavors have blended.

TESTERS' NOTES
• This isn't a Chinese dish at all. Rather, it was a favorite in American cafeterias, diners, and automats in the 1950s and '60s: a ground beef and pasta casserole stocked with vegetables and served in bowls. We've added okra and spiced it up a bit.

(continued)

• The bell pepper should be sliced into thin strips, each no more than ¼ inch wide.

• Switch out other shapes of whole wheat pasta you prefer (or as your pantry allows): ziti, rotini, fusilli, rotelle, or radiatori. But don't use small pasta shapes like orzo—or any sort of noodle. Both will dissolve too quickly into the sauce.

SHORTCUTS Use frozen bell pepper strips and frozen sliced okra, thawing them completely before adding to the slow cooker.

ground beef and vegetable "stir-fry"

EFFORT: **NOT MUCH** • PREP TIME: **15 MINUTES** • COOK TIME: **3 TO 4 HOURS** • KEEPS ON WARM: **2 HOURS** • SERVES: **3 TO 10**

INGREDIENTS	2- TO 3½-QT	4- TO 5½-QT	6- TO 8-QT
Lean ground beef, preferably 93% lean	1 pound	1¾ pounds	3 pounds
Soy sauce	2 tblsp	3 tblsp	6 tblsp
Rice vinegar	1 tblsp	2 tblsp	3 tblsp
Worcestershire sauce	1 tblsp	2 tblsp	3 tblsp
Asian red chile paste (see page 139)	1 tsp	½ tblsp	2 tsp
Five-spice powder	1 tsp	½ tblsp	2 tsp
Garlic powder	½ tsp	1 tsp	½ tblsp
Frozen mixed vegetables for stir-fries, thawed (without seasoning packet)	1 pound	1¾ pounds	3 pounds

1 Stir the ground beef with the soy sauce, vinegar, Worcestershire sauce, chile paste, five-spice powder, and garlic powder in the slow cooker until the ground beef is broken up and coated in the spices. Add the vegetables and toss gently.

2 Cover and cook on low, stirring once halfway through the cooking, for 3 hours in a small slow cooker, 3½ hours in a medium slow cooker, or 4 hours in a large slow cooker, or until the ground beef is cooked through and the spices have blended into a sauce.

TESTERS' NOTES

• Okay, this one's hardly authentic, but the classic flavors can be made into an easy casserole without having to heat up the stove.

• We reduced the cooking time here a bit so that the vegetables have a chance to stay crisp. Don't worry: the ground beef will be cooked through, provided you broke it into small bits as you stirred in the condiments and spices.

• Use any blend of frozen mixed vegetables, although the stir-fry blends will keep the dish more in line with the wok original. Just make sure the blend is not already spiced or sauced.

Serve It Up! This casserole isn't all that soupy, so if you serve it with cooked rice, offer a condiment like hoisin sauce or even bottled hot sauce on the side.

INGREDIENTS EXPLAINED Five-spice powder is a ground spice mix said to incorporate five basic flavor components: sour, sweet, bitter, savory, and salty. What's in any given bottle can vary, but look for cinnamon or cassia, star anise, and cloves; the mix may or may not include salt. You can also make your own: Toast 1 tablespoon black peppercorns, 1 tablespoon fennel seeds, 4 whole cloves, 2 star anise, and a 2-inch cinnamon stick broken into several pieces in a dry skillet set over medium heat, stirring constantly, until aromatic and even lightly browned, 4 to 5 minutes. Cool to room temperature (about 1 hour), then grind the spices in a spice grinder or mini food processor until powdery, producing about ¼ cup powder. Seal in a jar and store at room temperature for up to 6 months.

ALL-AMERICAN KNOW-HOW Are frozen vegetables *real* food? You bet. Vegetables to be frozen are often picked at the height of their ripeness because they will have no time to ripen in transport. They sometimes even have a higher vitamin and nutrition signature, thanks to quick-freezing methods in the fields.

ground beef stew with pumpkin and bacon

EFFORT: **A LOT** • PREP TIME: **40 MINUTES** • COOK TIME: **6 HOURS** • KEEPS ON WARM: **3 HOURS** • SERVES: **3 TO 10**

INGREDIENTS	2- TO 3½-QT	4- TO 5½-QT	6- TO 8-QT
Shelled green pumpkin seeds (pepitas)	3 tblsp	⅓ cup	⅔ cup
Slab bacon, diced into ¼-inch pieces	3 ounces	6 ounces	12 ounces
Halved and thinly sliced yellow onion	½ cup	1 cup	2 cups (about 1 large)
Minced garlic	1 tsp	2 tsp	1 tblsp
Lean ground beef, preferably 93% lean	¾ pound	1½ pounds	3 pounds
Peeled, seeded, and cubed pumpkin	2 cups	4 cups	8 cups
Reduced-sodium chicken broth	1 cup	2 cups	4 cups (1 quart)
Ripe tomatoes, chopped	¼ pound	½ pound	1 pound
Ancho chile powder (see page 147)	Up to 3 tblsp	Up to 6 tblsp	Up to ⅔ cup
Ground cinnamon	1 tsp	2 tsp	1 tblsp plus 1 tsp
Ground cloves	½ tsp	1 tsp	2 tsp
Ground allspice	½ tsp	1 tsp	2 tsp
Salt	¼ tsp	½ tsp	1 tsp

1 Spread the pumpkin seeds in a large, dry skillet and toast them over medium heat, stirring occasionally, until they brown and start to pop, about 4 minutes. Pour them into the slow cooker.

2 Set the skillet back over the heat; scatter the bacon bits inside. Cook, stirring occasionally, until the bacon is a little crunchy, between 5 and 8 minutes. Use a slotted spoon to transfer the bacon to the slow cooker (leaving the drippings behind).

3 Add the onion to the skillet. Cook, stirring occasionally, until softened, even a little browned in places, between 4 and 7 minutes. Stir in the garlic and cook for a few seconds. Grab that slotted spoon again and transfer the onion to the cooker.

4 Brown the ground beef in the skillet, stirring once in a while, until there's no hint of raw color anywhere, up to 8 minutes for a big batch. Scrape the beef into the slow cooker.

5 Stir in the pumpkin, broth, tomatoes, ancho chile powder, cinnamon, cloves, allspice, and salt. Cover and cook on low for 6 hours, or until the stew has thickened a bit and the pumpkin pieces are spoon-tender.

(continued)

• This spectacular ground beef stew is good enough for a dinner party, particularly on a chilly evening.
• Toasted pumpkin seeds offer a musky sweetness, a sophisticated bite in this otherwise straightforward fare.
• There's no set amount of ancho chile powder here, so you can determine the heat level.
• We tried this stew with beef broth, but the results were too heavy. Lighter, brighter chicken broth lets the more complex flavors come through with clarity.

Serve It Up! This stew is perhaps best served over rice—but go beyond the standard. Try medium-grain brown rice or even firmer red rice, quite nutty and aromatic. Or skip the rice entirely and serve it over warmed, canned, drained hominy or even cooked wheatberries. To gussy up the presentation, pass several condiments at the table for embellishing individual bowls: plain yogurt or sour cream, chopped cilantro leaves, diced red onion, and even diced mango.

INGREDIENTS EXPLAINED Green pumpkin seeds, often called by the Spanish name pepitas (*peh-PEE-tahs*), are the hulled bits from inside more standard, beige pumpkin seeds. (They can also be the hulled seeds of certain other winter squash varieties.) Look for them with the nuts or in the produce section of larger supermarkets.

ALL-AMERICAN KNOW-HOW To cube a pumpkin, cut the gourd into wedge-shaped chunks, then use a serrated spoon or a small paring knife to scrape the seeds and the damp membranes from the flesh. Use a vegetable peeler to remove the rind from each chunk, and cut the wedges into smaller bits, here about 1 inch each.

creamy meat sauce for pasta

EFFORT: **NOT MUCH** • PREP TIME: **20 MINUTES** • COOK TIME: **8 HOURS** • KEEPS ON WARM: **4 HOURS** • SERVES: **4 TO 12 (OVER COOKED PASTA)**

INGREDIENTS	2- TO 3½-QT	4- TO 5½-QT	6- TO 8-QT
Olive oil	1½ tblsp	2 tblsp	3 tblsp
Lean ground beef, preferably 93% lean	1 pound	1¾ pounds	3 pounds
Minced yellow onion	⅔ cup	1 cup (about 1 large)	1¾ cups
Minced celery	⅔ cup	1 cup (about 2½ medium ribs)	1¾ cups
Minced carrots	⅔ cup	1 cup (about 2 medium)	1¾ cups
No-salt-added canned crushed tomatoes	1¾ cups	3 cups	5⅓ cups
Dry white wine (such as Pinot Grigio) or dry vermouth	⅓ cup	½ cup	1 cup
Heavy cream	⅓ cup	½ cup	1 cup
Minced fresh basil leaves	1½ tblsp	2 tblsp	3½ tblsp
No-salt-added tomato paste	2 tsp	1 tblsp	2 tblsp
Minced fresh oregano leaves	2 tsp	1 tblsp	2 tblsp
Minced fresh rosemary leaves	2 tsp	1 tblsp	2 tblsp
Grated nutmeg	¼ tsp	½ tsp	1 tsp
Salt	¼ tsp	½ tsp	1 tsp
Ground black pepper	¼ tsp	½ tsp	1 tsp

1 Warm a large skillet over medium heat for a couple of minutes, then swirl in the oil. Crumble the ground beef into the skillet and cook, stirring occasionally, until lightly browned, with no raw color anywhere, between 4 and 10 minutes. Use a slotted spoon to transfer the ground beef to the slow cooker.

2 Stir in the onion, celery, carrots, tomatoes, wine, cream, basil, tomato paste, oregano, rosemary, nutmeg, salt, and pepper.

3 Cover and cook on low for 8 hours, stirring twice, or until the sauce is thick, creamy, decadent, and ready for pasta.

TESTERS' NOTES

• There may be no more quintessential Italian-American dish than a meat sauce like this one, a slow cooker riff on the classic ragù bolognese. All the components blend into a luscious sauce, ready to be ladled onto a plate of warm pasta—or layered in a baked pasta casserole.

• For a more sophisticated finish, substitute unsalted butter for the olive oil, or use a combination of the two.

• Use only fresh herbs for their bright, summery taste—a better foil to the complex, rich flavors.

• The sauce freezes exceptionally well. Cool for 20 minutes in the cooker, then ladle it into plastic or glass containers to be sealed and frozen for up to 6 months.

Serve It Up! Any pasta will do, although fettuccini or pappardelle are the traditional choices. Serve some finely grated Parmigiano-Reggiano cheese to sprinkle on every bowlful.

ALL-AMERICAN KNOW-HOW Mincing carrots can be a chore, especially when they roll around the cutting board. The best technique is to peel them, then slice them across into 4- or 5-inch segments. Cut these segments in half lengthwise, then each part in half again, and then keep slicing them until you whittle them all down into long, thin matchsticks. Gather several matchsticks together and slice them crosswise into tiny bits, each about ⅛ inch long.

meat sauce
with black olives and basil

EFFORT: **A LITTLE** • PREP TIME: **25 MINUTES** • COOK TIME: **8 HOURS** • KEEPS ON WARM: **4 HOURS** • SERVES: **3 TO 10 (WITH COOKED PASTA)**

INGREDIENTS	2- TO 3½-QT	4- TO 5½-QT	6- TO 8-QT
Olive oil	1 tsp	2 tsp	1 tblsp
Hot Italian sausage, any casings removed	¼ pound	½ pound	¾ pound
Lean ground beef, preferably 93% lean or ground round	½ pound	1 pound	1½ pounds
No-salt-added canned crushed tomatoes	1¾ cups	3½ cups	5 cups
Yellow onion, finely chopped	¾ cup	1½ cups	2 cups
Carrots, shredded	½ cup	1 cup	1½ cups
Medium celery ribs, finely chopped	1	2	3
Thinly sliced pitted black olives, preferably oil-cured	¼ cup	½ cup	¾ cup
No-salt-added tomato paste	2 tblsp	¼ cup	6 tblsp
Dried oregano	1 tsp	2 tsp	1 tblsp
Fennel seeds	½ tsp	1 tsp	1½ tsp
Sugar	½ tsp	1 tsp	1½ tsp
Salt	½ tsp	1 tsp	1¼ tsp
Minced fresh basil leaves	¼ cup	½ cup	¾ cup

1 Warm a large skillet over medium heat for a few minutes, then pour in the oil and tilt the skillet to slick the hot surface. Crumble in the sausage meat; cook, stirring often, until browned, no raw spots visible, between 4 and 6 minutes, depending on how much sausage you have and how big your skillet is. Use a

(continued)

slotted spoon to transfer the browned sausage meat to the slow cooker.

2 Crumble the ground beef into the skillet, still set over medium heat. Cook, stirring occasionally, until the beef loses any trace of pink and just begins to brown, between 4 and 8 minutes. Use a slotted spoon to transfer the beef to the slow cooker, leaving the rendered fat (which you can discard after you get the slow cooker going).

3 Stir the tomatoes, onion, carrots, celery, olives, tomato paste, oregano, fennel seeds, sugar, and salt into the cooker until the tomato paste dissolves and everything's mixed.

4 Cover and cook on low for 8 hours, or until the sauce has thickened and the flavors have blended. Stir in the basil just before serving.

TESTERS' NOTES
• This meat sauce is more aromatic than the previous incarnation, thanks in large part to the olives and dried spices. It uses two kinds of meat, both pork sausage and ground beef—the former for a distinct sweetness, the latter for a savory satisfaction. The sauce also mimics a more authentic Italian sensibility—more like a condiment for the cooked pasta than a sauce heaped into the bowls. You'll find you use less than you might normally.
• Shred the peeled carrots through the large holes of a box grater or with the shredding blade of a food processor.
• Don't mince the vegetables. Instead, cut them into small bits, each about ¼ inch. You want vegetables in every spoonful, but not so small they melt into the sauce.

Serve It Up! This hearty sauce is best on thick pasta noodles like pappardelle or even mafaldina. Or you can skip the pasta altogether: make long noodles from zucchini by running a vegetable peeler down their length, creating wide thin strips. Mound these in a bowl, then ladle the hot sauce on top.

lasagna

EFFORT: **A LOT** • PREP TIME: **30 MINUTES** • COOK TIME: **6 HOURS** • KEEPS ON WARM: **1 HOUR** • SERVES: **3 TO 8**

INGREDIENTS	2- TO 3½-QT	4- TO 5½-QT	6- TO 8-QT
Olive oil	1 tblsp	2 tblsp	3 tblsp
Lean ground beef, preferably 93% lean	½ pound	¾ pound	1¼ pounds
Mild Italian sausage, any casings removed	¼ pound	½ pound	¾ pound
No-salt-added canned crushed tomatoes	1½ cups	2½ cups	4 cups
Dried oregano	¾ tsp	½ tblsp	2 tsp
Crushed dried rosemary	¾ tsp	½ tblsp	2 tsp
Salt	⅛ tsp	¼ tsp	½ tsp
Ground black pepper	⅛ tsp	¼ tsp	½ tsp
Ricotta (regular or low-fat)	¾ cup	1¼ cups	2 cups
Large egg/yolk	1 yolk	1 whole	1 whole plus 1 yolk
Grated nutmeg	⅛ tsp	¼ tsp	½ tsp
Mozzarella cheese (regular or low-fat), shredded	3 ounces (about ¾ cup)	5 ounces (about 1¼ cups)	8 ounces (about 2 cups)
Dried lasagna noodles	4	6	10
Parmigiano-Reggiano cheese, finely grated	½ ounce (about 2 tblsp)	¾ ounce (about 3 tblsp)	1 ounce (about ¼ cup)

1 Set a large skillet over medium heat for a few minutes, swirl in the oil, and crumble in the ground beef and the sausage meat. Cook, stirring constantly, until thoroughly browned and broken into tiny bits, between 5 and 10 minutes. Stir in the tomatoes, oregano, rosemary, salt, and pepper. Set aside.

2 Stir the ricotta, egg, and nutmeg in a large bowl until the egg is thoroughly mixed into the cheese.

3 Layer in the slow cooker in this order: the meat sauce, the ricotta mixture, the mozzarella, and the noodles, breaking the noodles to fit the basic shape of your cooker and patching any holes with shards of the dried noodles. Because of varying shapes and sizes of slow cookers, there's no exact number for the number of layers; just begin and end with the meat sauce and make at least two full sets of layers. Sprinkle the top with the grated Parmigiano-Reggiano.

4 Cover and cook on low for 6 hours, or until the casserole has set and you can cut it with a knife. Turn the cooker off and let stand, covered, for 15 minutes. Serve the lasagna by slicing portions with a nonstick-safe knife or spatula, then lifting them out with a large, flat spatula.

TESTERS' NOTES
• Italian sausage meat will provide many of the classic seasonings for the meat sauce. But we also added some dried spices to give it a wintry, comfort-food feel, a nice balance to the summery tomatoes.
• If you're preparing this for a large slow cooker, the meat and vegetables may not fit in even the largest skillet. Use two skillets, set over separate burners, dividing the ingredients between them.
• Dried rosemary won't blend evenly through a casserole like this one because the individual leaves are too large and tough. By crushing the leaves under a rolling pin or even with your fingers, you'll be able to distribute the flavor evenly.
• Yes, you'll need to break the noodles to get them to fit. Here's the rule: you want decent coverage but you don't need to get obsessive.

porcupine meatballs

EFFORT: **A LOT** • PREP TIME: **1 HOUR 15 MINUTES (INCLUDES SOAKING THE RICE)** • COOK TIME: **2½ HOURS** • KEEPS ON WARM: **NO** • SERVES: **2 TO 6**

INGREDIENTS	2- TO 3½-QT	4- TO 5½-QT	6- TO 8-QT
Uncooked short-grain or sushi white rice	¾ cup	1 cup	2 cups
Lean ground beef, preferably 93% lean or ground round	6 ounces	½ pound	1 pound
Drained, rinsed, and chopped canned water chestnuts	¼ cup	6 tblsp	¾ cup
Minced scallion (white part only)	2 tsp	1 tblsp	2 tblsp
Minced peeled fresh ginger	1 tsp	½ tblsp	1 tblsp
Five-spice powder (see page 122)	¼ tsp	½ tsp	1 tsp
Soy sauce	1½ tblsp	2 tblsp	¼ cup
Reduced-sodium chicken broth	2 tblsp	3 tblsp	6 tblsp
Dry sherry	2 tsp	1 tblsp	2 tblsp
Rice vinegar	2 tsp	1 tblsp	2 tblsp

1 Place the rice in a large bowl, cover with water, and soak for 1 hour.

2 Set the ground beef, water chestnuts, scallion, ginger, five-spice powder, and half the soy sauce in a second large bowl. Using your clean, dry hands, work the mixture into an evenly spiced and uniform meatball mélange. Form the mixture into small meatballs, using 3 tablespoons per ball. Set the meatballs on a large plate or cutting board.

(continued)

3 Drain the rice in a colander set in the sink. Spread the rice in a thin layer on a plate. Roll the meatballs in the rice to coat them before placing them in a single layer in the slow cooker.

4 Whisk the remainder of the soy sauce with the broth, sherry, and rice vinegar in a small bowl. Pour the mixture over the meatballs, taking care not to knock off the rice kernels.

5 Cover and cook on high for 2½ hours, or until the rice is tender and the meatballs are cooked through. Serve the meatballs with some of the sauce drizzled over the top.

TESTERS' NOTES
• This Asian-inspired recipe makes very few meatballs, since they must stay small to cook properly yet still fit in a single layer in the slow cooker.
• The rice studding the meatballs give rise to their name, as the grains look like small quills. Don't worry; the rice will get tender. However, the meatballs will be a bit fragile. Scoop them out with a slotted spoon.
• For a more authentic flavor, substitute Shaoxing (a Chinese rice wine often used for cooking) for the dry sherry. Also whisk up to 1 teaspoon toasted sesame oil into the braising liquids in step 4.

Serve It Up! Since there's already rice on the meatballs, serve them over baby spinach leaves cooked with a little broth, some minced fresh ginger, and very thin garlic slivers in a covered, large skillet over medium heat. As a bonus, the soy sauce–laced sauce for the meatballs will add plenty of flavor to the wilted spinach.

meatballs in tomato sauce
with peppers

EFFORT: **A LITTLE** • PREP TIME: **20 MINUTES** • COOK TIME: **6 HOURS** • KEEPS ON WARM: **4 HOURS** • SERVES: **3 TO 8**

INGREDIENTS	2- TO 3½-QT	4- TO 5½-QT	6- TO 8-QT
Ground beef sirloin	¾ pound	1¼ pounds	2 pounds
Panko breadcrumbs	¼ cup	⅓ cup	½ cup
Parmigiano-Reggiano cheese, finely grated	½ ounce (about 2 tblsp)	¾ ounce (about 3 tblsp)	1¼ ounces (about ⅓ cup)
Dried basil	1 tblsp	1½ tblsp	2 tblsp
Grated nutmeg	⅛ tsp	¼ tsp	½ tsp
Red pepper flakes	⅛ tsp	¼ tsp	½ tsp
Fennel seeds	⅛ tsp	¼ tsp	½ tsp
Cubanelle pepper, stemmed, seeded, and cut into ½-inch rings (see page 47)	1 medium	1 large	3 medium
No-salt-added canned crushed tomatoes	1 cup plus 2 tblsp	2 cups	3½ cups
No-salt-added tomato paste	3 tblsp	⅓ cup	½ cup
Balsamic vinegar	1½ tblsp	2½ tblsp	¼ cup
Dried marjoram	¾ tsp	½ tblsp	2 tsp
Crushed dried rosemary	¾ tsp	½ tblsp	2 tsp
Dried oregano	¾ tsp	½ tblsp	2 tsp
Salt	⅛ tsp	¼ tsp	½ tsp

1 Use your clean, dry hands to mix the ground beef, breadcrumbs, cheese, basil, nutmeg, red pepper flakes, and fennel seeds in a large bowl, until the seasonings are evenly distributed in the ground beef.

2 Form the mixture into meatballs, each about 2 inches in diameter. Set them in the slow cooker; sprinkle the pepper rings around the meatballs.

3 Whisk the tomatoes, tomato paste, vinegar, marjoram, rosemary, oregano, and salt in a second large bowl; pour over the meatballs.

4 Cover and cook on low for 6 hours, or until the meatballs are firm to the touch but nonetheless tender when pierced with a fork.

TESTERS' NOTES
• We used ground sirloin because we wanted very little fat in this aromatic sauce. It's even slightly sour, thanks to both the tomatoes and the vinegar. Ground sirloin also gives the meatballs a firmer texture, more knife-and-fork than fork-and-spoon.
• Work gently with the ground meat mixture. Massage the spices and other ingredients into it without completely destroying its "ground" texture.

Serve It Up! There's quite a bit of sauce around these meatballs, so serve them in bowls with soup spoons for savoring every drop. Some crusty bread would also be great. (It would be even better if some fell into the bowls.) For a side dish, try chilled blanched green beans dressed with olive oil, balsamic vinegar, minced basil leaves, and sea salt.

ALL-AMERICAN KNOW-HOW To seed and cut cubanelle peppers into rings, first slice off the stem and about ¼ inch of the pepper below it. Use a small knife or your finger to reach inside and remove the seeds and the white membranes that attach them to the inside walls. Set the pepper on its side on a cutting board and slice it into thin rings about ¼ inch thick. If any of the rings are too large to fit neatly on a spoon, slice these in half for fewer drips on your shirt later.

meatballs with white beans and dill

EFFORT: **A LITTLE** • PREP TIME: **25 MINUTES** • COOK TIME: **6 HOURS** • KEEPS ON WARM: **1 HOUR** • SERVES: **4 TO 12**

INGREDIENTS	2- TO 3½-QT	4- TO 5½-QT	6- TO 8-QT
FOR THE MEATBALLS			
Lean ground beef, preferably round or sirloin	1 pound	2 pounds	3 pounds
Uncooked long-grain white rice	2 tblsp	¼ cup	6 tblsp
Dried plain whole wheat breadcrumbs	2 tblsp	¼ cup	6 tblsp
Minced fresh dill fronds	1½ tblsp	3 tblsp	⅓ cup
Finely grated lemon zest	½ tblsp	1 tblsp	2½ tblsp
Drained, rinsed, and minced capers	1 tsp	2 tsp	1 tblsp
Onion powder	1 tsp	2 tsp	1 tblsp
Salt	¼ tsp	½ tsp	¾ tsp
Ground black pepper	¼ tsp	½ tsp	¾ tsp
Drained and rinsed canned cannellini beans	1½ cups	3 cups	4½ cups
FOR THE SAUCE			
Reduced-sodium chicken broth	1 cup	2 cups	3 cups
All-purpose flour	2 tblsp	¼ cup	6 tblsp
No-salt-added tomato paste	1 tblsp	2 tblsp	3 tblsp
Fresh lemon juice	1 tblsp	2 tblsp	3 tblsp
Salt	¼ tsp	½ tsp	¾ tsp
Ground black pepper	¼ tsp	½ tsp	¾ tsp

(continued)

1 To make the meatballs, place the ground beef, rice, breadcrumbs, dill, lemon zest, capers, onion powder, salt, and pepper into a large bowl. Mix gently with clean dry hands until mixture is a uniform amalgam. Form this mixture into balls, using a scant ¼ cup per meatball. Set these in the slow cooker; sprinkle the beans around the meatballs.

2 To make the sauce, whisk the broth, flour, tomato paste, lemon juice, salt, and pepper in a large bowl until the flour dissolves. Pour over the meatballs.

3 Cover and cook on low for 6 hours, or until the meatballs are still firm but cooked through and nonetheless tender.

TESTERS' NOTES
• These meatballs have a Greek palette. They're somewhat sour from the lemon zest and capers, but also quite sweet from the beans and rice—and naturally so, with no added sugar in the mix.
• Make sure the lemon zest is minced into tiny bits. Nobody wants to get a big bite of lemon in a meatball!
• Jarred capers should always be rinsed before using. They're loaded with sodium and so can add a shocking amount to a final dish.
• If you like, add very small cubes of feta to the meatballs. Use a firm block of feta, stored in brine. Form each meatball around a small cube of cheese to hide this little surprise.

Serve It Up! Since this is a Greek-inspired recipe, serve it over **Mediterranean Mashed Potatoes:** While they are still hot, mash the potatoes with lots of minced garlic, a little olive oil, some chicken broth, a pinch of salt, and plenty of ground black pepper.

ALL-AMERICAN KNOW-HOW It's sometimes tough to tell when meatballs are done. You can take one out of the cooker and slice it open to see the texture, but the old-fashioned method still may not be an accurate gauge, given how the slow cooker works. (The meatballs may look pink inside, even when cooked through.) For complete assurance, use an instant-read meat thermometer; a meatball at its center should register 165°F.

INGREDIENTS EXPLAINED We don't call for seasoned breadcrumbs in this book because (1) the seasonings are sometimes of inferior quality, (2) the blend is often not in the recipe's best interest, and (3) there's sometimes too much salt in the mix. Instead, we prefer plain dry breadcrumbs so we can season the dish properly. By the way, plain breadcrumbs are sometimes labeled "unseasoned breadcrumbs."

easy cheesy meatballs

EFFORT: **NOT MUCH** • PREP TIME: **15 MINUTES** • COOK TIME: **6 HOURS** • KEEPS ON WARM: **1 HOUR** • SERVES: **3 TO 8**

INGREDIENTS	2- TO 3½-QT	4- TO 5½-QT	6- TO 8-QT
Italian-seasoned tomato paste	2 tblsp	3 tblsp	¼ cup
Full-bodied red wine, such as a California Zinfandel	2 tblsp	3 tblsp	¼ cup
Red wine vinegar	½ tblsp	2 tsp	1 tblsp
Lean ground beef, preferably 93% lean	¾ pound	1¼ pounds	2 pounds
Provolone cheese, finely shredded	2 ounces (about ½ cup)	3 ounces (about ¾ cup)	4 ounces (about 1 cup)
Uncooked long-grain white rice	¼ cup	⅓ cup	½ cup
Dried oregano	½ tsp	1 tsp	1¼ tsp
Dried thyme	½ tsp	¾ tsp	1 tsp
Crushed fennel seeds	¼ tsp	½ tsp	¾ tsp

1 Whisk the tomato paste, wine, and vinegar in a shallow bowl.

2 Mix the ground beef, cheese, rice, oregano, thyme, and fennel seeds in a large bowl until the cheese and seasonings are evenly distributed throughout the ground beef.

3 Form the mixture into balls, using about ⅓ cup for each fairly large meatball. As the meatballs are made, roll them in the tomato paste mixture, coating them lightly and evenly, then set them in the slow cooker in a single layer.

4 Once all the meatballs are made, cover the cooker and cook on low for 6 hours, or until the meatballs are firm and cooked through.

TESTERS' NOTES
• There's very little sauce here, just some juices in the slow cooker. In fact, we designed these to be sort of a meatball version of meatloaf.
• Substitute other cheeses for the provolone—Asiago, Swiss, or even dried Pecorino-Romano for a more assertive taste. In fact, packaged shredded provolone may well have to be minced on a cutting board to get the larger threads into tiny bits. If you really want to go easy, try a shredded Italian cheese blend.

Serve It Up! Serve these meatballs over pasta—or stack them plus any bits of sauce in baked potatoes!

SHORTCUTS Substitute an equivalent amount of Italian seasoning for the oregano, thyme, and crushed fennel seeds. Use a blend with only herbs in the mix, no preservatives or chemical fillers—and perhaps no salt, given how much is in the cheese.

ALL-AMERICAN KNOW-HOW To form meatballs, dampen your hands occasionally to keep the sticky meat from clumping to your fingers. However, don't go overboard; you can actually add enough natural moisture from your hands that the meatballs won't cohere.

stuffed meatloaf
with onion gravy

EFFORT: **A LOT** • PREP TIME: **40 MINUTES** • COOK TIME: **6 TO 8 HOURS** • KEEPS ON WARM: **2 HOURS** • SERVES: **3 TO 10**

INGREDIENTS	2- TO 3½-QT	4- TO 5½-QT	6- TO 8-QT
Fresh, plain breadcrumbs	⅓ cup	⅔ cup	1 cup
White button mushrooms, thinly sliced	2 ounces (about ⅓ cup)	4 ounces (about 1¼ cups)	6 ounces (about 1¾ cups)
Fresh thyme leaves, stripped from stem	½ tsp	1¼ tsp	2 tsp
Salt	⅛ tsp	¼ tsp	½ tsp
Ground black pepper	⅛ tsp	¼ tsp	¼ tsp
Lean ground beef, preferably 93% lean	1 pound	2 pounds	3 pounds
Toasted wheat germ	2 tblsp	¼ cup	⅓ cup
Dijon mustard	2 tsp	1½ tblsp	2 tblsp
Worcestershire sauce	2 tsp	1½ tblsp	2 tblsp
Onion powder	¼ tsp	½ tsp	½ tsp
Garlic powder	¼ tsp	½ tsp	½ tsp
Unsalted butter	1 tblsp	1½ tblsp	2 tblsp
Yellow onions, halved and thinly sliced	1 medium	2 medium	2 large
Mild paprika	¼ tsp	½ tsp	1 tsp
Celery seeds	¼ tsp	½ tsp	1 tsp
Reduced-sodium beef broth	½ cup	1 cup	1½ cups

1 Place the breadcrumbs, mushrooms, thyme, salt, and pepper in a large food processor fitted with the chopping blade. Pulse until a

(continued)

coarse amalgam forms, like wet sand or grainy dough, almost a paste. Scrape down and remove the blade.

2 Put the ground beef, wheat germ, mustard, Worcestershire sauce, onion powder, and garlic powder in a large bowl; mix with your hands (or a wooden spoon) until the wheat germ and other ingredients are spread throughout the ground meat.

3 Press half the meat mixture into a flattened loaf in the slow cooker, leaving a 1-inch gap between the loaf and the cooker's sides. Top with an even layer of all the breadcrumb stuffing, leaving a ½-inch border around the perimeter of the meat. Flatten out the remaining meat mixture like a top pie crust and place it over the filling. Press down to seal the sides together so that no juices can leak out. Seal any cracks by pressing the meat mixture together.

4 Melt the butter in a large skillet over medium heat. Dump in the onions and cook, stirring occasionally, until soft and golden, between 5 and 8 minutes, depending on the size of the batch. Stir in the paprika and celery seeds, then spoon the contents of the skillet over the meatloaf. Pour the beef broth on and around the meatloaf, taking care not to displace any onions.

5 Cover and cook on low for 6 hours in a small cooker, 7 hours in a medium cooker, or 8 hours in a large cooker, or until the meatloaf is cooked through and somewhat firm. Slice into wedges using a nonstick-safe knife or spatula, serving them with bits of the caramelized onions and any sauce in the cooker.

TESTERS' NOTES
• Here's a holiday-worthy meatloaf, great for any family gathering. The mushrooms will give the dish plenty of moisture, keeping it juicy and tender. Make sure you spread the ground mushroom mixture evenly across the meat to get the best reward for your effort.
• Admittedly, this meatloaf works best in an oval cooker, rather than a round one; but it can be done in both. You'll simply need to shape the meatloaf to your cooker—and then cut it into slices or pie wedges, depending on which sort of cooker you're working with.
• If your cooker doesn't have a nonstick finish, give it a spritz with nonstick cooking spray before building the meatloaf inside.

Serve It Up! Mashed roasted sweet potatoes would make a fine side for this sort of comfort food. Or bake the sweet potatoes, split them open, mush the insides with the tines of a fork, and lay the slices and sauce right on top.

INGREDIENTS EXPLAINED We use a fair amount of Worcestershire sauce in our cooking. Yes, it's an anchovy sauce—but mostly it's a complex bit of savory saltiness, a great match to beef of all sorts. While almost everyone knows the standard bottling, there are more complex, artisanal versions of this British classic available these days. Or go all out and make your own. We've got a knockout recipe on our website, www.bruceandmark.com.

balsamic braised meatloaf

EFFORT: **A LITTLE** • PREP TIME: **25 MINUTES** • COOK TIME: **8 HOURS** • KEEPS WELL WARM: **2 HOURS** • SERVES: **3 TO 10**

INGREDIENTS	2- TO 3½-QT	4- TO 5½-QT	6- TO 8-QT
Lean ground beef, preferably 93% lean	1 pound	2 pounds	3 pounds
Minced yellow onion	2½ tblsp	⅓ cup	½ cup
Plain dry breadcrumbs	2½ tblsp	⅓ cup	½ cup
Parmigiano-Reggiano cheese, finely grated	½ ounce (2 tblsp)	¾ ounce (3 tblsp)	1 ounce (¼ cup)
Minced garlic	1 tsp	½ tblsp	2 tsp
Large egg/yolk, well beaten in a small bowl	1 yolk	1 whole	1 whole plus 1 yolk
Dried basil	1 tsp	2 tsp	1 tblsp
Dried oregano	1 tsp	2 tsp	1 tblsp
Dried marjoram	1 tsp	2 tsp	1 tblsp
Salt	¼ tsp	½ tsp	1 tsp
Ground black pepper	¼ tsp	½ tsp	¾ tsp
Medium green bell peppers, stemmed, seeded, and cut into thin strips	1	2	3
White button mushrooms, thinly sliced	5 ounces (1½ cups)	8 ounces (2½ cups)	14 ounces (4 cups)
No-salt-added canned crushed tomatoes	⅓ cup	⅔ cup	1 cup
Reduced-sodium beef broth	⅓ cup	⅔ cup	1 cup
Balsamic vinegar	1½ tblsp	2½ tblsp	¼ cup
No-salt-added tomato paste	1 tblsp	2 tblsp	3 tblsp

1 Mix the ground beef, onion, breadcrumbs, cheese, garlic, egg, basil, oregano, marjoram, salt, and pepper in a large bowl until the cheese and spices are evenly distributed.

2 Gather the mixture into a ball, then transfer it to a cutting board. Form it into a tapered loaf, like a football cut in half lengthwise and no larger than the length and width of your slow cooker canister. Transfer it to the slow cooker. Spread the bell peppers and mushrooms over and around the meatloaf.

3 Whisk the tomatoes, broth, vinegar, and tomato paste in a large bowl until smooth. Pour over the meatloaf and vegetables.

4 Cover and cook on low for 8 hours, or until the meatloaf is cooked through and an instant-read meat thermometer inserted into its center registers 165°F. Serve slices with the sauce and vegetables ladled on top.

TESTERS' NOTES
• Braising a meatloaf in balsamic vinegar creates a wonderful meal—a little sour, a little sweet, yet quite sophisticated.
• Getting the meatloaf into the slow cooker can be a challenge. Work with a couple of large metal spatulas. If it tears or breaks, you can put it back together in the cooker.
• Don't use your best balsamic vinegar, aged for years. Instead, use a moderately sour, fairly economical bottling.
• Mince the onion into tiny bits so it distributes evenly in the meatloaf, almost melting as it bakes.
• Although you can try to lift a meatloaf out of a slow cooker when it's done, you might also end up with meatloaf shrapnel on your floor. It's best to use nonstick-safe spatulas and knives to cut it right in the cooker.

ALL-AMERICAN KNOW-HOW Braising is a low-moisture cooking technique in which low or moderate heat is applied to a mixture of ingredients not fully covered by any liquids. Think of a culinary continuum running from less liquid to more: braise, stew, soup.

italian-style stuffed bell peppers

EFFORT: **A LOT** • PREP TIME: **30 MINUTES** • COOK TIME: **6 HOURS** • KEEPS ON WARM: **2 HOURS** • SERVES: **3 TO 8**

INGREDIENTS	2- TO 3½-QT	4- TO 5½-QT	6- TO 8-QT
Lean ground beef, preferably 93% lean	½ pound	¾ pound	1½ pounds
Mild Italian sausage, any casings removed	5 ounces	½ pound	1 pound
Rolled oats (not quick-cooking or steel-cut)	⅓ cup	½ cup	1 cup
Parmigiano-Reggiano cheese, finely grated	1 ounce (about ¼ cup)	2 ounces (about ½ cup)	4 ounces (about 1 cup)
Minced fresh oregano leaves	½ tblsp	2 tsp	1½ tblsp
Minced fresh rosemary leaves	½ tblsp	2 tsp	1½ tblsp
Red pepper flakes	¼ tsp	½ tsp	Up to 1 tsp
Medium red or yellow bell peppers, tops sliced off and discarded, the ribs and seeds removed	3	4	8
No-salt-added canned crushed tomatoes	⅓ cup	½ cup	1 cup
Red wine	⅓ cup	½ cup	1 cup
Minced garlic	½ tsp	1 tsp	2 tsp
Salt	¼ tsp	½ tsp	¾ tsp
Grated nutmeg	⅛ tsp	¼ tsp	½ tsp
Balsamic vinegar	2 tsp	1 tblsp	2 tblsp

1 Mix the ground beef, sausage meat, oats, cheese, oregano, rosemary, and red pepper flakes in a large bowl until quite uniform, the spices distributed throughout.

2 Stuff the meat mixture evenly into the bell peppers; stand them up in the slow cooker, wedging them gently to fit as necessary.

3 Whisk the tomatoes, wine, garlic, salt, and nutmeg in a large bowl; pour over and around the stuffed peppers.

4 Cover and cook on low for 6 hours, or until the meat mixture in the peppers is cooked through and the peppers' flesh is fork-tender.

5 Use a big, slotted spoon to move the stuffed peppers to serving plates or shallow serving bowls. Skim any surface fat from the sauce in the cooker, then pour the strained sauce into a saucepan. Stir in the balsamic vinegar as you bring the sauce to a boil over high heat. Boil, stirring often, until reduced by half, from 4 to 7 minutes. Spoon the sauce over the stuffed peppers to serve.

TESTERS' NOTES

• Stuffed peppers are a homey weeknight dinner made easier by the slow cooker. What's better, the cooker softens the peppers themselves without drying them out, giving you more juicy bits per bite.
• Stuff the peppers the night before (or even the day before), then save them, covered, in the fridge until you're ready to get them cooking.
• The oats in these stuffed peppers stand in for the more traditional egg binder. The oats will absorb more of the juices in the peppers (there won't be any evaporation) and so render them succulent without being wet.
• For a leaner dish, use mild Italian turkey sausage. For a richer dish, you could substitute half the ground beef with ground pork.

Serve It Up! As a side, make a simple green salad with **Mustard Dressing:** For four servings, whisk a minced small shallot (or one lobe of a medium shallot) in a large bowl with ⅓ cup olive oil, 1½ tablespoons white wine vinegar, ½ tablespoon Dijon mustard, and ½ teaspoon salt. Add the salad greens and toss well.

ALL-AMERICAN KNOW-HOW "Reduced" means that a sauce has boiled or simmered until some of the water has evaporated, leaving a higher concentration of flavors with perhaps even some basic deepening or mellowing of those flavors. It all sounds fancy, but it essentially means that you keep a sauce bubbling until you hit the desired consistency: until a third or half its original volume (still watery but much more concentrated), until somewhat thickened (beyond half its original volume, starting to get some velvety texture), until a glaze (the point at which a wooden spoon run through it creates a line that holds its shape for a couple of seconds before the sauce flows back into place), or until a thick glaze (that line holds its shape even if you tilt the skillet or saucepan a bit).

stuffed cabbage in tomato sauce

EFFORT: **A LOT** • PREP TIME: **45 MINUTES** • COOK TIME: **8 HOURS** • KEEPS ON WARM: **1 HOUR** • SERVES: **5 TO 12**

INGREDIENTS	2- TO 3½-QT	4- TO 5½-QT	6- TO 8-QT
FOR THE STUFFED CABBAGE			
Savoy cabbage leaves	10	16	24
Lean ground beef, preferably 93% lean	14 ounces	1⅓ pounds	2 pounds
Minced yellow onion	3 tblsp	⅓ cup	½ cup
Uncooked long-grain white rice	3 tblsp	⅓ cup	½ cup
Chopped golden raisins	3 tblsp	⅓ cup	½ cup
Minced garlic	¾ tsp	½ tblsp	2 tsp
Dried thyme	¼ tsp	¾ tsp	1 tsp
Caraway seeds	¼ tsp	¾ tsp	1 tsp
Ground black pepper	¼ tsp	¾ tsp	1 tsp
Salt	⅛ tsp	¼ tsp	½ tsp
FOR THE SAUCE			
No-salt-added canned crushed tomatoes	1¼ cups	2⅓ cups	3½ cups
Cider vinegar	2 tblsp	¼ cup	6 tblsp
Packed light brown sugar	1 tblsp	2 tblsp	3 tblsp
No-salt-added tomato paste	1 tblsp	2 tblsp	3 tblsp
Dried dill	¼ tsp	½ tsp	1 tsp
Salt	⅛ tsp	¼ tsp	½ tsp
Ground black pepper	⅛ tsp	¼ tsp	½ tsp

1 Bring a large pot of water to a boil over high heat. Working in batches to prevent overcrowding, blanch the cabbage leaves in the boiling water for 3 minutes, then transfer them to a colander set in the sink. Run cool tap water over the batches to return them to room temperature; pat them dry individually and lay them out on a paper towel–lined work surface.

2 To make the stuffing, mix the ground beef, onion, rice, raisins, garlic, thyme, caraway seeds, pepper, and salt in a large bowl.

3 Cut out and discard the tough center stem from the bottom of each cabbage leaf. Fill each leaf with approximately ¼ cup meat stuffing. Roll them up, tucking the ends underneath. Place the rolls seam side down in the slow cooker, layering them as necessary but making sure those seams stay closed.

4 To make the sauce, whisk the crushed tomatoes, vinegar, brown sugar, tomato paste, dill,

(continued)

salt, and pepper in a large bowl until the brown sugar dissolves. Pour over the rolls in the cooker.

5 Cover and cook on low for 8 hours, or until the rice is tender in the rolls and the ground beef has cooked through. Serve by scooping the stuffed cabbage rolls out of the cooker with a large spoon and drizzling the sauce around them in the serving bowls.

TESTERS' NOTES
• Here's an Old World dish that's pretty foolproof in the slow cooker. The only real task is cutting the veins out of the cabbage leaves: take out the thick, triangular section at the base of each leaf, as well as a bit up the center vein itself, just until the leaf is pliable enough to be rolled up. Don't cut out too much or the leaf won't roll correctly. It may be best to have a couple of extra leaves, just to guard against mistakes. Why don't you cut the vein from the leaves before you boil them? Because those woody centers hold the leaves together in the pot.
• There's really no way to tell if the rolls are cooked through except to take one out, cut it open, and peek inside. That said, failing some malfunction in your cooker, they will indeed be done after 8 hours.

no-fuss chili

EFFORT: **NOT MUCH** • PREP TIME: **15 MINUTES** • COOK TIME: **8 HOURS** • KEEPS ON WARM: **4 HOURS** • SERVES: **4 TO 12**

INGREDIENTS	2- TO 3½-QT	4- TO 5½-QT	6- TO 8-QT
Beef top round, cut into ½-inch pieces	1¼ pounds	2 pounds	3½ pounds
Drained no-salt-added canned diced tomatoes	1¼ cups (about one 15-ounce can)	2 cups	3½ cups
Drained and rinsed canned pinto beans	1 cup	1¾ cups	3 cups
Green bell pepper, seeded, stemmed, and chopped	1 small	1 medium	1 large
Yellow onion, chopped	1 small	1 medium	1 large
Chili powder	3 tblsp	¼ cup	⅓ cup
Minced garlic	½ tsp	1 tsp	½ tblsp
Salt	¼ tsp	½ tsp	¾ tsp

Stir all the ingredients in the slow cooker. Cover and cook on low for 8 hours, or until the beef is quite tender.

TESTERS' NOTES
• Exceptionally clear-cut in its preparation, this chili is a great way to start experimenting with what a slow cooker can do for cuts of beef beyond ground.
• No ground beef in this chili? Nope. Call us purists (of a sort, since there are indeed beans in the mix). We feel the bottom round gives the chili better texture, a little chewiness to stand up to the spices.
• By the way, *chile* is the word for the pepper; *chili*, the stew.

Serve It Up! The success of this simple chili lies partly in the garnishes: shredded Cheddar cheese, jarred jalapeño rings, sour cream, minced red onion, and diced avocado.

INGREDIENTS EXPLAINED Beef round is a primal butcher cut, taken from the top of the back leg. The area gets a workout during a cow's life; so the meat is lean but also tough. It tenderizes with moist, long cooking (hello, slow cookers!) or with quick, high-heat searing. Here are some common cuts from the round that are used in the next several recipes. Although from the same part of the cow, they're not interchangeable, given cooking times and liquid levels in the dishes.

• *Bottom round.* A fairly tough but flavorful cut, often braised or roasted. It's sometimes left whole as a bottom round roast or even a rump roast (in which it comes to a pointy tip).

• *Eye of round*. A boneless roast often from the bottom round. It's fairly tough, often cut into small sections to be pounded even thinner.
• *Round steak*. A very lean cut, not quite as tender as bottom round.
• *Top round*. A lean cut, often used in braises and stews.

three-chile mole chili

EFFORT: **A LOT** • PREP TIME: **40 MINUTES** • COOK TIME: **6 HOURS** • KEEPS ON WARM: **4 HOURS** • SERVES: **4 TO 12**

INGREDIENTS	2- TO 3½-QT	4- TO 5½-QT	6- TO 8-QT
Dried ancho chiles	2	4	8
Dried mulato chiles	2	4	6
Dried pasilla chiles	2	4	6
Raisins	¼ cup	⅓ cup	½ cup
Unsweetened cocoa powder	1 tblsp	2 tblsp	3½ tblsp
Ground cumin	½ tblsp	1 tblsp	1 tblsp plus 1 tsp
Ground cinnamon	1 tsp	2 tsp	1 tblsp
Minced garlic	1 tsp	2 tsp	1 tblsp
Salt	½ tsp	1 tsp	½ tblsp
Beef bottom round, cut into ¼-inch pieces	1½ pounds	3 pounds	5 pounds
Reduced-sodium beef broth	¾ cup	1½ cups	2½ cups
Unsweetened apple juice	2 tblsp	¼ cup	⅓ cup
Yellow cornmeal	½ tblsp	1 tblsp	1½ tblsp

1 Bring a small pan of water to a boil over high heat. Stem the chiles, then open them up and scrape out the seeds and the pale membranes. Tear the chiles into small bits, place them in a large bowl, and cover with boiling water. Soak for 20 minutes.

2 Drain the chiles in a colander set over a bowl, reserving the soaking liquid. Place the softened chiles in a large blender; add the raisins, cocoa powder, cumin, cinnamon, garlic, and salt, as well as 1 tablespoon of the soaking liquid. Blend into a coarse paste, adding more soaking liquid as necessary to grind the chiles and raisins, scraping down the inside of the canister occasionally to make sure the paste has no chunks in it.

3 Scrape every drop of paste into the slow cooker. Stir in the beef, broth, apple juice, and cornmeal.

4 Cover and cook on low for 6 hours, or until the beef is quite tender and the sauce has thickened somewhat.

TESTERS' NOTES
• Although mole is a traditional Oaxacan sauce, there are thousands of variations. This one is modeled on one version of *mole negro* (black mole). The sauce makes a great braising medium for the slightly fattier beef bottom round.
• Cocoa powder may seem an odd ingredient, but it's a common addition in some forms of mole—a bit of bitter sophistication in an otherwise sweet and spicy sauce.
• The cornmeal acts as a thickening agent and gives the stew extra sweetness, a counterbalance to the cocoa powder and chiles. For the best results, use finely ground yellow cornmeal.
• The cooking time for this chili is slightly less than that given for the other two chilis, partly because the beef is cut into smaller bits.

INGREDIENTS EXPLAINED These three kinds of chiles are the holy trinity of *mole negro*:

(continued)

- *Ancho chiles* are dried poblano chiles, providing fruity, acidic notes.
- *Mulato chiles* are related to poblanos; they offer chocolate and licorice notes, as well as a moderate level of heat.
- *Pasilla chiles* are mild, fingerlike dried chilaca chiles with a pronounced citrus note. Pasillas are sometimes labeled as black chiles (*chile negro*). If possible, search out *pasilla de Oaxaca*, a smoked version of the standard pasilla.

ALL-AMERICAN KNOW-HOW Capsaicin is the fiery chemical present in varying degrees in every chile, from mild bell peppers to insanely hot habaneros. It's not water soluble, so the burn cannot be controlled by iced tea or even beer. Rather, capsaicin is fat soluble, so a buttered tortilla is a better flame retardant. Or sour cream. Or even diced avocado.

Given that chemistry, you can remove the threat of a burn from your hands by rubbing some canola, vegetable, or olive oil on them, massaging the oil under your fingertips and between your fingers, then washing your hands with soap and warm water.

swiss steak with onions and carrots

EFFORT: **A LITTLE** • PREP TIME: **20 MINUTES** • COOK TIME: **8 HOURS** • KEEPS ON WARM: **3 HOURS** • SERVES: **3 TO 10**

INGREDIENTS	2- TO 3½-QT	4- TO 5½-QT	6- TO 8-QT
Unsalted butter	1 tblsp	2 tblsp	3 tblsp
Yellow onions, chopped	2 small	2 medium	2 large
Medium carrots, thinly sliced	1	2	4
Dried thyme	¾ tsp	1¼ tsp	2 tsp
Salt	⅛ tsp	¼ tsp	½ tsp
Ground black pepper	⅛ tsp	¼ tsp	½ tsp
Beef eye of round steaks, about ½ inch thick	1 pound	2 pounds	3 pounds
Reduced-sodium beef broth	⅔ cup	1⅓ cups	2 cups
All-purpose flour	2 tblsp	¼ cup	⅓ cup
White wine vinegar	1 tsp	2 tsp	1 tblsp

1 Melt the butter in a large skillet set over medium heat. Add the onions and carrots; cook, stirring often, until the onions soften and turn translucent, about 5 minutes. Stir in the thyme, salt, and pepper. Remove from the heat to cool for 10 minutes.

2 Layer the vegetable mixture and steaks in the slow cooker: start with a ½-inch layer of the vegetables, add a layer of steak (without overlap, even a few holes between the steaks), and continue layering until you reach a final thin layer of vegetables.

3 Whisk the broth and flour in a large bowl until the flour has dissolved. Pour over the ingredients in the cooker.

4 Cover and cook on low for 8 hours, until the beef steaks are fork-tender. Use a fork to transfer the steaks to serving plates and a slotted spoon to pick up all the vegetables, leaving the juicy sauce behind. Pour the sauce into a fat separator and stir in the vinegar. (You can also skim off the fat from the surface of the sauce with a spoon.) Drizzle the skimmed sauce over the servings.

TESTERS' NOTES

• Round steaks are sometimes pounded even thinner for this American classic (which has nothing to do with Switzerland). It's a rich braise for a relatively affordable cut of beef. Best of all, the slow cooker works its magic without your needing to beat the steaks senseless.
• We've pumped up the veggies to increase the flavor quite a bit. For the best texture, use ½-inch pieces of onion but very thin carrot rounds.

ALL-AMERICAN KNOW-HOW What is "fork-tender"? It's not a culinary cliché. It means that a meat fork, inserted into a cut, encounters no resistance *as it is pulled back out*. If you insert a meat fork into a cut and feel you have to tug to get it out, or indeed, if you encounter any but the slightest resistance, the meat is not yet fork-tender.

orange beef "stir-fry"

EFFORT: **A LITTLE** • PREP TIME: **20 MINUTES** • COOK TIME: **6½ HOURS** • KEEPS ON WARM: **4 HOURS THROUGH STEP 3** • SERVES: **3 TO 10**

INGREDIENTS	2- TO 3½-QT	4- TO 5½-QT	6- TO 8-QT
Eye of round steaks, about ½ inch thick, cut into finger-wide strips	1 pound	2 pounds	3 pounds
Whole medium scallions, minced	1	2	3
Minced peeled fresh ginger	1 tblsp	2 tblsp	3 tblsp
Finely shredded orange zest	1 tblsp	2 tblsp	3 tblsp
Minced garlic	2 tsp	1 tblsp	4 tsp
Soy sauce	2 tblsp	¼ cup	6 tblsp
Fresh orange juice	2 tblsp	¼ cup	6 tblsp
Rice vinegar	1 tblsp	2 tblsp	3 tblsp
Packed light brown sugar	1 tblsp	2 tblsp	3 tblsp
Asian red chile paste	1 tsp	2 tsp	1 tblsp
Snow peas, trimmed	5 ounces (about 2 cups)	10 ounces (about 4 cups)	1 pound (about 6 cups)

1 Toss the beef, scallions, ginger, orange zest, and garlic in the slow cooker until the meat is coated in the aromatics.

2 Whisk the soy sauce, orange juice, rice vinegar, brown sugar, and chile paste in a large bowl until the sugar has dissolved. Pour over the ingredients in the slow cooker.

3 Cover and cook on low for 6 hours.

4 Stir the contents of the slow cooker and sprinkle the snow peas over the top. Turn the heat to high, cover, and cook for 30 minutes, or until the beef is tender but the snow peas are still a bit firm.

TESTERS' NOTES
• Barely authentic with no wok in sight, this slow cooker version of the traditional dish is nonetheless an easy workday dinner with spot-on flavors from the original.
• If the snow peas are very large, you'll need to remove the fibrous string that runs along the concave curve. Grab it at one end and zip it down the snow pea.

Serve It Up! Although cooked white or brown rice might be the standard, serve this aromatic braise over wilted Swiss chard.

SHORTCUTS Use beef cut into strips for stir-fry, available in the meat case of most supermarkets.

INGREDIENTS EXPLAINED Asian red chile paste is actually the name for an array of condiments, some soupy, most fiery, many incendiary. Look for bottles and jars in the Asian aisle of your supermarket. You can substitute sambal oelek (see page 404) or even Sriracha for a brighter, less complex heat.

beer-house beef and pickle rolls

EFFORT: **A LOT** • PREP TIME: **40 MINUTES** • COOK TIME: **6 HOURS** • KEEPS ON WARM: **3 HOURS** • SERVES: **4 TO 8**

INGREDIENTS	2- TO 3½-QT	4- TO 5½-QT	6- TO 8-QT
Eye of round steaks, about 4 ounces each, pounded to ¼-inch thickness	4	6	8
Coarse-grained mustard	2 tblsp	3 tblsp	¼ cup
Thin bacon strips, cut in half crosswise	4	6	8
Dill pickle spears	4	6	8
Yellow onions, chopped	1 medium	2 medium	2 large
Unsalted butter, melted and cooled for a few minutes	2 tblsp	3 tblsp	4 tblsp (½ stick)
Caraway seeds	½ tsp	¾ tsp	1 tsp
Mild paprika	1 tsp	½ tblsp	2 tsp
Reduced-sodium beef broth	1 cup	1½ cups	2 cups

1 Spread a flattened piece of steak out on a cutting board and smear with ½ tablespoon mustard. Top with 2 bacon pieces and a dill pickle spear, laying them so they run the length of the steak and are parallel to one another. Roll up the beef so that the pickle runs along the tube's length. Use butchers' twine to tie the roll in two or three places. Set aside and continue making more rolls.

2 Toss the onions and butter in the slow cooker until the onions are coated. Sprinkle the caraway seeds over the onions, then nestle the beef rolls seam side down into the cooker. Sprinkle these rolls with paprika; pour the broth into the cooker, taking care not to knock the paprika off the beef.

3 Cover and cook on low for 6 hours, or until the beef is tender and the onions have begun to break down into a sauce.

TESTERS' NOTES
- Good enough for a dinner party, these beef rolls are salty, peppery, and buttery—in other words, heaven. Break out the beer!
- Use fairly thin pickle spears so the rolls hold together.
- The beef may shrink as it cooks and so can fall apart as you lift the rolls out of the cooker. Use a large, wide metal spatula.
- To tie the rolls, make two or three loops around them, knotting each. Don't pull the butchers' twine so tight that it squeezes the roll—just tight enough to hold it. Snip the twine off when you serve the rouladen—or let everyone cut his or her own off at the table.

Serve It Up! Although mashed potatoes seem like a natural side for this dish, consider steaming peeled and cubed celery root or rutabaga before mashing the vegetables with some broth and butter.

INGREDIENTS EXPLAINED Butchers' twine is a sturdy, food-safe twine sold at larger supermarkets and many hardware stores. Don't use any twine or string that may have been manufactured with harmful dyes or solvents.

ALL-AMERICAN KNOW-HOW To flatten round steaks, set one between two sheets of wax paper on your work surface, then use the smooth side of a meat mallet or the bottom of a heavy saucepan to whack the beef to the desired thickness. But don't just strike it willy-nilly; instead, strike it near the center with a glancing blow, arching your swing so it moves out toward the edge of the steak, pushing the meat toward the perimeter. Peel off the wax paper and flatten more steaks between more sheets of wax paper.

wine-braised round roast with porcinis

EFFORT: **A LOT** • PREP TIME: **45 MINUTES** • COOK TIME: **4 TO 7 HOURS** • KEEPS ON WARM: **4 HOURS** • SERVES: **3 TO 10**

INGREDIENTS	2- TO 3½-QT	4- TO 5½-QT	6- TO 8-QT
Dried porcini mushrooms	¼ ounce	½ ounce	1 ounce
Unsalted butter	1 tblsp	1½ tblsp	3 tblsp
Pancetta, diced (see page 354)	1 ounce	2½ ounces	4 ounces
Eye of round roast	1 pound	2½ pounds	4 pounds
Thinly sliced yellow onions	⅓ cup	1¼ cups (about 1 medium)	1¾ cups
Shredded carrots	½ cup	1¼ cups	2 cups (about ¾ pound)
4-inch fresh rosemary stalks	1	2	3
Bay leaves	1	2	3
Red wine, such as a Barolo or Syrah	½ cup	1¼ cups	2 cups
No-salt-added tomato paste	1½ tblsp	¼ cup	⅓ cup
Ground black pepper	½ tsp	1 tsp	½ tblsp

1 Bring a saucepan of water to a boil over high heat. Place the mushrooms in a large bowl and fill the bowl at least halfway with boiling water. Soak for 30 minutes.

2 Meanwhile, melt the butter in a large skillet set over medium heat. Drop in the pancetta and fry, stirring often, until crisp, particularly at the corners of each piece, between 4 and 8 minutes, depending on the size of the batch.

Use a slotted spoon to transfer the pancetta to the slow cooker.

3 Set the eye of round roast in the skillet, still over medium heat. Brown on all sides, letting the roast sit for a few minutes, turning it a bit, then browning some more, up to 15 minutes, until dark brown blotches mottle the cut. Use tongs or a metal spatula to transfer the roast to the slow cooker.

4 Dump the onions into the skillet and cook, stirring often, until they soften, between 4 and 7 minutes, depending on the size of the batch. Scrape the contents of the skillet over and around the beef.

5 Add the carrots to the cooker, nestling them around the roast, not on it. Nestle the rosemary and bay leaves in the cooker to the sides of the roast.

6 Drain the soaked mushrooms in a colander set over a large bowl, catching and reserving the soaking liquid. Sprinkle the mushrooms around the cooker, not on the beef.

7 Whisk the wine, tomato paste, and pepper in a large bowl until smooth; whisk in 1 cup of the mushroom-soaking liquid for a small slow cooker, 2¼ cups for a medium model, or 3½ cups for a large one. Pour into the cooker.

8 Cover and cook on low for 4½ hours for a small slow cooker, 5½ hours for a medium slow cooker, or 7 hours for a large slow cooker, or until the beef is fork-tender.

9 Transfer the roast to a cutting board; let it stand for 10 minutes. Use a spoon to skim off any fat from the sauce in the cooker. Slice the roast into steak rounds about ¼ inch thick. Serve the steak with the sauce and vegetables on the side.

(continued)

TESTERS' NOTES

• Make sure you get all the dried porcini bits out of the bag, even the dust in the bottom. You don't want to miss any flavor.

• A fat separator will require a lot of work. Ladle all the vegetables, mushrooms, and sauce through a fine-mesh sieve and into a fat separator. Place the vegetables and mushrooms in a serving bowl, then wait a few minutes, until the fat indeed separates from the sauce.

Serve It Up! Since you don't want to miss a drop of that sauce, how about serving this on a bed of creamy polenta? In fact, there's a recipe for Parmesan Polenta on page 451, if you've got a second cooker on hand.

INGREDIENTS EXPLAINED Eye of round roasts vary in shape, from those that are uniform tubs of beef to those that taper at one end. For slow cooker dishes, try to get the most uniform roast so it cooks evenly throughout.

ropa vieja

EFFORT: **A LITTLE** • PREP TIME: **20 MINUTES** • COOK TIME: **9 HOURS** • KEEPS ON WARM: **6 HOURS** • SERVES: **4 TO 12**

INGREDIENTS	2- TO 3½-QT	4- TO 5½-QT	6- TO 8-QT
Drained no-salt-added canned diced tomatoes	⅔ cup	1⅓ cups	2 cups
Thinly sliced yellow onion	½ cup	1 cup	1¼ cups (about 1 medium)
Medium celery ribs, thinly sliced	1	2	4
Stemmed, seeded, and thinly sliced cubanelle peppers (see page 47)	⅓ cup	⅔ cup	1 cup (about 1 large)
Thinly sliced pitted green olives	3 tblsp	⅓ cup	½ cup
Golden raisins	1 tblsp	2 tblsp	3 tblsp
No-salt-added tomato paste	2 tsp	4 tsp	1½ tblsp
Dried oregano	½ tblsp	1 tblsp	1½ tblsp
Ground cumin	1 tsp	2 tsp	2½ tsp
Salt	¼ tsp	½ tsp	¾ tsp
Bay leaf	1	1	2
Skirt steak	1 pound	2 pounds	3 pounds
Sherry vinegar	2 tsp	4 tsp	2 tblsp

1 Stir the tomatoes, onion, celery, peppers, olives, raisins, tomato paste, oregano, cumin, salt, and bay leaf in the slow cooker until the tomato paste dissolves into the mix.

2 Nestle the skirt steak(s) into the sauce, cutting large steaks to fit the size of your slow cooker and overlapping them as necessary without folding the steaks over onto themselves. In the end, they should all be submerged in the sauce.

3 Cover and cook on low for 9 hours, or until the beef is so tender it can be shredded with a fork. Remove the bay leaf and use two forks to shred the meat completely. Stir in the vinegar before serving.

TESTERS' NOTES

• Here's a rather well-known beef dish, originally from the Canary Islands and now popular across the Caribbean and the southern United States, particularly around Miami. The name (*ROH-pah vee-AY-hah*) means "old clothes" and refers to the way the meat shreds into strings—an unflattering way to describe a terrific meal.

• We used skirt steak, rather than the more traditional flank steak, because the skirt steak will end up in shorter threads and be easier to eat. Also, it's a far more flavorful cut.

(continued)

Serve It Up! Ropa Vieja is most often served with white rice and a pot of tender, saucy black beans.

INGREDIENTS EXPLAINED Prized for its good flavor, like a steak version of a chuck roast, a skirt steak is from a group of muscles on the underbelly in front of the cow's flank. This long, thin steak is familiar as the original cut used for fajitas; it was also called "Roumanian tenderloin" in old-school delis.

stuffed flank steak

EFFORT: **A LOT** • PREP TIME: **40 MINUTES** • COOK TIME: **6 HOURS** •
KEEPS ON WARM: **2 HOURS** • SERVES: **3 TO 8**

INGREDIENTS	2- TO 3½-QT	4- TO 5½-QT	6- TO 8-QT
Flank steaks	1 pound	1½ pounds	3 pounds
Red wine vinegar	1 tblsp	2 tblsp	¼ cup
Minced garlic	1 tsp	2 tsp	4 tsp
Dried thyme	1 tsp	2 tsp	4 tsp
Salt	¼ tsp	½ tsp	1 tsp
Packed baby spinach leaves	4 cups (a little more than 4 ounces)	7 cups (about 8 ounces)	14 cups (about 1 pound)
Shallots, thinly sliced	2 ounces	4 ounces	8 ounces
Pine nuts	2½ tblsp	⅓ cup	⅔ cup
Red pepper flakes	½ tsp	1 tsp	2 tsp
Olive oil	½ tblsp	1 tblsp	2 tblsp
Reduced-sodium beef broth	1 cup	2 cups	4 cups (1 quart)

1 Lay a flank steak on your cutting board; insert the tip of your knife into the middle of the thickest side, then slice to the outside edge. Repeat on the other side to the opposite outside edge. Keep doing this until you can open the steak up flat; do not cut through the back, but instead leave it securely attached, like a book binding. Cover the steak with wax paper; use the smooth side of a meat mallet or the bottom of a heavy saucepan to pound the opened steak to ¼-inch thickness, starting at the middle and working your way out to the edges. Repeat with any other steaks as necessary.

2 Drizzle the steaks with the vinegar, garlic, thyme, and salt. Make a layer of spinach leaves across the cut surface, then top with the shallots before sprinkling with the pine nuts and red pepper flakes. (Apportion these stuffing ingredients evenly if you're working with more than one steak.)

3 Roll up the steak into a spiraled log, like a jelly roll. Tie the roll closed with butchers' twine in three or four places along its length.

4 Heat a skillet over medium-high heat. Swirl in the oil, then add one of the tied-up steaks. Brown it all around for a couple minutes, then turn it slightly to continue browning more surface area. Set aside and continue browning more steaks as necessary.

5 Set the steaks in the slow cooker, then pour in the broth. Cover and cook on low for 6 hours, or until each steak is quite tender when pierced. Use a wide metal spatula to transfer the steak to a cutting board; let stand for 10 minutes. Slice into ½-inch-thick rounds.

(continued)

TESTERS' NOTES

• This recipe is a little over the top, sure, but it also brings out the best in the cut, rendering the meat luxuriously flavorful.

• Flank steaks range from 1 to 2 pounds. If you're working with a large cooker, buy two 1½-pound flank steaks and wedge them side by side into the cooker. If they won't fit, you'll need to stack them, then reverse them halfway through the cooking so they both get time in the liquid.

• If you really want to go all out, cover the cut surface of the steak with thin slices of prosciutto before adding the spinach leaves and rolling them up. You can even add thin slices of provolone! (If you do, cut the spinach by about half so the steak is still easy to roll closed.)

• The cooking time is conservative because you want the meat to have some chew, the better to be able to slice these rolls into rounds.

• Pine nuts can be crazy-expensive if you buy them in those little jars. Instead, look for them in bulk or at least in larger quantities with the other nuts or in the produce section.

SHORTCUTS Ask your market's butcher to butterfly and pound the steaks for you, then skip step 1. The flank steak is a fairly fatty bit taken from the underside of the cow toward the back. Sometimes called the "bavette," it's also one of the tougher cuts of beef—and thus, long braising in a slow cooker comes to the rescue!

ALL-AMERICAN KNOW-HOW The trick to proper browning in a skillet is quite simple: you have to leave the meat alone until its surface crusts and even dries out a bit. After that, the meat can pop off the hot surface with a gentle prod from a spatula. If you find that pieces of meat are tearing as you try to turn them, you haven't let them brown enough.

skirt steak with pickled onions and green peppercorns

EFFORT: **NOT MUCH** • PREP TIME: **15 MINUTES** • COOK TIME: **7 HOURS** • KEEPS ON WARM: **2 HOURS** • SERVES: **3 TO 10**

INGREDIENTS	2- TO 3½-QT	4- TO 5½-QT	6- TO 8-QT
Reduced-sodium beef broth	⅓ cup	¾ cup	1½ cups
Dry sherry	2 tblsp	⅓ cup	½ cup
No-salt-added tomato paste	2 tsp	1 tblsp	2 tblsp
Soy sauce	2 tsp	1 tblsp	2 tblsp
Drained and rinsed pickled cocktail onions	6 tblsp	1 cup	1½ cups
Thinly sliced pitted green olives	¼ cup	⅔ cup	1 cup
Green peppercorns	½ tblsp	1 tblsp	2 tblsp
Skirt steaks, cut into 6-inch sections	1 pound	2 pounds	4 pounds

1 Whisk the broth, sherry, tomato paste, and soy sauce in the slow cooker until the tomato paste dissolves. Stir in the onions, olives, and peppercorns. Submerge the pieces of steak in the sauce.

2 Cover and cook on low for 7 hours, or until the steak is fork-tender. Transfer the beef to a cutting board; cool for 10 minutes. Slice the steaks into thin strips widthwise, then serve in bowls with the sauce ladled on top.

TESTERS' NOTES

• A fine dish for a dinner party, this hearty stew offers great contrasting flavors, particularly if you take extra care to slice the olives thin so you can get one in every bite.

• Skirt steaks do have a little fat on their external surfaces, but you needn't trim it off. The steaks themselves are quite lean; any extra fat will only enhance their already mild flavor.

Serve It Up! Because the sauce skews to the sour, serve this dish with a somewhat sweeter side, like a rice or barley pilaf stocked with vegetables.

INGREDIENTS EXPLAINED Green peppercorns are black peppercorns that have not been dried. The green version has a brighter and more acidic, if slightly muskier, flavor than its black and red counterparts.

barbecued brisket

EFFORT: **NOT MUCH** • PREP TIME: **15 MINUTES** • COOK TIME: **10 TO 12 HOURS** • KEEPS ON WARM: **4 HOURS** • SERVES: **6 TO 18**

INGREDIENTS	2- TO 3½-QT	4- TO 5½-QT	6- TO 8-QT
Beef brisket, preferably first-cut or flat-cut, trimmed	2 pounds	4 pounds	6 pounds
No-salt-added canned tomato puree	1 cup	2 cups	3 cups
No-salt-added tomato paste	3 tblsp	6 tblsp	9 tblsp
Cider vinegar	3 tblsp	6 tblsp	9 tblsp
Packed dark brown sugar	3 tblsp	6 tblsp	9 tblsp
Mild smoked paprika	1 tblsp	2 tblsp	3 tblsp
Worcestershire sauce	1 tsp	2 tsp	1 tblsp
Ground allspice	½ tsp	1 tsp	½ tblsp
Ground cloves	½ tsp	1 tsp	½ tblsp
Ground coriander	½ tsp	1 tsp	½ tblsp
Celery seeds	¼ tsp	½ tsp	1 tsp
Dry mustard (see page 392)	¼ tsp	½ tsp	1 tsp
Ground black pepper	¼ tsp	½ tsp	1 tsp
Garlic powder	¼ tsp	½ tsp	¾ tsp
Salt	¼ tsp	½ tsp	½ tsp

1 Set the brisket in the slow cooker. (If you can't fit the cut without folding, slice the brisket in half and set one piece on top of the other.)

2 Whisk the tomato puree, tomato paste, vinegar, brown sugar, paprika, Worcestershire sauce, allspice, cloves, coriander, celery seeds, mustard, pepper, garlic powder, and salt in a large bowl; pour over the brisket.

3 Cover and cook on low for 10 hours in a small cooker, 11 hours in a medium cooker, or 12 hours in a large cooker, or until the brisket is tender enough to slice without shredding. If you've stacked two pieces of brisket, you'll need to swap them halfway through cooking to make sure each piece spends time submerged in the sauce.

4 Transfer the meat to a cutting board and let stand for 10 minutes before slicing against the grain into ¼-inch-thick strips. Skim some of the fat from the sauce with a spoon before serving it on the side.

TESTERS' NOTES
• Here's an all-American slow cooker version of the American backyard favorite, given more oomph here with a homemade barbecue sauce. No, the meat's not truly *barbecued*. Let go of the culinary jargon; the flavors are the same.
• The sweet-and-savory barbecue sauce will set off the tender beef perfectly. Consider making a double batch of the sauce; save the remainder in a covered plastic or glass container in the freezer for up to 4 months, a boon for your next backyard cookout—or slow cooker brisket!

(continued)

INGREDIENTS EXPLAINED Cut from the cow's breast, a brisket is a rather stringy cut that tenderizes beautifully after long cooking with moist heat. When butchered into smaller, more manageable pieces, the leanest section is called the *first cut* or the *flat cut*. The first cut does have a layer of fat on top of the meat. We suggest trimming the fat, but leave it in place for a richer dinner.

ALL-AMERICAN KNOW-HOW For both tenderness and flavor, beef should be sliced "against the grain"—that is, with the most fibers exposed in each slice so that the pieces hold together, rather than turn to shards. In American butchering technique, the fibers always run through the cuts (not along their surface planes, as in European butchering). When it comes to brisket, you can see the fibers on the outside of the cut. Slice ninety degrees to their direction (that is, not with their direction but perpendicular to—or *against*—it).

For other cuts, you may need to run your fingers along the surface to tell which way the fibers are running, pulling the meat slightly apart to see what's what. And once in a great while, it's pure trial and error: slice a small piece off the end of the meat and look at the fibers inside.

sweet and spicy pulled brisket

EFFORT: **A LITTLE** • PREP TIME: **15 MINUTES** • COOK TIME: **10 TO 12 HOURS** • KEEPS ON WARM: **8 HOURS** • SERVES: **6 TO 14**

INGREDIENTS	2- TO 3½-QT	4- TO 5½-QT	6- TO 8-QT
Thinly sliced yellow onion	¾ cup	1¼ cups (about 1 medium)	2⅔ cups
First-cut or flat-cut beef brisket, trimmed	1½ pounds	3 pounds	4½ pounds
No-salt-added canned diced tomatoes	1¾ cups	3½ cups	5¼ cups
Molasses, preferably unsulphured	2 tblsp	¼ cup	6 tblsp
Balsamic vinegar	2 tblsp	¼ cup	6 tblsp
Minced garlic	2 tsp	1 tblsp	1½ tblsp
Canned chipotle chiles in adobo sauce, stemmed and minced	1	2	3
Ground coriander	1 tsp	2 tsp	1 tblsp
Ground cumin	1 tsp	2 tsp	1 tblsp
Ancho chile powder	1 tsp	2 tsp	1 tblsp
Salt	¼ tsp	½ tsp	½ tsp
Ground black pepper	¼ tsp	½ tsp	½ tsp
Bay leaves	1	2	3

1 Make an even layer of half the onions in the slow cooker. Set the brisket on top. (Slice the brisket into pieces if it won't fit easily.)

2 Stir the remainder of the onions with the tomatoes, molasses, vinegar, garlic, chipotles, coriander, cumin, chile powder, salt, pepper, and bay leaves in a large bowl, until the molasses dissolves into the mixture. Pour over the brisket.

3 Cover and cook on low for 10 hours in a small cooker, 11 hours in a medium cooker, or 12 hours in a large cooker, or until the brisket is so tender it can be shredded with a fork.

4 Discard the bay leaves. Shred the brisket right in the slow cooker, using two forks to pull it into shards and pieces; stir these into the sauce.

• If you're not from Texas, you may not have heard of pulled brisket. Just think of it as the cow equivalent of pulled pork. Better still, this sauce is even bolder than that for Basic Pulled Pork (see page 183)—aromatic and laced with warm spices.

• There's a lot of heat here, what with the chipotles and the ancho chile powder. Seed the chipotles, if you're concerned. Just make sure you use one, two, or three canned chiles, *not* one, two, or three cans of chiles.

• Use a sturdy, flavorful, low-grade balsamic vinegar, not the best stuff.

Serve It Up! You'll want hamburger buns or Kaiser rolls as a start—and then shredded iceberg lettuce, chopped tomatoes, jarred pickle relish, and/or jarred chow-chow to top the sandwiches. We've even been known to heap the brisket into buns and top it all with coleslaw!

INGREDIENTS EXPLAINED Standard supermarket chili powder is a blend of powdered dried chiles, ground cumin, and dried oregano. If possible, use a blend without added salt—or omit the salt from the recipe if your bottle is so laced.

Pure chile powder, like the ancho chile powder used here, omits all the other ingredients and so contains nothing but powdered, dried chiles. These varieties are always labeled by the type of chile: ancho, chipotle, or what have you.

wine-braised brisket

EFFORT: **A LITTLE** • PREP TIME: **10 MINUTES** • COOK TIME: **8 TO 10 HOURS** • KEEPS ON WARM: **4 HOURS** • SERVES: **4 TO 10**

INGREDIENTS	2- TO 3½-QT	4- TO 5½-QT	6- TO 8-QT
First-cut or flat-cut beef brisket, trimmed	1½ pounds	3 pounds	4½ pounds
Mild paprika	1 tsp	2 tsp	1 tblsp
Garlic powder	½ tsp	¾ tsp	1 tsp
Salt	½ tsp	¾ tsp	1 tsp
Ground black pepper	½ tsp	¾ tsp	1 tsp
Medium carrots, peeled and cut into 1-inch sections	2	4	6
Thinly sliced yellow onions	1 cup	2 cups (about 1 large)	3 cups
Medium celery ribs, thinly sliced	2	3	5
Bay leaves	1	2	3
Fruit-forward red wine, such as Pinot Noir	⅓ cup	⅔ cup	1 cup
Worcestershire sauce	1 tblsp	1½ tblsp	2 tblsp

1 Sprinkle both sides of the brisket with the paprika, garlic powder, salt, and pepper; set it in the slow cooker.

2 Sprinkle the carrots, onions, celery, and bay leaves around and on the brisket. Pour in the wine and Worcestershire sauce.

3 Cover and cook on low for 8 hours in a small cooker, 9 hours in a medium cooker, or 10 hours in a large cooker, or until the brisket is tender but can still be sliced into pieces without shredding.

(continued)

4 Transfer to a cutting board; cool for 10 minutes for the best flavor. Discard the bay leaves. Slice the meat against the grain into ¼-inch-thick pieces (see page 146). Ladle the vegetables and sauce into the bowls with the slices.

TESTERS' NOTES

• This braised brisket is a version of the traditional one made for Passover and some other Jewish holidays—although we've nixed the tomatoes and gone with a French vegetable mélange.

• Don't get hung up on timing—brisket is notorious for getting tender at its own rate. Start checking at the 7-hour mark and see where you are. If dinner is at an exact hour without leeway, consider making this the day before, storing it covered in the fridge, and reheating it in a tightly sealed foil packet or a tightly covered roasting pan in a 350°F oven for 20 minutes.

Serve It Up! For a more substantial sauce, remove all the meat and vegetables from the liquid in the slow cooker, then strain that liquid through a fine-mesh colander or sieve into a bowl. (Work in the sink to avoid a messy cleanup.) Bring the strained sauce to a boil in a saucepan set over medium-high heat. Boil for 1 or 2 minutes to concentrate the flavors, then stir in 1 to 2 teaspoons red wine vinegar to brighten the flavors.

INGREDIENTS EXPLAINED Bay leaves are considered a dried food ingredient. If you're lucky enough to have fresh bay leaves, cut the suggested amount in half unless you're fond of the aromatic punch they provide. Even fresh bay leaves should be discarded from a dish before serving.

barbecued beef ribs

EFFORT: **NOT MUCH** • PREP TIME: **15 MINUTES** • COOK TIME: **9 HOURS** • KEEPS ON WARM: **4 HOURS** • SERVES: **2 TO 8**

INGREDIENTS	2- TO 3½-QT	4- TO 5½-QT	6- TO 8-QT
Packed dark brown sugar	1 tsp	2 tsp	1 tblsp
Mild smoked paprika	½ tsp	1 tsp	2 tsp
Ground cumin	¼ tsp	½ tsp	1 tsp
Dried thyme	¼ tsp	½ tsp	1 tsp
Ground black pepper	¼ tsp	½ tsp	1 tsp
Onion powder	⅛ tsp	¼ tsp	½ tsp
Garlic powder	⅛ tsp	¼ tsp	½ tsp
Salt	⅛ tsp	¼ tsp	½ tsp
Bone-in beef back ribs	1 pound	2 pounds	4 pounds

1 Mix the brown sugar, paprika, cumin, thyme, pepper, onion powder, garlic powder, and salt in a small bowl.

2 Prepare the ribs by separating the rack into individual bones, then cut each bone in half widthwise if you have a round cooker rather than an oval one. (You might need a food-safe hacksaw for the latter task, or you can ask the butcher at your market to saw the ribs in half for you.)

3 Massage the rub into the ribs, pile them into the slow cooker, cover, and cook on low for 9 hours, or until the meat is tender at the bone yet still juicy.

- Who says you can't barbecue ribs in the slow cooker? Well, okay, you can't *barbecue* them. But you can make them taste like good barbecue.
- Beef ribs are far bigger—and meatier—than pork ribs. They're the bones that lie underneath a standing rib roast. Despite this pedigree, they're none too common in the barbecuing repertoire.
- Consider making a double or triple batch of this smoky and aromatic rub. Store the extra in a sealed glass container in your spice drawer or rack. Use it as a rub the next time you grill steaks—or mix it right into ground beef as a hamburger spice.

short ribs
with fennel and rosemary

EFFORT: **A LITTLE** • PREP TIME: **15 MINUTES** • COOK TIME: **8 HOURS** • KEEPS ON WARM: **4 HOURS** • SERVES: **3 TO 8**

INGREDIENTS	2- TO 3½-QT	4- TO 5½-QT	6- TO 8-QT
Unsalted butter	2 tsp	1 tblsp	1½ tblsp
English-cut beef short ribs	1¼ pounds	2¾ pounds	4¼ pounds
Salt	¼ tsp	½ tsp	¾ tsp
Ground black pepper	¼ tsp	½ tsp	¾ tsp
Shaved fennel bulb (see page 211)	1¾ cups	2⅔ cups	4¼ cups
Light-bodied, fruity red wine, such as from Fruili	1 cup	1½ cups	2½ cups
Fresh orange juice	½ cup	¾ cup	1¼ cups
Crushed dried rosemary	½ tblsp	2½ tsp	4 tsp

1 Melt the butter in a large skillet over medium heat. Season the short ribs with the salt and pepper, then set a few of them in the skillet. Brown them on all sides, leaving them for 2 to 3 minutes per side to make sure you get a brown crust. Transfer them to the slow cooker and continue to brown more as needed.

2 Add the fennel, wine, orange juice, and rosemary to the slow cooker. Cover and cook on low for 8 hours, or until the meat has pulled back from the bone and is tender when pierced with a fork. Use a spoon to skim any fat from the surface of the sauce before serving it on the side.

TESTERS' NOTES
- Short ribs are one of the best cuts of beef for the slow cooker: you get the luscious texture of a fairly fatty but sweet cut of beef, combined with the earthier flavor of the bone penetrating the meat.
- Braising meat or fish in a combination of red wine and orange juice is a technique that dates back to at least the seventeenth century. The finish this combo creates is sweet and mild, not acidic at all, and so a great match to the beef.
- For any of these short rib recipes, you can substitute buffalo short ribs, although they may take up to 2 hours longer to get tender because of the additional collagen. However, you'll be rewarded with a less sweet, more savory dish, better suited to a pile of mashed potatoes.

INGREDIENTS EXPLAINED Beef short ribs, sometimes called *thin ribs*, are cut from just behind the cow's primal chuck (and even sometimes a bit into that chuck in modern butchering techniques). Thus, short ribs combine the best of the fatty chuck with the milder flavors of the loin. We work with three types of short ribs in this book: the so-called *English cut*, in which the short ribs are sliced 4 to 5 inches long with a mound of meat along one side; *boneless* short ribs, simply English-cut short ribs without bones, allowing for a much sweeter finish; and *flanken cut,* in which the ribs are sliced crosswise, resulting in a 6- to 9-inch strip of meat with small oval bones lying along its length.

short ribs with orange marmalade and basil

EFFORT: **A LITTLE** • PREP TIME: **20 MINUTES** • COOK TIME: **9 HOURS** • KEEPS ON WARM: **3 HOURS** • SERVES: **3 TO 8**

INGREDIENTS	2- TO 3½-QT	4- TO 5½-QT	6- TO 8-QT
Unsalted butter	1 tblsp	1½ tblsp	3 tblsp
English-cut beef short ribs	1½ pounds	3 pounds	4½ pounds
Orange marmalade	½ cup	1 cup	1½ cups
Full-bodied white wine, such as white Bordeaux	¼ cup	½ cup	¾ cup
Minced fresh basil leaves	2 tblsp	¼ cup	6 tblsp
Salt	¼ tsp	½ tsp	¾ tsp
Ground black pepper	¼ tsp	½ tsp	¾ tsp

1 Melt the butter in a large skillet set over medium heat. Add three or four short ribs to the skillet; brown them on all sides, working to get good color with plenty of patience and turning them only after a few minutes on each side, perhaps 12 minutes per batch. Use tongs to transfer them into the slow cooker when they're ready, and continue browning more as necessary.

2 Whisk the marmalade, wine, basil, salt, and pepper in a big bowl until the marmalade has thinned out into a sauce. Pour this mixture over the short ribs in the cooker.

3 Cover and cook on low for 9 hours, or until the meat is fork-tender and has pulled back from the bones a bit. Transfer the short ribs to individual bowls; use a ladle or flatware spoon to skim any fat off the top of the sauce before serving.

TESTERS' NOTES
• Braising beef in white wine? You bet! The final dish is brighter, more summery than one with a braise prepared with red wine.
• The quality of the marmalade will directly affect the final dish. However, many high-end brands include large chunks of fruit, even stacked in rings in the jar. If you've got such a wonder on hand, mince the candied fruit so it distributes evenly in the sauce.

ALL-AMERICAN KNOW-HOW Forget the myth: all the alcohol in a recipe does not cook out of a dish, no matter what technique you use, but especially when you're working with a no-evaporation slow cooker. If you'd like an alcohol-free preparation, substitute a combination of chicken broth and unsweetened apple cider for the wine. You can also use a mixture of beef broth, unsweetened pomegranate juice, and a pinch of sugar for heartier braises.

short ribs in port with cabbage and vanilla

EFFORT: **A LOT** • PREP TIME: **30 MINUTES** • COOK TIME: **7 HOURS** • KEEPS ON WARM: **3 HOURS** • SERVES: **3 TO 10**

INGREDIENTS	2- TO 3½-QT	4- TO 5½-QT	6- TO 8-QT
Unsalted butter	½ tblsp	1 tblsp	2 tblsp
Pancetta, chopped (see page 354)	4 ounces	6 ounces	12 ounces
Boneless beef short ribs	1½ pounds	2½ pounds	4 pounds

Thinly sliced yellow onions	1/3 cup	1 cup (about 1 small)	2 cups
Minced garlic	2 tsp	4 tsp	2 tblsp plus 2 tsp
Thinly sliced and cored green cabbage, separated into strands	2½ cups	4 cups (about a 1-pound head)	7 cups
Non-vintage tawny port	2/3 cup	1 cup	2 cups
Reduced-sodium beef broth	6 tblsp	¾ cup	1½ cups
No-salt-added tomato paste	2½ tblsp	¼ cup	½ cup
Fennel seeds	½ tsp	1 tsp	2 tsp
Ground allspice	¼ tsp	½ tsp	1 tsp
Ground black pepper	¼ tsp	½ tsp	1 tsp
4-inch rosemary sprig	½	1	2
4-inch cinnamon stick	½	1	1
Vanilla bean, split in half lengthwise	½	1	1

1 Melt the butter in a large skillet over medium heat, then add the pancetta bits. Cook, stirring often, until frizzled and well browned, 4 to 6 minutes. Use a slotted spoon to transfer the pancetta to the slow cooker, leaving the skillet (and any drippings) over the heat.

2 Set up to five boneless short ribs in the skillet; brown them on all sides, taking care to leave them alone until you get good color, maybe 2 minutes per side, then turning them to another side and leaving them be. As they're ready, use the slotted spoon to transfer them to the cooker; continue browning as necessary.

3 Dump the onions into the skillet; cook, stirring often, until they soften and turn golden, 4 to 6 minutes. Add the garlic, stir about half a minute, and scrape the contents of the skillet into the slow cooker.

4 Dump the cabbage into the cooker. Whisk the port, broth, tomato paste, fennel seeds, allspice, and pepper in a bowl; pour over the meat and vegetables. Nestle the rosemary, cinnamon, and vanilla bean into the liquid in the cooker.

5 Cover and cook on low for 7 hours, or until the meat is extremely tender when pierced with a fork and the cabbage has begun to melt into the sauce. Discard the rosemary, cinnamon stick, and vanilla bean before skimming the sauce for fat and then serving.

TESTERS' NOTES
• Although port, vanilla, and cabbage may sound like a strange grouping, they meld into a fairly sweet, slightly grassy sauce spiked with just a hint of bitterness for a bit of sophistication—in other words, a great sauce for beef.
• Slice the onions and cabbage so the strips of both are about the same width, the better to meld into the dish.
• For the best taste, skip the presliced pancetta and go to the deli counter to ask for a single hunk of pancetta. At home, slice it into ½-inch-thick rounds, then cut into smaller cubes. There's no additional salt needed here because there's plenty in the pancetta.

Serve It Up! You'll need mashed potatoes as a bed, but don't think good ol' milk and butter as the additions to the boiled or steamed spuds. Instead, how about vegetable broth, sour cream, and a little minced orange zest?

korean-style barbecue short ribs

EFFORT: **A LITTLE** • PREP TIME: **15 MINUTES** • COOK TIME: **8 HOURS** • KEEPS ON WARM: **4 HOURS** • SERVES: **4 TO 10**

INGREDIENTS	2- TO 3½-QT	4- TO 5½-QT	6- TO 8-QT
Soy sauce	¼ cup	⅓ cup	⅔ cup
Packed dark brown sugar	¼ cup	⅓ cup	⅔ cup
Toasted sesame oil (see page 196)	1 tblsp	1½ tblsp	2½ tblsp
Minced peeled fresh ginger	1½ tblsp	2 tblsp	2½ tblsp
Rice vinegar	1 tblsp	1½ tblsp	2½ tblsp
Minced garlic	2 tsp	1 tblsp	1½ tblsp
Sambal oelek or Asian hot sauce (see page 404)	½ tblsp	2 tsp	1 tblsp
Flanken-cut beef short ribs (see page 149)	2 pounds	3 pounds	5 pounds
Medium scallions, thinly sliced, white and green parts kept separate	3	4	7
Toasted white sesame seeds	2 tsp	1 tblsp	2 tblsp

1 Mix the soy sauce, brown sugar, sesame oil, ginger, vinegar, garlic, and sambal oelek in the slow cooker. Nestle the short ribs and the white parts of the scallions into this sauce.

2 Cover and cook on low for 8 hours, or until the meat is so fork-tender that you don't even need to open the drawer with the knives. Sprinkle the green parts of the scallions and the sesame seeds over everything in the slow cooker before serving (or over individual servings in bowls).

TESTERS' NOTES
• This barbecue is actually modeled on a Korean recipe, a sticky-sweet mix that's perfect for these meaty short ribs.
• Bring plenty of napkins to the table because this is ideal finger food for gnawing. Everyone should pick up the bones and slurp the sauce.

SHORTCUTS Of course, asking for fresh ginger doesn't mean you can't use jarred—just don't use ground or crystallized (candied) ginger. If you buy minced ginger in a jar, look for pale beige bits without browning or excess liquid. Once opened, store it, sealed, in the refrigerator for several months.

chuck roast with tomatoes and autumn spices

EFFORT: **A LITTLE** • PREP TIME: **25 MINUTES** • COOK TIME: **5 TO 8 HOURS** • KEEPS ON WARM: **3 HOURS** • SERVES: **3 TO 10**

INGREDIENTS	2- TO 3½-QT	4- TO 5½-QT	6- TO 8-QT
Olive oil	½ tblsp	1 tblsp	1½ tblsp
Boneless beef chuck roast, trimmed	1½ pounds	3 pounds	4½ pounds
Drained no-salt-added canned whole tomatoes	1 cup	2 cups	3 cups
Chopped yellow onion	¼ cup	½ cup	¾ cup (about 1 small)
No-salt-added tomato paste	1½ tblsp	3 tblsp	⅓ cup
Ground allspice	¼ tsp	½ tsp	1 tsp
Ground black pepper	¼ tsp	½ tsp	1 tsp

Ground cloves	⅛ tsp	¼ tsp	½ tsp
Salt	¼ tsp	½ tsp	½ tsp
Ground mace	Pinch	⅛ tsp	¼ tsp
4-inch cinnamon sticks	2	3	5

1 Warm a big skillet over medium heat, then swirl in the olive oil. Set the chuck roast in the skillet and brown all sides, turning it only after it has deepened in color, about 15 minutes in all. Set the roast in the slow cooker.

2 Pour the tomatoes into a big bowl. With clean hands, a pastry cutter, or even kitchen shears, break up the tomatoes into rough, uneven bits. Stir in the onion, tomato paste, allspice, pepper, cloves, salt, and mace until the tomato paste dissolves. Pour into the slow cooker, scraping the bowl to get every drop. Nestle the cinnamon sticks around the roast.

3 Cover and cook on low for 5 hours in a small slow cooker, 7 hours in a medium slow cooker, or 8 hours in a large slow cooker, or until the chuck roast is ridiculously tender when pierced with a fork but not yet falling apart at the seams. Transfer to a cutting board and wait for 10 or 15 minutes so the juices reincorporate into the meat's fibers. Discard the cinnamon sticks. Chunk up the roast, skim the sauce for any surface fat, and serve in bowls.

TESTERS' NOTES

• Here, tomatoes pair with familiar flavors from mulled cider or even apple pie to create a warm but mellow sauce for the chuck roast.

• Cinnamon sticks lose their punch during long storage. Figure on a year at most in a dry, cool, dark pantry. After that, you'll need to swap them for fresh sticks to get the best results.

• If you let one side of the roast get really brown, almost crunchy, over the heat in the skillet, it will easily pop off the hot surface when you slip a thin spatula underneath it.

INGREDIENTS EXPLAINED Chuck roasts are found over the cow's front legs, an area stocked with collagen and connective tissue—all the stuff that melts to bathe the roast in its own juices. There are actually several boneless cuts from this area that can stand in for a chuck roast: the cross-rib roast, the top blade roast, the shoulder roast, or any sort of arm roast. These come in a variety of shapes: flat slabs, rounded mounds, or even misshapen lumps. Any will work in all these chuck recipes.

chuck roast with mushrooms and thyme

EFFORT: **A LITTLE** • PREP TIME: **35 MINUTES** • COOK TIME: **5 TO 7 HOURS** • KEEPS ON WARM: **3 HOURS** • SERVES: **4 TO 8**

INGREDIENTS	2- TO 3½-QT	4- TO 5½-QT	6- TO 8-QT
Unsalted butter	½ tblsp	1 tblsp	2 tblsp
Boneless beef chuck roast, trimmed	1½ pounds	2½ pounds	3½ pounds
Salt	¼ tsp	½ tsp	¾ tsp
Ground black pepper	¼ tsp	½ tsp	¾ tsp
White button mushrooms, sliced	12 ounces (about 3¾ cups)	1 pound (about 5 cups)	1½ pounds (about 7½ cups)
Dry vermouth	¼ cup	⅓ cup	½ cup
Dried thyme	½ tsp	1 tsp	½ tblsp
Apple jelly	⅓ cup	½ cup	¾ cup

1 Melt the butter in a large skillet set over medium heat. Season the roast with salt and

(continued)

pepper, then set it in the skillet. Brown on all sides for about 15 minutes, turning it only after you've got good coloring on the meat. Transfer the roast to a slow cooker.

2 Add the mushrooms to the skillet, still set over the heat. Stir once in a while until they release their liquid and it reduces to a thick glaze, between 4 and 8 minutes, depending on how many mushrooms you're working with.

3 Increase the heat to medium-high. Pour in the vermouth, add the thyme, and continue boiling, stirring once in a while, until the liquid in the skillet is again a thick glaze, 3 to 6 minutes. Stir in the apple jelly until it dissolves, then scrape the contents of the skillet into the slow cooker.

4 Cover and cook on low for 5 hours in a small slow cooker, 6 hours in a medium slow cooker, or 7 hours in a large cooker, or until the roast is fork-tender. Transfer the roast to a cutting board; leave it alone for 10 to 15 minutes. Cut it into serving-sized chunks; serve in bowls with the sauce and the mushrooms ladled on top.

TESTERS' NOTES

• The slow cooker may have been invented for a chuck roast; in low heat and a moist environment, the cut can be cooked to utter perfection.

• The apple jelly gives the sauce a luxurious sheen, a foil to the earthy mushrooms and thyme.

• When you prepare to serve a pot roast, look for the natural seams in the meat. Pull these apart, then look for the grain in each chunk, often running at a slight angle to the rift you just made.

• Substitute buffalo or venison chuck roasts for the beef, but increase the cooking time by as much as 25 percent. The buffalo chuck will be quite savory, a more intense contrast with the apple jelly; the venison chuck is musky, even gamy, suitable for even some additional apple jelly or perhaps apple chutney as a garnish for the bowls.

ALL-AMERICAN KNOW-HOW Reducing a sauce to a thick glaze is merely a matter of patience. Turn up the heat and let the liquids simmer at a good bubble. The sauce is the right consistency when you can pull a wooden spoon through the liquid and its path remains behind without the liquid flowing into place.

chuck roast with rutabaga and sour cream

EFFORT: **A LITTLE** • PREP TIME: **25 MINUTES** • COOK TIME: **5 TO 7 HOURS** • KEEPS ON WARM: **3 HOURS** • SERVES: **3 TO 8**

INGREDIENTS	2- TO 3½-QT	4- TO 5½-QT	6- TO 8-QT
Unsalted butter	2 tsp	1 tblsp	2 tblsp
Boneless beef chuck roast, trimmed	1¼ pounds	2¼ pounds	3½ pounds
Salt	⅛ tsp	¼ tsp	½ tsp
Ground black pepper	⅛ tsp	¼ tsp	½ tsp
Yellow onion, chopped	1 small	1 medium	2 medium
Ground allspice	1 tsp	½ tblsp	2 tsp
Dried dill	½ tsp	¾ tsp	1 tsp
Rutabaga, peeled and cubed	1¼ pounds (about 3½ cups)	2 pounds (about 5½ cups)	3 pounds (about 8 cups)
Reduced-sodium beef broth	½ cup	⅔ cup	1 cup
Sour cream (regular, low-fat, or fat-free)	½ cup	⅔ cup	1 cup

1 Melt the butter in a large skillet over medium heat. Season the beef with salt and pepper, set it in the skillet, and brown on all sides, not being too quick to turn it before it has gotten brown and even a bit crusty, about 12 minutes in all. Transfer to the slow cooker.

2 Add the onion to the skillet and cook, stirring often, until soft and sweet, about 5 minutes. Stir in the allspice and dill, then scrape the contents of the skillet over and around the roast.

3 Dot the rutabaga cubes around the roast, then pour in the broth. Cover and cook on low for 5 hours in a small slow cooker, 6 hours in a medium cooker, or 7 hours in a large one, or until the roast is fork-tender. Transfer the roast to a cutting board; leave it alone for 10 to 15 minutes.

4 Use a spoon to skim the fat from the sauce in the cooker; stir in the sour cream. Chunk up the beef and serve it in bowls along with the sauce and plenty of rutabaga cubes.

TESTERS' NOTES
• Feel free to use frozen chopped onion here, since the flavor is more important than the texture.
• To make this meal a day in advance, skip adding the sour cream and refrigerate the pot roast and its sauce separately. The next day, wrap the roast in foil and reheat it for 20 minutes at 325°F; bring the sauce and vegetables to a full simmer in a saucepan; remove the pan from the heat and stir in the sour cream just before serving.

INGREDIENTS EXPLAINED Rutabagas, sometimes called *yellow turnips* or even *Swedes* (because of their Scandinavian heritage), are a starchy root vegetable, a cross between a cabbage and a turnip. They are often coated in a food-safe wax to preserve freshness. Peel a rutabaga with a vegetable peeler; slice the root into 1-inch-thick rings, then cut into 1-inch chunks.

chuck roast with figs and pearl onions

EFFORT: **A LITTLE** • PREP TIME: **25 MINUTES** • COOK TIME: **5 TO 8 HOURS** • KEEPS ON WARM: **3 HOURS** • SERVES: **3 TO 9**

INGREDIENTS	2- TO 3½-QT	4- TO 5½-QT	6- TO 8-QT
Olive oil	1 tsp	2 tsp	1 tblsp
Boneless beef chuck roast, trimmed	1 pound	2 pounds	4 pounds
Peeled small fresh pearl onions, or frozen pearl onions, thawed	½ cup	1 cup	2 cups
Reduced-sodium beef broth	½ cup	1 cup	2 cups
Full-bodied, lush red wine, such as Côtes-du-Rhône	⅓ cup	¾ cup	1½ cups
Dried figs, stemmed and quartered	2	4	8
Stemmed fresh thyme leaves	1 tsp	2 tsp	1½ tblsp
Ground allspice	⅛ tsp	¼ tsp	½ tsp
Salt	⅛ tsp	¼ tsp	½ tsp
Ground black pepper	⅛ tsp	¼ tsp	½ tsp

1 Set a large skillet over medium heat for a couple of minutes; drizzle in the oil and swirl the skillet to coat the hot surface. Add the roast and brown it on all sides, waiting patiently until a good crust forms, 3 to 5 minutes per side. Make sure you also brown the ends or the perimeter, depending on how the roast is cut. When it's right and ready, transfer it to the slow cooker.

2 Add the pearl onions to the skillet, still set over the heat. Stir until you get some nice caramelization on several sides, about 5 minutes or so. Scrape the onions into the slow cooker.

(continued)

Then stir in the broth, wine, figs, thyme, allspice, salt, and pepper.

3 Cover and cook on low for 5 hours in a small slow cooker, 6 hours in a medium slow cooker, or 8 hours in a large one, or until the meat is quite tender but not yet falling apart along its seams.

TESTERS' NOTES
• This chuck roast recipe was developed based on a traditional French flavor profile of figs and thyme in red wine. If you want an even more Gallic air, substitute unsalted butter for the olive oil.
• There's really only one way to know if a chuck roast is tender: cut off a little chunk and taste-test it. It should be soft, quite luscious, with just the hint of a firm chew left in the meat.

chuck roast with coffee and allspice

EFFORT: **A LITTLE** • PREP TIME: **20 MINUTES** • COOK TIME: **5 TO 8 HOURS** • KEEPS ON WARM: **3 HOURS** • SERVES: **4 TO 10**

INGREDIENTS	2- TO 3½-QT	4- TO 5½-QT	6- TO 8-QT
Unsalted butter	½ tblsp	1 tblsp	1½ tblsp
Thinly sliced yellow onion	¾ cup	1⅓ cups (about 1 medium)	2½ cups
Strong, freshly brewed dark roast coffee	½ cup	1 cup	1½ cups
Molasses, preferably unsulphured	1 tsp	2 tsp	1 tblsp
Finely grated orange zest	½ tblsp	1 tblsp	1½ tblsp
Medium garlic cloves, slivered	1	2	3
4-inch cinnamon stick	½	1	1½
Boneless beef chuck roast, trimmed	1½ pounds	3 pounds	4½ pounds
Salt	½ tsp	1 tsp	1¼ tsp
Ground black pepper	¼ tsp	½ tsp	¾ tsp
Ground allspice	¼ tsp	½ tsp	¾ tsp

1 Melt the butter in a large skillet over medium heat. Spill the onion slices into the skillet, reduce the heat to very low, and cook, stirring often, until they turn yellow, soft, and sweet, about 20 minutes. If they begin to brown, stir more frequently and reduce the heat even further.

2 Scrape the contents of the skillet into the slow cooker. Stir in the coffee, molasses, orange zest, and garlic. Put the cinnamon stick in the mixture.

3 Rub the roast with salt, pepper, and allspice. Set it into the cooker, mounding the onion up around the sides.

4 Cover and cook on low for 5 hours in a small slow cooker, 7 hours in a medium slow cooker, or 8 hours in a large one, or until the roast is quite tender when pierced with a fork. If you're in doubt, give it another 30 minutes.

5 Transfer the roast to a cutting board; let it alone for 10 to 15 minutes. Discard the cinnamon stick; if necessary, skim the sauce of any surface fat. Cut the roast into chunks and serve in bowls with that sauce ladled over each portion.

TESTERS' NOTES
• Coffee, orange zest, cinnamon, and allspice make a sophisticated and elegant sauce, probably not for the

elementary-school set, but definitely a crowd-pleaser among the adults.

• Of any of these chuck roast recipes, this one requires that the beef be well trimmed. Too much dissolved fat will not work with the coffee in the sauce, muting many of the distinct, bitter and sweet notes it will bring to the beef.

Serve It Up! Make **Croutons** for the bowls. Cut a baguette into 2-inch cubes, toss them with a little olive oil on a rimmed baking sheet, and toast in a 350°F oven until brown and crunchy, about 15 minutes, stirring occasionally. Pour the stew over these when serving.

ALL-AMERICAN KNOW-HOW The zest of a citrus fruit is the more colorful, outer layer of its skin, not deep at all. The rind, by contrast, includes both the zest and the white pith underneath. Use a microplane—originally developed to grate hard cheese—to remove the sweet-and-sour zest without pushing down into the bitter pith. Failing that, try a vegetable peeler, but don't apply much pressure. You'll also need to mince these strips.

chuck stew with bacon, beer, and mustard

EFFORT: **A LITTLE** • PREP TIME: **35 MINUTES** • COOK TIME: **6 HOURS** • KEEPS ON WARM: **4 HOURS** • SERVES: **4 TO 12**

INGREDIENTS	2- TO 3½-QT	4- TO 5½-QT	6- TO 8-QT
Slab bacon, cut into ½-inch pieces	4 ounces	8 ounces	1 pound
Boneless beef chuck, cut into 1-inch cubes	1½ pounds	3 pounds	4½ pounds

	3 ounces (about 1 cup)	6 ounces (about 2 cups)	9 ounces (about 3 cups)
Cremini or brown button mushrooms, thinly sliced	3 ounces (about 1 cup)	6 ounces (about 2 cups)	9 ounces (about 3 cups)
Chopped yellow onion	¼ cup	½ cup	1 cup (about 1 medium)
Medium carrots, thinly sliced	2	3	4
Dark beer, preferably brown ale	½ cup	1 cup	1½ cups (or one 12-ounce bottle)
Coarse-grained mustard	1 tblsp	2 tblsp	3 tblsp
Ground black pepper	1 tsp	2 tsp	1 tblsp
Caraway seeds	1 tsp	2 tsp	2½ tsp

1 Heat a large skillet over medium-high heat, then add the bacon bits, working in batches to prevent overcrowding. Brown them on all sides, stirring only occasionally so the pieces get a sizzling crust, about 7 minutes per batch. Use a slotted spoon to transfer them to the slow cooker and continue frying more as needed.

2 Do the same with the pieces of beef chuck: brown them in batches in the rendered bacon fat, about 8 minutes per batch. Transfer the meat to the slow cooker and soldier on until you've browned them all.

3 Reduce the heat under the skillet to medium-low; dump in the mushrooms and onion. (You may have to do this in two batches if you're working with a large slow cooker.) Cook, stirring often, until the onion softens and begins to brown, about 6 minutes.

4 Scrape the contents of the skillet into the slow cooker. Stir in the carrots, beer, mustard, pepper, and caraway seeds.

(continued)

5 Cover and cook on low for 6 hours, or until the beef is tender enough that you don't have to think about setting the table with knives.

TESTERS' NOTES

• Yep, there's lots of browning required for this dish, but you need to put that bacon fat to good use! And it will pay off in a satisfying stew that needs little else except a glass of brown ale to go with it.

• The beer will foam when you pour it into the slow cooker. Stir gently to reduce the froth.

SHORTCUTS For this and other recipes in this book that call for beef chuck cut into chunks, you can substitute already cubed beef stew meat. However, all your work may not be done. Make sure you cut those cubes into the size required by the recipe you've chosen.

chuck, vegetable, and guinness stew

EFFORT: **A LITTLE** • PREP TIME: **25 MINUTES** • COOK TIME: **8 HOURS** • KEEPS ON WARM: **4 HOURS** • SERVES: **3 TO 12**

INGREDIENTS	2- TO 3½-QT	4- TO 5½-QT	6- TO 8-QT
Olive oil	1 tblsp	2 tblsp	¼ cup
Boneless beef chuck, cut into 2-inch cubes	1 pound	3 pounds	5 pounds
Salt	¼ tsp	½ tsp	¾ tsp
Thinly sliced yellow onion	¾ cup	2 cups (about 1 large)	3½ cups
Carrots, peeled and cut into 1-inch sticks	¼ pound	¾ pound	1¼ pounds
Turnips, peeled and cubed	¼ pound	½ pound	1 pound
Eggplant, cut into cubes	¼ pound	½ pound	¾ pound
Finely grated orange zest	1 tsp	1 tblsp	1½ tblsp
Minced garlic	1 tsp	2 tsp	1 tblsp
Fresh thyme sprigs	1	3	5
Bay leaves	1	2	3
Guinness or other stout beer	¾ cup	2 cups	3½ cups

1 Set a large skillet over medium heat for a few minutes, then pour in the oil. Salt the beef and brown it in the skillet (without crowding) on all sides, turning only when you have to, about 8 minutes per batch; transfer to the slow cooker and continue browning more.

2 Add the onion to the skillet. Stir until it softens and even browns a bit, 4 to 7 minutes, depending on how much you've got. Scrape all the onion into the slow cooker.

3 Stir in the carrots, turnips, eggplant, orange zest, garlic, thyme sprigs, and bay leaves. Pour the beer over everything.

4 Cover and cook on low for 8 hours, or until the vegetables and beef chunks are all fork-tender.

TESTERS' NOTES

• Guinness or another stout beer offers a savory bitterness just at the back of the complex flavors in their hearty stew. One note: don't use a flavored stout, which will unnecessarily complicate the dish.

• There's no need to peel the eggplant before chopping it into cubes for this stew.

• When you're browning cubed meat for large slow cookers, divide the oil, using a little for each batch.

chuck stew with briny breadcrumbs

EFFORT: **A LOT** · PREP TIME: **30 MINUTES** · COOK TIME: **7 HOURS** ·
KEEPS ON WARM: **4 HOURS THROUGH STEP 3** · SERVES: **3 TO 14**

INGREDIENTS	2- TO 3½-QT	4- TO 5½-QT	6- TO 8-QT
Olive oil	2 tsp	2 tblsp	3 tblsp
Boneless beef chuck or beef stew meat, cut into 1½-inch pieces	1 pound	3 pounds	5 pounds
Yellow onions, chopped	1 small	2 medium	3 medium
Ripe tomatoes, chopped	10 ounces	1 pound	1 pound 10 ounces
Moderately sweet white wine, such as Viognier	⅔ cup	2 cups	3⅓ cups
Dried thyme	½ tsp	1 tsp	2½ tsp
Fennel seeds	½ tsp	1 tsp	2½ tsp
Dried sage	½ tsp	1 tsp	2 tsp
Ground allspice	¼ tsp	½ tsp	1¼ tsp
Salt	¼ tsp	½ tsp	1 tsp
Bay leaves	1	2	4
Plain fresh breadcrumbs	⅓ cup	1 cup	1⅔ cups
Hazelnuts, toasted and skinned	¼ cup	½ cup	1 cup
Halved pitted green olives	¼ cup	½ cup	1 cup
Packed fresh parsley leaves	3 tblsp	½ cup	1 cup
Drained and rinsed capers	1 tsp	1 tblsp	2 tblsp
Medium garlic cloves, peeled	1	2	4

1 Set a large skillet over medium heat for a few minutes, then swirl in the oil. Brown the meat in the skillet, working in batches, until deeply browned on all sides, about 8 minutes per batch. Transfer the cubes of meat to the slow cooker; continue browning as necessary.

2 Add the onions to the skillet, then stir occasionally until they begin to brown and get really soft, 5 to 7 minutes. Scrape into the slow cooker.

3 Stir in the tomatoes, wine, thyme, fennel seeds, sage, allspice, salt, and bay leaves. Cover and cook on low for 7 hours, or until the beef is very tender when you poke it with a fork.

4 As the stew cooks, place the breadcrumbs, hazelnuts, olives, parsley, capers, and garlic in a food processor. Process until finely chopped, about like wet sand.

5 When the stew is ready, discard the bay leaves. Place about ⅓ cup of the breadcrumb mixture in each serving bowl, then ladle the stew on top.

TESTERS' NOTES

• This aromatic stew is thickened by the intensely flavored breadcrumb mixture in the bowls. The seasoning pairs with the white wine, soaks up most of the moisture, and adds lighter, piquant notes to the stew's deep taste.

• Only use fresh breadcrumbs, not dried. To make your own, grind several slices of stale bread in a food processor until the crumbs are about the consistency of fine gravel. You can also look for fresh breadcrumbs in the bakery section of most large supermarkets.

ALL-AMERICAN KNOW-HOW To toast hazelnuts, spread them on a rimmed baking sheet and set them in a 350°F oven for about 10 minutes, stirring often, until lightly browned and aromatic. To skin them, cool them on the baking sheet for 15 minutes, then dump them into a clean kitchen towel. Gather the towel together with the nuts inside, then massage the towel over the hazelnuts, thereby removing much of their papery, outer husks. No need to get off every speck—just the majority of it.

sichuan-style chuck stew

EFFORT: **NOT MUCH** • PREP TIME: **20 MINUTES** • COOK TIME: **7 HOURS** • KEEPS ON WARM: **4 HOURS** • SERVES: **4 TO 12**

INGREDIENTS	2- TO 3½-QT	4- TO 5½-QT	6- TO 8-QT
Boneless beef chuck, cut into 1-inch cubes	1¼ pounds	2½ pounds	4 pounds
Carrots, cut into 1-inch sections	1 pound	1½ pounds	2¼ pounds
Dry sherry	¼ cup	½ cup	¾ cup plus 2 tblsp
Julienned peeled fresh ginger	1½ tblsp	3 tblsp	6 tblsp
Soy sauce	¼ cup	½ cup	¾ cup plus 2 tblsp
Packed light brown sugar	¼ cup	½ cup	¾ cup plus 2 tblsp
Star anise	1	3	4
Sichuan peppercorns (optional)	½ tsp	1 tsp	2 tsp
Dried chiles de árbol or other small dried Asian chiles	3	6	10

1 Mix everything in the slow cooker.

2 Cover and cook on low for 7 hours, or until the beef is quite tender. Discard the star anise before serving.

TESTERS' NOTES
• This stew mimics the classic Chinese braising method called "red cooking," so named because fine soy sauce, when long simmered, can take on a slightly red cast.
• If you want a more authentic taste, substitute Shaoxing (Chinese rice wine) for the sherry.

• The star anise pods may fall apart as they cook. Fish out the small bits if possible; although they are edible, someone may end up with a big hit of the spice.

Serve It Up! You'll need cooked white or brown rice. Try a medium-grain rice such as Arborio for a nice textural contrast.

INGREDIENTS EXPLAINED Sichuan peppercorns are actually not peppercorns at all, but the cracked hulls of the seed of a citrus plant. They're available in many large supermarkets or always from Chinese grocery stores, whether brick-and-mortar or online. The so-called peppercorns have a lemony, peppery bite with a slight mouth-numbing quality.

smoky black bean and chuck stew

EFFORT: **A LITTLE** • PREP TIME: **10½ HOURS (INCLUDES SOAKING THE BEANS)** • COOK TIME: **8 HOURS** • KEEPS ON WARM: **3 HOURS** • SERVES: **4 TO 12**

INGREDIENTS	2- TO 3½-QT	4- TO 5½-QT	6- TO 8-QT
Dried black beans	1 cup	2 cups	3 cups
Slab bacon, diced	2 ounces	4 ounces	6 ounces
Boneless beef chuck, cut into 2-inch pieces	1 pound	2 pounds	3 pounds
Reduced-sodium chicken broth	1½ cups	3 cups	4½ cups
Yellow onions, finely chopped	1 medium	2 medium	2 large
Minced fresh oregano leaves	1 tblsp	2 tblsp	3 tblsp
Minced garlic	2 tsp	1 tblsp	1½ tblsp

	8 ounces	1 pound	1½ pounds
Smoked pork hocks	8 ounces	1 pound	1½ pounds
Cider vinegar	½ tblsp	1 tblsp	1½ tblsp

1 Cover the beans with cool tap water in a large bowl, and set on the counter to soak overnight, or for at least 10 hours.

2 Drain the beans in a colander; pour them into the slow cooker.

3 Heat a large skillet over medium heat, then add the bacon. Cook, stirring often, until browned and crisp, 3 to 6 minutes. Use a slotted spoon to transfer the bacon bits to the cooker.

4 Use the bacon fat in the skillet to brown the beef chunks, working in batches over medium heat as necessary to prevent overcrowding, 8 to 10 minutes per batch. Transfer the browned cubes to the cooker and continue browning more until finished.

5 Stir in the broth, onions, oregano, and garlic; nestle the hocks into the stew.

6 Cover and cook on low for 8 hours, or until the beef is fork-tender and the pork shreds off the hocks.

7 Transfer the hocks to a cutting board and cool the pork for 10 minutes. Keep the slow cooker covered and set on warm. Shred the meat off the bones with two forks; discard the bones, chop the pork into small bits, and stir these along with the vinegar into the stew.

TESTERS' NOTES
• Here's a warming meal for a chilly night when you want real food but don't want to spend too long making it. The dried beans cook down until they are rich and chewy.
• You want the bits of onion small (¼-inch pieces at most) so they can melt into the sauce.

• Don't be tempted to use dried oregano; fresh adds a bit of springtime brightness to an otherwise dark and mellow meal.

Serve It Up! Doctor sour cream with a little ground cumin, some minced cilantro leaves, and a squeeze of lime juice, then dollop this concoction onto the stew in the bowls.

beef bourguignon

EFFORT: **A LOT** • PREP TIME: **11 HOURS (INCLUDES MARINATING THE BEEF)** • COOK TIME: **7 HOURS** • KEEPS ON WARM: **4 HOURS** • SERVES: **3 TO 16**

INGREDIENTS	2- TO 3½-QT	4- TO 5½-QT	6- TO 8-QT
Boneless beef chuck, cut into 1½-inch cubes	1 pound	3 pounds	5 pounds
Dry red wine, such as French Burgundy or Pinot Noir	1 cup	3 cups	5 cups
Fresh thyme sprigs	1	3	5
Medium garlic cloves, peeled and smashed	1	2	4
Salt	¼ tsp	½ tsp	1 tsp
Ground black pepper	¼ tsp	½ tsp	¾ tsp
Bay leaves	1	2	4
Slab bacon, chopped	2 ounces	6 ounces	10 ounces
Small fresh pearl onions, peeled, or frozen pearl onions, thawed	⅔ cup	2 cups	3 cups
Carrots, peeled and cut into 1-inch sections	¼ pound	10 ounces	1 pound
All-purpose flour	1 tblsp	3 tblsp	⅓ cup

(continued)

1 Seal the beef, wine, thyme, garlic, salt, pepper, and bay leaves in a very large zip-closed plastic bag. Massage the wine onto the beef through the plastic, then set the bag in the refrigerator for at least 10 hours (or up to 16 hours).

2 Remove the beef pieces from the bag and pat them dry with paper towels. Set them out on the counter to come back to room temperature while you complete the next step.

3 Strain the marinade from the bag through a fine-mesh sieve or colander into a bowl, catching the liquid below. Dig out the thyme sprigs, bay leaves, and garlic cloves and add these to the cooker. Reserve the marinade.

4 Fry the bacon in a large skillet set over medium heat until crisp, stirring occasionally, 4 to 7 minutes, depending on how much is in the skillet. Use a slotted spoon to transfer the crunchy bits to the slow cooker.

5 Brown the pieces of beef in the bacon fat in the skillet, working with just a handful of pieces at a time, about 8 minutes per batch, turning them onto all sides. Use that slotted spoon to transfer them to the cooker, then continue browning more.

6 Once the beef's done, scatter the pearl onions in the skillet; cook, stirring often, until they begin to brown a bit on all sides, 4 to 7 minutes. Once again, use that slotted spoon to get them into the slow cooker.

7 Pour ½ cup of the strained marinade into the skillet; bring to a boil, scraping up any browned bits in the skillet with a spoon. Pour and scrape the contents of the skillet into the slow cooker. Stir in the carrots.

8 Whisk the remainder of the strained marinade with the flour in a large bowl until the flour dissolves. Pour into the slow cooker.

9 Cover and cook on low for 7 hours, or until the beef cubes are wonderfully tender and succulent. Discard the bay leaves before serving.

TESTERS' NOTES

• If you're going to do it, you might as well do it right! This is undoubtedly a complicated recipe, a slow cooker version of the classic, complete with a wine marinade and endless layering of flavors to build the stew.
• Make sure the bag with the beef and marinade is well sealed to avoid a messy cleanup. Consider setting the bag in a large bowl, just to make sure you're not a victim of drips and spills.

Serve It Up! Although often served over mashed potatoes (with plenty of butter, whole milk, salt, and ground black pepper), this stew also works well over cooked pasta, particularly wide noodles like pappardelle, or even over homemade croutons (see page 157).

beef goulash with mushrooms and potatoes

EFFORT: **NOT MUCH** • PREP TIME: **20 MINUTES** • COOK TIME: **8 HOURS** • KEEPS ON WARM: **3 HOURS** • SERVES: **4 TO 16**

INGREDIENTS	2- TO 3½-QT	4- TO 5½-QT	6- TO 8-QT
Boneless beef chuck, cut into 2-inch pieces	1¼ pounds	2½ pounds	4½ pounds
Cremini or brown button mushrooms, thinly sliced	½ pound (about 2½ cups)	1 pound (about 5 cups)	1 pound 10 ounces (about 8 cups)

Russet or other baking potatoes, peeled and shredded through the large holes of a box grater	5 ounces	10 ounces	1 pound
Moderately sweet white wine, such as Pinot Blanc	¼ cup	½ cup	¾ cup plus 2 tblsp
No-salt-added tomato paste	1 tblsp	2 tblsp	3½ tblsp
Mild paprika	1 tblsp	2 tblsp	3½ tblsp
Caraway seeds	¼ tsp	½ tsp	1 tsp
Salt	¼ tsp	½ tsp	1 tsp
Ground black pepper	¼ tsp	½ tsp	1 tsp
Bay leaf	1	1	2
Sherry vinegar	1 tblsp	2 tblsp	3½ tblsp
Sour cream (regular, low-fat, or fat-free)	¼ cup	½ cup	1 cup

1 Stir the beef, mushrooms, shredded potatoes, wine, tomato paste, paprika, caraway seeds, salt, pepper, and bay leaves in the slow cooker until the pieces of meat are evenly coated with the tomato mixture and spices.

2 Cover and cook on low for 8 hours, or until the beef is meltingly tender. Stir in the vinegar; dollop 1 tablespoon sour cream onto the individual servings in the bowls.

TESTERS' NOTES

• This is the American version of the Hungarian classic, modified for the slow cooker. The potatoes are the secret thickener; they'll deliver plenty of starch.

• The sour cream is added only as a garnish since it can break if cooked for hours.

Serve It Up! Ladle the stew into bowls with cooked, wide egg noodles that have been tossed with poppy seeds (and maybe a little butter).

beef tagine with butternut squash

EFFORT: **NOT MUCH** • PREP TIME: **20 MINUTES** • COOK TIME: **8 HOURS** • KEEPS ON WARM: **3 HOURS** • SERVES: **3 TO 10**

INGREDIENTS	2- TO 3½-QT	4- TO 5½-QT	6- TO 8-QT
Mild paprika	2 tsp	1½ tblsp	2 tblsp
Ground cinnamon	1 tsp	2 tsp	4 tsp
Ground coriander	½ tsp	1 tsp	½ tblsp
Ground ginger	½ tsp	1 tsp	½ tblsp
Red pepper flakes	½ tsp	1 tsp	½ tblsp
Salt	½ tsp	1 tsp	½ tblsp
Boneless beef chuck, cut into 2-inch pieces	1 pound	2 pounds	3½ pounds
Butternut squash, peeled, seeded, and cut into 2-inch cubes	1 pound	1½ pounds	2¼ pounds
Ripe tomatoes, chopped	½ pound	1 pound	1½ pounds
Shallots, peeled and quartered	4	8	10
Medium garlic cloves, peeled and slivered	2	4	6
Reduced-sodium chicken broth	½ cup	1 cup	1⅔ cups
Minced fresh cilantro leaves	¼ cup	½ cup	¾ cup

1 Mix the paprika, cinnamon, coriander, ginger, red pepper flakes, and salt in the slow cooker, then add the beef and stir until the cubes are coated in the spices. Dump in the butternut squash, tomatoes, shallots, and garlic; pour in the broth and stir well.

2 Cover and cook on low for 8 hours, or until the beef and butternut squash are meltingly tender. Stir in the cilantro just before serving.

(continued)

TESTERS' NOTES
- A tagine is a Moroccan casserole, long-simmered in a shallow pan under a conical lid. While this is not a true tagine, it does replicate the traditional flavors.
- Don't seed those tomatoes. They'll add lots of essential moisture.
- We used chicken broth for a lighter finish that lets the complexity of those spices come through.

thai beef curry

EFFORT: **A LOT** • PREP TIME: **45 MINUTES** • COOK TIME: **7 HOURS** • KEEPS ON WARM: **4 HOURS** • SERVES: **4 TO 10**

INGREDIENTS	2- TO 3½-QT	4- TO 5½-QT	6- TO 8-QT
Dried New Mexican red chiles	1	2	3
Thinly sliced lemongrass, white and pale green parts only (see page 273)	2 tblsp	¼ cup	6 tblsp
Minced peeled fresh ginger	1 tblsp	2 tblsp	3 tblsp
Minced garlic	1 tsp	2 tsp	1 tblsp
Ground cinnamon	½ tsp	1 tsp	½ tblsp
Ground coriander	⅛ tsp	¼ tsp	½ tsp
Grated nutmeg	⅛ tsp	¼ tsp	¼ tsp
Boneless beef chuck, cut into 1-inch pieces	1¼ pounds	2½ pounds	3¾ pounds
4-inch cinnamon sticks	½	1	1½
Cardamom seeds	½ tsp	1 tsp	½ tblsp
Whole cloves	5	10	15
White potatoes, peeled and cut into 1-inch cubes	1 pound (about 3½ cups)	2 pounds (about 7 cups)	3 pounds (about 10½ cups)
Coconut milk	¾ cup	1½ cups	2¼ cups
Reduced-sodium beef broth	¼ cup	½ cup	¾ cup
Packed light brown sugar	2 tblsp	¼ cup	6 tblsp
Fish sauce (see page 96)	1½ tblsp	3 tblsp	⅓ cup
Tamarind paste	1½ tblsp	3 tblsp	⅓ cup
Chopped roasted peanuts	⅓ cup	⅔ cup	1 cup

1 Bring a pan of water to a boil over high heat. Stem and seed the chiles, then tear the flesh into small bits. Set the torn chiles in a bowl and pour boiling water over them. Soak for 20 minutes.

2 Drain the chile bits in a colander set over a bowl, catching the liquid in a bowl below. Scrape the softened chiles into a large blender; add the lemongrass, ginger, garlic, cinnamon, coriander, and nutmeg. Blend into a grainy paste, adding just enough of the soaking liquid to keep the blade moving through the paste.

3 Scrape the chile mixture into the slow cooker, add the beef, and toss to make sure every piece of meat is coated.

4 Set a large skillet over medium heat for a couple of minutes. Add the cinnamon stick, cardamom, and cloves. Toast until aromatic, stirring often, about 3 minutes. Pour the spices into the cooker; stir in the potatoes.

5 Whisk the coconut milk, broth, brown sugar, fish sauce, and tamarind paste in a bowl until the sugar has dissolved. Pour this mixture over everything in the cooker; toss well.

6 Cover and cook on low for 8 hours, or until the meat and potatoes are very tender when pierced with a fork. Sprinkle the chopped peanuts over the stew or over individual bowlfuls when serving.

TESTERS' NOTES

• This recipe is actually a slow-cooker version of Thai massaman curry, so named because the dish was heavily influenced by spices and techniques from the food carried in caravans from as far away as Iran (thus, *massaman,* or Moslem). Rather than using a packaged Thai curry paste, we went all out and built the curry from scratch.

• Use only fresh lemongrass or jarred lemongrass packed in water, not dried lemongrass. If there are any dried-out or desiccated bits on the spears, peel them off until you get down to a moist core.

• Use white potatoes like Irish creamers, not the starchier Russets or baking potatoes.

INGREDIENTS EXPLAINED Tamarind paste is the boiled down, sticky, sweet-and-sour juice from the fruit of a tree indigenous to northern Africa. The paste is now used worldwide in dishes—and is an ingredient in Worcestershire sauce. Look for small jars of tamarind paste in the international aisle of most supermarkets.

east indian beef curry

EFFORT: **NOT MUCH** • PREP TIME: **15 MINUTES** • COOK TIME: **8 HOURS** • KEEPS ON WARM: **4 HOURS** • SERVES: **4 TO 16**

INGREDIENTS	2- TO 3½-QT	4- TO 5½-QT	6- TO 8-QT
Ground cardamom	½ tsp	½ tblsp	2½ tsp
Ground coriander	½ tsp	½ tblsp	2½ tsp
Ground cumin	½ tsp	½ tblsp	2½ tsp
Ground mace	½ tsp	1 tsp	½ tblsp
Cayenne	⅛ tsp	½ tsp	¾ tsp
Salt	⅛ tsp	½ tsp	¾ tsp

Boneless beef chuck, cut into 2-inch pieces	1½ pounds	3½ pounds	5½ pounds
Unsalted butter	½ tblsp	1½ tblsp	2 tblsp
Shallots, thinly sliced	3 ounces	8 ounces	12 ounces
Reduced-sodium beef broth	¼ cup	⅔ cup	1 cup
Sweet white wine, such as Riesling or Spätlese	1½ tblsp	⅓ cup	½ cup

1 Mix the cardamom, coriander, cumin, mace, cayenne, and salt in the slow cooker. Add the beef cubes and stir until they are coated in the spices.

2 Melt the butter in a large skillet set over medium heat. Add the shallots; cook, stirring often, until softened and sweet, 4 to 6 minutes. Scrape the contents of the skillet into the slow cooker.

3 Stir in the broth and wine. Cover and cook on low for 8 hours, or until the beef bits are quite tender, irresistibly so.

TESTERS' NOTES

• Here's a wonderfully aromatic spice blend, far better than many of the versions of curry powder available in supermarkets. Make a triple batch and save it in a small, sealed jar for curries down the road.

• The sophistication to this rather straightforward dish comes from the shallots fried in butter.

INGREDIENTS EXPLAINED Curries are not one thing, but a multitude of dishes—each one with a blend of spices that creates an individual, even idiosyncratic flavor profile, which is a far cry from that yellow spice blend often used heavy-handedly in recipes. It's safe to say that there are as many kinds of curry as there are mindful Indian cooks.

oxtails braised in red wine with carrots and prunes

EFFORT: **A LOT** • PREP TIME: **40 MINUTES** • COOK TIME: **10 HOURS** • KEEPS ON WARM: **4 HOURS** • SERVES: **4 TO 12**

INGREDIENTS	2- TO 3½-QT	4- TO 5½-QT	6- TO 8-QT
Unsalted butter	1½ tblsp	2½ tblsp	4 tblsp (½ stick)
Beef oxtails	2 pounds	4 pounds	6 pounds
Salt	¼ tsp	½ tsp	1 tsp
Ground black pepper	¼ tsp	½ tsp	¾ tsp
Small fresh pearl onions, peeled, or frozen, thawed	⅔ cup	2½ cups	4 cups
Medium carrots, cut into 1-inch pieces	1	2	4
Pitted prunes	⅓ cup	⅔ cup	1 cup
Minced garlic	1 tsp	½ tblsp	2 tsp
Dried oregano	¾ tsp	1¼ tsp	2 tsp
Crushed dried rosemary	¾ tsp	1¼ tsp	2 tsp
Dried thyme	¾ tsp	1¼ tsp	2 tsp
Bold dry red wine, such as Mouvedre or Granache	½ cup	1 cup	1½ cups
Reduced-sodium beef broth	½ cup	1 cup	1½ cups
All-purpose flour	1½ tblsp	2½ tblsp	¼ cup

1 Melt the butter in a large skillet set over medium heat. Season the oxtails with the salt and pepper, then set as many in the skillet as will comfortably fit. Brown them on both sides, turning only after a few minutes. Transfer them to the slow cooker and brown more as necessary.

2 Dump the pearl onions into the skillet, still over medium heat. Cook, stirring often, until browned on at least two sides, between 4 and 8 minutes. Scrape the contents of the skillet into the cooker. Add the carrots, prunes, garlic, oregano, rosemary, and thyme. Pour in the wine and stir well.

3 Whisk the broth and flour in a bowl until the flour dissolves; pour over the ingredients in the cooker.

4 Cover and cook on low for 10 hours, or until the meat has shrunk back from the bones and is quite tender.

TESTERS' NOTES

• For those who like bones with their beef, there may be no finer stew. Oxtails release lots of collagen and sticky protein, enriching the stew into a ridiculously satisfying meal. You'll want to have plenty of napkins at the table: everyone's going to want to pick up the bones and slurp off the sauce.

• If the prunes are larger than bite-size, slice them in half before adding them to the slow cooker.

• If you have a set of marrow spoons, now is the time to use them! Dig out the soft, luxurious bits in some of the larger bones, then spread it on crunchy bread—or simply let it dissolve into the stew.

INGREDIENTS EXPLAINED Oxtails are, well, the cow's tail cut into bony segments. They're an old-fashioned cut, more from your grandmother's day than yours, but they deserve a comeback. The best are in small pieces, each just one bone long, chock full of meat in the nooks and crannies.

oxtails braised
with gigantes
beans

EFFORT: **A LOT** • PREP TIME: **10½ HOURS (INCLUDES SOAKING THE BEANS)** • COOK TIME: **10 HOURS** • KEEPS ON WARM: **2 HOURS** • SERVES: **4 TO 12**

INGREDIENTS	2- TO 3½-QT	4- TO 5½-QT	6- TO 8-QT
Dried gigantes beans	⅓ cup	⅔ cup	1 cup
Olive oil	½ tblsp	1½ tblsp	2 tblsp
Beef oxtails (see page 166)	1½ pounds	3 pounds	4½ pounds
Yellow onion, chopped	1 small	1 medium	1 large
Dry white wine, such as Chardonnay	¼ cup	⅓ cup	½ cup
Water	1⅓ cups	2⅔ cups	4 cups (1 quart)
Worcestershire sauce	½ tblsp	1½ tblsp	2 tblsp
Dried thyme	½ tsp	1 tsp	½ tblsp
Ground black pepper	¼ tsp	½ tsp	¾ tsp

1 Soak the gigantes beans in a large bowl of water for 10 hours (or up to 16 hours).

2 Set a large skillet over medium heat for a few minutes, then swirl in the oil. Add the oxtails in batches to brown them, 6 to 8 minutes per batch, turning once. Transfer them to the slow cooker and continue browning more as necessary.

3 Add the onion to the skillet, still set over medium heat. Cook, stirring often, until lightly browned on a few sides, between 4 and 7 minutes. Transfer the onion to the slow cooker.

4 Pour the wine into the skillet; bring to a rolling boil. Scrape up any browned bits in the skillet; pour and scrape the contents of the skillet into the slow cooker.

5 Drain the beans in a colander in the sink; pour them into the cooker. Stir in the water, Worcestershire sauce, thyme, and pepper.

6 Cover and cook on low for 10 hours, or until the meat has pulled back from the bones and even the cartilage around the meat is tender.

TESTERS' NOTES

• Oxtails and gigantes beans add up to a rich stew, quite hearty for a cold evening's meal.

• We used water here, not broth. We found the dish to be so rich, it didn't need any added push. The water also allows the other flavors to come through without complication.

INGREDIENTS EXPLAINED Gigantes beans, also called *gigandes beans* or *yigandes beans,* or even *gigandes plaki,* are something of a Greek staple, often stewed with tomatoes, olive oil, and parsley, then served as one of several small plates (*meze*) for a lighter meal. If you can't find gigantes beans, substitute dried large lima beans.

pork

These recipes are some of the simplest in this book. That should come as no surprise, since the sweet and *umami* flavors of pork seem to get even better in a slow cooker. There's no need to fuss it up!

It's hard to imagine that pork was once subjected to a host of culinary indignities. The meat itself had become pretty tasteless and was often cooked to ridiculously high internal temperatures in a wrong-headed bid for safety. But thanks to both a resurgence of heritage pig breeds and better cooking techniques, as well as more sensible internal temperature guidelines from the USDA, there's been something of a pork renaissance. It's the go-to meat for every foodie in the land. And probably for a lot of families, too.

Even quick-cooking cuts like pork chops and pork tenderloin do well in the slow cooker, partly because of the way the meat is evenly marbled. Yes, you can overcook it; but most of the time, you don't have to worry about doing so in the high-moisture world of a slow cooker.

We start with those chops, then make our way to the tenderloin before turning to the (ahem) meat of the chapter: the pork loin and shoulder. Both are seemingly made for what the slow cooker can do best: mellow flavors, blend them, and make dinner without too much work. Okay, we've got a few high-effort recipes, too. Everyone should stuff a pork loin just once! But for the most part, pork doesn't need fancy techniques.

We'll round out this section with ham recipes and some pork meatballs in Italian and Chinese incarnations, all solid American fare. And we'll take a glance at some lesser used cuts like belly and hocks. Did you know you can even make baby back ribs in the slow cooker?

Most of these recipes freeze well, partly for the same reasons that pork is easy to cook: the finished products are loaded with plenty of fat and flavor. Consider setting up a slow cooker this weekend, if only to make a batch of Basic Pulled Pork (page 183) or Italian Sunday Gravy (page 199). After you've relished every bite you can, squirrel away smaller servings in your freezer.

And one cautionary note before you get started: as you move through these recipes, pay particular attention to the differences between bone-in and boneless cuts. The amount of liquids and the cooking times have been calibrated to fit a specific cut. A recipe for a boneless pork loin simply will not work with the bone-in variety.

So stock up—not only at home but at the store, too. Just remember: when freezing meat at home, remove it from the supermarket packaging, then store the pork in large zip-closed plastic bags, sealed tightly with all the air let out. A well-stocked freezer and a slow cooker are hog heaven.

pork chops with dried fruit and honey

EFFORT: **NOT MUCH** • PREP TIME: **15 MINUTES** • COOK TIME: **5 HOURS** • KEEPS ON WARM: **1 HOUR** • SERVES: **2 TO 6**

INGREDIENTS	2- TO 3½-QT	4- TO 5½-QT	6- TO 8-QT
Unsweetened chunky applesauce	¼ cup	½ cup	¾ cup
Dried cranberries	¼ cup	½ cup	¾ cup
Golden raisins	¼ cup	½ cup	¾ cup
Chopped dried apricots	¼ cup	½ cup	¾ cup
Minced red onion	2 tblsp	¼ cup	6 tblsp
Honey	1 tblsp	2 tblsp	3 tblsp
White wine vinegar	½ tblsp	1 tblsp	1½ tblsp
4-inch cinnamon stick	1	1	1½
Fresh thyme sprigs	2	3	5
1-inch-thick bone-in pork rib or loin chops (about 12 ounces each), trimmed	2	4	6
Salt	¼ tsp	½ tsp	1 tsp
Ground black pepper	¼ tsp	½ tsp	1 tsp

1 Stir the applesauce, cranberries, raisins, apricots, onion, honey, and vinegar in the slow cooker. Nestle the cinnamon stick and thyme sprigs into the sauce. Season the chops with salt and pepper; tuck them into the sauce.

2 Cover and cook on low for 5 hours, or until the pork is tender and the sauce has begun to thicken a bit. Discard the cinnamon sticks and thyme sprigs before serving.

TESTERS' NOTES
• Pork chops present a problem for the slow cooker. They're first-rate quick-cookers; therefore, they can dry out fast. We solve that by (1) using bone-in chops (never boneless) and (2) calling for chops slightly larger than the usual, all in a bid to make dinner as tasty as it can be.
• Trim the pork chops by cutting off most of the fat that rings the chops. Leave a small bit for flavor, but not enough to create a grease slick in the sauce.

ALL-AMERICAN KNOW-HOW Bone-in pork chops may not fit neatly in one layer. If not, make a slit in one side of the meat to bend the chops open a bit so they'll fit in the cramped quarters. They can overlap; they shouldn't be stacked.

pork chops with cranberry, orange, and sage

EFFORT: **A LITTLE** • PREP TIME: **20 MINUTES** • COOK TIME: **5 HOURS** • KEEPS ON WARM: **2 HOURS** • SERVES: **2 TO 6**

INGREDIENTS	2- TO 3½-QT	4- TO 5½-QT	6- TO 8-QT
Unsalted butter	1 tblsp	2 tblsp	2½ tblsp
1-inch-thick bone-in pork rib or loin chops (about 12 ounces each), trimmed	2	4	6
Salt	¼ tsp	½ tsp	1 tsp
Ground black pepper	¼ tsp	½ tsp	1 tsp
Whole-berry cranberry sauce	¾ cup	1½ cups	2¼ cups

Finely chopped yellow onion	¼ cup	½ cup	¾ cup (about 1 small)
Finely chopped celery	¼ cup	½ cup	¾ cup (about 2 medium ribs)
Dijon mustard	½ tblsp	1 tblsp	1½ tblsp
Minced sage leaves	½ tblsp	1 tblsp	1½ tblsp
Finely grated orange zest	½ tsp	1 tsp	½ tblsp

1 Melt the butter in a large skillet over medium heat. Season the pork chops with salt and pepper; slip them into the skillet. Brown on both sides, 3 to 4 minutes per side. (If your skillet isn't large enough to hold all the chops comfortably, work in batches, using half the butter for each batch.) Transfer the chops to the slow cooker.

2 Stir the cranberry sauce, onion, celery, mustard, sage, and orange zest in a bowl until the cranberry sauce begins to dissolve into the sauce. Pour the mixture over the chops.

3 Cover and cook on low for 5 hours, or until the meat is fork-tender, particularly at the bone. Serve with the sauce on the side.

TESTERS' NOTES
• Use only spicy, smooth Dijon mustard. You need its nose-spank to balance the cranberry sauce.
• Smooth (or jellied) cranberry sauce is too sweet. Use a cranberry sauce with berry chunks in the mix.

Serve It Up! To make use of the rich sauce, serve the chops in a hot baked sweet potato that's been split open. Or place them over buttered noodles—or even mashed, roasted, or steamed root vegetables.

pork chops with peppers and vinegar

EFFORT: **A LITTLE** • PREP TIME: **25 MINUTES** • COOK TIME: **5 HOURS** • KEEPS ON WARM: **2 HOURS** • SERVES: **2 TO 6**

INGREDIENTS	2- TO 3½-QT	4- TO 5½-QT	6- TO 8-QT
Green or red bell peppers, stemmed, seeded, and thinly sliced	2 small	3 medium	3 large
Minced red onion	2 tblsp	¼ cup	⅓ cup
Dry white wine, such as a Pinot Grigio or Chardonnay, or dry vermouth	½ cup	1 cup	1½ cups
White wine vinegar	1 tblsp	2 tblsp	2½ tblsp
Minced fresh oregano leaves	1 tsp	2 tsp	1 tblsp
Sugar	½ tsp	1 tsp	1¼ tsp
Olive oil	½ tblsp	1 tblsp	1½ tblsp
1 inch-thick bone-in pork rib or loin chops (about 12 ounces each), trimmed	2	4	6
Mild paprika	½ tsp	1 tsp	½ tblsp
Salt	¼ tsp	½ tsp	1 tsp
Ground black pepper	¼ tsp	½ tsp	1 tsp

1 Stir the bell peppers, onion, wine, vinegar, oregano, and sugar in the slow cooker until the sugar dissolves.

2 Heat a large skillet over medium heat for a few minutes, then swirl in the olive oil. Season the pork chops with paprika, salt, and pepper; slide them into the skillet. Brown on both sides, between 3 to 4 minutes per side. (If you have to work in batches, divide the oil among

(continued)

those batches.) Transfer the chops to the slow cooker as they're ready, setting them into the sauce.

3 Cover and cook on low for 5 hours, or until the pork is luxuriously tender. Transfer the chops to serving plates, then spoon the sauce on top.

TESTERS' NOTES
• Fresh bell peppers give the sauce a better texture than frozen peppers.
• For a brighter, more aromatic flavor, substitute marjoram for the oregano.
• For a spicier dish, add some cayenne with the paprika.

pork sirloin with peppers and olives

EFFORT: **A LITTLE** • PREP TIME: **15 MINUTES** • COOK TIME: **8 HOURS** • KEEPS ON WARM: **1 HOUR** • SERVES: **3 TO 8**

INGREDIENTS	2- TO 3½-QT	4- TO 5½-QT	6- TO 8-QT
Olive oil	½ tblsp	1 tblsp	1½ tblsp
Boneless pork sirloin roast	1 pound	2 pounds	3½ pounds
Sliced pitted black olives	2½ tblsp	⅓ cup	½ cup
White wine vinegar	2 tblsp	¼ cup	⅓ cup
Cubanelle peppers, stemmed, seeded, and sliced into 1-inch-thick rings (see page 47)	2	4	7
Finely grated lemon zest	1 tsp	2 tsp	1 tblsp
Minced garlic	½ tsp	1 tsp	½ tblsp
Ground black pepper	¼ tsp	½ tsp	1 tsp
4-inch rosemary sprig	1	1	2

1 Set a large skillet over medium heat for a couple of minutes, then swirl in the oil. Slip the roast into the skillet; brown it on both sides, 4 to 5 minutes a pop.

2 Transfer the roast to the slow cooker. Add the olives, vinegar, pepper rings, lemon zest, garlic, pepper, and rosemary. Make sure the rosemary is submerged in the vegetables and sauce.

3 Cover and cook on low for 8 hours, or until the pork is quite tender but not falling apart.

4 Transfer the roast to a cutting board; let stand for 10 minutes. Carve against the grain into thin, ½-inch slices (see page 146). Discard the rosemary, skim the sauce for surface fat, and serve the sauce with the pork.

TESTERS' NOTES
• A pork sirloin roast is fairly lean and so it benefits from the long, slow moist heat.
• There's no salt in this recipe because the olives will leach plenty into the sauce.
• Use the best-quality olives you can comfortably afford, usually found on the salad or antipasto bar at the supermarket. Avoid any olives with seasonings that compete with those in the sauce.

INGREDIENTS EXPLAINED A pork sirloin roast is from the back of the pig, a lean and economical cut, near the legs (and thus the ham). Often sold bone-in, with bits of the hip and backbone, it can prove difficult to carve. You won't get even rounds; work around the bones to yield chunks of meat that you can cut down to size. Ask for it to be boned at the meat counter.

slow-roasted rack of pork

EFFORT: **NOT MUCH** • PREP TIME: **15 MINUTES** • COOK TIME: **4 TO 8 HOURS** • KEEPS ON WARM: **1 HOUR** • SERVES: **2 TO 6**

INGREDIENTS	4- TO 5½-QT	6- TO 8-QT
Minced fresh rosemary leaves	1½ tblsp	3 tblsp
Finely minced lemon zest	1 tblsp	2 tblsp
Minced garlic	2 tsp	1 tblsp
Kosher salt	1 tsp	2 tsp
Ground black pepper	½ tsp	1 tsp
Bone-in pork rib roast	2 to 3 bones (2½ to 4 pounds)	4 to 6 bones (4½ to 6 pounds)

1 Mix the rosemary, lemon zest, garlic, salt, and pepper in a small bowl. Rub this mixture over the pork roast; set it bone side down in the slow cooker.

2 Cover and cook on low for 4 to 6 hours in a medium cooker, 6 to 8 hours in a large cooker, or until the meat is tender at the bone and an instant-read meat thermometer inserted into the center of the roast without touching bone registers 150°F.

3 Transfer the roast to a cutting board; let it rest for 10 minutes. To serve, slice between the bones, dividing the chops from each other.

TESTERS' NOTES

• Yes, you can roast a whole pork rib roast in a slow cooker—just not in a small slow cooker. There's not enough room.
• This recipe is easier in an oval cooker than a round one. In fact, the roast may not fit at all in some round cookers. Check the dimensions of your model before you plunk down money at the grocery store.
• The roast won't brown and crisp as it does in an oven. Instead, it becomes almost pork confit, an outstanding preparation, juicy and mellow.
• We don't advocate trimming the rack because we prize that luxurious confit consistency the slow cooker produces. However, the juices in the slow cooker will be too fatty for a good sauce.
• All those aromatics should be minced into small bits about the size of the grains of salt to get evenly distributed across the roast.

pineapple teriyaki pork tenderloin

EFFORT: **A LITTLE** • PREP TIME: **15 MINUTES** • COOK TIME: **6 HOURS** • KEEPS ON WARM: **NO** • SERVES: **3 TO 8**

INGREDIENTS	2- TO 3½-QT	4- TO 5½-QT	6- TO 8-QT
Canned crushed pineapple	2 tblsp	¼ cup	⅓ cup
Soy sauce	2 tblsp	3½ tblsp	5 tblsp
Dry white wine, such as Chardonnay	1 tblsp	2 tblsp	3 tblsp
Packed dark brown sugar	1 tblsp	2 tblsp	3 tblsp
Minced peeled fresh ginger	½ tblsp	1 tblsp	1¼ tblsp
Toasted sesame oil (see page 196)	2 tsp	1½ tblsp	2 tblsp
Minced garlic	1 tsp	2 tsp	2½ tsp
Pork tenderloin	1 pound	2 pounds	3½ pounds

(continued)

1 Stir the pineapple, soy sauce, wine, brown sugar, ginger, sesame oil, and garlic in the slow cooker until the brown sugar dissolves. Tuck the pork tenderloin into the sauce.

2 Cover and cook on low for 6 hours, or until the pork is fork-tender. Transfer the tenderloin to a cutting board; slice into rounds about ½ inch thick to serve.

TESTERS' NOTES

• The pork tenderloin is a small, delicately flavored tidbit from the pig, a favorite for quick cooking but doable in the slow cooker if you follow our timings exactly and don't allow the cooker to flip over onto a "keep warm" setting.

• Making your own teriyaki sauce from scratch ensures there aren't a lot of funky chemicals in the mix! And the pineapple flavor will be much more naturally sweet, better for mingling with the tangy soy sauce.

• The pork tenderloins should not be browned because they would be almost cooked through (then rendering them dry in the cooker). Instead, the poaching liquid will turn them velvety and rich.

honey mustard pork tenderloin

EFFORT: **A LITTLE** • PREP TIME: **20 MINUTES** • COOK TIME: **6 HOURS** • KEEPS ON WARM: **NO** • SERVES: **3 TO 8**

INGREDIENTS	2- TO 3½-QT	4- TO 5½-QT	6- TO 8-QT
Brussels sprouts	½ pound	1 pound	1¾ pounds
Ground allspice	¼ tsp	½ tsp	¾ tsp
Salt	¼ tsp	½ tsp	¾ tsp
Ground black pepper	¼ tsp	½ tsp	¾ tsp
Dry white wine, such as white Bordeaux	2 tblsp	¼ cup	6 tblsp
Honey mustard	2 tsp	1½ tblsp	2½ tblsp
Worcestershire sauce	1 tsp	2 tsp	1 tblsp
Pork tenderloin	1 pound	2 pounds	3½ pounds

1 Cut the stem ends off the Brussels sprouts, then thinly shred them. Stir into the cooker along with the allspice, salt, and pepper; drizzle with the wine.

2 Mix the honey mustard and Worcestershire sauce in a small bowl; smear over the pork. Nestle the meat into the shredded sprouts.

3 Cover and cook on low for 6 hours, or until the pork is quite tender when pierced with a fork. Transfer to a carving board; slice into ½-inch-thick rounds. Mound the Brussels sprouts and sauce on the plates or a serving platter, then set the carved pork on top of each mound.

TESTERS' NOTES

• Some people shy away from Brussels sprouts because of their bitter earthiness. If that's a concern in your crowd, remember the rule: the smaller the sprout, the less assertive its flavor.

• For quicker prep but more cleanup, use the 4mm slicing blade of a food processor to shred the Brussels sprouts.

• For larger slow cookers, use more than one pork tenderloin. You may need to slice them to get them to fit. Don't stack them; make an even layer of tenderloin pieces.

apple-spiced pork tenderloin

EFFORT: **A LITTLE** • PREP TIME: **15 MINUTES** • COOK TIME: **6 HOURS** • KEEPS ON WARM: **NO** • SERVES: **3 TO 8**

INGREDIENTS	2- TO 3½-QT	4- TO 5½-QT	6- TO 8-QT
Frozen unsweetened apple juice concentrate, thawed	2 tblsp	¼ cup	⅓ cup
Ground cinnamon	¼ tsp	½ tsp	¾ tsp
Ground cumin	¼ tsp	½ tsp	¾ tsp
Salt	¼ tsp	½ tsp	¾ tsp
Ground black pepper	¼ tsp	½ tsp	¾ tsp
Ground cloves	⅛ tsp	¼ tsp	½ tsp
Cayenne	⅛ tsp	¼ tsp	½ tsp
Pork tenderloin	1 pound	2 pounds	3½ pounds
Unsalted butter, at room temperature	1 tblsp	2 tblsp	3 tblsp

1 Mix the apple juice concentrate, cinnamon, cumin, salt, pepper, cloves, and cayenne in the slow cooker.

2 Smear the pork with the butter; set it into the liquid.

3 Cover and cook on low for 6 hours, or until the pork is fork-tender. Transfer the tenderloin to a cutting board and slice into ½-inch-thick rounds.

TESTERS' NOTES
• The poaching liquid is not really a sauce as is. However, you can ladle it into a saucepan and boil it down over high heat, stirring often, until it's syrupy like a glaze.
• For some heat, mix a dash of cayenne into the butter before smearing it on the meat.

• Once again, you may need to work with more than one pork tenderloin to fill out the appropriate weight for the recipe. Slice them in pieces to fit in one layer.

Serve It Up! For a side dish, place small white or yellow new potatoes in a steamer basket or vegetable steamer set over 1 or 2 inches of simmering water. Cover and steam until tender, 15 to 20 minutes.

sichuan-style pork loin with chestnuts

EFFORT: **NOT MUCH** • PREP TIME: **15 MINUTES** • COOK TIME: **8 HOURS** • KEEPS ON WARM: **2 HOURS** • SERVES: **3 TO 10**

INGREDIENTS	2- TO 3½-QT	4- TO 5½-QT	6- TO 8-QT
Boneless pork loin, cut into 1½-inch cubes	1 pound	2¼ pounds	4 pounds
Jarred roasted chestnuts	1 cup	3 cups	5 cups
Thinly sliced whole scallions	3 tblsp	½ cup	¾ cup
Packed dark brown sugar	2 tsp	2 tblsp	3½ tblsp
Minced peeled fresh ginger	2 tsp	2 tblsp	3½ tblsp
Minced garlic	1 tsp	2 tsp	1 tblsp
Sichuan peppercorns (see page 160)	1 tsp	2 tsp	1 tblsp
Grated nutmeg	¼ tsp	½ tsp	¾ tsp
Soy sauce	2 tblsp	⅓ cup	½ cup
Dark rum, such as Myers's	2 tblsp	⅓ cup	½ cup
Reduced-sodium chicken broth	2 tblsp	⅓ cup	½ cup

(continued)

1 Toss the pork loin chunks, chestnuts, scallions, brown sugar, ginger, garlic, Sichuan peppercorns, and nutmeg in the slow cooker. Stir in the soy sauce, rum, and broth until the brown sugar dissolves.

2 Cover and cook on low for 7 hours, or until the sauce is intensely flavored and the pork is velvety tender.

TESTERS' NOTES
• This easy braise is all about the balance of aromatics, the way they meld into a sauce over time.
• When shopping for jarred chestnuts, look for them in clear containers so you can see what you're getting. The chestnuts should be whole, not chipped apart; they should also be firm and rounded, not squished onto each other. Chestnuts are a common ingredient in Chinese cooking, a starchy addition to many braises. Although available in almost every supermarket, they're much less expensive in Asian grocery stores or from the online sites.

Serve It Up! Have bowls of white rice ready. But instead of standard long-grain rice, use a medium grain for a chewier, moister side dish.

pesto-crusted pork loin

EFFORT: **NOT MUCH** • PREP TIME: **15 MINUTES** • COOK TIME: **5 TO 8 HOURS** • KEEPS ON WARM: **2 HOURS** • SERVES: **3 TO 10**

INGREDIENTS	2- TO 3½-QT	4- TO 5½-QT	6- TO 8-QT
Packed basil leaves	1¼ cups	2½ cups	4 cups
Pine nuts	2½ tblsp	⅓ cup	½ cup
Parmigiano-Reggiano cheese, finely grated	1 ounce (about 2 tblsp)	2 ounces (about ¼ cup)	3 ounces (about 6 tblsp)
Olive oil	1½ tblsp	2½ tblsp	¼ cup
White wine vinegar	1 tblsp	2 tblsp	3 tblsp
Salt	¼ tsp	½ tsp	1 tsp
Ground black pepper	¼ tsp	½ tsp	1 tsp
Boneless pork loin	1¼ pounds	2½ pounds	4 pounds

1 Process the basil, pine nuts, cheese, olive oil, vinegar, salt, and pepper in a large food processor fitted with the chopping blade until there's a coarse paste with some graininess still in the mix. Smear this pesto all over the pork loin and set it in the slow cooker.

2 Cover and cook on low for 5 hours in a small slow cooker, 6 hours in a medium cooker, or 8 hours in a large cooker, or until the pork is fork-tender. Lift the pork to a cutting board; cool for 10 minutes. Carve it into ½-inch-thick rounds.

TESTERS' NOTES
• A pork loin is one of the few relatively lean cuts that take to the slow cooker without much fuss or care. Here, a simple pesto coats the roast to protect it during the long cooking.
• Large basil leaves can have a somewhat tough, fibrous stem. Remove these before packing the leaves into the measuring cups.
• For a deeper taste, toast the pine nuts in a dry skillet set over medium-low heat, stirring often, until lightly browned, about 5 minutes.

INGREDIENTS EXPLAINED A pork loin is the very definition of eating high on the hog—that is, eating the lean choice cuts, this one the juicy bit right under the ribs. The pork loin can come with the bones attached—and in fact does come that way in butcher shops—which is why we call for a *boneless* pork loin. It may also have a small amount of fat along its exterior surface. You can trim it off, but we don't advise it, since the melting fat will keep basting the rather lean meat as it cooks.

ALL-AMERICAN KNOW-HOW Assuming the slow cooker works properly and the size of the meat is within the recipe's requirements, a pork loin will be cooked through in the stated time. However, to be certain, take the internal temperature of the pork by inserting an instant-read meat thermometer into the loin's center and make sure the gauge registers at least 145°F for safe but still pink pork, or 155°F for a more cooked-through finish.

hours in a large cooker, or until the pork loin is fork-tender. Transfer the loin to a cutting board, let it be for 10 minutes, and slice it into ½-inch-thick rounds.

TESTERS' NOTES

• In this fairly straightforward recipe for a hearty Sunday supper, the flavors of the pork stand out, even with the big combo of balsamic vinegar and Dijon mustard.

• The juices in the cooker don't make a successful sauce. Instead, have more Dijon mustard at the table for smearing on individual servings.

• This pork loin makes excellent sandwiches the next day, topped with a little mayonnaise, some chopped iceberg lettuce, and thinly sliced cucumber, all served on multi-grain bread.

balsamic-glazed pork loin

EFFORT: **NOT MUCH** • PREP TIME: **15 MINUTES** • COOK TIME: **5 TO 9 HOURS** • KEEPS ON WARM: **3 HOURS** • SERVES: **3 TO 8**

INGREDIENTS	2- TO 3½-QT	4- TO 5½-QT	6- TO 8-QT
Packed dark brown sugar	2 tblsp	¼ cup	½ cup
Balsamic vinegar	1 tblsp	2 tblsp	¼ cup
Dijon mustard	1 tblsp	2 tblsp	¼ cup
Minced garlic	1 tsp	2 tsp	4 tsp
Ground cinnamon	½ tsp	1 tsp	2 tsp
Ground black pepper	½ tsp	1 tsp	2 tsp
Boneless pork loin	1½ pounds	2½ pounds	5 pounds

1 Stir the brown sugar, vinegar, mustard, garlic, cinnamon, and pepper in a bowl until it's a loose paste. Smear the mixture over the pork loin; set it in the slow cooker.

2 Cover and cook on low for 5 hours in a small cooker, 6 hours in a medium one, or 9

fruit-stuffed pork loin

EFFORT: **A LOT** • PREP TIME: **30 MINUTES** • COOK TIME: **6 TO 9 HOURS** • KEEPS ON WARM: **3 HOURS** • SERVES: **4 TO 10**

INGREDIENTS	2- TO 3½-QT	4- TO 5½-QT	6- TO 8-QT
Boneless pork loin	2 pounds	3½ pounds	5 pounds
Salt	¼ tsp	½ tsp	1 tsp
Ground black pepper	¼ tsp	½ tsp	1 tsp
Dried apricots	6	10	14
Pitted prunes	6	10	14
Olive oil	2 tsp	1 tblsp	1½ tblsp
Stemmed fresh rosemary leaves	1 tblsp	2 tblsp	3 tblsp
Dry vermouth	⅓ cup	½ cup	¾ cup

(continued)

1 Start by opening up the pork loin. If your butcher has not done this task for you, lay it on a clean, dry work surface and make a cut along the length of the pork loin, about three-quarters of the way through the meat, so that you can open up the loin like a book.

2 Season the meat all over with salt and pepper. Lay it cut side up on the cutting board. Arrange the apricots and prunes in rows on half of the cut side. Fold the pork loin closed; tie it in four to six places with butchers' twine to hold the meat in a tube-like shape.

3 Set a large skillet over medium heat for a couple of minutes, then pour in the oil. Set the stuffed loin in the skillet; brown it on all sides, taking care to let each surface get a deep golden color before turning, about 10 minutes in all.

4 Transfer the pork loin to the slow cooker, sprinkle the rosemary on and around it; pour in the vermouth. Cover and cook on low for 6 hours in a small slow cooker, 7 hours in a medium cooker, or 9 hours in a large one, or until the pork is quite tender but still holds its shape when pierced with a fork. Use a large, wide spatula to transfer the pork to a cutting board; let it alone for 10 minutes. Slice it into 1-inch-thick rounds; ladle the sauce from the cooker onto these slices.

TESTERS' NOTES
• Evenly sized dried fruit are easier to roll up and close in the loin. Slice large pieces in half to fit.
• If possible, use the bright orange California apricots rather than the paler Turkish ones. The former are a tart spark against the sweet prunes.
• If you're rosemary averse, substitute a similar amount of thyme.

Serve It Up! For a sophisticated side dish, melt a minced anchovy or two in a large skillet over medium heat with olive oil, red pepper flakes, and a little salt. Toss in trimmed green beans and cook just until blistered, stirring frequently, up to 5 minutes. Serve warm with balsamic vinegar and grated Parmigiano-Reggiano on top.

pulled pork loin and vegetables

EFFORT: **A LITTLE** • PREP TIME: **20 MINUTES** • COOK TIME: **7 TO 10 HOURS** • KEEPS ON WARM: **4 HOURS THROUGH STEP 4** • SERVES: **3 TO 10**

INGREDIENTS	2- TO 3½-QT	4- TO 5½-QT	6- TO 8-QT
Mild smoked paprika	½ tblsp	1 tblsp	2 tblsp
Packed light brown sugar	½ tblsp	1 tblsp	2 tblsp
Dry mustard (see page 392)	½ tsp	1 tsp	2 tsp
Dried thyme	¼ tsp	½ tsp	1 tsp
Salt	¼ tsp	½ tsp	1 tsp
Ground black pepper	¼ tsp	½ tsp	1 tsp
Ground cloves	⅛ tsp	¼ tsp	½ tsp
Celery seeds	⅛ tsp	¼ tsp	½ tsp
No-salt-added canned crushed tomatoes	¾ cup	1½ cups	3 cups
Balsamic vinegar	1 tsp	½ tblsp	1 tblsp
Boneless pork loin	1 pound	2 pounds	4 pounds
Frozen mixed vegetables, thawed	1 cup	2 cups	4 cups

1 Mix the paprika, brown sugar, mustard, thyme, salt, pepper, cloves, and celery seeds in a small bowl. Massage this mixture all over the pork loin; set it in the slow cooker.

2 Pour the tomatoes and balsamic vinegar around the pork loin, taking care not to wash off its spice rub.

3 Cover and cook on low for 6 hours in a small slow cooker, 7 hours in a medium cooker, or 9 hours in a large cooker, or until the meat is falling-apart tender.

4 Turn the cooker to high. Use two forks to shred the pork right in the cooker. Stir in the vegetables, cover, and cook on high for 1 hour to heat through.

TESTERS' NOTES
• Here's a healthier version of the Basic Pulled Pork (page 183). This one calls for leaner pork loin and includes a hearty serving of vegetables in the mix.
• Use just about any blend of vegetables, but avoid using those specifically designed for stir-fries, as well as any spiced or sauced blends.
• The frozen mixed vegetables must be thawed before they're stirred into the cooker; otherwise, they'll drop the temperature. Set them out on the counter for a few hours as the pork cooks.

Serve It Up! Although pulled pork is often served on hamburger buns, this version would be less successful that way because of the vegetables in the mix. Serve it as open-faced sandwiches, atop toasted whole wheat or multigrain bread. Have some sour cream to dollop on each serving—and perhaps some grated cheese.

seed-crusted pork loin and potatoes

EFFORT: **NOT MUCH** • PREP TIME: **15 MINUTES** • COOK TIME: **5 TO 8 HOURS** • KEEPS ON WARM: **2 HOURS** • SERVES: **3 TO 10**

INGREDIENTS	2- TO 3½-QT	4- TO 5½-QT	6- TO 8-QT
Medium yellow potatoes (such as Yukon Gold), quartered	3	5	11
Olive oil	1 tsp	2 tsp	1 tblsp
Caraway seeds	¼ tsp	½ tsp	1 tsp
Coriander seeds	¼ tsp	½ tsp	1 tsp
Fennel seeds	¼ tsp	½ tsp	1 tsp
Yellow mustard seeds	¼ tsp	½ tsp	1 tsp
Salt	¼ tsp	½ tsp	1 tsp
Ground black pepper	¼ tsp	½ tsp	1 tsp
Boneless pork loin	1 pound	2 pounds	4 pounds

1 Toss the potato quarters and oil in the slow cooker.

2 Mix all the seeds with the salt and pepper in a small bowl. Spread this mixture on a cutting board, then roll the pork in it, coating the meat thoroughly, even pressing down a bit to get the seeds to stick. Set the pork loin on top of the potatoes.

3 Cover and cook on low for 5 hours in a small slow cooker, 6 hours in a medium cooker, or 8 hours in a large cooker, or until the pork is cooked through and the potatoes are tender. Transfer the pork to a cutting board, let stand for 10 minutes, then slice it into ½-inch-thick rings. Serve with the potatoes on the side.

(continued)

TESTERS' NOTES

• A slow cooker lets you do some things an oven never could, like roasting a pork loin coated in so many seeds. They'd turn bitter in the oven, but they stay aromatic in the slow cooker.

• Make the bed of potatoes as even as you can so the meat rests securely on top. Yukon Gold potatoes are a little starchier than red-skinned potatoes and make a creamier contrast to the crunchy seeds.

• A large pork loin may not fit in a large round slow cooker. Slice off whatever sized piece that will let the meat fit securely in the cooker, then wedge the remainder in the space to the side of the larger piece.

INGREDIENTS EXPLAINED Look for an evenly shaped piece of boneless pork loin for better cooking (and serving). The center section is lean; the larger end is marbled and may better suit your taste. Ask your butcher to help you make a selection.

pork loin with apples and thyme

EFFORT: **A LITTLE** • PREP TIME: **20 MINUTES** • COOK TIME: **4 TO 8 HOURS** • KEEPS ON WARM: **2 HOURS** • SERVES: **3 TO 8**

INGREDIENTS	2- TO 3½-QT	4- TO 5½-QT	6- TO 8-QT
Unsalted butter	½ tblsp	1 tblsp	2 tblsp
Boneless pork loin	1 pound	2 pounds	4 pounds
Tart apples (such as Empire or Northern Spy), peeled, cored, and thinly sliced	1 small	1 medium	2 medium
Yellow onion, thinly sliced	1 small	1 medium	2 medium

	2- TO 3½-QT	4- TO 5½-QT	6- TO 8-QT
Dry white wine, such as Albariño	¼ cup	⅓ cup	¾ cup
Honey	1 tsp	½ tblsp	1 tblsp
Fresh thyme sprigs	2	4	6
Salt	¼ tsp	½ tsp	1 tsp
Ground black pepper	¼ tsp	½ tsp	1 tsp

1 Melt the butter in a large skillet over medium heat. Add the pork loin and sear, turning only once, until each side is lightly browned, about 10 minutes in all. Transfer the pork loin to a slow cooker.

2 Add the apples and onion to the skillet. Cook, stirring often, until both begin to soften, about 5 minutes.

3 Remove the skillet from the heat; stir in the wine, honey, thyme, salt, and pepper. Pour and scrape the contents of the skillet over the pork loin.

4 Cover and cook on low for 4 hours in a small slow cooker, 6 hours in a medium cooker, or 8 hours in a large one, or until the pork is tender but cooked through.

5 Discard the thyme sprigs. Transfer the pork to a carving board; cool for 10 minutes before slicing into ½-inch-thick rounds. Serve with the apples and sauce from the cooker.

TESTERS' NOTES

• Browning a pork loin is really just a matter of patience. Each side should sit on the hot surface until it gets a golden crust—nothing too brown for most of these recipes, but still well beyond any depressing shades of gray.

• A 4-pound pork loin may be bigger than your largest skillet. If so, cut it in half and work in batches, using a tablespoon of butter for each browning. You can then squeeze these halves to fit in your slow cooker.

Serve It Up! Offer **Roasted Potatoes** as a side dish: Quarter red-skinned potatoes, then toss them with olive oil, salt, and pepper on a large, rimmed baking sheet. Bake in a 400°F oven for about 1 hour, tossing occasionally, until browned, crunchy on the outside but still tender on the inside.

chile-peanut pork loin

EFFORT: **NOT MUCH** • PREP TIME: **15 MINUTES** • COOK TIME: **4 TO 8 HOURS** • KEEPS ON WARM: **3 HOURS** • SERVES: **3 TO 8**

INGREDIENTS	2- TO 3½-QT	4- TO 5½-QT	6- TO 8-QT
Thinly sliced red onion	½ cup (about 1 small)	1 cup	2 cups
Chunky natural-style peanut butter	¼ cup	½ cup	1 cup
Packed dark brown sugar	2 tblsp	¼ cup	½ cup
Soy sauce	2 tblsp	¼ cup	6 tblsp
Rice vinegar	2 tblsp	¼ cup	6 tblsp
Asian red chile paste (see page 139)	1 tsp	2 tsp	4 tsp
Minced garlic	1 tsp	2 tsp	4 tsp
Minced peeled fresh ginger	1 tsp	2 tsp	4 tsp
Boneless pork loin	1 pound	2 pounds	4 pounds
Limes, quartered	1	2	4

1 Spread the onion in an even layer in the bottom of the slow cooker.

2 Whisk the peanut butter, brown sugar, soy sauce, vinegar, chile paste, garlic, and ginger in a small bowl. Slather the mixture over the pork loin; set the loin on top of the onion.

3 Cover and cook on low for 4 hours in a small slow cooker, 6 hours in a medium cooker, or 8 hours in a large cooker, or until the pork is cooked through and the onion has softened.

4 Transfer the pork loin to a cutting board; leave it alone for 10 minutes. Slice it into ½-inch-thick rounds. Ladle the sauce over the slices on serving plates and offer the lime quarters on the side for squeezing fresh juice over the pork

TESTERS' NOTES
• Because there's already brown sugar in the rub, use a natural peanut butter to cut down on the overall sweetness of the dish.
• You can use a bottled hot sauce like sambal oelek (see page 404) in the rub, although there's an astounding array of Asian red chile sauces available in most supermarkets, not to mention even more at Asian grocery stores or from online suppliers.

Serve It Up! How about stir-frying broccoli florets in a very hot wok with a little toasted sesame oil, a splash of soy sauce, and some red pepper flakes?

cold pork in garlic sauce

EFFORT: **A LOT** • PREP TIME: **12½ HOURS (INCLUDES CHILLING THE PORK)** • COOK TIME: **5 TO 8 HOURS** • KEEPS ON WARM: **NO** • SERVES: **4 TO 12**

INGREDIENTS	2- TO 3½-QT	4- TO 5½-QT	6- TO 8-QT
Boneless pork loin	1 pound	2 pounds	4 pounds
Whole scallions, halved lengthwise	4	7	14
Half-inch-thick slices of peeled fresh ginger	¼ cup	½ cup	1 cup
Salt	1 tsp	½ tblsp	1 tblsp
Soy sauce	2 tblsp	¼ cup	½ cup
Minced garlic	1½ tblsp	2½ tblsp	⅓ cup
Toasted sesame oil (see page 196)	1 tblsp	2 tblsp	¼ cup
Balsamic vinegar	2½ tsp	1½ tblsp	3 tblsp
Worcestershire sauce	2½ tsp	1½ tblsp	3 tblsp
Rice vinegar	2½ tsp	1½ tblsp	3 tblsp
Sugar	2½ tsp	1½ tblsp	3 tblsp
Chile oil	1 tsp	½ tblsp	1 tblsp
Thinly sliced peeled cucumber	1 cup	2 cups	4 cups

1 Tie the pork loin with butchers' twine about every 2 inches along its length to hold its shape as it braises. Set it in the slow cooker; add cool tap water until it is submerged by 1 inch. Sprinkle the scallions, ginger, and salt around the meat.

2 Cover and cook on low for 5 hours in a small slow cooker, 6 hours in a medium cooker, or 8 hours in a large one, or until the pork is cooked through but still firm, not yet shreddable.

3 Transfer the pork loin to a large high-sided baking dish; ladle the poaching liquid and all the aromatics around the pork loin. Cover and refrigerate for at least 12 hours or up to 48 hours.

4 Whisk the soy sauce, garlic, sesame oil, balsamic vinegar, Worcestershire sauce, rice vinegar, sugar, and chile oil in a small bowl until the sugar dissolves.

5 Transfer the pork loin to a cutting board; discard the poaching liquid and the aromatics. Slice the loin into ¼-inch-thick rounds. Arrange the cucumber slices on a serving platter; set the pork loin slices on top. Ladle a little of the soy sauce mixture over the rounds and pass the extra on the side.

TESTERS' NOTES
• Here's a pork loin dish you can make ahead and then serve at a cocktail party. Your slow cooker can even replace your oven this summer! The chilled pork continues to absorb the flavorful sauce as it chills, resulting in a firmer, denser texture.
• If your slow cooker has a removable insert, lift it right out of the cooker, keep the lid in place, and set the whole thing with the pork and poaching liquid in the fridge. Set a towel underneath the insert if it's at all hot.
• For a heartier meal, or if you're feeding a crowd, add chilled cooked soba noodles on the platter.

INGREDIENTS EXPLAINED Chile oil is an Asian condiment, made by soaking chiles in a neutral vegetable oil. Other spices like Sichuan peppercorns and garlic may also be in the mix. Some oils are strained; others retain a dusky, red sediment of ground chiles. In the case of these recipes, we call for the strained oil.

texas-style pork chili

EFFORT: **NOT MUCH** • PREP TIME: **20 MINUTES** • COOK TIME: **7 HOURS** • KEEPS ON WARM: **3 HOURS** • SERVES: **3 TO 8**

INGREDIENTS	2- TO 3½-QT	4- TO 5½-QT	6- TO 8-QT
Boneless pork loin, cut into 1-inch cubes	1¼ pounds	2 pounds	3½ pounds
Packed dark brown sugar	5 tsp	2 tblsp	3½ tblsp
Salt	½ tsp	1 tsp	½ tblsp
No-salt-added canned diced tomatoes	1¼ cups	2 cups	3½ cups
Yellow onion, chopped	1 small	1 medium	1 large
Drained and chopped jarred roasted red pepper (pimiento)	2½ tblsp	¼ cup	⅓ cup
Chili powder	3 tblsp	¼ cup	⅓ cup
Ground cumin	2 tsp	1 tblsp	5 tsp
Minced garlic	½ tblsp	2 tsp	1 tblsp
Canned chipotle chile in adobo sauce, stemmed, seeded, and minced	½	1	2
Adobo sauce from the can	1½ tblsp	2 tblsp	3½ tblsp

1 Toss the pork cubes with the brown sugar and salt in the slow cooker until well coated.

2 Dump the tomatoes, onion, red pepper, chili powder, cumin, garlic, minced chipotle, and adobo sauce into the slow cooker; stir gently until the meat is good and slathered.

3 Cover and cook on low for 8 hours, or until the pork is meltingly, irresistibly tender.

TESTERS' NOTES
• Texans are pretty insistent that chili doesn't have beans, so here's a legume-free recipe, an all-pork take on the classic Lone Star rib-sticker—even if pork loin makes it a tad healthier than the more standard pork shoulder.
• Don't confuse one canned chipotle in adobo sauce with a whole can of chiles; otherwise, the chili will be too hot to eat.

ALL-AMERICAN KNOW-HOW The easiest way to chunk up a pork loin is to halve it lengthwise, then set the halves cut side down on your cutting board. Slice them into long spears about the width you need, then slice these spears crosswise into chunks.

basic pulled pork

EFFORT: **NOT MUCH** • PREP TIME: **15 MINUTES** • COOK TIME: **6 TO 10 HOURS** • KEEPS ON WARM: **4 HOURS** • SERVES: **3 TO 10**

INGREDIENTS	2- TO 3½-QT	4- TO 5½-QT	6- TO 8-QT
Chili sauce, such as Heinz	⅓ cup	¾ cup	1¼ cups
Red wine vinegar	1 tblsp	2½ tblsp	¼ cup
Packed dark brown sugar	1 tblsp	2½ tblsp	¼ cup
Worcestershire sauce	1 tsp	1 tblsp	1½ tblsp
Dijon mustard	1 tsp	1 tblsp	1½ tblsp
Molasses, preferably unsulphured	1 tsp	1 tblsp	1½ tblsp
Ancho chile powder (see page 147)	1 tsp	1 tblsp	1½ tblsp
Ground cumin	¼ tsp	¾ tsp	1 tsp
Ground cloves	¼ tsp	½ tsp	1 tsp
Bone-in pork shoulder	1½ pounds	3 pounds	5 pounds

(continued)

1 Mix the chili sauce, vinegar, brown sugar, Worcestershire sauce, mustard, molasses, chile powder, cumin, and cloves in the slow cooker until the brown sugar and molasses dissolve. Set the pork shoulder in the cooker, turning it once to coat it with the sauce.

2 Cover and cook on low for 6 hours in a slow small cooker, 8 hours in a medium cooker, or 10 hours in a large cooker, or until the meat is quite literally falling off the bone.

3 Use a spoon to skim the fat from the surface of the cooking liquid, then shred the meat by pulling it apart with two forks. Discard the bones and stir well before serving.

TESTERS' NOTES
• Skip manning the grill all day. With a slow cooker, you can make a terrific pulled pork without much fuss.
• Treat the timing as a suggestion: the pork has to be meltingly tender, no longer able to adhere to the bone. All that collagen melt will make the meat moist and irresistible, so cook as long as you need to until you find the meat perfectly tender.
• There's no smoke flavor in this pulled pork. We wanted the sweeter, more elemental taste of pork to be at the front of the dish. However, if you want a smokier taste, use a smoked bone-in pork shoulder.

Serve It Up! Have toasted Kaiser or onion rolls on hand, as well as a platter of thinly sliced vegetables for sandwich toppers: tomatoes, radishes, cucumbers, and red onion. Pickled jalapeño rings or hot chow-chow would also be a welcome addition.

INGREDIENTS EXPLAINED A pork shoulder is a highly marbled hunk of meat from just over the pig's front legs. It's the standard choice for pulled pork, although you can substitute another cut from the front shoulder, the so-called *picnic ham* (which is not a ham at all, since it doesn't come from the back leg). Some pork shoulders are sold with the rind (that is, the skin) and a thick layer of fat attached. Have the butcher at your market slice off

both for the recipes in this book. You may also need to ask him or her to cut the pork shoulder into smaller chunks to fit a smaller slow cooker.

alabama-style pulled pork with white sauce

EFFORT: **A LITTLE** • PREP TIME: **15 MINUTES** • COOK TIME: **6 TO 10 HOURS** • KEEPS ON WARM: **4 HOURS** • SERVES: **3 TO 8**

INGREDIENTS	2- TO 3½-QT	4- TO 5½-QT	6- TO 8-QT
FOR THE PULLED PORK			
Mild smoked paprika	1 tsp	2 tsp	1 tblsp
Packed dark brown sugar	1 tsp	2 tsp	1 tblsp
Ground cumin	1 tsp	½ tblsp	1 tblsp
Garlic powder	¼ tsp	½ tsp	1 tsp
Onion powder	¼ tsp	½ tsp	1 tsp
Ground black pepper	¼ tsp	½ tsp	1 tsp
Bone-in pork shoulder	1¼ pounds	2½ pounds	4 pounds
Liquid smoke	1 tblsp	1½ tblsp	2 tblsp
FOR THE WHITE SAUCE			
Mayonnaise	¼ cup	½ cup	1 cup
White vinegar	1 tblsp	2 tblsp	¼ cup
Ground black pepper	1 tsp	½ tblsp	1 tblsp

1 Mix the paprika, brown sugar, cumin, garlic powder, onion powder, and pepper in a small bowl. Massage the pork with the liquid smoke, then coat it with the spice mixture. Set the meat in the slow cooker.

2 Cover and cook on low for 6 hours in a small slow cooker, 8 hours in a medium cooker, or 10 hours in a large one, or until the meat is so tender it will fall off the bone into bits with almost no prodding.

3 Remove and discard the bones; shred the meat using two forks, bathing it in the cooking juices. Use tongs to transfer the meat to a serving platter, leaving at least some of those juices behind for your cardiologist's sake.

4 To make the white sauce, whisk the mayonnaise, vinegar, and black pepper in a small bowl; serve on the side for drizzling over the pulled pork.

TESTERS' NOTES
• Alabama pulled pork is a thing of beauty! This is a drier version than Basic Pulled Pork (page 183), with less sauce but nonetheless ramped up with the smoky spices and white sauce.
• Yep, that sauce is just mayonnaise thinned with plain, white vinegar and spiked with black pepper. Don't use anything fancier!
• Give the pork sauce more oomph by using cracked black peppercorns. Use even more than we suggest for a mouth-poppingly hot sauce.
• Make this dish up to two days in advance. Refrigerate the pork and sauce separately, but cover both tightly. Reheat the pork in a tightly sealed aluminum foil packet in a 325°F oven for 20 to 25 minutes.

Serve It Up! You'll need toasted buns, a platter of deviled eggs, and lots of napkins! Avoid spiking the sandwiches with pickled jalapeño rings or anything very hot, since the black pepper in the sauce will provide the spark.

pork cacciatore

EFFORT: **A LOT** • PREP TIME: **40 MINUTES** • COOK TIME: **6 TO 10 HOURS** • KEEPS ON WARM: **3 HOURS** • SERVES: **3 TO 10**

INGREDIENTS	2- TO 3½-QT	4- TO 5½-QT	6- TO 8-QT
Slab bacon, chopped	2 ounces	4 ounces	8 ounces
Bone-in pork shoulder	1¼ pounds	2½ pounds	5 pounds
Thinly sliced cremini or brown button mushrooms	½ cup (about 1½ ounces)	1 cup (about 3 ounces)	2 cups (about 6 ounces)
Chopped yellow onion	6 tblsp	¾ cup (about 1 small)	1½ cups
Stemmed, seeded, and chopped green bell pepper	6 tblsp	¾ cup (about 1 small)	1½ cups
Thinly sliced carrot	⅓ cup	½ cup (about 1 medium)	1 cup
Drained no-salt-added canned diced tomatoes	⅔ cup	1¼ cups	2½ cups
Dry white wine, such as Verdicchio	¼ cup	½ cup	1 cup
No-salt-added tomato paste	1½ tblsp	3 tblsp	6 tblsp
Minced fresh oregano leaves	1 tsp	½ tblsp	2 tsp
Minced fresh rosemary leaves	½ tsp	1 tsp	2 tsp
Stemmed fresh thyme leaves	½ tsp	1 tsp	2 tsp
Ground black pepper	⅛ tsp	¼ tsp	½ tsp

1 Brown the bacon in a large skillet set over medium heat until crisp at the edges, between 4 and 8 minutes depending on the size of the batch. Use a slotted spoon to transfer the bacon to the cooker, leaving its rendered fat behind.

(continued)

2 With the skillet (and the luscious rendered fat) still over medium heat, brown the pork shoulder on all sides, turning it only after you've got a dark brown sheen with some crunchy bits on each side, about 15 minutes in all. Transfer the pork to a cutting board.

3 Add the mushrooms to the skillet, stirring often, until they release their liquid and it bubbles away, between 5 and 8 minutes. Scrape the contents of the skillet into the cooker.

4 Add the onion, bell pepper, and carrot to the slow cooker. Set the pork shoulder into the vegetables.

5 Stir the tomatoes, wine, tomato paste, oregano, rosemary, thyme, and pepper in a bowl until the tomato paste dissolves; pour over the pork shoulder and vegetables.

6 Cover and cook on low for 6 hours in a small slow cooker, 8 hours in a medium model, or 10 hours in a large one, or until the meat easily chunks into bits off the bone. Uncover and cool for 10 minutes. Use a fork to pry off hunks of the pork, place them in serving bowls, and spoon the vegetables and sauce over each serving.

TESTERS' NOTES

• Cacciatora ("hunter style") is a popular Italian-American dish, a rustic stew of meat, tomatoes, and vegetables in an aromatic sauce. It's often made with chicken, although we think it's a particularly bright and yet hearty combination of flavors that match well with pork.

• This dish is most often made with pancetta, an unsmoked but cured pork product; however, we like the smoky taste of bacon better. Switch back to the original for a lighter taste.

• You can try to lift the pork shoulder out of the slow cooker to carve it at the table, but you'll need good strength, large utensils, and a steady hand to keep it from falling apart (or to the floor). Send any children or pets out of the room before attempting this complicated maneuver.

jerk pork shoulder

EFFORT: **A LITTLE** • PREP TIME: **20 MINUTES** • COOK TIME: **6 TO 10 HOURS** • KEEPS ON WARM: **2 HOURS** • SERVES: **4 TO 12**

INGREDIENTS	2- TO 3½-QT	4- TO 5½-QT	6- TO 8-QT
Whole medium scallions, thinly sliced	1	2	3
Chopped pickled jalapeño rings	2 tsp	4 tsp	2 tblsp
Garlic cloves, peeled	1	2	3
Cider vinegar	2 tsp	4 tsp	2 tblsp
Peeled and minced fresh ginger	1 tsp	2 tsp	1 tblsp
Packed dark brown sugar	1 tsp	2 tsp	1 tblsp
Molasses, preferably unsulphured	1 tsp	2 tsp	1 tblsp
Dried thyme	¼ tsp	½ tsp	1 tsp
Ground allspice	¼ tsp	½ tsp	1 tsp
Ground coriander	¼ tsp	½ tsp	1 tsp
Salt	¼ tsp	½ tsp	1 tsp
Ground black pepper	¼ tsp	½ tsp	1 tsp
Boneless pork shoulder	1½ pounds	3 pounds	4½ pounds
Medium sweet potatoes, peeled and cut into 2-inch pieces	1	2	3

1 Place the scallions, jalapeños, garlic, vinegar, ginger, brown sugar, molasses, thyme, allspice, coriander, salt, and pepper in a food processor fitted with the chopping blade; process until you have a coarse paste, scraping down the inside of the canister once or twice.

2 Rub the spice paste onto the pork shoulder. Set the pork in the slow cooker; distribute the sweet potato cubes around the pork.

3 Cover and cook on low for 6 hours in a small slow cooker, 8 hours in a medium cooker, or 10 hours in a large cooker, or until the meat is so tender that it offers no resistance to a fork.

TESTERS' NOTES
• This jerk paste is more aromatic than fiery. Give it more heat by adding up to 1 teaspoon cayenne.
• The pork shoulder for this recipe should be *boneless*; it's most likely been tied at the supermarket to hold its shape. Remove the twine before serving (but not before cooking). However, if the meat comes in a netted bag, remove that bag; the roast may fall into large chunks, but these chunks can be cooked in the same manner as a whole roast.

Serve It Up! For a **Green Bean Salad:** Steam green beans until crisp-tender, then chop them into 1-inch pieces. Toss with diced pitted green olives and thinly sliced shallot. Add plenty of olive oil, some balsamic vinegar, salt and pepper, and a pinch of sugar, then toss one last time.

milk-braised pork shoulder

EFFORT: **A LOT** • PREP TIME: **30 MINUTES** • COOK TIME: **6 TO 10 HOURS** • KEEPS ON WARM: **2 HOURS** • SERVES: **3 TO 10**

INGREDIENTS	2- TO 3½-QT	4- TO 5½-QT	6- TO 8-QT
Dry white wine, such as Pinot Grigio	⅓ cup	⅔ cup	1 cup
Milk	¾ cup	1½ cups	2 cups
Heavy cream	3 tblsp	⅓ cup	½ cup
Garlic cloves, peeled and smashed	1	2	3
Fresh sage leaves	4	8	12
Grated nutmeg	⅛ tsp	¼ tsp	½ tsp
Salt	⅛ tsp	¼ tsp	½ tsp
Ground black pepper	⅛ tsp	¼ tsp	½ tsp
Bone-in pork shoulder	1½ pounds	3 pounds	5 pounds

1 Bring the wine to a boil in a medium saucepan set over high heat. Boil until reduced to a thick glaze, then pour in the milk and cream. Bring back to a boil, stirring often. Boil for 1 minute. Pour the mixture into the slow cooker and cool for 10 minutes.

2 Stir the garlic, sage, nutmeg, salt, and pepper into the milk mixture. Add the pork shoulder to the slow cooker; turn to coat.

3 Cover and cook on low for 6 hours in a small slow cooker, 8 hours in a medium cooker, or 10 hours in a large model, or until the meat falls in chunks off the bone.

4 Break the meat into serving-size chunks and move them to a serving platter. Discard the bones and any cartilage.

5 Puree the sauce: either use an immersion blender right in the slow cooker or pour the sauce into a large blender, cover, remove the center from the lid, place a clean kitchen towel over said lid, and blend until smooth, scraping down the inside of the canister at least once. Pour the pureed sauce into a large saucepan; bring to a boil over high heat. Boil for up to 3 minutes, stirring occasionally, to make a richer sauce.

(continued)

• Because of negative charges among the molecules, milk is one of the few protein-based substances that can be boiled without coagulating. Thus, it's a rich braising medium for pork, a rather old-fashioned Italian technique.
• Make sure the slow cooker insert is scrupulously clean before you start; the presence of just a speck of vinegar can lead to curdled milk in the sauce. That said, the blender will take care of the unsightly problem in step 5.

Serve It Up! Serve these chunks over cooked egg noodles tossed with butter and poppy seeds.

ALL-AMERICAN KNOW-HOW Keep in mind there's a difference between grated and ground nutmeg. The grated spice is shaved off the whole nutmeg with a microplane or a nutmeg grater; it has a bright, clean fragrance, a bit woody as well as floral. The ground spice is usually jarred and has a much earthier flavor. If substituting ground nutmeg for grated, use only half the stated amount.

pork carnitas

EFFORT: **NOT MUCH** • PREP TIME: **20 MINUTES** • COOK TIME: **8 HOURS** • KEEPS ON WARM: **4 HOURS** • SERVES: **4 TO 10**

INGREDIENTS	2- TO 3½-QT	4- TO 5½-QT	6- TO 8-QT
Boneless pork shoulder, cut into 2-inch pieces	2 pounds	3½ pounds	5 pounds
Chopped canned green chiles, hot or mild	½ cup	¾ cup	1¼ cups
Fresh orange juice	¼ cup	⅓ cup	⅔ cup
Fresh lime juice	¼ cup	⅓ cup	⅔ cup
Minced garlic	1 tblsp	1½ tblsp	2½ tblsp
Ground cumin	1 tsp	½ tblsp	1 tblsp

1 Mix the cubed pork, chiles, orange juice, lime juice, garlic, and cumin in the slow cooker.

2 Cover and cook on low for 8 hours, or until the pork is quite tender.

3 Transfer the pork chunks to a bowl; strain the fat from the sauce, either by spooning it from the surface or by pouring the sauce into a fat separator. Pour the strained sauce into a saucepan and bring to a boil over high heat, stirring occasionally. Boil until reduced by half. Cool a few minutes, then pour the sauce over the pork in the bowl.

TESTERS' NOTES
• Here's a reinvention of the Tex-Mex favorite, developed specifically for the slow cooker.
• There's no additional salt needed here, because there's plenty in the canned chiles.

Serve It Up! Have flour tortillas at the ready, along with sour cream, minced cilantro leaves, diced avocado, sliced olives, and sliced radishes. For the best taste, warm the tortillas over an open gas flame, about 10 seconds per side, until browned and even a little charred in a few places.

ALL-AMERICAN KNOW-HOW To peel garlic cloves before you mince them, lay them on a cutting board, set the side of a large knife on top, and give the flat surface of the blade a whack. The garlic cloves underneath will split open—no big deal, since you're going to mince them anyway. More important, the papery hulls will slip right off.

pork mole rojo
with plantains

EFFORT: **A LOT** • PREP TIME: **1 HOUR** • COOK TIME: **8 HOURS** •
KEEPS ON WARM: **2 HOURS** • SERVES: **3 TO 8**

INGREDIENTS	2- TO 3½-QT	4- TO 5½-QT	6- TO 8-QT
Dried ancho chiles (see page 138)	6	8	12
Olive oil	½ tblsp	1 tblsp	1½ tblsp
Boneless pork shoulder, cut into 2-inch pieces	1½ pounds	2½ pounds	4 pounds
Chopped yellow onion	½ cup	¾ cup	1¼ cups
Minced garlic	2 tsp	1 tblsp	5 tsp
Reduced-sodium chicken broth	½ cup	¾ cup	1¼ cups
Red wine vinegar	2 tblsp	3 tblsp	⅓ cup
Worcestershire sauce	1 tblsp	1½ tblsp	2½ tblsp
Dried oregano	1 tsp	½ tblsp	2½ tsp
Dried thyme	1 tsp	½ tblsp	2½ tsp
Ground cloves	½ tsp	¾ tsp	1¼ tsp
Ground black pepper	½ tsp	¾ tsp	1¼ tsp
Ripe plantains, peeled and cut into 2-inch pieces	1 pound	2 pounds	2½ pounds
Bay leaves	1	2	3

1 Bring a small saucepan of water to a boil over high heat. Seed the chiles by tearing them open and discarding their seeds and white membranes. Remove and discard the stems, then tear the flesh into small pieces and place it in a bowl. Cover with boiling water; set aside to soak for 20 minutes.

2 Meanwhile, heat a large skillet over medium heat for a few minutes, then swirl in the oil. Set the pork shoulder in the skillet; brown it on all sides, which may take up to 15 minutes depending on how much pork you have. Transfer the pork shoulder to the slow cooker.

3 Brown the onion in the skillet, stirring until it's soft, about 4 minutes. Add the garlic, stir over the heat a few seconds, then scrape the contents of the skillet into the slow cooker with the pork.

4 Drain the chiles in a colander set in the sink. Place these softened chiles in a large food processor; add the broth, vinegar, Worcestershire sauce, oregano, thyme, cloves, and pepper. Process until you have a fairly smooth paste, scraping down the inside of the canister once or twice. Pour the sauce over the pork and vegetables.

5 Push the plantains and bay leaves into the sauce in and around the pork. Cover and cook on low for 8 hours, or until the pork is ridiculously tender.

TESTERS' NOTES
• Mole rojo (*MOH-lay RO-hoh*) is a red chile sauce, sour from the vinegar but balanced with plenty of herbs. It's one of the world's best braising mixtures.
• Feel free to mix up the chiles in this sauce, substituting a few dried New Mexican chiles for a few of the anchos and ending up with a brighter sauce that's a little more sour.

Serve It Up! Mole rojo does best with a sweeter side dish. How about a salad of orange slices and mango chunks, tossed with minced cilantro, salt, and a splash of aged balsamic vinegar?

pork shoulder
with coriander and fenugreek

EFFORT: **A LOT** • PREP TIME: **30 MINUTES** • COOK TIME: **7 TO 10 HOURS** • KEEPS ON WARM: **4 HOURS THROUGH STEP 3** • SERVES: **3 TO 8**

INGREDIENTS	2- TO 3½-QT	4- TO 5½-QT	6- TO 8-QT
Minced garlic	½ tblsp	1 tblsp	2 tblsp
Kosher salt	¾ tsp	½ tblsp	1 tblsp
Ground coriander	½ tsp	1 tsp	2 tsp
Ground fenugreek	½ tsp	¾ tsp	½ tblsp
Boneless pork butt	1¼ pounds	2½ pounds	4 pounds
Olive oil	½ tblsp	1 tblsp	2 tblsp
Minced fresh cilantro leaves	2 tblsp	¼ cup	½ cup
Cider vinegar	½ tblsp	2½ tsp	1½ tblsp

1 Make a coarse, dry paste by stirring the garlic, salt, coriander, and fenugreek in a small bowl. Use a paring knife to make slits all over the roast; smear the paste into these openings.

2 Heat a large skillet over medium heat for a few minutes, then swirl in the oil. Place the pork butt into the skillet. Brown it on all sides—which is easier said than done, given its shape. Be patient and precise, leaving each side over the heat until you get some fairly dark bits. The whole process may take up to 20 minutes.

3 Put the roast in the slow cooker. Cover and cook on low for 7 hours in a small slow cooker, 9 hours in a medium model, or 10 hours in a large one, or until the meat is fork-tender but not yet falling apart at the bone.

4 Transfer it to a cutting board using tongs and a large spatula. As the meat rests for 10 minutes, skim the fat from the juices in the slow cooker either by running a flatware spoon along their surface or by pouring them into a fat separator and leaving them be for a few minutes. Pour the skimmed juices into a medium saucepan; stir in the cilantro and vinegar. Bring to a boil over high heat; then continue boiling until reduced by half, between 5 and 10 minutes, stirring occasionally. Carve the roast into slices for serving and pass the sauce on the side.

TESTERS' NOTES
• Maybe now's the time to get the kids involved in cooking! Small fingers are needed to get the spice paste into the slits without tearing the meat.
• These flavors are modeled on roasts from southwestern Russia and nearby Georgia. The meal is savory, even a little muskier than some preparations for pork butt. It'll pair well with a sweet white wine or even beer at the table.

ALL-AMERICAN KNOW-HOW When you carve a pork butt, make those slices against the grain (see page 146). However, the grain's direction can be hard to determine, since several muscle groups make up a pork butt. Make a slice, note the grain inside, and turn the cut so that the grain runs perpendicular to your knife as you carve. That said, some pieces may just chunk off whole onto the cutting board. Small ones can be served whole; larger ones can be sliced against the grain.

curried pork shoulder with raisins and walnuts

EFFORT: **A LITTLE** • PREP TIME: **25 MINUTES** • COOK TIME: **7 HOURS** • KEEPS ON WARM: **3 HOURS** • SERVES: **3 TO 10**

INGREDIENTS	2- TO 3½-QT	4- TO 5½-QT	6- TO 8-QT
Ground coriander	1 tsp	2 tsp	4 tsp
Ground cinnamon	½ tsp	1 tsp	2 tsp
Ground cumin	½ tsp	1 tsp	2 tsp
Ground ginger	½ tsp	1 tsp	2 tsp
Ground black pepper	¼ tsp	½ tsp	1 tsp
Ground cardamom	⅛ tsp	¼ tsp	½ tsp
Saffron	Pinch	⅛ tsp	¼ tsp
Boneless pork shoulder, cut into 1-inch pieces	1¼ pounds	2½ pounds	5 pounds
Unsalted butter	½ tblsp	1 tblsp	2 tblsp
Thinly sliced yellow onion	½ cup (about 1 small)	1 cup	2 cups
Chopped toasted walnuts	2½ tblsp	⅓ cup	⅔ cup
Chopped golden raisins	2 tblsp	¼ cup	½ cup
Chopped preserved lemon, rind only	1½ tblsp	3 tblsp	6 tblsp
Sweet white wine, such as Spätlese	2 tblsp	¼ cup	½ cup

1 Mix the coriander, cinnamon, cumin, ginger, pepper, cardamom, and saffron in a large bowl. Add the chunks of pork; stir until every piece is coated in the spices. Scrape the contents of the bowl—and every last grain of spice—into the slow cooker.

2 Melt the butter in a large skillet over low heat. Add the onion, reduce the heat even further, and cook until very soft and sweet, 15 to 20 minutes, stirring occasionally. If the onion starts to brown, reduce the heat still more and stir more frequently. If it is truly browning, remove the skillet from the heat and cool for a couple of minutes before proceeding.

3 Scrape the contents of the skillet into the slow cooker. Stir in the walnuts, raisins, and preserved lemon. Toss well, pour in the wine, and stir again.

4 Cover and cook on low for 7 hours, or until the flavors have blended and the pork is beyond fork-tender, even spoon-tender.

TESTERS' NOTES
• Here's an aromatic curry, with warming spices instead of hot, the perfect antidote to a chilly evening. Note that the pork is cut into smaller chunks than in some other recipes. Good knife work will pay off with a better dinner—and a faster cooking time here.
• You're not caramelizing the onion in step 2; you're simply cooking it until it is sweet, browning the batch as little as possible.

SHORTCUTS If you have a no-turmeric, no-salt curry blend (thus, not the standard yellow curry powder), you can substitute it for the first six ingredients; use 1 tablespoon in a small slow cooker, 2 tablespoons in a medium cooker, or 3½ tablespoons in a large one.

INGREDIENTS EXPLAINED Preserved lemons are a Middle Eastern specialty: little lemons preserved in a brine of their own juices and water. The pulp is soft and squishy but the rind retains more texture. Look for them in the international aisle of most supermarkets.

pork shoulder
with tomatillos and chiles

EFFORT: **A LITTLE** • PREP TIME: **25 MINUTES** • COOK TIME: **8 HOURS** • KEEPS ON WARM: **3 HOURS** • SERVES: **4 TO 10**

INGREDIENTS	2- TO 3½-QT	4- TO 5½-QT	6- TO 8-QT
Tomatillos, husks removed, rinsed (see page 49)	1½ pounds	3 pounds	4½ pounds
Fresh serrano or small jalapeño chiles	2	4	6
Boneless pork shoulder, cut into 2-inch chunks	1¼ pounds	2½ pounds	4 pounds
Minced yellow onion	¼ cup	½ cup	¾ cup
Minced garlic	1 tsp	2 tsp	1 tblsp
Cumin seeds	½ tsp	1 tsp	½ tblsp
Fennel seeds	½ tsp	1 tsp	½ tblsp
Minced cilantro leaves	2 tblsp	¼ cup	6 tblsp
Fresh lime juice	1 tblsp	2 tblsp	3 tblsp
Salt	¼ tsp	½ tsp	½ tsp

1 Position the rack 4 to 6 inches from the broiler; preheat the broiler. Halve the tomatillos and set them cut side down on a large rimmed baking sheet along with the chiles. Broil the tomatillos and chiles until they begin to blister and brown, about 5 minutes, turning the chiles once. Remove the tray from the broiler and cool on a wire rack for 15 minutes.

2 Stem and seed the chiles, then chop them and the tomatillos. Scrape both into the slow cooker, and stir in the pork, onion, garlic, cumin seeds, and fennel seeds.

3 Cover and cook on low for 8 hours, or until the pork is tender enough to be cut with your worst knife. Stir in the cilantro, lime juice, and salt before serving.

TESTERS' NOTES
• This pork is stewed, not braised. Expect a lot of liquid here—it's not a soup, but definitely is soupy.
• Don't be tempted to use canned tomatillos. Their flavors will have dulled too far. Most large supermarkets carry tomatillos in the summer; almost all Latin American markets carry them year round.
• There's plenty of flavor in those caramelized brown bits still on the baking sheet. If you want, add a tablespoon or two of chicken broth while the pan is still hot and stir well to dissolve, then pour it all into the slow cooker along with the other ingredients.

Serve It Up! This Southwestern stew makes a fine dinner with cornbread or polenta. But it would also be great as a breakfast. Make it overnight, then serve it in bowls with poached eggs set on top.

INGREDIENTS EXPLAINED Beware enhanced meat! Many markets inject pork shoulders and other larger cuts with a briny solution of broth, salt, monosodium glutamate (MSG, which can be labeled as "natural flavors" in the United States), and other additives, always shown as containing some "percent of a solution." It's all supposed to create a juicier, more flavorful roast; but this chemical engineering is unnecessary when you're working with a slow cooker, which holds the juices at a low temperature, tenderizing the meat without losing flavor. You can almost always avoid this problem with organic meat, but read labels carefully in any event. If you do use injected pork, you may well end up with a much soupier dinner.

pork shoulder in creamy mushroom sauce

EFFORT: **A LOT** • PREP TIME: **30 MINUTES** • COOK TIME: **8 HOURS** •
KEEPS ON WARM: **3 HOURS THROUGH STEP 3** • SERVES: **3 TO 8**

INGREDIENTS	2- TO 3½-QT	4- TO 5½-QT	6- TO 8-QT
Unsalted butter	½ tblsp	1 tblsp	2 tblsp
Boneless pork shoulder, cut into 2-inch cubes	1 pound	2 pounds	4 pounds
Salt	¼ tsp	½ tsp	1 tsp
Ground black pepper	¼ tsp	½ tsp	1 tsp
Chopped yellow onion	¼ cup	½ cup	1 cup (about 1 medium)
Reduced-sodium chicken broth	¼ cup	½ cup	1 cup
Thinly sliced cremini or brown button mushrooms	1 cup (about 3 ounces)	1½ cups (about 5 ounces)	3 cups (about 10 ounces)
Fresh thyme sprigs	2	3	4
4-inch rosemary sprigs	1	1	2
Heavy cream	2 tblsp	¼ cup	½ cup
Minced chives	2 tsp	1 tblsp	2 tblsp

1 Melt the butter in a large skillet over medium heat. Season the pork chunks with salt and pepper; brown them in batches, turning them only after they've got a golden color, about 8 minutes per batch. Transfer the chunks to the slow cooker and continue browning as necessary.

2 Dump the onion into the skillet. Stir a few times, then pour in the broth. Raise the heat to medium-high and bring the broth to a simmer, scraping up any browned bits in the skillet. Pour the contents of the skillet into the slow cooker. Stir in the mushrooms; push the thyme and rosemary into the sauce.

3 Cover and cook on low for 8 hours, or until the pork is gorgeously tender.

4 Transfer the pork chunks to a serving bowl or platter. Discard the rosemary and thyme sprigs. Defat the sauce in the cooker, using a flatware spoon to skim its surface.

5 Pour the sauce into a medium saucepan; bring to a boil over medium-high heat, stirring occasionally. Stir in the cream and chives; boil for 2 minutes, stirring quite often. Spoon some sauce over the meat and pass more at the table.

TESTERS' NOTES
• The mushrooms aren't cooked down to lose their moisture before they go into the slow cooker. That extra juice helps create the sauce—which is further concentrated after the pork has cooked.
• The onion is not softened in the skillet, just warmed; instead, it is partly stewed in the broth, giving it a more assertive flavor, a better match with the sweet cream.

orange-glazed pork butt

EFFORT: **NOT MUCH** • PREP TIME: **10 MINUTES** • COOK TIME: **6 TO 10 HOURS** • KEEPS WELL WARM: **3 HOURS** • SERVES: **3 TO 8**

INGREDIENTS	2- TO 3½-QT	4- TO 5½-QT	6- TO 8-QT
Boneless pork butt	1 pound	2 pounds	4 pounds
Orange marmalade	2 tblsp	¼ cup	½ cup
Soy sauce	4 tsp	2½ tblsp	⅓ cup
No-salt-added tomato paste	½ tblsp	1 tblsp	2 tblsp
Cider vinegar	1 tsp	½ tblsp	1 tblsp
Ground cloves	⅛ tsp	¼ tsp	½ tsp
Red pepper flakes	⅛ tsp	¼ tsp	½ tsp

1 Set the pork butt in the slow cooker. Whisk the marmalade, soy sauce, tomato paste, vinegar, cloves, and red pepper flakes in a bowl until fairly smooth; smear the mixture over the exposed bits of the pork.

2 Cover and cook on low for 6 hours in a small slow cooker, 8 hours in a medium cooker, or 10 hours in a large one, or until the meat is quite tender but not yet shreddable. Let rest for 10 minutes uncovered with the cooker turned off, then portion the meat into large chunks, or transfer it to a cutting board and slice it into more manageable pieces.

TESTERS' NOTES

• A pork butt is often used interchangeably with a pork shoulder. However, we feel the shoulder bone imparts great flavor to pulled pork and other dishes; we save the somewhat fattier, more decadent boneless pork butt for over-the-top roasts like this one.

• They'll be plenty of juice in the cooker after the pork roasts, but it's mostly fat and a little too oily for a good gravy.

INGREDIENTS EXPLAINED Despite an evocative name, the pork butt is taken from nowhere near the back end of a pig; instead, it's from the front quarter, a fairly fatty cut. To be specific, the butt is the slightly thicker section of meat from the front shoulder, rather than the more pyramidal bit often called (confusingly!) the pork shoulder. Despite some minor differences, a Boston butt is just about the same thing as a pork butt; either will work here.

pork butt with whiskey and sage

EFFORT: **A LOT** • PREP TIME: **12½ HOURS (INCLUDES MARINATING THE PORK)** • COOK TIME: **7 TO 11 HOURS** • KEEPS ON WARM: **4 HOURS** • SERVES: **3 TO 10**

INGREDIENTS	2- TO 3½-QT	4- TO 5½-QT	6- TO 8-QT
Small garlic cloves, peeled	3	5	10
Fresh sage leaves	3	5	10
Boneless pork butt	1¼ pounds	2½ pounds	5 pounds
Coarse-grained mustard	1 tblsp	2 tblsp	¼ cup
Packed dark brown sugar	1 tblsp	2 tblsp	¼ cup
Blended whiskey	½ tblsp	1 tblsp	2 tblsp
Worcestershire sauce	½ tsp	1 tsp	2 tsp

1 Halve the garlic cloves and sage leaves. Count the total number of pieces you've got (12, 20, or 40). Use the tip of a paring knife to make that number of small, thin slits all over the pork butt; insert a piece of garlic or a folded sage leaf into each hole.

2 Mix the mustard, brown sugar, whiskey, and Worcestershire sauce in a small bowl until the brown sugar almost dissolves. Smear the mixture all over the pork. Set it in a large baking dish; cover tightly with plastic wrap. Refrigerate for at least 12 hours or up to 24 hours.

3 Unwrap the pork roast and set it out on the counter for 30 minutes.

4 Put the roast in the slow cooker, cover, and cook on low for 7 hours in a small slow cooker, 9 hours in a medium cooker, or 11 hours in a large cooker, or until the meat is fork-tender but not yet completely falling apart.

5 Using large tongs or a spatula, transfer the roast to a cutting board and let it rest for 10 minutes. Carve it into slices for serving, even those pieces that fall off.

TESTERS' NOTES
• Use a blended whiskey here, a sturdy, fairly dry mix without a lot of aged oakiness in tow. Do not substitute bourbon—too sweet a finish.
• Dijon mustard is simply too assertive and won't let the other flavors come through. A coarse-grained mustard still gives that piquant hit without overpowering subtler notes.

INGREDIENTS EXPLAINED Technically, *whiskey* comes from the United States or Ireland; *whisky* comes from everywhere else, from Scotland to India, Canada to New Zealand. Use an American or Irish blended whiskey, sturdier in its flavor to stand up to the long cooking, rather than a fancy single malt.

chinatown barbecue pork

EFFORT: **A LITTLE** • PREP TIME: **15 MINUTES** • COOK TIME: **7 TO 12 HOURS** • KEEPS ON WARM: **5 HOURS** • SERVES: **4 TO 12**

INGREDIENTS	2- TO 3½-QT	4- TO 5½-QT	6- TO 8-QT
Soy sauce	¼ cup	½ cup	¾ cup
Hoisin sauce	¼ cup	½ cup	¾ cup
Honey	¼ cup	½ cup	¾ cup
No-salt-added tomato paste	2 tblsp	¼ cup	6 tblsp
Rice vinegar	1 tblsp	2 tblsp	3 tblsp
Toasted sesame oil	2 tsp	1½ tblsp	2 tblsp
Minced garlic	2 tsp	4 tsp	2 tblsp
Minced peeled fresh ginger	2 tsp	4 tsp	2 tblsp
Five-spice powder (see page 122)	½ tsp	1 tsp	½ tblsp
Celery seeds	½ tsp	1 tsp	1¼ tsp
Ground cloves	½ tsp	1 tsp	1¼ tsp
Boneless pork butt	2 pounds	4 pounds	6 pounds

1 Whisk the soy sauce, hoisin sauce, honey, tomato paste, vinegar, sesame oil, garlic, ginger, five-spice powder, celery seeds, and cloves in the slow cooker until the honey and tomato paste have dissolved. Set the pork in the slow cooker; turn to coat all sides.

2 Cover and cook on low for 7 hours in a small slow cooker, 9 hours in a medium cooker, or 12 hours in a large cooker, or until the meat is far beyond tender, well into the fabled realm of pulled pork.

(continued)

3 Transfer the pork from the cooker to a large cutting board. Take care: it can come apart at the seams.

4 Skim the fat off the sauce in the slow cooker; pour the skimmed juices into a large saucepan and bring to a boil over high heat, stirring frequently. Boil the juices until they thicken into a sauce, stirring fairly often, between 3 and 8 minutes.

5 Shred the pork with two forks; transfer the shredded meat to a serving bowl. Drizzle the sauce over the meat and pass extra on the side for dunking and dipping.

TESTERS' NOTES
• This is a sweet, sticky barbecue, best served over white rice. Also, have some rice vinegar on the table for sprinkling on the meat.
• You can chop the meat into small bits to stuff into pork buns or pork dumplings. Or freeze any leftovers and thaw them for a day when you're feeling ambitious.

Serve It Up! Have a salad on the side, made from thinly sliced radishes, thinly sliced mango, and jícama matchsticks, dressed with a little toasted sesame oil, white wine vinegar, red pepper flakes, and crunchy sea salt.

INGREDIENTS EXPLAINED Sesame oil is available in two varieties: toasted and untoasted (or sometimes called "dark" and "light"). The former is more aromatic, tastier in fact; the latter, a tad more esoteric, available at high-end supermarkets and Asian grocery stores. We call for only *toasted sesame oil*.

Because of complex chemical interactions, it can go rancid rather quickly. Open the bottle when you get it home from the supermarket. If you detect a funky, musky tang, take the bottle back for a refund. Once opened, refrigerate it, sealed, for up to 6 months. It will solidify after being chilled; run the sealed jar under warm tap water to loosen up as much as you need.

sweet and sticky country-style ribs

EFFORT: **NOT MUCH** • PREP TIME: **5 MINUTES** • COOK TIME: **8 HOURS** • KEEPS ON WARM: **2 HOURS** • SERVES: **3 TO 10**

INGREDIENTS	2- TO 3½-QT	4- TO 5½-QT	6- TO 8-QT
Bone-in country-style pork ribs	2 pounds	4 pounds	6 pounds
Maple syrup	2 tblsp	¼ cup	6 tblsp
Soy sauce	2 tblsp	¼ cup	6 tblsp
Onion powder	½ tsp	1 tsp	½ tblsp
Ground allspice	¼ tsp	½ tsp	½ tblsp
Ground cinnamon	¼ tsp	½ tsp	½ tblsp
Ground cloves	¼ tsp	½ tsp	1¼ tsp
Ground black pepper	¼ tsp	½ tsp	1¼ tsp

1 Put the ribs in the slow cooker. Whisk the maple syrup, soy sauce, onion powder, allspice, cinnamon, cloves, and pepper in a bowl; pour over the ribs.

2 Cover and cook on low for 8 hours, or until the pork is falling-off-the-bone tender.

TESTERS' NOTES
• Break out the napkins! This sauce turns these economical pork ribs into a decadent feast.
• Layer the country-style ribs as evenly as possible in the slow cooker so they all have an equal chance to be smothered in the sauce. If some are stacked out of the sauce, swap their places halfway through cooking, particularly in a round slow cooker.

INGREDIENTS EXPLAINED Country-style pork ribs, cut from the sirloin end of the pork loin, are meaty ribs, not at all like those used for the standard barbecued pork ribs or baby back ribs, but more like fatty, narrow pork chops. Country-style ribs are sold both bone-in and boneless—we prefer the bone-in variety in most slow cooker recipes because the bone imparts so much flavor. Country-style ribs are often sold in a large slab, particularly at big-box stores. These should be divided into individual ribs, each with a bone (you can ask the butcher to do it for you). Plan on each bone-in country-style rib weighing about ½ pound.

smoky country-style ribs with apples and peppers

EFFORT: **NOT MUCH** • PREP TIME: **15 MINUTES** • COOK TIME: **8 HOURS** • KEEPS ON WARM: **2 HOURS** • SERVES: **3 TO 10**

INGREDIENTS	2- TO 3½-QT	4- TO 5½-QT	6- TO 8-QT
Medium apples (such as Empire or Granny Smith), peeled, cored, and thinly sliced	1	2	3
Red bell peppers, stemmed, seeded, and thinly sliced	1 small	1 medium	2 medium
Yellow onion, thinly sliced	1 small	1 medium	1 large
Bone-in country-style pork ribs	2 pounds	3½ pounds	5 pounds
Reduced-sodium chicken broth	6 tblsp	⅔ cup	1 cup
Mild smoked paprika	½ tblsp	1 tblsp	1½ tblsp
Caraway seeds	1 tsp	2 tsp	1 tblsp
Ground cumin	1 tsp	2 tsp	1 tblsp
Ground cinnamon	½ tsp	1 tsp	1¼ tsp
Salt	½ tsp	¾ tsp	1 tsp
Ground black pepper	½ tsp	¾ tsp	1 tsp

1 Toss the apple, bell pepper, and onion in the slow cooker; make an even layer across the bottom. Lay the ribs on top, overlapping as necessary.

2 Whisk the broth, paprika, caraway seeds, cumin, cinnamon, salt, and pepper in a bowl; pour over the ribs.

3 Cover and cook on low for 8 hours, or until the pork is fork-tender right at the bone.

4 Transfer the ribs to a cutting board. Use a slotted spoon to fish out and then mound the vegetables on a serving platter as a bed for the ribs; set the ribs on top. Skim the sauce in the cooker for any surface fat, then dribble the sauce on top of the ribs.

TESTERS' NOTES
• Country-style ribs are incredibly forgiving, what with all that wonderful fat and collagen melting into the sauce. The best preparations use simple techniques to meld big flavors.
• These ribs freeze exceptionally well. Seal portions in containers and store in the freezer for up to 6 months. Thaw, then reheat the ribs, sauce, and everything else in a microwave-safe bowl or tightly sealed aluminum foil packet in a 350°F oven for 20 minutes.

INGREDIENTS EXPLAINED Smoked paprika is a Spanish and Portuguese favorite, now common in all supermarkets in North America. It's made from dried

(continued)

smoked chiles. It actually comes in several varieties, based on the heat of those chiles as well as the fineness of the grind. We call for only finely ground sweet smoked paprika in this book. Smoked paprika will last about 9 months if stored in a sealed container in a dry, cool place, before the intense flavors begin to fade.

country-style ribs with orange and thyme

EFFORT: **A LITTLE** • PREP TIME: **15 MINUTES** • COOK TIME: **8 HOURS** • KEEPS ON WARM: **4 HOURS** • SERVES: **3 TO 10**

INGREDIENTS	2- TO 3½-QT	4- TO 5½-QT	6- TO 8-QT
Orange, thinly sliced into rings and seeded	1 small	1 medium	2 medium
Fresh thyme sprigs	2	4	6
Fennel seeds	1 tsp	1¾ tsp	2½ tsp
Olive oil	1 tblsp	2 tblsp	3 tblsp
Bone-in country-style pork ribs	2 pounds	3½ pounds	5 pounds
Salt	½ tsp	¾ tsp	1 tsp
Ground black pepper	½ tsp	¾ tsp	1 tsp
Dry red wine, such as Syrah	1 cup	1¾ cups	2½ cups
Honey	2 tsp	1½ tblsp	2 tblsp

1 Lay the orange slices in the bottom of the slow cooker. Lay the thyme sprigs on top and sprinkle the fennel seeds evenly over both.

2 Set a large skillet over medium heat for a few minutes, then swirl in the olive oil. Season the ribs with salt and pepper then slip in a few—as many as will fit without crowding—to brown on all four sides, about 10 minutes per batch. Transfer the ribs to the slow cooker and continue browning as necessary.

3 Pour the wine over everything in the slow cooker, then cover and cook on low for 8 hours, or until the meat almost separates from the bone on each rib. If some ribs sit in the juices while others are more exposed, switch their places halfway through cooking.

4 Transfer the ribs to a serving platter or plates. Remove and discard the orange slices and thyme from the slow cooker; skim the fat off the sauce or pour it into a fat separator, and wait a couple of minutes. In any event, pour the strained sauce into a small sauce-pan, stir in the honey, and bring to a boil over medium-high heat, stirring occasionally. Boil until reduced by half, stirring frequently; then spoon the sauce over the ribs.

TESTERS' NOTES
• We brown the country-style ribs in this recipe to pump up the flavors a bit, a better match for the more assertive ingredients that make up the sauce.
• Feel free to substitute rosemary or marjoram sprigs for the thyme.

italian sunday gravy

EFFORT: **A LOT** • PREP TIME: **1 HOUR** • COOK TIME: **12 HOURS**
• KEEPS ON WARM: **4 HOURS THROUGH STEP 3** • SERVES: **4 TO 12 (OVER COOKED PASTA)**

INGREDIENTS	2- TO 3½-QT	4- TO 5½-QT	6- TO 8-QT
Bone-in country-style pork ribs	1 pound	2 pounds	3 pounds
No-salt-added canned crushed tomatoes	1¼ cups	2⅓ cups	3½ cups
Italian-seasoned canned diced tomatoes	1¼ cups	2⅓ cups	3½ cups
Thinly sliced yellow onions	⅔ cup	1⅓ cups	2 cups
Seeded, stemmed, and thinly sliced green bell peppers	⅔ cup	1⅓ cups	2 cups
Dry white wine, such as Pinot Grigio	⅓ cup	⅔ cup	1 cup
No-salt-added tomato paste	2 tblsp	¼ cup	6 tblsp
Dried oregano	2 tsp	4 tsp	2 tblsp
Dried basil	2 tsp	4 tsp	2 tblsp
Garlic cloves, peeled and thinly sliced	2	3	4
Dried rosemary	1 tsp	2 tsp	1 tblsp
Dried thyme	1 tsp	2 tsp	1 tblsp
Salt	¼ tsp	½ tsp	1 tsp
Ground black pepper	¼ tsp	½ tsp	1 tsp
Grated nutmeg	⅛ tsp	¼ tsp	½ tsp

1 Position the rack in the center of the oven; heat the oven to 450°F. Set the ribs on a large, rimmed baking sheet. Brown them in the oven for about 20 minutes, turning occasionally, until the rendered fat on the tray is beginning to sizzle.

2 Use tongs to transfer the ribs to the slow cooker. Stir in the tomatoes, diced tomatoes, onions, bell peppers, wine, tomato paste, oregano, basil, garlic, rosemary, thyme, salt, pepper, and nutmeg.

3 Cover and cook on low for 10 hours, or until the meat won't even stay on the bones.

4 Use tongs and a big spoon to transfer the ribs from the cooker to a large cutting board. Take care—they may well fall apart. Cool for 10 minutes. Keep the slow cooker covered and on low.

5 Debone the meat and chop it into small bits. Stir it back into the sauce in the cooker.

6 Cook on high, uncovered, for 2 hours, or until the entire stew has thickened somewhat.

TESTERS' NOTES

• A recipe just like your *nonna* used to make, this is the classic pasta sauce reconstructed for the slow cooker. It takes all day, just as her sauce would. But you don't have to stir as frequently.

• The ribs are browned in the oven, not just in a skillet on the stovetop, in an attempt to burn some flavor into the bones themselves, not just brown the meat.

• Only dried herbs will do here; don't be tempted to use fresh. The dried ones have a subtler, milder, somewhat darker taste.

• Take care that you pick all the bones out of the ribs, including any extraneous bits left from careless butchering.

• This sauce freezes well. Cool for about 30 minutes, then ladle it into zip-closed bags or plastic containers, seal, and store in the freezer for up to 6 months. Thaw in the fridge overnight, then reheat in a covered saucepan set over low heat until hot and bubbling.

Serve It Up! You'll need cooked pasta—pappardelle, spinach fettuccini, or perhaps a shape like farfalle or ziti. And add lots of freshly grated Parmigiano-Reggiano.

spicy country-style ribs with fried garlic

EFFORT: **A LITTLE** • PREP TIME: **35 MINUTES** • COOK TIME: **8 HOURS** • KEEPS ON WARM: **3 HOURS** • SERVES: **3 TO 10**

INGREDIENTS	2- TO 3½-QT	4- TO 5½-QT	6- TO 8-QT
Yellow onion, chopped	1 small	1 medium	1 large
Cider vinegar	1½ tblsp	2½ tblsp	⅓ cup
Minced peeled fresh ginger	1 tblsp	4 tsp	2½ tblsp
Ground coriander	1 tsp	½ tblsp	2½ tsp
Ground cumin	1 tsp	½ tblsp	2½ tsp
Dry mustard (see page 392)	1 tsp	½ tblsp	2¼ tsp
Salt	½ tsp	1 tsp	1¼ tsp
Ground cardamom	¼ tsp	½ tsp	¾ tsp
Cayenne	¼ tsp	½ tsp	¾ tsp
Ground cloves	⅛ tsp	¼ tsp	½ tsp
Bone-in country-style pork ribs	2 pounds	3½ pounds	5 pounds
Peanut oil	2 tsp	1 tblsp	2 tblsp
Thinly sliced peeled garlic	¼ cup	⅓ cup	½ cup
Sweet white wine, such as German Auslese	¼ cup	6 tblsp	⅔ cup

1 Mix the onion, vinegar, ginger, coriander, cumin, mustard, salt, cardamom, cayenne, and cloves in the slow cooker. Add the ribs; toss repeatedly to coat thoroughly.

2 Heat the oil in a large skillet over medium heat for a few minutes. Add the garlic and cook, stirring often, until the garlic blisters and even browns a bit at its edges. Spoon the contents of the skillet over everything in the slow cooker. Drizzle the wine on top.

3 Cover and cook on low for 8 hours, or until the pork is aromatic, sweet, and ridiculously tender. Transfer the pork ribs to a serving platter or plates; skim any fat off the sauce in the cooker and serve it on the side.

TESTERS' NOTES
• Blistering the garlic takes it beyond the sweet, adding bitter notes. These will mellow in the cooker but still provide a bit of sophistication in a very aromatic dish.
• Although this dish freezes fairly well, the texture of the pork is uncompromised after the thaw but the spices will dull a bit. Stir lemon juice or white wine vinegar into portions before reheating to brighten the flavors.

Serve It Up! Can't get enough garlic? Fry slivered garlic and cumin seeds in peanut oil in a skillet over medium heat until the garlic browns and the cumin seeds start to pop, stirring often. Spoon this over the top of the stew.

country-style ribs with red ale and roots

EFFORT: **A LITTLE** • PREP TIME: **12 HOURS 15 MINUTES (INCLUDES MARINATING THE RIBS)** • COOK TIME: **8 HOURS** • KEEPS ON WARM: **2 HOURS** • SERVES: **3 TO 8**

INGREDIENTS	2- TO 3½-QT	4- TO 5½-QT	6- TO 8-QT
Bone-in country-style pork ribs	1½ pounds	2½ pounds	4 pounds
Red ale	½ cup	1 cup	2 cups

Minced fresh rosemary leaves	1 tblsp	2 tblsp	3 tblsp
Finely grated lemon zest	1 tsp	2 tsp	1 tblsp
Minced garlic	1 tsp	2 tsp	1 tblsp
Carrots, peeled and cut into 1-inch pieces	½ pound	¾ pound	1¼ pounds
Parsnips, peeled and cut into 1-inch pieces	½ pound	¾ pound	1¼ pounds
Salt	¼ tsp	½ tsp	¾ tsp
Ground black pepper	¼ tsp	½ tsp	¾ tsp

1 Combine the ribs, ale, rosemary, lemon zest, and garlic in a big bowl. Cover and refrigerate for 12 hours or up to 16 hours, tossing occasionally so the ribs swap places in the marinade.

2 Pour everything from the bowl into the slow cooker; let stand uncovered at room temperature for 20 minutes.

3 Stir in the carrots, parsnips, salt, and pepper.

4 Cover and cook on low for 8 hours, or until the pork is fork-tender, particularly at the bone. Use tongs or a large slotted spoon to transfer the ribs and vegetables to a serving platter or plates. Defat the sauce by skimming it with a spoon; drizzle it over the ribs and vegetables.

TESTERS' NOTES
• If you have a slow cooker with a removable insert, marinate the ribs in the ale and aromatics overnight, covered, in the fridge. Since the container itself will be chilly, let it all stand at room temperature for 30 minutes before proceeding with the recipe. You may also have to add up to 1 hour to the cooking time, depending on how quickly your appliance takes the chill off everything.
• If you find rosemary too assertive in this dish, try minced marjoram leaves.

• Use a red ale, not a red cola! The best red ales come from Ireland or Belgium, although a few U.S. producers have gotten into the game. They add a pleasing, herbaceous bitterness to a very smooth, moderately sweet finish.

rum-glazed baby back ribs

EFFORT: **A LITTLE** • PREP TIME: **20 MINUTES** • COOK TIME: **8 HOURS** • KEEPS ON WARM: **2 HOURS** • SERVES: **2 TO 8**

INGREDIENTS	2- TO 3½-QT	4- TO 5½-QT	6- TO 8-QT
Packed dark brown sugar	1½ tblsp	1 tblsp	2 tblsp
Mild smoked paprika	½ tsp	1 tsp	2 tsp
Dry mustard (see page 392)	¼ tsp	½ tsp	1 tsp
Ground ginger	¼ tsp	½ tsp	1 tsp
Salt	¼ tsp	½ tsp	1 tsp
Baby back ribs, cut into 2- or 4-bone sections	1½ pounds	3½ pounds	6 pounds
Thinly sliced yellow onion	½ cup (about 1 small)	1 cup	1½ cups
4-inch cinnamon stick	½	1	2
Dark rum, such as Myers's	¼ cup	½ cup	¾ cup
No-salt-added tomato paste	1 tblsp	2 tblsp	3 tblsp
Honey	1 tblsp	2 tblsp	3 tblsp
Cider vinegar	½ tblsp	1 tblsp	1½ tblsp

1 Mix the brown sugar, paprika, mustard, ginger, and salt in a small bowl; rub the mixture onto the ribs. Set them in the slow cooker, stacking them with a little airspace between

(continued)

the ribs, standing them on their sides or over-lapping as necessary.

2 Add the onion and cinnamon stick to the cooker, placing them on and around the ribs.

3 Whisk the rum, tomato paste, honey, and vinegar in a small bowl; pour over the ribs.

4 Cover and cook on low for 8 hours, or until the ribs are very tender and can be pulled apart at the base of each section.

5 Move the ribs to a serving platter. Discard the cinnamon stick. Defat the sauce in the cooker by skimming it with a spoon, then pour the sauce into a medium saucepan. Bring to a boil over high heat, stirring often. Boil until reduced by half, continuing to stir with even a little more urgency, then drizzle some of the sauce on the ribs and pass the rest on the side for the dippers in the crowd.

TESTERS' NOTES
• This sticky, sweet barbecue sauce is a great match for pork ribs. Best of all, you don't have to make the sauce stovetop; it melds into a sauce right in the cooker.
• We cut the ribs into sections so they'll fit into any shape cooker. Although it's easy to separate the racks into individual ribs once the connective tissue has melted, it can be tough work separating them while they're still raw. It you want to simplify the job, have the supermarket's butcher do it for you—although you'll have to know the approximate dimensions of your cooker so you can tell him just how many ribs to leave connected in each section.

INGREDIENTS EXPLAINED Baby back ribs—also called *loin ribs* or *Canadian back ribs*—are the ribs right off the backbone, above the spare ribs but often taken from smaller hogs. They have become the quintessential rib rack in the United States. Baby back ribs offer sweet, fatty bits of meat between the rib bones, perfect for gnawing. So take your time! Some wet paper towels will come in handy at the table.

apricot-glazed ham

EFFORT: **A LITTLE** • PREP TIME: **40 MINUTES** • COOK TIME: **8 TO 10 HOURS** • KEEPS ON WARM: **3 HOURS** • SERVES: **6 TO 12**

INGREDIENTS	4- TO 5½-QT	6- TO 8-QT
Chopped dried apricots	⅓ cup	½ cup
Packed light brown sugar	⅓ cup	½ cup
Dijon mustard	2 tblsp	3 tblsp
Ground cinnamon	½ tsp	¾ tsp
Ground cloves	¼ tsp	¼ tsp
Grated nutmeg	¼ tsp	¼ tsp
Bone-in smoked ham, butt or shank end	4 pounds	8 pounds

1 Bring a small saucepan of water to a boil over high heat. Put the apricots in a small bowl; cover with boiling water. Set aside for 30 minutes.

2 Drain the apricots in a fine-mesh sieve or small-holed colander set in the sink. Set them in a small bowl; add the brown sugar, mustard, cinnamon, cloves, and nutmeg. Use a spoon to mash the ingredients into a paste.

3 Place the ham cut side down—or any way that will fit—in the slow cooker. Smear the exposed meat with the apricot paste.

4 Cover and cook on low for 8 hours in a medium cooker or 10 hours in a large cooker, or until the tender meat has pulled away from the bone but still holds its shape when sliced. If you make a slice into the ham in the cooker, you'll be able to tell its consistency.

5 Transfer the ham to a carving board; let stand for 10 minutes before slicing.

TESTERS' NOTES
• This tangy paste is made even better if you use bright orange California apricots, which are more sour than the pale Turkish ones.
• Don't have any dried apricots on hand? Use chopped pitted prunes or stemmed dried figs for a sweeter glaze. Or try pitted dates (but soak them in the hot water for only 10 minutes).

INGREDIENTS EXPLAINED A ham is the hindquarter of the pig. A whole ham is actually the hip joint, part of the buttocks, and a part of the thigh. It's almost never sold in this gargantuan state but is instead sliced in half, creating the butt and shank ends. The former, higher up on the hog, has a complex structure of bones and more fat; the latter, the traditional version shown in Norman Rockwell paintings, has a single bone running through its center and tapers to one end.

ALL-AMERICAN KNOW-HOW Slow cookers and hams are not necessarily a match made in heaven—because of fit, not technique. To make sure you can complete a ham recipe, measure the depth and width of your model before you head to the supermarket. Take the tape measure with you and measure the hams in the case. You may find a slightly smaller ham will fit—or even a slightly larger one. Adjust the cooking time proportionally.

Serve It Up! To carve a shank-end ham, make thin slices around the thigh bone, starting at the large end of the roast and cutting into the meat perpendicular to that bone. Of course, you'll never get a whole slice off. Rather, slice a few thin pieces from one side, then turn the ham over and slice a few more from another spot, all the time working your way around that bone. Occasionally, run your knife along the surface plane of the bone to loosen more meat from it as you carve.

When you carve a butt-end ham, you'll end up with some slices, but also with chunks and ends. Look for the larger sections of meat and slice down, creating thin slices, some of which may fall apart because of the way the muscles are shaped. If you find your cuts are falling into too many pieces at any point, hack off a whole quadrant and slice it into thin pieces and irregular chunks on the carving board.

pork and beans

EFFORT: **NOT MUCH** • PREP TIME: **10 MINUTES** • COOK TIME: **10 HOURS** • KEEPS ON WARM: **4 HOURS THROUGH STEP 2** • SERVES: **5 TO 10**

INGREDIENTS	4- TO 5½-QT	6- TO 8-QT
Water	3 cups	6 cups
Chili powder	1 tblsp	2 tblsp
Dried oregano	½ tblsp	1 tblsp
Ground cumin	½ tblsp	1 tblsp
Onion powder	½ tblsp	1 tblsp
Chopped pickled jalapeño rings	2 tblsp	¼ cup
Dried pinto beans	1 cup	2 cups
Bone-in smoked ham	2½ pounds	4 pounds
Salt (optional)	¼ tsp	½ tsp

1 Mix the water, chili powder, oregano, cumin, and onion powder in the slow cooker. Stir in the pinto beans. Nestle the ham into the mixture.

2 Cover and cook on low for 10 hours, or until the meat falls from the bone and is completely shreddable.

(continued)

3 Move the ham from the cooker to a carving board (you may need to do this in pieces, as the meat will fall apart). Let stand for 10 minutes. Keep the cooker covered and on low.

4 Shred the meat off the bones and discard the bones. Scoop about 1 cup of beans from the cooker with a slotted spoon and pour them into a small bowl. Mash them into a paste with the back of a wooden spoon. Stir this paste and the shredded meat (as well as the salt, if desired) into the cooker to serve.

TESTERS' NOTES
• There's no denying that a smoked ham makes the best pork and beans, far leaner but also more tasty than hocks or the random bits of meat used in commercial productions.
• The mashed beans help thicken the stew. If you like, cover and cook on low for an additional 30 minutes to make sure everything's hot when served.
• The amount of ham here is actually a bit less than the previous ham recipe. Have the butcher cut a ham down to size; freeze the other parts for more pork and beans in the months to come.
• Nope, you can't really make this dish in a small slow cooker. You'll almost never find a bone-in ham small enough. That said, you could make it with bone-in ham steaks. Use 1½ pounds and half the stated amounts for the other ingredients as listed for a 4- to 5½-quart slow cooker.

Serve It Up! This is a meal, not a side dish—and best for bowls. Have warmed flour tortillas, sour cream, grated cheese, and even pickle relish for accoutrements.

chinese-style braised pork belly

EFFORT: **A LITTLE** • PREP TIME: **12 HOURS 20 MINUTES (INCLUDES MARINATING THE PORK BELLY)** • COOK TIME: **8 HOURS** • KEEPS ON WARM: **4 HOURS** • SERVES: **4 TO 12**

INGREDIENTS	2- TO 3½-QT	4- TO 5½-QT	6- TO 8-QT
Fresh pork belly, any rind removed	1½ pounds	3 pounds	4½ pounds
Soy sauce	5 tblsp	⅔ cup	1 cup
Packed dark brown sugar	¼ cup	½ cup	¾ cup
Dry sherry	2 tblsp	¼ cup	6 tblsp
Reduced-sodium chicken broth	⅓ cup	⅔ cup	1 cup
Minced peeled fresh ginger	1 tblsp	2 tblsp	3 tblsp
Whole medium scallions, cut into 1-inch pieces	6	12	18
Garlic cloves, peeled and smashed	2	4	5
Serrano chiles, stemmed and halved	1	2	2
4-inch cinnamon sticks	1	2	2
Star anise	1	2	2

1 Cut the pork belly into 2-inch chunks. Set them in a large bowl and toss with the soy sauce, brown sugar, and sherry until evenly coated. Cover and refrigerate for at least 12 hours or up to 16 hours.

2 Remove the meat from the marinade (reserve any juice in the bowl). Pat the chunks dry with paper towels. Heat a large skillet over medium heat; add a batch of pork chunks to the skillet, just enough so there's no crowding.

Brown on all sides, about 10 minutes per batch. As they're ready, transfer them to the slow cooker and continue browning more.

3 Scrape any reserved marinade from the bowl into the cooker. Stir in the broth, ginger, scallions, garlic, chiles, cinnamon sticks, and star anise.

4 Cover and cook on low for 8 hours, or until very tender.

5 Use a slotted spoon to move the chunks of pork belly to a heat-safe serving bowl or platter. Spoon or ladle the sauce through a strainer and into a fat separator. Discard the aromatics and set aside for 10 minutes. Pour the skimmed sauce into a small saucepan, bring it to a boil over high heat, and reduce to half its volume, about 3 to 8 minutes. Pour the sauce over the pork belly.

TESTERS' NOTES
• This Asian-style preparation yields aromatic chunks of fatty meat with a rich, heady broth.
• Dry the marinated cubes well so they'll brown properly. For even better browning, let them sit out of the marinade at room temperature for 20 minutes before browning.

Serve It Up! Have bowls of cooked medium-grain white or brown rice at everyone's place. Use chopsticks or a spoon to reach into the cooker to pull out a few pieces at a time and set them on the rice. Drip bits of the sauce over the pork in the bowls, if desired.

INGREDIENTS EXPLAINED Pork belly is about the most ridiculously decadent cut of pork you can find. Most of it is cured for bacon. For this recipe, choose a large fresh (that is, *uncured*) slab to cut into chunks. Make sure the butcher has removed any rind. While you're at it, look for a slab of pork belly with plenty of meat, not just rifts of fat.

hoppin' john

EFFORT: **A LITTLE** • PREP TIME: **12 HOURS 20 MINUTES (INCLUDES SOAKING THE PEAS)** • COOK TIME: **9 HOURS** • KEEPS ON WARM: **NO** • SERVES: **2 TO 8**

INGREDIENTS	2- TO 3½-QT	4- TO 5½-QT	6- TO 8-QT
Dried black-eyed peas	½ cup	1 cup	2 cups
Reduced-sodium chicken broth	1 cup	2 cups	4 cups (1 quart)
Drained no-salt-added canned diced tomatoes	6 tblsp	¾ cup	1½ cups
Minced yellow onion	6 tblsp	¾ cup	1½ cups
Stemmed, seeded, and minced green bell pepper	6 tblsp	¾ cup	1½ cups
Minced celery	¼ cup	½ cup	1 cup
Cajun seasoning blend	1 tsp	½ tblsp	1 tblsp
Smoked ham hocks	1	1	2
Long-grain white rice	¼ cup	½ cup	1 cup
Thinly sliced whole scallions	1 tblsp	2 tblsp	¼ cup

1 Put the black-eyed peas in a large bowl, fill the bowl about two-thirds with cool tap water, and soak for at least 12 hours or up to 20 hours.

2 Drain the peas in a colander set in the sink; scatter them in the slow cooker. Stir in the broth, tomatoes, onion, bell pepper, celery, and Cajun seasoning; nestle in the ham hock.

3 Cover and cook on low for 8 hours, or until the meat easily falls off the bones. Move the hock to a cutting board (a wooden spoon in the other hand helps for balance). Keep the slow cooker covered and on low.

(continued)

4 Cool the meat for a couple of minutes, then shred it off the bones. Discard the bones (look for little bits and chips), then chop the meat and stir it back into the stew in the slow cooker.

5 Stir in the rice and scallions. Cover and cook on high for 1 hour, or until the rice is tender and the stew has thickened considerably.

TESTERS' NOTES

• Hoppin' John is a West African dish that has long been a staple in Southern kitchens. It's a mix of rice, black-eyed peas, and vegetables, sometimes made with fatback, but here with the somewhat leaner ham hock.

• Some hocks are kept luridly pink, thanks to lots of saltpeter and other preservatives. If you want to skip this chemical treatment, look for nitrate-free smoked ham hocks or uncured smoked ham hocks. There's no additional salt required here since the hock will have plenty.

Serve It Up! Hoppin' John is sometimes served on New Year's Day, a harbinger of good luck for the year ahead. Serve it with steamed or sautéed greens (particularly collard greens) for a more substantial meal.

lion's head meatballs

EFFORT: **A LOT** • PREP TIME: **45 MINUTES** • COOK TIME: **6 HOURS** • KEEPS ON WARM: **2 HOURS** • SERVES: **2 TO 6**

INGREDIENTS	2- TO 3½-QT	4- TO 5½-QT	6- TO 8-QT
Dried shiitake mushrooms	8	10	16
Cored and shredded napa cabbage	4 cups	6 cups	10 cups
Chopped canned water chestnuts	¾ cup	1 cup	1¾ cups
Sliced scallion greens, in ½-inch pieces	½ cup	⅔ cup	1 cup
Peeled and minced fresh ginger	2 tblsp	3 tblsp	⅓ cup
Lean ground pork	1 pound	1½ pounds	2½ pounds
Minced scallion whites	¼ cup	6 tblsp	1 cup
Ground ginger	1 tsp	½ tblsp	2 tsp
Soy sauce	3 tblsp	⅓ cup	½ cup
Worcestershire sauce	1 tblsp	1½ tblsp	2½ tblsp
Balsamic vinegar	1 tblsp	1½ tblsp	2½ tblsp

1 Bring a pan of water to a boil over high heat. Set the dried mushrooms in a bowl; fill the bowl about two-thirds with boiling water. Set aside to steep for 20 minutes.

2 Drain the mushrooms in a colander set over a bowl to catch the soaking liquid (now a mushroom stock). Cut off and discard the shiitake stems. Slice the caps into thin strips; toss with the cabbage, water chestnuts, scallion greens, and fresh ginger in the slow cooker.

3 Mix the ground pork, scallion whites, and ground ginger in a large bowl. Form the mixture into one large meatball for a small slow cooker, two for a medium one, or three for a large one. Set the meatballs in the cabbage mixture.

4 Whisk the soy sauce, Worcestershire sauce, and balsamic vinegar in a large bowl. Whisk in 1 cup reserved mushroom stock for a small slow cooker, 1½ cups for a medium cooker, or 2½ cups for a large cooker. Pour over the meatballs and vegetables in the cooker.

5 Cover and cook on low for 6 hours, or until the pork is cooked through and the cabbage is tender. Serve by cutting the meatball into pie-shaped wedges and offering these atop the vegetables and sauce.

TESTERS' NOTES

• These large meatballs are a specialty of Cantonese cooking—and so of American Chinese cooking as well.
• The big meatballs—said to look like a lion's head with a cabbage mane around it—can sometimes fall apart when poached on the stovetop. The slow cooker solves that problem with its even, low heat.

pork and sausage meatballs with pasta sauce

EFFORT: **A LITTLE** • PREP TIME: **20 MINUTES** • COOK TIME: **10 HOURS** • KEEPS ON WARM: **1 HOUR** • SERVES: **4 TO 8**

INGREDIENTS	2- TO 3½-QT	4- TO 5½-QT	6- TO 8-QT
Cremini or brown button mushrooms, sliced	6 ounces (about 2 cups)	10 ounces (about 3 cups)	13 ounces (about 4 cups)
No-salt-added canned diced tomatoes	1¾ cups	2⅔ cups	3½ cups
No-salt-added tomato paste	¾ cup	1 cup plus 2 tblsp	1½ cups
Chopped yellow onion	⅓ cup	⅔ cup	1 cup (about 1 medium)
Stemmed, seeded, and chopped green bell pepper	⅓ cup	⅔ cup	1 cup (about 1 medium)
Full-bodied red wine, such as Syrah or Zinfandel	⅓ cup	⅔ cup	1 cup
Minced fresh basil leaves	2 tblsp	3 tblsp	¼ cup
Dried oregano	1 tsp	½ tblsp	2 tsp
Dried rosemary	1 tsp	½ tblsp	2 tsp
Dried thyme	1 tsp	½ tblsp	2 tsp
Salt	¼ tsp	½ tsp	1 tsp
Ground black pepper	¼ tsp	½ tsp	1 tsp
Grated nutmeg	⅛ tsp	¼ tsp	½ tsp
Lean ground pork	6 ounces	½ pound	¾ pound
Mild Italian sausage, any casings removed	6 ounces	½ pound	¾ pound
Pine nuts	2 tblsp	3 tblsp	¼ cup
Plain dry breadcrumbs	2 tblsp	3 tblsp	¼ cup

1 Mix the mushrooms, tomatoes, tomato paste, onion, bell pepper, wine, basil, oregano, rosemary, thyme, salt, pepper, and nutmeg in the slow cooker until the tomato paste dissolves in the mix.

2 Mix the ground pork, sausage meat, pine nuts, and breadcrumbs in a large bowl. Use your clean dry hands to form this mixture into meatballs, each with a scant ¼ cup. Put the meatballs into the sauce in the cooker.

3 Cover and cook on low for 10 hours, or until the sauce has thickened a bit and the meatballs are cooked through.

TESTERS' NOTES

• This is a complex dish, packed with herbs and spices. Classic comfort food, sophisticated flavors, and a fairly easy technique—what could be better?

(continued)

• We've used two kinds of pork here: the standard ground pork for its luxurious sweetness and Italian-style pork sausage for its flavorings and somewhat coarser texture.
• For even more flavor, toast the pine nuts in a dry skillet over medium-low heat until lightly browned, stirring often, about 5 minutes. Cool for 30 minutes before using them.

SHORTCUTS Use frozen chopped onion and bell pepper. Make sure the vegetables are thoroughly thawed—if not even at room temperature—before adding them.

Serve It Up! Have some cooked pasta already in the bowls when the meal is ready. For more flavor, first toss the hot, drained pasta with a little crumbled goat cheese.

kielbasa with sauerkraut and apples

EFFORT: **NOT MUCH** • PREP TIME: **15 MINUTES** • COOK TIME: **6 HOURS** • KEEPS ON WARM: **2 HOURS** • SERVES: **2 TO 6**

INGREDIENTS	2- TO 3½-QT	4- TO 5½-QT	6- TO 8-QT
Packaged sauerkraut	½ pound	1 pound	2½ pounds
Dry white wine or dry vermouth	¾ cup	1½ cups	3½ cups
Shredded cored apple	¾ cup	1½ cups	3½ cups
Peeled and shredded Russet potatoes	¾ cup	1½ cups	3½ cups
Caraway seeds	¼ tsp	½ tsp	1¼ tsp
Ground black pepper	¼ tsp	½ tsp	1¼ tsp
Smoked kielbasa, cut into 6-inch lengths	¾ pound	1½ pounds	4 pounds

1 Drain the sauerkraut in a colander set in the sink; squeeze it by handfuls over the sink before dropping it into the slow cooker. Stir in the wine, apple, potatoes, caraway seeds, and pepper. Press the sausage into the mixture.

2 Cover and cook on low for 6 hours, or until the kielbasa is hot and the potatoes in the mix are quite tender.

TESTERS' NOTES
• For the best taste, use the packaged sauerkraut in plastic bags at the deli counter, the kind that must be refrigerated in a dated package. Avoid the canned stuff.
• There's no need to peel the apples. Shred them through the large holes of a box grater, stopping when you get down to the tough core.
• Use only Russet potatoes. They have the right balance of starch and moisture to thicken the sauce without leaving it too wet or too dry. Shred them through the large holes of a box grater.

lamb

Lamb was once a no-no on the American dinner table. Still is, for many of us. Frankly, the meat has suffered from taste and texture problems. It even has had seasonal issues. Like turkey, it was a holiday dish, best served, not in the fall, but the spring. Who makes lamb in June?

We do. Everyone should. True, lamb is a bigger taste than beef or pork, but that's to our advantage. We can ramp up the garlic and still not overshadow the meat.

That said, lamb shouldn't have to be off-putting. A dank funkiness is a sign that the lamb was older than nine months—almost mutton—or that the meat hasn't been sold quickly enough from the supermarket. Good-quality, young lamb should be aromatic, even sweet, with only a bit of earthy complexity. If you're ever in doubt, ask to smell the raw lamb at the supermarket. You'll be able to tell if the lamb is sweet the moment the butcher opens the package for you. Look for a clean, fresh, light aroma with the barest hint of minerality.

Of any meat, lamb affords the most leeway in its cooking time. And this, even more than its taste, may be the reason it's often considered right for a holiday dish, or for a day when you're not tied to the clock. A lamb stew may take 6 to 8 hours to finish up in the slow cooker; a leg of lamb, 7 to 10 hours to get tender. Such swings are based on many factors: how old the lamb was, what it was fed, how stressed it was in its life, and even when it was purchased. Start checking a stew an hour before it should be done; a larger cut, two hours before. And be prepared to keep cooking it until the meat is tender and juicy. You'll know by that tried-and-true fork test: a fork should go into and *come out of* the meat without much resistance. If you've got to push *or* pull, you've got to cook it longer.

So fire up the slow cooker! It's time this maligned meat got its due.

lamb chops with apricots and pumpkin seeds

EFFORT: **NOT MUCH** • PREP TIME: **15 MINUTES** • COOK TIME:
8 HOURS • KEEPS ON WARM: **3 HOURS** • SERVES: **3 TO 9**

INGREDIENTS	2- TO 3½-QT	4- TO 5½-QT	6- TO 8-QT
Bone-in lamb shoulder chops, cut into 2- to 3-inch chunks	1½ pounds	2½ pounds	4½ pounds
Thinly sliced red onion	⅓ cup	1 cup (about 1 small)	1¾ cups
Dried apricots, halved	3	8	14
Green pumpkin seeds (pepitas; see page 124), toasted	1½ tblsp	¼ cup	7 tblsp
Minced garlic	1 tsp	2 tsp	1 tblsp
Cider vinegar	1 tblsp	3 tblsp	5 tblsp
Ground cumin	½ tsp	1½ tsp	2½ tsp
Ground coriander	½ tsp	1 tsp	1½ tsp
Ground ginger	½ tsp	1 tsp	1½ tsp
Ground cinnamon	¼ tsp	½ tsp	1 tsp
Fennel seeds	¼ tsp	½ tsp	1 tsp
Saffron	⅛ tsp	¼ tsp	½ tsp
Salt	⅛ tsp	¼ tsp	½ tsp
Ground black pepper	⅛ tsp	¼ tsp	½ tsp
Reduced-sodium chicken broth	3 tblsp	½ cup	1 cup
No-salt-added tomato paste	2½ tsp	2 tblsp	3½ tblsp
Packed dark brown sugar	1 tsp	2 tsp	1 tblsp

1 Dump the cut-up chops, onion, apricots, pumpkin seeds, and garlic into the slow cooker.

2 Stir the vinegar, cumin, coriander, ginger, cinnamon, fennel seeds, saffron, salt, and pepper into a paste in a small bowl. Scrape the paste into the cooker, then use your clean, dry hands to toss everything until the meat and other ingredients are evenly coated in the paste.

3 Clean and dry your hands again. Whisk the broth, tomato paste, and brown sugar in a large bowl until the brown sugar dissolves. Pour this mixture over everything in the cooker.

4 Cover and cook on low for 8 hours, or until the meat is quite tender, particularly at the bone.

TESTERS' NOTES

• An aromatic—rather than spicy—curry blend, this one complements the lamb, making a comfort-food meal quick and easy.
• If you're not comfortable working with your hands in step 2, use two wooden spoons, although you'll have to use quite a bit of elbow grease to get the meat coated in the spices.
• Lamb shoulder chops can be quite fatty, but we don't advise trimming them because you'll then lose the collagen and connective tissue, both of which melt into the sauce to make it richer and more satisfying.

Serve It Up! For a **Grilled Corn Side Salad:** Grill ears of corn and slices of red onion until lightly browned (or use a grill pan and swab the vegetables with a little olive oil). Slice the kernels off the ears; chop the onions into kernel-sized bits. Toss them both in a bowl with olive oil, lime juice, salt, and red pepper flakes.

INGREDIENTS EXPLAINED A lamb shoulder chop is the most economical sort of lamb chop, taken from up near the front of the animal rather than off the ribs or back near the loin. There's a complex structure of bones in the chops, so chunk them up by trying to get a bit of bone in each piece. By the way, we don't recommend rib or loin lamb chops in the slow cooker. They're just too expensive to braise—and terrific quick-cookers, to boot!

lamb chops
with sun-dried tomatoes and chickpeas

EFFORT: **NOT MUCH** • PREP TIME: **15 MINUTES** • COOK TIME:
8 HOURS • KEEPS ON WARM: **4 HOURS** • SERVES: **3 TO 9**

INGREDIENTS	2- TO 3½-QT	4- TO 5½-QT	6- TO 8-QT
Drained and rinsed canned chickpeas	1 cup	1¾ cups	3 cups
Fennel bulbs, trimmed and chopped	5 ounces (about ⅔ cup)	½ pound (about 1 cup)	1 pound (about 2 cups)
Leeks (white and pale green part only), halved lengthwise, washed to remove internal grit, and thinly sliced	3 ounces (about ⅓ cup)	¼ pound (about ½ cup)	½ pound (about 1 cup)
Chopped sun-dried tomatoes	3½ tblsp	⅓ cup	½ cup
Fresh orange juice	1 tblsp	2 tblsp	3 tblsp
Dijon mustard	2 tsp	4 tsp	2 tblsp
Finely grated orange zest	1 tsp	½ tblsp	2 tsp
Salt	¼ tsp	½ tsp	1 tsp
Ground black pepper	¼ tsp	½ tsp	1 tsp
Garlic cloves, peeled and slivered	2	4	6
Bone-in lamb shoulder chops, cut into 2- to 3-inch pieces	1½ pounds	2½ pounds	4½ pounds

1 Stir the chickpeas, fennel, leeks, sun-dried tomatoes, orange juice, mustard, orange zest, salt, pepper, and garlic in the slow cooker. Add the lamb chops; toss well.

2 Cover and cook on low for 8 hours, or until the meat is wonderfully tender and sweet.

TESTERS' NOTES
• Canned chickpeas can range in quality: inferior brands are mushy and tasteless; better-quality ones are firm with a delicate earthiness. Here, their flavors blend with the vegetables and orange juice to tip the dish toward a southern Mediterranean flavor.
• Use dry sun-dried tomatoes, often found in the produce section, rather than those packed in oil.
• Choose an organically grown orange, since you'll be using the peel. As a rule, take the zest from a fruit *before* you take the juice.

ALL-AMERICAN KNOW-HOW Fennel bulbs must be trimmed *before* they can be chopped. Take off the feathery fronds as well as the stalks that come out of the bulb. (Both can be stored in the freezer to be added to soups, stews, or stocks.) Cut off any browned or discolored areas as well as the tough, dried-out bottom of the bulb. Slice the bulb in half from the fronds to the root, then set the halves cut side down on your cutting board. Slice them into thin strips, then turn these strips sideways and slice crosswise into the segments you need.

hunan lamb

EFFORT: **NOT MUCH** • PREP TIME: **15 MINUTES** • COOK TIME:
8 HOURS • KEEPS ON WARM: **4 HOURS** • SERVES: **3 TO 9**

INGREDIENTS	2- TO 3½-QT	4- TO 5½-QT	6- TO 8-QT
Bone-in lamb shoulder chops, cut into 2- or 3-inch pieces	1½ pounds	2½ pounds	4½ pounds
Leeks (white and pale green part only), halved lengthwise, washed for grit, and thinly sliced	¾ pound	1¼ pounds	2 pounds
Minced whole scallions	¼ cup	⅓ cup (about 1 medium)	½ cup
Soy sauce	2 tblsp	3 tblsp	⅓ cup
Dry sherry	2 tblsp	3 tblsp	⅓ cup
Asian chile oil (see page 182)	½ tblsp	2 tblsp	3 tblsp
Minced peeled fresh ginger	2 tsp	1 tblsp	2 tblsp
Minced garlic	2 tsp	1 tblsp	2 tblsp
Cumin seeds	2 tsp	1 tblsp	2 tblsp
Ground black pepper	¼ tsp	½ tsp	¾ tsp

1 Toss the cut-up lamb, leeks, scallions, soy sauce, sherry, chile oil, ginger, garlic, cumin seeds, and pepper in the slow cooker until the meat is coated in the liquids and aromatics.

2 Cover and cook on low for 8 hours, or until the stew is irresistibly aromatic.

TESTERS' NOTES
• This Hunan dish is, yes, spicy, but it's actually far more fragrant thanks to all those cumin seeds. Believe it or not, we've actually held back on their number to accommodate American palates. If you want an even more authentic taste, add up to 50 percent more.

• Why leeks and scallions? Leeks add a subtle, slightly dull sweetness, while scallions offer a bright springtime spark.
• Pass extra chile oil or sambal oelek (see page 404) at the table to spice things up even more.

lamb chops with red wine, carrots, and prunes

EFFORT: **A LITTLE** • PREP TIME: **20 MINUTES** • COOK TIME: **8 HOURS**
• KEEPS ON WARM: **4 HOURS** • SERVES: **2 TO 8**

INGREDIENTS	2- TO 3½-QT	4- TO 5½-QT	6- TO 8-QT
Olive oil	½ tblsp	1 tblsp	2 tblsp
Bone-in lamb shoulder chops, cut into 2- to 3-inch pieces	1 pound	2 pounds	4 pounds
Salt	¼ tsp	½ tsp	1 tsp
Ground black pepper	⅛ tsp	¼ tsp	½ tsp
Large shallots, peeled and halved	2	4	8
Full-bodied dry red wine, such as Côtes-du-Rhône or Cabernet Franc	¾ cup	1½ cups	3 cups
Baby carrots	6	10	16
Pitted prunes, halved	2	4	8
4-inch rosemary sprigs	1	2	4
Fresh thyme sprigs	1	1	2

1 Heat a large skillet over medium heat for a couple of minutes, then swirl in the oil. Season the lamb chunks with salt and pepper, then set enough of them in the skillet that they can brown properly without overcrowding. Turn after 2 or 3 minutes, and continue browning on the other side. Transfer the browned chops to the slow cooker.

2 Place the shallots in the skillet, still set over medium heat. Cook until browned, turning only occasionally, 4 to 5 minutes. Transfer the shallots to the slow cooker.

3 Pour the wine into the hot skillet, still over the heat. Bring to a full boil, scraping up any browned bits in the skillet. Scrape and pour its contents into the slow cooker.

4 Stir in the carrots and prunes; toss well. Tuck the rosemary and thyme sprigs into the mixture.

5 Cover and cook on low for 8 hours, or until the meat is quite tender.

TESTERS' NOTES
• Red wine, carrots, and prunes are a classic combination in French cooking—and a good match to savory lamb.
• You can use peeled regular carrots, but cut them into segments about as long and wide as baby carrots.
• For a richer and more complex preparation, substitute unsalted butter or even walnut oil for the olive oil.

INGREDIENTS EXPLAINED Thyme sprigs are always a bit of a problem, given how wispy they are. A sprig is actually not just one of the tendril-like threads but instead a group of those threads with the harder stem at the bottom. If you've only got wispy threads on hand, double or triple the amount to match what would be on the sprigs.

best-ever lamb navarin

EFFORT: **A LOT** • PREP TIME: **40 MINUTES** • COOK TIME: **8½ HOURS** • KEEPS ON WARM: **3 HOURS** • SERVES: **3 TO 9**

INGREDIENTS	2- TO 3½-QT	4- TO 5½-QT	6- TO 8-QT
Unsalted butter	1 tblsp	1½ tblsp	2 tblsp
Boneless lamb shoulder, cut into 2-inch pieces	1 pound	2 pounds	3 pounds
Chopped yellow onion	½ small	1 small	1 medium
Carrots, peeled and cut into 1-inch pieces	5 ounces	10 ounces	1 pound
Turnips, peeled and cut into 1-inch pieces	5 ounces	10 ounces	1 pound
Dry white wine, such as Chardonnay	⅓ cup	⅔ cup	1 cup
Salt	¼ tsp	½ tsp	1 tsp
Ground black pepper	¼ tsp	¼ tsp	½ tsp
Fresh tarragon sprigs	1	2	3
Fresh thyme sprigs	1	2	2
Potato starch	1 tsp	2 tsp	1 tblsp

1 Melt the butter in a large skillet over medium heat. Slip some lamb chunks into the skillet—as many as will fit without crowding. Brown on all sides, giving them only a slight beige color, about 8 minutes per batch. Transfer the cubes to the slow cooker, adding more to keep going through the whole batch.

2 Dump the onion into the skillet, still set over medium heat. Cook, stirring often, until softened and pale yellow, about 4 minutes. Scrape the contents of the skillet into the slow cooker. *(continued)*

3 Stir in the carrots, turnips, wine, salt, and pepper. Tuck the tarragon and thyme sprigs into the sauce.

4 Cover and cook on low for 8 hours, or until the meat is fork-tender.

5 Use a slotted spoon to transfer the lamb and vegetables to a big bowl. Cover the cooker and set it to high. Defat the sauce in the cooker, either by skimming it with a flatware spoon or pouring it into a fat strainer. Whisk 2 table-spoons of the sauce with the potato starch in a small bowl, then whisk this mixture back into the slow cooker. Stir into the meat and vegetables.

6 Cover the slow cooker and cook on high for 30 minutes, or until the sauce has thickened a bit.

TESTERS' NOTES
• A *navarin* is a French stew, usually made with turnips (*navet* in French). If there are other vegetables in the mix (as here), it's really a *navarin printanier*.
• Boneless lamb shoulder is our preferred cut for this dish because the flavor will be milder and sweeter than the same cuts with bits of bone in them.
• Sear the lamb in the skillet, but don't get carried away. You want a delicate flavor, not deep or complicated.

Serve It Up! While mashed potatoes seem a given, try this stew over homemade croutons (see page 157) or even over whole-grain grits (which have a more rustic texture than standard polenta).

INGREDIENTS EXPLAINED Potato starch is an old-fashioned thickener; it's the fluffy starch extracted from potatoes, prized for the silky texture it brings to sauces and less gummy than cornstarch. Look for potato starch in the baking aisle.

gin-braised leg of lamb

EFFORT: **A LITTLE** • PREP TIME: **25 MINUTES** • COOK TIME: **7 TO 9 HOURS** • KEEPS ON WARM: **3 HOURS** • SERVES: **4 TO 10**

INGREDIENTS	2- TO 3½-QT	4- TO 5½-QT	6- TO 8-QT
Boneless leg of lamb, tied into a roast	1½ pounds	2½ pounds	4½ pounds
Medium garlic cloves, thinly slivered	1	2	3
Crushed juniper berries	½ tsp	1 tsp	½ tblsp
Olive oil	2 tsp	1 tblsp	2 tblsp
Thinly sliced yellow onion	⅔ cup	1 cup	1¾ cups
Reduced-sodium chicken broth	⅓ cup	½ cup	1 cup
Gin	3 tblsp	¼ cup	⅓ cup
Stemmed, seeded, and thinly sliced green or red bell pepper	⅓ cup	½ cup	¾ cup
Dried porcini mushrooms	¼ ounce	½ ounce	¾ ounce
Fresh thyme sprigs	3	4	7
Bay leaves	1	2	3

1 Use a paring knife to make small slits across the meat; fill each slit with a garlic sliver or a piece of a juniper berry.

2 Heat a large skillet over medium heat for a couple of minutes, then pour in the oil. Swirl the skillet to coat the hot surface, then add the leg of lamb and brown on all sides, about 5 minutes per side, taking care to get fairly dark spots mottled across the meat. Transfer the leg of lamb to the slow cooker.

3 Pour the onion into the skillet, still set over medium heat with the lamb fat in the pan.

Cook, stirring often, until softened, about 4 minutes. Spread the onion over and around the leg of lamb. Add the broth, gin, pepper strips, and porcini; tuck the thyme and bay leaves into the liquid.

4 Cover and cook on low for 7 hours in a small slow cooker, 8 hours in a medium cooker, and 9 hours in a large cooker, or until the meat is quite tender although still capable of being sliced into pieces that don't shred or fall apart.

5 Transfer the meat to a cutting board; let stand for 10 minutes. Discard the thyme sprigs and bay leaves; skim the surface fat off the sauce with a spoon. Carve the meat against the grain (page 146); serve with the sauce on the side.

TESTERS' NOTES

• A bone-in leg of lamb will not necessarily fit in a slow cooker, no matter the appliance's size; but a boneless leg will fit almost every time. Buy these roasts already tied at almost all supermarkets, or ask the butcher to bone a leg of lamb and tie the meat into a compact roast.

• Gin is an amazing braising medium—sweet, even a little sticky, and fantastically aromatic. Use a moderately high-quality gin. (No amount of aromatics can cover the taste of cheap booze.)

Serve It Up! For an elegant side dish, roast whole shallots with plenty of olive oil in a covered pan in a 350°F oven for 25 minutes. Quarter radicchio heads through the root, then add them to the pan with a bit more olive oil, tossing everything well. Uncover the pan and roast about 20 more minutes, tossing occasionally, until the radicchio is lightly browned. Let the vegetables cool, then chop them and toss in a large bowl with balsamic vinegar and salt.

leg of lamb with tons of garlic

EFFORT: **A LITTLE** • PREP TIME: **20 MINUTES** • COOK TIME: **7 TO 9 HOURS** • KEEPS ON WARM: **4 HOURS** • SERVES: **4 TO 12**

INGREDIENTS	2- TO 3½-QT	4- TO 5½-QT	6- TO 8-QT
Olive oil	½ tblsp	1 tblsp	2 tblsp
Boneless leg of lamb, tied into a roast	1¼ pounds	2½ pounds	5 pounds
Moderately sweet white wine, such as Pinot Blanc or Sauvignon Blanc	¼ cup	½ cup	1 cup
Whole garlic cloves (still in their husks)	10	20	40
4-inch fresh rosemary sprigs	2	4	8
Fresh thyme sprigs	2	4	8
Bay leaves	2	4	8
Ground black pepper	½ tsp	1 tsp	2 tsp
Salt	½ tsp	1 tsp	1½ tsp

1 Heat a large skillet over medium heat for a couple of minutes, then swirl in the oil. Set the leg of lamb in the skillet and brown on all sides, about 4 minutes per side, taking care to get good brown bits all over the meat. Transfer to the slow cooker.

2 Pour the wine over the lamb. Sprinkle the garlic, rosemary, thyme, bay leaves, pepper, and salt on and around the leg of lamb.

3 Cover and cook on low for 7 hours in a small slow cooker, 8 hours in a medium cooker, and 9 hours in a large cooker, or until the meat is fork-tender.

(continued)

4 Transfer the roast to a cutting board; let stand for 10 minutes. Remove and discard the rosemary, thyme, and bay leaves. Fish the garlic cloves out and set them on a serving platter. Skim or strain the fat from the sauce. Carve the lamb, place the slices on the serving platter, and serve with the sauce on the side.

TESTERS' NOTES

• If you love garlic, this is the recipe for you! The lamb also braises in lots of aromatic herbs, yielding a rich sauce.
• The garlic softens so much, you can squeeze it out of its husks onto the finished meat, and serve it like a condiment, or have slices of toasted bread on hand and use that soft garlic pulp as the spread.
• While some of the thyme or rosemary can sit up on top of the roast, make sure the bay leaves are submerged in the wine.

shawarma-roasted leg of lamb

EFFORT: **A LITTLE** • PREP TIME: **25 MINUTES** • COOK TIME: **7 TO 9 HOURS** • KEEPS ON WARM: **3 HOURS** • SERVES: **4 TO 12**

INGREDIENTS	2- TO 3½-QT	4- TO 5½-QT	6- TO 8-QT
Unsalted butter	1 tblsp	2 tblsp	3 tblsp
Yellow onion, thinly sliced	1 small	1 medium	2 medium
Olive oil	2 tsp	4 tsp	2 tblsp
Minced garlic	2 tsp	4 tsp	2 tblsp
Kosher salt	½ tsp	1 tsp	1½ tsp
Ground cardamom	½ tsp	1 tsp	1½ tsp
Ground mace	½ tsp	1 tsp	1½ tsp
Mild paprika	½ tsp	1 tsp	1½ tsp
Ground cinnamon	¼ tsp	½ tsp	1 tsp
Cayenne	Pinch	⅛ tsp	¼ tsp
Boneless leg of lamb, tied into a roast	1½ pounds	3 pounds	5 pounds

1 Melt the butter in a large skillet over low heat. Add the onion, drop the heat down further if possible, and cook, stirring frequently, until soft and very sweet, 15 to 20 minutes. If the onion begins to brown, reduce the heat still further and stir even more often. Scrape the contents of the skillet into the slow cooker.

2 Make a paste of the olive oil, garlic, salt, cardamom, mace, paprika, cinnamon, and cayenne in a small bowl. Smear the paste all over the leg of lamb; set it on top of the onion in the cooker.

3 Cover and cook on low for 6 hours in a small slow cooker, 8 hours in a medium cooker, or 10 hours in a large cooker, or until the meat is fork-tender, easily cut into thin slices.

4 Transfer the meat to a carving board; let stand for 10 minutes to become even juicier. Carve against the grain into thin slices (see page 146) or small chunks and serve with the softened onion on the side.

TESTERS' NOTES

• The spice rub here mimics that on Middle-Eastern *shawarma*—except with the flavors bumped up a bit to match the way the slow cooker works without much browning.
• Make sure you get the spice rub into the cracks and crannies of the roast—however, remember that the rub is *hot*. Don't touch your eyes or nose before you rub the oil all over your hands and wash up well with warm water and soap.

Serve It Up! Serve the slices in pita pockets with chopped lettuce and tomato. Make an easy **Tzatziki Sauce:** Mix a diced cucumber, a little lemon juice, minced dill, salt, and pepper into Greek yogurt.

spicy lamb stew
with ginger and peanuts

EFFORT: **NOT MUCH** • PREP TIME: **15 MINUTES** • COOK TIME: **8 HOURS** • KEEPS ON WARM: **3 HOURS** • SERVES: **3 TO 10**

INGREDIENTS	2- TO 3½-QT	4- TO 5½-QT	6- TO 8-QT
Boneless leg of lamb, cut into 1-inch pieces	1¼ pounds	2 pounds	4 pounds
Red bell pepper, stemmed, seeded, and thinly sliced	1 small	1 medium	2 medium
Yellow onion, thinly sliced	1 small	1 medium	2 medium
Roasted unsalted peanuts	3 tblsp	¼ cup	½ cup
Julienned peeled fresh ginger	3 tblsp	¼ cup	½ cup
Minced garlic	½ tblsp	2 tsp	1½ tblsp
Soy sauce	⅓ cup	½ cup	1 cup
Black bean chile sauce	3 tblsp	¼ cup	½ cup
Rice vinegar	2 tblsp	3 tblsp	6 tblsp
Creamy natural-style peanut butter	1½ tblsp	2 tblsp	¼ cup
Packed dark brown sugar	1½ tblsp	2 tblsp	¼ cup

1 Combine the lamb chunks, bell pepper, onion, peanuts, ginger, and garlic in the slow cooker.

2 Whisk the soy sauce, chile sauce, vinegar, peanut butter, and brown sugar in a bowl until smooth. Pour over the ingredients in the slow cooker; toss well.

3 Cover and cook on low for 8 hours, or until the meat is fork-tender.

TESTERS' NOTES
• This Asian-inspired sauce mellows dramatically as it cooks. Consider it an easy wok-style braise from the slow cooker.
• It's important that the chunks of lamb be fairly small, about 1 inch each. That way, you'll need only spoons at the table, not an entire place setting.

Serve It Up! Yes, you can offer it over cooked rice (white or brown). But also try this very aromatic stew over cooked white or red quinoa that has been mixed with finely diced cucumber and seasoned with a splash of rice vinegar.

INGREDIENTS EXPLAINED Black bean chile sauce is an Asian condiment prized for its salty heat. Not the same as Chinese black bean sauce, black bean *chile* sauce can be quite red and looks more like a chile sauce with some preserved black beans added to the mix for a musky pop. Look for this condiment in jars in the Asian aisle; keep it refrigerated for up to 6 months after opening.

ALL-AMERICAN KNOW-HOW To julienne fresh ginger, peel a 2-inch chunk with a vegetable peeler, then cut the piece into very thin slices no wider than a matchstick. Slice each of these pieces into very thin strips.

lamb ragù

EFFORT: **NOT MUCH** • PREP TIME: **20 MINUTES** • COOK TIME:
8 HOURS • KEEPS ON WARM: **4 HOURS** • SERVES: **4 TO 12**

INGREDIENTS	2- TO 3½-QT	4- TO 5½-QT	6- TO 8-QT
Boneless leg of lamb, diced into ½-inch pieces	1 pound	1½ pounds	3 pounds
Yellow onion, chopped	1 small	1 medium	2 medium
Chopped carrots	⅔ cup	1 cup	2 cups
Minced fresh sage leaves	2 tblsp	3 tblsp	5 tblsp
Minced garlic	2 tsp	4 tsp	2 tblsp
Minced fresh rosemary leaves	2 tsp	1 tblsp	1½ tblsp
Salt	¼ tsp	½ tsp	1 tsp
Ground black pepper	¼ tsp	½ tsp	1 tsp
Dry vermouth	⅔ cup	1 cup	2 cups
No-salt-added tomato paste	6 tblsp	½ cup plus 2 tblsp	1¼ cups
All-purpose flour	1 tsp	2 tsp	1½ tblsp
Dried rotini, cooked and drained	8 ounces	1 pound	1½ pounds

1 Mix the lamb, onion, carrots, sage, garlic, rosemary, salt, and pepper in the slow cooker.

2 Whisk the vermouth, tomato paste, and flour in a bowl until the flour dissolves and the mixture is fairly smooth. Pour over the other ingredients; stir well.

3 Cover and cook on low for 8 hours, or until the flavors have mellowed and the meat is incredibly tender. Serve the ragù over the cooked pasta.

TESTERS' NOTES
• The real effort here is dicing the meat: it needs to be in tiny bits so they form a ground-beef-like sauce when long cooked.
• The flavors of this ragù are more intense than the standard ground-beef version. For an even more intense bump, add up to ½ teaspoon ground cinnamon with the herbs.

Serve It Up! Ladle the stew over spinach fettuccini, then sprinkle with crumbled feta—or go really over the top and use an aged crumbly goat cheese.

lamb shanks with white wine and tomatoes

EFFORT: **A LITTLE** • PREP TIME: **20 MINUTES** • COOK TIME: **9 HOURS** • KEEPS ON WARM: **4 HOURS** • SERVES: **2 TO 8**

INGREDIENTS	2- TO 3½-QT	4- TO 5½-QT	6- TO 8-QT
Almond or olive oil	½ tblsp	1 tblsp	2 tblsp
Lamb shanks, about 12 ounces each	2	4	8
Salt	¼ tsp	½ tsp	1 tsp
Ground black pepper	¼ tsp	½ tsp	1 tsp
Peeled small fresh pearl onions, or frozen, thawed	½ cup	1 cup	2 cups
Ripe tomatoes, chopped	½ pound	1 pound	2 pounds
Dry white wine, such as Chardonnay	½ cup	1 cup	2 cups
Minced fresh basil leaves	2 tblsp	¼ cup	½ cup
Bay leaf	1	1	2

1 Heat a large skillet over medium heat for a couple of minutes, then swirl in the oil. Season the shanks with salt and pepper, set them in the skillet, and brown them on all sides, up to 12 minutes per shank. (Do this task in stages if you can't fit all the shanks comfortably in your skillet; divide the almond oil among the batches as necessary.) Transfer the browned shanks to the slow cooker.

2 Scrape the pearl onions into the skillet, still set over the heat. Cook, stirring often, until softened and barely translucent but not yet browned, about 3 minutes. Pour the onions from the skillet into the slow cooker.

3 Add the tomatoes, wine, basil, and bay leaf to the slow cooker. Cover and cook on low for 9 hours, or until the meat is pulling away from the bones and quite tender.

4 Discard the bay leaf. Use a slotted spoon to transfer a shank and some vegetables to each serving bowl. Skim the sauce for fat and pour it over the shanks.

TESTERS' NOTES
• Almond oil offers a sweet, velvety finish to the stew, but you can substitute olive oil at will.
• Lamb shanks are big-time comfort food. In a slow cooker, the meat takes on a luxurious quality, an almost confit-like texture.
• Lamb shanks work better in an oval slow cooker than a round one. Stack them so they lean on each other without one sitting in the liquid and the others resting above it. It may help to alternate them, one meat side down, another meat side up. If so, swap them around halfway through cooking to make sure everything takes a plunge in the liquid below.

lamb shanks
with red wine and carrots

EFFORT: **A LOT** • PREP TIME: **25 MINUTES** • COOK TIME: **9 HOURS** • KEEPS ON WARM: **4 HOURS** • SERVES: **2 TO 8**

INGREDIENTS	2- TO 3½-QT	4- TO 5½-QT	6- TO 8-QT
Olive oil	½ tblsp	1 tblsp	2 tblsp
Lamb shanks, about 12 ounces each	2	4	8
Thinly sliced yellow onion	½ cup	1 cup (about 1 small)	2 cups
Chopped carrots	½ cup	1 cup	2 cups
Chopped celery	½ cup	1 cup	2 cups
Minced garlic	1 tsp	2 tsp	1½ tblsp
Reduced-sodium chicken broth	¼ cup	½ cup	1 cup
Dry red wine, such as Shiraz, Syrah, or light Pinor Noir	½ cup	1 cup	2 cups
No-salt-added tomato paste	2 tblsp	¼ cup	½ cup
Dried thyme	½ tsp	1 tsp	2 tsp
Salt	¼ tsp	½ tsp	1 tsp
Ground black pepper	¼ tsp	½ tsp	1 tsp

1 Heat a large skillet over medium heat, then pour in the oil. Swirl to coat, then add the lamb shanks. Brown on all sides, about 12 minutes per shank. (Only brown as many as will fit comfortably in the skillet at a time, adding more as space opens up.) Transfer the browned shanks to the slow cooker.

2 Add the onion, carrots, celery, and garlic to the skillet, still set over the heat. Cook, stirring often, until the onion begins to turn translucent, about 3 minutes.

3 Use a slotted spoon to transfer the vegetables to the slow cooker. Pour the broth into the skillet, raise the heat to high, and stir until simmering, scraping up any browned bits in the skillet. Pour the contents of the skillet into the slow cooker.

4 Whisk the wine, tomato paste, thyme, salt, and pepper in a bowl; pour over the contents of the slow cooker.

5 Cover and cook on low for 9 hours, or until the meat has pulled back from the bone and is fork-tender.

TESTERS' NOTES

• To balance the more assertive tastes in this stew, get all the browning flavor in the skillet into the slow cooker—an extra step, sure, but clearly worth it.

• This is a hearty, French-inspired preparation, stocked with plenty of vegetables. You can even make it ahead, debone the meat, stir it back into the stew, and save it in the freezer as a terrific stew for some future evening.

Serve It Up! For a **Wax Bean Salad:** Blanch wax beans in boiling water for 1 minute, then drain and refresh under cool tap water. Toss them with diced tomatoes, sliced green olives, minced shallots, olive oil, lemon juice, salt, and ground black pepper.

veal and rabbit

Boredom at the plate leads to mindless overeating. If you want to lose weight, you have to eat a wider variety of things—otherwise, you'll be eating more of the same ol' things to find any satisfaction. So here's to veal and rabbit, two slow cooker meats we might not consider all that often.

Veal is sweet and tender, about the best meat in the supermarket. We suspect everyone who's had osso buco knows that, although they may not have known they were eating veal. You can skip the guilt that comes with eating veal now that there are small-production veal farmers with calves in the fields. Pastured veal is not white but pink; the meat is mellow and marbled, perfect for the slow cooker. Rabbit, by contrast, is more assertive, rich and mineraly, like a cross between pork tenderloin and dark-meat turkey. But don't expect to pick any buckshot out of your teeth: today's rabbits are raised on farms.

That said, there can be a problem with both veal and rabbit. They're not the most popular meats in the supermarket, so they have a tendency to sit on the shelf. If you're in doubt, ask the butcher to open a package for you, especially when you're buying rabbit. Take a whiff; make sure it's not off.

After that, cooking rabbit and veal is all about the braise. When it comes to veal, all that talk about good browning technique gets tossed out of the window. You don't want to brown the meat very much—just get it beige with a few brown bits. Too much browning, and the overall flavor will become too bitter and assertive. And no, we don't have a recipe for veal scaloppini; it would be a waste in the slow cooker. Instead, we have multiple recipes for veal stew meat and veal shanks, as well as several recipes that call for a whole rabbit cut into eight or nine parts.

So eat more things. You'll find yourself more quickly satisfied and you may even eat less in the long run. No guarantees, though. These dishes are pretty tasty.

veal shoulder
with artichokes and lemon

EFFORT: **A LITTLE** • PREP TIME: **25 MINUTES** • COOK TIME: **6 TO 8 HOURS** • KEEPS ON WARM: **2 HOURS** • SERVES: **2 TO 8**

INGREDIENTS	2- TO 3½-QT	4- TO 5½-QT	6- TO 8-QT
Unsalted butter	1 tsp	2 tsp	1 tblsp
Olive oil	1 tsp	2 tsp	1 tblsp
Bone-in veal shoulder roast	1¼ pounds	2½ pounds	4 pounds
Salt	⅛ tsp	¼ tsp	½ tsp
Ground black pepper	⅛ tsp	¼ tsp	½ tsp
Peeled small fresh pearl onions, or frozen, thawed	¼ cup	½ cup	1 cup
Trimmed and quartered fresh baby artichokes, or frozen quartered artichoke hearts, thawed	¾ cup	1½ cups	3 cups
Finely grated lemon zest	½ tsp	1 tsp	2 tsp
Minced fresh rosemary leaves	½ tsp	1 tsp	2 tsp
Minced garlic	½ tsp	1 tsp	2 tsp
Slightly sweet white wine, such as Pinot Gris	About ½ cup	About 1 cup	About 2 cups

1 Melt the butter in the olive oil in a large skillet set over medium heat. Season the roast with salt and pepper, set it in the skillet, and brown it on all sides, not letting it get too dark but allowing it to get some decidedly beige patches, about 10 minutes. Transfer to the slow cooker.

2 Add the pearl onions; stir them around the skillet until lightly browned, about 5 minutes. Pour into the slow cooker.

3 Add the artichoke hearts, lemon zest, rosemary, and garlic, sprinkling all these on and around the roast. Pour in the wine until it comes about a third of the way up the roast. Cover and cook on low for 6 hours in a small slow cooker, 7 hours in a medium cooker, or 8 hours in a large cooker, or until the meat is fork-tender.

4 Transfer the roast to a cutting board; let stand for 10 minutes before carving into slices and chunks against the grain (see page 146).

TESTERS' NOTES
• Since a shoulder roast is a fairly large cut, it may not fit into your specific slow cooker model. Take the width and length measurements of your crock before you head to the store. If nothing fits with room to spare for the braising liquid, consider veal shoulder chops as a substitute.
• If you use fresh baby artichokes, peel off almost all the outer leaves, taking the artichoke down to the heart before quartering it.

Serve It Up! Slice Yukon Gold potatoes into quarters; toss them with olive oil, salt, and pepper in a heavy roasting pan; and bake at 375°F until crunchy and brown, between 45 minutes and 1 hour 15 minutes, stirring occasionally.

veal and tomato stew

EFFORT: **A LITTLE** • PREP TIME: **30 MINUTES** • COOK TIME: **8 HOURS** • KEEPS ON WARM: **4 HOURS** • SERVES: **2 TO 8**

INGREDIENTS	2- TO 3½-QT	4- TO 5½-QT	6- TO 8-QT
Olive oil	2 tsp	1 tblsp	2 tblsp
Bone-in veal shoulder chops, cut into 2-inch chunks	1 pound	2½ pounds	4½ pounds
Salt	¼ tsp	½ tsp	1 tsp
Ground black pepper	¼ tsp	½ tsp	1 tsp
Full-bodied, mildly sweet red wine, such as California Zinfandel	¾ cup	1 cup	2 cups
Drained no-salt-added canned diced tomatoes	¾ cup	2 cups	2¾ cups
No-salt-added tomato paste	1½ tblsp	¼ cup	⅓ cup
Worcestershire sauce	2 tsp	1 tblsp	2 tblsp
Whole garlic cloves, peeled	2	4	7
4-inch rosemary sprigs	1	2	4

1 Set a large skillet over medium heat for a few minutes; swirl in the oil. Season the veal chunks with salt and pepper, then add some to the skillet, working in batches as necessary; lightly brown on all sides, turning occasionally, 6 to 8 minutes. Use tongs to transfer the chunks to a slow cooker and keep browning more.

2 Raise the heat to high; pour the wine into the skillet. Bring to a full boil, stirring once in a while to scrape up any browned bits. Continue boiling until the liquid in the skillet has reduced by half, between 3 and 6 minutes. Pour the wine reduction over the veal.

3 Stir the tomatoes, tomato paste, and Worcestershire sauce in a bowl until the tomato paste dissolves; stir into the ingredients in the slow cooker. Nestle the garlic cloves and rosemary into the sauce.

4 Cover and cook on low for 8 hours, or until the sauce is very aromatic and the veal is tender when pierced with a fork. Discard the rosemary before serving.

TESTERS' NOTES
• Although veal is traditionally browned in butter, olive oil adds a brighter, slightly sour flavor, a better contrast to the sweetness in the wine.
• When you cut up the veal, try to keep a bone in each chunk—at least where possible.
• You won't want to miss those garlic cloves. They'll have softened enough after cooking that you can smear them onto pieces of crunchy bread.

INGREDIENTS EXPLAINED Veal shoulder chops, cut from above the front legs, offer marbled, delicate meat. There can be plenty of bones in the chops—or just a few, depending on how they were butchered.

stuffed boneless breast of veal

EFFORT: **A LOT** • PREP TIME: **1 HOUR** • COOK TIME: **10 HOURS** •
KEEPS ON WARM: **3 HOURS** • SERVES: **8**

INGREDIENTS	6- TO 8-QT
Dry vermouth	1 cup
Chopped dried apricots	½ cup
Golden raisins	½ cup
Russet potatoes, peeled and shredded	½ pound
Carrots, peeled and shredded	6 ounces
Dried thyme	2 tsp
Dried sage	2 tsp
Salt	½ tsp
Ground black pepper	½ tsp
Boneless breast of veal, a pocket-like slit made into the thick side	4 pounds
Olive oil	2 tblsp
Dry white wine, such as Pinot Grigio	1 cup
Fresh sage sprigs	2
Garlic cloves, peeled	2
Bay leaf	1

1 Stir the vermouth, apricots, and raisins in a small saucepan; bring to a simmer over high heat, stirring occasionally. Cover, reduce the heat to low, and simmer for 20 minutes, until the fruit has softened. Uncover the pan, raise the heat to medium-high, and boil until the liquid has reduced to a glaze, about 6 minutes, stirring occasionally. Set aside to cool for 30 minutes.

2 Pour the contents of the saucepan into a bowl; stir in the potato, carrot, thyme, sage, salt, and pepper. Stuff the potato mixture into the pocket in the breast of veal (see Testers' Notes for how to make the pocket). Sew the opening of the pocket closed using a sterilized trussing needle or even a large tapestry needle and butchers' twine.

3 Heat a large skillet over medium heat for a few minutes; swirl the oil in the skillet. Add the stuffed veal and brown on both sides, 6 to 8 minutes per side. Transfer the stuffed veal to the slow cooker, pour in the wine, and tuck the sage sprigs, garlic cloves, and bay leaf into the liquid around the meat.

4 Cover and roast on low for 10 hours, or until the meat is fork-tender. Transfer to a cutting board; let stand for 10 minutes. Slice into ½-inch strips of meat.

TESTERS' NOTES
• A breast of veal is a luxurious cut laced with lots of collagen—and so perfect for the slow cooker. Because the cut of meat is so large, this recipe can only be made in a large slow cooker.
• Shred the potatoes and carrots through the large holes of a box grater or with the shredding blade of a large food processor.
• To make a pocket in the side of the breast of veal, insert the tip of a large knife into the center of the thick side, the blade turned so that the flat surface is parallel to your work surface. Make a small slice in one direction, remove the knife, and make a slice in the opposite direction. Continue on, making cuts back and forth until a pocket opens up in the meat without breaking through any side. (You can also ask the butcher at your supermarket to do it for you.)

Serve It Up! Make an **Apple and Radish Salad:** Shred peeled apples and whole radishes through the large holes of a box grater. Toss these shreds with lemon juice, olive oil, stemmed thyme leaves, crunchy sea salt, and ground black pepper.

chile-braised veal sirloin

EFFORT: **NOT MUCH** • PREP TIME: **15 MINUTES** • COOK TIME: **6 TO 9 HOURS** • KEEPS ON WARM: **4 HOURS** • SERVES: **3 TO 10**

INGREDIENTS	2- TO 3½-QT	4- TO 5½-QT	6- TO 8-QT
Boneless veal sirloin roast	1¼ pounds	2½ pounds	4 pounds
Drained and rinsed canned black beans	1 cup	1¾ cups	3 cups
Drained canned mandarin orange segments, packed in water	¼ cup	½ cup	¾ cup
Fresh orange juice	2 tblsp	¼ cup	6½ tblsp
Finely grated orange zest	½ tblsp	1 tblsp	1 tblsp plus 2 tsp
Honey	½ tblsp	1 tblsp	1 tblsp plus 2 tsp
Thinly sliced serrano chile	½ tblsp	1 tblsp	1½ tblsp
Minced garlic	1 tsp	2 tsp	1 tblsp
Cumin seeds	½ tsp	1 tsp	1½ tsp
Dried oregano	½ tsp	1 tsp	1½ tsp
Ground cinnamon	¼ tsp	½ tsp	¾ tsp
Ground black pepper	¼ tsp	½ tsp	¾ tsp
Ground cloves	⅛ tsp	¼ tsp	½ tsp
Salt	⅛ tsp	¼ tsp	½ tsp

1 Set the roast in the slow cooker; sprinkle the beans on and around the roast.

2 Stir the orange segments, juice, zest, honey, serranos, garlic, cumin seeds, oregano, cinnamon, pepper, cloves, and salt in a bowl; pour over and around the roast.

3 Cover and cook on low for 6 hours in a small slow cooker, 8 hours in a medium cooker, and 9 hours in a large cooker, or until the roast is fork-tender but still will hold its shape when sliced. (You may have to slice a small bit off to see how it holds together.)

4 Transfer to a cutting board and let it rest for 10 minutes while you skim the sauce for any surface fat. Slice into thin strips against the grain (see page 146); nap with the sauce.

TESTERS' NOTES
• A veal sirloin roast is a luxurious cut, but it still needs a slow braise to become meltingly tender.
• Because of varying amounts of collagen in the meat, you may find that your particular roast takes a little longer than suggested—perhaps another hour before it's wonderfully tender.

ALL-AMERICAN KNOW-HOW If desired, make your own orange suprêmes—wedge-shaped pieces of citrus with no pith or veins. Cut thin slices off the stem end and the opposite end of an orange. Stand the fruit cut side down on a cutting board. Cut off the rind by slicing down and following the fruit's curve, removing any pith without taking off much flesh. Hold the peeled fruit in your hand over a bowl; cut along the white membranes in V-shaped wedges, removing the individual sections. (Do not slice down into your hand!) Let the sections fall into the bowl below; pick out any seeds; discard the pith and peels. Now you'll have both orange juice and orange supremes.

pineapple-glazed veal ribs

EFFORT: **NOT MUCH** • PREP TIME: **15 MINUTES** • COOK TIME: **8 HOURS** • KEEPS ON WARM: **2 HOURS** • SERVES: **2 TO 6**

INGREDIENTS	2- TO 3½-QT	4- TO 5½-QT	6- TO 8-QT
Bone-in veal ribs, cut into 2-bone sections	2 pounds	4 pounds	6 pounds
Drained canned crushed pineapple packed in juice	⅔ cup	1⅓ cups	2 cups
Soy sauce	2 tblsp	3½ tblsp	⅓ cup
Packed dark brown sugar	2 tblsp	3½ tblsp	⅓ cup
Dry sherry	1 tblsp	2 tblsp	3 tblsp
Minced peeled fresh ginger	½ tblsp	1 tblsp	1½ tblsp
Toasted sesame oil (see page 196)	1 tsp	2 tsp	1 tblsp
Medium garlic cloves, peeled and quartered	1	2	3

1 Set the ribs in the slow cooker. Stir the pineapple, soy sauce, brown sugar, sherry, ginger, sesame oil, and garlic in a bowl; pour over the ribs.

2 Cover and cook on low for 8 hours, or until the meat is so tender that it is almost falling off the bone.

TESTERS' NOTES
• Veal ribs are not quite as meaty as beef ribs—and the taste is milder, sweeter.
• To cut the ribs into two-bone sections, use a sharp, heavy cleaver to press down between the bones and through the connective bits at the bottom of the rack. (Or ask the butcher to do this.)

osso buco with apples and cream

EFFORT: **A LITTLE** • PREP TIME: **30 MINUTES** • COOK TIME: **9 TO 10 HOURS** • KEEPS ON WARM: **3 HOURS THROUGH STEP 4** • SERVES: **2 TO 6**

INGREDIENTS	2- TO 3½-QT	4- TO 5½-QT	6- TO 8-QT
Slab bacon, cut into ½-inch cubes	¼ pound	6 ounces	10 ounces
1½-inch-thick veal osso buco slices (about 12 ounces each), tied	2	4	6
Leeks (white and pale green part only), halved lengthwise, washed thoroughly to remove any grit, and thinly sliced	4 ounces	8 ounces	12 ounces
Brandy	¼ cup	6 tblsp	½ cup
Minced fresh sage leaves	½ tblsp	1 tblsp	1½ tblsp
Ground allspice	½ tsp	¾ tsp	1 tsp
Ground black pepper	¼ tsp	½ tsp	1 tsp
Tart apples (like Granny Smith), peeled, cored, and cut into 3-inch chunks	1 large	2 large	3 large
Dry white wine, such as an Albarino or Chardonnay	½ cup	1 cup	1½ cups
Heavy cream	3 tblsp	¼ cup	⅓ cup

1 Fry the bacon cubes in a large skillet set over medium heat until well browned and even a little crunchy at the edges, between 5 and 8 minutes. Use a slotted spoon to transfer them to the slow cooker.

2 Slip the osso buco into the bacon fat–filled skillet, still set over the heat. Add only as many as will comfortably fit, browning them on both sides in batches, about 8 minutes, turning once. Transfer the browned meat to the slow cooker, arranging them in one layer with as little overlap as possible.

3 Add the leeks to the skillet and cook until wilted and aromatic, about 4 minutes, stirring frequently. Pour in the brandy; if the liquid ignites, quickly cover the skillet and move it off the heat for 2 minutes before uncovering and proceeding. As the liquid in the skillet comes to a full boil, scrape up any browned bits on the hot surface. Stir in the sage, allspice, and pepper, then scrape the contents of the skillet into the slow cooker. Add the apples and wine.

4 Cover and cook on low for 9 hours, or until the meat is gorgeously tender at the bone.

5 Use a slotted spoon to transfer the portions of veal to serving bowls. Remove the twine. Skim the surface fat off the sauce in the cooker; pour the sauce and all the vegetables into a large saucepan. Bring to a boil over high heat, stir in the cream, and cook for 1 minute, stirring all the while. Ladle the sauce and vegetables over the portions in the bowls.

TESTERS' NOTES
• The secret to a good cream sauce is (1) not to use too much cream and (2) to boil it down a bit so that it loses that "raw" taste.
• Feel free to substitute venison osso buco for the veal. The bold flavors of this recipe will make a nice match to the richer, gamier meat.

INGREDIENTS EXPLAINED Osso buco is made from sliced veal shanks, a tough, fairly fatty bit of the calf that becomes wonderfully tender when braised for a long time. The name—pronounced *oh-soh BOO-coh*—literally means "bone [with a] hole," a reference to the piece of bone marrow often found in the center of the shank (or shin) bone. If you've got them, put marrow spoons on the table to mine the bones' incredibly delectable centers.

ALL-AMERICAN KNOW-HOW To tie osso buco, wrap butchers' twine once or twice around the circumference, positioning the twine in the middle of the area. The portions must be tied or the meat will quite literally fall off the bone, as the fatty connective tissue melts during braising. You can snip the twine away just before you ladle the sauce over the cooked pieces.

osso buco with coffee and chiles

EFFORT: **A LITTLE** • PREP TIME: **20 MINUTES** • COOK TIME: **10 HOURS** • KEEPS ON WARM: **3 HOURS** • SERVES: **2 TO 6**

INGREDIENTS	2- TO 3½-QT	4- TO 5½-QT	6- TO 8-QT
Olive oil	2 tsp	4 tsp	2 tblsp
1½-inch-thick veal osso buco slices (about 12 ounces each), tied	2	4	6
Salt	⅛ tsp	¼ tsp	½ tsp
Ground black pepper	⅛ tsp	¼ tsp	½ tsp
Yellow onion, thinly sliced	1 medium	1 large	2 large
Ancho chile powder (see page 147)	2 tsp	4 tsp	2 tblsp
Finely grated fresh orange zest	1 tsp	2 tsp	1 tblsp
Minced garlic	1 tsp	2 tsp	1 tblsp
Strong drip or French-press coffee	½ cup	¾ cup	1 cup
Moderately sweet white wine, such as Sauvignon Blanc	½ cup	¾ cup	1 cup

(continued)

1 Heat a large skillet over medium heat, then swirl in the oil. Season the osso buco with salt and pepper, then slip as many as will comfortably fit into the skillet. Brown on both sides, turning once, about 8 minutes. Transfer the rounds to the slow cooker and continue browning more as necessary. Fit them in one layer in the slow cooker, as little overlap as possible.

2 Add the onion to the skillet, still set over the heat. Stir until lightly golden, about 5 minutes. Spoon the onion on top of the osso buco.

3 Sprinkle the onion with the chile powder, orange zest, and garlic. Pour the coffee and wine over everything.

4 Cover and cook on low for 10 hours, or until the meat is fork-tender. Transfer the osso buco to serving bowls; snip and discard the twine. Skim the sauce for any surface fat, then ladle the sauce and onion over the osso buco.

TESTERS' NOTES
• Coffee, chiles, and orange zest are a complex, sophisticated combination—sweet, bitter, and spicy.
• Use freshly brewed coffee; otherwise, this can add stale, burned notes to this elegant meal. There's no need for espresso. Simply add another scoop of grounds to your usual batch of coffee to make it a bit stouter.

osso buco with mushrooms and black olives

EFFORT: **A LOT** • PREP TIME: **30 MINUTES** • COOK TIME: **9 TO 10 HOURS** • KEEPS ON WARM: **3 HOURS** • SERVES: **2 TO 6**

INGREDIENTS	2- TO 3½-QT	4- TO 5½-QT	6- TO 8-QT
Dried porcini mushrooms	¼ ounce	½ ounce	1 ounce
Unsalted butter	1 tsp	½ tblsp	1 tblsp
Olive oil	1 tsp	½ tblsp	1 tblsp
1½-inch-thick veal osso buco slices (about 12 ounces each), tied (see page 227)	2	4	6
Thinly sliced yellow onion	½ cup	1 cup (about 1 small)	1½ cups
Minced garlic	2 tsp	1 tblsp	1½ tblsp
Dry white wine, such as Chardonnay	⅔ cup	1⅓ cups	2 cups
Chopped sun-dried tomatoes	⅓ cup	⅔ cup	1 cup
Pitted small oil-cured black olives	2 tblsp	¼ cup	6 tblsp
Minced fresh rosemary leaves	1 tblsp	1½ tblsp	2 tblsp
Salt	⅛ tsp	¼ tsp	½ tsp
Ground black pepper	⅛ tsp	¼ tsp	½ tsp

1 Bring a saucepan of water to a boil over high heat. Set the dried porcini in a medium bowl; fill the bowl about two-thirds full with boiling water. Soak for 20 minutes.

2 Strain the dried mushrooms in a colander set over a second bowl, thereby catching and saving the mushroom soaking liquid.

3 Melt the butter with the oil in a large skillet set over medium heat. Slip as many of the osso buco pieces into the skillet as will comfortably fit. Brown them on both sides, about 8 minutes per batch, turning once. If possible, make one layer of the osso buco in the slow cooker, squeezing to fit (although you can also tilt a couple of the pieces up to help with space).

4 Brown the onion in the same skillet, still set over the heat. Stir until the onion is limp and even a little browned in places, 5 to 10 minutes. Add the garlic, stir well for a few seconds, then scrape the contents of the skillet into the slow cooker.

5 Add the mushrooms, wine, sun-dried tomatoes, olives, rosemary, salt, and pepper to the cooker. Pour in the mushroom-soaking liquid until the total sauce in the cooker comes about halfway up the osso buco pieces.

6 Cover and cook on low for 9 hours, or until the meat is quite tender, especially right next to the bone. Use a large, slotted spoon and tongs to transfer the osso buco to serving bowls. Remove the twine. Skim the surface fat off the sauce, then ladle the liquid into the bowls.

TESTERS' NOTES
• Although not the most classic preparation of osso buco, this recipe showcases Mediterranean flavors with some of the richest veal you can eat.
• Oil-cured olives are particularly rich—and salty. Look for them on the salad or olive bar at larger supermarkets, rather than in a can or jar. If you're concerned about salt, omit any additional and pass extra flaked sea salt at the table.

Serve It Up! Osso buco is often served with risotto, mashed potatoes, polenta, or even cooked and drained pasta, particularly fettuccini. We've also served this dish over black Venere rice, a sticky-sweet specialty grain from Italy.

rabbit cacciatore

EFFORT: **A LOT** • PREP TIME: **30 MINUTES** • COOK TIME: **6 HOURS** • KEEPS ON WARM: **3 HOURS** • SERVES: **3 TO 10**

INGREDIENTS	2- TO 3½-QT	4- TO 5½-QT	6- TO 8-QT
Slab bacon, chopped	3 ounces	6 ounces	12 ounces
Rabbit, cut into pieces, or packaged rabbit legs	1½ pounds	3 pounds	6 pounds
Peeled and quartered shallots	½ cup	1 cup	2 cups
Minced garlic	1 tsp	2 tsp	4 tsp
Drained no-salt-added canned diced tomatoes	1½ cups	3 cups	6 cups
Moderately dry white wine, such as Sauvignon Blanc	¼ cup	½ cup	1 cup
All-purpose flour	1 tblsp	2 tblsp	¼ cup
Dried basil	1 tsp	2 tsp	4 tsp
Dried thyme	½ tsp	1 tsp	2 tsp
Ground black pepper	½ tsp	1 tsp	2 tsp

1 Fry the bacon in a large skillet over medium heat until crisp, stirring often, between 4 and 7 minutes. Use a slotted spoon to transfer the bacon to the slow cooker.

(continued)

2 Brown the rabbit pieces in stages in the bacon fat in the skillet, turning each piece only after 3 or 4 minutes, but taking care never to crowd the skillet. As they're done, transfer the rabbit pieces to the slow cooker and continue browning more.

3 Toss the shallots into the skillet, still over the heat, and cook until lightly browned and a bit translucent on the outside, about 5 minutes. Add the garlic to the skillet, cook a few seconds, then scrape the contents of the skillet into the slow cooker.

4 Pour the tomatoes over the contents of the slow cooker. Whisk the wine, flour, basil, thyme, and pepper in a bowl until the flour has dissolved, then pour the wine mixture into the slow cooker.

5 Cover and cook on low for 6 hours, or until the rabbit is tender but juicy. Use tongs to transfer the pieces to serving bowls. Skim the sauce for fat and slather it over the rabbit pieces.

TESTERS' NOTES
• This tomato-rich, heavily herbed braise is best on a cold, winter evening.
• Pour the diced tomatoes into a strainer in the sink to drain them thoroughly. If there's too much liquid, the sauce can become overpoweringly heavy.
• There's a lot of flavor left in that skillet when you're done browning. If you want to capture it for a side sauce, save ¼ to ½ cup of the juice from the canned tomatoes. Pour it into the skillet when you're done browning the shallots, crank the heat up to high, and boil the juice down to a thick glaze, stirring often to get up every crusty bit in the skillet.

ALL-AMERICAN KNOW-HOW With less fat and a firmer texture than chicken, rabbit makes a wonderful meal. However, its anatomy can be tricky. Unless you're sure of its bone structure, ask the butcher to cut the rabbit into 8 to 10 pieces. Most rabbits weigh between 2 and

3½ pounds, more than you'll need for a small slow cooker. Although you can sometimes find a small rabbit, also look for packaged rabbit legs and buy a similar amount as the recipe requires.

rabbit with pancetta and prunes

EFFORT: **A LOT** • PREP TIME: **30 MINUTES** • COOK TIME: **5½ HOURS** • KEEPS ON WARM: **3 HOURS** • SERVES: **3 TO 10**

INGREDIENTS	2- TO 3½-QT	4- TO 5½-QT	6- TO 8-QT
Pancetta, chopped (see page 354)	4 ounces	6 ounces	8 ounces
Rabbit, cut into pieces, or packaged rabbit legs	1½ pounds	3 pounds	6 pounds
Brandy	2 tblsp	¼ cup	⅓ cup
Carrots, peeled and cut into 1-inch sections	¼ pound	½ pound	¾ pound
Yellow onion, chopped	½ small	1 small	1 medium
Pitted prunes, halved	2	4	8
Fresh thyme sprigs	1	2	4
Fresh sage leaves	3	6	12
Ground black pepper	¼ tsp	½ tsp	1 tsp
Moderately light but dry red wine, such as Petit Syrah	1 cup	2 cups	One 750-ml bottle
Unsalted butter, at room temperature	1 tblsp	2 tblsp	3 tblsp
All-purpose flour	1 tblsp	2 tblsp	3 tblsp

1 Fry the pancetta in a large skillet over medium heat until crisp, between 5 and 10 minutes. Use a slotted spoon to transfer the pancetta bits to the slow cooker.

2 Brown the rabbit in the same skillet, still set over the heat. Taking care not to over-crowd the skillet, make sure each has some light golden spots across the surface, 6 to 8 minutes per batch. Transfer the rabbit pieces to the slow cooker.

3 Pour the brandy into the skillet. If the li-quor ignites, quickly cover the skillet and take it off the heat for 2 minutes before returning to the heat, uncovered. When the liquid in the skillet is boiling, scrape up any browned bits on the hot surface, then scrape the contents of the skillet into the slow cooker.

4 Add the carrots, onion, prunes, thyme, sage, and pepper to the cooker. Pour in the wine. (The liquid should come about three-quarters of the way up the rabbit and vegetables in the cooker. If not, add water to compensate.)

5 Cover and cook on low for 5 hours, until the meat is tender but not falling off the bone.

6 Use tongs to transfer the rabbit pieces to a large bowl. Cover the cooker and set the temperature on high. Mash the butter into the flour in a small bowl until the mixture forms a paste. Whisk the paste into the sauce in the cooker in dribs and drabs to dissolve it. Return the rabbit pieces to the cooker and cook on high for 30 more minutes, until the sauce has thickened slightly.

TESTERS' NOTES

• This one's a *civet* (*see-VAY*)—a rich wine-based stew traditionally thickened with blood, but here with a beurre manié (*burr mahn-YAY*), a paste of butter and flour that gives the sauce a velvety finish.

• If you don't want to use brandy, substitute chicken broth for a less-worrisome technique.

ALL-AMERICAN KNOW-HOW Liquor can ignite in a hot skillet or pan—or at least, the volatilizing gas-ses can ignite, causing a nasty fire. Follow a few safety precautions:

• Turn off any exhaust vent so that flames don't get sucked up into it.

• Never pour directly from the bottle. Fumes can ignite even in its neck. Pour the needed amount into a measur-ing cup first.

• Have a lid nearby to cover the skillet quickly.

• Make sure all children and pets are out of the room, in case of flare-ups.

• Be steady and patient, never quick or harried.

• Keep a charged fire extinguisher in your kitchen.

rabbit with whiskey and lima beans

EFFORT: **NOT MUCH** • PREP TIME: **15 MINUTES** • COOK TIME: **6 HOURS 15 MINUTES** • KEEPS ON WARM: **3 HOURS** • SERVES: **2 TO 8**

INGREDIENTS	2- TO 3½-QT	4- TO 5½-QT	6- TO 8-QT
No-salt-added canned diced tomatoes, including juices	1 cup	1¾ cups	3½ cups
Frozen lima beans, thawed	¾ cup plus 2 tblsp	1½ cups	3 cups
Corn kernels, fresh cut from cob, or frozen, thawed	⅔ cup	1 cup	2 cups
Stemmed, seeded, and chopped green bell pepper	⅓ cup	½ cup	1 cup (about 1 medium)
Whiskey, preferably American blended	¼ cup	⅓ cup	½ cup
Reduced-sodium chicken broth	¼ cup	⅓ cup	½ cup
Dried thyme	1 tsp	½ tblsp	1 tblsp
Dried rosemary	¾ tsp	1 tsp	2 tsp
Salt	¼ tsp	½ tsp	1 tsp
Celery seeds	⅛ tsp	¼ tsp	½ tsp
Ground black pepper	⅛ tsp	¼ tsp	½ tsp
Cayenne	Pinch	⅛ tsp	¼ tsp
Rabbit, cut into pieces, or packaged rabbit legs	1¼ pounds	2 pounds	4 pounds
No-salt-added tomato paste	1 tblsp	1½ tblsp	2½ tblsp

1 Mix the tomatoes, lima beans, corn, bell pepper, whiskey, broth, thyme, rosemary, salt, celery seeds, pepper, and cayenne in the slow cooker. Smear the rabbit pieces with the tomato paste; nestle them into the vegetable mixture.

2 Cover and cook on low for 6 hours, or until very tender.

3 Use tongs to remove the rabbit pieces from the cooker to a cutting board, working with a spatula underneath each piece so that it doesn't fall apart. Cover the cooker and continue cooking on low. Cool the rabbit pieces for 10 minutes.

4 Debone the rabbit and shred the meat. Stir it back into the sauce in the cooker. Cover and cook on low for 15 minutes to heat through.

TESTERS' NOTES
• This hearty stew is stocked with vegetables, the better to set off the mild, sweet rabbit.
• Take care that you do not drain the canned tomatoes unless the recipe specifically instructs you to do so. As here, that extra juice is often necessary to the recipe's success.

rabbit with carrots and nutmeg

EFFORT: **A LITTLE** • PREP TIME: **25 MINUTES** • COOK TIME: **6 HOURS** • KEEPS ON WARM: **3 HOURS** • SERVES: **3 TO 10**

INGREDIENTS	2- TO 3½-QT	4- TO 5½-QT	6- TO 8-QT
Carrots, peeled and shredded	¾ pound	1¼ pounds	2¼ pounds
Golden raisins	3 tblsp	6 tblsp	¾ cup
Dried thyme	½ tsp	1 tsp	2 tsp
Ground allspice	¼ tsp	½ tsp	1 tsp
Grated nutmeg	¼ tsp	½ tsp	¾ tsp
Unsalted butter	½ tblsp	1 tblsp	2 tblsp
Rabbit, cut into pieces, or packaged rabbit legs	1½ pounds	3 pounds	6 pounds
Salt	¼ tsp	½ tsp	1 tsp
Ground black pepper	¼ tsp	½ tsp	1 tsp
Reduced-sodium chicken broth	½ cup	1 cup	2 cups

1 Mix the carrots, raisins, thyme, allspice, and nutmeg in the slow cooker. Spread the mixture into a bed.

2 Melt the butter in a large skillet set over medium heat. Season the rabbit with salt and pepper, then lay as many of the rabbit pieces in the skillet as will fit leaving a couple of inches of space between each. Brown on both sides, about 8 minutes, turning once.

3 Transfer the browned rabbit pieces to the slow cooker, nestling the pieces into the carrot mixture. Brown the remainder of the rabbit pieces, still working in batches to prevent overcrowding, and then transfer these pieces to the slow cooker.

4 Pour the broth over everything in the cooker. Cover and cook on low for 6 hours, or until the rabbit is tender without necessarily falling off the bone.

TESTERS' NOTES
• This is a fairly simple Old World stew, a great way to introduce yourself to rabbit if you've never given it a try.
• When you're working stovetop, you don't want any dark brown patches on the rabbit pieces; rather, some golden bits work best with this fairly mild, sweet meat.

poultry

CHANCES ARE, IF YOU'RE MAKING DINNER TONIGHT, IT'S SOME
piece of a bird—probably boneless skinless chicken breasts or boneless chicken thighs, but maybe ground turkey. We Americans cook more pounds of bird per person than we do of beef or pork—and certainly more than fish. And after a brief lull in poultry consumption in the early 2000s, we're back to new heights year after year.

      This poultry tendency is sort of strange, given how difficult birds can be to raise (ever tried to chase one that gets loose?) and the small yield of meat. But over the millennia, birds have been on the right side of every trend: the nomadic life epoch, the settle-down-in-groups movement, the chicken-in-every-pot era, the low-fat craze, the low-carb panic, and even the high-fat, throw-cholesterol-to-the-wind barbecue mania. They've even made a comeback among the hipsters who raise chickens on their rooftops.

Birds have long been a human staple because they're tasty, easy to cook, and nutritious. They're perfect for a slow cooker: lots of interstitial fat that slowly melts into the sauce, bringing a braise or stew to a fine fullness without much fuss.

All this culinary hero worship belies an Achilles' heel for us: chicken skin. Although it may be delicious when fried or roasted, it wins few awards in a slow cooker, turning soft and spongy. When there's no evaporation, things can't get crisp. Thus, poultry skin, long a favorite of bird eaters everywhere, almost comes to naught.

Fear not. There are ways around this dilemma: sure, by using skinless pieces of poultry when it doesn't matter; but also by taking an extra step to crisp that skin when it does. Carefully follow the requirements for skin-on or skinless birds in these recipes. There's no reason you'll want that skin in a long stew; there's every reason you'll want it in an intense braise.

Remember, too, that most slow cooker recipes are incredibly forgiving. Got a quarter pound more or less of the bird than the recipe requires? No problem! Another little bit won't make any difference to most of these stews. And if you have the small end of the large slow cookers (a 6-quart appliance), feel free to use the amounts for a stew or braise in a medium cooker for fewer servings.

A note on shopping: if you're buying chicken pieces in a Styrofoam container under plastic wrap, take them out of this packaging when you get them home, particularly if you intend to freeze them for a later use. That packaging can freeze to the pieces and allow bacterial contamination during refrigeration. Remove the absorbent pad and slip the chicken parts into a zip-closed bag to be stored in the fridge for no more than 2 days or in the freezer for up to 4 months.

So here's to our most popular sort of meal. And here's to more ways that you can prepare chicken without resorting to canned-this and processed-that. We'll be eating even more poultry next year. Count on it.

chicken

You'd expect lots of recipes for chicken in a slow cooker book, but you might not expect the range we've got here. Sure, there are plenty of braises and stews. But there's much more. A slow cooker is hardly a backyard fire pit, but the appliance does cook up some tasty barbecue. The meat stays so moist there's little danger of its drying out while the flavors—mostly smoked paprika and fiery chiles—soak in. No, you'll never fool true barbecue mavens with our Pulled Chicken (page 246) or Honey-Barbecued Chicken Drumsticks (page 259); but you might not need to. They'll be too busy wiping their mouths.

What's more, if we futz with the definition of roasting, we can turn our small countertop appliance into a grown-up's version of an Easy-Bake oven: no fuss, no mess, and pretty convenient all around. Yes, we must sometimes take care of the browning problem—sometimes by searing the chicken before it goes into the cooker and sometimes by crisping it under the broiler after it comes out. But we don't have to. And voilà: we can roast chicken breasts, chicken legs, and even whole chickens.

We do take exception to one common slow cooker practice: dropping frozen chicken breasts or thighs into the cooker and letting them go for 8 to 10 hours. The meat doesn't go from thawed to cooked quickly enough. It passes—for a long while—into a danger zone that lets nasty bacteria grow. These pests chow down and produce (ahem) residue often as toxic as the bacteria themselves. Suffice it to say, frozen chicken in a slow cooker is not a safe practice.

This section is divided by the basic chicken parts: we start with the tenders, then move on to the breasts (first boneless, then bone-in), then to the thighs (boneless before bone-in), before we get to the legs, wings, and finally the whole birds, sometimes cut up and a few left whole. We round it out with some recipes for ground chicken, several for the meat from a purchased rotisserie bird, and a recipe that uses chicken sausage.

When you're shopping for chicken, follow these basic guidelines:

- Choose chicken by weight, buying what the recipe requires.

- Look for supple skin with a pale, pink cast, neither leathery nor spongy.

- Check the expiration date and note whether it's a "sell by" (which gives you a couple more days) or a "use by" date.

- Rely on your sense of smell. A fresh chicken should have little odor—if any, bright and bracing, not sulfurous or metallic.

- Read the label. Some processed chicken is injected with a saline solution in a chicken-broth base. Juiced birds have a higher sodium content—and may not be to your liking for a variety of reasons, including so-called natural flavorings, which can include monosodium glutamate. If you've got injected chicken meat, reduce the salt in the recipe.

You should—as always—feel free to use these recipes for not only DIY road maps but also inspiration, altering spices and shifting vegetables. If you keep the bits of chicken the same as the recipe requires, you'll end up with a fine meal: always the best expectation.

chicken tenders with spicy apple butter

EFFORT: NOT MUCH • PREP TIME: **10 MINUTES** • COOK TIME: **2½ TO 3½ HOURS** • KEEPS ON WARM: **30 MINUTES** • SERVES: **3 TO 10**

INGREDIENTS	2- TO 3½-QT	4- TO 5½-QT	6- TO 8-QT
Uncoated, unseasoned chicken tenders	1½ pounds	3 pounds	4 pounds
Unsweetened apple butter	1 cup	2 cups	3 cups
Minced garlic	2 tsp	4 tsp	2 tblsp
Apple cider vinegar	1 tblsp	2 tblsp	3 tblsp
Red pepper flakes	1 tsp	2 tsp	1 tblsp
Ground cinnamon	½ tsp	1 tsp	½ tblsp
Salt	½ tsp	1 tsp	½ tblsp
Ground black pepper	½ tsp	1 tsp	½ tblsp
Grated nutmeg	¼ tsp	½ tsp	¾ tsp

1 Stir the chicken, apple butter, garlic, vinegar, red pepper flakes, cinnamon, salt, pepper, and nutmeg in the slow cooker.

2 Cover and cook on low for 2½ hours in a small slow cooker, 3 hours in a medium cooker, or 3½ hours in a large model, or until the chicken is cooked through and the sauce has thickened a bit.

TESTERS' NOTES
• Yep, you can cook white meat chicken in the slow cooker; you just can't cook it for long. Don't keep this dish warm for more than 30 minutes; the chicken will become unappealingly dry.
• By adding lots of warm spices like cinnamon and nutmeg to apple butter, as well as a little vinegar for kick, you can turn the jarred favorite into a down-home braising sauce.
• Apple butter is sweet by nature; the apples have been cooked down, even caramelized. You don't need added sugar in it, nor spices like cinnamon. Read the label carefully.
• When you stir the chicken and sauce in the slow cooker, make sure every piece of meat is well coated, most submerged.

INGREDIENTS EXPLAINED Sometimes called *chicken strips* or *chicken fingers*, chicken tenders are boneless, skinless strips of chicken meat. Years back, they were almost always the section of breast meat that hangs below the main lump on the bone; these days, they're sometimes taken from the breast but are also compressed from various bits from the bird.

apricot and jalapeño chicken tenders

EFFORT: NOT MUCH • PREP TIME: **15 MINUTES** • COOK TIME: **2½ TO 3½ HOURS** • KEEPS ON WARM: **1 HOUR** • SERVES: **3 TO 10**

INGREDIENTS	2- TO 3½-QT	4- TO 5½-QT	6- TO 8-QT
Uncoated, unseasoned, chicken tenders	1½ pounds	3 pounds	4½ pounds
Dried oregano	½ tblsp	1 tblsp	1½ tblsp
Salt	1 tsp	1½ tsp	2 tsp
Ground black pepper	½ tsp	1 tsp	1½ tsp
Garlic powder	¼ tsp	½ tsp	¾ tsp
All-fruit apricot spread	½ cup	1 cup	1½ cups

Minced jarred pickled jalapeño rings	Up to 2 tblsp	Up to ¼ cup	Up to 6 tblsp
Soy sauce	1 tblsp	2 tblsp	3 tblsp
Honey	1 tblsp	2 tblsp	3 tblsp
Fresh lemon juice	1 tblsp	2 tblsp	3 tblsp

1 Stir the chicken, oregano, salt, pepper, and garlic powder in the slow cooker until the meat is coated in the spices.

2 Whisk the all-fruit spread, jalapeño, soy sauce, honey, and lemon juice in a large bowl; pour over the tenders.

3 Cover and cook on low, stirring once halfway through cooking, for 2½ hours in a small slow cooker, 3 hours in a medium model, or 3½ hours in a large one, or until the chicken is no longer pink in the middle and the sauce is bubbling.

TESTERS' NOTES
• Apricots and jalapeños are a match made in heaven! Here's a mash-up based on a sweet-and-sour Asian sauce that's a new twist on comfort food.
• Use an all-fruit spread, not a jar of sugary jam or preserves. All-fruit spreads are always placed in the grocery store near the jams and jellies.

ALL-AMERICAN KNOW-HOW White-meat chicken can dry out in the cooker, mostly because it's so low in fat. The trick is to cook the meat beyond the first stage of dryness, until there's some collagen melt between the fibers. In our tests, the chicken tenders were officially "done" about an hour before our stated times, then turned dry 30 minutes later, and finally became moist again at the stated times because of collagen melt.

chicken breasts
with pears and fennel

EFFORT: **NOT MUCH** • PREP TIME: **15 MINUTES** • COOK TIME: **4 TO 5 HOURS** • KEEPS ON WARM: **1 HOUR** • SERVES: **3 TO 8**

INGREDIENTS	2- TO 3½-QT	4- TO 5½-QT	6- TO 8-QT
Fennel bulbs, trimmed and chopped (see page 211)	1 pound (about 2 cups)	1½ pounds (about 3½ cups)	2¼ pounds (about 5 cups)
Chopped dried pears	1 cup	1¾ cups	2½ cups
Fresh thyme sprigs	4	7	10
Ground black pepper	1 tsp	2 tsp	1 tblsp
Grated nutmeg	½ tsp	1 tsp	1½ tsp
Salt	½ tsp	1 tsp	1½ tsp
Boneless skinless chicken breasts	1½ pounds	2¾ pounds	4 pounds
Dry white wine, such as Pinot Grigio	¾ cup	1¼ cups	2 cups
Honey	1 tblsp	5 tsp	2½ tblsp

1 Mix the fennel, pears, and thyme sprigs in the slow cooker.

2 Stir the pepper, nutmeg, and salt in a small bowl; rub into the chicken breasts. Nestle them into the fennel mixture.

3 Whisk the wine and honey in a bowl; pour around (not over) the meat.

4 Cover and cook on low for 4 hours in a small slow cooker, 4½ hours in a medium one, or

(continued)

5 hours in a large model, or until the chicken is tender and the fennel is in a sweet, herbaceous sauce. Discard the thyme sprigs. Serve the chicken, fennel, and sauce in bowls.

TESTERS' NOTES
• Here's a light dinner, sweet but with complex flavors, and a great way to prepare chicken breasts.
• If you pour the liquids directly onto the chicken, you'll knock off the spice coating.
• For a nonalcoholic version, substitute unsweetened pear nectar for the wine.

Serve It Up! Pair these chicken breasts with cooked wild rice, seasoned with butter, ground cinnamon, and salt.

prosciutto-wrapped chicken on shredded carrots

EFFORT: **A LITTLE** • PREP TIME: **25 MINUTES** • COOK TIME: **4 TO 5 HOURS** • KEEPS ON WARM: **2 HOURS** • SERVES: **4 TO 12**

INGREDIENTS	2- TO 3½-QT	4- TO 5½-QT	6- TO 8-QT
Carrots, shredded	¾ pound	1¼ pounds	2 pounds
Balsamic vinegar	1 tblsp	2 tblsp	3 tblsp
Minced fresh rosemary leaves	2 tsp	1½ tblsp	2 tblsp
Worcestershire sauce	½ tblsp	1 tblsp	1½ tblsp
Paper-thin prosciutto slices	4	8	12
Fresh sage leaves	8	16	24
Boneless skinless chicken breasts	4	8	12

1 Combine the carrots, vinegar, rosemary, and Worcestershire sauce in the slow cooker; make an even bed of the mixture across the bottom of the cooker.

2 Put a piece of prosciutto on your work surface. Top with 2 sage leaves; then lay the chicken breasts on top so that their lengths run the same direction as the pieces of prosciutto. Fold the prosciutto over the chicken and set it seam side down on top of the carrot mixture. Continue making more, squeezing them to fit in one layer as much as possible.

3 Cover and cook on low for 4 hours in a small slow cooker, 4½ hours in a medium cooker, or 5 hours in a large one, or until the chicken is cooked through and the carrots have softened considerably. Serve in bowls with the broth around the chicken.

TESTERS' NOTES
• Shred the carrots through the large holes of a box grater—or with the shredding blade of a large food processor.
• If possible, fit these chicken breasts in one layer, even if you have to force them a bit, so that one side of the prosciutto stays out of the liquid, thereby improving its texture as it cooks.
• There's no need for aged balsamic vinegar here—a less expensive, full-flavored bottling will do.
• For a sweeter dish, substitute finely chopped onion for half the shredded carrots.

SHORTCUTS Shredded carrots are sometimes available in the refrigerator case of your supermarket's produce section.

INGREDIENTS EXPLAINED Prosciutto (*proh-SHOO-toe*), more properly *prosciutto crudo,* is cured bone-in ham, hung to age in barns or climate-controlled facilities until it's a salty, porky wonder. The best prosciutto is shaved right off the bone at the deli counter rather than sold sliced in packages. Keep the slices tightly sealed and in the fridge until you're ready to use them. The salty but subtle flavors hold up very well in a slow cooker.

chicken tikka masala with cucumber salad

EFFORT: **NOT MUCH** • PREP TIME: **15 MINUTES** • COOK TIME: **4 TO 5 HOURS** • KEEPS ON WARM: **1 HOUR** • SERVES: **3 TO 10**

INGREDIENTS	2- TO 3½-QT	4- TO 5½-QT	6- TO 8-QT
Boneless skinless chicken breasts, cut into 2-inch pieces	1½ pounds	3½ pounds	5 pounds
No-salt-added canned crushed tomatoes	1½ cups	2¼ cups	5 cups
No-salt-added tomato paste	¼ cup	⅔ cup	¾ cup plus 1 tblsp
Garam masala (see page 252)	1 tblsp	2½ tblsp	3½ tblsp
Minced peeled fresh ginger	1 tblsp	2½ tblsp	3½ tblsp
Minced garlic	2 tsp	1½ tblsp	2½ tblsp
Peeled and diced cucumbers	2 cups	4½ cup	7 cups
Minced fresh cilantro leaves	¼ cup	⅔ cup	1 cup
Rice vinegar	2 tblsp	5 tblsp	7 tblsp
Red pepper flakes	½ tsp	1¼ tsp	2 tsp
Sugar	½ tsp	1¼ tsp	2 tsp
Greek yogurt	¼ cup	⅔ cup	¾ cup

1 Mix the chicken, tomatoes, tomato paste, garam masala, ginger, and garlic in the slow cooker until the tomato paste dissolves and the chicken pieces are thoroughly coated.

2 Cover and cook on low for 3 hours in a small slow cooker, 3½ hours in a medium cooker, or 4 hours in a large one, or until the chicken is tender and the sauce is bubbling.

3 Meanwhile, mix the cucumbers, cilantro, rice vinegar, red pepper flakes, and sugar in a large bowl.

4 Stir the yogurt into the ingredients in the slow cooker until the sauce is creamy. Dish up the stew and serve the cool-but-spicy cucumber salad on top.

TESTERS' NOTES
• A slow cooker makes perfect *tikka masala*, a tomato-rich stew for chicken.
• You may find many blends of garam masala in the international aisle of your supermarket. You'll find even more at East Indian markets or their online outlets.
• There's no need to seed those cucumbers; the extra juice around those seeds will add to the stewiness of the final dish.

Serve It Up! Toss cooked, still-hot white basmati rice with toasted sliced almonds, chopped golden raisins, and a smidgen of unsalted butter to make a bed in the bowls for the stew.

ALL-AMERICAN KNOW-HOW In many of these recipes for boneless skinless chicken breasts, the meat is cut into specific sizes or chunks. Follow that measurement closely: it determines the cooking time, the amount of liquid used, and the overall effect of the dish.

chicken, rice, mushrooms, and cranberries

EFFORT: **NOT MUCH** • PREP TIME: **10 MINUTES** • COOK TIME: **5½ TO 7 HOURS** • KEEPS ON WARM: **1 HOUR** • SERVES: **3 TO 8**

INGREDIENTS	2- TO 3½-QT	4- TO 5½-QT	6- TO 8-QT
Boneless skinless chicken breasts, cut into 1½-inch pieces	1 pound	1¾ pounds	3 pounds
Thinly sliced cremini or brown button mushrooms, thinly sliced	1¼ cups (about 4 ounces)	2 cups (about 6 ounces)	3½ cups (about 11 ounces)
Low-sodium chicken broth	1 cup	1½ cups	2½ cups
Medium celery ribs, thinly sliced	2	3	4
Uncooked long-grain brown rice, such as brown basmati	½ cup	¾ cup	1¼ cups
Chopped yellow onion	⅓ cup	½ cup	1 cup (about 1 medium)
Dried cranberries	¼ cup	⅓ cup	⅔ cup
Sliced almonds	¼ cup	⅓ cup	⅔ cup
Dried sage	½ tsp	1 tsp	2 tsp
Salt	¼ tsp	½ tsp	1 tsp

1 Mix the chicken, mushrooms, broth, celery, rice, onion, cranberries, almonds, sage, and salt in the slow cooker.

2 Cover and cook on low for 5½ hours in a small slow cooker, 6 hours in a medium one, or 7 hours in a large one, or until the chicken is cooked through and the rice is tender. Let stand for 10 minutes, covered but unplugged, before serving.

TESTERS' NOTES
• We pumped up the flavors of the weeknight chicken casserole, adding cranberries and almonds, as well as lots of sage.
• Brown rice adds good texture—and whole-grain health—to this simple but hearty fare. Make sure the individual grains are submerged in the liquid before cooking.
• For more flavor, toast the sliced almonds in a dry skillet over medium-low heat until aromatic and lightly browned, about 4 minutes, tossing often.

ALL-AMERICAN KNOW-HOW Because of concerns associated with *Bacillius cereus* and rice, never let cooked rice stand at room temperature for more than 20 minutes—and never let it sit on the "keep warm" cycle of a slow cooker for more than 1 hour. Refrigerate any leftovers promptly.

chicken and dumplings

EFFORT: **A LOT** • PREP TIME: **35 MINUTES** • COOK TIME: **4½ TO 5 HOURS** • KEEPS ON WARM: **2 HOURS THROUGH STEP 2** • SERVES: **3 TO 9**

INGREDIENTS	2- TO 3½-QT	4- TO 5½-QT	6- TO 8-QT
FOR THE STEW			
Low-sodium chicken broth	1 cup	1¾ cups	3 cups
Sour cream (regular or low-fat)	¼ cup	½ cup	¾ cup
All-purpose flour	2½ tblsp	¼ cup	7 tblsp
Poultry seasoning	¼ tsp	½ tsp	1 tsp
Boneless skinless chicken breasts, cut into 1-inch pieces	1 pound	1¾ pounds	3 pounds

	1 small	1 large	2 large
Yellow onion, chopped	1 small	1 large	2 large
Medium celery ribs, chopped	3	4	6
Carrot, thinly sliced	1 small	1 medium	2 medium
FOR THE DUMPLINGS			
All-purpose flour	¼ cup	½ cup	¾ cup
Dry mustard (see page 392)	¼ tsp	½ tsp	¾ tsp
Baking soda	¼ tsp	½ tsp	¾ tsp
Salt	¼ tsp	½ tsp	¾ tsp
Milk	2 tblsp plus 2 tsp	⅓ cup	½ cup
Unsalted butter, melted	1 tblsp	1½ tblsp	2 tblsp plus 1 tsp

1 Whisk the broth, sour cream, flour, and poultry seasoning in the slow cooker until the flour has dissolved and the mixture is smooth. Stir in the chicken, onion, celery, and carrot until well coated.

2 Cover and cook on low for 4 hours in a small or medium slow cooker, or for 4½ hours in a large cooker.

3 Switch the cooker to high. Make the dumplings by whisking the flour, mustard, baking soda, and salt in a big bowl; stir in the milk and butter to form a sticky batter. Drop by tablespoonfuls onto the stew, each scoop about the size of a walnut in its shell. Cover the stew evenly with the small dumplings.

4 Cover and cook on high for 30 minutes, or until the dumplings are set and somewhat firm.

TESTERS' NOTES
• Since these dumplings are usually cooked over a bubbling stew, the slow cooker is the perfect tool to make this comfort food easy.

• Chop the vegetables into ½- to 1-inch pieces so they provide some texture.
• The dumpling batter is sticky. Coat a flatware tablespoon with nonstick spray so the gluey stuff will release better—or use your finger to thwack it onto the stew.

INGREDIENTS EXPLAINED Poultry seasoning is a blend of dried spices, popular in Southern cooking. You can make your own, skipping any salt, MSG, or even less savory additives that are in some mixes. Combine 3 tablespoons dried sage, 1½ tablespoons dried thyme, 1 tablespoon dried marjoram, ½ tablespoon ground black pepper, and 1 teaspoon ground cloves in a small bowl. Stir well, then store in a small glass jar or plastic container at room temperature in a cool, dark place for up to 1 year.

honey-mustard chicken breasts

EFFORT: **A LOT** • PREP TIME: **30 MINUTES** • COOK TIME: **4 HOURS/ 6 HOURS** • KEEPS ON WARM: **2 HOURS THROUGH STEP 4** • SERVES: **2 TO 6**

INGREDIENTS	2- TO 3½-QT	4- TO 5½-QT	6- TO 8-QT
Yellow potatoes (such as Yukon Gold), quartered	¾ pound	1¼ pounds	1¾ pounds
Honey	2 tblsp	¼ cup	⅓ cup
Dijon mustard	2 tblsp	¼ cup	⅓ cup
Bone-in skin-on chicken breasts (12 ounces each)	2	4	6
Mild paprika	¼ tsp	½ tsp	¾ tsp
Salt	¼ tsp	½ tsp	¾ tsp
Ground black pepper	¼ tsp	½ tsp	¾ tsp
Olive oil	½ tblsp	1 tblsp	1½ tblsp

(continued)

1 Make an even layer of the potato quarters across the bottom of the slow cooker.

2 Whisk the honey and mustard in a small bowl until creamy. Loosen the skin on the chicken breasts; rub the honey-mustard mixture both under the skin (thus, onto the meat) and over the skin of each breast.

3 Sprinkle the paprika, salt, and pepper over the skin of the breasts. Set them skin side up on the potatoes, squishing them to fit in one layer.

4 Cover and cook on high for 4 hours or on low for 6 hours, or until an instant-read meat thermometer inserted into the meat of a breast without touching bone registers 165°F.

5 Position the oven rack 6 inches from the broiler and turn on your broiler to warm it up. Use tongs to transfer the breasts, skin side up, onto a rimmed baking sheet.

6 Brush the olive oil over the skin. Broil the chicken breasts until brown and a bit crisp, about 3 minutes. Serve with the braised potatoes on the side.

TESTERS' NOTES
• Bone-in chicken breasts can indeed be prepared in the slow cooker, so long as you lift them up a bit off the produced fat (or submerge them in a sauce, as in some other recipes in this book).
• Because it's difficult to tell when these large breasts are done, you'll need to use an instant-read meat thermometer for safety's sake. That kitchen gadget is your best tool for avoiding most pathogens you might face from undercooked meat.
• As you lift the skin off the raw meat, be on the lookout for any blobs of fat that you can pull out and throw away. Otherwise, they'll melt and overwhelm the potatoes below.

INGREDIENTS EXPLAINED Bone-in chicken breasts often have a bit of rib meat hanging down off one side.

For almost all recipes, this should be sliced off and discarded—or saved in a zip-closed plastic bag in the freezer for making Chicken Stock (see page 110).

ALL-AMERICAN KNOW-HOW To loosen the skin from a chicken breast, start at the pointy, narrow end of the breast and run a clean, dry finger under the line where the skin meets the meat. Run your finger back and forth, enlarging this space, fitting in a second finger and working gently until you get near the thicker end. Lift the skin off the meat without stretching it too much or tearing it loose.

chicken jambalaya

EFFORT: **A LITTLE** • PREP TIME: **15 MINUTES** • COOK TIME: **5 HOURS** • KEEPS ON WARM: **1 HOUR** • SERVES: **2 TO 6**

INGREDIENTS	2- TO 3½-QT	4- TO 5½-QT	6- TO 8-QT
Boneless skinless chicken breasts, cut into 1-inch cubes	¾ pound	1¼ pounds	2½ pounds
Smoked sausage, preferably Cajun andouille, cut into ½-inch pieces	5 ounces	8 ounces	1 pound
No-salt-added canned diced tomatoes	1¾ cups	3½ cups	7 cups
Chopped yellow onion	⅓ cup	¾ cup (about 1 small)	1½ cups
Stemmed, seeded, and chopped green bell pepper	⅓ cup	¾ cup (about 1 small)	1½ cups
Uncooked long-grain white rice	6 tblsp	¾ cup	1½ cups
Thinly sliced celery	6 tblsp	½ cup	1 cup

Dried thyme	½ tsp	1 tsp	2 tsp
Dried sage	¼ tsp	½ tsp	1¼ tsp
Celery seeds	¼ tsp	½ tsp	1¼ tsp
Hot pepper sauce, such as Tabasco	¼ tsp	½ tsp	1 tsp
Bay leaves	1	2	3

1 Stir the chicken, sausage, tomatoes, onion, bell pepper, rice, celery, thyme, sage, celery seeds, hot sauce, and bay leaves.

2 Cover and cook on low for 5 hours, or until the rice is tender and the stew has thickened a bit. Discard the bay leaves before ladling the stew into bowls.

TESTERS' NOTES
• There are actually two types of jambalaya. As a general rule, the Creole version has tomatoes, the Cajun version doesn't. This is a streamlined, slow cooker morph of the former.
• The rice is more of a thickener than a main component of the casserole. (We didn't use brown rice here because it doesn't have enough stickiness to get the job done.)
• Add up to 1 cup frozen cut okra, thawed, with the other vegetables.
• Substitute smoked turkey sausage for the andouille for a somewhat healthier meal.

SHORTCUTS Omit the dried thyme, sage, and celery seeds; substitute a bottled Cajun seasoning blend: 1 teaspoon for a small slow cooker, 2 teaspoons for a medium batch, and 1½ tablespoons for a large one. If your bottled blend includes cayenne, consider omitting the hot sauce as well.

INGREDIENTS EXPLAINED Cajun andouille sausage is a coarse-grained smoked sausage made with pork, onion, garlic, and seasonings. It should not be confused with the French andouille, made from tripe and other innards. If Cajun andouille proves hard to find, substitute smoked kielbasa.

apricot and buttermilk curry chicken breasts

EFFORT: **A LITTLE** • PREP TIME: **25 MINUTES** • COOK TIME: **4 HOURS 15 MINUTES/6 HOURS 15 MINUTES** • KEEPS ON WARM: **2 HOURS THROUGH STEP 5** • SERVES: **2 TO 6**

INGREDIENTS	2- TO 3½-QT	4- TO 5½-QT	6- TO 8-QT
Low-sodium chicken broth	⅓ cup	⅔ cup	1 cup
All-fruit apricot spread	1½ tblsp	2½ tblsp	¼ cup
Diced dried apricots	1½ tblsp	2½ tblsp	¼ cup
Ground turmeric	¾ tsp	1¼ tsp	2 tsp
Ground cumin	¾ tsp	1¼ tsp	2 tsp
Ground coriander	¾ tsp	1¼ tsp	2 tsp
Chili powder	¾ tsp	1¼ tsp	2 tsp
Ground cinnamon	¼ tsp	½ tsp	¾ tsp
Salt	¼ tsp	½ tsp	¾ tsp
Cayenne	Pinch	⅛ tsp	¼ tsp
Unsalted butter	1 tblsp	1½ tblsp	2 tblsp
Bone-in skinless chicken breasts (12 ounces each), sliced in half widthwise	2	4	6
Yellow onion, chopped	1 small	1 medium	2 medium
Minced peeled fresh ginger	1 tblsp	1½ tblsp	2 tblsp
Minced garlic	1 tsp	2 tsp	1 tblsp
Dry white wine, such as Chardonnay	2 tblsp	¼ cup	6 tblsp
Stemmed, seeded, and chopped green bell pepper	⅓ cup	⅔ cup	1 cup (about 1 medium)
Buttermilk	2 tblsp	¼ cup	⅓ cup

(continued)

1 Whisk the broth, apricot spread, dried apricots, turmeric, cumin, coriander, chili powder, cinnamon, salt, and cayenne in the slow cooker until the spread is dissolved.

2 Melt the butter in a large skillet over medium heat. Add a few of the chicken pieces, skin side down, and cook, 5 or 6 minutes, until well browned. Transfer to the slow cooker skin side up and continue browning more pieces. (If you'll be working in several batches, divide the butter among them so that there's always some fat in the skillet.)

3 Dump the onion into the skillet, still set over the heat; stir until translucent, 2 to 4 minutes, depending on the size of the batch.

4 Stir in the ginger and garlic, cook for a few seconds, then pour in the wine. Bring to a boil, scraping up any browned bits in the skillet. Scrape the contents of the skillet into the cooker over the breasts. Sprinkle the bell pepper over everything.

5 Cover and cook on high for 4 hours or on low for 6 hours, or until the chicken is tender and an instant-read meat thermometer inserted into the thickest piece of chicken breast without touching bone registers 165°F.

6 Transfer the chicken breasts to a serving bowl or platter; tent loosely with foil to keep warm. Stir the buttermilk into the sauce in the cooker. Cover and cook on high for 15 minutes to heat through.

TESTERS' NOTES
• This dish is actually modeled on a South African curry, which is sweet, sour, and spicy. The buttermilk adds a tangy finish.
• Here's a trade-off: soften the onion for sweetness; don't soften the bell pepper for a peppery bite. They balance each other in this rather rich and heavily spiced sauce.

INGREDIENTS EXPLAINED Chickens have only one breast in the barnyard—that is, the large, meaty chest above their legs. However, in the kitchen we divide the breast into two sections or lobes, each on one side of the breast bone; we then refer to each of these as a "breast." It would be far more accurate, however, to say "chicken breast halves."

pulled chicken

EFFORT: **NOT MUCH** • PREP TIME: **20 MINUTES** • COOK TIME: **4 HOURS/6 HOURS** • KEEPS ON WARM: **2 HOURS** • SERVES: **3 TO 8**

INGREDIENTS	2- TO 3½-QT	4- TO 5½-QT	6- TO 8-QT
No-salt-added canned crushed tomatoes	½ cup	1 cup	1⅔ cup
Chopped canned green chiles, hot or mild	¼ cup	½ cup	¾ cup
Red wine vinegar	1½ tblsp	2½ tblsp	⅓ cup
Honey	1 tblsp	2 tblsp	3½ tblsp
Mild smoked paprika	1 tblsp	2 tblsp	¼ cup
No-salt-added tomato paste	2 tsp	1 tblsp	2½ tblsp
Worcestershire sauce	½ tblsp	2 tsp	1½ tblsp
Ancho chile powder (see page 147)	1 tsp	2 tsp	4 tsp
Dry mustard (see page 392)	1 tsp	2 tsp	4 tsp
Ground cloves	¼ tsp	¼ tsp	½ tsp
Boneless skinless chicken thighs	1¼ pounds	2¼ pounds	4 pounds

Chopped yellow onion	¼ cup	½ cup	¾ cup (about 1 small)
Minced garlic	1 tsp	2 tsp	1 tblsp

1 Mix the tomatoes, chiles, vinegar, honey, paprika, tomato paste, Worcestershire sauce, chile powder, mustard, and cloves in the slow cooker until the tomato paste dissolves and the spices are evenly blended throughout. Add the chicken, onion, and garlic; toss well to coat.

2 Cover and cook on high for 4 hours or on low for 6 hours, or until the meat is beyond tender, truly falling apart. Use two forks to shred the chicken into threads right in the cooker; stir well to mix with the sauce.

TESTERS' NOTES

• We love the glories of pulled pork; however, by altering spices to consider the somewhat more savory flavor of chicken and adjusting liquids to account for its slightly drier texture, we can make a fine (and more economical) version with chicken thighs.

• Even boneless skinless chicken thighs may have some fat clinging to the meat. Trim this off for a healthier meal. (Given how the slow cooker makes all meat luxuriously moist, you won't notice the difference.)

Serve It Up! We prefer toasted whole wheat buns—or even slices of toasted multigrain bread—for this pulled chicken. Pickled jalapeño rings and deli mustard would make great condiments. Since the sandwiches are messy, cut children's sandwiches into tiny bites or wrap the sections in wax paper to catch the drips.

chicken mole rojo

EFFORT: **A LITTLE** • PREP TIME: **15 MINUTES** • COOK TIME: **4 HOURS/7 HOURS** • KEEPS ON WARM: **2 HOURS** • SERVES: **3 TO 10**

INGREDIENTS	2- TO 3½-QT	4- TO 5½-QT	6- TO 8-QT
Dried New Mexican red chiles	1	2	4
Drained no-salt-added canned diced tomatoes	1 cup	2 cups	4¼ cups
Chopped yellow onion	¼ cup	½ cup	1 cup (about 1 medium)
Canned chipotle chile in adobo sauce, stemmed and seeded	½	1	2
Chili powder	2½ tsp	2 tblsp	5 tblsp
Garlic cloves, peeled and quartered	1	2	4
Ground cumin	½ tsp	1 tsp	2¼ tsp
Ground cinnamon	½ tsp	1 tsp	2¼ tsp
Salt	¼ tsp	½ tsp	1 tsp
Bone-in skinless chicken breasts	1¾ pounds	3½ pounds	7 pounds

1 Stem and seed the chiles, removing any bits of membrane that attach the seeds to the skin. Mince that skin and put the tiny bits in a big blender.

2 Add the tomatoes, onion, chipotle, chili powder, garlic, cumin, cinnamon, and salt. Cover and blend until smooth, scraping down the inside of the canister occasionally.

3 Set the chicken in the slow cooker, squishing them to fit in one layer. Pour the sauce

(continued)

from the blender over and around them, scraping every last drop out of that blender.

4 Cover and cook on high for 4 hours or on low for 7 hours, or until the meat is falling-off-the-bone tender.

TESTERS' NOTES
• *Mole rojo* is a nonchocolate version of the famed Oaxacan sauce, thick with tomatoes and aromatics. It's also a great braising medium for bone-in chicken breasts.
• The chiles are not soaked in this version but instead used dry. The best way to mince the skin is with a pair of kitchen shears, working over the blender as you snip off tiny bits.

ALL-AMERICAN KNOW-HOW While the threat of salmonella need not be sensationalized, a good cook takes a few precautions:

• Never rinse chicken before cooking: doing so can cause cross-contamination through random splatters or run-off in your sink. (Besides, bacteria are killed by heat, not water.)
• After working with raw poultry, wash your hands with soap under very warm water for 10 seconds.
• Wash all cutting boards and utensils with hot soapy water, preferably in the dishwasher.
• Wash all kitchen surfaces with a bleach-based cleaner.

INGREDIENTS EXPLAINED A cultivar of the Anaheim chile, the New Mexican chile is prized in Southwestern cooking for its bright, slightly sour pop and contrasting, sweet burn. Look for these chiles dried in bags at most supermarkets, often in the produce section, or in more copious supply, often fresh, at Latin American markets. The dried chiles should be pliable and red, not desiccated or dusty brown; they should have an earthy, fruity aroma.

chicken mole negro

EFFORT: **A LOT** • PREP TIME: **40 MINUTES** • COOK TIME: **4 HOURS/ 7 HOURS** • KEEPS ON WARM: **2 HOURS** • SERVES: **3 TO 10**

INGREDIENTS	2- TO 3½-QT	4- TO 5½-QT	6- TO 8-QT
Dried ancho chiles (see page 138)	1	2	4
Dried mulato chiles (see page 138)	1	2	4
Dried pasilla chiles (see page 138)	1	2	4
Sliced almonds	2 tblsp	¼ cup	½ cup
Drained no-salt-added canned diced tomatoes	6 tblsp	¾ cup	1½ cups
No-salt-added tomato paste	1½ tblsp	2 tblsp plus 2 tsp	⅓ cup
White sesame seeds	2½ tsp	1½ tblsp	3 tblsp
Dried figs, stemmed and halved	1	2	3
Bittersweet chocolate, finely grated	¼ ounce	½ ounce	1 ounce
Minced garlic	½ tsp	1 tsp	2 tsp
Ground cumin	½ tsp	1 tsp	2 tsp
Dried oregano	½ tsp	1 tsp	2 tsp
Ground cloves	¼ tsp	½ tsp	1 tsp
Salt	¼ tsp	½ tsp	1 tsp
Bone-in skinless chicken breasts	1¾ pounds	3½ pounds	7 pounds

1 Bring a pan of water to a boil over high heat. Stem the chiles and scrape out the seeds, as well as any desiccated bits of the pale white membranes. Tear the cleaned chiles into smaller bits, place these in a large bowl, and fill the bowl about halfway with boiling water. Set aside for 20 minutes.

2 Meanwhile, toast the sliced almonds in a dry skillet over medium-low heat until fragrant and lightly browned, between 4 and 6 minutes, stirring frequently. Pour the almonds into a large food processor or a large blender.

3 Drain the plumped-up chiles in a colander set in the sink, discarding the soaking liquid, and add them to the processor or blender. Also dump in the tomatoes, tomato paste, sesame seeds, figs, chocolate, garlic, cumin, oregano, cloves, and salt. Cover and process or blend until a smooth puree, scraping down the inside of the canister a few times to make sure every bit of those chiles gets mushed up.

4 Place the chicken breasts in the cooker as evenly as possible; pour the sauce over and around them.

5 Cover and cook on high for 4 hours or on low for 7 hours, or until the chicken is very tender, certainly falling off the bone.

TESTERS' NOTES
• If you can't already tell, we're nuts about *mole negro*, the famed Oaxacan chile sauce, and this is a fairly authentic presentation.
• For the best flavor, use bone-in chicken breasts. However, there's no need for the skin—it'll just turn gummy. Better to coat them in that luxurious sauce and let them get tender in their naked state.
• Grate the chocolate with a microplane so that it's in the finest possible threads.
• The total amount of sauce made for a large slow cooker may well override the capacity for a large food processor. Work in batches to avoid messy cleanups.

Serve It Up! For a bed in the bowls, try **Mashed Plantains**, a Latin American favorite: Cut unpeeled semi-ripe (no brown spotting) plantains into 3-inch sections and boil them in water for 30 minutes. Drain, cool, and peel, then mash the plantains with a potato masher or a fork. Mince some garlic and cook until lightly browned in plenty of olive oil over medium-low heat. Stir this mixture into the mashed plantains and season with salt and ground black pepper.

teriyaki-glazed chicken thighs

EFFORT: **NOT MUCH** • PREP TIME: **10 MINUTES** • COOK TIME: **3 HOURS/5 HOURS** • KEEPS ON WARM: **1 HOUR** • SERVES: **2 TO 8**

INGREDIENTS	2- TO 3½-QT	4- TO 5½-QT	6- TO 8-QT
Boneless skinless chicken thighs	1 pound	2½ pounds	4 pounds
Mirin	3 tblsp	7 tblsp	¾ cup
Soy sauce	2 tblsp	5 tblsp	½ cup
Packed dark brown sugar	1 tblsp	2½ tblsp	¼ cup
Minced peeled fresh ginger	2 tsp	5 tsp	2½ tblsp
Red pepper flakes	½ tsp	1¼ tsp	2 tsp

1 Toss the chicken, mirin, soy sauce, brown sugar, ginger, and red pepper flakes in the slow cooker until the brown sugar has dissolved and coated the meat.

2 Cover and cook on high for 3 hours or on low for 6 hours, or until the chicken is lacquered yet tender.

(continued)

TESTERS' NOTES

• Rather than using a bottled teriyaki sauce (with too many preservatives), we prefer this streamlined version, a mix of only five ingredients.

• For the best glazing effect, arrange the chicken thighs in one layer even if you have to squish them to fit.

• Since the glaze is sticky, consider lightly oiling the inside of your slow cooker canister if it doesn't have a nonstick finish or has had food burned onto it in the past.

INGREDIENTS EXPLAINED Mirin is a Japanese rice wine, sweet and aromatic, mostly used in cooking, although finer bottlings are sometimes drunk straight. If you can't find it among the Asian products or cooking wines at your supermarket, substitute white wine but add ¼ teaspoon granulated sugar for every 3 tablespoons wine.

buttery and spicy chicken thighs

EFFORT: **NOT MUCH** • PREP TIME: **15 MINUTES** • COOK TIME: **6 HOURS** • KEEPS ON WARM: **2 HOURS** • SERVES: **3 TO 12**

INGREDIENTS	2- TO 3½-QT	4- TO 5½-QT	6- TO 8-QT
Boneless skinless chicken thighs	1½ pounds	3 pounds	6 pounds
Thinly sliced yellow onion	½ cup	1 cup (about 1 small)	2 cups
Moderately dry white wine, such as Viognier	2 tblsp	¼ cup	½ cup
Minced peeled fresh ginger	1 tblsp	2 tblsp	¼ cup
Unsalted butter, melted	1 tblsp	2 tblsp	¼ cup
Minced jarred pickled jalapeño rings	1 tblsp	2 tblsp	¼ cup
Minced garlic	½ tblsp	1 tblsp	2 tblsp
Green cardamom pods	4	8	16
Whole cloves	4	8	16
Coriander seeds	½ tsp	1 tsp	2 tsp
Cumin seeds	¼ tsp	½ tsp	1 tsp
4-inch cinnamon stick	½	½	1

1 Mix the chicken, onion, wine, ginger, butter, jalapeño, garlic, cardamom pods, cloves, coriander seeds, cumin seeds, and cinnamon stick in the slow cooker.

2 Cover and cook on low for 6 hours, or until the meat is velvety tender and the flavors have blended. Discard the cardamom pods, cloves, and cinnamon stick before serving.

TESTERS' NOTES

• This casserole is quite aromatic, thanks to all those spices, and the butter adds a rich silkiness. It's like a sophisticated, grown-up take on Buffalo chicken.

• You'll have to go trawling for the whole spices when the dish is done. (No one wants the pop of a whole clove with their chicken.)

• If you like tamer fare and don't want all these pungent spices, halve the amount of cardamom and cloves.

Serve It Up! Make **Farro Salad:** Combine cooked, drained, and cooled farro (preferably either whole-grain or *semi-perlato*), chopped fennel, chopped red bell pepper, olive oil, stemmed thyme leaves, white balsamic vinegar, and salt in a large serving bowl.

chicken, chorizo, and brown rice

EFFORT: **A LITTLE** • PREP TIME: **25 MINUTES** • COOK TIME: **5 HOURS**
• KEEPS ON WARM: **1 HOUR** • SERVES: **3 TO 8**

INGREDIENTS	2- TO 3½-QT	4- TO 5½-QT	6- TO 8-QT
Olive oil	1 tblsp	2 tblsp	3 tblsp
Dried chorizo, or other spicy pork sausage, sliced into 2-inch pieces	¼ pound	6 ounces	10 ounces
Boneless skinless chicken thighs	1 pound	2 pounds	3 pounds
No-salt-added canned diced tomatoes	1¾ cups	3½ cups	5 cups
Drained and rinsed canned chickpeas	1 cup	1¾ cups	2⅔ cups
Frozen green peas, thawed	¾ cup	1½ cups	2 cups
Yellow onion, chopped	1 medium	1 large	2 medium
Chopped jarred roasted red pepper (pimiento)	¾ cup	1½ cups	2¼ cups
Uncooked medium-grain white rice, such as Arborio	⅔ cup	1⅓ cups	2 cups
Minced garlic	1 tsp	2 tsp	1 tblsp
Dried oregano	1 tsp	2 tsp	1 tblsp
Dried thyme	1 tsp	2 tsp	1 tblsp
Mild smoked paprika	1 tsp	2 tsp	1 tblsp
Salt	½ tsp	1 tsp	½ tblsp
Saffron	⅛ tsp	¼ tsp	½ tsp
Bay leaves	1	2	3

1 Set a large skillet over medium heat for a few minutes, then add the oil. Slip the sausage pieces into the skillet and cook on both sides, turning once, until lightly browned with plenty of fat in the skillet, 3 to 6 minutes. Use a slotted spoon to move the chorizo to a large plate next to the stove.

2 Slip the chicken into the skillet—as many as will fit. Brown on both sides, turning once, about 6 minutes. Transfer the browned thighs to the plate with the chorizo; add more chicken to the skillet and keep browning as necessary.

3 Stir the tomatoes, chickpeas, peas, onion, red pepper, rice, garlic, oregano, thyme, paprika, salt, saffron, and bay leaves in the slow cooker. Tuck the chicken pieces and chorizo into this mixture.

4 Cover and cook on low for 5 hours, or until almost all of the liquid has been absorbed and the rice is tender. Discard the bay leaves and let stand in the covered (but unplugged) appliance for 10 minutes before serving.

TESTERS' NOTES
• This casserole is sort of like *arroz con pollo*, a Spanish favorite.
• Store leftovers quickly in a sealed container in the fridge.
• Chop up the leftover chicken and sausage, stir them back into the rice mixture, add a beaten egg or two, and form the mixture into 4-inch cakes that you can fry in unsalted butter or olive oil in a large skillet the next day.

INGREDIENTS EXPLAINED Jarred roasted red peppers are sometimes called *pimientos*—and are sold both whole and chopped. The smaller bits can be too squishy; the whole peppers in jars have a firmer texture. If you don't want to spring for a whole jar, look for these roasted red peppers on the salad bar at your supermarket. One medium roasted red pepper will yield about ¾ cup chopped pepper.

chicken rogan josh

EFFORT: **A LITTLE** • PREP TIME: **20 MINUTES** • COOK TIME: **5 HOURS** • KEEPS ON WARM: **1 HOUR** • SERVES: **2 TO 8**

INGREDIENTS	2- TO 3½-QT	4- TO 5½-QT	6- TO 8-QT
Plain Greek yogurt	½ cup	1 cup	1¾ cups
Yellow onion, chopped	1 small	1 medium	1 large
Minced peeled fresh ginger	5 tsp	3 tblsp	5 tblsp
Minced garlic	1 tsp	2 tsp	4½ tsp
Fennel seeds	½ tsp	1 tsp	2 tsp
Whole cloves	½ tsp	1 tsp	2 tsp
Cumin seeds	½ tsp	1 tsp	2 tsp
Ground turmeric	¼ tsp	½ tsp	1 tsp
Cayenne	¼ tsp	½ tsp	1 tsp
Ground cinnamon	¼ tsp	½ tsp	1 tsp
Boneless skinless chicken thighs	1¼ pounds	2½ pounds	4½ pounds
Unsalted butter, melted and cooled	1 tblsp	2 tblsp	3 tblsp
Garam masala	½ tsp	1 tsp	2 tsp

1 Stir the yogurt, onion, ginger, garlic, fennel seeds, cloves, cumin seeds, turmeric, cayenne, and cinnamon in the slow cooker until the sauce is uniformly colored.

2 Toss the chicken, butter, and garam masala in a large bowl until the meat is coated in the spice mixture. Tuck the thighs into the yogurt mixture, then scrape every last drop of spices and butter into the cooker.

3 Cover and cook on low for 5 hours, or until the meat is tender and cooked through.

TESTERS' NOTES

• Thoroughgoing comfort food, Rogan Josh is a Kashmiri dish, usually made with lamb, although we prefer it with chicken in the slow cooker for a cleaner, brighter taste.

• Although Rogan Josh is traditionally made with shallots, not onions, we prefer the latter's slightly more earthy taste in this long-cooked version.

• If you don't have Greek yogurt, strain regular plain yogurt in a coffee-filter–lined or cheesecloth-lined colander set in the refrigerator over a bowl to catch the drips. It takes two to three times the amount of regular yogurt to yield the necessary amount of strained yogurt.

Serve It Up! Make an easy rice dish by tossing together long-grain white or brown basmati rice, minced peeled cucumber, minced red onion, corn kernels, and a little rice vinegar for a tart spark.

INGREDIENTS EXPLAINED Garam masala is a blend of ground spices from northern India—technically a curry, although with less flexibility among the chosen spices and so a category on its own. The name means "warm spices," a bow to its alleged warming properties. Look for brands that contain cloves, cinnamon, cumin, and cardamom.

ALL-AMERICAN KNOW-HOW Make your own **Garam Masala:** Blend 3 tablespoons ground coriander, 1½ tablespoons ground cinnamon, 1½ tablespoons ground cumin, 1 tablespoon ground ginger, 1 teaspoon ground cloves, 1 teaspoon ground fenugreek, 1 teaspoon ground black pepper, ¾ teaspoon ground cardamom, and ½ teaspoon turmeric in a small bowl. Store it, covered, in a small glass bottle or a small plastic container in your spice cabinet or drawer for up to 4 months.

sticky chicken thighs with apricots

EFFORT: **NOT MUCH** • PREP TIME: **10 MINUTES** • COOK TIME: **5 HOURS** • KEEPS ON WARM: **3 HOURS** • SERVES: **2 TO 8**

INGREDIENTS	2- TO 3½-QT	4- TO 5½-QT	6- TO 8-QT
Bone-in skinless chicken thighs	1 pound	2½ pounds	4 pounds
Quartered dried apricots	⅓ cup	¾ cup	1⅓ cups
Shelled unsalted pistachios	3 tblsp	½ cup	¾ cup
Packed dark brown sugar	4 tsp	3 tblsp	⅓ cup
Minced peeled fresh ginger	4 tsp	3 tblsp	⅓ cup
Ground cinnamon	¼ tsp	1 tsp	1¾ tsp
Ground coriander	¼ tsp	1 tsp	1¾ tsp
Ground cumin	¼ tsp	1 tsp	1¾ tsp
Salt	⅛ tsp	½ tsp	1 tsp

1 Mix the chicken, apricots, pistachios, brown sugar, ginger, cinnamon, coriander, cumin, and salt in the slow cooker until the sugar has melted into a coating for the meat.

2 Cover and cook on low for 6 hours, or until the chicken is falling-off-the-bone tender.

TESTERS' NOTES
• As a hearty meal with nonetheless bright flavors, you might consider this for your next Memorial Day picnic. Just drag the slow cooker right out to the deck. Take that, barbecue mavens!
• Leaving the meat on the bone will give the chicken a texture more reminiscent of a roasted dish, less like a braised casserole. There's no extra liquid here, so the chicken thighs become glazed in the sauce.

• If you can find only chicken thighs with the skin attached, you'll need to skin each before adding it slow cooker, as well as removing any globs of fat.

chicken and sweet potato stew

EFFORT: **NOT MUCH** • PREP TIME: **20 MINUTES** • COOK TIME: **6 HOURS** • KEEPS ON WARM: **3 HOURS** • SERVES: **3 TO 8**

INGREDIENTS	2- TO 3½-QT	4- TO 5½-QT	6- TO 8-QT
Bone-in skinless chicken thighs	1½ pounds	2½ pounds	4 pounds
Medium sweet potatoes, each peeled and cut into 6 spears	1 pound	2 pounds	3 pounds
White button mushrooms, thinly sliced	3 ounces (about 1 cup)	7 ounces (about 2 cups)	10 ounces (about 3 cups)
Large shallots, peeled and halved	3	6	10
Garlic cloves, peeled	6	12	20
Dry vermouth	½ cup	1 cup	1¾ cups
All-purpose flour	1 tblsp	2 tblsp	3 tblsp
Minced fresh rosemary leaves	½ tblsp	1 tblsp	1½ tblsp
Salt	¼ tsp	½ tsp	¾ tsp
Ground black pepper	¼ tsp	½ tsp	¾ tsp

1 Combine the chicken, sweet potato spears, mushrooms, shallots, and garlic cloves in the slow cooker, tossing a few times.

(continued)

2 Whisk the vermouth, flour, rosemary, salt, and pepper in a bowl until the flour dissolves; pour over the chicken and vegetables.

3 Cover and cook on low for 6 hours, or until the chicken is cooked through and the stew is very fragrant.

TESTERS' NOTES
• In this easy stew, the sweet potatoes stay firmer because they're in large pieces, a good match with the thighs.
• Sweet potatoes and mushrooms are a fine pairing—sweet with earthy; bright with a mild *umami* presence.
• The shallots and garlic will soften until creamy, a real treat when smeared on a piece of crunchy bread.

chicken thighs
with celery root and sour cream

EFFORT: **A LOT** • PREP TIME: **30 MINUTES** • COOK TIME: **5½ HOURS**
• KEEPS ON WARM: **2 HOURS THROUGH STEP 5** • SERVES: **3 TO 8**

INGREDIENTS	2- TO 3½-QT	4- TO 5½-QT	6- TO 8-QT
Thin bacon slices, chopped	2	4	7
Bone-in skinless chicken thighs	1¼ pounds	2½ pounds	4 pounds
Yellow onion, chopped	1 small	1 medium	1 large
Celery root, peeled and cut into 2-inch cubes (see page 81)	½ pound	1 pound	1²/₃ pounds
Medium carrots, cut into 2-inch sections	1	2	3
Minced garlic	2 tsp	1 tblsp	4 tsp
Fresh thyme sprigs	2	4	6
Moderately dry white wine, such as Sauvignon Blanc	1 cup	1¾ cups	3 cups
Coarse-grained mustard	1 tblsp	2 tblsp	3 tblsp
Bay leaves	1	2	3
Sour cream (regular or low-fat)	2 tblsp	¼ cup	⅓ cup

1 Fry the bacon in a large skillet over medium-high heat until crisp, stirring occasionally, between 3 and 5 minutes. Use a slotted spoon to transfer the bacon bits to the slow cooker.

2 Brown the thighs in the rendered bacon fat, adding as many as will fit comfortably in the skillet, about 6 minutes, turning once. Transfer the thighs to the cooker and continue browning more as necessary.

3 Keep the skillet over the heat and add the onion. Cook, stirring frequently, until translucent, between 3 and 5 minutes. Either use the slotted spoon to transfer the onion bits to the cooker or scrape the contents (fat and all) from the skillet into the cooker.

4 Stir in the celery root, carrot, garlic, and thyme sprigs. Whisk the wine and mustard in a medium bowl, pour into the cooker, and tuck the bay leaves into the sauce.

5 Cover and cook on low for 5½ hours, or until the chicken is tender but not yet falling off the bone.

6 Use tongs or a slotted spoon to transfer the thighs to a big bowl. Stir the sour cream into the sauce in the slow cooker. Return the thighs to the sauce and cook on high for 10 minutes to bring everything up to serving temperature. Discard the thyme sprigs and bay leaves before serving.

TESTERS' NOTES
• Bacon, wine, mustard, thyme, sour cream—this dish is like a European countryside classic amped up with more assertive American proportions.
• Cut the celery root and carrot into slightly larger pieces so they've got better texture after the long cooking.

spicy chicken thighs with plantains

EFFORT: **A LOT** • PREP TIME: **12 HOURS 20 MINUTES (INCLUDES MARINATING THE CHICKEN)** • COOK TIME: **6 HOURS** • KEEPS ON WARM: **4 HOURS** • SERVES: **3 TO 9**

INGREDIENTS	2- TO 3½-QT	4- TO 5½-QT	6- TO 8-QT
Medium whole scallions, trimmed and thinly sliced	1	3	5
Garlic cloves, peeled	1	2	3
Balsamic vinegar	1 tblsp	2 tblsp	3½ tblsp
Honey	½ tblsp	1 tblsp	2 tblsp
Bottled ginger juice	1 tsp	2 tsp	1 tblsp
Red pepper flakes	Up to ½ tsp	Up to 1 tsp	Up to ½ tblsp
Ground coriander	½ tsp	1 tsp	½ tblsp
Dried thyme	½ tsp	1 tsp	½ tblsp
Salt	½ tsp	1 tsp	½ tblsp
Ground cinnamon	¼ tsp	½ tsp	1 tsp
Ground allspice	¼ tsp	½ tsp	¾ tsp
Grated nutmeg	¼ tsp	½ tsp	¾ tsp
Bone-in skinless chicken thighs	1½ pounds	3 pounds	4½ pounds
Large ripe plantains, peeled and sliced into 2-inch pieces	1	2	3
Frozen apple juice concentrate, thawed	1 tblsp	2 tblsp	3 tblsp

1 Place the scallions, garlic, vinegar, honey, ginger juice, red pepper flakes, coriander, thyme, salt, cinnamon, allspice, and nutmeg in a food processor fitted with the chopping blade. Cover and process, scraping down the inside of the canister once or twice, until a coarse paste comes together.

2 Place the chicken thighs in a large bowl. Scrape the spice paste into the bowl; toss well to coat. Cover and refrigerate for at least 12 hours or up to 16 hours, tossing at least one more time.

3 Set the chicken thighs in the slow cooker; scrape every drop from the bowl into the cooker as well. Dump in the plantain, pour in the apple juice concentrate, and stir well.

4 Cover and cook on low for 6 hours, or until the thighs are tender, especially at the ends where there's plenty of cartilage near the bone.

TESTERS' NOTES
• This dish is a riff on Jamaican jerk chicken, made with a fresh, fiery rub rather than a bottled sauce.
• Consider making a double quantity of this rub, saving the remainder in a sealed plastic container in the fridge for up to 4 months.
• The amounts of spices and aromatics for a small slow-cooker version may well be too small for some food processors to grind properly. Use a mini food processor or a large spice grinder.

(continued)

- The peels of ripe plantains are mottled with many brown patches, even soft in some places. There certainly shouldn't be green anywhere—or even any large, unbroken patch of yellow.

Serve It Up! For a side dish for four people, stem and shred green cabbage, then toss it into a wok set over medium-high heat with some olive oil. Stir until the cabbage wilts, then add drained and rinsed canned kidney beans as well as a healthy splash of vegetable broth. Cover, reduce the heat to low, and cook until the cabbage is tender, about 10 minutes, stirring occasionally. Season with salt and perhaps more red pepper flakes for an even more fiery dinner.

ALL-AMERICAN KNOW-HOW Bottled ginger juice is available in almost every supermarket. However, you can make your own by pressing chopped peeled fresh ginger through a garlic press.

chicken and chickpea stew

EFFORT: **A LITTLE** • PREP TIME: **20 MINUTES** • COOK TIME: **4 HOURS/7 HOURS** • KEEPS ON WARM: **3 HOURS** • SERVES: **3 TO 10**

INGREDIENTS	2- TO 3½-QT	4- TO 5½-QT	6- TO 8-QT
Drained no-salt-added canned diced tomatoes	⅔ cup	1¼ cups	2½ cups
Drained and rinsed canned chickpeas	⅔ cup	1¼ cups	2½ cups
Chopped yellow onion	½ cup	¾ cup (1 small)	1¼ cups
Chopped fresh parsley leaves	2 tblsp	¼ cup	½ cup
Mild smoked paprika	½ tsp	1 tsp	2 tsp
Ground cloves	¼ tsp	½ tsp	1 tsp
Ground cinnamon	⅛ tsp	¼ tsp	½ tsp
Saffron	⅛ tsp	¼ tsp	½ tsp
Ground black pepper	⅛ tsp	¼ tsp	½ tsp
Minced fresh oregano leaves	½ tblsp	1 tblsp	2 tblsp
Olive oil	½ tblsp	1 tblsp	2 tblsp
Minced garlic	1 tsp	2 tsp	1 tblsp
Salt	¼ tsp	½ tsp	1 tsp
Bone-in skinless chicken thighs	1½ pounds	3 pounds	6 pounds

1 Stir the tomatoes, chickpeas, onion, parsley, paprika, cloves, cinnamon, saffron, and pepper in the slow cooker.

2 Mix the oregano, olive oil, garlic, and salt in a small bowl; smear this paste over the chicken thighs. Set them into the cooker so they're submerged about halfway.

3 Cover and cook on high for 4 hours or on low for 7 hours, or until the meat is almost falling off the bone.

TESTERS' NOTES
- Half curry, half tagine, and with a little Italian flair (and fresh oregano) thrown in for good measure, this stew is a melting pot of flavors.
- Stemming parsley leaves (as well as rosemary, thyme, and cilantro) can be a pain; however, those stems, if even slightly fibrous, may not get tender in the long haul.
- Mince the oregano so that it is small enough to help form the herb paste. If desired, use kosher or sea salt for even more flavor and texture.

Trail Mix Porridge (*page 28*)

CLOCKWISE FROM TOP LEFT: Sour Cream Chocolate Chip Coffee Cake (*page 37*), Tomatillo Sauce for Eggs (*page 49*), and Bacon and Onion Hash Browns (*page 48*).

OPPOSITE: Beef Short Rib and Red Cabbage Soup (*page 97*).

soups

CLOCKWISE FROM TOP LEFT: French Onion Soup (*page 59*), Creamy Tomato Soup (*page 57*), Lima Bean and Kale Soup (*page 75*), and Quinoa and Squash Soup (*page 81*).

Alabama-Style Pulled Pork with
White Sauce *(page 184)*

CLOCKWISE FROM TOP LEFT: Slow-Roasted Rack of Pork (*page 173*), Barbecued Brisket (*page 145*), Easy Cheesy Meatballs (*page 130*), and Barbecued Beef Ribs (*page 148*).

OPPOSITE: Roast Chicken with Potatoes, Lemon, and Rosemary (*page 272*).

poultry

CLOCKWISE FROM TOP LEFT: Turkey Thighs with Chestnuts and Marmalade (*page 290*), Stuffed Turkey Breast (*page 282*), Chicken Brunswick Stew (*page 268*), and Prosciutto-Wrapped Chicken on Shredded Carrots (*page 240*).

OPPOSITE: Chicken Mole Negro (*page 248*).

fish & shellfish

CLOCKWISE FROM TOP LEFT: Mussels with Beer, Chorizo, and Chipotles (*page 379*), Bass in Fennel Broth (*page 354*), Thin Fish Fillets in Packets with Tomatoes and Squash (*page 332*), and Crab Legs with Butter, Garlic, and Dill (*page 385*).

OPPOSITE: Cajun Shrimp Boil (*page 366*).

CLOCKWISE FROM TOP LEFT: Three-Bean Chili (*page 443*), Mac and Cheese (*page 391*), and Curried Eggs (*page 414*).

OPPOSITE: Sesame Beans (*page 430*) and Candied Sweet Potatoes (*page 417*).

CLOCKWISE FROM LEFT: Raspberry Cream Cheese Puddings *(page 479)*, Cherry-Almond Rice Pudding *(page 485)*, and Chewy Brown Sugar Chocolate Chip Oat Cake *(page 470)*.

OPPOSITE: Apple Walnut Crisp *(page 490)*.

desserts

Fudgy Brownie Cake *(page 461)*

chicken thighs
with parsnips and figs

EFFORT: **A LITTLE** • PREP TIME: **25 MINUTES** • COOK TIME: **6 HOURS**
• KEEPS ON WARM: **3 HOURS** • SERVES: **2 TO 6**

INGREDIENTS	2- TO 3½-QT	4- TO 5½-QT	6- TO 8-QT
Unsalted butter	1 tblsp	2 tblsp	3 tblsp
Bone-in, skin-on chicken thighs	1 pound	2 pounds	4½ pounds
Parsnips, peeled and cut into 1-inch sections	½ pound	1 pound	2 pounds
Dried Turkish figs, stemmed and halved	4	8	16
Finely grated fresh orange zest	½ tblsp	1 tblsp	2½ tblsp
Caraway seeds	¼ tsp	½ tsp	1¼ tsp
Ground allspice	¼ tsp	½ tsp	1¼ tsp
Salt	¼ tsp	½ tsp	1¼ tsp
Ground black pepper	¼ tsp	½ tsp	1¼ tsp
Dry white wine, such as Sancerre or Chablis	¾ cup	1½ cups	3¼ cups

1 Melt the butter in a large skillet over medium heat, tilting to coat the hot surface. Work with as many chicken thighs as will fit without crowding. Set them skin side down in the skillet and cook on one side only until deeply browned, between 4 and 6 minutes. Transfer to the slow cooker and continue browning more. If browning in batches, divide the butter among the batches.

2 Add the parsnips, figs, orange zest, caraway seeds, allspice, salt, and pepper to the slow cooker. Stir well, then drizzle the wine over everything.

3 Cover and cook on low for 6 hours, or until the chicken and parsnips are wonderfully tender.

TESTERS' NOTES
• Look for firm dried figs that are nonetheless plump with lots of juice.
• Substitute peeled turnips or rutabaga for the parsnips, although the final dish won't be as aromatic as the original.

---

chicken thighs
with shallots and peppers

EFFORT: **A LITTLE** • PREP TIME: **30 MINUTES** • COOK TIME:
4 HOURS/6 HOURS • KEEPS ON WARM: **3 HOURS** • SERVES: **3 TO 8**

INGREDIENTS	2- TO 3½-QT	4- TO 5½-QT	6- TO 8-QT
Thick-cut bacon slices	3	4	6
Whole small shallots, peeled	8	12	18
Bone-in skin-on chicken thighs	1¼ pounds	2 pounds	4 pounds
Thinly sliced jarred roasted red peppers (pimiento)	⅓ cup	⅔ cup	1 cup
Halved pitted green olives	⅓ cup	⅔ cup	1 cup
Red wine vinegar	1 tsp	2 tsp	1 tblsp
Ground black pepper	¼ tsp	½ tsp	½ tsp
Fresh thyme sprigs	2	3	4
Red sweet vermouth	3 tblsp	5 tblsp	½ cup

1 Fry the bacon slices in a large skillet set over medium heat, turning when brown and

(continued)

crisp, 5 to 6 minutes in all. Transfer the bacon slices to a plate, leaving the fat in the pan.

2 Add the shallots to the skillet, still set over medium heat. Brown the shallots in the bacon fat, stirring occasionally, about 4 minutes. Use a slotted spoon to transfer the shallots to the slow cooker.

3 Set several of the chicken thighs skin side down in the bacon fat–filled skillet. Brown well on one side, letting the thighs rest for 5 to 6 minutes before popping them off the hot surface. Transfer them to the slow cooker and then continue browning until all thighs are finished. Crumble the crisp bacon into the cooker as well.

4 Add the red peppers, olives, vinegar, and pepper. Toss well, then tuck the thyme sprigs among the vegetables. Drizzle the vermouth over everything.

5 Cover and cook on high for 4 hours or on low for 6 hours, or until the chicken thighs are gloriously tender at the bone. Discard the thyme sprigs before serving.

TESTERS' NOTES
• This is a fairly sweet dish, thanks to the sweet vermouth. However, the olives and bacon hold off that sweetness nicely, letting the delicious chicken flavor come through.
• If possible, avoid rather tasteless canned olives. Look for better choices on your supermarket's salad bar or at the olive bar. Avoid stuffed olives or those coated with herbs or spices.

INGREDIENTS EXPLAINED Red vermouth is sometimes called *sweet vermouth* or *Italian vermouth*, and sometimes labeled simply *rosso*. It's mildly sweet, even a tad bitter, and shockingly red. Although we prefer it in cocktails rather than cooking, it can be balanced with red wine vinegar and aromatics to make a sweet, sophisticated sauce.

chicken thighs
with olives and prunes

EFFORT: **A LITTLE** • PREP TIME: **25 MINUTES** • COOK TIME: **4 HOURS/ 6 HOURS** • KEEPS ON WARM: **3 HOURS** • SERVES: **3 TO 10**

INGREDIENTS	2- TO 3½-QT	4- TO 5½-QT	6- TO 8-QT
Olive oil	1 tblsp	2 tblsp	3 tblsp
Bone-in skin-on chicken thighs	1¼ pounds	2½ pounds	5 pounds
Whole pitted green olives	¼ cup	½ cup	1 cup
Whole pitted prunes	¼ cup	½ cup	1 cup
White wine vinegar	1 tblsp	2 tblsp	3 tblsp
Packed dark brown sugar	1 tblsp	2 tblsp	3 tblsp
Dried oregano	1 tblsp	2 tblsp	3 tblsp
Minced garlic	½ tblsp	1 tblsp	2 tblsp
Drained and rinsed capers	½ tblsp	1 tblsp	2 tblsp
Bay leaves	1	2	3
Dry white wine, such as Pinot Grigio	¼ cup	½ cup	1 cup

1 Warm a large skillet set over medium heat, then swirl in the olive oil. Add the chicken thighs skin side down, as many as will fit in the pan without crowding. Brown well on one side, until the skin is dark brown, between 4 and 6 minutes. Transfer the thighs, and continue browning in batches.

2 Stir the olives, prunes, vinegar, brown sugar, oregano, garlic, and capers into the slow cooker. Tuck the bay leaves among the ingredients. Pour the wine over everything.

3 Cover and cook on high for 4 hours or on low for 6 hours, or until the meat is tender enough to pull away from the bone. Discard the bay leaf or leaves before serving.

TESTERS' NOTES
• This is our slow cooker homage to the famed Chicken Marbella, a staple from the *Silver Palate Cookbook*.
• You can use chicken with the skin on in the slow cooker, but you have to brown that skin very well to crisp it, give it good color (nobody wants a horrid-looking dinner), and render some of the fat.
• Use high-quality green olives, preferably fat ones off of the supermarket's salad or olive bar.

Serve It Up! To add a thickener in the bowl, grind plain dry breadcrumbs with toasted sliced almonds and a pinch of cinnamon in a large food processor fitted with the chopping blade. Ladle the stew over a couple of tablespoons of this mixture in the bowls.

honey-barbecued chicken drumsticks

EFFORT: **A LITTLE** • PREP TIME: **15 MINUTES** • COOK TIME: **3½ HOURS/6 HOURS** • KEEPS ON WARM: **3 HOURS** • SERVES: **3 TO 10**

INGREDIENTS	2- TO 3½-QT	4- TO 5½-QT	6- TO 8-QT
No-salt-added tomato paste	3 tblsp	6 tblsp	¾ cup
Honey	1 tblsp	2 tblsp	¼ cup
Packed dark brown sugar	1 tblsp	2 tblsp	¼ cup
Cider vinegar	4 tsp	1½ tblsp	3 tblsp
Worcestershire sauce	4 tsp	1½ tblsp	3 tblsp
Dijon mustard	2 tsp	1 tblsp	2 tblsp
Chili powder	2 tsp	1 tblsp	2 tblsp
Ground cloves	¼ tsp	½ tsp	1 tsp
Salt	⅛ tsp	¼ tsp	½ tsp
Skinless chicken drumsticks	1½ pounds	3 pounds	5 pounds

1 Mix the tomato paste, honey, brown sugar, vinegar, Worcestershire sauce, mustard, chili powder, cloves, and salt in the slow cooker. Add the chicken drumsticks and toss to coat well.

2 Cover and cook on high for 3½ hours or on low for 6 hours, or until the meat is quite tender, particularly at the thick end of the drumsticks with the cartilage.

TESTERS' NOTES
• Although there's not much required to make these kid-friendly, sweet and spicy drumsticks, we felt we had to up the effort level to *a little* since you'll need to skin those legs.
• If you wish, use only standard chili powder, rather than our chili-clove mixture, for a slightly muskier, milder flavor.

Serve It Up! Make an easy **Quinoa Pilaf** by mixing shredded carrot, finely diced zucchini, and some melted butter into a saucepan of still-warm cooked white quinoa. Cover and set aside for 10 minutes to blend the flavors.

ALL-AMERICAN KNOW-HOW To skin chicken legs, pick up a paper towel and grasp the small end of the leg with it. With a second paper towel in your other hand, peel the skin off from the large end down to the small end, and yank off and discard.

raspberry chipotle chicken drumsticks

EFFORT: **A LITTLE** • PREP TIME: **15 MINUTES** • COOK TIME: **3½ HOURS/6 HOURS** • KEEPS ON WARM: **2 HOURS** • SERVES: **3 TO 10**

INGREDIENTS	2- TO 3½-QT	4- TO 5½-QT	6- TO 8-QT
Chili sauce, such as Heinz	⅓ cup	½ cup	¾ cup plus 2 tblsp
Seedless raspberry jam or preserves	3 tblsp	¼ cup	7 tblsp
Rice vinegar	2 tblsp	3 tblsp	5 tblsp
Molasses, preferably unsulphured	1½ tblsp	2 tblsp	3½ tblsp
Soy sauce	1½ tblsp	2 tblsp	3½ tblsp
Sugar	2½ tsp	1 tblsp	5 tsp
Minced garlic	2½ tsp	1 tblsp	5 tsp
Canned chipotle chiles in adobo sauce, stemmed and minced	Up to 1	Up to 1½	Up to 2
Ground cumin	¼ tsp	½ tsp	1 tsp
Skinless chicken drumsticks	1¾ pounds	3 pounds	5 pounds

1 Stir the chili sauce, raspberry jam, vinegar, molasses, soy sauce, sugar, garlic, chipotle, and cumin in the slow cooker. Set the drumsticks in the sauce and turn to coat on all sides.

2 Cover and cook on high for 3½ hours or on low for 6 hours, or until the meat is tender and the sauce has thickened a bit.

TESTERS' NOTES
• This chipotle-laced mixture eventually becomes a thick, spicy, but sweet glaze for chicken legs.
• What's left in the cooker isn't very good as a side sauce on mashed potatoes or such. However, you can pour it into a saucepan and boil it down over medium-high heat to a barbecue-sauce-like glaze for the drumsticks.

INGREDIENTS EXPLAINED Molasses can be extracted from either young or mature sugarcane. The young sugarcane is doped with sulfur dioxide, a preservative; the older canes don't receive (or need) such treatment and so the molasses is labeled *unsulphured*—our preference. There are three grades of molasses: mild (sometimes called *Barbados molasses*), dark (sometimes called *second molasses*), and the dense, dank *blackstrap molasses*. Either of the first two will work in all of these recipes. (You can also substitute black treacle or dark sorghum syrup for molasses in most braising and stewing recipes.)

garlic-roasted chicken drumsticks

EFFORT: **A LITTLE** • PREP TIME: **15 MINUTES** • COOK TIME: **6 HOURS** • KEEPS ON WARM: **3 HOURS** • SERVES: **3 TO 8**

INGREDIENTS	2- TO 3½-QT	4- TO 5½-QT	6- TO 8-QT
Skinless chicken drumsticks	1½ pounds	3 pounds	4½ pounds
Olive oil	1 tblsp	2 tblsp	3 tblsp
Minced fresh rosemary leaves	2 tsp	1 tblsp	1½ tblsp
Finely grated lemon zest	2 tsp	1 tblsp	1½ tblsp

Ground black pepper	1 tsp	2 tsp	1 tblsp
Salt	½ tsp	¾ tsp	1 tsp
Whole garlic cloves, peeled	10	16	24
Dry vermouth	2 tblsp	¼ cup	6 tblsp

1 Rub the chicken drumsticks with the olive oil. Mix the rosemary, lemon zest, pepper, and salt in a bowl; sprinkle evenly over the legs.

2 Lay the chicken legs in the slow cooker; sprinkle the garlic cloves around them. Drizzle the vermouth slowly over the top, taking care not to disturb the herb and zest rub.

3 Cover and cook on low for 6 hours, or until the chicken is fork-tender and the garlic cloves are soft and spreadable.

TESTERS' NOTES

• A slow-cooker variation on the theme of chicken with forty cloves of garlic, this braise is rich and aromatic, best on a wintry evening.

• Even dry white wine is a tad too sweet here; we prefer the more herbaceous dry vermouth.

• If you want to skip the alcohol-laced liquids, substitute reduced-sodium chicken broth but also add ½ teaspoon sugar to a small slow cooker, 1 teaspoon sugar to a medium model, or 1 teaspoon to a large.

• The garlic cloves, once softened in the cooker, can be spread on bread like butter. Or beat a few into mashed potatoes with plenty of sour cream. Any you don't eat can be saved back for a spread in wraps or on sandwiches the next day.

chicken leg quarters with mushrooms and leeks

EFFORT: **A LITTLE** • PREP TIME: **25 MINUTES** • COOK TIME: **6 HOURS 10 MINUTES** • KEEPS ON WARM: **3 HOURS THROUGH STEP 3** • SERVES: **3 TO 9**

INGREDIENTS	2- TO 3½-QT	4- TO 5½-QT	6- TO 8-QT
Cremini or brown button mushrooms, sliced	6 ounces (about 2 cups)	13 ounces (about 4 cups)	1 pound 3 ounces (about 6 cups)
Leeks (white and green part only), halved lengthwise, washed, and thinly sliced	¾ pound (about 1¼ cups)	1¼ pounds (about 2¾ cups)	2 pounds (about 4 cups)
All-purpose flour	1½ tblsp	2½ tblsp	¼ cup
Stemmed fresh thyme leaves	2 tsp	1½ tblsp	2 tblsp
Minced fresh sage leaves	2 tsp	1½ tblsp	2 tblsp
Salt	¼ tsp	½ tsp	1 tsp
Ground black pepper	⅛ tsp	¼ tsp	½ tsp
Skinned chicken leg-and-thigh quarters	1½ pounds	3 pounds	4½ pounds
Dry white wine, such as white Burgundy or Chardonnay	⅓ cup	⅔ cup	1 cup
Low-sodium chicken broth	⅓ cup	⅔ cup	1 cup
Heavy cream	2 tblsp	3 tblsp	5 tblsp

1 Mix the mushrooms, leeks, flour, thyme, sage, salt, and pepper in the slow cooker until the flour coats the vegetables completely.

(continued)

2 Nestle the chicken into the vegetables; pour the wine and broth over and around them.

3 Cover and cook on low for 6 hours, or until the chicken is falling off the bone.

4 Transfer the chicken pieces to a serving platter; turn the cooker to high. Skim off the sauce for any surface fat with a flatware spoon, then stir in the cream. Return the chicken to the cooker and cook on high for 10 minutes to heat thoroughly.

TESTERS' NOTES
• This braise is modeled on a classic French dish, *poulet grand-mère*, but here enriched with cream to pair with the mushrooms and thyme. We've also added sage as a twist to give the sauce a savory edge.
• With a dish this rich, every ingredient should be at its best. If you've made your own chicken stock (see page 110), by all means use it here!

Serve It Up! Separate the thighs from the legs for those who want less meat. White rice or noodles may be the classic medium for this dish, but also consider a bed of cooked and drained wheatberries, rye berries, triticale berries, or farro.

INGREDIENTS EXPLAINED Chicken leg quarters are the thigh and leg of the bird—the whole swath of dark meat. They are sometimes called *whole chicken legs*, since the leg would naturally include the thigh. They can be tricky to skin. Follow the procedure for skinning chicken legs (page 259), then continue peeling the skin off the larger thigh. Or ask the butcher at your supermarket to do the task for you.

chicken leg quarters with tomatoes and basil

EFFORT: **A LOT** • PREP TIME: **30 MINUTES** • COOK TIME: **6 HOURS** • KEEPS ON WARM: **3 HOURS** • SERVES: **3 TO 9**

INGREDIENTS	2- TO 3½-QT	4- TO 5½-QT	6- TO 8-QT
All-purpose flour	½ cup	1 cup	2 cups
Salt	1 tsp	2 tsp	1 tblsp
Ground black pepper	1 tsp	2 tsp	1 tblsp
Skinless chicken leg-and-thigh quarters	1½ pounds	3 pounds	4½ pounds
Olive oil	1½ tblsp	3 tblsp	⅓ cup
Full-bodied rosé wine, such as Grenache rosé	½ cup	1 cup	1½ cups
No-salt-added canned crushed tomatoes	¾ cup	1½ cups	2½ cups
Thinly sliced pitted black olives	¼ cup	½ cup	¾ cup
Chopped fresh parsley leaves	¼ cup	½ cup	¾ cup
Diced red onion	2½ tblsp	⅓ cup	½ cup (about 1 small)
Minced garlic	1 tsp	2 tsp	1 tblsp
Minced fresh basil leaves	2 tblsp	¼ cup	6 tblsp

1 Mix the flour, salt, and pepper on a large plate, then dredge the chicken pieces in the seasoned flour, coating all sides.

2 Set a large skillet over medium heat for a few minutes, then pour in the oil. Tilt the skillet so the oil coats the hot surface. Slip the several dredged chicken pieces into the skillet, as many as will fit without crowding; brown well, about 6 minutes, turning only after you've achieved a fairly dark color. Use tongs to move the browned pieces to a plate and soldier on, dredging and browning more as needed.

3 Add some of the seasoned flour to the skillet, still set over medium heat: 1 tablespoon for a small slow cooker, 2 tablespoons for a medium one, or 3 tablespoons for a large cooker. Stir until the flour begins to brown, about 2 minutes. Pour in the wine and stir until the flour dissolves, the browned bits come up off the bottom of the skillet, and the mixture thickens a bit to create a sauce. Pour the sauce into the cooker.

4 Stir the tomatoes, olives, parsley, onion, and garlic into the slow cooker. Tuck the browned chicken pieces into the cooker, stacking them if possible so that some of the pieces are in the sauce.

5 Cover and cook on low for 6 hours, or until the chicken is wonderfully tender. Transfer the chicken pieces to a serving platter, skim the sauce for surface fat, and stir in the basil. Serve the sauce on the side.

TESTERS' NOTES
• The rosé wine adds a light touch to this stew.
• Remove as much fat from the chicken pieces as possible when you skin them. (You can also make this dish with skinless bone-in chicken thighs. Use the stated amount by weight.)
• Coat the chicken evenly but thoroughly in the seasoned flour. Every surface counts! And don't skimp on the browning step. Not only will it add flavor, but the crust will also dissolve in the sauce to thicken it.

ALL-AMERICAN KNOW-HOW The secret to browning the chicken, skin on or off, is to leave it alone; only then can the natural sugars caramelize and the proteins tighten, causing the meat or skin to brown. Once the chemical reaction is well under way, the pieces can almost be popped off the skillet's hot surface with a spatula, rather than pried off and torn up.

---

soy sauce–braised chicken leg quarters

EFFORT: **A LITTLE** • PREP TIME: **20 MINUTES** • COOK TIME: **7 HOURS** • KEEPS ON WARM: **3 HOURS** • SERVES: **4 TO 10**

INGREDIENTS	2- TO 3½-QT	4- TO 5½-QT	6- TO 8-QT
Low-sodium chicken broth, plus additional as necessary	2 cups	3½ cups	5 cups
Soy sauce	¼ cup	½ cup	¾ cup plus 2 tblsp
Oyster sauce	2 tblsp	¼ cup	⅓ cup
Dry sherry	2 tblsp	¼ cup	½ cup
Whole scallions, cut into 1-inch pieces	2 medium	3 medium	4 medium
Minced peeled fresh ginger	2 tblsp	¼ cup	⅓ cup
Medium garlic cloves, slivered	1	2	4
Peanut oil	1 tblsp	2 tblsp	3 tblsp
Skin-on chicken leg-and-thigh quarters	2 pounds	3½ pounds	5 pounds

1 Mix the measured amount of broth plus the soy sauce, oyster sauce, and sherry in the slow cooker. Stir in the scallions, ginger, and garlic.

(continued)

2 Set a large skillet over medium heat; after a couple of minutes, swirl in the oil. Slip a couple of the leg quarters skin side down into the skillet; cook on one side until well browned, about 4 minutes. Without turning, transfer the quarters skin side up to the slow cooker; continue browning more quarters as necessary.

3 Check to make sure the liquid covers the chicken at least halfway, if not three-fourths of the way; add more broth as necessary. Cover and cook on low for 7 hours, or until the chicken is quite tender, particularly in the joint.

TESTERS' NOTES

• This is a traditional Chinese technique, a salty but aromatic broth that slowly poaches the chicken to tenderness.
• Soy sauce mellows as it cooks, but you will also immediately notice the quality of the brand you've used, so buy smart. Better brands have a brewed, slightly fermented taste, not at all like salty water. These more complex flavors will shine in a dish like this.

Serve It Up! Serve this dish hot or cold. Traditionally, the meat would be sliced into bits, then served with a mixture of salt, black pepper, and ground Sichuan peppercorns (see page 160) as a dip at the table. Or skim the sauce for fat and use the sauce as a dip.

INGREDIENTS EXPLAINED Oyster sauce is a thick, brown, pasty Chinese condiment—somewhat sweet, quite salty, and (in the best bottlings) a little musky. Once made from oyster stew that was boiled down to a viscous paste, it is now mostly a combination of sugar, salt, thickeners, and oyster "extract." Look for it in the international aisle of almost all supermarkets.

chicken confit

EFFORT: **A LOT** • PREP TIME: **24 HOURS 15 MINUTES** • COOK TIME: **8 HOURS** • KEEPS ON WARM: **NO** • SERVES: **2 TO 8**

INGREDIENTS	2- TO 3½-QT	4- TO 5½-QT	6- TO 8-QT
Skin-on chicken leg-and-thigh quarters	1½ pounds	2½ pounds	4 pounds
Bay leaves	4	6	8
Medium garlic cloves, peeled and halved	2	3	4
Kosher salt	1 tblsp	1½ tblsp	2 tblsp
Olive oil	Up to 6 cups (1½ quarts)	Up to 10 cups (2½ quarts)	Up to 14 cups (3½ quarts)

1 Lay the leg quarters on a large rimmed baking sheet. Slip a bay leaf and a halved garlic clove under each leg. Sprinkle the chicken quarters with the salt. Cover and refrigerate for 24 hours.

2 Rinse the salt off the quarters; pat them dry. Put the bay leaves and garlic in the slow cooker; lay the chicken quarters on top.

3 Pour enough olive oil over the quarters so they're submerged by 1 inch. Cover and cook on low for 8 hours, or until the meat is quite tender.

4 Use large tongs and a spatula to remove the fragile chicken quarters from the fat and transfer them to a large baking dish, roasting pan, or bowl. Discard the garlic and bay leaves. Ladle the fat from the cooker over the legs, submerging them fully. Cover and refrigerate for at least 2 days or up to 2 weeks—or store in sealed smaller containers and freeze in the fat for up to 3 months.

TESTERS' NOTES

• If you've never had confit (*con-FEET*), you're in for a treat. By slow-poaching the chicken in olive oil, the meat becomes meltingly soft, the height of luxury.

• For more flavor, add a rosemary or thyme sprig for each quarter.

• Try to arrange the quarters in one layer in the slow cooker; if not, you'll need even more olive oil to get them fully submerged.

• There's no need to use high-quality extra-virgin olive oil in this dish; a sturdy, flavorful store brand is fine.

• The legs must be submerged in the fat before they're stored in the fridge; otherwise, there's the threat of oxidation and bacterial contamination. Use as deep a dish as you have and be prepared to pour in a little more olive oil in order to submerge the quarters completely.

Serve It Up! To serve chicken confit, chip one or two of the quarters out of the fat; scrape off almost all the adhering fat. Set them skin side up on a large rimmed baking sheet; bake in a heated 400°F oven until crisp. Serve them whole or shred the meat and serve it with a lentil salad, on a green salad, or as a special first course with crunchy bread slices and a fruit-laced chutney.

sesame chicken wings

EFFORT: **A LOT** • PREP TIME: **20 MINUTES** • COOK TIME: **4 TO 5 HOURS** • KEEPS ON WARM: **NO** • SERVES: **4 TO 12**

INGREDIENTS	2- TO 3½-QT	4- TO 5½-QT	6- TO 8-QT
Packed dark brown sugar	¼ cup	½ cup	¾ cup
Soy sauce	2 tblsp	3½ tblsp	⅓ cup
White sesame seeds	1 tblsp	5 tsp	2½ tblsp
Ground ginger	1 tsp	2 tsp	1 tblsp
Toasted sesame oil (see page 196)	2 tblsp	3½ tblsp	⅓ cup
Chicken wings, cut into drumlets and winglets, flappers removed and discarded	2 pounds	4 pounds	6 pounds
Rice vinegar	1 tblsp	1½ tblsp	2½ tblsp
Ground black pepper	2 tsp	1 tblsp	1½ tblsp

1 Mix the brown sugar, soy sauce, sesame seeds, and ginger in the slow cooker until the brown sugar is partially dissolved.

2 Set a large skillet over medium heat for a few minutes and swirl in the sesame oil. Add as many wing parts as will fit without crowding; brown, turning once, about 5 minutes. Transfer to the slow cooker and continue browning more as necessary. At the end, scrape every bit of oil and juice from the skillet into the cooker as well. Toss the wings in the sauce.

3 Cover and cook on low for 4 hours in a small slow cooker, 4½ hours in a medium model, or 5 hours in a large one, or until the meat is tender and cooked through, but not yet falling off the bone.

4 Transfer the wings to a serving platter. Skim any surface fat from the sauce in the cooker, then pour the sauce into a medium saucepan. Stir in the vinegar and pepper; bring to a full boil over high heat, stirring often. Boil until reduced to a thick glaze, between 3 and 6 minutes. Drizzle this glaze over the wings before serving.

(continued)

• Chicken wings are a bit of indulgence in the slow cooker—especially since you can't really skin them. Brown the skin well so it doesn't turn too gummy as it cooks.

• Unfortunately, chicken wings require exact timing in the slow cooker: they don't keep well on warm; the meat turns too soft, almost gelatinous. So remove the wings to a platter as soon as you're sure they're cooked through.

• Don't shortcut the process in step 4. You want a thick, sticky sauce for the wings.

INGREDIENTS EXPLAINED Barring some mishap, every chicken has two wings; and each wing has three parts. There's the pointed wing tip—that is, the *flapper* in butcher talk. It should be discarded for all these recipes. Then there are the other two bits: the *drumlet* (named because it looks like a little drumstick) and the double-boned *winglet*.

To divide the parts of a chicken wing on your own, hold it against a cutting board and pull any two of the three sections apart until the joint is revealed. Insert the tip of a knife into the joint, pretty straight down, then slice through the ligaments and tendons until the joint comes in half. Slice through the skin to separate; repeat with the other joint.

You can often find separate packages of drumlets and winglets at the grocery store. Buy whichever suits your taste—or mix and match for larger batches.

ALL-AMERICAN KNOW-HOW To know for sure if chicken wings are tender in a slow cooker, insert a large carving or meat fork into the thickest part of the wing. If the fork can be pulled out with resistance—and certainly without the wing coming up with the fork—then the meat is indeed ready to eat.

orange-ginger barbecued wings

EFFORT: **A LITTLE** • PREP TIME: **20 MINUTES** • COOK TIME: **4 TO 5 HOURS** • KEEPS ON WARM: **NO** • SERVES: **4 TO 12**

INGREDIENTS	2- TO 3½-QT	4- TO 5½-QT	6- TO 8-QT
No-salt-added tomato paste	3 tblsp	5 tblsp	½ cup
Frozen orange juice concentrate, thawed	2 tblsp	¼ cup	6 tblsp
Honey	2 tblsp	¼ cup	6 tblsp
White wine vinegar	1 tblsp	2 tblsp	3 tblsp
Minced peeled fresh ginger	1 tblsp	2 tblsp	3 tblsp
Ground cloves	½ tsp	¾ tsp	1¼ tsp
Ground cinnamon	½ tsp	¾ tsp	1¼ tsp
Salt	½ tsp	¾ tsp	1¼ tsp
Celery seeds	¼ tsp	½ tsp	¾ tsp
Unsalted butter	1 tblsp	2 tblsp	3 tblsp
Chicken wings, cut into drumlets and winglets, flappers removed and discarded	2 pounds	4 pounds	6 pounds

1 Whisk the tomato paste, orange juice concentrate, honey, vinegar, ginger, cloves, cinnamon, salt, and celery seeds in the slow cooker until the tomato paste dissolves.

2 Melt the butter in a large skillet over medium heat, then add enough wing parts to fill but not crowd the pan. Brown, turning once, about 5 minutes. Transfer them to the slow cooker and continue browning more until finished. (You can divide the butter into smaller bits for multiple batches.) Toss the wings in the sauce to coat them thoroughly and evenly.

3 Cover and cook on low for 4 hours in a small slow cooker, 4½ hours in a medium model, or 5 hours in a large cooker, or until the meat is tender at the bone.

TESTERS' NOTES

• This sweet barbecue sauce calls out for a dark beer! So make a slow cooker of wings before the game or your next party, then break out the bottles.

• Use orange juice concentrate, not orange drink or squeezed orange juice. The concentrate has more pronounced flavors, the better to stand up to the vinegar and spices.

• We used a very dark buckwheat honey in testing this recipe, and it offered a slightly bitter, more tannic taste to the glaze.

spicy pomegranate-glazed chicken wings

EFFORT: **A LITTLE** • PREP TIME: **20 MINUTES** • COOK TIME: **4 TO 5 HOURS** • KEEPS ON WARM: **NO** • SERVES: **4 TO 12**

INGREDIENTS	2- TO 3½-QT	4- TO 5½-QT	6- TO 8-QT
Pomegranate molasses (see page 399)	¼ cup	½ cup	¾ cup
Hot pepper sauce, such as Sriracha or Frank's	3 tblsp	⅓ cup	½ cup
Minced garlic	1 tblsp	2 tblsp	3 tblsp
Coriander seeds	2 tsp	1 tblsp	1½ tblsp
Ground black pepper	1 tsp	½ tblsp	2½ tsp
Mild paprika	1 tsp	2 tsp	1 tblsp
Salt	½ tsp	1 tsp	½ tblsp
Unsalted butter	2 tblsp	4 tblsp (½ stick)	6 tblsp (¾ stick)
Chicken wings, cut into drumlets and winglets, flappers removed and discarded	2 pounds	4 pounds	6 pounds

1 Stir the pomegranate molasses, chili sauce, garlic, coriander seeds, pepper, paprika, and salt in the slow cooker until fairly smooth.

2 Melt the butter in a large skillet over medium heat, then brown a batch of the chicken wing parts, turning once, about 5 minutes. (Divide the butter among several batches for the larger set of ingredients but use it all.) Transfer the wings to the slow cooker as they're ready. At the end, scrape any remaining butter in the skillet into the slow cooker and toss everything well.

3 Cover and cook on low for 4 hours in a small slow cooker, 4½ hours in a medium cooker, or 5 hours in a large cooker, or until the meat is quite tender at the bone.

TESTERS' NOTES

• Hot and buttery, these spicy, sweet-and-sour wings actually get their zing from the pomegranate molasses and coriander. Teenagers will scarf them down.

• Don't use a chili sauce like Heinz; rather, use a thick red pourable hot sauce—*not* a searingly hot sauce like Tabasco, but something thicker. (Of the sauces we recommend, Sriracha, a Thai sauce sometimes called *rooster sauce*, is far hotter than Frank's.)

spicy chicken
stewed with peanuts

EFFORT: **NOT MUCH** • PREP TIME: **15 MINUTES** • COOK TIME: **6 HOURS** • KEEPS ON WARM: **3 HOURS** • SERVES: **3 TO 10**

INGREDIENTS	2- TO 3½-QT	4- TO 5½-QT	6- TO 8-QT
Whole chicken, cut into pieces and skinned, any giblets or neck removed	1½ pounds	3 pounds	5 pounds
No-salt-added canned crushed tomatoes	1 cup	2 cups	3½ cups
Finely chopped roasted unsalted peanuts	½ cup	1 cup	1¾ cups
Diced yellow onion	2 tblsp	¼ cup	½ cup (about 1 small)
Canned chipotle chiles in adobo sauce, stemmed, seeded, and minced	Up to 2	Up to 3	Up to 5
Ground allspice	¼ tsp	½ tsp	1 tsp
Ground cloves	¼ tsp	½ tsp	1 tsp
Salt	¼ tsp	½ tsp	¾ tsp
Ground black pepper	¼ tsp	½ tsp	¾ tsp
4-inch cinnamon stick	½	1	2

1 Put the chicken pieces in the slow cooker, layering them so that as much of each piece as possible will be in the sauce.

2 Whisk the tomatoes, peanuts, onion, chipotle, allspice, cloves, salt, and pepper in a bowl; pour over the chicken pieces. Tuck in the cinnamon stick.

3 Cover and cook on low for 6 hours, or until the chicken is tender at the bone. Discard the cinnamon stick before serving.

TESTERS' NOTES
• This aromatic stew works best if there's a mix of white and dark meat chicken. That way, it won't be too oily—and will please everyone!
• For a thick stew to be spooned over cooked rice, remove the chicken pieces, cool in a colander set in the sink for a few minutes, then shred the meat from the bones and stir it back into the slow cooker. Maintain the slow cooker's low heat while you're working with the chicken, then cook on high for 10 minutes to heat through.

chicken brunswick stew

EFFORT: **A LITTLE** • PREP TIME: **30 MINUTES** • COOK TIME: **6 HOURS** • KEEPS ON WARM: **3 HOURS** • SERVES: **3 TO 10**

INGREDIENTS	2- TO 3½-QT	4- TO 5½-QT	6- TO 8-QT
Olive oil	1 tblsp	2 tblsp	3 tblsp
Whole chicken, cut into pieces, with skin on, giblets and neck removed	1½ pounds	3 pounds	5 pounds
Salt	½ tsp	1 tsp	½ tblsp
Ground black pepper	½ tsp	1 tsp	½ tblsp
Frozen pearl onions, thawed, or small fresh, peeled	⅔ cup	1¼ cups	2 cups
Drained no-salt-added canned diced tomatoes	1 cup	2 cups	3½ cups
Frozen sliced okra, thawed, or fresh, trimmed and sliced into 1-inch bits	½ cup	1 cup	2 cups
Corn kernels, fresh cut from cob, or frozen, thawed	½ cup	1 cup	2 cups

			1½ cups (about 1 medium)
Red bell pepper strips	½ cup	1 cup	
No-salt-added tomato paste	1 tblsp	2 tblsp	¼ cup
Minced fresh sage leaves	1 tsp	2 tsp	1 tblsp
Minced fresh oregano leaves	1 tsp	2 tsp	1 tblsp
Minced garlic	1 tsp	2 tsp	1 tblsp

1 Warm a large skillet over medium heat, then swirl in the oil. Season the chicken pieces with salt and pepper, then add a few to the skillet to brown them on both sides, about 6 minutes, turning once. Transfer to the slow cooker and continue browning more as necessary.

2 Pour the onions into the skillet; brown, stirring often, about 5 minutes. Pour them into the slow cooker.

3 Stir the tomatoes, okra, corn, bell pepper strips, tomato paste, sage, oregano, and garlic in a bowl until the tomato paste coats almost everything. Dump the mixture into the slow cooker and toss well.

4 Cover and cook on low for 6 hours, or until the chicken is fork-tender.

TESTERS' NOTES
• Brunswick stew, a Southern tradition, is often made with rather obscure meats. Squirrel, anyone? We simplified things a bit, added a few veggies, and dropped the spicy heat. You can pass the hot pepper sauce at the table.
• Make sure you brown that chicken well, since the skin is going right into the stew. The more color, the more flavor—and the less rendered fat that will actually make it into the final dish.
• Use any color of bell pepper you like—or a variety for more color in the dish.
• Large sage leaves can have a fibrous stem. Remove this before mincing.

• For a more authentic presentation, remove the meat from the cooker and cool a bit, then debone and chop the meat and stir it back into the stew. Cover and cook on high for 15 minutes to heat through.

Serve It Up! Brunswick stew is often thickened with bread. Replicate that by putting a mixture of finely ground fresh breadcrumbs, red pepper flakes, and black pepper in the serving bowls before dishing up the stew. Drizzle the bowls with high-quality olive oil as a finishing touch.

SHORTCUT Feel free to use frozen bell pepper strips. They must be completely thawed. And they must not include any added spices or sauce.

INGREDIENTS EXPLAINED Some of these recipes call for the pieces of a whole chicken. A bird usually is cut into eight or nine pieces (two legs, two thighs, two breasts, two wings, and a back—or other permutations, depending on the knife technique). You can buy the chicken cut up, or you can do it yourself. That said, a small slow cooker will not take a whole chicken—more like half a whole one: a leg, a thigh, a breast, a wing. If you're working with a small slow cooker, save the rest of the meat for another dish.

chicken with fennel and pancetta

EFFORT: **A LITTLE** • PREP TIME: **25 MINUTES** • COOK TIME: **7 HOURS**
• KEEPS ON WARM: **3 HOURS** • SERVES: **3 TO 10**

INGREDIENTS	2- TO 3½-QT	4- TO 5½-QT	6- TO 8-QT
Olive oil	2 tsp	1 tblsp	2 tblsp
Pancetta, chopped (see page 354)	2 ounces	4 ounces	6 ounces
Whole chicken, cut into parts and skinned, any giblets or neck removed	1½ pounds	3 pounds	5 pounds
Cremini or brown button mushrooms, thinly sliced	3 ounces (about 1 cup)	6 ounces (about 2 cups)	10 ounces (about 3½ cups)
Yellow onion, chopped	1 small	1 medium	1 large
Fennel bulbs, trimmed and diced (see page 211)	¼ pound (about ½ cup)	½ pound (about 1 cup)	1 pound (about 2 cups)
Ripe tomatoes, chopped	¼ pound (about ½ cup)	½ pound (about 1 cup)	1 pound (about 2 cups)
No-salt-added tomato paste	2 tblsp	¼ cup	7 tblsp
Minced fresh oregano leaves	2 tsp	1 tblsp	2 tblsp
Minced fresh basil leaves	2 tsp	1 tblsp	2 tblsp
Stemmed fresh thyme leaves	1 tsp	2 tsp	1 tblsp
Fennel seeds	½ tsp	1 tsp	2 tsp
Red pepper flakes	¼ tsp	½ tsp	1 tsp

1 Set a large skillet over medium heat for a couple of minutes, then swirl in the oil. Add the pancetta pieces; cook, stirring often, until browned on all sides, 3 to 5 minutes. Use a slotted spoon to move the pancetta to the slow cooker.

2 Slip a few pieces of chicken at a time into the skillet and brown them, turning once, about 6 minutes. Move them to the slow cooker and continue browning more pieces as needed.

3 Add the mushrooms, onion, fennel, tomatoes, tomato paste, oregano, basil, thyme, fennel seeds, and red pepper flakes. Toss well to coat the meat in the tomato paste.

4 Cover and cook on low for 7 hours, or until the sauce is bubbling and the chicken is meltingly tender at the bone.

TESTERS' NOTES

• This Italian-inspired stew is fairly delicately flavored, a good match for an Easter dinner.
• Although we're fans of chicken skin, it proved too assertive and oily for this rather delicate, dramatic stew.
• Substitute skinless bone-in chicken thighs, if desired.
• Leave the vegetables in fairly large chunks, at least ½ inch. There needs to be plenty of body and texture in the sauce.
• To make a light ragù to serve over polenta or spaghetti, cool the stew, then bone and chop the chicken meat. Stir it back into the sauce, cook on high for 20 minutes to heat through, then dish it up!

roast chicken
with parsnips and tomatoes

EFFORT: **NOT MUCH** • PREP TIME: **20 MINUTES** • COOK TIME: **5 TO 6 HOURS** • KEEPS ON WARM: **2 HOURS** • SERVES: **4 TO 6**

INGREDIENTS	6- TO 8-QT
Parsnips, peeled and cut into 2-inch segments	1 pound
Ripe cherry tomatoes	½ pound
Fresh thyme sprigs	6
Lemon pepper	1 tblsp
Mild paprika	1 tsp
Whole chicken, skin on, any giblets and neck removed, the bird trussed (see page 272)	3½ to 5 pounds

1 Arrange the parsnips, tomatoes, and thyme as a single layer in the bottom of the slow cooker.

2 Mix the lemon pepper and paprika in a small bowl; rub all over the chicken, even in the cavity. Set on top of the parsnip mixture.

3 Cover and cook on high for 5 to 6 hours, depending on the size of chicken, until an instant-read meat thermometer inserted into the thickest part of the thigh without touching bone registers 165°F.

4 Unplug the appliance, uncover, and let stand for 10 minutes. Transfer the chicken to a carving board; slice into eight or nine pieces. Discard the thyme sprigs before serving the parsnips and tomatoes.

TESTERS' NOTES

• Yes, you can roast a whole chicken in a slow cooker—just not in a small model, or even a medium model, for that matter. However, if you find a small chicken and can get it comfortably inside a medium cooker without squeezing it tight against the sides, then go for it. But there must be breathing space around the bird in the insert.

• Lemon pepper usually includes salt in the mixture. If the one you have is salt-free, add up to 1 teaspoon salt to the seasoning blend.

• The parsnips and tomatoes become wonderfully rich after sitting in the chicken fat. If you want to make this a healthier meal, skin the bird *after* you cook it (but not before).

• There's only one way to know if a bird is cooked through: an instant-read meat thermometer.

• Letting the bird rest in the cooker for 10 minutes both reincorporates the juices and lets the joints firm up, so the bird doesn't fall to pieces when you try to lift it out of the cooker. The best tool for getting a whole bird out of a cooker is a pair of oven-safe silicone baking mitts.

ALL-AMERICAN KNOW-HOW To make lemon pepper seasoning, position the rack in the center of the oven and heat the oven to 175°F. Line a large rimmed baking sheet with parchment paper or a silicone baking mat. Use a microplane to grate the zest from 5 medium lemons; mix with ⅓ cup crushed black peppercorns. Spread in an even layer on the baking sheet. Bake until very dried, between 1 and 1½ hours, stirring once. Cool completely on a wire rack, then process in a mini food processor with ¼ cup kosher salt until the consistency of coarse sand. (You can also grind the mixture with the salt in batches in a spice grinder.) Store in a sealed glass jar or plastic container for up to 1 month or freeze for up to 6 months.

roast chicken
with potatoes, lemon, and rosemary

EFFORT: **A LITTLE** • PREP TIME: **25 MINUTES** • COOK TIME: **5 TO 6 HOURS** • KEEPS ON WARM: **2 HOURS** • SERVES: **4 TO 6**

INGREDIENTS	6- TO 8-QT
Medium yellow potatoes (such as Yukon Gold), quartered	4
Finely grated fresh lemon zest	1 tblsp
Minced garlic	1 tblsp
Salt	½ tsp
Ground black pepper	½ tsp
4-inch fresh rosemary sprigs	4
Unsalted butter	2 tblsp
Whole chicken, skin on, the giblets and neck removed, the bird trussed	3½ to 5 pounds
Dry white wine, such as Pinot Grigio	1 cup

1 Arrange the potato quarters in one layer in the slow cooker. Toss with the lemon zest, garlic, salt, and pepper. Lay the rosemary sprigs on top of the mixture.

2 Melt the butter in a large skillet over medium heat. Set the chicken in the skillet and brown on all sides, splattering everything in sight and working patiently to get good color across the bird. Once done, set the chicken, breast side up, on top of the rosemary. Drizzle the wine on and around the chicken.

3 Cover and cook on high for 5 to 6 hours, until an instant-read meat thermometer inserted into the thickest part of the thigh, without touching the bone, registers 165°F.

4 Unplug the appliance, uncover, and let stand for 10 minutes. Transfer the chicken to a carving board, slice off and discard the twine, and then slice the bird into eight or nine pieces. Discard the rosemary sprigs before serving the potatoes and any juices in the slow cooker.

TESTERS' NOTES
• Because the bird is browned before it is put in the slow cooker, it must be trussed to hold together in the skillet.
• For a richer sauce, transfer the potatoes to a serving bowl and strain the sauce in the cooker into a small saucepan. Bring to a boil over high heat, then whisk in 1 or 2 tablespoons unsalted butter. Drizzle over the chicken and potatoes.

ALL-AMERICAN KNOW-HOW A trussed chicken is one that has been tied with butchers' twine to hold its shape as it cooks. The butcher at your supermarket can do this for you—or you can do it yourself. Use only dye-free, food-safe butchers' twine, available at all cooking supply stores and most hardware and grocery stores. To truss the bird, pull the wings close to the breast to protect the white meat, then tie them in place by wrapping the twine around the bird a couple of times before knotting it. Bring the legs together over the large opening, crossing them over each other before winding the twine around their ends and knotting the twine securely, thereby mostly closing the large opening.

chicken meatballs in thai coconut curry

EFFORT: **A LITTLE** • PREP TIME: **20 MINUTES** • COOK TIME: **5 HOURS** • KEEPS ON WARM: **2 HOURS** • SERVES: **3 TO 10**

INGREDIENTS	2- TO 3½-QT	4- TO 5½-QT	6- TO 8-QT
Coconut milk	⅔ cup	1 cup	2⅓ cups
Low-sodium chicken broth	¼ cup	⅔ cup	1½ cups
Yellow Thai curry paste	½ tblsp	1 tblsp	2 tblsp plus 1 tsp
Fish sauce (see page 96)	1 tsp	2 tsp	5 tsp
Packed light brown sugar	1 tsp	2 tsp	5 tsp
Ground chicken	1 pound	1½ pounds	3½ pounds
Minced red onion	¼ cup	⅓ cup	¾ cup
Minced trimmed lemongrass (white and pale green part only)	2 tblsp	3 tblsp	7 tblsp
Minced fresh cilantro leaves	2 tblsp	3 tblsp	7 tblsp
Minced garlic	1 tsp	2 tsp	5 tsp

1 Whisk the coconut milk, broth, chile paste, fish sauce, and brown sugar in the slow cooker until the brown sugar dissolves.

2 Mix the ground chicken, onion, lemongrass, cilantro, and garlic in a large bowl. Use your clean, dry hands to form this mixture into meatballs using ¼-cup increments. Drop them into the coconut sauce.

3 Cover and cook on low for about 5 hours, until an instant-read meat thermometer inserted into the center of one meatball registers 165°F and the sauce is aromatic and rich.

TESTERS' NOTES

• This spicy meatball dish is made even better with yellow chile paste. Look for a brand that isn't just chiles, but instead is stocked with aromatics.

• Mince the vegetables and herbs well so they meld evenly into the meatballs.

• Some coconut milk is so thick it needs to be stirred in the can before you can use it in a recipe.

• Timing in a ground chicken recipe is a tad less exact because the ground meat needs to reach a safe temperature. Various slow cookers operate at different temperatures on the low setting, so you may find you need to crank the machine to high for the last 30 minutes or so to get the meatballs done. If you're working with an older model (and thus it has a lower "low" setting), you may need to cook all the ground chicken recipes on high, adjusting the timing down a bit to compensate.

INGREDIENTS EXPLAINED Lemongrass is a slightly sour, lemony, perfume-laced grass highly prized in Southeast Asian cooking. It's available in whole stalks at larger, high-end supermarkets. Choose the moistest and most pliable stalks of the bunch; then trim off the roots, peel off the outer layers, and use only the pale white or purple bits near the roots. Otherwise, the white sections of lemongrass stalks are often available in plastic containers near the other fresh herbs—or sometimes in jars in the spice rack or in the international aisle.

ALL-AMERICAN KNOW-HOW To make your own yellow Thai curry paste, start by mincing two 2-inch-long pieces of trimmed lemongrass (only the white or purple bits near the root). Place these in a large spice grinder or a mini food processor with 1 or 2 seeded, stemmed, and chopped serrano chiles; 2 peeled, quartered garlic cloves; 4 whole cloves, 2 tablespoons cumin seeds, 1 tablespoon coriander seeds, and 2 teaspoons ground cinnamon. Grind or process the ingredients, scraping down the interior of the container occasionally, until a coarse paste forms. Use as much as you need, then transfer this paste to a small glass jar or plastic container and store in the freezer for up to 3 months.

stuffed cannelloni with chicken and spinach

EFFORT: **A LITTLE** • PREP TIME: **20 MINUTES** • COOK TIME: **4 HOURS** • KEEPS ON WARM: **NO** • SERVES: **3 TO 5**

INGREDIENTS	4- TO 5½-QT	6- TO 8-QT
Boned, skinned, and chopped supermarket rotisserie chicken meat	½ cup	1 cup
Gruyère cheese, shredded	5 ounces (about 1¼ cups)	10 ounces (about 2½ cups)
Frozen chopped spinach, thawed and squeezed of excess moisture	⅓ cup	⅔ cup
Minced yellow onion	2½ tblsp	⅓ cup
Dried thyme	1 tsp	2 tsp
Garlic powder	¼ tsp	½ tsp
Salt	¼ tsp	½ tsp
Dry white wine, such as Chardonnay	2 to 3 tblsp	3 to 4 tblsp
Large uncooked dried cannelloni	Up to 6	Up to 10
Low-sodium chicken broth	1¼ cups	2½ cups
Sour cream (regular or low-fat)	¼ cup	½ cup
All-purpose flour	2½ tblsp	⅓ cup
Hot pepper sauce, such as Tabasco	½ tsp	¾ tsp
Parmigiano-Reggiano cheese, finely grated	2 ounces (about ¼ cup)	4 ounces (about ½ cup)

1 Mix the chicken, Gruyère, spinach, onion, thyme, garlic powder, and salt in a large bowl. Stir in just enough wine that the mixture coheres without turning soupy.

2 Gently stuff the chicken mixture into the cannelloni tubes, using your clean fingers to push the filling into the still-hard tubes; lay the stuffed tubes in one layer in the slow cooker.

3 Whisk the broth, sour cream, flour, and hot pepper sauce in a second bowl, then pour over the tubes. Sprinkle with the grated Parmigiano-Reggiano.

4 Cover and cook on low for 4 hours, or until the sauce is bubbling and the filling is heated through.

TESTERS' NOTES
• There are no ingredient amounts for a small slow cooker here because the effort seemed beyond the norm to make two stuffed tubes.
• Squeeze the spinach in small handfuls to get rid of the extra water, which can ruin the sauce.
• Work with only as many shells as will fit easily in the bottom of the cooker. (You'll want to test it out before you start filling them.) If you find you must stack them a bit on each other, remember: (1) those shells on the bottom may collapse, so they won't be neat servings; and (2) those shells on the top must be covered with sauce, in which case you may need to whisk together a little more.
• Don't use fat-free sour cream; it can break during the long cooking.

INGREDIENTS EXPLAINED Gruyère is a hard Swiss cheese, prized for its sweet, salty flavor as well as for its ability to melt into perfect gooeyness. For almost all cooking and baking recipes, the less aged, slightly softer, and less expensive Gruyère is preferred to the older, cracked, and more assertive varieties.

red chicken enchilada casserole

EFFORT: **A LOT** • PREP TIME: **20 MINUTES** • COOK TIME: **4 HOURS** •
KEEPS ON WARM: **NO** • SERVES: **3 TO 8**

INGREDIENTS	2- TO 3½-QT	4- TO 5½-QT	6- TO 8-QT
Dried New Mexican chiles (see page 248)	8	12	20
Olive oil	½ tblsp	1 tblsp	1½ tblsp
Yellow onion, chopped	1 small	1 medium	1 large
Minced garlic	1 tblsp	1½ tblsp	2½ tblsp
Low-sodium chicken broth	1⅓ cups	2 cups	3⅓ cups
Packed fresh oregano leaves	2 tsp	1 tblsp	2 tblsp
Salt	½ tsp	1 tsp	½ tblsp
Ground black pepper	¼ tsp	½ tsp	1 tsp
Drained and rinsed canned black beans	⅔ cup	1 cup	1⅔ cups
Chopped walnuts	⅔ cup	1 cup	1⅔ cups
Ground cinnamon	½ tsp	1 tsp	½ tblsp
8-inch flour tortillas	4	6	10
Boned, skinned, and chopped supermarket rotisserie chicken meat	1⅓ cups	2 cups	3⅓ cups
Cheddar cheese, preferably mild, shredded	7 ounces (about 1¾ cup)	10 ounces (about 2½ cups)	1 pound (about 4 cups)

1 Bring a pan of water to a boil over high heat. Stem and seed the chiles, taking care to remove the pale inner membranes. Tear the chile flesh into bits and set them in a large bowl and fill the bowl at least halfway with boiling water. Set aside to steep for 20 minutes.

2 Heat a large skillet over medium heat for a few minutes, then pour in the oil. Add the onion and cook, stirring often, until translucent, about 2 minutes. Stir in the garlic and remove the skillet from the heat.

3 Drain the softened chiles in a colander set in the sink. Scrape them into a large food processor fitted with the chopping blade; add the onion and garlic to the food processor as well. Add the broth, oregano, salt, and pepper. Cover and process until a fairly smooth puree forms, scraping down the inside of the container once or twice. (If you're working with a very large batch, it may overflow your food processor—work in two batches, if you're at all concerned.)

4 Stir the beans, walnuts, and cinnamon together in a second bowl.

5 Layer the chile sauce, tortillas, chicken, bean mixture, and the cheese in the slow cooker. Repeat, making as many layers as you can in that order and depending on the size of your cooker.

6 Cover and cook on low for 4 hours, or until the cheese has melted. Unplug the appliance, uncover it, and let stand for 10 minutes before cutting into wedges or scooping out with a large spoon.

TESTERS' NOTES
• A bit complicated, no doubt, but this recipe yields satisfying family fare—or a retro kick.
• For a more intense flavor, toast the walnut pieces in a dry skillet over medium-low heat until aromatic and lightly browned, about 4 minutes.

(continued)

• Cut the tortillas so they'll make single layers in the cooker, using the extra bits to fill in any gaps.

SHORTCUTS Skip making the enchilada sauce in steps 1 through 3, and instead use 2 cups purchased enchilada sauce for a small slow cooker, 3 cups for a medium cooker, or 5 cups for a large cooker.

southwestern chicken and mac casserole

EFFORT: **NOT MUCH** • PREP TIME: **15 MINUTES** • COOK TIME: **4 HOURS** • KEEPS ON WARM: **NO** • SERVES: **2 TO 8**

INGREDIENTS	2- TO 3½-QT	4- TO 5½-QT	6- TO 8-QT
Boned, skinned, and chopped supermarket rotisserie chicken meat	1¼ cups	3 cups	5 cups
Low-sodium vegetable broth	1 cup	2½ cups	4 cups
Chopped drained canned tomatillos	½ cup	1¼ cups	2 cups
Corn kernels, fresh cut from the cob, or frozen, thawed	½ cup	1¼ cups	2 cups
Yellow or red bell peppers, stemmed, seeded, and chopped	1 small	1 medium	2 medium
Chopped fresh cilantro leaves	2 tblsp	⅓ cup	½ cup
Dried oregano	½ tsp	1 tsp	½ tblsp
Ground cumin	¼ tsp	½ tsp	1 tsp
Salt	¼ tsp	½ tsp	1 tsp
Dried whole wheat farfalle (bow-tie pasta)	3 ounces	7 ounces	12 ounces

1 Stir the chicken, broth, tomatillos, corn, bell pepper, cilantro, oregano, cumin, and salt in the slow cooker. Pour in the pasta and stir well.

2 Cover and cook on low for 4 hours, stirring once or twice while cooking, or until the pasta is tender and the flavors have blended.

TESTERS' NOTES
• This easy casserole is a great way to gussy up supermarket rotisserie chicken meat. The fresh cilantro does much of the heavy lifting; the tomatillos give the dish a slightly sour spark.
• We use vegetable broth to give the casserole a lighter, brighter finish. Substitute chicken broth for a more classic, comfort-food taste.
• For more oomph, add a small amount of crumbled soft goat cheese with the other ingredients.

ALL-AMERICAN KNOW-HOW Let a rotisserie chicken cool for 20 minutes (that is, the time probably equal to the ride or walk home) before beginning to work with it. Cut the chicken into pieces—legs, thighs, breast, wings—then peel off the skin. The meat should come straight off the bones, but check thoroughly for stray bits of cartilage or small bones. Your best tools for this entire operation are your clean, dry hands.

Serve It Up! Make a **Southwestern Bean Salad** as a side dish for four people: Drain and rinse a can of black beans, then mix those beans with about 1 cup chopped jarred roasted red pepper and some minced red onion. Stir in 2 tablespoons lime juice, 1½ tablespoons walnut oil, ½ teaspoon chili powder, and ½ teaspoon salt.

chicken sausage and winter squash

EFFORT: **A LITTLE** • PREP TIME: **25 MINUTES** • COOK TIME: **5 HOURS**
• KEEPS ON WARM: **2 HOURS** • SERVES: **2 TO 6**

INGREDIENTS	2- TO 3½-QT	4- TO 5½-QT	6- TO 8-QT
Unsalted butter	1 tblsp	2 tblsp	3 tblsp
Chicken sausage, cut into 2-inch lengths	1 pound	2 pounds	3½ pounds
Winter squash (such as butternut), peeled, seeded, and cubed	½ pound	1 pound	3 pounds
Yellow onion, chopped	1 small	1 medium	1 large
Golden raisins	¼ cup	½ cup	¾ cup
Ground coriander	½ tsp	1 tsp	½ tblsp
Ground ginger	½ tsp	1 tsp	½ tblsp
Cayenne	¼ tsp	½ tsp	¾ tsp
Saffron	⅛ tsp	¼ tsp	½ tsp
4-inch cinnamon stick	½	1	2
Low-sodium chicken broth	1 cup	1¾ cups	3 cups

1 Melt the butter in a large skillet over medium heat. Add the sausage pieces (as much as will fit). Brown on several sides, turning occasionally, about 6 minutes. (If necessary, divide the butter among several batches.) Transfer to the slow cooker and continue browning as needed.

2 Add the squash, onion, raisins, coriander, ginger, cayenne, saffron, and cinnamon stick to the slow cooker. Toss everything together, then pour the broth over the mixture.

3 Cover and cook on low for 5 hours, or until the squash is tender and the chicken sausage is cooked through.

TESTERS' NOTES
• Vary this dish by using another type of winter squash you prefer, perhaps buttercup, hubbard, or even pumpkin. (Shoot, you can even use cubed sweet potatoes.) By the way, acorn and delicata squash don't need to be peeled, just seeded.
• Since there are plenty of spices for the squash, use a fairly mild chicken sausage, which will be flavored mostly by the aromatics used in this recipe.

turkey

Turkey suffers from an unconscionable holiday hangover—and so quietly withdraws from the scene for the rest of the year. Except for the occasional sliced deli turkey sandwich, or maybe the lamentable appearance of turkey bacon when we're feeling that we've overindulged, the noble fowl Ben Franklin wanted as the national bird is a culinary no-show. Few people make turkey for a run-of-the-mill weeknight.

Too bad. Turkey is, yes, very lean—and contains far less of that alleged sleep-inducing L-tryptophan than eggs. But more importantly, it's perhaps the tastiest bird from the supermarket. It also cooks more evenly than chicken—and proves more versatile, thanks to the ways the meat absorbs and revamps essential flavors, muting sweet notes in favor of the savory. With a slow cooker, that sort of magic is all the easier. But don't think we've forgotten about Thanksgiving or any other holiday. We've even got a recipe for a whole roast turkey from the slow cooker—provided you've got a large model of the appliance in the cupboard.

However, we might as well admit it up front: there are some problems. Since turkey is low in fat, it can be a quick-cooking meat, particularly when the bones and joints have been removed, as in a boneless breast roast or even turkey cutlets. Neither is a good choice for us here—unless we're willing to make some adjustments. (We are.) Boneless white meat needs protection, whether that's with a lot of vegetables offering their moisture to a braise or a rich, moist stuffing for cutlets.

Of course, there's little necessary fandango when it comes to the dark meat bits: thighs, legs, and wings. These take well to braises, to slow-cooker roasts, even to barbecue. Just take a look at our three basic turkey thigh braises: with cherries and orange zest, with chestnuts and marmalade, and with mustard and white wine. Turkey can stand up to that wide range of flavors!

We round out our turkey compendium with recipes using ground turkey as well as a few recipes for leftover turkey. We hope these will be welcome problem-solvers for after the holiday meal.

However, even if we're on a mission to bring turkey back to the weeknight table, your supermarket may not be on board our campaign. While turkey wings and legs are often available ready-to-cook in the meat case, breasts and whole birds are too often dropped in the deep freeze for year-round storage. So practice good thawing procedures. Set the turkey on a plate in the refrigerator to catch drips. A 5-pound turkey breast can take up to two full days to thaw properly; a larger bird, up to four days. If you're pressed for time, use the quick-thaw method: set the bird in its wrapping in a large bowl and fill the bowl with cool water. Set on the counter and change the water every 20 minutes to keep it from getting warm. You'll be able to thaw even a whole bird in a few hours.

So let's plan on a ham this Thanksgiving and make every other day Turkey Day.

turkey breast
over butternut squash and chard

EFFORT: **A LITTLE** • PREP TIME: **25 MINUTES** • COOK TIME: **4 TO 5½ HOURS** • KEEPS ON WARM: **1 HOUR** • SERVES: **5 TO 10**

INGREDIENTS	4- TO 5½-QT	6- TO 8-QT
Unsalted butter	3 tblsp	5 tblsp
Yellow onion, chopped	1 small	1 large
Swiss chard, stemmed, chopped, and packed	¾ pound	1½ pounds
Dry white wine, such as Albariño	2 tblsp	3 tblsp
Butternut squash, peeled, seeded, and cut into cubes	1 pound	2 pounds
Maple syrup	2 tblsp	¼ cup
Ground cinnamon	½ tsp	1 tsp
Bone-in, skin-on turkey breast	2½ pounds	5 to 6 pounds
Fresh sage leaves	6	12
Salt	½ tsp	1 tsp
Ground black pepper	½ tsp	¾ tsp

1 Melt the butter in a large skillet over medium-low heat. Dump in the onion, drop the heat to low, and cook slowly, stirring frequently, until golden and somewhat sweet, about 10 minutes.

2 Raise the heat to medium, add the chard, and stir well to begin the wilting process. Add the wine and keep stirring until the chard fully wilts.

3 Scrape the contents of the skillet into the slow cooker; stir in the squash cubes, maple syrup, and cinnamon.

4 Loosen the skin over the turkey breast by running your clean, dry fingers between the skin and the meat. Slip the sage leaves between the skin and the meat. Pat the skin back into place and set the breast skin side up in the slow cooker. Sprinkle with the salt and pepper.

5 Cover and cook on low for 4 hours in a medium slow cooker or 5½ hours in a large one, until an instant-read meat thermometer inserted in the meat (without touching the bone) registers 165°F.

6 Transfer the turkey breast to a cutting board. Use a slotted spoon to transfer the vegetables to a serving bowl. Pour the liquid in the cooker into a medium saucepan; bring to a boil over high heat, stirring occasionally, and cook until the sauce has reduced to a glaze, perhaps 3 to 5 minutes. Carve the turkey breast into thin slices and serve the sauce and vegetables on the side.

TESTERS' NOTES
• Wash the chard leaves, then cut out the large veins that run along their centers. Don't worry about drying the leaves after chopping; the extra moisture will help them wilt quickly.
• Although the onion is not yet caramelized after only 10 minutes, it does show the brilliance of the slow cooker. You can start the caramelization on the stove, then let it continue in the appliance until the onion is ridiculously sweet, the same as if you'd let it go an hour stovetop, stirring frequently.
• There is no recipe here for a small slow cooker because you'll never find a bone-in turkey breast small enough to fit in one. Okay, someone is surely going to prove us wrong, but everyone else should consider a larger model.

boneless turkey breast with dried fruit

EFFORT: **A LITTLE** • PREP TIME: **20 MINUTES** • COOK TIME: **4½ TO 5½ HOURS** • KEEPS ON WARM: **3 HOURS** • SERVES: **3 TO 10**

INGREDIENTS	2- TO 3½-QT	4- TO 5½-QT	6- TO 8-QT
Packed dark brown sugar	2½ tblsp	⅓ cup	⅔ cup
Minced peeled fresh ginger	2 tsp	1 tblsp	2 tblsp
Ground cinnamon	¼ tsp	½ tsp	1 tsp
Salt	¼ tsp	½ tsp	1 tsp
Ground black pepper	¼ tsp	½ tsp	1 tsp
Boneless skinless turkey breast	1 pound	2 pounds	4 pounds
Butternut squash, peeled, seeded, and cubed	½ pound (1½ cups)	1 pound (3 cups)	1¾ pounds (5 cups)
Chopped dried apricots	¼ cup	½ cup	1 cup
Chopped pitted prunes	¼ cup	½ cup	1 cup
4-inch rosemary sprigs	1	2	3

1 Mix the brown sugar, ginger, cinnamon, salt, and pepper in a small bowl.

2 Wind butchers' twine around the turkey breast in two to four places to form a fairly compact roast before tying securely. Rub the brown sugar mixture all over the roast. Set it in the slow cooker. Sprinkle the squash, apricots, and prunes around the roast. Tuck in the rosemary sprigs.

3 Cover and cook on low for 4½ hours in a small slow cooker, 5 hours in a medium one, or 5½ hours in a large appliance, until an instant-read meat thermometer inserted into the center of the meat registers 165°F. Transfer to a cutting board; let stand for 10 minutes.

4 Snip off the butchers' twine, then carve the meat into ½-inch-thick slices. Discard the rosemary sprigs. Fish the squash and fruit out of the cooker with a slotted spoon to serve on the side.

TESTERS' NOTES

• Although you may not be able to fit a bone-in turkey breast in a small slow cooker, you can certainly get a boneless breast in there. This sweet rub slowly caramelizes on the roast, seeping down into the vegetables below to morph them into true comfort food.

• Substitute any other variety of winter squash, like buttercup, red kuri, or pumpkin. The squash cubes should be about ½ inch—which may be smaller than those of the prepared butternut squash in the produce section. Slice those bigger pieces to the proper size.

• Always follow the rule for dried fruit: it should smell sweet and fragrant, a bit like a concentrated version of its fresh kin. It should also be moist and pliable despite being dried. If your supermarket only has inferior offerings, you should consider taking your hard-earned dollars elsewhere.

stuffed turkey breast

EFFORT: **A LOT** • PREP TIME: **40 MINUTES** • COOK TIME: **4 TO 5 HOURS** • KEEPS ON WARM: **NO** • SERVES: **3 TO 6**

INGREDIENTS	2- TO 3½-QT	4- TO 5½-QT	6- TO 8-QT
Boneless skinless turkey breast	1 pound	1½ pounds	2½ pounds
Crumbled day-old corn muffins	1 cup	1½ cups	2½ cups
Minced shallots	3 tblsp	⅓ cup	½ cup
Minced celery	2 tblsp	⅓ cup	½ cup
Dry white wine, such as Chardonnay	3 tblsp	⅓ cup	½ cup
Large egg yolks, well beaten in a small bowl	1	2	3
Poultry seasoning (see page 243)	1 tsp	½ tblsp	2½ tsp
Salt	½ tsp	¾ tsp	1¼ tsp
Ground black pepper	½ tsp	¾ tsp	1¼ tsp
Unsalted butter	2 tblsp	3 tblsp	5 tblsp
Low-sodium chicken broth	2 cups	3 cups	5 cups
Potato starch	1 tsp	½ tblsp	2½ tsp

1 Lay the turkey breast on a large cutting board and butterfly it by splitting in half lengthwise without cutting through all the way and opening it up something like a book. Cover with plastic wrap and use the smooth side of a meat mallet or the bottom of a heavy saucepan to flatten to ¼ inch thick.

2 Combine the crumbled muffins, shallots, celery, wine, egg yolk(s), poultry seasoning, salt, and pepper in a large bowl. Stir gently but stop before the corn muffins break down into a paste. Spread over the turkey breast, leaving a ½-inch margin.

3 Roll the breast closed and tie it with butchers' twine in at least three places, perhaps more. Knot securely but not too tight.

4 Melt the butter in a large skillet set over medium heat. Slip the turkey breast into the pan and brown on all sides, turning occasionally, about 6 minutes. Transfer to the slow cooker; pour in the broth over the top.

5 Cover and cook on low for 4 hours in a small slow cooker, 5 hours in a medium or large model, or until an instant-read meat thermometer inserted into the center of the breast registers 165°F. Use a large spatula to move the turkey breast to a cutting board. Let stand while you make the sauce.

6 Ladle the juices from the cooker into a large saucepan; bring to a boil over high heat. Boil for 1 minute. Whisk the potato starch into a little water in a small bowl (just enough water to get it to dissolve, no more than a tablespoon or so), then whisk into the broth. Boil for a few seconds until the sauce has thickened. Remove the sauce from the heat. Slice the stuffed turkey breast into ½-inch-thick rings, and serve with the sauce on the side.

TESTERS' NOTES

• Though it takes a bit of work, this recipe nonetheless yields a showstopper, turkey and dressing all in one.
• When you're mixing that stuffing, stir only until it's the consistency of traditional cornbread dressing (that is, not mushy).
• Some purchased corn muffins are unbearably sweet. Look for ones without much sugar in the mix—or even none at all, if you can find them (probably at a higher-end bakery).
• Unfortunately, there's no real way to tell how many purchased corn muffins you'll need to crumble into bits to make the required amount. Buy more than you think you'll

need, then freeze the rest for the next time you intend to make a stuffing like this.

SHORTCUTS Ask the butcher at your supermarket to butterfly a turkey breast for you. He or she may be unwilling to do so unless you buy a whole breast. Freeze the remainder in a sealed plastic bag to dice or chop for other turkey recipes.

shredded balsamic barbecued turkey

EFFORT: **NOT MUCH** · PREP TIME: **15 MINUTES** · COOK TIME: **6 TO 8 HOURS** · KEEPS ON WARM: **4 HOURS** · SERVES: **3 TO 10**

INGREDIENTS	2- TO 3½-QT	4- TO 5½-QT	6- TO 8-QT
No-salt-added canned tomato sauce	⅔ cup	1 cup	2⅓ cups
Canned chopped green chiles, mild or hot	¼ cup	½ cup	1 cup plus 2 tblsp
Balsamic vinegar	2 tblsp	3 tblsp	7 tblsp
Packed dark brown sugar	2 tblsp	3 tblsp	7 tblsp
Mild smoked paprika	5 tsp	2 tblsp	4½ tblsp
No-salt-added tomato paste	1½ tblsp	2 tblsp	4½ tblsp
Worcestershire sauce	2 tsp	1 tblsp	2 tblsp plus 1 tsp
Chili powder	2 tsp	1 tblsp	2 tblsp plus 1 tsp
Dry mustard (see page 392)	1¼ tsp	2 tsp	4½ tsp
Onion powder	¼ tsp	½ tsp	1¼ tsp
Salt	¼ tsp	½ tsp	1¼ tsp
Garlic powder	⅛ tsp	¼ tsp	½ tsp
Ground cloves	⅛ tsp	¼ tsp	½ tsp
Boneless skinless turkey breast	1½ pounds	2½ pounds	4½ pounds

1 Whisk the tomato sauce, chiles, balsamic vinegar, brown sugar, paprika, tomato paste, Worcestershire sauce, chili powder, mustard, onion powder, salt, garlic powder, and cloves in the slow cooker until the tomato paste dissolves and the sauce is uniform.

2 Set the turkey breast in the sauce. Cover and cook on low for 6 hours in a small slow cooker, 7 hours in a medium cooker, or 8 hours in a large one, or until the meat can be easily shredded with a fork. Then do just that: use a fork (or two) to shred the meat into small bits. Stir the meat into the sauce to serve.

TESTERS' NOTES
• Because of varying densities among the turkey's muscle groups, as well as residual moisture in that meat, a turkey breast may or may not become shreddable in the time stated. Start checking about an hour early, then keep cooking the meat until it's the right *consistency* (not, as is usually the case, the right temperature).
• Use a good-quality but inexpensive balsamic vinegar, not a syrupy, aged bottling.

Serve It Up! Although you can serve this on toasted buns with chopped lettuce and tomato, you might consider it in soft tacos made from whole wheat tortillas, shredded Cheddar cheese, sliced radishes, and minced cilantro.

turkey chili with raisins and cinnamon

EFFORT: **NOT MUCH** • PREP TIME: **15 MINUTES** • COOK TIME:
3 HOURS/5 HOURS • KEEPS ON WARM: **4 HOURS** • SERVES: **3 TO 10**

INGREDIENTS	2- TO 3½-QT	4- TO 5½-QT	6- TO 8-QT
Boneless skinless turkey breast or breast cutlets, cut into ¼-inch pieces	1 pound	2½ pounds	4½ pounds
Canned diced tomatoes with chiles (such as Rotel)	1¾ cups	4 cups	7 cups
Drained and rinsed canned pinto beans	1¾ cups	4 cups	7 cups
Raisins	¼ cup	⅔ cup	1 cup plus 2 tblsp
Canned chipotles in adobo sauce, stemmed and minced	Up to 1½	Up to 2½	Up to 4
Ground cinnamon	½ tsp	1¼ tsp	2¼ tsp
Salt	½ tsp	1¼ tsp	2 tsp

1 Dump the turkey, tomatoes, beans, raisins, chipotles, cinnamon, and salt into the slow cooker. Stir well.

2 Cover and cook on high for 3 hours or on low for 5 hours, or until the chili has thickened a bit and the flavors have blended.

TESTERS' NOTES
• A simple meal, its success relies on your knife technique: cut the turkey into tiny bits. But don't be tempted to use ground turkey, which can clump.
• Slice the raisins in half if you want them more evenly distributed in the sauce. Or substitute dried currants.

Serve It Up! Have shredded Monterey Jack, chopped avocado, shredded tart apples, sour cream, and/or crumbled bacon bits for condiments at the table.

turkey tetrazzini

EFFORT: **NOT MUCH** • PREP TIME: **15 MINUTES** • COOK TIME:
4 HOURS • KEEPS ON WARM: **NO** • SERVES: **2 TO 6**

INGREDIENTS	2- TO 3½-QT	4- TO 5½-QT	6- TO 8-QT
Boneless skinless turkey breast or breast cutlets, cut into ½-inch pieces	⅔ pound	1 pound	1¾ pounds
Cremini or brown button mushrooms, thinly sliced	4 ounces (about 1⅓ cups)	7 ounces (about 2 cups)	11 ounces (about 3½ cups)
Dried whole wheat ziti	4 ounces (1⅓ cups)	6 ounces (2 cups)	10 ounces (3⅓ cups)
Low-sodium chicken broth	⅔ cup	1 cup	1¾ cups
Dry sherry	⅓ cup	½ cup	1 cup
Sour cream (regular or low-fat)	⅓ cup	½ cup	¾ cup
All-purpose flour	4 tsp	2 tblsp	3½ tblsp
Dijon mustard	½ tblsp	2 tsp	3½ tsp
Mild paprika	½ tblsp	2 tsp	3½ tsp
Salt	¼ tsp	½ tsp	1 tsp

1 Stir the diced turkey, mushrooms, and ziti in the slow cooker.

2 Whisk the broth, sherry, sour cream, flour, mustard, paprika, and salt in a large bowl until the flour dissolves; pour over the ingredients in the slow cooker and stir well to coat.

3 Cover and cook on low, stirring twice, for 4 hours, or until the pasta is tender and the sauce has thickened.

TESTERS' NOTES

• Here's a slow-cooker version of the creamy casserole. Stirring it twice during cooking will keep the pasta from clumping together.

• The required amount of diced turkey may not represent all the meat from a breast. Our advice? Buy an equivalent amount of turkey breast cutlets and dice what you need, or dice a larger boneless breast and freeze the rest in a zip-closed plastic bag for the next time you want comfort food like this.

• Whole wheat pasta will stand up better to the long cooking; it will also offer a firmer bite, better against the creamy sauce.

• Don't use fat-free sour cream; it can break and cause the sauce to appear to have curdled.

italian-style turkey and peppers

EFFORT: **A LITTLE** • PREP TIME: **20 MINUTES** • COOK TIME:
3 HOURS/5 HOURS • KEEPS ON WARM: **4 HOURS** • SERVES: **3 TO 8**

INGREDIENTS	2- TO 3½-QT	4- TO 5½-QT	6- TO 8-QT
Olive oil	1 tblsp	2 tblsp	3 tblsp
Italian turkey sausages, sweet or hot	½ pound	1 pound	1¾ pounds
Italian-style canned diced tomatoes	1 cup	1¾ cups	3 cups
Italian-style tomato paste	⅓ cup	⅔ cup	1¼ cups
Fennel seeds	½ tsp	1 tsp	2 tsp
Red pepper flakes	¼ tsp	½ tsp	¾ tsp
Salt (optional)	¼ tsp	½ tsp	¾ tsp
Cubanelle peppers, stemmed, seeded, and sliced (see page 47)	2 medium	3 large	5 large
Turkey breast cutlets, cut into ½-inch strips	½ pound	1 pound	1¾ pounds
Whole medium scallions, chopped	2	3	5

1 Set a large skillet over medium heat for a few minutes, then pour in the oil. Add the sausages, working in batches as necessary, turning them to brown to get good color on the casings, 4 or 5 minutes, then transfer to a cutting board and continue browning more as necessary. Once done, cool the sausages for 5 minutes, then slice into 2-inch pieces.

2 Stir the tomatoes, tomato paste, fennel seeds, red pepper flakes, and salt (if desired) in the slow cooker until the tomato paste dissolves.

3 Set the sausage pieces in the slow cooker; add the cubanelle peppers, turkey strips, and scallions. Toss well.

4 Cover and cook on high for 3 hours or on low for 5 hours, or until the sausage is cooked through and the sauce has thickened a bit.

TESTERS' NOTES

• Although you can use turkey sausage links for this dish, full-size turkey sausages are often more flavorful. Look for them in the meat case of your supermarket.

(continued)

- We tested this recipe with Italian-seasoned turkey sausage, but you could use other flavors as desired so long as you keep in mind that the overall dish should be oriented toward traditional Italian flavorings. Sage and lemon turkey sausage would work; Asian-flavored turkey sausages wouldn't.
- The salt is optional because those canned seasoned tomatoes are often loaded with sodium.

Serve It Up! Steam or boil white potatoes like Irish creamers, then peel them and mash with equal parts cream cheese, sour cream, milk, and butter. Season the potatoes with salt and ground black pepper, then plop some in every bowl and dish up the stew on top.

cider-braised turkey drumsticks

EFFORT: **A LITTLE** • PREP TIME: **30 MINUTES** • COOK TIME: **5 HOURS/8 HOURS** • KEEPS ON WARM: **3 HOURS** • SERVES: **2 TO 8**

INGREDIENTS	2- TO 3½-QT	4- TO 5½-QT	6- TO 8-QT
Thin strips of bacon, chopped	2 ounces	4 ounces	8 ounces
Skin-on turkey drumsticks	2	4	8
Carrots, chopped	½ pound (about 1½ cups)	1 pound (about 3 cups)	2 pounds (about 6 cups)
Leeks (white and pale green part only), halved lengthwise, washed carefully for interior grit, and thinly sliced	¼ pound (about ½ cup)	½ pound (about 1 cup)	1 pound (about 2 cups)
Packed light brown sugar	2 tblsp	¼ cup	½ cup
Stemmed fresh thyme leaves	2 tsp	1½ tblsp	3 tblsp
Bay leaves	1	2	3
Ground black pepper	½ tsp	1 tsp	2 tsp
Unsweetened apple cider	1 cup	2 cups	4 cups (1 quart)

1 Fry the bacon pieces in a large skillet set over medium heat until crisp, stirring often, between 4 and 8 minutes. Use a slotted spoon to move those bits into the slow cooker.

2 Set a few drumsticks into the hot bacon fat in the skillet; cook over medium heat, turning occasionally, until well browned, about 8 minutes. Move the drumsticks to the slow cooker; continue browning more as needed.

3 Mix the carrots, leeks, brown sugar, and thyme in a big bowl until the brown sugar coats everything; pour into the slow cooker. Tuck the bay leaves among the vegetables. Sprinkle with pepper; pour in the cider.

4 Cover and cook on high for 5 hours or on low for 8 hours, or until the meat is wonderfully tender. Use tongs to transfer the turkey drumsticks to a large platter. Discard the bay leaves; use a slotted spoon to transfer the carrots and leeks to a serving bowl. Skim the sauce for fat on its surface, then serve the sauce on the side with the drumsticks and vegetables.

TESTERS' NOTES
- It's all about the browning. If you don't take your time to brown the drumsticks properly, the skin will turn unappealingly spongy.
- For a somewhat less sweet, more sweet-and-sour dish, add up to 2 tablespoons apple cider vinegar with the cider.

Serve It Up! Make an easy side salad by tossing small broccoli florets, seedless green grape halves, chopped celery, and salted sunflower seeds with some mayonnaise, some plain yogurt, a little white wine vinegar, a pinch of sugar, and a little salt.

kir-braised turkey drumsticks

EFFORT: **A LITTLE** • PREP TIME: **20 MINUTES** • COOK TIME: **5 HOURS/8 HOURS** • KEEPS ON WARM: **3 HOURS** • SERVES: **2 TO 8**

INGREDIENTS	2- TO 3½-QT	4- TO 5½-QT	6- TO 8-QT
Unsalted butter	1 tblsp	2 tblsp	3 tblsp
Skin-on turkey drumsticks	2	4	8
Frozen pearl onions, thawed, or fresh, peeled	½ cup	1 cup	1²/₃ cups
Light but dry white wine, such as Pouilly Fumé	½ cup	1 cup	2½ cups
Crème de Cassis or other black currant liqueur	2 tblsp	3 tblsp	7 tblsp
Salt	¼ tsp	¼ tsp	½ tsp
Ground black pepper	½ tsp	1 tsp	2 tsp

1 Melt the butter in a large skillet set over medium heat. Add a few of the turkey drumsticks and brown on all sides, turning occasionally, about 8 minutes. (If working with several batches, divide the butter among them and melt more each time.) Transfer the drumsticks to the slow cooker.

2 Dump the pearl onions into the skillet; brown, stirring occasionally, between 4 to 8 minutes, depending on the size of the batch. Scrape these into the slow cooker. Pour the wine and cassis over the legs and onions; sprinkle with salt and pepper.

3 Cover and cook on high for 5 hours or on low for 8 hours, or until the meat is falling-apart tender, particularly at the thick end of each leg. Transfer the drumsticks to a serving platter; tent with foil to keep warm.

4 Skim the fat from the juices in the slow cooker (by way of a flatware spoon or a fat separator). Pour the juices into a large saucepan. Bring to a boil over high heat, stirring occasionally. Boil furiously until reduced to about two-thirds the original volume, until a glaze-like sauce, between 3 and 8 minutes. Serve on the side with the drumsticks.

TESTERS' NOTES
• A kir (*keer*) is a classic cocktail made from white wine and cassis, a syrupy black currant liqueur. Here, that combo becomes a braising medium for chewy, meaty turkey drumsticks, a sweet pop of flavor balanced by butter and salt.
• Brown the drumsticks well. That caramelization will provide essential bitter and even sour notes to balance the sweet liqueur.

INGREDIENTS EXPLAINED Crème de cassis (*crem duh cah-SEES*) is a black currant liqueur. The name indicates a product of France, though any domestic black currant liqueur will work as well. Do not use black currant *eau de vie,* which is too strong for this dish.

turkey pot pie

EFFORT: **A LOT** • PREP TIME: **20 MINUTES** • COOK TIME: **7 HOURS 12 MINUTES** • KEEPS ON WARM: **3 HOURS THROUGH STEP 3** • SERVES: **4 TO 12**

INGREDIENTS	2- TO 3½-QT	4- TO 5½-QT	6- TO 8-QT
Skinless turkey thighs	1¼ pounds	2 pounds	3½ pounds
Cremini or brown button mushrooms, thinly sliced	3 ounces (about ¾ cup)	5 ounces (about 1½ cups)	7 ounces (about 2 cups)
Diced red-skinned potatoes (in about ¼-inch pieces)	½ cup	1 cup	1½ cups (about ½ pound)
Thinly sliced carrot	½ cup	⅔ cup	1¼ cup (about ½ pound)
Chopped yellow onion	⅓ cup	½ cup	¾ cup (about 1 small)
Thinly sliced celery	¼ cup	⅓ cup (about 1 medium rib)	¾ cup
Dried cranberries	¼ cup	⅓ cup	½ cup
All-purpose flour	1½ tblsp	2½ tblsp	¼ cup
Poultry seasoning (see page 243)	½ tblsp	2 tsp	1 tblsp
Salt	¼ tsp	½ tsp	1 tsp
Ground black pepper	¼ tsp	½ tsp	1 tsp
Low-sodium chicken broth	¾ cup	1¼ cups	2 cups
4-inch squares of frozen puff pastry, thawed	4	8	12

1 Cut the meat off the bones of the turkey thighs. Discard any cartilage, joints, and the bones themselves. Chop the meat into ½-inch pieces.

2 Stir the turkey meat with the mushrooms, potatoes, carrot, onion, celery, cranberries, flour, poultry seasoning, salt, and pepper in the slow cooker. Pour the broth over this mixture.

3 Cover and cook on low for 7 hours, or until the stew is thickened and rich, the vegetables are tender, and the meat is still juicy. Switch the cooker to warm.

4 As the appliance keeps the stew warm, preheat the oven to 400°F. Lay the puff pastry squares on a large baking sheet; bake until browned and (indeed) puffed, about 12 minutes.

5 Ladle the stew into serving bowls; top each with one of the puff pastry squares.

TESTERS' NOTES
• There's a bit of work to do here, what with chopping all those vegetables and deboning the turkey thighs. Still, you'll end up with a rib-sticker that just might be the perfect dinner solution for weekend guests.
• While this dish is definitely better with dark-meat turkey, you can substitute diced boneless turkey breast cutlets for an easier (if chewier) dinner.
• Yes, we cheated and baked the puff pastry in the oven. But it'll never brown in the slow cooker; it would turn gummy and inedible. Such cheating seems a small price for pot pie.

INGREDIENTS EXPLAINED The quality of frozen puff pastry varies dramatically. Some are honest-to-goodness butter-and-flour affairs; others are just an excuse for lots of tasteless hydrogenated fats. Read the labels to find the best product you can comfortably afford.

turkey thighs
with garlic and potatoes

EFFORT: **A LITTLE** • PREP TIME: **20 MINUTES** • COOK TIME:
4 HOURS/6 HOURS • KEEPS ON WARM: **3 HOURS** • SERVES: **4 TO 10**

INGREDIENTS	2- TO 3½-QT	4- TO 5½-QT	6- TO 8-QT
Packed stemmed fresh sage leaves	1 tblsp	2 tblsp	3 tblsp
Minced garlic	2 tsp	4 tsp	2 tblsp
Finely grated lemon zest	½ tblsp	1 tblsp	1½ tblsp
Salt	½ tsp	1 tsp	½ tblsp
Ground black pepper	½ tsp	1 tsp	½ tblsp
Olive oil	1½ tblsp	3 tblsp	¼ cup
Skinless turkey thighs	1½ pounds	4½ pounds	6 pounds
Medium yellow potatoes (such as Yukon Gold), cut into 1-inch wedges	2	4	6
White wine vinegar	2 tsp	1 tblsp	1½ tblsp

1 Mince the sage, garlic, lemon zest, salt, and pepper on a clean cutting board. Add half the olive oil; rock the knife through the ingredients, gathering them again into a pile until they become a coarse paste.

2 Make small, thin slits all over the meat of the turkey thighs. Scoop up the herb paste and rub it both *onto* the meat and *into* the slits. Set the thighs into the slow cooker.

3 Pile the potato wedges in the slow cooker; toss with the remaining olive oil as well as the vinegar. Scatter around the thighs.

4 Cover and cook on high for 4 hours or on low for 6 hours, or until the meat is fork-tender, particularly at the knuckle-like joints. Scoop the thighs into bowls and serve with the potatoes on the side.

TESTERS' NOTES
• Skin turkey thighs by grabbing the loose flap of skin at one end with paper towels and pulling it off the meat. Also remove any obvious globs of fat.
• There's not much of a sauce here; it's mostly rendered fat and olive oil with some of the turkey juices underneath. You can drizzle it over the meat or you can discard it.
• You *can* use a mini food processor to create the paste for the meat, but chopping the ingredients with a knife gives them a juicy, paste-like consistency that you cannot achieve with the convenience appliance.

Serve It Up! Make a **Brussels Sprouts Hash**: Shred Brussels sprouts by removing the stem ends and slicing them into thin strips. Cook these in a little unsalted butter with chopped pecans or walnuts, minced green onion, and a little minced mint. Season with salt and pepper—and add some crumbled, crunchy bacon, if you like.

turkey thighs
with chestnuts and marmalade

EFFORT: **A LITTLE** • PREP TIME: **20 MINUTES** • COOK TIME:
4 HOURS/6 HOURS • KEEPS ON WARM: **2 HOURS** • SERVES: **4 TO 10**

INGREDIENTS	2- TO 3½-QT	4- TO 5½-QT	6- TO 8-QT
Unsalted butter	1½ tblsp	2½ tblsp	3 tblsp
Skinless turkey thighs	2 pounds	4½ pounds	6 pounds
Orange marmalade	¼ cup	½ cup	¾ cup
Jarred peeled roasted chestnuts	1 cup	2 cups	3 cups
Low-sodium chicken broth	½ cup	1 cup	1½ cups
Stemmed fresh thyme leaves	2 tsp	4 tsp	2 tblsp
Ground black pepper	½ tsp	1 tsp	1½ tsp
Salt	½ tsp	1 tsp	1¼ tsp

1 Melt the butter in a large skillet over medium heat. Add a batch of the thighs and brown on both sides, 4 to 7 minutes, turning once, before transferring them to the slow cooker. Brown more as needed. (If you're working with the largest batch, consider dividing the butter in half or even thirds so there's plenty of fat for each batch.) When you're done, scrape any of the remaining butter from the skillet into the cooker as well.

2 Smear the thighs with the marmalade, then sprinkle the chestnuts around them. Whisk the broth, thyme, pepper, and salt in a big bowl and pour *around* the thighs (not on them, to avoid knocking off the marmalade).

3 Cover and cook on high for 4 hours or on low for 6 hours, or until the meat is fork-tender and glazed with marmalade.

TESTERS' NOTES
• Fairly simple, this braise offers a lot of flavor for a relatively small amount of work. Use the highest-quality orange marmalade you can comfortably afford; you'll want the sour pop of the good stuff.
• With *skin-on* turkey thighs, the sauce gets too oily, no matter how much the thighs are browned. Skinless offers a more straightforward taste, a better match to the few ingredients.

Serve It Up! Here's a quick and innovative side dish for this fairly sweet main course. Steam peeled and sliced carrots and parsnips until tender, then mash them with reduced-sodium vegetable broth, a little nut oil, a sprinkle of salt, and a pinch of cayenne.

ALL-AMERICAN KNOW-HOW Stem thyme leaves by holding the sprig in one hand by its thick end and running the fingers of your other hand along the stem but "against the grain"—that is, from the thinnest part to the thickest, knocking off the leaves to the cutting board below.

turkey thighs
with mustard and white wine

EFFORT: **A LITTLE** • PREP TIME: **20 MINUTES** • COOK TIME:
4 HOURS/6 HOURS • KEEPS ON WARM: **3 HOURS** • SERVES: **4 TO 10**

INGREDIENTS	2- TO 3½-QT	4- TO 5½-QT	6- TO 8-QT
Unsalted butter	2 tsp	2 tblsp	3 tblsp
Olive oil	2 tsp	1 tblsp	2 tblsp
Skinless turkey thighs	2 pounds	4½ pounds	6 pounds
Chopped yellow onion	½ cup	⅔ cup (about 1 small)	1¼ cups
Chopped fresh parsley leaves	2 tblsp	5 tblsp	½ cup
Minced garlic	1 tsp	2½ tsp	1½ tblsp
Low-sodium chicken broth	1 cup	2 cups	3 cups
Dry white wine, such as Chardonnay	½ cup	1 cup	1½ cups
All-purpose flour	1½ tblsp	3 tblsp	5 tblsp
Dijon mustard	1 tblsp	2 tblsp	3 tblsp

1 Melt the butter with the oil in a large skillet set over medium heat. Slip a batch of thighs into the skillet and brown on both sides, 4 to 6 minutes, turning once, before moving them to the slow cooker. Continue browning more as necessary.

2 Dump the onion into the skillet, still set over medium heat. Cook, stirring often, until softened and translucent, about 3 minutes. Scrape the contents of the skillet into the slow cooker. Sprinkle everything with the parsley and garlic.

3 Whisk the broth, wine, flour, and mustard in a large bowl until the flour dissolves. Pour over the other ingredients.

4 Cover and cook on high for 4 hours or on low for 6 hours, or until the sauce has thickened somewhat and the meat is fork-tender.

TESTERS' NOTES
• The slightly sour flavors of this simple braise are balanced by the parsley. After long cooking, the wine provides most of the sweetness.
• Make sure you whisk the flour with the liquids until every grain dissolves. If your forearm technique isn't up to snuff, whisk in half the flour, then add the remaining and continue whisking.

Serve It Up! Make a quick rustic **applesauce** as a side dish: For four servings, stir into a large saucepan 2 cups peeled, cored, and chopped sweet apples (like Gala or Pippin); 2 cups peeled, cored, and chopped tart apples (like Granny Smith or Empire); 3 tablespoons packed dark brown sugar; 1½ teaspoons finely grated lemon zest; ½ teaspoon ground cinnamon; ½ teaspoon vanilla extract; and ¼ teaspoon salt. Simmer over low heat about 20 minutes, stirring often, until tender but chunky. Stir in 1½ tablespoons crème fraîche or sour cream before serving.

turkey thighs
with apples and brandy

EFFORT: **A LITTLE** • PREP TIME: **20 MINUTES** • COOK TIME:
4 HOURS/6 HOURS • KEEPS ON WARM: **3 HOURS** • SERVES: **3 TO 12**

INGREDIENTS	2- TO 3½-QT	4- TO 5½-QT	6- TO 8-QT
Unsalted butter	½ tblsp	1 tblsp	2½ tblsp
Olive oil	1 tsp	1 tblsp	4 tsp
Skinless turkey thighs	1½ pounds	4½ pounds	6 pounds
Moderately sweet apples (such as Jonagold or Pippin), peeled, cored, and chopped	1 medium	3 medium	4 medium
Yellow onion, chopped	1 small	1 medium	1 large
Thinly sliced carrot	⅓ cup	1 cup (about 1 medium)	1⅓ cups
Minced garlic	1 tsp	1 tblsp	1½ tblsp
Stemmed fresh thyme leaves	1 tsp	1 tblsp	1½ tblsp
Ground allspice	¼ tsp	½ tsp	1 tsp
Salt	¼ tsp	½ tsp	1 tsp
Ground black pepper	¼ tsp	½ tsp	1 tsp
Low-sodium chicken broth	½ cup	1¼ cups	2 cups
Brandy	2 tblsp	5 tblsp	½ cup
Bay leaves	1	2	3

1 Melt the butter in the olive oil in a large skillet set over medium heat. Slip several of the turkey thighs into the skillet and brown on both sides, turning once, about 6 minutes. Transfer them to the slow cooker and continue browning more as needed.

2 Stir the apples, onion, carrot, garlic, thyme, allspice, salt, and pepper in a large bowl, then pour into the slow cooker. Whisk the broth and brandy in that same bowl; pour into the slow cooker as well. Tuck the bay leaves among the vegetables.

3 Cover and cook on high for 4 hours or on low for 6 hours, or until the meat is very tender right at the joints of the turkey thighs. Remove the bay leaves. Serve in bowls with the vegetables and juices ladled around the thighs.

TESTERS' NOTES
• If you don't want to pull the skin off with a paper towel, there's a second method to skin the thighs. Beginning at one end of the thigh, snip a bit of the skin free with clean kitchen shears, and then peel off the skin, snipping it loose in places as necessary.
• There's no need to soften the apples or onion before they go into the cooker, since they'll leach their juices to make the sauce.
• Don't want to use brandy? Try unsweetened apple cider and a drop or two of brandy flavoring.

turkey pot roast

EFFORT: **A LOT** • PREP TIME: **25 MINUTES** • COOK TIME: **6 HOURS** •
KEEPS ON WARM: **3 HOURS** • SERVES: **3 TO 8**

INGREDIENTS	2- TO 3½-QT	4- TO 5½-QT	6- TO 8-QT
Unsalted butter	1 tblsp	2 tblsp	3 tblsp
Bone-in skin-on turkey thighs	1½ pounds	3 pounds	4½ pounds
Salt	½ tsp	1 tsp	½ tblsp
Ground black pepper	½ tsp	1 tsp	½ tblsp
Brandy	2 tblsp	3 tblsp	¼ cup
Small yellow onions, peeled and quartered	1	2	3
Baby carrots	1 cup	2¼ cups	3 cups
Yellow potatoes (such as Yukon Gold), cut into 1-inch cubes	6 ounces	10 ounces	1 pound
Finely grated lemon zest	½ tblsp	2½ tsp	1½ tblsp
Ground allspice	¼ tsp	½ tsp	1 tsp
Fresh thyme sprigs	1	2	3
Bay leaves	1	2	3
Low-sodium chicken broth	¼ cup	7 tblsp	¾ cup

1 Melt the butter in a large skillet over medium heat. Season the turkey thighs with salt and pepper and slip several pieces, skin side down, into the skillet. Cook until nicely browned but without turning, 3 to 4 minutes. Transfer them to the slow cooker and continue browning until finished. (Consider dividing the amount of butter in half or even thirds for large batches of turkey thighs.)

2 Once all the thighs are in the cooker, pour the brandy into the skillet and quickly scrape up any browned bits on the hot surface. (Take care: the brandy may well ignite. Have a skillet lid close at hand; cover the skillet and set off the heat for a couple of minutes if the stuff goes up in flames.) Scrape the contents of the skillet into the slow cooker.

3 Sprinkle the onions, carrots, potatoes, lemon zest, and allspice over and around the thighs. Tuck the thyme sprigs and bay leaves into the vegetables. Pour the broth into the slow cooker.

4 Cover and cook on low for 6 hours, or until the meat is fork-tender. Discard the thyme sprigs and bay leaves before ladling the braise into bowls.

TESTERS' NOTES
• Move over, beef! Turkey thighs can make a fine pot roast, provided you brighten the flavors a bit with lemon zest and shift the herbs to a lighter palette.
• Substitute peeled and cubed turnips or rutabaga for the potatoes.

SHORTCUTS If you wish, omit the brandy (and thus all of step 2). The flavors won't be as intense (you'll miss all the browned bits in the skillet), but you'll have less of a chance of setting your kitchen on fire.

barbecued turkey wings

EFFORT: **A LITTLE** • PREP TIME: **20 MINUTES** • COOK TIME: **6 HOURS** • KEEPS ON WARM: **2 HOURS** • SERVES: **3 TO 10**

INGREDIENTS	2- TO 3½-QT	4- TO 5½-QT	6- TO 8-QT
Skin-on turkey wings, each sliced at the joints into sections	4	7	10
Liquid smoke	2 tsp	3½ tsp	5 tsp
Worcestershire sauce	2 tsp	3½ tsp	5 tsp
Packed dark brown sugar	2 tblsp	3 tblsp	4½ tblsp
Mild paprika	1½ tblsp	2 tblsp	3½ tblsp
Dried thyme	1 tsp	½ tblsp	2 tsp
Salt	1 lsp	½ tblsp	2 tsp
Onion powder	½ tsp	¾ tsp	1 tsp
Ground black pepper	½ tsp	¾ tsp	1 tsp
Garlic powder	⅛ tsp	¼ tsp	½ tsp

1 Spread the turkey wing pieces on a large baking sheet in one layer. Stir the liquid smoke and Worcestershire sauce in a small bowl, then rub the mixture onto the wings.

2 Mix the brown sugar, paprika, thyme, salt, onion powder, pepper, and garlic powder in a small bowl; sprinkle this mixture evenly over both sides of the wing pieces. Pile them into the slow cooker.

3 Cover and cook on low for 6 hours, or until the meat is falling-off-the-bone tender.

TESTERS' NOTES

• This dry roast achieves a moist barbecue. That's what the slow cooker does best when there isn't a stew or braise involved.

• Slice the wings exactly as you would chicken wings. See page 266 for a fuller explanation.

• Some of those turkey wings will sit down in the accumulating liquid as they cook. Consider rearranging their position after the first three hours so some don't sit in the juices the whole time.

• If you want a crisp skin on those wings, transfer them to a large rimmed baking sheet when done and broil for 3 to 4 minutes per side 4 to 6 inches from a heated element.

Serve It Up! Toss brown rice with a little lime juice and toasted sesame oil for an easy side dish.

smoked turkey wings with beans and rice

EFFORT: **NOT MUCH** • PREP TIME: **15 MINUTES** • COOK TIME: **5 HOURS** • KEEPS ON WARM: **NO** • SERVES: **2 TO 6**

INGREDIENTS	2- TO 3½-QT	4- TO 5½-QT	6- TO 8-QT
Low-sodium chicken broth	2 cups	3 cups	5 cups
Drained and rinsed canned black beans	1¼ cups	1¾ cups	3 cups
Uncooked long-grain white rice	⅔ cup	1⅓ cups	2¼ cups
Chopped yellow onion	2½ tblsp	¼ cup	⅓ cup

Chopped celery	2½ tblsp	¼ cup	⅓ cup
Chopped, seeded, and cored green bell pepper	2½ tblsp	¼ cup	⅓ cup
Finely grated orange zest	2½ tsp	1 tblsp	5 tsp
Dried sage	1 tsp	1½ tsp	2 tsp
Dried thyme	¾ tsp	1 tsp	1½ tsp
Celery seeds	½ tsp	¾ tsp	1 tsp
Ground allspice	⅛ tsp	¼ tsp	½ tsp
Hot pepper sauce, such as Tabasco	½ tsp	1 tsp	½ tblsp
Smoked turkey wings, each sliced at the joints into sections	1 pound	1½ pounds	2½ pounds

1 Mix the broth, beans, rice, onion, celery, bell pepper, orange zest, sage, thyme, celery seeds, allspice, and hot sauce in the slow cooker. Nestle the wings in the mixture.

2 Cover and cook on low for 5 hours, or until the rice is tender and the meat can fall off the bones.

TESTERS' NOTES
• You'll need smoked turkey wings for this one-pot meal—and you'll need them to fit your slow cooker's size and shape. Slice them at the joint, pulling them open before dividing them with a heavy, sharp knife.
• If the smoked turkey wings still have the long flappers attached, don't throw these out. Add them for flavor to the mix!
• If you can't find smoked turkey wings, slice turkey wings into sections, brown them in a bit of butter over medium heat, and coat them lightly with smoked paprika before adding them to the cooker. The flavor will be far less intense, but we wouldn't want you to miss out on this meal!

SHORTCUTS Skip the dried sage, dried thyme, celery seeds, ground allspice, and bottled hot sauce, and instead use a bottled Cajun seasoning blend: 2½ teaspoons for a

small slow cooker, 1 tablespoon for a medium one, or 5 teaspoons for a large cooker.

Serve It Up! While that slow cooker is going, make **Slow-Roasted Tomatoes** in the same amount of time. Cut plum tomatoes in half lengthwise, then season their cut sides with a mixture of equal parts sugar and olive oil, plus salt, dried basil, and ground black pepper. Roast on an oiled rimmed baking sheet in a preheated 225°F oven for about 5 hours, until tender and a bit shriveled.

hot cherry-glazed turkey wings

EFFORT: **A LITTLE** • PREP TIME: **20 MINUTES** • COOK TIME: **6 HOURS** • KEEPS ON WARM: **2 HOURS** • SERVES: **3 TO 10**

INGREDIENTS	2- TO 3½-QT	4- TO 5½-QT	6- TO 8-QT
Olive oil	1 tblsp	2 tblsp	2½ tblsp
Skin-on turkey wings, each sliced at the joints into sections	4	7	10
Sour cherry preserves	¼ cup	½ cup	⅔ cup
Cored, seeded, and minced red bell pepper	¼ cup	⅓ cup	½ cup
Minced garlic	2 tsp	3½ tsp	5 tsp
Red pepper flakes	½ tsp	1 tsp	½ tblsp
Salt	¼ tsp	½ tsp	¾ tsp
Fresh lime juice	2 tsp	3½ tsp	5 tsp

(continued)

1 Warm a large skillet over medium heat, then pour in the oil. Slip in several of the wing pieces and cook, turning once, until well browned, about 5 minutes. Transfer to the slow cooker and continue browning the rest of the lot.

2 Use a fork to mash the cherry preserves, bell pepper, garlic, red pepper flakes, and salt in a small bowl until it's a thick, sticky paste. Smear—nay, massage—the mixture on the turkey wings.

3 Cover and cook on low for 6 hours, until the meat is fork-tender, particularly in the thick bits of the drumlets.

4 Use tongs or a slotted spoon to transfer the wings to a serving platter. Skim the sauce in the cooker of its surface fat, then pour the sauce into a medium saucepan. Bring to a simmer over medium-high heat, stirring often. Stir in the lime juice and boil for 1 or 2 minutes, until just slightly thickened. Drizzle the sauce over the wings before serving.

TESTERS' NOTES
• These sweet-and-spicy turkey wings would be a welcome addition to the half-time show during the game.
• Cherry preserves will have bits of cherries in them—which will then end up in the sauce. If you want a smoother drizzle, use cherry jam.

Serve It Up! Have crunchy kale chips on the side. Stem kale leaves and cut them into 2-inch pieces. Lay them on a large baking sheet, drizzle with olive oil, add salt, and toss well. Spread them out again in a single layer, then bake in a 275°F oven for 20 minutes, turning once, or until crunchy. Cool on a wire rack a few moments before removing from the tray and serving.

tequila lime turkey chili

EFFORT: **NOT MUCH** • PREP TIME: **20 MINUTES** • COOK TIME: **4 HOURS/6 HOURS** • KEEPS ON WARM: **4 HOURS** • SERVES: **3 TO 10**

INGREDIENTS	2- TO 3½-QT	4- TO 5½-QT	6- TO 8-QT
Olive oil	2 tblsp	3 tblsp	¼ cup
Ground turkey meat	1½ pounds	2½ pounds	4½ pounds
Canned fire-roasted diced tomatoes	3½ cups	7 cups	10½ cups
Tequila	¼ cup	½ cup	¾ cup
No-salt-added tomato paste	¼ cup	½ cup	¾ cup
Chili powder	3 tblsp	⅓ cup	½ cup
Minced garlic	1 tblsp	2 tblsp	3 tblsp
Minced fresh oregano leaves	2 tsp	4 tsp	2 tblsp
Honey	2 tsp	4 tsp	2 tblsp
Finely grated lime zest	2 tsp	4 tsp	2 tblsp

1 Warm a large skillet over medium heat for a few minutes, then swirl in the oil. Crumble in the turkey and cook, stirring often, until there are no pink, raw-looking bits left, between 4 and 7 minutes. Scrape the contents of the skillet into the slow cooker.

2 Stir in the tomatoes, tequila, tomato paste, chili powder, garlic, oregano, honey, and lime zest until the tomato paste dissolves in the mix.

3 Cover and cook on high for 4 hours or low for 6 hours, stirring once or twice during the cooking, until the chili thickens a bit and the flavors meld.

TESTERS' NOTES

• You don't want to use an aged, oaky *añejo* tequila, best for sipping; instead, try a high-quality, floral *reposado*. Just remember: no amount of high-quality ingredients can ever cover the taste of cheap alcohol.

• There's quite a bit of chili powder here—it serves not only as the flavoring agent but also the thickener.

• Stirring the chili once or twice will keep the ground turkey from clumping.

INGREDIENTS EXPLAINED According to USDA guidelines, the label on ground turkey tells the whole tale. "Ground turkey" means the package includes ground meat, skin, fat, and even cartilage; "ground turkey meat" means there's only meat in the mix. White-meat ground turkey must be so labeled, with the above strictures still in force (thus, the ridiculously complex "white meat ground turkey meat" on some packages). For the slow cooker, we prefer a mix of white and dark meat without skin and fat—thus, look for *ground turkey meat* at the store.

turkey, ricotta, and basil meatballs

EFFORT: **A LITTLE** • PREP TIME: **20 MINUTES** • COOK TIME: **4 HOURS**
• KEEPS ON WARM: **1 HOUR** • SERVES: **2 TO 6**

INGREDIENTS	2- TO 3½-QT	4- TO 5½-QT	6- TO 8-QT
Ground turkey meat	1 pound	1½ pounds	2 pounds
Plain dry breadcrumbs	¼ cup	½ cup	¾ cup
Ricotta (regular or low-fat)	¼ cup	6 tblsp	½ cup
Large egg yolk, beaten in a small bowl	1	1	2
Finely minced lemon zest	2 tsp	1 tblsp	1½ tblsp
Dried oregano	½ tsp	¾ tsp	1 tsp
Dried marjoram	½ tsp	¾ tsp	1 tsp
Grated nutmeg	¼ tsp	¼ tsp	½ tsp
Salt	¼ tsp	¼ tsp	½ tsp
Red pepper flakes	1 tsp	½ tblsp	2 tsp

1 Mix the turkey, breadcrumbs, ricotta, egg yolk, lemon zest, oregano, marjoram, nutmeg, and salt in a large bowl until the spices are uniform throughout and there are no pockets of unblended ricotta.

2 Use your clean, dry hands to make fairly hefty meatballs, using about ¼ cup of the meat mixture for each. Set them in one layer in the slow cooker; sprinkle the red pepper flakes over the meatballs.

3 Cover and cook on low for 4 hours, or until the meatballs are cooked through and until an instant-read meat thermometer inserted into the center of one meatball registers 165°F. Use a slotted spoon to transfer the meatballs to bowls to serve.

TESTERS' NOTES

• These are rich, dense meatballs, thanks to the bread and cheese. You'll want a green salad with a spiky vinaigrette afterward!

• Use full-fat or low-fat ricotta for this dish. Fat-free may become too watery during the long cooking—and thus cause the meatballs to fall apart.

Serve It Up! Although fine on their own, you can put the meatballs on a bed of cooked and drained spaghetti, tossed with olive oil and white wine vinegar. Pour the cooking juices in the slow cooker into a fat separator, then drizzle these over the servings.

turkey meatloaf
with cranberries

EFFORT: **A LOT** • PREP TIME: **50 MINUTES** • COOK TIME: **4½ TO 6 HOURS** • KEEPS ON WARM: **2 HOURS** • SERVES: **3 TO 9**

INGREDIENTS	2- TO 3½-QT	4- TO 5½-QT	6- TO 8-QT
Plain couscous	6 tblsp	¾ cup	1½ cups
Ground turkey meat	¾ pound	1½ pounds	3 pounds
Minced yellow onion	⅓ cup	⅔ cup	1¼ cups
Finely chopped dried cranberries	¼ cup	½ cup	1 cup
Minced celery	2 tblsp	¼ cup	½ cup
Stemmed fresh thyme leaves	1 tblsp	2 tblsp	3½ tblsp
Minced fresh sage leaves	1 tsp	2 tsp	3½ tsp
Salt	½ tsp	1 tsp	½ tblsp
Ground black pepper	½ tsp	1 tsp	½ tblsp
Smooth jellied cranberry sauce	1 tblsp	2 tblsp	¼ cup
Red wine vinegar	1 tsp	2 tsp	4 tsp

1 Set a tea kettle full of water to boil. Pour the couscous into a large bowl and cover it with boiling water. Cover with a plate or plastic wrap and set aside for 10 minutes, or until the water has been absorbed. Break up the couscous grains with a fork and cool, uncovered, for 30 minutes.

2 Add the turkey, onion, cranberries, celery, thyme, sage, salt, and pepper to the bowl; stir well until the spices and vegetables are evenly distributed throughout.

3 Dribble a little olive oil into the slow cooker and wipe it around with a paper towel, coating the bottom and the bend at the sides. Form the meat mixture into a smooth, fairly compact mound in the cooker, leaving a ½-inch border between it and the slow cooker's perimeter.

4 Use a fork to mash the cranberry sauce and vinegar into a paste in a small bowl; smear over the top of the meatloaf.

5 Cover and cook on low for 4½ hours in a small slow cooker, 5 hours in a medium cooker, or 6 hours in a large one, or until an instant-read meat thermometer inserted into the center of the meatloaf registers 165°F. Uncover, turn the slow cooker off, and cool for 10 minutes. Use a nonstick-safe knife or large spatula to cut the meatloaf into ½-inch-thick slices right in the cooker.

TESTERS' NOTES
• The onion, celery, and cranberries need to be minced into fine bits so they almost melt into the meatloaf.
• Turkey meatloaf, even in a slow cooker, can turn frustratingly dry. Couscous to the rescue! It adds and even binds in necessary moisture, keeping the overall texture more satisfying.

ALL-AMERICAN KNOW-HOW There's no doubt: you'll cry when chopping onions. Natural defenses of the plant are released as a gas and combine with your tears to make a mess in your eyes. Everyone has a solution: chopping the onion underwater (which waterlogs the vegetable), wearing protective eyeglasses (which can fog up), or holding your breath (which doesn't help). The only way to avoid the tears? Ask someone to do the job for you.

spicy turkey meatballs with pinto beans

EFFORT: **A LITTLE** • PREP TIME: **20 MINUTES** • COOK TIME: **5 HOURS**
• KEEPS ON WARM: **1 HOUR** • SERVES: **3 TO 8**

INGREDIENTS	2- TO 3½-QT	4- TO 5½-QT	6- TO 8-QT
Canned fire-roasted diced tomatoes	1½ cups	3 cups	4½ cups
Dark beer, such as Negro Model	½ cup	1 cup	1½ cups
No-salt-added tomato paste	¼ cup	½ cup	¾ cups
Chili powder	2 tblsp	¼ cup	6 tblsp
Drained and rinsed canned pinto beans	1½ cups	3 cups	4½ cups
Ground turkey meat	1 pound	2 pounds	3 pounds
Spicy Italian pork sausage, casings removed	½ pound	1 pound	1½ pounds

1 Whisk the tomatoes, beer, tomato paste, and chili powder in the slow cooker until the tomato paste dissolves. Stir in the beans.

2 Mix the turkey and sausage meat in a large bowl; form into golf ball-size meatballs, tucking them into the sauce in the cooker as you make them.

3 Cover and cook on low for 5 hours, or until the meatballs are cooked through, until an instant-read meat thermometer inserted into the center of more than one registers 165°F each time. Ladle the meatballs, beans, and sauce into bowls.

TESTERS' NOTES

• Because turkey is a low-fat meat, these meatballs can't stay warm for a long time in the cooker without drying out. Be prepared to eat them soon after they're ready.
• If you can't find canned fire-roasted tomatoes at your market, use regular canned diced tomatoes and add ¼ teaspoon mild smoked paprika to a small slow cooker, ½ teaspoon to a medium slow cooker, and ¾ teaspoon to a large one.
• Add up to 1 tablespoon minced fresh oregano leaves with the chili powder for a brighter pop of flavor.
• Although we prefer the spice blend in Italian sausage here, you could substitute Cajun or even Southwestern pork sausage at will. Just remove any casings and crumble the meat into small bits to mix with the ground turkey.

Serve It Up! Serve this stew over cornbread squares—or even split-open and toasted corn muffins.

turkey meatloaf with brown sugar glaze

EFFORT: **A LITTLE** • PREP TIME: **20 MINUTES** • COOK TIME: **4½ TO 6 HOURS** • KEEPS ON WARM: **2 HOURS** • SERVES: **2 TO 8**

INGREDIENTS	2- TO 3½-QT	4- TO 5½-QT	6- TO 8-QT
Ground turkey meat	1 pound	2 pounds	4 pounds
Shredded carrots	½ cup	1 cup	2 cups (about 10 ounces)
Plain dry breadcrumbs	¼ cup	½ cup	1 cup
Large eggs/white, well beaten in a small bowl	1 white	1 whole egg	2 whole eggs
Dried thyme	½ tsp	1 tsp	2 tsp
Dried sage	½ tsp	1 tsp	2 tsp
Salt	½ tsp	1 tsp	2 tsp
Ground black pepper	½ tsp	1 tsp	2 tsp
Ground allspice	¼ tsp	½ tsp	1 tsp
Packed light brown sugar	2 tblsp	¼ cup	½ cup
Dijon mustard	2 tsp	4 tsp	2½ tblsp
Worcestershire sauce	1 tsp	2 tsp	4 tsp

1 Mix the turkey, carrots, breadcrumbs, egg, thyme, sage, salt, pepper, and allspice in a large bowl until the carrots and spices are even through the mixture.

2 Pour a little olive oil into the slow cooker's canister, then use a paper towel to smooth it around, greasing the bottom of the cooker as well as the bend where the walls meet the bottom.

3 With your clean, dry hands, gather the meat mixture into a smooth, fairly compact mound in the slow cooker, leaving a ½-inch clearance between the loaf and the walls.

4 Whisk the brown sugar, mustard, and Worcestershire sauce in a small bowl; smear over the meatloaf.

5 Cover and cook on low for 4½ hours in a small slow cooker, 5 hours in a medium one, or 6 hours in a large model, or until an instant-read meat thermometer inserted into the center of the meatloaf registers 165°F. Uncover the cooker, turn it off, and let the meatloaf stand for 10 minutes. Use a nonstick-safe knife or a large nonstick-safe spatula to cut the meatloaf into ½-inch-thick slices for serving.

TESTERS' NOTES
• Shredded carrots add moisture to this meatloaf. Shred them through the large holes of a box grater or with the shredding blade of a food processor.
• You can lift this meatloaf out of the cooker before slicing it; but you'll need exceptionally large spatulas and good shoulder strength to do it, particularly if you're working in a large slow cooker.

Serve It Up! Try **Smoky Brussels Sprouts** on the side: For four servings, fry 2 pieces of bacon in a large skillet until very crisp. Remove them, then add ½ cup chicken broth, 1 tablespoon dark brown sugar, and 1 teaspoon salt. Stir until it comes to a boil, then dump in about 1¼ pounds trimmed and halved small Brussels sprouts. Cover and cook until tender, about 4 minutes. Use a slotted spoon to transfer the Brussels sprouts to a serving bowl and crumble the bacon on top.

turkey and dressing casserole

EFFORT: **NOT MUCH** • PREP TIME: **15 MINUTES** • COOK TIME: **5 HOURS** • KEEPS ON WARM: **NO** • SERVES: **3 TO 10**

INGREDIENTS	2- TO 3½-QT	4- TO 5½-QT	6- TO 8-QT
Chopped skinless and boneless cooked turkey	2¼ cups	4 cups	5½ cups
Crumbled day-old cornbread	1¾ cups	3 cups	4¼ cups
Small cubes of day-old baguette	1¾ cups	3 cups	4¼ cups
Chopped yellow onion	½ cup	¾ cup (about 1 small)	1 cup
Medium celery ribs, chopped	2	3	4
Unsalted butter, melted	4 tblsp (½ stick)	6 tblsp (¾ stick)	9 tblsp
Dried sage	1¼ tsp	2 tsp	3½ tsp
Dried thyme	½ tsp	1 tsp	½ tblsp
Salt	½ tsp	1 tsp	½ tblsp
Ground black pepper	¼ tsp	½ tsp	¾ tsp
Low-sodium chicken broth	1¾ cups	3 cups	4¼ cups
Large eggs	2	3	4 whole plus 1 yolk

1 Mix the turkey, cornbread, baguette, onion, celery, butter, sage, thyme, salt, and pepper in the slow cooker until the vegetables and meat are evenly distributed throughout.

2 Whisk the broth and eggs in a large bowl until smooth; pour over the ingredients in the cooker, pressing down to make sure everything gets soaked.

3 Cover and cook on low for 5 hours, or just until the cornbread mixture is set without being wet or jiggly. Serve by spooning up portions onto the plates.

TESTERS' NOTES
• Here's a whole Thanksgiving dinner from the slow cooker! Just add steamed broccoli and roasted sweet potatoes on the side.
• You don't have to wait until you have leftover turkey to make this meal. Look for house-roasted whole turkey or turkey breast in the deli case of your supermarket.

turkey bolognese pasta sauce

EFFORT: **NOT MUCH** • PREP TIME: **10 MINUTES** • COOK TIME:
3 HOURS/5 HOURS • KEEPS ON WARM: **3 HOURS** • SERVES: **2 TO 6**

INGREDIENTS	2- TO 3½-QT	4- TO 5½-QT	6- TO 8-QT
No-salt-added canned crushed tomatoes	2 cups	3½ cups	5¾ cups
Chopped skinless and boneless cooked turkey	1¾ cups	3 cups	5 cups
Chopped yellow onion	⅓ cup	½ cup	1 cup (about 1 medium)
Shredded carrots	⅓ cup	½ cup	1 cup (about 5 ounces)
Minced celery	⅓ cup	½ cup	1 cup
Minced fresh basil leaves	2½ tblsp	¼ cup	⅓ cup
Minced fresh oregano leaves	2 tsp	1 tblsp	5 tsp
Minced garlic	½ tblsp	2 tsp	3½ tsp
Fennel seeds	½ tsp	1 tsp	½ tblsp
Red pepper flakes	¼ tsp	½ tsp	¾ tsp
Salt	¼ tsp	½ tsp	¾ tsp

1 Stir the crushed tomatoes, turkey, onion, carrots, celery, basil, oregano, garlic, fennel seeds, red pepper flakes, and salt in the slow cooker.

2 Cover and cook on high for 3 hours or on low for 5 hours, or until the sauce has thickened a bit and is bubbling hot.

TESTERS' NOTES
• This easy slow cooker ragù is perfect for the night after a holiday meal when you have lots of leftover turkey on hand.
• The sauce is a bit thinner than a traditional ragù: we left out the tomato paste for a cleaner, brighter flavor, more in keeping with an easy dinner after a big meal.

Serve It Up! Serve the sauce over cooked ziti or farfalle rather than spaghetti.

turkey shepherd's pie

EFFORT: **A LITTLE** • PREP TIME: **25 MINUTES** • COOK TIME: **6 HOURS**
• KEEPS ON WARM: **3 HOURS** • SERVES: **3 TO 8**

INGREDIENTS	2- TO 3½-QT	4- TO 5½-QT	6- TO 8-QT
Chopped skinless and boneless cooked turkey	3 cups	4½ cups	7 cups
Green peas, thawed frozen, or shelled fresh	½ cup	¾ cup	1¼ cups
Chopped yellow onion	¼ cup	6 tblsp	⅔ cup (about 1 small)
All-purpose flour	5 tsp	2½ tblsp	¼ cup
Unsalted butter, melted	1½ tblsp	2 tblsp	3 tblsp
Poultry seasoning (see page 243)	1¼ tsp	2 tsp	1 tblsp
Salt	¼ tsp	½ tsp	1 tsp
Ground black pepper	¼ tsp	½ tsp	1 tsp
Low-sodium fat-free chicken broth	1½ cups	2½ cups	3½ cups
Worcestershire sauce	4 tsp	2 tblsp	3 tblsp
Sweet potatoes, peeled and shredded	¼ pound	½ pound	¾ pound
Cheddar cheese (regular or low-fat), shredded	2 ounces (about ½ cup)	4 ounces (about 1 cup)	6 ounces (about 1½ cups)

1 Mix the turkey, peas, onion, flour, butter, poultry seasoning, salt, and pepper in the slow cooker until the flour coats everything in a uniform mix.

2 Stir the broth and Worcestershire sauce in a large bowl; pour over the turkey mixture.

3 Toss the sweet potatoes and Cheddar in the same bowl; sprinkle evenly over the casserole.

4 Cover and cook on low for 6 hours, or until the cheese has melted into a topping and the filling is bubbling hot.

TESTERS' NOTES
• This is our take on shepherd's pie, usually made with ground lamb or beef and mashed potatoes. We've mixed it up a bit with turkey and sweet potatoes, but kept it a one-pot meal.
• If you're making this with purchased turkey from the deli counter, ask for the thighs and legs from the in-house roasted turkey. Because the meat is not encased in a sauce or stuffing, it can dry out as it cooks. Dark meat will solve the problem, and yield a better dinner.
• A casserole like this one is a fine time to pull out the frozen, chopped onions. Just defrost them first so their chill doesn't alter the cooking time.

Serve It Up! Have a tangy **Mustard Slaw** on the side: Mix bagged shredded cabbage with thinly sliced red onion and shredded carrots, then make a dressing with two parts white wine vinegar, one part mayonnaise, one part mustard, and one part sugar, seasoned with salt and ground black pepper. Toss it and sprinkle with mild paprika or a smidgen of cayenne.

whole roast turkey

EFFORT: **A LITTLE** • PREP TIME: **30 MINUTES** • COOK TIME: **5 HOURS** • KEEPS ON WARM: **3 HOURS** • SERVES: **10 TO 12**

INGREDIENTS	6- TO 8-QT
Whole bone-in skin-on turkey, giblets removed and the bird trussed (see page 272)	8 to 9 pounds
Tart medium green apple (such as Granny Smith), quartered	1
Medium yellow onion, quartered	1
Olive oil	¼ cup
Salt	1 tsp
Ground black pepper	1 tsp
Onion powder	½ tsp
Garlic powder	½ tsp
Mild paprika	½ tsp

1 Stuff the large cavity with the apple and onion. Rub the outside of the bird with the olive oil.

2 Mix the salt, pepper, onion powder, garlic powder, and paprika in a small bowl; massage this mixture over the outside of the bird.

3 Set the bird breast side up in the slow cooker. Cover and cook on high for 5 hours, or until an instant-read meat thermometer inserted into both the breast and the thigh (without touching bone) registers 165°F.

4 Lift the bird out of the slow cooker using a couple of large spatulas—and indeed maybe an extra pair of hands equipped with some kitchen tongs for balance and support. Transfer to a carving board, scoop out the apple and onion (these can be discarded), and let stand for 10 minutes before carving.

TESTERS' NOTES

• If you roast a whole turkey in a slow cooker, you will free up your oven on a holiday for everything else! However, we've got one warning: the bird won't get a crunchy skin. If that matters, set the cooked turkey in a heavy-duty roasting pan, then broil it six to eight inches from the heated element to crisp the skin, turning the whole bird to get each side browned, about 15 minutes in all.

• You don't need to peel or even core the apple since it's in the bird for flavor, not for eating.

• Note that the cooking temperature here is *high*, not low. You need that higher temperature to get such a huge bird done expeditiously for safety's sake.

• Don't be tempted to cook a bird larger than 9 pounds. The larger birds will not get out of the danger zone for bacterial growth quickly enough. However, you can certainly use a smaller one, down to about 7 pounds—although the timing will be shortened by as much as an hour.

• Check the internal temperature after 3 hours to see where you are, then continue cooking to the proper internal temperature for safety and tenderness.

game hens, duck, and capon

There's something almost iconic about eating birds, about bringing food down from the heavens. Sure, almost all the birds in our supermarket were raised on farms; very few migrated south, paddled around ponds, or even scratched in the dirt. But that doesn't mean it's not woven into the fabric of our souls that dinner can indeed fall from the sky, a bountiful gift. No wonder birds make it to our sacred meals: Sunday lunch, Shabbat dinner, and all sorts of festivity.

Yet despite their status as culinary icons, birds on the table can bring on lots of boredom. We've seen them so often; we've made so many. If you still want to connect with your roots, you might consider one of these—not only because they're rarities for most of us but also because they bring back the excitement of *the bird,* that elemental, slightly oily deliciousness that made us first look to the heavens for dinner.

You'll notice that there are no duck *breast* recipes here. First, there's no way to keep them rare or medium-rare; cooked-through duck breasts are tough. Second, you'd have to remove the skin and fat, thus leaving the more delicate meat too exposed to the heat. And finally, duck breasts are like beef tenderloin: a quick cooker that's far better on the grill than in the slow cooker.

Maybe we originally brought dinner down from the sky partly because we ourselves are so landlocked, because we envied the birds their ability to fly, to take off into the blue in ways we never could. Once we got them back on land, we turned them into some of the best meals for our tables. Flightless, we soar.

rotisserie-style cornish game hens

EFFORT: **A LITTLE** • PREP TIME: **20 MINUTES** • COOK TIME:
3 HOURS/5 HOURS • KEEPS ON WARM: **1 HOUR** • SERVES: **2 TO 4**

INGREDIENTS	2- TO 3½-QT	6- TO 8-QT
Mild paprika	1 tsp	2 tsp
Mild smoked paprika	1 tsp	2 tsp
Salt	1 tsp	2 tsp
Dried thyme	½ tsp	1 tsp
Onion powder	½ tsp	1 tsp
Celery seeds	¼ tsp	½ tsp
Ground allspice	¼ tsp	½ tsp
Garlic powder	¼ tsp	½ tsp
Ground black pepper	¼ tsp	½ tsp
Cornish game hens (about 2 pounds each), skinned, giblets or neck removed	1	2
Small yellow onions, peeled and quartered	1	2
Medium garlic cloves, peeled	4	8

1 Mix both paprikas, the salt, thyme, onion powder, celery seeds, allspice, garlic powder, and black pepper in a small bowl.

2 Dab a little olive oil on a paper towel and all over the outside of the game hens. Spread and pat the spice mixture over the birds. Stuff the bits of onions and garlic inside the birds. Set them in the slow cooker, squeezing to fit.

3 Cover and cook on high for 3 hours or on low for 5 hours, or until the meat is tender at the bone, particularly where the thighs join the body.

4 Use tongs to transfer the birds to a cutting board; let stand for 5 minutes. Remove the onions and garlic inside the body cavities. Cut the birds in half lengthwise to serve.

TESTERS' NOTES
• Here's the easiest way to prepare game hens so they're still moist and juicy but have the same flavoring as the best rotisserie chickens.
• Since this is a recipe for whole birds, there's no instruction for a medium cooker—not because you can't prepare this recipe in one but because the shape of a medium cooker's canister will determine whether you can cook one or two birds in it. Discover which yours can fit and prepare the recipe accordingly. In general, round models will fit one game hen, and oblong ones will fit two.

Serve It Up! These game hens make a great nibble before a dinner party or even a TV snack during the game. Cook them as directed, then slice them into smaller pieces, as you would a roast chicken. Lay these on a platter and offer a creamy dip on the side.

INGREDIENTS EXPLAINED Despite its name, a Cornish game hen is not a game bird. According to the USDA, it's a young chicken, less than five weeks old, weighing between 1½ and 2½ pounds depending on the exact breed, often a cross of a Cornish chicken with more standard breeds. And despite claiming to be a hen, a Cornish game hen can be male or female.

cornish game hens with butter and sage

EFFORT: **A LITTLE** • PREP TIME: **20 MINUTES** • COOK TIME: **3 HOURS/5 HOURS** • KEEPS ON WARM: **1 HOUR** • SERVES: **2 TO 4**

INGREDIENTS	2- TO 3½-QT	6- TO 8-QT
Cornish game hens (about 2 pounds each), skin on, giblets or neck removed	1	2
Small fresh sage leaves	16	32
Salt	1 tsp	2 tsp
Ground black pepper	½ tsp	1 tsp
Garlic powder	¼ tsp	½ tsp
Olive oil	1 tblsp	2 tblsp
Unsalted butter, at room temperature	2 tblsp	4 tblsp (½ stick)

1 Loosen the skin from the birds (see page 244). Slip the sage leaves between the skin and the meat.

2 Mix the salt, pepper, and garlic powder in a small bowl; rub over the birds.

3 Warm a large skillet over medium heat for a few minutes, then swirl in the oil (or half the oil if you're working with two birds). Slip one bird into the skillet; brown well on all sides, about 8 minutes, turning occasionally, but letting it sit against the heat a while so that the skin browns, even caramelizes. Set the bird in the slow cooker. If you've got a second bird, pour the remaining oil into the skillet; brown that bird as well. Make sure both birds are breast side up in the cooker.

4 Smear the butter over the birds. Cover and cook on high for 3 hours or on low for 5 hours, or until the meat is tender and juicy and the joints are quite loose. Transfer to a cutting board, let stand for 10 minutes, then slice in half lengthwise to serve.

TESTERS' NOTES

• There's plenty of flavor in these birds, thanks to the butter and sage. Make sure you brown them well so that the skin doesn't go boggy in the cooker.

• As in the last recipe, the shape of a medium cooker's canister will determine whether you can cook one or two birds. Follow this recipe accordingly for the number of birds you can prepare.

Serve It Up! For a whole-grain side dish, mix warm cooked wild rice with chopped pecans and dried cranberries. Season with salt, ground allspice, and butter.

ALL-AMERICAN KNOW-HOW The best tool for moving Cornish game hens out of a slow cooker is a pair of large kitchen tongs. However, the interior of the birds may be full of hot juices. Pick up the bird and tip it forward, draining the juices out of the large cavity and into the slow cooker—then tip it the other way to pour any juices out of the smaller cavity in the back.

honey-spiced cornish game hens

EFFORT: **NOT MUCH** • PREP TIME: **20 MINUTES** • COOK TIME: **6 HOURS** • KEEPS ON WARM: **2 HOURS** • SERVES: **2 TO 4**

INGREDIENTS	2- TO 3½-QT	4- TO 5½-QT	6- TO 8-QT
Finely grated yellow onion	2 tblsp	3 tblsp	¼ cup
Honey	1½ tblsp	2 tblsp	3 tblsp
Minced garlic	½ tblsp	2 tsp	1 tblsp
Ground turmeric	½ tsp	½ tsp	1 tsp
Ground coriander	½ tsp	½ tsp	1 tsp
Ground cinnamon	¼ tsp	¼ tsp	½ tsp
Salt	¼ tsp	¼ tsp	½ tsp
Ground allspice	⅛ tsp	⅛ tsp	¼ tsp
Cayenne	⅛ tsp	⅛ tsp	¼ tsp
Cornish game hens (about 2 pounds each), skinned, giblets and neck removed, the birds sliced in half lengthwise (see page 309)	1	1½	2
Drained no-salt-added canned diced tomatoes	1 cup	1½ cups	2 cups

1 Mix the onion, honey, garlic, turmeric, coriander, cinnamon, salt, allspice, and cayenne in a bowl; rub all over the game hens.

2 Set them in the slow cooker, overlapping as necessary but creating as close to one layer as you can. Pour the tomatoes on and around the game hens without knocking off the spice rub.

3 Cover and cook on low for 6 hours, or until the meat is almost falling-off-the-bone tender.

Serve in big bowls with the tomatoes and juices ladled around the birds.

TESTERS' NOTES
• This recipe is based on a Moroccan set of flavorings, an aromatic mélange that slowly melts into the meat with traces of warm spices and a little kick from the heat.
• Grate the peeled onion through the small holes of a box grater, creating something very much like onion mush; it will then fuse with the spices as the meat cooks and sweetens.
• The cooking time here is slightly longer, so that the birds will become so tender that the meat practically falls off the bone, a little bit of luxury among the spicy aromatics.

orange-glazed cornish game hens

EFFORT: **A LITTLE** • PREP TIME: **20 MINUTES** • COOK TIME: **5 HOURS** • KEEPS ON WARM: **1 HOUR THROUGH STEP 3** • SERVES: **2 TO 6**

INGREDIENTS	2- TO 3½-QT	4- TO 5½-QT	6- TO 8-QT
Cornish game hens (about 2 pounds each), skinned, giblets and neck removed, the birds split in half lengthwise	1	2	3
Fresh orange juice	⅓ cup	⅔ cup	1 cup
Dry white wine, such as Chardonnay	⅓ cup	⅔ cup	1 cup
Honey	2 tblsp	¼ cup	⅓ cup
Soy sauce	2 tsp	4 tsp	2 tblsp
Ground cinnamon	Pinch	⅛ tsp	¼ tsp
Grated nutmeg	Pinch	⅛ tsp	¼ tsp

1 Pack the birds cut side down into the slow cooker, overlapping as necessary but making as even a single layer as possible.

2 Whisk the orange juice, wine, honey, soy sauce, cinnamon, and nutmeg in a bowl; pour over the hens.

3 Cover the slow cooker and cook on low for 5 hours, or until the joints are loose and the meat is quite tender.

4 Transfer the birds to a cutting board; leave them for 10 minutes. Skim the sauce for surface fat, then pour it into a medium saucepan and bring to a boil over high heat. Stir frequently as it reduces to a glaze. Drizzle the glaze over the game hens when serving.

TESTERS' NOTES
• This meal will blow through a pile of napkins—the only way to eat these sweet, sticky hens is to use your fingers!
• Swirl at most 1 tablespoon unsalted butter into the sauce for a slightly more savory but certainly more elegant sauce.

Serve It Up! Since the game hens are in a sweet sauce, have **Spiky Poppyseed Dressing** for the salad: puree 3 tablespoons white wine vinegar, 2 tablespoons sugar, ½ tablespoon minced onion, ¼ teaspoon mild paprika, and ¼ teaspoon Worcestershire sauce in a blender. With the blender running, drizzle ½ cup olive oil into the mixture; process until smooth. Stir in 1 tablespoon poppy seeds.

ALL-AMERICAN KNOW-HOW To slice a game hen in half lengthwise, set it breast side up on your work surface and insert a chef's knife into the large opening. Locate the spinal column running straight at you along what's now the bottom of the bird; slice down on either side of that spine, then remove it. Turn the bird over, press it open a bit, and slice down through the breast bone.

red currant–glazed cornish game hens

EFFORT: **A LOT** • PREP TIME: **30 MINUTES** • COOK TIME: **5 HOURS** • KEEPS ON WARM: **1 HOUR** • SERVES: **2 TO 6**

INGREDIENTS	2- TO 3½-QT	4- TO 5½-QT	6- TO 8-QT
Cornish game hens (about 2 pounds each), skin on, giblets and neck removed, birds split in half	1	2	3
Salt	1 tsp	½ tblsp	1 tblsp
Ground black pepper	1 tsp	½ tblsp	1 tblsp
Unsalted butter	1 tblsp	2 tblsp	3 tblsp
Full-bodied rosé wine, such as Grenache rosé	6 tblsp	¾ cup	1¼ cups
Red currant jelly	2 tblsp	¼ cup	6 tblsp
Chopped peeled shallots	2 tblsp	¼ cup	6 tblsp
Stemmed fresh thyme leaves	½ tblsp	1 tblsp	1½ tblsp

1 Season the game hens with the salt and pepper. Melt 1 tablespoon butter in a large skillet set over medium heat, then add the two halves of one bird. Brown on both sides, turning once, about 8 minutes in all. Slip these halves into the slow cooker, then continue browning game hens, adding another tablespoon of butter for each batch.

2 Set the game hens skin side up in the slow cooker in as close to one layer as you can manage, some overlapping possible so long as the birds are fairly even in their placement.

3 Bring the wine, jelly, shallots, and thyme to a boil in a small or medium saucepan set over

(continued)

medium-high heat, stirring often. Reduce the heat and simmer slowly for 3 minutes, stirring often; then pour this sauce over the birds.

4 Cover and cook on low for 5 hours, or until the meat is tender at the bone and the sauce is starting to glaze the meat. Use tongs to pluck the birds out of the slow cooker and move them to a serving platter or plate. If desired, skim the sauce in the cooker of surface fat and use the sauce as a "gravy" for the meat.

TESTERS' NOTES

• Somewhat tart red currant jelly makes a classic glaze for birds of all kinds—but perhaps none to such success as when paired with the naturally sweet flavor of Cornish game hens.
• That gravy would be even better if you brought it to a simmer in a saucepan and whisked a tablespoon or two of butter into it. (Or skip the butter and add up to ¼ cup heavy cream.) If you'd like it a little thicker, mix 1 teaspoon potato starch with some water and whisk it into the bubbling sauce until thickened.

lemony cornish game hens

EFFORT: **A LITTLE** • PREP TIME: **25 MINUTES** • COOK TIME: **3 HOURS/5 HOURS** • KEEPS ON WARM: **1 HOUR** • SERVES: **2 TO 6**

INGREDIENTS	2- TO 3½-QT	4- TO 5½-QT	6- TO 8-QT
Cornish game hens (about 2 pounds each), skin on, giblets and neck removed, the birds split in half lengthwise (see page 309)	1	2	3
Salt	1 tsp	2 tsp	1 tblsp
Ground black pepper	1 tsp	2 tsp	1 tblsp
Lemon marmalade	3 tblsp	⅓ cup	½ cup
Fresh lemon juice	3 tblsp	⅓ cup	½ cup
4-inch rosemary sprigs	1	2	3
Olive oil	1 tblsp	1½ tblsp	2 tblsp

1 Season the game hens with the salt and pepper. Lay them skin side up on a large rimmed baking sheet. Position the oven rack 4 to 6 inches from the broiler and heat the element. Broil the hens until brown, about 4 minutes. Transfer them to the slow cooker, arranging them skin side up in as even a layer as possible.

2 Whisk the lemon marmalade and lemon juice in a bowl; drizzle over the game hens. Tuck the rosemary sprigs among them. Drizzle all with olive oil.

3 Cover and cook on high for 3 hours or on low for 5 hours, or until the meat is juicy-tender but cooked through. Serve with plenty of napkins!

TESTERS' NOTES

• This sweet-and-sour preparation makes for a fantastic meal: sticky, sour, sweet, and near perfect. Broiling the hens, rather than browning them in a skillet, gives them a gentler, milder taste, better in keeping with the sauce here.
• Look for lemon marmalade among the preserves and jams or in the international aisle.

garlicky cornish game hens

EFFORT: **A LITTLE** • PREP TIME: **15 MINUTES** • COOK TIME: **3 HOURS/5 HOURS** • KEEPS ON WARM: **1 HOUR THROUGH STEP 3** • SERVES: **2 TO 6**

INGREDIENTS	2- TO 3½-QT	4- TO 5½-QT	6- TO 8-QT
Cornish game hens (about 2 pounds each), skinned, giblets and neck removed, birds cut in half lengthwise (see page 309)	1	2	3
Salt	½ tsp	1 tsp	½ tblsp
Ground black pepper	½ tsp	1 tsp	½ tblsp
Medium garlic cloves (hulls on)	3	6	10
Fresh thyme sprigs	2	2	4
Sweet white wine, such as Riesling or Spätlese	2 tblsp	¼ cup	½ cup
White balsamic vinegar (see page 77)	½ tblsp	1 tblsp	2 tblsp

1 Season the birds with salt and pepper, then lay them bone side down in the slow cooker in as neat an overlapped layer as you can.

2 Tuck the garlic cloves and thyme sprigs among the hens. Pour the wine and vinegar gently on and around them (to moisten them but keep the salt and pepper in place).

3 Cover and cook on high for 3 hours or on low for 5 hours, or until the joints are loose and the meat is fork-tender.

4 Transfer the birds to a serving platter or serving plates. Discard the thyme sprigs, then use a flatware spoon to skim the sauce of any surface fat. Squeeze the soft pulp from the garlic hulls and use a fork to mash it into the juices in the cooker, thickening the sauce a bit. Stir well and spoon over the game hens.

TESTERS' NOTES
• The very sweet wine will balance the garlic and even the vinegar. Better yet, save back that wine and serve the rest, well-chilled, with dinner.
• You'll want plenty of crunchy bread on hand to mop up this sour, garlicky sauce.
• To give the meat a bit more texture, consider omitting the salt from the recipe and instead garnishing portions with flaked sea salt.

Serve It Up! Here's a **Warm Bean Salad** for a side dish: Heat drained and rinsed chickpeas and black beans with some vegetable broth, minced pickled jalapeño, minced parsley, salt, and pepper in a covered saucepan over medium heat for a few minutes. Stir in finely chopped stemmed chard; continue cooking, covered, until tender, no more than a few minutes. Stir in some grated Parmigiano-Reggiano or aged Asiago before serving.

lacquered cornish game hens

EFFORT: **A LOT** • PREP TIME: **15 MINUTES** • COOK TIME: **5 HOURS** • KEEPS ON WARM: **1 HOUR THROUGH STEP 4** • SERVES: **2 TO 4**

INGREDIENTS	2- TO 3½-QT	4- TO 5½-QT	6- TO 8-QT
Cornish game hens (about 2 pounds each), skin on, giblets or neck removed, birds cut in half lengthwise (see page 309)	1	1½	2
Soy sauce	½ cup	¾ cup	1 cup
Hoisin sauce	½ cup	¾ cup	1 cup
Dry sherry	¼ cup	6 tblsp	½ cup
Worcestershire sauce	1 tblsp	1½ tblsp	2 tblsp
Balsamic vinegar	1 tblsp	1½ tblsp	2 tblsp
Unsulfured molasses	1 tblsp	1½ tblsp	2 tblsp
Packed dark brown sugar	1 tblsp	1½ tblsp	2 tblsp
Whole medium scallions, trimmed	1	2	3
Slivered peeled fresh ginger	½ tblsp	2 tsp	1 tblsp
Star anise	½	1	1
Toasted sesame oil	1 tsp	½ tblsp	2 tsp

1 Arrange the birds skin side down in the slow cooker in as close to a single layer as possible, overlapping as necessary.

2 Whisk the soy sauce, hoisin sauce, sherry, Worcestershire sauce, vinegar, molasses, and brown sugar in a bowl until smooth. Pour over the birds in the cooker.

3 Tuck the scallions, ginger, and star anise around the birds. Drizzle with sesame oil.

4 Cover and cook on low for 5 hours, or until the birds are cooked through and deeply lacquered by the sauce.

5 Use tongs to transfer the birds skin side up to a large baking sheet. Brush generously with the sauce in the cooker. Position the rack 4 to 6 inches from the broiler and heat the element. Broil the birds until a bit crunchy, brushing one more time with the sauce, about 5 minutes.

TESTERS' NOTES
• Slowly poaching in a sweet but aromatic blend, these game birds become finger-food heaven. "Lacquered" is a Western way to describe an Asian cooking technique, perhaps a tad unappetizing but certainly descriptive of the mahogany sheen the meat takes on.
• The juices in the cooker are really too salty to make a good sauce on the plates. However, the sugars burn a bit under the broiler, muting the saltiness and creating a rich coating on the birds.

cornish game hens in saffron rice

EFFORT: **A LOT** • PREP TIME: **30 MINUTES** • COOK TIME: **6 HOURS** • KEEPS ON WARM: **NO** • SERVES: **2 TO 4**

INGREDIENTS	2- TO 3½-QT	4- TO 5½-QT	6- TO 8-QT
Uncooked long-grain white rice, such as basmati	⅔ cup	1 cup	1⅓ cups
Low-sodium chicken broth	1¼ cups	1¾ cups	2½ cups

Diced, cored, and seeded red bell pepper	¼ cup	6 tblsp	½ cup
Minced yellow onion	¼ cup	6 tblsp	½ cup
Frozen peas, thawed, or fresh peas, shelled	¼ cup	6 tblsp	½ cup
Minced garlic	1 tsp	½ tblsp	2 tsp
Salt	½ tsp	1 tsp	½ tblsp
Ground black pepper	½ tsp	1 tsp	½ tblsp
Saffron	⅛ tsp	¼ tsp	½ tsp
Unsalted butter	1 tblsp	1½ tblsp	2 tblsp
Cornish game hens (about 2 pounds each), skin on, giblets or neck removed, birds split in half lengthwise (see page 309)	1	1½	2

1 Mix the rice, broth, bell pepper, onion, peas, garlic, salt, pepper, and saffron in the slow cooker.

2 Melt the butter in a large skillet over medium heat. Add the game hens and cook on all sides, turning occasionally, until well browned, about 8 minutes. Transfer the hens to the slow cooker, nestling them down into the broth mixture.

3 Cover and cook on low for 6 hours, or until the rice is tender and almost all the liquid has been absorbed and the meat is falling off the bone.

TESTERS' NOTES

• For our money, this is the best chicken and rice on the market. The rice will get tender at its own rate. It could take up to an extra hour, depending on how much residual moisture is in each grain after sitting on the shelf.

• For more flavor, add up to 1½ cups cooked sliced mushrooms to the rice mixture before you add the game hens. (Raw mushrooms will release too much moisture, turning the dish watery.)

duck leg quarters
with cherries and brandy

EFFORT: **A LITTLE** • PREP TIME: **30 MINUTES** • COOK TIME: **4 HOURS/6 HOURS** • KEEPS ON WARM: **2 HOURS** • SERVES: **2 TO 8**

INGREDIENTS	2- TO 3½-QT	4- TO 5½-QT	6- TO 8-QT
All-purpose flour	1 cup	1½ cups	3 cups
Olive oil	1 tblsp	1½ tblsp	¼ cup
Duck leg quarters, skin removed	2	4	8
Minced shallots	¼ cup	½ cup	1¼ cups
Brandy	¼ cup	½ cup	1 cup
Dried cherries	½ cup	1 cup	2 cups
Honey	2 tsp	1½ tblsp	3 tblsp
Herbes de Provence (see page 90)	½ tblsp	1 tblsp	2 tblsp
Salt	¼ tsp	½ tsp	1 tsp
Ground black pepper	¼ tsp	½ tsp	1 tsp
Low-sodium chicken broth	½ cup	1 cup	2¼ cups

1 Spread the flour on a large plate. Warm a skillet over medium heat for a few minutes, then swirl in the oil. Dredge several of the duck quarters in the flour, coating all sides, then slip them into the hot oil. Cook, turning once, until well browned, about 5 minutes. Continue browning more duck quarters as necessary to get the job done. (If you've got several batches, divide the oil among them.)

2 Add the shallots to the skillet, still set over the heat. Stir until softened, about 2 minutes.

(continued)

3 Pour the brandy into the skillet. (Take care: the alcohol may ignite. If so, cover the skillet and set it off the heat for several minutes—then uncover and return to low heat.) Stir until the browned bits are scraped up from the bottom of the skillet, just a few seconds.

4 Pour everything from the skillet into the slow cooker. Add the cherries, honey, herbes de Provence, salt, and pepper. Stir well, then pour the broth over everything.

5 Cover and cook on high for 4 hours or on low for 6 hours, or until the legs are tender at the pliable joint. Dish the quarters and sauce into bowls to serve.

TESTERS' NOTES

• We might as well start our slow cooker duck recipes with a cherry-laced classic—one well worth a reinterpretation for the slow cooker.

• Although some subsequent recipes use skin-on duck quarters, a few (like this one) work best without that protective coating—here, so those cherry flavors can lacquer the meat.

• Make sure you have a skillet lid at the ready in case that brandy ignites.

• Look for dried cherries without any added sugar. If you want more of a sweet-sour finish to the dish, used dried sour cherries, sometimes called Montmorency cherries.

INGREDIENTS EXPLAINED Duck leg quarters are the leg and thigh portion of the duck; the quarters are often sold individually shrink-wrapped. Moulard duck leg quarters are larger than those of other duck breeds—eight Moulard quarters may overflow even the largest slow cooker, so cut down the amount by one or two quarters.

ALL-AMERICAN KNOW-HOW You'll most likely need to skin the duck quarters yourself. Peel off both the skin and the substantial layer of subcutaneous fat over the meat. Don't worry—there's plenty of interstitial fat to keep those duck quarters moist and juicy.

duck leg quarters
with acorn squash and figs

EFFORT: **A LITTLE** • PREP TIME: **30 MINUTES** • COOK TIME: **6 HOURS** • KEEPS ON WARM: **1 HOUR** • SERVES: **2 TO 8**

INGREDIENTS	2- TO 3½-QT	4- TO 5½-QT	6- TO 8-QT
Duck leg quarters, skin on	2	4	8
Acorn squash, seeded and cut into 2-inch cubes	¾ pound	1¼ pounds	2 pounds
Halved stemmed dried figs	¾ cup	1½ cups	2¾ cups
Minced yellow onion	¼ cup	½ cup	1¼ cups
Minced garlic	1 tsp	½ tblsp	1 tblsp
Fresh thyme sprigs	2	4	8
Star anise	1	2	3
Low-sodium chicken broth	1½ cups	3 cups	6¼ cups
White wine vinegar	1 tblsp	2 tblsp	¼ cup

1 Set a large skillet over medium heat, then slip in several of the duck leg quarters skin side down. Cook until well browned, until much of the fat has begun to render out, about 5 minutes. Turn over the leg quarters, brown a few minutes on the other side, and transfer to the slow cooker. Continue browning more duck leg quarters in the same way.

2 Add the squash, figs, onion, garlic, thyme sprigs, and star anise. Toss well so that the vegetables are under, around, and on top of the duck. Pour the broth and vinegar evenly over everything.

3 Cover and cook on low for 6 hours, or until the squash is tender and the meat is tender at the bone.

4 Use a slotted spoon to transfer the meat, vegetables, and figs to a serving platter or individual bowls. Discard the thyme and star anise. Use a flatware spoon to skim the sauce of surface fat or pour it in a fat separator and let it settle for a couple of minutes. Serve the sauce on the side with the duck and veggies.

TESTERS' NOTE

• The skin on acorn squash is perfectly edible—and will soften beautifully in the slow cooker.

duck leg quarters with port and cabbage

EFFORT: **A LITTLE** • PREP TIME: **30 MINUTES** • COOK TIME: **7 HOURS** • KEEPS ON WARM: **1 HOUR** • SERVES: **2 TO 8**

INGREDIENTS	2- TO 3½-QT	4- TO 5½-QT	6- TO 8-QT
Duck leg quarters, skin on	2	4	8
Port wine, preferably a non-vintage ruby or tawny port	⅓ cup	⅔ cup	2 cups
Red cabbage, cored and shredded	½ pound	1 pound	1¾ pounds
Chopped red onion	¼ cup	½ cup	1¼ cups
Golden raisins	¼ cup	½ cup	1 cup
Stemmed fresh thyme leaves	½ tblsp	1 tblsp	2 tblsp
Salt	¼ tsp	½ tsp	1 tsp
Ground black pepper	¼ tsp	½ tsp	1 tsp
Low-sodium chicken broth	½ cup	1 cup	2¼ cups

1 Set a large skillet over medium heat for a few minutes, then add several of the duck leg quarters skin side down. Cook until browned enough to pop off the hot surface without tearing, about 4 minutes. Turn, then lightly brown on the nonskin side, perhaps 2 minutes. Transfer to a cutting board and continue browning more in the rendered duck fat, eventually getting all those quarters stacked on that cutting board.

2 Pour off the (very!) hot fat, then set the skillet back over the heat and pour in the port. Stir quickly until the blackened bits in the skillet melt. Pour into the cooker. Stir in the cabbage, onion, raisins, thyme, salt, and pepper. Toss well to combine.

3 Nestle the browned duck quarters into the cabbage mixture. (You may have to tuck them this way and that to get them evenly distributed throughout the vegetables, in as many layers as necessary with vegetables still covering the meat.) Pour the broth over the top.

4 Cover and cook on low for 7 hours, or until the meat is falling-off-the-bone tender. Serve by transferring the quarters to serving bowls and topping with the vegetables and sauce.

TESTERS' NOTES

• Here's a surprisingly complex dish, despite the rather simple ingredients. Golden raisins are slightly less sweet than standard black raisins and so offer a brighter pop.
• The cooking time is a little longer here so that the meat can quite literally fall off the bone.
• It can take up to 15 minutes to render the fat from those leg quarters. No, you don't have to get every speck. But patience will pay off in a better, less oily meal. That said, don't waste the rendered duck fat in the skillet. Pour it into a glass container, seal, and freeze for up to 3 months; it's great for the next time you want to make roasted potatoes or even fried eggs.

duck leg quarters
with dried fruit and red wine

EFFORT: **A LOT** • PREP TIME: **30 MINUTES** • COOK TIME: **6 HOURS** • KEEPS ON WARM: **2 HOURS** • SERVES: **2 TO 8**

INGREDIENTS	2- TO 3½-QT	4- TO 5½-QT	6- TO 8-QT
All-purpose flour	1 cup	1½ cups	3 cups
Olive oil	1 tblsp	1½ tblsp	¼ cup
Duck leg quarters, skin removed	2	4	8
Frozen pearl onions, thawed, or fresh pearl onions, peeled	½ cup	1 cup	2 cups
Bold dry red wine, such as a Cabernet Franc or a Merlot	½ cup	1 cup	2 cups
Chopped dried fruit	½ cup	1 cup	2 cups
Dried thyme	½ tsp	1 tsp	2¼ tsp
Ground allspice	¼ tsp	½ tsp	1¼ tsp
Salt	¼ tsp	½ tsp	1 tsp
Ground black pepper	¼ tsp	½ tsp	¾ tsp
Low-sodium chicken broth	Up to ½ cup	Up to 1 cup	Up to 2 cups

1 Spread the flour on a large plate. Set a large skillet over medium heat, then pour in the olive oil. Dredge a few of the duck leg quarters in the flour to coat, shake off any excess flour, and slip them into the skillet. Cook until browned on both sides, about 6 minutes, turning once. Remove them from the skillet and continue browning more. (If you're working with a large batch, divide the oil among the batches.)

2 Pour the pearl onions into the skillet, still set over medium heat. Cook until lightly brown, between 4 and 7 minutes, stirring often.

3 Pour the wine into the skillet; bring to a full simmer, stirring constantly to lift any browned bits off the skillet's hot surface. Pour and scrape the contents of the skillet into the slow cooker.

4 Stir in the dried fruit, thyme, allspice, salt, and pepper; toss well. Pour enough broth into the slow cooker so that the duck leg quarters are covered by about a third.

5 Cover and cook on low for 6 hours, or until the meat is tender at the bone, particularly in the joint of the quarters.

TESTERS' NOTES
• This traditional braise shouldn't be too soupy so the dried fruit stays moist and flavorful, not watery and thus overshadowed.
• You can use any combination of dried fruit you like: red plums, pluots, nectarines, peaches, or figs. We'd suggest avoiding raisins, currants, and prunes, merely because you might want to experiment with other dried fruits that offer brighter flavors. But steer clear of dried tropical fruits (bananas, pineapple, papaya, or mango), as well as dried berries.

ALL-AMERICAN KNOW-HOW Dredging meat in flour is a fairly simple process—so long as you remember to shake off any excess flour that can gum up the sauce. Rather than passing the meat through the flour, set it into it, press gently, turn it over, press again, and push a little flour against the sides. Then lift the piece up and tap it to knock that excess flour back onto the plate. The meat should be coated in white, no bald spots anywhere, but with a thin enough coating that the meat's color shows through.

duck leg quarters
with tomatoes and herbs

EFFORT: **A LITTLE** • PREP TIME: **30 MINUTES** • COOK TIME:
4½ HOURS/7 HOURS • KEEPS ON WARM: **2 HOURS** • SERVES: **2 TO 8**

INGREDIENTS	2- TO 3½-QT	4- TO 5½-QT	6- TO 8-QT
Duck leg quarters, skin removed	2	4	8
Salt	¼ tsp	½ tsp	1 tsp
Ground black pepper	¼ tsp	½ tsp	1 tsp
Olive oil	1 tblsp	2 tblsp	¼ cup
Chopped yellow onions	6 tblsp	¾ cup (about 1 small)	1¾ cups
Chopped carrots	6 tblsp	¾ cup (about ¼ pound)	1½ cups
Minced garlic	1 tsp	2 tsp	1 tblsp
Drained no-salt-added canned diced tomatoes	¾ cup	1½ cups	3 cups
Dry white wine, such as Chardonnay	¼ cup	½ cup	1 cup
No-salt-added tomato paste	1 tblsp	2 tblsp	¼ cup
Dried oregano	1 tsp	½ tblsp	1 tblsp
Dried rosemary	½ tsp	1 tsp	2 tsp
Fennel seeds	¼ tsp	½ tsp	1¼ tsp

1 Season the duck leg quarters with salt and pepper. Warm a large skillet over medium heat for a few minutes, then swirl in the oil. Add several of the duck quarters and brown well on both sides, about 5 minutes, turning once. Transfer these browned quarters to the slow cooker and keep at it as necessary.

2 Dump the onions and carrots into the skillet, still set over the heat. Cook, stirring often, until the onions are translucent and the carrots are just beginning to get tender, 2 to 3 minutes. Stir in the garlic for a few seconds, then scrape everything into the slow cooker.

3 Whisk the tomatoes, wine, tomato paste, oregano, rosemary, and fennel seeds in a bowl; pour over the duck and vegetables.

4 Cover and cook on high for 4½ hours or on low for 7 hours, or until the joints in the duck are loose and pliable and the meat is fork-tender. Serve it in bowls with plenty of the sauce and vegetables napped over each piece of meat.

TESTERS' NOTES
• We've had a few sweet duck braises, but you'll be surprised how a savory preparation with tomatoes and white wine changes the taste of the duck. This dish is fairly elemental: a little gamy, but also better suited to a spring or summer day.
• Drain the canned tomatoes so that they don't bog down the sauce.

duck leg quarters
with pears and
saffron

EFFORT: **A LITTLE** • PREP TIME: **30 MINUTES** • COOK TIME: **6 HOURS**
• KEEPS ON WARM: **2 HOURS** • SERVES: **2 TO 8**

INGREDIENTS	2- TO 3½-QT	4- TO 5½-QT	6- TO 8-QT
Duck leg quarters, skin removed	2	4	8
Mild smoked paprika	½ tblsp	1 tblsp	2 tblsp
Salt	¼ tsp	½ tsp	1¼ tsp
Ground black pepper	¼ tsp	½ tsp	1 tsp
Olive oil	1 tblsp	2 tblsp	3 tblsp
Firm medium aromatic Bosc pears, cored and chopped	1 medium	2 medium	4 medium
Chopped jarred roasted red peppers (pimientos)	½ cup	1 cup	2¼ cups
Frozen peas, thawed, or fresh peas, shelled	¼ cup	½ cup	1 cup
Dried oregano	1 tsp	½ tblsp	1 tblsp
Saffron	⅛ tsp	¼ tsp	½ tsp
Low-sodium chicken broth	¾ cup	1½ cups	3¼ cups
Sherry vinegar	½ tblsp	1 tblsp	2 tblsp

1 Rub the duck leg quarters with the paprika, salt, and pepper. Set a large skillet over medium heat for a few minutes, then swirl in the oil. Slip several of the leg quarters into the skillet and cook, turning once, until browned, about 5 minutes in all. Transfer them to the slow cooker and continue browning more leg quarters as required.

2 Add the pears, red pepper, peas, oregano, and saffron to the cooker; toss well so that the duck pieces are scattered evenly among the vegetables. Pour the broth and vinegar over the top.

3 Cover and cook on low for 6 hours, or until the meat is fork-tender and the saffron has melted into the sauce. Serve by scooping up portions in big bowls.

TESTERS' NOTES
• The pears should be firm so they don't melt into the sauce. However, they must be aromatic to add any flavor at all.
• Although there's plenty of flavor left in the browned bits in the skillet, the extra fat can weigh down a light, aromatic sauce. Better—in rare instances like this one—to leave it behind.

Serve It Up! If you want to make this for a dinner party, put out plates of olives, hummus, and marinated anchovies as nibbles beforehand.

easy cassoulet

EFFORT: **A LOT** • PREP TIME: **12 HOURS 20 MINUTES (INCLUDES SOAKING THE BEANS OVERNIGHT)** • COOK TIME. **9 HOURS** • KEEPS ON WARM: **3 HOURS** • SERVES: **2 TO 6**

INGREDIENTS	2- TO 3½-QT	4- TO 5½-QT	6- TO 8-QT
Dried white beans	¾ cup	1¼ cups	2½ cups
Duck leg quarters, skin removed	1	2	3
Chicken or duck sausage	½ pound	¾ pound	1¼ pounds
Unsalted butter	½ tblsp	1 tblsp	2 tblsp
Low-sodium chicken broth	1½ cups	2½ cups	5 cups
Yellow onion, chopped	1 medium	1 large	2 large
Medium carrots, cut into 1-inch slices	1	2	4
Medium celery ribs, sliced	1	2	4
Minced garlic	½ tblsp	2½ tsp	1½ tblsp
Dried rosemary	½ tsp	¾ tsp	1¼ tsp
Dried sage	¼ tsp	½ tsp	1 tsp
Dried thyme	¼ tsp	½ tsp	1 tsp
Salt	¼ tsp	½ tsp	¾ tsp
Ground black pepper	¼ tsp	½ tsp	1 tsp
Bay leaves	1	2	2

1 Pour the beans into a large bowl; fill the bowl about two-thirds full with cool tap water. Soak overnight, about 12 hours, at least 10 hours but not more than 16 hours.

2 Divide the legs from the thighs of the duck quarters; slice the sausage into 2-inch pieces. Melt the butter in a large skillet over medium heat. Add the duck and sausage pieces, as many as will fit without any crowding. Cook until browned, about 5 minutes, turning once, then transfer to the slow cooker. Continue browning and transferring more until you've completed the batch.

3 Drain the beans in a colander and clatter them into the slow cooker. Add the broth, onion, carrots, celery, garlic, rosemary, sage, thyme, salt, pepper, and bay leaves. Stir well.

4 Cover and cook on low for 9 hours, or until the beans are tender and the duck meat is falling off the bone. Discard the bay leaves, then serve by scooping big spoonfuls into bowls.

TESTERS' NOTES

• Although not authentic, this streamlined version of the French classic is a one-pot meal, a delicious treat on a chilly evening.
• Use smoked bratwurst or Cajun andouille (see page 245) for this dish. Avoid any big flavoring blends or cheese in the sausage.
• While you can use great northern or cannellini beans, you can also use pinto, cranberry, or pink beans.

shredded chinatown duck

EFFORT: **A LITTLE** • PREP TIME: **20 MINUTES** • COOK TIME: **7 TO 8 HOURS** • KEEPS ON WARM: **2 HOURS THROUGH STEP 3** • SERVES: **3 TO 6**

INGREDIENTS	4- TO 5½-QT	6- TO 8-QT
Whole duck, skin on, giblets removed, neck removed and saved	3½ to 4½ pounds	5 to 6 pounds
Honey	3 tblsp	¼ cup
Five-spice powder (see page 122)	2 tsp	1 tblsp
Whole medium scallions, trimmed	8	12
Soy sauce	2 tsp	1 tblsp

1 Rub the duck inside and out with the honey; sprinkle the outside with the five-spice powder.

2 If the duck you bought has its neck in the body cavity, place that neck in the slow cooker; cover with the scallions. Otherwise, make a bed of scallions in the slow cooker, bending some to fit into a single layer. Set the duck breast side up on the scallions. Drizzle the duck with the soy sauce.

3 Cover and cook on low for 7 hours in a medium slow cooker or 8 hours in a large one, or until the meat is tender at the bone, almost falling apart.

4 Use tongs and a large spatula to transfer the duck to a cutting board; cool for 10 minutes.

5 Meanwhile, pick out and discard the scallions in the sauce. Pour the sauce into a fat separator and let settle for several minutes. Pour the defatted sauce into a saucepan and bring to a boil over high heat, stirring occasionally. Boil until reduced by half.

6 Skin the duck, then cut it into smaller pieces. Pull the meat off the bones; shred it into small bits. Pour some of the sauce over the shredded meat, toss well, and serve with more sauce on the side.

TESTERS' NOTES
• Call this a slow-cooker variation of Peking duck, that Chinatown favorite.
• The duck poaches in the slowly rendering fat, thereby becoming almost a confit—a luxurious, soft, and tasty meal.
• A large duck will fit in a large oval slow cooker but perhaps not in a round one. You will probably have to use the medium-size ingredients in your large round cooker.

Serve It Up! Serve with flour tortillas, lavash, or lefse (a Norwegian flatbread), as well as hoisin sauce and shredded radishes to make wraps at the table.

INGREDIENTS EXPLAINED Most of the ducks sold in the United States are Long Island ducklings, a specific breed of mallard duck. Also known as Peking (or Pekin) ducks, these white-feathered, big-breasted fowl trace their heritage to four ducks imported from China in 1873. The Long Island farms have since been eaten up by residential real estate; almost all Long Island ducklings are now raised in the Midwest.

By contrast, muscovy ducks come from Latin or South America. They have been crossbred with mallard ducks and are sometimes available at high-end supermarkets. The meat is less fatty and also gamier. Muscovies are smaller than Long Island ducklings. Moulards, a French specialty, are extra-large, meaty ducks often sold for a premium.

capon braised with figs and prosciutto

EFFORT: **A LITTLE** • PREP TIME: **20 MINUTES** • COOK TIME: **4 HOURS/6 HOURS** • KEEPS ON WARM: **2 HOURS** • SERVES: **3 TO 8**

INGREDIENTS	2- TO 3½-QT	4- TO 5½-QT	6- TO 8-QT
Olive oil	1 tblsp	2 tblsp	3½ tblsp
Thinly sliced prosciutto, chopped	2 ounces	4 ounces	7 ounces
Mixed capon pieces, skin removed	1½ pounds	3 pounds	5 pounds
Ground black pepper	½ tsp	1 tsp	½ tblsp
Yellow onion, chopped	1 small	1 medium	1 large
Trimmed and chopped fennel (see page 211)	½ cup	1 cup	1⅓ cups (about ½ pound)
Stemmed and chopped dried figs	⅓ cup	⅔ cup	1 cup
Minced garlic	1 tsp	2 tsp	2½ tsp
Minced fresh sage leaves	2 tsp	4 tsp	5 tsp
Red pepper flakes	½ tsp	1 tsp	1¼ tsp
Fruit-forward red wine, such as California Zinfandel	½ cup	1 cup	1⅓ cups
Low-sodium chicken broth	¼ cup	½ cup	¾ cup

1 Set a large skillet over medium heat for a few minutes, then swirl in the oil. Add the prosciutto bits and cook, stirring often, until lightly browned and even crisp, between 3 and 5 minutes. Use a slotted spoon to get them from the skillet to the slow cooker.

2 Season the capon pieces with pepper, then slip several into the skillet, just so there's no crowding. Cook, turning once, until browned, 5 minutes. Transfer them to the slow cooker and continue working your way through.

3 Toss the onion, fennel, figs, garlic, sage, and red pepper flakes with the other ingredients in the slow cooker, making sure everything's equally distributed.

4 Whisk the wine and broth in a big bowl; pour over the other ingredients.

5 Cover and cook on high for 4 hours or on low for 6 hours, or until the meat is fork-tender and an instant-read meat thermometer inserted into a couple of the pieces without touching bone registers 165°F. Serve heaping spoonfuls in big bowls.

TESTERS' NOTES
• Before chopping the prosciutto, oil a knife or give it a spritz with nonstick spray to make the job easier.
• The fried prosciutto should be crisp, not only for the more pronounced taste but also to render out some fat.

INGREDIENTS EXPLAINED A capon is a gelded rooster. These birds pick up extra fat and are thick around the middle. You get a meaty fowl that's larger than a chicken but not as large as a turkey—and with a taste that's a cross between the two.

capon braised with lemon and red currant jelly

EFFORT: **A LITTLE** • PREP TIME: **30 MINUTES** • COOK TIME:
4 HOURS/6 HOURS • KEEPS ON WARM: **1 HOUR** • SERVES: **4 TO 9**

INGREDIENTS	2- TO 3½-QT	4- TO 5½-QT	6- TO 8-QT
Unsalted butter	1 tblsp	2 tblsp	3 tblsp
Mixed capon pieces, skin on	2 pounds	4 pounds	6 pounds
Yellow onion, chopped	1 medium	2 medium	2 large
Fresh lemon juice	¼ cup	½ cup	¾ cup
Red currant jelly	2 tblsp	¼ cup	6 tblsp
Low-sodium chicken broth	¾ cup	1½ cups	2¼ cups
Finely grated lemon zest	2 tsp	4 tsp	2 tblsp
Salt	½ tsp	1 tsp	1½ tsp
Ground black pepper	½ tsp	1 tsp	1¼ tsp
4-inch rosemary sprigs	1	2	3

1 Melt the butter in a large skillet set over medium heat. Add a few of the capon pieces, as many as will fit without any sign of crowding. Cook, turning once, until well browned, 6 to 7 minutes. Transfer the pieces to the slow cooker and continue browning more as needed.

2 Add the onion to the skillet, still set over the heat. Cook, stirring often, until translucent, between 3 and 6 minutes, depending on the side of the batch.

3 Stir the lemon juice and red currant jelly into the onion; as the mixture comes to a boil, scrape up any browned bits in the skillet. Pour and scrape the contents of the skillet into the slow cooker.

4 Pour the broth over everything. Sprinkle the lemon zest, salt, and pepper over the ingredients. Tuck the rosemary sprigs into the sauce.

5 Cover and cook on high for 4 hours or on low for 6 hours, or until the meat is falling-off-the-bone tender and an instant-read meat thermometer inserted into one or two pieces without touching bone registers 165°F. Use tongs to transfer the capon pieces to serving bowls, discard the rosemary sprigs, skim the sauce for surface fat, and dish up the vegetables and sauce around the capon pieces.

TESTERS' NOTES
• There's quite a bit of lemon juice here. We wanted to keep this a true sweet-and-*sour* recipe, not one of those preparations where the sour is no more than a mere wish in the name.
• For the best overall texture and flavor, grate the lemon zest with a microplane, taking just the top yellow bits without scraping down into the white pith.

Serve It Up! Try this with a creamy rice salad on the side. Mix cooked long-grain white rice with chopped and seeded cucumber and apple, as well as a little minced red onion and some grated carrot. Dress with plain yogurt, a little sugar, and some salt, pepper, and red pepper flakes.

capon roasted over sauerkraut and potatoes

EFFORT: **NOT MUCH** • PREP TIME: **20 MINUTES** • COOK TIME: **5½ TO 6 HOURS** • KEEPS ON WARM: **2 HOURS** • SERVES: **6 TO 8**

INGREDIENTS	6- TO 8-QT
Thinly sliced bacon	4 ounces
Sauerkraut, squeezed of excess moisture	4 cups
Chopped red-skinned potatoes	3 cups (about 1 pound)
Chopped red onion	¼ cup
Caraway seeds	½ tblsp
Dried dill	1 tsp
Mild paprika	1 tblsp
Onion powder	1 tsp
Salt	½ tsp
Ground black pepper	½ tsp
Capon, skin on, giblets and neck removed	7 pounds

1 Fry the bacon in a skillet over medium heat until brown and crisp. Transfer a paper towel–lined plate to drain for a few minutes, then crumble the pieces into the slow cooker.

2 Mix in the sauerkraut, potatoes, onion, caraway seeds, and dill. Stir well and form an even yet not compact layer.

3 Mix the paprika, onion powder, salt, and pepper in a small bowl; spread and pat this mixture onto the capon. Set the capon in the slow cooker, pushing it down into the vegetables.

4 Cover and cook on high for 5½ to 6 hours, until the meat is tender at the bone and an instant-read meat thermometer inserted into the thickest part of the thigh without touching bone registers 165°F. Transfer the bird to a cutting board; let stand for 10 minutes. Carve and serve with the sauerkraut mixture on the side.

TESTERS' NOTES

• Here's a German-inspired preparation for a capon. The bird is fairly meaty and the flavor is more pronounced than that of a standard chicken, so these bold tastes will melt into a meal that needs a glass or two of dark beer.

• For the best taste, look for refrigerated sauerkraut in the deli case at your supermarket.

fish & shellfish

QUICK, HEALTHY, AND FLAVORFUL—THAT'S THE SKINNY ON FISH.
Then there's the bad news: the ocean's fish population is being depleted as overfishing booms; chemical contaminants are tainting whole species as governments do nothing. It sounds dire. It *is* dire. But the bad news is really the good news: it forces us to make better fish-buying decisions at the supermarket, which then allow us to make healthier meals in the slow cooker. No, you can't approach fish with a know-nothing smugness. The sustainability of fish is an ongoing and difficult discussion. There are a host of websites dedicated to the subject, perhaps none better than that by the Monterey Bay Aquarium, which has a phone app to help you make good decisions right in the supermarket (or at a restaurant). And you should be informed. When you are, you'll realize that this whole category—from tilapia to shrimp, orange roughy to scallops, tuna to clams—needn't inspire fear.

There was a time when supermarkets slapped fish fillets onto Styrofoam platters, wrapped them in cellophane, and put them at the end of the meat case. These days, even small supermarkets have dedicated fish counters. Chances are, between your work and your home, there's a supermarket with a decent selection. If not, consider an Asian market you might find in your journeys. The array will be astounding.

Some of the best fish and shellfish is found frozen. Indeed, much of what gets sold in your supermarket has been defrosted in the back. You might as well avoid the markup and buy the frozen fillets or scallops. When you're planning a dinner, place as much as you need in a bowl in the fridge, leave it to thaw until the next day, and you'll be able to whip up tasty fare with your slow cooker.

If you are intent on buying fresh fish or shellfish, you'll need to pick it up on your way home. Fish should be cooked the same day you buy it—or maybe the next day, but no later.

Store what you bought in the fridge, but don't expect it to last very long.

And let's also be clear about the leftovers. Short ribs can easily be reheated for a quick meal. But to reheat a fish casserole or a shellfish stew? Not so easy. Fish doesn't linger well, so you'll want to eat it all the night you make it. If you're going to get serious about fish, you might want to buy a smaller slow cooker. Sure, these recipes are scaled up for the big models as well, but you might not be ready to eat 6 pounds of mussels in a sitting. (Then again, a mussels party, complete with a batch of homemade french fries, might be the perfect solution.)

In the end, we hope you'll get hooked on fish and shellfish done in your slow cooker. True, few of these recipes are all-day affairs. They're probably best for Sundays, when you can put something into the slow cooker in the afternoon and have it for dinner a few hours later. But they'll also provide some of the lightest and brightest fare in this book. There's no bad news there.

fish

Slow cooker fish? Isn't that an oxymoron? After all, fish fillets rank among the world's best quick-cookers; many are done in under 10 minutes. So why use a slow cooker?

Because you need a sauce. Fish off of a baking tray or out of a frying pan is notoriously dull, nothing more than a dab of this herb or a dash of that condiment to make it palatable. Here's where a slow cooker helps out. You can build a deep, rich sauce in the cooker, then put in the fish fillets to poach for a few minutes. Since most sauces take time to build their layers of flavor, you might as well hand the job over to the slow cooker. When you come home from work, you can slip the fish into that sauce and have dinner ready almost before you can pour the first glass of wine.

However, there are a couple of problems lurking around the corner. The availability of any one type of fish in your supermarket isn't guaranteed. Because of production quotas, shipping traffic, and routine commodity auctions among suppliers, no one can ever be sure there will be red snapper fillets (or sole or tilapia, or what have you) lying on the ice at the fish counter on any given day.

To solve that problem, we've designed many of these recipes to be quite flexible. We've got a whole set designed to work with any number of thin fish fillets—anything from perch to flounder to rockfish. While there are subtle differences among the flavors of these fish, the various sauces we've created should smooth out any rough spots. And the same goes for thick fish fillets: haddock, pollock, halibut, cod, and the rest. We've crafted a second set of recipes to work with these. You can pick a recipe and walk into the supermarket, confident that you'll find what you need among the many possibilities there.

About two-thirds of the way through this section of the book, we get into some recipes for specific types of fish: salmon, tuna, and swordfish most prominently, but also monkfish and black cod, available more sporadically. We felt that these fish stand apart from the watery herd: they have such a pronounced flavor and textural profile that they warrant their own creations.

All that said, there's one last problem—and it's fully yours to solve when you're standing at the fish counter. How do you select a fresh fish fillet? Here are the four clues:

- The flesh should be firm with no desiccated bits where the meat is pulling into distinct planes or where there are withered bits at the edges.

- There should be no milky liquid on its surface, the first sign of rot.

- There should be no opalescent sheen, a sign that the fillet is beyond its prime.

- Most important, the fillet should have no fishy odor but rather a clean, bracing smell like ocean spray on a early spring morning at high tide.

Armed with that knowledge, you're now ready to step away from the country-style pork ribs or skinless chicken thighs and cook some fish in your slow cooker.

thin fish fillets
with zucchini and olives

EFFORT: **NOT MUCH** • PREP TIME: **20 MINUTES** • COOK TIME:
2 HOURS 20 MINUTES (AT MOST) • KEEPS ON WARM: **1 HOUR**
THROUGH STEP 1 • SERVES: **2 TO 8**

INGREDIENTS	2- TO 3½-QT	4- TO 5½-QT	6- TO 8-QT
Shredded zucchini, squeezed to remove moisture	1 cup (about 1 medium)	2 cups (about 2 medium)	3½ cups (about 2 large)
Low-sodium vegetable broth	¼ cup	½ cup	1 cup
Minced shallot	1½ tblsp	3 tblsp	⅓ cup
Sliced pitted black olives	1½ tblsp	3 tblsp	⅓ cup
Minced fresh dill fronds	½ tblsp	1 tblsp	1½ tblsp
Olive oil	½ tblsp	1 tblsp	1½ tblsp
Fresh lemon juice	½ tblsp	1 tblsp	1½ tblsp
Salt	⅛ tsp	¼ tsp	¾ tsp
Freshly ground black pepper	⅛ tsp	¼ tsp	¾ tsp
Skinless thin white-fleshed fish fillets, fresh or frozen, thawed	1 pound, cut into 2 or 3 pieces	1¾ pounds, cut into 4 or 5 pieces	3 pounds, cut into 7 or 8 pieces

1 Stir the zucchini, broth, shallot, olives, dill, olive oil, lemon juice, salt, and pepper in the slow cooker. Cover and cook on high for 2 hours, or until the mixture is bubbling and the vegetables have begun to get tender.

2 Nestle the fish fillets in the sauce. Cover and continue cooking on high for 15 to 20 minutes, or until the fish flakes when scraped with a fork.

3 Transfer the fillets to serving bowls using a wide spatula, then spoon the sauce over each.

TESTERS' NOTES
• This fresh sauce offers an Italian flair to fish. If you're using frozen fillets, they should be thoroughly thawed before they hit the sauce.
• Shred the zucchini through the large holes of a box grater, then squeeze it firmly by small handfuls to get rid of excess moisture.
• Fresh dill has a bit more heft to stand up to the sauce. If you can only find dried, use half the stated amount.
• The fillets don't need to be fully submerged; they can even overlap a bit, provided that you put the thin part of one over the thick part of another, rather than vice versa.

Serve It Up! Have **baked potatoes** at the ready. Wash and dry medium-sized Russet or baking potatoes, then microwave them two at a time on high for 5 minutes. Remove them from the microwave oven (they're hot!) and rub with olive oil. Bake on the rack in a 400°F oven for about 30 minutes, until the skins are crisp and the insides are soft. Split them open on plates or spoon the sauce on top.

INGREDIENTS EXPLAINED Thin white-fleshed fish fillets that will work with all these recipes include tilapia, snapper, flounder, fluke, turbot, freshwater bass, largemouth bass, catfish, rockfish, perch, and crappie.

ALL-AMERICAN KNOW-HOW The easiest way to tell when fish fillets are done is to use a fork to pull at the meat, particularly at the thickest point. The flesh should separate into distinct shards—not easily (there should be a modicum of resistance to avoid pabulum) but certainly without effort. Always keep the cardinal rule for fish fillets in mind: they're done in a matter of minutes, even in a slow cooker. We've given their cooking time a range because catfish are thicker than perch, fluke is thicker than freshwater bass, and so on. Check all of them after 15 minutes to make your decision about when they're done to your satisfaction.

sweet-and-sour thin fish fillets

EFFORT: **A LITTLE** • PREP TIME: **25 MINUTES** • COOK TIME: **2 HOURS 20 MINUTES (AT MOST)** • KEEPS ON WARM: **3 HOURS THROUGH STEP 1** • SERVES: **2 TO 7**

INGREDIENTS	2- TO 3½-QT	4- TO 5½-QT	6- TO 8-QT
Low-sodium chicken broth	⅓ cup	½ cup	¾ cup
Minced celery	2½ tblsp	¼ cup	6 tblsp
Minced carrot	2½ tblsp	¼ cup	6 tblsp
Minced scallion (white part only)	2 tblsp	3 tblsp	¼ cup
Rice vinegar	2 tblsp	3 tblsp	¼ cup
Sugar	2 tblsp	3 tblsp	¼ cup
Soy sauce	4 tsp	2 tblsp	3 tblsp
Minced peeled fresh ginger	2 tsp	1 tblsp	1½ tblsp
Minced garlic	½ tsp	1 tsp	1¼ tsp
Water	2 tsp	1 tblsp	1½ tblsp
Cornstarch	1¼ tsp	2 tsp	1 tblsp
Skinless thin white-fleshed fish fillets, fresh or frozen, thawed (see page 328)	1 pound, cut into 2 or 3 pieces	1¾ pounds, cut into 4 or 5 pieces	2½ pounds, cut into 6 or 7 pieces

1 Stir the broth, celery, carrot, scallion, rice vinegar, sugar, soy sauce, ginger, and garlic in the slow cooker. Cover and cook on high for 2 hours.

2 Whisk the water and cornstarch in a small bowl until dissolved. Stir into the sauce in the cooker until thoroughly incorporated. Nestle the fish fillets in the sauce.

3 Cover and continue cooking on high for 15 to 20 minutes, or until the fish flakes when scraped at the thickest part with a fork. Use a wide spatula to transfer the fillets to individual bowls; spoon the sauce over each.

TESTERS' NOTES

• Mince the vegetables into tiny bits so that you can get a mound of them with each bite of fish.

• Chicken broth and fish fillets? Yep, it's a compromise, mostly because there's very little good-quality fish broth on the market. That said, you can make your own fish stock and store it in the freezer for just such an emergency (see page 112).

• Whisk the water and cornstarch until there's not a trace of undissolved cornstarch—which could fall out of suspension and end up burned on the bottom of the crock.

• As you stir the cornstarch slurry into the sauce, the liquid will thicken quickly, almost instantly. Don't be alarmed—just get the fillets into the sauce, cover, and continue cooking.

Serve It Up! Put the cooked fish and sauce over cooked long-grain white rice in the bowls.

ALL-AMERICAN KNOW-HOW Most thin white-fleshed fish fillets are sold skinless. That said, you can often find snapper fillets and some others with the skin on. That skin can add a lot of briny taste to the dish; but it can also curl as it cooks, becoming unsightly and even shredding the meat. To solve that problem, score the skin with two or three diagonal cuts across each piece, cutting through the skin without cutting into the flesh below. If you are cooking skin-on fillets, always set them skin side down in the slow cooker.

thin fish fillets
in red wine with peppers and oregano

EFFORT: **A LITTLE** • PREP TIME: **20 MINUTES** • COOK TIME: **2 HOURS 20 MINUTES (AT MOST)** • KEEPS ON WARM: **3 HOURS THROUGH STEP 2** • SERVES: **2 TO 8**

INGREDIENTS	2- TO 3½-QT	4- TO 5½-QT	6- TO 8-QT
Drained and chopped jarred roasted red bell pepper (pimiento)	⅓ cup	½ cup	1 cup
Medium-bodied, fruity red wine, such as Oregon Pinot Noir	¾ cup	1½ cups	2⅓ cups
Drained and rinsed canned chickpeas	½ cup	⅔ cup	1¼ cups
Thinly sliced pitted black olives	2½ tblsp	¼ cup	7 tblsp
Minced red onion	2½ tblsp	¼ cup	7 tblsp
Minced garlic	½ tblsp	2 tsp	1 tblsp
Minced fresh oregano leaves	½ tblsp	2 tsp	1 tblsp
Saffron	⅛ tsp	¼ tsp	¼ tsp
4-inch cinnamon stick	½	1	1
Minced fresh cilantro leaves	2 tblsp	3 tblsp	⅓ cup
Skinless thin white-fleshed fish fillets, fresh or frozen, thawed (see page 328)	1 pound, cut into 2 or 3 pieces	2 pounds, cut into 4 or 5 pieces	3 pounds, cut into 7 or 8 pieces

1 Place the red pepper in a blender or a mini food processor. Blend or process, scraping down the inside of the container occasionally, until a smooth paste forms. Add a little juice from the jar if you need help getting the blades going. Scrape the puree into the slow cooker.

2 Stir in the wine, chickpeas, olives, onion, garlic, oregano, saffron, and cinnamon stick. Cover and cook on high for 2 hours, until hot and even bubbling.

3 Discard the cinnamon stick. Stir in the cilantro; slip the fish fillets into the hot sauce. Cover and continue cooking on high for 15 to 20 minutes, or until the fish flakes when the thick part is scraped with a fork.

TESTERS' NOTES
• The red pepper puree will thicken the sauce a bit, giving it some body to balance all the aromatics.
• We might not think so now, but red wine has been a classic braising medium for fish since the Renaissance. It offers a tart pop, more satisfying in many ways than the finish white wine gives.

Serve It Up! Serve this meal over **Roasted Romaine Lettuce Sections**: Heat an oven to 400°F. Remove the outer leaves from a head of romaine lettuce, then slice the head into ½-inch-thick sections through the root end. Generously rub a large baking sheet with oil, lay the slices on the baking sheet, and generously coat them in the oil. Bake, turning once, until softened and a little browned, about 15 minutes. Sprinkle with salt before transferring these slices to serving bowls or plates to be a bed for the fish and sauce.

thin fish fillets
in spicy coconut milk

EFFORT: **A LITTLE** • PREP TIME: **20 MINUTES** • COOK TIME: **2 HOURS 20 MINUTES (AT MOST)** • KEEPS ON WARM: **2 HOURS THROUGH STEP 2** • SERVES: **2 TO 8**

INGREDIENTS	2- TO 3½-QT	4- TO 5½-QT	6- TO 8-QT
Almond or canola oil	½ tblsp	1 tblsp	2 tblsp
Thinly sliced shallot	2 tblsp	¼ cup (about 1 ounce)	6 tblsp
Thinly sliced garlic	1 tsp	2 tsp	1 tblsp
Coconut milk	½ cup	1 cup	2 cups
Low-sodium chicken broth	¼ cup	½ cup	1 cup
Fresh lime juice	1 tblsp	2 tblsp	3 tblsp
Minced peeled fresh ginger	1 tblsp	2 tblsp	¼ cup
Red Thai curry paste	1 tsp	2 tsp	4 tsp
Shredded fresh basil leaves	2 tblsp	¼ cup	½ cup
Skinless thin white-fleshed fish fillets, fresh or frozen, thawed (see page 328)	¾ pound, cut into 2 pieces	1½ pounds, cut into 4 pieces	3 pounds, cut into 8 pieces

1 Set a large skillet over medium heat for a few minutes, then swirl in the oil. Add the shallot and garlic; cook, stirring often, until lightly browned and frizzled at the edges, about 5 minutes. Scrape the contents of the skillet into the slow cooker.

2 Stir in the coconut milk, broth, lime juice, ginger, and curry paste. Cover and cook on high for 2 hours, until simmering.

3 Stir in the basil; slip the fish fillets into the sauce, overlapping them only as necessary. Cover and continue cooking on high for 15 to 20 minutes, or until the fish flakes when a thick part is scraped with a fork.

TESTERS' NOTES
• This spicy Thai curry is embellished with tons of aromatics: fried garlic, shallots, and basil.
• The garlic should brown a bit in the oil, even blister. It'll pick up bitter notes that will work against the curry and the sweet coconut milk.

INGREDIENTS EXPLAINED Although packaged red Thai curry paste is a convenient shortcut, you can make your own. Start by stemming and seeding 4 dried New Mexican red chiles; tear the flesh into bits and cover with boiling water to steep for 20 minutes. Drain the soaked chiles, then dump them into a large heavy-duty spice grinder or large mortar. Add 1 quartered medium shallot, 2 two-inch pieces of lemongrass, 1 tablespoon coriander seeds, 1 tablespoon minced peeled fresh ginger, 1 tablespoon minced garlic, 1 tablespoon packed cilantro stems, 1 teaspoon black peppercorns, and ½ teaspoon salt. Grind or crush the ingredients into a coarse paste. Scrape into a glass jar and store, sealed, in the fridge for a week or so or in the freezer for up to 3 months.

ALL-AMERICAN KNOW-HOW For a perfect fish dinner, invest in a wide spatula, one that will fit in the cooker but still slip under the fillets—which can break into pieces once they're cooked. Consider warming the serving bowls or plates, either by setting them in a 250°F oven for no more than 10 minutes or running hot water into them and then drying them completely.

thin fish fillets in packets with tomatoes and squash

EFFORT: **A LITTLE** • PREP TIME: **20 MINUTES** • COOK TIME: **1½ TO 2 HOURS** • KEEPS ON WARM: **NO** • SERVES: **2 TO 6**

INGREDIENTS	2- TO 3½-QT	4- TO 5½-QT	6- TO 8-QT
Skinless thin white-fleshed fish fillets, fresh or frozen, thawed (see page 328)	12 ounces, cut into 2 pieces	1½ pounds, cut into 4 pieces	2¼ pounds, cut into 6 pieces
Yellow or other summer squash, diced	5 ounces (about 1 cup)	10 ounces (about 2 cups)	1 pound (about 3 cups)
Cherry tomatoes, halved	4	8	12
Dry white wine, such as Pinot Grigio	2 tblsp	¼ cup	6 tblsp
Salt	¼ tsp	½ tsp	½ tsp
Ground black pepper	¼ tsp	½ tsp	½ tsp
Fresh thyme sprigs	2	4	6

1 Cover the slow cooker and heat on high while you prepare the fish.

2 Tear off two lengths of aluminum foil, each three times as long as the length of your slow cooker. Set them on top of each other on your counter. Place the fish fillets in the center of the foil, then top them with the squash, tomatoes, wine, salt, pepper, and thyme sprigs. Fold the ends over the fillets and other ingredients, making a packet, taking care to crimp the central seam closed as well as to fold and even crush the ends to seal the whole thing tightly.

3 Set the packet in the slow cooker. Cover and cook on high for 1½ hours in a small slow cooker, 1 hour 45 minutes in a medium one, or 2 hours in a large model.

4 Transfer the packet to a serving platter; cool for 10 minutes. Open the packet and discard the thyme sprigs before dishing up individual servings onto plates.

TESTERS' NOTES
• Cooking fish fillets in packets is one of the best methods to be sure they don't dry out over the long haul. The packet should be well crimped to seal in every drop, creating a steam chamber to poach the fish.
• If you have concerns about placing fish and other food items directly on foil, you can top a piece with a similarly sized piece of parchment paper, thereby putting a layer between the food and the foil.
• If possible, choose a mild fish such as snapper or flounder, fillets that won't compete with the aromatic but delicate sauce.

Serve It Up! Lifting the packet from the slow cooker can be a chore because the juices inside are hot; should the packet open, you can get scalded. Use a large spatula; put any children or pets out of the room. Open the packet on your counter to transfer the fillets to individual plates. Serve the fish and sauce right on top of mashed potatoes, garnished with olive oil rather than butter.

thin fish fillets
in packets with coconut and peanuts

EFFORT: **A LITTLE** • PREP TIME: **20 MINUTES** • COOK TIME: **1½ TO 2 HOURS** • KEEPS ON WARM: **NO** • SERVES: **2 TO 6**

INGREDIENTS	2- TO 3½-QT	4- TO 5½-QT	6- TO 8-QT
Skinless thin white-fleshed fish fillets, fresh or frozen, thawed (see page 328)	12 ounces, cut into 2 pieces	1½ pounds, cut into 4 pieces	2¼ pounds, cut into 6 pieces
Red bell peppers, cored, seeded, and diced	1 small	1 medium	2 medium
Minced shallots	2 tblsp	¼ cup	6 tblsp
Chopped roasted unsalted peanuts	2 tblsp	¼ cup	6 tblsp
Shredded unsweetened coconut	2 tblsp	¼ cup	6 tblsp
Fresh lime juice	1 tblsp	2 tblsp	3 tblsp
Soy sauce	1 tblsp	2 tblsp	3 tblsp
Fresh cilantro sprigs	4	8	12

1 Cover the cooker and set it to high to heat while you prepare the fish fillets.

2 Tear off two lengths of aluminum foil, each three times as long as the length of your slow cooker. Set them on top of each other on your counter. Set the fish fillets in the center of the foil; top with the bell pepper, shallots, peanuts, coconut, lime juice, soy sauce, and cilantro. Fold the ends over the fillets and other ingredients, making a packet, taking care to crimp the central seam closed as well as to fold and even crush the ends to seal tightly.

3 Set the packet in the crock, cover, and cook on high for 1½ hours in a small slow cooker, 1 hour 45 minutes in a medium cooker, or 2 hours in a large cooker. Transfer the packet to a serving platter; cool for 10 minutes. Open the packet and discard the cilantro sprigs before dishing up individual servings onto plates.

TESTERS' NOTES
• Because the packet is sealed, there's no real way to know when the fillets are done. Never fear: they will be, given the amount of steam created inside.
• For a little spicy heat, add some red pepper flakes to the mix or sprinkle the cooked fillets with a little sambal oelek (see page 404).
• If possible, choose fillets with a more assertive flavor such as tilapia or catfish.

Serve It Up! Although the flavors skew Asian, you might want to serve these fillets over steamed or skillet-wilted spinach—or even over steamed broccoli florets. For more flavor, toss either of these green vegetables with finely grated lemon zest and coarse salt.

thick fish fillets
with tomatoes and cinnamon

EFFORT: **NOT MUCH** • PREP TIME: **10 MINUTES** • COOK TIME:
2 HOURS 40 MINUTES (AT MOST) • KEEPS ON WARM: **3 HOURS**
THROUGH STEP 1 • SERVES: **2 TO 7**

INGREDIENTS	2- TO 3½-QT	4- TO 5½-QT	6- TO 8-QT
Drained no-salt-added canned diced tomatoes	1 cup	1½ cups	2¼ cups
Low-sodium vegetable broth	3 tblsp	¼ cup	6 tblsp
Minced shallot	2½ tblsp	¼ cup	6 tblsp
Unsalted butter	2 tblsp	3 tblsp	5 tblsp
Fennel seeds	¼ tsp	½ tsp	¾ tsp
Salt	⅛ tsp	¼ tsp	½ tsp
Ground black pepper	⅛ tsp	¼ tsp	½ tsp
4-inch cinnamon stick	½	1	1
Thick white-fleshed fish fillets, skin removed	1 pound, cut into 2 or 3 pieces	1¾ pounds, cut into 4 or 5 pieces	2½ pounds, cut into 6 or 7 pieces

1 Mix the tomatoes, broth, shallot, butter, fennel seeds, salt, pepper, and cinnamon stick in the slow cooker. Cover and cook on high for 2 hours, or until fragrant and bubbling.

2 Stir the sauce well to incorporate the butter. Slip the fish fillets into the sauce. Cover and continue cooking for 30 to 40 additional minutes, or until the fish is firm and opaque. Remove the cinnamon stick before serving.

TESTERS' NOTES
• Although thicker fillets take longer to cook, they're still done fairly quickly. If you like the fish a little less dry, a little more velvety, consider removing the fillets after at most 30 minutes, maybe even 25 minutes.
• Butter, cinnamon, and tomatoes are an excellent, Old World trio—a savory indulgence in this easy sauce.
• Although the fillets needn't be submerged, they shouldn't be sitting on top of the sauce. Make little wells with a spoon, then settle the fish into those indentations, spooning a little of the sauce over them. Or you can simply slide them into the sauce, thinner end first.

Serve It Up! These fillets—and particularly this sauce—are terrific served over homemade croutons (see page 157).

INGREDIENTS EXPLAINED Thick white-fleshed fish fillets include cod, scrod, haddock, grouper, sturgeon, sea bass, black cod (or sable), pollock, and halibut. Almost all are sold skinned. If not, ask the fishmonger to take the skin off for you.

ALL-AMERICAN KNOW-HOW Many thicker white-fleshed fish fillets won't flake when done in the same way that, say, tilapia will. Although these fillets will certainly be done by the timings given here (barring some maladjustment in your cooker), there is one tried-and-true method for testing them: take a metal skewer or cake tester, insert it into the center of the thickest part of a fillet, and hold it there for 5 seconds. Remove it and touch it to your lips. It should be warm, not cool or even room temperature.

thick fish fillets
with peppers and lime

EFFORT: **NOT MUCH** • PREP TIME: **15 MINUTES** • COOK TIME:
2 HOURS 40 MINUTES (AT MOST) • KEEPS ON WARM: **2 HOURS
THROUGH STEP 1** • SERVES: **2 TO 8**

INGREDIENTS	2- TO 3½-QT	4- TO 5½-QT	6- TO 8-QT
Chopped cubanelle peppers (see page 47)	1 cup	2 cups	4 cups
Drained no-salt-added canned diced tomatoes	1 cup	2 cups	4 cups
Minced whole scallion	2 tblsp	¼ cup	½ cup
Fresh lime juice	1 tblsp	2 tblsp	3 tblsp
Drained and minced capers	½ tblsp	1 tblsp	2 tblsp
Minced fresh oregano leaves	½ tblsp	1 tblsp	2 tblsp
Minced garlic	½ tsp	1 tsp	2 tsp
Salt	¼ tsp	½ tsp	1 tsp
Thick white-fleshed fish fillets, skin removed (see page 334)	¾ pound, cut into 2 pieces	1½ pounds, cut into 4 pieces	3 pounds, cut into 8 pieces

1 Stir the peppers, tomatoes, scallion, lime juice, capers, oregano, garlic, and salt in the slow cooker. Cover and cook on high for 2 hours, or until the sauce is bubbling.

2 Slip the fillets into the sauce. Cover and continue cooking on high for 30 to 40 minutes, or until the fish is opaque and firm.

TESTERS' NOTES
• Once you slip the fillets into the sauce, spoon just a bit of it over them so they'll cook more evenly and become infused with that flavor throughout.

Serve It Up! This sauce is so aromatic, it needs a sweet side dish for balance. We recommend serving the fillets and sauce over creamy polenta.

thick fish fillets
poached in a corn relish

EFFORT: **A LITTLE** • PREP TIME: **20 MINUTES** • COOK TIME: **2 HOURS
40 MINUTES (AT MOST)** • KEEPS ON WARM: **3 HOURS THROUGH
STEP 1** • SERVES: **2 TO 7**

INGREDIENTS	2- TO 3½-QT	4- TO 5½-QT	6- TO 8-QT
Corn kernels, fresh cut off the cob, or frozen, thawed	1¼ cups	2 cups	3¼ cups
Red bell pepper, stemmed, seeded and chopped	1 small	1 medium	1 large
Low-sodium chicken broth	⅓ cup	½ cup	¾ cup
Minced red onion	3 tblsp	⅓ cup	½ cup
Minced fresh parsley leaves	2½ tblsp	¼ cup	6 tblsp
Cider vinegar	2 tblsp	3 tblsp	¼ cup
Sugar	1½ tblsp	2 tblsp	3 tblsp
Unsalted butter	1½ tblsp	2 tblsp	3 tblsp
Thick white-fleshed fish fillets, skin removed (see page 334)	1 pound, cut into 3 pieces	1¾ pounds, cut into 4 or 5 pieces	2½ pounds, cut into 6 or 7 pieces

1 Stir the corn, bell pepper, broth, onion, parsley, vinegar, sugar, and butter in the slow

(continued)

cooker. Cover and cook on high for 2 hours, or until the butter melts and the sauce is bubbling.

2 Nestle the fillets in the sauce. Cover and continue cooking on high for an additional 30 to 40 minutes, or until the fish is firm and opaque.

TESTERS' NOTES

• A juicy corn relish makes an excellent poaching sauce for fish fillets, particularly thick ones that need a little extra cooking and so can stand up to the time it takes to get the relish to the right consistency.
• For heat, add up to 2 teaspoons red pepper flakes with the corn kernels.

Serve It Up! Transfer the fillets to serving plates, then spoon the sauce into hot, split-open baked potatoes.

thick fish fillets with apples and cumin vinaigrette

EFFORT: **A LOT** • PREP TIME: **30 MINUTES** • COOK TIME: **3 HOURS 40 MINUTES (AT MOST)** • KEEPS ON WARM: **1 HOUR THROUGH STEP 1** • SERVES: **2 TO 6**

INGREDIENTS	2- TO 3½-QT	4- TO 5½-QT	6- TO 8-QT
Cored and shredded savoy cabbage	1¼ cups	2 cups	4 cups (about a 1-pound head)
Peeled, cored, and shredded tart firm apple, such as Empire or Granny Smith	⅓ cup	½ cup	1 cup (about 1 large)
Drained and rinsed canned chickpeas	⅔ cup	1 cup	1¾ cups
Chopped red onion	3 tblsp	¼ cup	½ cup (about 1 small)
Salt	⅛ tsp	¼ tsp	½ tsp
Ground black pepper	⅛ tsp	¼ tsp	½ tsp
Fresh thyme sprigs	1	2	4
Dry white wine, such as Chardonnay	½ cup	¾ cup	1½ cups
Thick white-fleshed fish fillets, skin removed (see page 334)	¾ pound, cut into 2 pieces	1¼ pounds, cut into 3 or 4 pieces	2½ pounds, cut into 5 or 6 pieces
Olive oil	1½ tblsp	2 tblsp	¼ cup
Minced shallot	2 tsp	1 tblsp	2 tblsp
Crushed cumin seeds	¼ tsp	½ tsp	1 tsp
White balsamic vinegar (see page 77)	2 tsp	1 tblsp	1½ tblsp
Fresh lime juice	½ tsp	1 tsp	2 tsp

1 Mix the cabbage, apple, chickpeas, onion, salt, pepper, and thyme sprigs in the slow cooker. Pour the wine over the top. Cover and cook on high for 3 hours, or until the mixture is like a thick stew.

2 Nestle the fish in the cabbage mixture. Cover and continue cooking on high for 30 to 40 minutes, or until the fillets are firm and opaque.

3 As the fish cooks, whisk the olive oil, shallot, cumin seeds, vinegar, and lime juice in a small bowl. Transfer the fillets and the cabbage mixture to serving plates; drizzle the vinaigrette over each serving.

TESTERS' NOTES

• Here's a slow cooker fish that's good enough for a Christmas Eve dinner. The drizzled aromatic dressing takes the whole thing right over the top.

- Shred the apple through the large holes of a box grater. The shredding blade of a food processor can "juice" the apple, making it dry in the sauce.
- Crush the cumin seeds on a cutting board under a large saucepan or heavy pot.

fish ragù

EFFORT: **A LOT** • PREP TIME: **25 MINUTES** • COOK TIME: **4 HOURS 20 MINUTES** • KEEPS ON WARM: **4 HOURS THROUGH STEP 2** • SERVES: **4 TO 10 OVER COOKED PASTA**

INGREDIENTS	2- TO 3½-QT	4- TO 5½-QT	6- TO 8-QT
Olive oil	¼ cup	6 tblsp	½ cup
Chopped celery	½ cup (about 2 medium ribs)	¾ cup	1¼ cups
Chopped carrots	½ cup	¾ cup	1¼ cups (about ½ pound)
Chopped yellow onion	½ cup	¾ cup	1 cup (about 1 medium)
Minced garlic	1 tsp	½ tblsp	2 tsp
No-salt-added canned diced tomatoes	3½ cups	5¼ cups	9¾ cups
Drained, rinsed, and chopped capers	1 tblsp	1½ tblsp	2½ tblsp
Dried oregano	2 tsp	1 tblsp	2 tblsp
Dried marjoram	1 tsp	½ tblsp	1 tblsp
Red pepper flakes	½ tsp	¾ tsp	1 tsp
Thick white-fleshed fish fillets, skin removed (see page 334)	1 pound	1½ pounds	2½ pounds
Chopped fresh parsley leaves	¼ cup	6 tblsp	⅔ cup
Fettuccini, pappardelle, or mafaldine, cooked and drained	12 ounces	1½ pounds	2¼ pounds

1 Heat a large skillet over medium heat for a couple of minutes. Swirl in the oil, then add the celery, carrots, and onion. Cook, stirring often, until the onion turns translucent and softens a bit, between 4 and 7 minutes. Stir in the garlic and cook for a few seconds, until aromatic.

2 Scrape the contents of the skillet into the slow cooker. Stir in the tomatoes, capers, oregano, marjoram, and red pepper flakes. Cover and cook on low for 4 hours.

3 Stir in the fish and parsley. Cover, set the heat on high, and cook for 20 minutes, or until the fish bits are cooked through and the flavors have blended. Serve the ragù over the cooked pasta in bowls.

TESTERS' NOTES
- This rib-sticking ragù would be great over wide noodles of almost any sort, or even over soba noodles.
- For a richer finish, replace half the stated olive oil quantity with unsalted butter.
- Because of the lack of evaporation, don't expect a reduced ragù. The sauce will be thinner than a ragù simmered on the stovetop. If that bothers you, you can partially drain the tomatoes before adding them.
- Chopping fish can be a chore; make sure your blade is sharp. If you notice any sticking, coat the blade with nonstick spray before continuing.
- Wider noodles are better here—no angel hair pasta, please, because it will just clump without melding with the sauce.

olive oil–poached salmon

EFFORT: **NOT MUCH** • PREP TIME: **10 MINUTES** • COOK TIME: **4 TO 5 HOURS** • KEEPS ON WARM: **4 HOURS THROUGH STEP 2** • SERVES: **4 TO 12**

INGREDIENTS	2- TO 3½-QT	4- TO 5½-QT	6- TO 8-QT
Olive oil	At least 6 cups	At least 8 cups (2 quarts)	At least 10 cups
Skin-on salmon fillet	1 pound	2 pounds	3 pounds
Medium garlic cloves, peeled and smashed	2	3	4
Finely grated lemon zest	1 tsp	2 tsp	1 tblsp
Fresh thyme sprigs	2	3	4

1 Pour the oil into the slow cooker. Slip the salmon into it to let the oil cover the fillet generously and fully. If it does not cover, add more oil until it does. Lift the fillet out of the oil, letting any excess oil drain back into the cooker. Set the fillet on a plate, cover loosely with plastic wrap, and refrigerate.

2 Stir the garlic, lemon zest, and thyme into the oil in the slow cooker. Cover and cook on high for 2 hours.

3 Slip the fillet skin side down back into the oil. Cover and cook on low for 2 hours in a small slow cooker, 2½ hours in a medium one, or 3 hours in a large model, or until the thickest part of the fillet will flake when pricked with a fork. Use a wide spatula (or two) to lift the fillet from the oil and onto a serving platter.

TESTERS' NOTES
• There's no better method for poaching salmon—and no richer fish dinner. You can serve it warm with a simple vinaigrette or even aïoli (see page 339); or you can refrigerate it, covered, for up to 2 days for a cold lunch or quick dinner.
• You place the oil and salmon in the slow cooker first to measure the exact amount of oil you'll need to keep the salmon submerged while it cooks.
• Don't use an expensive olive oil; instead, select a sturdy, first-cold-pressed version that has the distinct aroma of tart olives. Unfortunately, the poaching oil won't be much good afterward.
• Serve the salmon by lifting portions off the skin (which has a compromised, squishy texture after poaching).
• For olive oil–poached halibut, substitute an equivalent amount of skinless halibut fillet.

Serve It Up! For the best-ever salmon salad for sandwiches or wraps, flake some of the meat into a bowl and mix with mayonnaise, minced shallot, thinly sliced celery, and a dash of pickle relish.

wine-poached salmon

EFFORT: **NOT MUCH** • PREP TIME: **10 MINUTES** • COOK TIME: **2½ HOURS (AT MOST)** • KEEPS ON WARM: **4 HOURS THROUGH STEP 1** • SERVES: **2 TO 8**

INGREDIENTS	2- TO 3½-QT	4- TO 5½-QT	6- TO 8-QT
Dry white wine, such as Chardonnay	⅔ cup	1 cup	2 cups
Low-sodium vegetable broth	⅔ cup	1 cup	2 cups
Yellow onion, chopped	⅓ cup	½ cup	1 cup

Salt	½ tsp	1 tsp	½ tblsp
Ground black pepper	¼ tsp	½ tsp	¾ tsp
Celery seeds	⅛ tsp	¼ tsp	½ tsp
Fresh tarragon sprigs	2	3	6
Skin-on salmon fillet	1 pound, cut into 2 or 3 pieces	1½ pounds, cut into 4 or 5 pieces	2½ pounds, cut into 7 or 8 pieces

1 Stir the wine, broth, onion, salt, pepper, and celery seeds in the slow cooker. Tuck in the tarragon, then cover and cook on high for 2 hours.

2 Slip the salmon pieces into the sauce. Cover and continue cooking on high for 20 to 30 minutes, or until the flesh is opaque and easily flakes with a fork. Use a large, slotted spatula to transfer the pieces to serving plates or a serving platter. Discard the poaching liquid.

TESTERS' NOTES

• With this easy preparation, the fillets come out moist every time. Leaving the skin on the salmon not only adds a lot of flavor but also helps the sections hold together as they poach.

• There's a range of time here because salmon fillets have a range of thickness: very thin ones, no more than ½ inch thick, will certainly be done in 20 minutes; thicker portions may take a bit longer. In no case should you walk away from the cooker to do much more than set the table.

Serve It Up! The poaching liquid will be a tad too fishy to make a good sauce, so prepare a creamy, homemade **Aïoli** (*ay-OH-lee*): Whisk 2 large egg yolks, 2 teaspoons lemon juice, 1 teaspoon Dijon mustard, ½ teaspoon salt, and ½ teaspoon ground black pepper in a medium bowl until creamy and smooth. Press one or two peeled garlic cloves through a garlic press and into the mixture, then begin drizzling in olive oil as you whisk. The exact amount will

be determined by the density of the egg yolks and even ambient factors like humidity and temperature. However, you'll probably end up adding about 1 cup. Whisk all the while, dribbling the oil in the smallest stream, until you get a thick, rich, mayonnaise-like sauce. Save back any leftovers, covered, in the refrigerator for up to 3 days. You can even chill the salmon and serve it cold with the aïoli on the side.

pesto-rubbed salmon

EFFORT: **NOT MUCH** • PREP TIME: **15 MINUTES** • COOK TIME: **3 HOURS** • KEEPS ON WARM: **2 HOURS THROUGH STEP 1** • SERVES: **2 TO 8**

INGREDIENTS	2- TO 3½-QT	4- TO 5½-QT	6- TO 8 QT
Red onions, thinly sliced	2 medium	4 medium	4 large
Olive oil (for onions)	3 tblsp	6 tblsp	¾ cup
Packed fresh basil leaves	½ cup	1 cup	2 cups
Pine nuts	1½ tblsp	3 tblsp	⅓ cup
Medium garlic cloves, peeled	1	2	3
Parmigiano-Reggiano cheese, finely grated	1 ounce (about 2 tblsp)	2 ounces (about ¼ cup)	4 ounces (about ½ cup)
Olive oil (for pesto)	2 tblsp	¼ cup	½ cup
Freshly ground black pepper	¼ tsp	½ tsp	¾ tsp
Salmon fillet, skin removed	12 ounces, cut into 2 pieces	1½ pounds, cut into 4 pieces	3 pounds, cut into 8 pieces

(continued)

1 Toss the onions and oil in the slow cooker. Cover and cook on high until softened and sweet, about 2½ hours.

2 Set the basil leaves, pine nuts, and garlic on a cutting board; rock a large, heavy knife through them repeatedly, until the mixture is reduced to a thick paste. Scrape it into a bowl and stir in the cheese, olive oil, and pepper.

3 Rub the basil pesto all over the rounded side of the salmon pieces; set the pieces on top of the onions. Cover and cook on high for 30 minutes, or until opaque and warm. Serve by slipping a large spatula under the pieces to transfer them to serving plates without disturbing the pesto. Use a slotted spoon to scoop up some onions for a garnish on each serving.

TESTERS' NOTES

• The thicker the pesto, the more it will adhere to the salmon fillets. Fresh herbs have varying degrees of moisture content, based on the time of year and the lapse of time since they were picked. It's best to start with a little less oil and add more if you find this classic no-cook sauce isn't coming together.

• Although we suggest mincing the basil and other items on a cutting board, you can make the batch for the medium or large slow cooker in a mini food processor or even a blender.

• The salmon is skinless here so that it doesn't make the soft, delicious onions underneath taste too fishy.

SHORTCUTS Use purchased pesto instead of making your own: ¼ cup for the small slow cooker, ½ cup for the medium one, and 1 cup for the large.

INGREDIENTS EXPLAINED There's a bewildering array of salmon in our supermarkets. Almost all Atlantic salmon is farmed; much of the Pacific crop is wild (although a significant part is farmed as well). Farmed salmon is cheaper and so makes up 80 percent of U.S. consumption. Farmed salmon is fattier and to some people tastier; wild salmon has more beneficial omega-3s. In general, we use two rules when buying salmon: we ask questions at the fish counter (*What's fresh? What would work with the recipe?*) and we always ask to smell the salmon for freshness.

ALL-AMERICAN KNOW-HOW The easiest way to skin a salmon fillet is to ask the fishmonger at your supermarket to do it for you. If you must do it at home, set the fillet skin side down on a cutting board. Choose a long, thin, sharp knife and slice the skin free from the flesh at one corner of the fillet's small end. Hold the now-loose skin (not the fillet itself) with one hand, stretching that skin taut, then work the knife back and forth along the skin, always pressing the blade down toward the cutting board rather than up into the meat. Keep pulling the skin taut as you work your way down the fillet until the meat comes free.

salmon with tomatoes and black olives

EFFORT: **NOT MUCH** • PREP TIME: **20 MINUTES** • COOK TIME: **1½ HOURS** • KEEPS ON WARM: **NO** • SERVES: **3 TO 8**

INGREDIENTS	2- TO 3½-QT	4- TO 5½-QT	6- TO 8-QT
Grape tomatoes, halved	12	18	32
Chopped pitted black olives	3 tblsp	⅓ cup	½ cup
Minced garlic	1 tsp	½ tblsp	2 tsp
Olive oil	1 tblsp	2 tblsp	3 tblsp
Salmon fillet, skinned	1¼ pounds, cut into 3 pieces	2 pounds, cut into 5 pieces	3 pounds, cut into 8 pieces
Salt	¼ tsp	¾ tsp	1 tsp
Ground black pepper	¼ tsp	¾ tsp	1 tsp
Minced fresh oregano leaves	1 tblsp	1½ tblsp	2 tblsp

1 Pour a little oil into the slow cooker and grease the bottom and sides by rubbing it around with a paper towel. Stir the tomatoes, olives, and garlic in the slow cooker to create an even layer. Cover and cook on high for 45 minutes, or until the tomatoes soften and the sauce begins to bubble a bit.

2 Oil the fish fillets on both sides, then season the flesh with salt and pepper. Set them in the cooker on top of the tomatoes and other ingredients, then sprinkle with the oregano.

3 Cover and continue cooking on high for 45 minutes, or until the fish flakes when scraped with a fork. Use a large spatula to transfer the salmon to a cutting board, slice into servings, and top with the tomato mixture remaining in the slow cooker.

TESTERS' NOTES
• Here's the very definition of summer: light and delicious, the best of the slow cooker when the weather turns warm.
• If you can only find large cherry tomatoes, cut them into smaller pieces, perhaps into quarters, so the fillet will lie flat on top.

salsa-baked salmon

EFFORT: **A LITTLE** • PREP TIME: **15 MINUTES** • COOK TIME: **1 TO 1½ HOURS** • KEEPS ON WARM: **NO** • SERVES: **3 TO 8**

INGREDIENTS	2- TO 3½-QT	4- TO 5½-QT	6- TO 8-QT
Ripe tomatoes, chopped	½ pound	1¾ pounds	2 pounds
Chopped red onion	2 tblsp	3 tblsp	¼ cup
Minced seeded serrano chile	1 tblsp	4 tsp	2 tblsp
Fresh lime juice	1 tsp	½ tblsp	2 tsp
Minced garlic	½ tsp	¾ tsp	1 tsp
Chili powder	½ tsp	¾ tsp	1 tsp
Ground cumin	½ tsp	¾ tsp	1 tsp
Salt	¼ tsp	¼ tsp	½ tsp
Hot pepper sauce, such as Tabasco	¼ tsp	¼ tsp	½ tsp
Skin-on salmon fillet, in 1 piece	1 pound	1½ pounds	2½ pounds

1 Stir the tomatoes, onion, chile, lime juice, garlic, chili powder, cumin, salt, and hot sauce in a medium bowl.

2 Dab some olive oil on a paper towel and rub it around the interior of the slow cooker, coating the bottom particularly well. Lay the salmon fillet skin side down in the cooker. Spoon and spread the salsa over the salmon, even to the edges.

3 Cover and cook on high for 1 hour in a small slow cooker, 1 hour 15 minutes in a medium cooker, or 1½ hours in a large cooker, or until the fillet flakes when pierced with a fork.

TESTERS' NOTES
• For a chunkier salsa, do all the chopping and mincing by hand; for a smoother salsa, pulse the ingredients in a food processor until you get a very finely ground puree.
• It's better here to cook the salmon in one piece so that the salsa doesn't run off too many edges in the cooker. Once removed, you can slice the fish into sections—or fork the meat off the skin—for individual servings.

SHORTCUTS Use purchased salsa. For the best consistency, choose a thicker (rather than a runnier) variety; for the best flavor, choose a fairly straightforward salsa, perhaps with fire-roasted tomatoes and garlic in the mix. You'll need 1¼ cups for the small slow cooker, 1¾ cups for the medium cooker, or 2½ cups for a large one.

romesco-baked salmon

EFFORT: **A LOT** • PREP TIME: **25 MINUTES** • COOK TIME: **1½ HOURS** • KEEPS ON WARM: **NO** • SERVES: **3 TO 8**

INGREDIENTS	2- TO 3½-QT	4- TO 5½-QT	6- TO 8-QT
Olive oil	2 tblsp	3 tblsp	¼ cup
Medium garlic cloves, peeled and halved lengthwise	3	5	6
Cubes of baguette or Italian bread (1-inch pieces)	¾ cup	1 cup	1½ cups
Blanched almonds or skinned hazelnuts	¼ cup	6 tblsp	½ cup
Drained no-salt-added canned diced tomatoes, preferably fire-roasted	¾ cup plus 2 tblsp	1¼ cups	1¾ cups
Chopped jarred roasted red bell pepper (pimiento)	6 tblsp	⅔ cup	¾ cup
Mild smoked paprika	1 tsp	2 tsp	1 tblsp
Sherry vinegar	1 tsp	2 tsp	1 tblsp
Salt	⅛ tsp	¼ tsp	½ tsp
Skin-on salmon fillet, in 1 piece	1 pound	1½ pounds	2½ pounds

1 Set a large skillet over medium heat for a few minutes, then swirl in the oil. Add the garlic, bread cubes, and nuts. Stir over the heat until the bread begins to brown, between 2 and 4 minutes.

2 Scrape the contents of the skillet into a food processor fitted with the chopping blade. Add the tomatoes, pepper, paprika, vinegar, and salt. Pulse until a coarse mixture the texture of wet sand comes together.

3 Dab some olive oil on a paper towel and grease the inside of the slow cooker, particularly the bottom. Lay the fillet skin side down in the cooker; spread the bread mixture on top of the fish.

4 Cover and cook on high for 1 hour in a small slow cooker, 1 hour 15 minutes in a medium cooker, or 1½ hours in a large model, or until the fish flakes when pricked with a fork. Use a large spatula to lift the salmon onto a serving platter.

TESTERS' NOTES
• This coating is a simplified version of a classic Catalan sauce, often used to thicken fish stews. On the salmon, it's a luxurious accompaniment to the oily fish.
• If you don't have a spatula large enough to get the salmon out of the cooker in one piece, cut it in half or thirds with a flatware knife before lifting the pieces out. You may not be able to cut through the skin—and may have some sharding, too—but better that than bits of salmon all over the counter.

INGREDIENTS EXPLAINED
Sherry vinegar, called *vinagre de Jerez*, is exactly what it sounds like: vinegar made from sherry (with some brandy in the mix in lower-end bottlings). You'll definitely get what you pay for; cheaper bottlings can taste sharp and dry; better ones, mellow and oaky. However, you don't need a budget-buster for these recipes, just a flavorful vinegar without rank acidity.

maple, chipotle, and lime-glazed salmon

EFFORT: **A LITTLE** • PREP TIME: **15 MINUTES** • COOK TIME: **1 TO 1½ HOURS** • KEEPS ON WARM: **NO** • SERVES: **2 TO 8**

INGREDIENTS	2- TO 3½-QT	4- TO 5½-QT	6- TO 8-QT
Maple syrup	¼ cup	½ cup	¾ cup
Soy sauce	2 tblsp	¼ cup	6 tblsp
Fresh lime juice	1 tblsp	2 tblsp	3 tblsp
Canned chipotle chiles in adobo sauce, stemmed and minced	Up to ½	Up to 1	Up to 2
Minced garlic	1 tsp	2 tsp	1 tblsp
Minced peeled fresh ginger	½ tsp	1 tsp	½ tblsp
Skin-on salmon fillet	1 pound	1½ pounds	2½ pounds

1 Pour a little olive oil into the slow cooker, then smear it around with a wadded-up paper towel, coating the bottom thoroughly.

2 Whisk the maple syrup, soy sauce, lime juice, chiles, garlic, and ginger in a small bowl. Slip the salmon, skin side down, into the slow cooker; coat with the maple syrup mixture, right up to the edge of the meat.

3 Cover and cook on high for 1 hour in a small slow cooker, 1 hour 15 minutes in a medium cooker, or 1½ hours in a large cooker, or until the fish flakes when scraped with a fork. Use a large spatula to transfer the salmon to a serving platter or a carving board.

TESTERS' NOTES

• If you like a more sour finish, add up to 50 percent more lime juice.

• These "sauce" ingredients would also make a great barbecue rub for chicken or pork.

INGREDIENTS EXPLAINED Chipotle chiles are smoked jalapeños. They are often canned in adobo sauce, a blend of paprika, spices, salt, garlic, and vinegar, a mix popular in Spanish, Latin American, and Filipino cooking. The chiles need to be stemmed—and perhaps seeded if you want to lower the heat.

horseradish-crusted salmon with oranges

EFFORT: **A LITTLE** • PREP TIME: **20 MINUTES** • COOK TIME: **2 HOURS 45 MINUTES** • KEEPS ON WARM: **NO** • SERVES: **2 TO 8**

INGREDIENTS	2- TO 3½-QT	4- TO 5½-QT	6- TO 8-QT
Fennel bulb, trimmed and thinly sliced (see page 211)	¾ pound (about 2 cups)	1½ pounds (about 4 cups)	3 pounds (about 6 cups)
Medium oranges, made into suprêmes (see page 225)	1	2	4
Red onion, chopped	1 small	1 medium	1 large
Fresh tarragon sprigs	1	2	4
Jarred white horseradish	¼ cup	½ cup	1 cup
Minced fresh dill fronds	½ tsp	1 tsp	2 tsp
Salmon fillet, skin removed	¾ pound, cut into 2 pieces	1½ pounds, cut into 4 pieces	3 pounds, cut into 8 pieces

(continued)

1 Stir the fennel, orange supremes, onion, and tarragon in the slow cooker. Cover and cook on high for 2 hours, or until the fennel has softened and the liquid is bubbling.

2 Mix the horseradish and dill in a small bowl; spread on the salmon on the side opposite from which the skin was. Set coated side up on top of the fennel mixture in the slow cooker.

3 Cover and continue cooking on high for 45 minutes, or until the salmon can be flaked with a flatware fork. Transfer the pieces one by one to serving plates; spoon some of the fennel and orange sauce around the servings.

TESTERS' NOTES
• Believe it or not, spiky horseradish works well on delicate salmon, particularly as the spiky condiment mellows in the slow cooker.
• Use skin-on fillets if you prefer even more salmon flavor.
• Don't use dried herbs for the preparations. You need all the oomph of fresh ones to stand up to the other flavors in the mix.

Serve It Up! Serve this with **Mashed Celery Root**: Peel the root and cut it into 1-inch cubes. Place them in a large saucepan, cover with water, and bring to a boil over high heat. Cover, reduce the heat a bit, and cook until tender, about 15 minutes. Drain in a colander, then pour the cubes into a large bowl. Add butter, a little cream, salt, and pepper, and use an electric mixer at medium speed to whip into a fairly creamy puree.

roasted salmon steaks with mustard and dill

EFFORT: **NOT MUCH** • PREP TIME: **15 MINUTES** • COOK TIME: **1½ HOURS** • KEEPS ON WARM: **NO** • SERVES: **2 TO 6**

INGREDIENTS	2- TO 3½-QT	4- TO 5½-QT	6- TO 8-QT
Thin lemon slices	4	6	10
Olive oil	½ tblsp	1 tblsp	1½ tblsp
Dijon mustard	2 tblsp	¼ cup	6 tblsp
Minced fresh dill fronds	2 tsp	1½ tblsp	2½ tblsp
Fresh lemon juice	1 tsp	½ tblsp	2 tsp
Salmon steaks, about 8 ounces each, skin on	2	4	6

1 Smear some olive oil around the inside bottom and sides of the slow cooker canister. Cover the bottom with a layer of lemon slices.

2 Mix the olive oil, mustard, dill, and lemon juice in a small bowl; rub onto the salmon steaks. Set them in the slow cooker on top of the lemon slices.

3 Cover and cook on high for 1½ hours, or until the meat flakes when scraped with a fork.

TESTERS' NOTES
• The usual problem with salmon steaks is that the exterior bits dry out before the interior is cooked properly. But the slow cooker allows the fish to roast at a lower temperature, thereby ensuring it stays moist and delicate.
• It may be hard to check the steaks all the way through for doneness. You can try the knife trick (see page 334), or simply cut into one in the slow cooker to make sure.

• These steaks cook a bit longer because (1) the machine is not already heated when they make their appearance and (2) they are not submerged in an already hot liquid.

Serve It Up! Make an easy slaw by shredding red cabbage and moderately sweet, cored apples like Galas through the large holes of a box grater or with the shredding blade of a food processor. Mix them with mayonnaise, sour cream, a little cider vinegar, salt, pepper, celery seeds, and some minced parsley leaves.

salmon loaf

EFFORT: **A LOT** • PREP TIME: **30 MINUTES** • COOK TIME: **3 TO 4 HOURS** • KEEPS ON WARM: **NO** • SERVES: **2 TO 6**

INGREDIENTS	2- TO 3½-QT	4- TO 5½-QT	6- TO 8-QT
Medium shrimp, peeled and deveined	¼ pound	½ pound	¾ pound
Canned salmon, flaked	6 ounces	12 ounces	1 pound 2 ounces (18 ounces)
Plain dry breadcrumbs	¼ cup	½ cup	¾ cup
Minced yellow onion	2 tblsp	¼ cup	6 tblsp
Minced celery	2 tblsp	¼ cup	6 tblsp
Dijon mustard	1 tblsp	2 tblsp	3 tblsp
Large eggs, at room temperature	1	2	3
Dried dill	½ tsp	1 tsp	½ tblsp
Dried thyme	½ tsp	1 tsp	½ tblsp
Salt	¼ tsp	½ tsp	¾ tsp
Hot pepper sauce, such as Tabasco	¼ tsp	½ tsp	¾ tsp
Garlic powder	⅛ tsp	¼ tsp	¼ tsp
Milk	Up to ¼ cup	Up to ½ cup	Up to ¾ cup

1 Dab some olive oil on a paper towel and thoroughly grease the inside of a slow cooker.

2 Pulse the shrimp in a large food processor fitted with the chopping blade until a thick, sticky paste.

3 Scrape the shrimp paste into a large bowl; stir in the salmon, breadcrumbs, onion, celery, mustard, eggs, dill, thyme, salt, hot sauce, and garlic powder. Add the milk in tablespoon increments until you can form a wet paste that holds its shape.

4 Dump the salmon mixture into the slow cooker, then use your clean, wet hands to form it all into a loaf, keeping at least ½ inch free space between it and the side of the canister. Smooth the top of the loaf.

5 Cover and cook on low for 3 hours in a small slow cooker, 3½ hours in a medium cooker, or 4 hours in a large one, or until an instant-read meat thermometer inserted into the center of the loaf registers 165°F. Cool for 10 minutes before transferring to a serving platter. Cover and chill for at least 8 hours or up to 3 days.

TESTERS' NOTES

• Old-fashioned cocktail party fare, this rendition of salmon mousse can also be chilled and then sliced into wedges for sandwiches or served with bagels and cream cheese for breakfast—or with Aïoli (page 339) on a buffet spread.

• Canned salmon varies dramatically in quality. If possible, look for cans made with salmon fillets; otherwise, you may end up with skin and even small bones.

(continued)

- The amount of milk needed varies widely based on the relative moisture in the other ingredients. You'll need to add at least half of the stated amount to get the loaf to cohere, but you don't want that mixture to be too wet. Stop and assess; stir vigorously to break the salmon into the mixture.
- Because of the eggs and shrimp, the internal temperature of the loaf is crucial to alleviate food safety concerns. Because slow cookers have varying cooking temperatures, yours may take a little longer to get to the proper temperature. For this recipe, rely on the internal temperature, not the timing.

trout in buttery white wine sauce

EFFORT: **A LITTLE** • PREP TIME: **20 MINUTES** • COOK TIME: **3 HOURS**
• KEEPS ON WARM: **4 HOURS THROUGH STEP 1** • SERVES: **2 TO 6**

INGREDIENTS	2- TO 3½-QT	4- TO 5½-QT	6- TO 8-QT
Dry white wine, such as white Burgundy	1 cup	2 cups	3 cups
Low-sodium vegetable broth	1 cup	2 cups	3 cups
Shallots, peeled and chopped	2 ounces	4 ounces	6 ounces
Salt	¼ tsp	½ tsp	¾ tsp
Ground black pepper	¼ tsp	½ tsp	¾ tsp
Fresh tarragon sprigs	2	4	6
Whole trout, cleaned and boned	2	4	6
White wine vinegar	2 tsp	1½ tblsp	2 tblsp
Unsalted butter, at room temperature, cut into small pieces	4 tblsp (½ stick)	8 tblsp (1 stick)	12 tblsp (1½ sticks)

1 Stir the wine, broth, shallots, salt, and pepper in the slow cooker. Tuck the tarragon sprigs into the mixture, cover, and cook on high for 2 hours.

2 Slip the trout into the slow cooker, arranging them head to tail so they fit in a fairly tight group. Cover and continue cooking on high for 1 hour, or until the flesh can be flaked with a fork.

3 Use a large spatula to transfer the trout to a serving platter or individual serving plates. Tent with aluminum foil to keep warm. Strain the liquid in the slow cooker through a fine-mesh sieve or a cheesecloth-lined colander into a bowl below. Discard the strained solids.

4 Pour the strained liquid into a medium or large saucepan and bring to a boil over high heat, stirring occasionally. Reduce the heat a bit and boil until reduced to about ⅓ cup for 2 trout, ⅔ cup for 4 trout, or 1 cup for 6 trout. Whisk the vinegar into the sauce, then remove it from the heat and whisk in the butter until smooth. Drizzle the sauce over the trout to serve.

TESTERS' NOTES
- Trout make a healthy meal without much fuss at all. Unfortunately, the skin will not get crisp; but you can easily peel it back after the trout have poached.
- Buttery and rich, this sauce seems to cry out for mashed potatoes on the side. Make sure the butter is soft so that it blends quickly into the sauce.

INGREDIENTS EXPLAINED Although there are many varieties of trout available on the market, any will do here, including the bulk that are farm-raised. While we wouldn't recommend the oilier sea trout here, even it will work if you like a pronounced fish taste.

herb-stuffed trout with a peppery cream sauce

EFFORT: **A LITTLE** • PREP TIME: **20 MINUTES** • COOK TIME: **1½ HOURS** • KEEPS ON WARM: **NO** • SERVES: **2 TO 6**

INGREDIENTS	2- TO 3½-QT	4- TO 5½-QT	6- TO 8-QT
Ground black pepper	½ tsp	1 tsp	½ tblsp
Whole trout, cleaned and boned	2	4	6
Salt	¼ tsp	½ tsp	¾ tsp
Fresh dill sprigs	2	4	6
Fresh thyme sprigs	2	4	6
Dry white wine, such as Pinot Grigio	½ cup	1 cup	1½ cups
Heavy cream	3 tblsp	6 tblsp	½ cup

1 Grease the inside of the slow cooker canister with unsalted butter; sprinkle it with the pepper. Season the trout inside and out with salt, then lay a dill sprig and a thyme sprig inside each fish's body cavity.

2 Set the fish in the slow cooker, overlapping as necessary, head to tail to make an even layer. Pour the wine over the trout.

3 Cover and cook on high for 1½ hours, or until the flesh under the skin can be scraped into large pieces with a fork.

4 Use a large spatula to transfer the trout to a serving platter or serving plates; cover loosely with aluminum foil to keep warm.

5 Remove any aromatic herbs that have fallen into the slow cooker. Pour the poaching liquid into a saucepan, scraping out every last speck for the peppery bits. Stir in the cream, and bring to a boil over high heat. Reduce the heat a little and boil, stirring occasionally, until the volume of the liquid is about two-thirds its original amount. Drizzle the sauce over the fish to serve.

TESTERS' NOTES
• There's a fair amount of ground black pepper in this sauce—you can add even more, up to double the stated amount, if you really want that peppery bite. Just remember that black pepper has an "exponential" factor, turning into a mouth-burning pop with shocking abandon.
• The trout skin can easily be pulled back with the tines of a fork so you can check the flesh underneath to determine if it's cooked through.

Serve It Up! Spike some cooked couscous with drained canned mandarin orange segments and toasted sliced almonds, as well as a little salt and pepper. Better yet, search out whole-grain couscous, or the more esoteric but much more aromatic barley couscous, a global staple.

ALL-AMERICAN KNOW-HOW If you have squeamish diners at the table, remove the heads from the trout after cooking. Leaving the head on will keep the fish together as it cooks.

tuna noodle casserole

EFFORT: **A LITTLE** • PREP TIME: **15 MINUTES** • COOK TIME: **1½ HOURS** • KEEPS ON WARM: **NO** • SERVES: **3 TO 8**

INGREDIENTS	2- TO 3½-QT	4- TO 5½-QT	6- TO 8-QT
Dried farfalle (bow-tie pasta), preferably whole wheat	6 ounces	10 ounces	1 pound
Cheddar cheese, preferably mild, grated	6 ounces (about 1½ cups)	10 ounces (about 2½ cups)	1 pound (about 4 cups)
Canned tuna, drained	6 ounces	12 ounces (¾ pound)	18 ounces (1 pound 2 ounces)
All-purpose flour	2 tblsp	3 tblsp	⅓ cup
Milk	1½ cups	2½ cups	4 cups (1 quart)
Mild paprika	1 tsp	2 tsp	1 tblsp
Dried dill	½ tsp	¾ tsp	1 tsp
Onion powder	⅛ tsp	¼ tsp	½ tsp

1 Generously grease the inside of the slow cooker with unsalted butter, paying special attention to the seam where the side meets the bottom. Mix the pasta, cheese, tuna, and flour in a large bowl; pour into the cooker.

2 Whisk the milk, paprika, dill, and onion powder in that same bowl; pour evenly over the ingredients in the cooker.

3 Cover and cook on high for 45 minutes. Stir well, then cover and continue cooking on high for 45 minutes, or until the casserole is set and the pasta is tender.

TESTERS' NOTES

• Comfort food deluxe, this easy casserole makes great leftovers the next day. Although we usually prefer sharp Cheddar, a milder version will offer the more authentic taste and won't run interference with the taste of the tuna.
• Although tuna packed in water is healthier, tuna packed in oil is tastier. Our favorite canned tuna is light yellowfin, packed in olive oil.
• The sauce will appear to have broken about halfway through cooking. Stirring it will take care of the matter.
• There's no topping here, but that's what crumbled potato chips are for. Sprinkle them over individual servings.

tuna with tomatoes, potatoes, and peppers

EFFORT: **A LITTLE** • PREP TIME: **25 MINUTES** • COOK TIME: **3½ HOURS (AT MOST)** • KEEPS ON WARM: **1 HOUR THROUGH STEP 2** • SERVES: **3 TO 8**

INGREDIENTS	2- TO 3½-QT	4- TO 5½-QT	6- TO 8-QT
Tuna steaks, about 1½ inches thick	1 pound	1½ pounds	2½ pounds
Olive oil	1½ tblsp	2 tblsp	3½ tblsp
Mild smoked paprika	1½ tblsp	2 tblsp	3½ tblsp
Ripe tomatoes, chopped	10 ounces (1⅓ cups)	1 pound (2 cups)	1¼ pounds (2½ cups)
Yellow potatoes (such as Yukon Gold), diced	¼ pound (1⅓ cups)	½ pound (2 cups)	¾ pound (2½ cups)

Green or red bell peppers, cored, seeded, and diced	1 small	1 medium	1 large
Low-sodium chicken broth	⅔ cup	1 cup	1½ cups
Dry white wine, such as Chardonnay	6 tblsp	½ cup	⅔ cup
Minced fresh oregano leaves	2 tsp	1 tblsp	2 tblsp
Salt	½ tsp	¾ tsp	1 tsp

1 Rub the tuna steaks with olive oil and paprika. Cut them into 2-inch pieces, set them on a plate, cover, and refrigerate while you make the sauce.

2 Mix the tomatoes, potatoes, bell pepper, broth, wine, oregano, and salt in the slow cooker. Cover and cook on high for 3 hours.

3 Add the tuna pieces, nestling them in the vegetables. Cover and continue cooking on high for 15 to 30 minutes, or until the tuna is either pink in the center or cooked through. Serve by spooning the tuna chunks and vegetables with sauce into bowls.

TESTERS' NOTES
• We feel strongly that tuna should not be overcooked. We took these chunks out after 15 minutes but also recommended 30 minutes because most people like theirs more well done.
• Make sure you dice the potatoes into pieces no larger than ½-inch cubes. They'll need to cook relatively quickly (at least in slow-cooker terms).

INGREDIENTS EXPLAINED Tuna steaks sometimes have tough, fibrous white nerve tissue running through the meat. Try to choose steaks that are free of those streaks. Or ask the fishmonger to cut the larger ones out for you. If you like tuna as rare as we do, buy sushi-grade tuna steaks for safety's sake.

coconut and ginger–crusted black cod

EFFORT: **A LITTLE** • PREP TIME: **15 MINUTES** • COOK TIME: **1 HOUR 15 MINUTES** • KEEPS ON WARM: **NO** • SERVES: **3 TO 8**

INGREDIENTS	2- TO 3½-QT	4- TO 5½-QT	6- TO 8-QT
Unsweetened shredded coconut	½ cup	¾ cup plus 2 tblsp	1⅓ cups
Ground ginger	1 tsp	1¾ tsp	1 tblsp
Finely grated lime zest	1 tsp	1¾ tsp	1 tblsp
Salt	¼ tsp	½ tsp	¾ tsp
Cayenne	Up to ¼ tsp	Up to ½ tsp	Up to ¾ tsp
Black cod fillets, skin on or removed	1¼ pounds, cut into 3 pieces	2 pounds, cut into 4 or 5 pieces	3 pounds, cut into 6 to 8 pieces
Fresh lime juice	2 tblsp	3 tblsp	¼ cup

1 Generously grease the inside of the slow cooker canister with unsalted butter. Cover and cook on high while you prepare the dish.

2 Place the coconut, ginger, lime zest, salt, and cayenne in a large food processor fitted with the chopping blade; process until finely ground, about the texture of yellow cornmeal.

3 Rub the fish fillets with the lime juice, then pour the coconut mixture in the food processor onto a plate. Coat the fish in the coconut mixture, turning the fillets this way and that

(continued)

to get an even crust. Shake off any excess and set them in the slow cooker in one layer.

4 Lay overlapping lengths of paper towels on top of the slow cooker, covering the opening completely. Set the cover in place and cook on high for 1 hour 15 minutes, or until the fish is firm and opaque.

TESTERS' NOTES
• A dry-roasting technique allows this rich fish to condense a bit without the more uncompromising heat of the oven, thereby preserving moisture and ensuring better texture.
• The butter in the crock will not only keep the fish from sticking, it will also melt into a sauce. You won't want to miss it, even to dab bread in it.
• A "crust" is a bit of a misnomer. It's not crunchy but it will adhere to coat the fillets. The paper towels, however, will keep moisture from ruining the coating on the fish.
• Skinned black cod will be milder; skin-on will be much more assertive. Your call.

INGREDIENTS EXPLAINED Black cod, sometimes called *sablefish,* was once practically a giveaway, thought too oily to make a good meal, until it was allegedly "discovered" and made chic by chefs in the 1990s. Quite expensive, it should only be purchased from a reputable fishmonger who isn't trying to scam other substitutes.

Serve It Up! Black cod seems to demand a rice dish. Make **Fried Rice** in a wok: Scramble an egg or two in peanut oil over medium-high heat, breaking up the curds quickly as they form. Add minced scallions, ginger, garlic, and lots of white rice; toss well until heated through, then season with soy sauce and minced cilantro leaves.

salt cod with creamy white beans

EFFORT: **A LOT** • PREP TIME: **24 HOURS 20 MINUTES (INCLUDES SOAKING THE SALT COD)** • COOK TIME: **5 HOURS** • KEEPS ON WARM: **2 HOURS THROUGH STEP 2** • SERVES: **3 TO 9**

INGREDIENTS	2- TO 3½-QT	4- TO 5½-QT	6- TO 8-QT
Salt cod	½ pound	1 pound	1½ pounds
Drained and rinsed canned white beans	3 cups	6 cups	9 cups
Low-sodium vegetable broth	1½ cups	3 cups	4½ cups
Yellow onion, chopped	1 small	1 large	2 medium
Minced celery	½ cup	1 cup	1¼ cups
Shredded carrot	⅓ cup	⅔ cup	1 cup
Ground black pepper	½ tsp	1 tsp	½ tblsp
4-inch rosemary sprigs	1	2	3
Bay leaves	1	2	3
Heavy cream	½ cup	1 cup	1½ cups

1 Put the salt cod in a big bowl, cover completely with water, and refrigerate for 24 hours, changing the water twice.

2 Mix the beans, broth, onion, celery, carrot, and pepper in the slow cooker. Tuck in the rosemary sprigs and bay leaves. Cover and cook on high for 4 hours, or until the beans are ridiculously soft.

3 Bring the cream to a simmer in a small saucepan set over medium-high heat; set aside. Drain the salt cod and cut it into 1-inch chunks. Stir the cream and salt cod into the cooker.

4 Cover and continue cooking on high for 1 hour, or until the stew is aromatic and irresistible. Discard the rosemary sprigs and bay leaves before serving.

TESTERS' NOTES
• Long an economical staple, salt cod here becomes a rich addition to a rather simple stew. In order to balance the fish's oily flavor, cook the onion quite a bit, at a fairly low heat, so that its sweetness stands out.
• If you find rosemary too aggressive, substitute tarragon or even thyme sprigs.
• If you want to thicken this stew, scoop out about a third of the beans and mash them to a paste in a bowl with the back of a wooden spoon. Stir the puree back into the soup and cook on high for 10 minutes to warm through.

Serve It Up! Ladle this stew over cooked wide noodles, tossed with poppy seeds and a little butter.

INGREDIENTS EXPLAINED Traditionally called "dried and salted cod" (which explains exactly what it is), salt cod has provided cold-weather food for centuries. You must soak salt cod to rehydrate it as well as change the water while soaking to pull as much salt out as possible. These days, because of overfishing on a global scale, other white fish are often sold as salt cod, the words now more of a generic label. But there's no need to worry—any variety will work here.

swordfish with fennel and rosemary

EFFORT: **A LITTLE** • PREP TIME: **15 MINUTES** • COOK TIME: **2½ HOURS** • KEEPS ON WARM: **NO** • SERVES: **2 TO 8**

INGREDIENTS	2- TO 3½-QT	4- TO 5½-QT	6- TO 8-QT
No-salt-added canned diced tomatoes	1¾ cups	3½ cups	7 cups
Fennel bulbs, trimmed and chopped (see page 211)	6 ounces (about ¾ cup)	¾ pound (about 1½ cups)	1¼ pounds (about 2¾ cups)
Chopped red onion	¼ cup	½ cup (about 1 small)	1 cup
Chopped pitted black olives	¼ cup	½ cup	1 cup
No-salt-added tomato paste	1 tblsp	2 tblsp	6 tblsp
Drained, rinsed, and minced capers	½ tblsp	1 tblsp	2 tblsp
Minced fresh rosemary leaves	1 tsp	2 tsp	1½ tblsp
Minced garlic	1 tsp	2 tsp	1½ tblsp
Stemmed fresh thyme leaves	½ tsp	1 tsp	2 tsp
Swordfish steaks, about 6 ounces each, skin removed	2	4	8

1 Mix the tomatoes, fennel, onion, olives, tomato paste, capers, rosemary, garlic, and thyme in the slow cooker until the tomato paste has evenly coated everything. Cover and cook on high for 2 hours, or until bubbling and steamy.

2 Nestle the swordfish in the sauce. Cover and continue cooking on high for 30 minutes,

(continued)

or until the fish is firm and cooked through. Serve by transferring the steaks to a cutting board, mounding the vegetables and sauce in bowls, then topping with the fish.

TESTERS' NOTES
• Make sure the fennel and red onion are chopped into pieces no larger than ½ inch. They'll need a head start to soften and meld into a sauce.
• Substitute tuna steaks, if desired. Consider cooking them only 20 minutes for medium-rare.
• The only thing that would make this dish better would be bacon. So add some: cook up a few strips, crumble them in with the tomatoes, and have a go at it.

INGREDIENTS EXPLAINED Swordfish is an oily fish, a migratory predator, often cut into meaty steaks. The skin is tough and won't soften much in the slow cooker, so it should be removed. Ask the fishmonger to get rid of it for you.

swordfish with herbed butter

EFFORT: **A LITTLE** • PREP TIME: **20 MINUTES** • COOK TIME: **1½ HOURS** • KEEPS ON WARM: **NO** • SERVES: **3 TO 8**

INGREDIENTS	2- TO 3½-QT	4- TO 5½-QT	6- TO 8-QT
Red onion, thinly sliced	1 small	1 medium	1 large
Swordfish steaks, about 6 ounces each, skin removed	3	5	8
Minced fresh parsley leaves	4 tsp	2 tblsp	3½ tblsp
Minced fresh thyme leaves	2 tsp	1 tblsp	1½ tblsp
Minced garlic	1 tsp	2 tsp	2½ tsp
Finely minced lemon zest	1 tsp	2 tsp	2½ tsp
Salt	¼ tsp	½ tsp	¾ tsp
Ground black pepper	¼ tsp	½ tsp	¾ tsp
Unsalted butter	3 tblsp, cut into 3 pieces	5 tblsp, cut into 5 pieces	8 tblsp (1 stick), cut into 8 pieces

1 Grease the inside of the slow cooker canister with unsalted butter. Sprinkle the onion in an even layer in the crock, then set the swordfish steaks on top.

2 Sprinkle the fish with the parsley, thyme, garlic, lemon zest, salt, and pepper. Set a pat of butter on top of each fish steak.

3 Cover and cook on high for 1½ hours, or until the fish is cooked through without being dry.

TESTERS' NOTES
• Spoon every speck of sauce over these meaty steaks.
• Make sure the lemon zest is actually minced, not just grated. Otherwise, it won't soften quickly enough.
• The cooking time is longer here since the fish is dry-roasted, not put into a bubbling sauce.
• Substitute halibut steaks for the swordfish, if desired.

stuffed sole

EFFORT: **A LOT** • PREP TIME: **35 MINUTES** • COOK TIME: **1½ HOURS** • KEEPS ON WARM: **NO** • SERVES: **2 TO 6**

INGREDIENTS	2- TO 3½-QT	4- TO 5½-QT	6- TO 8-QT
Unsalted butter	2 tblsp	4 tblsp (½ stick)	6 tblsp
Minced shallot	2 tblsp	¼ cup	6 tblsp
Pine nuts	2 tblsp	¼ cup	6 tblsp

	2/3 cup	1 1/3 cups	2 cups
Fresh breadcrumbs	2/3 cup	1 1/3 cups	2 cups
Minced fresh parsley leaves	2 tblsp	1/4 cup	6 tblsp
Parmigiano-Reggiano cheese, finely grated	1/2 ounce (about 1 tblsp)	1 ounce (about 2 tblsp)	1 1/2 ounces (about 3 tblsp)
White balsamic vinegar (see page 77)	1 tblsp	2 tblsp	3 tblsp
Dijon mustard	1/2 tblsp	1 tblsp	1 1/2 tblsp
Sole fillets	4	8	12

1 Grease the inside of the slow cooker canister with unsalted butter, taking special care to coat the bottom generously.

2 Melt the butter in a large skillet over medium heat. Add the shallot and pine nuts; cook, stirring often, until the shallot softens, between 3 and 5 minutes.

3 Scrape the contents of the skillet into a large bowl. Stir in the breadcrumbs, parsley, cheese, vinegar, and mustard until everything is uniformly combined. Cool for 10 minutes.

4 Lay the sole fillets on a clean, dry work surface (or as many as will fit at one time). Top each fillet with 2 to 3 tablespoons of the breadcrumb mixture. Roll the fillets closed and set them seam side down in the cooker in one layer, squeezing to fit as you need to.

5 Cover and cook on high for 1 1/2 hours, or until the fish can be flaked when pricked with a fork. Use tongs and a small spatula to transfer the fillets to serving plates.

TESTERS' NOTES

• Because sole fillets can be small, sometimes less than 3 ounces, we figured two per serving was about right. If you find larger sole fillets, particularly those harvested along the Maine coast that can be 5 or 6 ounces each, you'll want to use half as many, but slice each in half lengthwise before stuffing.

• Dry breadcrumbs won't soften in the slow cooker to make a successful filling. You'll need to search out fresh ones in the bakery section of your supermarket, or pulse bits of a baguette in a food processor fitted with the chopping blade to make your own.

• You can make this dish even more decadent by reducing the mustard by half before adding up to 6 ounces of lump crab meat, picked over for shell and cartilage, to the breadcrumb mixture.

monkfish with pancetta and leeks

EFFORT: **A LITTLE** • PREP TIME: **20 MINUTES** • COOK TIME: **2 1/2 HOURS** • KEEPS ON WARM: **NO** • SERVES: **2 TO 8**

INGREDIENTS	2- TO 3 1/2-QT	4- TO 5 1/2-QT	6- TO 8-QT
Unsalted butter	1 1/2 tblsp	2 tblsp	3 tblsp
Pancetta, diced	4 ounces	6 ounces	10 ounces
Thinly sliced leek (white and pale green part only), washed carefully to remove internal sand	6 tblsp	1/2 cup	1 cup (about 1/2 pound)
Dry vermouth	2/3 cup	1 cup	1 2/3 cups
Minced fresh rosemary leaves	1/2 tblsp	2 tsp	1 tblsp
Bay leaf	1	1	2
Chopped fresh parsley leaves	1 1/2 tblsp	2 tblsp	1/4 cup
Monkfish fillets	1 pound, cut into 2 to 3 pieces	1 1/2 pounds, cut into 4 or 5 pieces	2 1/2 pounds, cut into 7 or 8 pieces

(continued)

1 Melt the butter in large skillet over medium heat. Add the pancetta and fry until crisp, stirring often, between 3 and 6 minutes.

2 Scrape the contents of the skillet into the slow cooker; stir in the leek, vermouth, rosemary, and bay leaf. Cover and cook on high for 2 hours, or until bubbling and aromatic.

3 Stir in the parsley, then nestle the monkfish in the sauce. Cover and continue cooking on high for 30 minutes, or until the fish is firm and opaque. Discard the bay leaf, cut the monkfish into individual servings, and offer them in bowls with the sauce.

TESTERS' NOTES
• Monkfish is an oily but surprisingly mild fish, once called "poor man's lobster" for its meaty texture and shellfish-like taste. Like lobster, monkfish can be quickly overcooked and turn rubbery. Start checking the fish after 20 minutes—it won't flake with a fork, but instead should cut easily with a knife, revealing an opaque if still slightly gelatinous center.
• Make sure the pancetta is cut into cubes no larger than ¼ inch. You want them to accent the fish, not compete with it on the fork.

INGREDIENTS EXPLAINED Pancetta is cured pork belly, not smoked like bacon. It is often rolled into a tight spiral and laced with cracked black peppercorns and sometimes other spices. A favorite in Italian cooking, pancetta sometimes is sold sliced in packages, found near the prosciutto. However, the best-tasting pancetta is sliced right at the deli counter for you. Ask for ¼-inch-thick slices, which you can then easily dice at home.

bass in fennel broth

EFFORT: **A LOT** • PREP TIME: **30 MINUTES** • COOK TIME: **4 HOURS 20 MINUTES TO 4 HOURS 40 MINUTES** • KEEPS ON WARM: **3 HOURS THROUGH STEP 2** • SERVES: **2 TO 8**

INGREDIENTS	2- TO 3½-QT	4- TO 5½-QT	6- TO 8-QT
Low-sodium chicken broth	1½ cups	2½ cups	4 cups (1 quart)
Fennel bulbs, trimmed and chopped (see page 211)	½ pound	1 pound	1½ pounds
Minced yellow onion	¼ cup	⅓ cup	½ cup
Minced celery	¼ cup	⅓ cup	½ cup
Salt	⅛ tsp	¼ tsp	½ tsp
Ground black pepper	⅛ tsp	¼ tsp	½ tsp
Dry white wine, such as white Chablis	2 tblsp	3 tblsp	¼ cup
Chopped fresh parsley leaves	2 tblsp	3 tblsp	¼ cup
Fennel seeds	¼ tsp	½ tsp	1 tsp
Striped bass, black bass, sea bass, or largemouth bass, skin on but scored	1 pound	1½ pounds	2½ pounds

1 Stir the broth, fennel, onion, celery, salt, and pepper in the slow cooker. Cover and cook on high for 3 hours.

2 Use a slotted spoon to remove all the solids from the broth; discard the solids. Stir in the wine, parsley, and fennel seeds. Cover and continue cooking on high for 1 hour.

3 Lay the fish in the broth. Cover and continue cooking on high for 20 minutes in a small slow cooker, 30 minutes in a medium cooker, or 40 minutes in a large cooker, until the bass flakes into meaty chunks when scraped with a fork. Use a wide spatula to get the fish into serving bowls, then ladle the poaching liquid on top.

TESTERS' NOTES
• Feel free to use the fennel fronds here as well, especially since you'll remove them before adding the fish.
• Substitute skin-on snapper fillets for the bass, if desired. Score the skin on these as well.

Serve It Up! Of course, you'll need crunchy bread to dip in the broth. Beyond that, consider a **Salad of Grilled Radicchio**: Slice the heads in half, then oil them and grill on an outdoor grill or in a grill pan set over medium-high heat. Lay the quarters on a platter and top with a creamy dressing that's a mixture of mayonnaise, minced dill, minced parsley leaves, a little lemon juice, and some pickle relish. Sprinkle crunchy sea salt or kosher salt over the platter.

bluefish and potato stew

EFFORT: **A LITTLE** • PREP TIME: **20 MINUTES** • COOK TIME: **6½ HOURS** • KEEPS ON WARM: **1 HOUR THROUGH STEP 2** • SERVES: **3 TO 8**

INGREDIENTS	2- TO 3½-QT	4- TO 5½-QT	6- TO 8-QT
Olive oil	2 tblsp	3 tblsp	⅓ cup
Yellow onion, chopped	1 small	1 medium	2 medium
Red bell pepper, cored, seeded, and chopped	1 small	1 medium	2 medium
Green bell pepper, cored, seeded, and chopped	1 small	1 medium	2 medium
Minced garlic	1 tsp	2 tsp	1 tblsp
Russet or other baking potatoes, peeled and diced	10 ounces	1¼ pounds	2 pounds
Drained no-salt-added canned diced tomatoes	1 cup	1¾ cups	2¾ cups
Red (sweet) vermouth (see page 258)	½ cup	¾ cup	1¼ cups
Bottled clam juice	½ cup	¾ cup	1¼ cups
Mild paprika	2 tsp	3½ tsp	2 tblsp
Stemmed fresh thyme leaves	2 tsp	3 tsp	5 tsp
Bluefish fillets, skin removed, cut into 1-inch pieces	1 pound	1¾ pounds	2¾ pounds

1 Set a large skillet over medium heat for a few minutes, then swirl in the oil. Add the onion and bell peppers. Cook, stirring often, until the onion softens, between 5 and 9 minutes.

2 Stir in the garlic, cook for a few seconds, and scrape the contents of the skillet into the slow cooker. Stir in the potatoes, tomatoes, vermouth, clam juice, paprika, and thyme. Cover and cook on low for 6 hours, or until the potatoes are quite tender.

3 Gently stir in the bluefish pieces. Cover, turn the heat to high, and cook for 30 minutes, or until the fish is cooked through.

TESTERS' NOTES
• This hearty stew would be best if you lived near the coast where you can sometimes find fresh, never-frozen bluefish at the supermarket.
• If you've got leftovers, save them in the fridge, tightly covered, for a day or so, then mix in some panko breadcrumbs and form them into patties. Fry in a skillet over medium heat with a little olive oil and unsalted butter.

(continued)

SHORTCUTS This recipe is perfect for frozen chopped onions and frozen chopped bell peppers. Plus, there's no need to thaw them. Just cook an extra minute or so in the skillet to make sure they're hot.

INGREDIENTS EXPLAINED Bluefish is an oily, strong-tasting fish, somewhat milder (though not very much so) than mackerel. It's common in fish markets along the eastern U.S. coastline.

seafood barley risotto

EFFORT: **A LITTLE** • PREP TIME: **20 MINUTES** • COOK TIME: **3 HOURS 50 MINUTES TO 4 HOURS 50 MINUTES** • KEEPS ON WARM: **NO** • SERVES: **2 TO 6**

INGREDIENTS	2- TO 3½-QT	4- TO 5½-QT	6- TO 8-QT
Low-sodium chicken broth	2½ cups	5¼ cups	7 cups
Pearled barley (see page 24)	1 cup plus 2 tblsp	1½ cups	2 cups plus 2 tblsp
Thinly sliced leek (white and pale green part only), washed carefully to remove interior sand	⅓ cup	1 cup (about ½ pound)	1¼ cups
Stemmed fresh thyme leaves	1 tsp	2 tsp	1 tblsp
Saffron	Up to ¼ tsp	Up to ½ tsp	Up to ¾ tsp
Cod fillets, cut into ½-inch pieces	5 ounces	¾ pound	1 pound
Bay scallops	3 ounces	½ pound	10 ounces
Pecorino-Romano cheese, finely grated	½ ounce (about 1 tblsp)	1 ounce (about 2 tblsp)	1½ ounces (about 3 tblsp)
Ground black pepper	½ tsp	¾ tsp	1 tsp

1 Combine the broth, barley, leek, thyme, and saffron in the slow cooker. Cover and cook on low for 3½ hours in a small slow cooker, 4 hours in a medium cooker, or 4½ hours in a large one, or until the barley is almost tender and much of the liquid has been absorbed.

2 Gently stir in the cod pieces and scallops. Cover, set the temperature to high, and continue cooking for 20 minutes. Stir in the cheese and pepper before serving.

TESTERS' NOTES
• Yes, there's a mix of seafood and shellfish here. You can't make a good seafood risotto without that combo!
• Tiny bay scallops can be hard to locate. If you can only find the larger sea scallops, cut them in half or even quarters to match the size of the cod pieces.

Serve It Up! You'll want a fairly simple salad to go with this more complex dish. Mix toasted walnut or pecan pieces with thinly sliced and cored apple and chopped romaine, then dress it with an emulsion of two parts white wine vinegar to five parts olive oil, plus a pinch of sugar and a very little bit of minced ginger, as well as some salt and ground black pepper.

INGREDIENTS EXPLAINED Pecorino is the name for a range of cheeses, all made from sheep's milk. Pecorino-Romano is the most common form found in North America, and the mildest of the bunch. All also come in soft and semi-soft varieties, but you're looking for the hard grating type for all of these recipes.

bouillabaisse

EFFORT: **A LITTLE** • PREP TIME: **30 MINUTES** • COOK TIME:
4½ HOURS • KEEPS ON WARM: **3 HOURS THROUGH STEP 1** •
SERVES: **2 TO 6**

INGREDIENTS	2- TO 3½-QT	4- TO 5½-QT	6- TO 8-QT
Drained no-salt-added canned diced tomatoes	1 cup	2 cups	3 cups
Moderately dry white wine, such as Viognier	¾ cup	1¾ cups	2½ cups
Fennel bulbs, trimmed and chopped (see page 211)	6 ounces	10 ounces	1 pound
Bottled clam juice	⅔ cup	1⅓ cups	2 cups
No-salt-added tomato paste	1 tblsp	2 tblsp	3 tblsp
Minced garlic	1 tsp	2 tsp	1 tblsp
Herbes de Provence (see page 90)	1 tsp	½ tblsp	2½ tsp
Saffron	Pinch	⅛ tsp	¼ tsp
Thick white fish fillets, skin removed (see page 334)	10 ounces	18 ounces (1 pound 2 ounces)	1¾ pounds
Sea scallops	¼ pound	½ pound	¾ pound
Large shrimp, peeled and deveined	¼ pound	½ pound	¾ pound

1 Mix the tomatoes, wine, fennel, clam juice, tomato paste, garlic, herbes de Provence, and saffron in the slow cooker until the tomato paste dissolves. Cover and cook on high for 4 hours.

2 Add the fish, scallops, and shrimp, submerging them in the sauce. Cover and continue cooking on high for 30 minutes.

TESTERS' NOTES
• This recipe won't win any authenticity awards, but it is a quick way to get an aromatic and satisfying fish stew on the table.
• Bottled clam juice is a less than perfect necessity in the absence of good fish stock in our supermarkets. If you find the latter, by all means use it, or make your own stock (see page 112).

Serve It Up! A proper bouillabaisse is always topped with a rouille (*roo-EE*), a thick sauce. To make your own, crush a garlic clove or two through a garlic press and into a large bowl, then whisk in a couple of large egg yolks as well as some salt, ground black pepper, and a pinch of cayenne. Now begin whisking in olive oil in the thinnest drizzle, whisking all the while, adding up to 1 cup oil (maybe a little more or less depending on the day's humidity and temperature) until you have a thick sauce, the consistency of mayonnaise. Frankly, we often forgo the rouille and grind up a mixture of fresh breadcrumbs, toasted and skinned hazelnuts, and celery leaves, ladling the soup in the bowls over this and topping it with a little Aïoli (page 339).

shellfish, mollusks, and the rest

Without a doubt, we've come to America's favorite seafood. We gulp
down over a billion pounds of shrimp a year, not to mention the legions of crabs, lobsters,
scallops, mussels, clams, and oysters that make it to our tables. And no wonder: shellfish
of all sorts is easy to prepare. Shrimp may well be the boneless, skinless chicken breasts
of the ocean.

Although many sorts of shellfish cost no more than fish fillets, they do pair more easily with bigger flavors. You'll notice that many of these recipes tilt toward the spicy or bold, partly because the naturally sweet flavors of shrimp and the rest can withstand a greater punch than tilapia or even pork. Consider Shrimp with Jalapeños and Thyme (page 360) or Red Curry Mussels (page 381).

However, we've got the same problem here that we've got with fish fillets: almost all these shellfish, mollusks, and their oceanic kin cook in no time. You can't put a pound of shelled shrimp in the slow cooker and head off to work for 8 hours. But just as you did with fish recipes, you can build a fairly complex sauce that will cook the shrimp in a matter of minutes. In fact, the slow cooker sauce will often be better than the one prepared on the stove because it will have had hours to blend and balance, providing a more complex palette for your favorite seafood.

As to buying various sorts of shellfish, keep this in mind: except for exceedingly rare occasions, almost all the shrimp sold in the United States have been frozen at harvest. Those lying on the ice at your supermarket may look fresh, but the chances are that they've been thawed in the back. So do what your fishmonger did: head to the freezer case and buy the more economical bags of frozen shrimp or scallops. You'll save money and end up with meals ahead when you stock up on a freezer sale.

To thaw shrimp, scallops, crab legs, and lobster tails, take out as many as you need, put them in a bowl, and store them in the fridge overnight. If you're really in a rush, thaw them on the counter in a bowl of cold water, changing the water for more cold (never warm!) water every 15 minutes until they're ready to go. *Never* put frozen or even half-frozen shrimp in the slow cooker. The gradual rise in temperature also gives rise to food safety issues. Your stomach will thank you for being careful.

As to mussels and clams, you'll need to buy them from a reputable fish counter. Here's the most important rule: if the place smells like fish (or if it smells of cleaning products, particularly ammonia), turn around and walk out. You buy bivalves live and you cook them live because they're prone to quick deaths and even quicker rot. We'll have some specific tips in the recipes ahead; for now, suffice it to say that buying mussels, clams, or oysters requires a level of trust between you and your supplier.

We've got a lot of shellfish to eat if we want to keep up with our annual quota. Let's get cracking.

shrimp with jalapeños and thyme

EFFORT: **NOT MUCH** • PREP TIME: **10 MINUTES** • COOK TIME: **2 HOURS 20 MINUTES** • KEEPS ON WARM: **2 HOURS THROUGH STEP 1** • SERVES: **3 TO 8**

INGREDIENTS	2- TO 3½-QT	4- TO 5½-QT	6- TO 8-QT
Dry white wine, such as Chardonnay	½ cup	1 cup	1¾ cups
Thinly sliced scallion greens	¼ cup	½ cup	¾ cup
Stemmed, seeded, and minced fresh jalapeño chile	Up to 2 tsp	Up to 1½ tblsp	Up to 2½ tblsp
Olive oil	2 tsp	1½ tblsp	2 tblsp
Ground black pepper	¼ tsp	½ tsp	1 tsp
Shell-on medium shrimp (about 30 per pound), deveined	1½ pounds	2½ pounds	4 pounds
Stemmed fresh thyme leaves	1 tsp	½ tblsp	1 tblsp

1 Mix the wine, scallions, jalapeño, oil, and pepper in the slow cooker. Cover and cook on high for 2 hours, or until bubbling and aromatic.

2 Stir in the shrimp and thyme. Cover and continue cooking on high for 20 minutes, or until the shrimp are pink and firm.

TESTERS' NOTES
• Fresh jalapeño chiles have a slightly sour, citruslike bite, a fine pairing to sweet shrimp.
• If desired, dress up the sauce. Strain it into a medium saucepan, removing the solids, then bring it to a boil over high heat. Cook until reduced by about a third from its original volume, then whisk in up to 3 tablespoons unsalted butter. For an even thicker sauce, use room-temperature butter mashed with an equal amount of flour, whisking this mixture into the sauce by tiny little dribs and drabs over very low heat.

Serve It Up! Since the sauce is fairly spicy, make a cooling side salad of diced cucumber, red bell pepper, and carrots, bound together with plain yogurt, a splash of rice vinegar, a pinch of sugar, and salt.

INGREDIENTS EXPLAINED Shrimp are always sold by size; however, the adjectives used to describe those sizes don't mean much. *Medium, large*, and *jumbo* are mere window-dressing. One store's *large* may be another's *jumbo*. For accuracy, purchase shrimp the way the fishmonger does: by how many make up a pound. About 30 shrimp per pound are medium size; over 40 per pound, fairly small; under 20 per pound, quite large; and under 5 per pound, lobster tails in shrimp drag.

ALL-AMERICAN KNOW-HOW Shrimp are easily overcooked. You're looking for the characteristic change of color to pinkish red, so you have firm but not rubbery meat. There's only one way to tell for sure: bite into one to try it.

Many of these recipes call for shrimp that have been *deveined*—a euphemism for the act of removing the digestive tract, the dark "vein" running along the outside curve of the tail. You devein shrimp by making a shallow cut along that curve and picking out the dark line with the tip of the paring knife. For a way out of this job, buy already deveined shrimp or ask the fishmonger at your market to do it for you.

buttery spicy shrimp

EFFORT: **NOT MUCH** • PREP TIME: **10 MINUTES** • COOK TIME: **2 HOURS 20 MINUTES** • KEEPS ON WARM: **2 HOURS THROUGH STEP 1** • SERVES: **3 TO 8**

INGREDIENTS	2- TO 3½-QT	4- TO 5½-QT	6- TO 8-QT
Unsalted butter	4 tblsp (½ stick)	8 tblsp (1 stick)	12 tblsp (1½ sticks)
Worcestershire sauce	2 tblsp	¼ cup	⅓ cup
Fresh lemon juice	2 tblsp	¼ cup	6 tblsp
Olive oil	1 tblsp	2 tblsp	3 tblsp
Bottled red pepper sauce or hot sauce	½ tblsp	1 tblsp	2 tblsp
Ground black pepper	1 tsp	2 tsp	1 tblsp
Shell-on medium shrimp (about 30 per pound), deveined	1½ pounds	2½ pounds	4 pounds
Minced fresh parsley leaves	1½ tblsp	3 tblsp	¼ cup

1 Mix the butter, Worcestershire sauce, lemon juice, olive oil, hot sauce, and black pepper in the slow cooker. Cover and cook on high for 2 hours.

2 Stir in the shrimp and parsley. Cover and continue cooking on high for 20 minutes, or until the shrimp are pink and firm.

TESTERS' NOTES

• Shell-on shrimp are an excellent choice to get the "Buffalo" treatment. There's lots of opportunity to slurp the sauce off those shells.

• We used Tabasco sauce. But chipotle hot sauce will give the dish a smoky flavor; a habanero sauce, a lethal spike.

shrimp in gingery wine sauce

EFFORT: **NOT MUCH** • PREP TIME: **10 MINUTES** • COOK TIME: **2 HOURS 50 MINUTES** • KEEPS ON WARM: **2 HOURS THROUGH STEP 1** • SERVES: **3 TO 8**

INGREDIENTS	2- TO 3½-QT	4- TO 5½-QT	6- TO 8-QT
Olive oil	¼ cup	½ cup	¾ cup
Dry white wine, such as Pinot Grigio	¼ cup	½ cup	¾ cup
Minced peeled fresh ginger	2 tblsp	¼ cup	6 tblsp
Minced garlic	2 tsp	1½ tblsp	2 tblsp
Fresh lemon wedges	3	6	10
Shell-on medium shrimp (about 30 per pound), deveined	1½ pounds	2½ pounds	4 pounds
Chopped fresh parsley leaves	2 tblsp	¼ cup	½ cup

1 Mix the olive oil, wine, ginger, garlic, and lemon wedges in the slow cooker. Cover and cook on high for 2½ hours, until fragrant and bubbling.

2 Stir in the shrimp and parsley. Cover and continue cooking on high for 20 minutes, or until the shrimp are pink and firm. Have a bowl ready to catch the shells as you suck the sauce off them and then peel them off, dipping the meat back into the sauce from the cooker.

TESTERS' NOTES

• The lemon wedges actually soften and cook in the sauce. They're delicious, especially if minced up on your plate and mixed into some white rice.

• Feel free to substitute small clams or even cockles for the shrimp.

(continued)

INGREDIENTS EXPLAINED These first recipes have been prepared with shell-on shrimp because they make excellent finger fare at the coffee table when a game or a movie is on. That said, you can make these dishes with peeled and deveined shrimp if you intend to serve them as a family meal at the table, where little fingers don't need any more help getting messy.

sweet chile shrimp

EFFORT: **A LOT** • PREP TIME: **30 MINUTES** • COOK TIME: **1 HOUR 50 MINUTES** • KEEPS ON WARM: **2 HOURS THROUGH STEP 3** • SERVES: **3 TO 10**

INGREDIENTS	2- TO 3½-QT	4- TO 5½-QT	6- TO 8-QT
Dried New Mexican chiles, stemmed, seeded, and torn into pieces	1	2	3
Minced whole scallion	2 tblsp	¼ cup	½ cup
Thinly sliced lemongrass (white and pale green parts only; see page 273)	2 tblsp	¼ cup	½ cup
Packed light brown sugar	1½ tblsp	3 tblsp	6 tblsp
Fish sauce (see page 96)	1 tblsp	2 tblsp	¼ cup
Minced peeled fresh ginger	½ tblsp	1 tblsp	2 tblsp
Medium garlic cloves, peeled	2	3	6
Stemmed and seeded serrano chiles, halved lengthwise	½	1	2
Shell-on medium shrimp (about 30 per pound), deveined	1¼ pounds	2½ pounds	5 pounds

1 Bring a small saucepan of water to a boil over high heat. Place the dried chile in a small bowl; cover with boiling water. Soak for 20 minutes, then drain in a colander set over a bowl, catching the soaking water below.

2 Put the soaked chile in a large blender along with the scallion, lemongrass, brown sugar, fish sauce, ginger, garlic, and fresh chile. Add a little of the soaking liquid, no more than a tablespoon or so, then blend until smooth, stopping the machine once or twice to scrape down the inside of the canister. (Add a little more of the soaking liquid, if necessary, to make sure things are blending well.)

3 Scrape the chile puree into the slow cooker. Cover and cook on high for 1½ hours, or until the sauce is bubbling.

4 Stir in the shrimp. Cover and continue cooking on high for 20 minutes, or until the shrimp are pink and firm.

TESTERS' NOTES
• Here's a Malaysian-inspired sauce for shrimp. Of course, you can use shelled shrimp, but eating them won't be as much fun. You can also use larger shrimp, even those coming in at 20 shrimp per pound, but you'll need to increase the cooking time by 5 or 10 minutes.
• The amount of chile-soaking liquid you'll need to create a smooth sauce varies widely. Start out with a little—you can always add more. You want a smooth sauce, not a sticky paste.
• If you want to get fancy, substitute grated palm sugar for the brown sugar for a more mellow, less tannic taste.

Serve It Up! Cook up a pot of short-grain sticky white rice, then ladle the shrimp and sauce over bowlfuls.

black pepper shrimp

EFFORT: **NOT MUCH** • PREP TIME: **10 MINUTES** • COOK TIME: **1 HOUR 50 MINUTES** • KEEPS ON WARM: **NO** • SERVES: **3 TO 8**

INGREDIENTS	2- TO 3½-QT	4- TO 5½-QT	6- TO 8-QT
Unsalted butter, cut into small bits	2 tblsp	4 tblsp (½ stick)	8 tblsp (1 stick)
Packed dark brown sugar	2 tblsp	¼ cup	½ cup
Minced peeled fresh ginger	1 tblsp	2 tblsp	¼ cup
Minced garlic	1 tblsp	2 tblsp	3 tblsp
Oyster sauce (see page 264)	1 tblsp	2 tblsp	3 tblsp
Soy sauce	1 tblsp	2 tblsp	3 tblsp
Coarsely ground black pepper	Up to 2 tsp	Up to 1 tblsp	Up to 2 tblsp
Shell-on medium shrimp (about 30 per pound), deveined	1¼ pounds	2½ pounds	4 pounds
Minced fresh basil leaves	2 tblsp	¼ cup	½ cup

1 Mix the butter, brown sugar, ginger, garlic, oyster sauce, soy sauce, and black pepper in the slow cooker. Cover and cook on high for 1½ hours, or until the butter has melted and begun to form a bubbling sauce.

2 Stir in the shrimp and basil. Cover and continue cooking on high for 20 minutes, or until the shrimp are pink and firm.

TESTERS' NOTES

• This is a slow cooker variation on a common Vietnamese dish, usually made with a burned caramel sauce and plenty of black pepper. The recipe actually calls for *coarsely* ground black pepper, rather than the more standard finely ground sort, so that the pepper doesn't just melt into the sauce. If you've only got finely ground on hand, use about half the stated amount.

• Here's a fine opportunity to substitute small clams or even mussels for the shrimp.

shrimp in asian black bean sauce

EFFORT: **NOT MUCH** • PREP TIME: **10 MINUTES** • COOK TIME: **2 HOURS 20 MINUTES** • KEEPS ON WARM: **2 HOURS THROUGH STEP 1** • SERVES: **3 TO 8**

INGREDIENTS	2- TO 3½-QT	4- TO 5½-QT	6- TO 8-QT
Low-sodium vegetable broth	½ cup	1 cup	1½ cups
Medium whole scallions, thinly sliced	2	3	4
Minced peeled fresh ginger	2 tblsp	¼ cup	7 tblsp
Dry sherry	2 tblsp	¼ cup	7 tblsp
Jarred Asian black bean sauce or chile sauce with preserved black beans (see page 217)	2 tblsp	¼ cup	7 tblsp
Soy sauce	1 tblsp	2 tblsp	3½ tblsp
Toasted sesame oil (see page 196)	1 tsp	2 tsp	1 tblsp
Shell-on medium shrimp (about 30 per pound), deveined	1¼ pounds	2½ pounds	4 pounds

1 Stir the broth, scallions, ginger, sherry, black bean sauce, soy sauce, and sesame oil in the slow cooker. Cover and cook on high for 2 hours, or until bubbling and aromatic.

2 Stir in the shrimp. Cover and continue cooking on high for 20 minutes, or until the shrimp are pink and firm.

(continued)

shrimp creole

EFFORT: **A LOT** · PREP TIME: **30 MINUTES** · COOK TIME: **2 HOURS 20 MINUTES** · KEEPS ON WARM: **2 HOURS THROUGH STEP 3** · SERVES: **2 TO 6**

INGREDIENTS	2- TO 3½-QT	4- TO 5½-QT	6- TO 8-QT
Peanut oil	2 tblsp	3½ tblsp	⅓ cup
Yellow onion, chopped	1 small	1 medium	1 large
Green bell pepper, stemmed, seeded, and chopped	1 small	1 medium	1 large
Medium celery ribs, chopped	1	2	4
Minced garlic	2 tsp	3½ tsp	2 tblsp
All-purpose flour	2 tblsp	5 tblsp	7 tblsp
Low-sodium chicken broth	1 cup	1⅔ cups	2⅔ cups
No-salt-added canned diced tomatoes	1¾ cups	2¾ cups	4½ cups
Mild paprika	1 tsp	2 tsp	1 tblsp
Dried sage	½ tsp	1 tsp	½ tblsp
Dried thyme	½ tsp	1 tsp	½ tblsp
Celery seeds	¼ tsp	½ tsp	¾ tsp
Salt	¼ tsp	½ tsp	¾ tsp
Cayenne (optional)	¼ tsp	½ tsp	¾ tsp
Medium shrimp (about 30 per pound), peeled and deveined	¾ pound	1¼ pounds	2 pounds

1 Put a large saucepan over medium heat for a few minutes, then pour in the oil. Tilt the pan to coat the bottom, then add the onion, bell pepper, and celery. Cook, stirring often, until the vegetables have begun to soften a bit, between 4 and 7 minutes.

2 Add the garlic, stir well over the heat, then sprinkle the flour over everything. Cook, stirring almost constantly, until the flour coating begins to brown, perhaps 5 minutes. Pour in the broth and stir constantly until bubbling and thickened slightly.

3 Scrape the contents of the saucepan into the slow cooker; stir in the tomatoes, paprika, sage, thyme, celery seeds, salt, and cayenne (if using). Cover and cook on high for 2 hours, or until bubbling and aromatic.

4 Stir in the shrimp. Cover and continue cooking on high for 20 minutes, or until the shrimp are pink and firm.

TESTERS' NOTES
• Yes, this dish is a complex mix of flavors—and perhaps even more complex when made with chicken broth, used here in the absence of good fish or shellfish stock (unless you make your own; see pages 112–113).
• Add a splash of Worcestershire sauce with the tomatoes and some chopped parsley leaves with the shrimp if you want to make the flavors even more ornate.
• The most important task here is properly browning the flour coating on the vegetables. Not only do you want to get rid of that raw flour taste, you also want to deepen its flavors to add a toasty note underneath the stew.

SHORTCUTS Omit the paprika, sage, thyme, celery seeds, and salt; instead, use 2½ teaspoons bottled Creole seasoning in a small batch, 4½ teaspoons in a medium batch, or 2½ tablespoons in a large one. Check the bottling and see if the blend includes hot stuff like cayenne. If so, omit the cayenne as well.

shrimp with olives, fennel, and capers

EFFORT: **NOT MUCH** • PREP TIME: **15 MINUTES** • COOK TIME: **2 HOURS 50 MINUTES** • KEEPS ON WARM: **1 HOUR THROUGH STEP 1** • SERVES: **3 TO 8**

INGREDIENTS	2- TO 3½-QT	4- TO 5½-QT	6- TO 8-QT
Trimmed and chopped fennel (see page 211)	½ cup	1 cup (about ½ pound)	1¾ cups
Low-sodium vegetable broth	½ cup	1 cup	1½ cups
Chopped yellow onion	⅓ cup	⅔ cup (about 1 small)	1¼ cups
Chopped celery	⅓ cup	⅔ cup (about 2½ medium ribs)	1¼ cups
Thinly sliced, pitted green olives	¼ cup	½ cup	¾ cup
Drained, rinsed, and minced capers	2 tblsp	3 tblsp	¼ cup
Herbes de Provence (see page 90)	2 tsp	1 tblsp	1½ tblsp
Medium shrimp (about 30 per pound), peeled and deveined	1½ pounds	2½ pounds	4 pounds

1 Stir the fennel, broth, onion, celery, olives, capers, and herbes de Provence in the slow cooker. Cover and cook on high for 2½ hours, or until the vegetables are tender and the sauce is bubbling.

2 Stir in the shrimp. Cover and continue cooking on high for 20 minutes, or until the shrimp are pink and firm.

TESTERS' NOTES
• More the foundation for a stew rather than a sauce, the vegetables here should retain a bit of their fresh crunch to stand up to the sweet shrimp.
• Shrimp are by nature salty. To keep the meal from being doped with sodium, make sure you rinse the capers before mincing them.
• Feel free to substitute small clams or even cockles for the shrimp.

Serve It Up! Rather than just standard garlic bread to dip into the stew, try this: rub thick slices of sourdough bread with quartered peeled garlic cloves and halved plum tomatoes (the tomato juice and pulp will seep into the bread). Toss out the used tomatoes and garlic, then drizzle the bread with olive oil and season it with salt and pepper before broiling on a large baking sheet until lightly browned and crunchy.

cajun shrimp boil

EFFORT: **NOT MUCH** • PREP TIME: **10 MINUTES** • COOK TIME: **4 HOURS 20 MINUTES** • KEEPS ON WARM: **NO** • SERVES: **2 TO 8**

INGREDIENTS	2- TO 3½-QT	4- TO 5½-QT	6- TO 8-QT
Water	About 3 cups	About 5 cups	About 8 cups (2 quarts)
Chopped yellow onion	1 tblsp	2 tblsp	¼ cup
Old Bay Seasoning	1 tblsp	2 tblsp	¼ cup
Medium celery ribs, cut into 2-inch pieces	2	4	8
Garlic cloves, peeled	1	2	3
Small red-skinned potatoes	½ pound	1 pound	2 pounds
Smoked sausage, cut into 1-inch pieces	¼ pound	½ pound	1 pound
Shell-on medium shrimp (about 30 per pound), deveined	¾ pound	1½ pound	3 pounds
4-inch pieces of husked and silked corn on the cob	2	4	8

1 Fill the slow cooker with water until it comes about a quarter of the way up the sides. Stir in the onion, Old Bay Seasoning, celery, and garlic.

2 Slip the potatoes and sausage into the water. Cover and cook on low for 4 hours, or until the potatoes are almost tender and the sausage is cooked through.

3 Stir in the shrimp and corn. Cover, set the heat to high, and cook for 20 minutes, or until the shrimp are pink and firm. Drain the stew into a large colander before dumping everything in a big serving bowl, or use tongs to transfer the shrimp, sausage, corn, and potatoes to a bowl.

TESTERS' NOTES
• There's really no substitute for Old Bay Seasoning, a mix of dry mustard, paprika, cinnamon, bay leaves, and other spices.
• We prefer smoked kielbasa in this boil. However, you can use other smoked sausages, even turkey or chicken sausages. Just do not use breakfast links or any sausage laced with cheese or ingredients not in the spirit of Louisiana.
• The garlic cloves are tender and edible, if strong. Mash and spread them on toast.

coconut curry shrimp

EFFORT: **NOT MUCH** • PREP TIME: **15 MINUTES** • COOK TIME: **2 HOURS 20 MINUTES** • KEEPS ON WARM: **1 HOUR THROUGH STEP 2** • SERVES: **3 TO 8**

INGREDIENTS	2- TO 3½-QT	4- TO 5½-QT	6- TO 8-QT
Coconut milk	1 cup	1½ cups	2⅔ cups
Yellow Thai curry paste (see page 273)	Up to 3 tblsp	Up to ¼ cup	Up to ½ cup
Fish sauce (see page 96)	2 tsp	1 tblsp	2 tblsp
Packed light brown sugar	2 tsp	1 tblsp	2 tblsp
Fresh shiitake mushrooms, stemmed and thinly sliced	3 ounces	6 ounces	9 ounces
Red bell pepper, stemmed, seeded, and chopped	1 medium	2 small	2 medium
Medium whole scallions, thinly sliced	1	2	3

	2 tsp	1 tblsp	2 tblsp
Minced peeled fresh ginger	2 tsp	1 tblsp	2 tblsp
Medium shrimp (about 30 per pound), peeled and deveined	1 pound	1½ pounds	2¾ pounds

1 Whisk the coconut milk, curry paste, fish sauce, and brown sugar in the slow cooker until the brown sugar melts.

2 Stir in the shiitakes, bell pepper, scallions, and ginger. Cover and cook on high for 2 hours, or until bubbling and hot.

3 Stir in the shrimp. Cover and continue cooking on high for 20 minutes, or until the shrimp are pink and firm.

TESTERS' NOTES

• You can use almost any size shrimp for this dish, from monsters at 10 per pound to small shrimp at around 50 per pound. Just don't use so-called baby shrimp or salad shrimp; they'll cook too quickly without absorbing enough flavor.

• Try this with crawfish tail meat instead of shrimp.

• Leave the bell peppers in ½-inch pieces, a little larger than usual, so that they don't soften too quickly.

• Yellow Thai curry paste can be quite fiery. Hang back a bit if you don't yet have the hang of it for your own taste.

Serve It Up! Rather than serving this stew over rice, try it alongside a cooling dish of shredded carrots and cucumbers, tossed with sesame oil, rice vinegar, and a pinch of sugar.

shrimp, artichoke, and barley pilaf

EFFORT: **A LITTLE** • PREP TIME: **20 MINUTES** • COOK TIME: **3 HOURS 20 MINUTES** • KEEPS ON WARM: **NO** • SERVES: **2 TO 6**

INGREDIENTS	2- TO 3½-QT	4- TO 5½-QT	6- TO 8-QT
Low-sodium vegetable broth	2 cups	3 cups	5 cups
Frozen artichoke heart quarters, thawed	1 cup	1½ cups	2½ cups
Pearled barley (see page 24)	⅔ cup	1 cup	1⅔ cups
Chopped yellow onion	½ cup	¾ cup (about 1 small)	1¼ cups
Minced garlic	1¼ tsp	2 tsp	1 tblsp
Minced fresh dill fronds	1¼ tsp	2 tsp	1 tblsp
Finely grated lemon zest	1¼ tsp	2 tsp	1 tblsp
Medium shrimp (about 30 per pound), peeled and deveined	⅔ pound	1 pound	1⅔ pounds
Aged Pecorino-Romano cheese, finely grated	½ ounce (about 2 tblsp)	1½ ounces (about ⅓ cup)	2 ounces (about ½ cup)
Ground black pepper	¼ tsp	½ tsp	1 tsp

1 Stir the broth, artichoke hearts, barley, onion, garlic, dill, and lemon zest in the slow cooker. Cover and cook on high for 3 hours, or until almost all the liquid has been absorbed.

2 Stir in the shrimp, cheese, and pepper. Cover and continue cooking on high for 20 minutes, or until the shrimp are pink and firm.

(continued)

• Rice proves too gummy, so barley makes a better alternative for a slow-cooker pilaf. The barley is also a bit savory, certainly not as sweet, and so better complements the shrimp.

• Frozen artichoke heart quarters are firmer than their jarred kin and thus better able to stand up to long cooking. That said, if you can only find the canned, use them at will.

• You can substitute semi-pearled (or *semi-perlato*) barley and have a bit more whole-grain goodness.

spicy garlic shrimp

EFFORT: **A LITTLE** • PREP TIME: **20 MINUTES** • COOK TIME: **3 HOURS 20 MINUTES** • KEEPS ON WARM: **NO** • SERVES: **3 TO 8**

INGREDIENTS	2- TO 3½-QT	4- TO 5½-QT	6- TO 8-QT
Moderately dry white wine, such as Sauvignon Blanc	⅓ cup	½ cup	¾ cup plus 1 tblsp
Minced peeled fresh ginger	1½ tblsp	2 tblsp	3½ tblsp
Stemmed, seeded, and minced fresh jalapeño chile	4 tsp	2 tblsp	3½ tblsp
Minced garlic	2 tsp	1 tblsp	2 tblsp
Ground cardamom	½ tsp	1 tsp	½ tblsp
Ground coriander	½ tsp	1 tsp	½ tblsp
Ground cumin	½ tsp	1 tsp	½ tblsp
Ground black pepper	½ tsp	1 tsp	½ tblsp
Ground cinnamon	¼ tsp	½ tsp	¾ tsp
Ground turmeric	¼ tsp	½ tsp	¾ tsp
Ground cloves	⅛ tsp	¼ tsp	½ tsp
Yellow onions, thinly sliced into rings	2 small	2 medium	2 large
Unsalted butter, cut into small bits	1½ tblsp	2 tblsp	3½ tblsp
Medium shrimp (about 30 per pound), peeled and deveined	1½ pounds	2½ pounds	4 pounds

1 Puree the wine, ginger, jalapeño, garlic, cardamom, coriander, cumin, pepper, cinnamon, turmeric, and cloves in a large blender, occasionally scraping down the inside of the canister until you get a wet, moderately smooth paste.

2 Scrape the paste into the slow cooker; stir in the onions and butter. Cover and cook on high for 3 hours, or until bubbling and aromatic.

3 Stir in the shrimp. Cover and continue cooking on high for 20 minutes, or until the shrimp are pink and firm.

TESTERS' NOTES

• You can also use ghee, or clarified butter, for this sauce, if you prefer no milk solids in the mix (which give slightly bitter notes to the dish). That said, we liked those notes and so felt it wasn't worth the effort to clarify any butter.

• For a hotter sauce, don't seed the chiles, and add some cayenne to the mix—up to 1 teaspoon for a large slow cooker.

Serve It Up! Although often served over rice, we like this lighter shrimp version of the classic curry over mashed sweet potatoes laced with butter, salt, pepper, and perhaps a little ground cumin for a savory pop.

jerk shrimp and plantains

EFFORT: **A LITTLE** • PREP TIME: **20 MINUTES** • COOK TIME: **3 HOURS 20 MINUTES** • KEEPS ON WARM: **NO** • SERVES: **3 TO 8**

INGREDIENTS	2- TO 3½-QT	4- TO 5½-QT	6- TO 8-QT
Medium whole scallions, thinly sliced	2	3	5
Medium serrano chiles, stemmed and minced	½	1	1½
Red wine vinegar	1½ tblsp	2 tblsp	3½ tblsp
Unsweetened apple juice	1½ tblsp	2 tblsp	3½ tblsp
Honey	2 tsp	1 tblsp	2 tblsp
Minced peeled fresh ginger	1¼ tsp	2 tsp	1 tblsp
Ground coriander	¾ tsp	1 tsp	1¾ tsp
Dried thyme	¾ tsp	1 tsp	1¾ tsp
Minced garlic	½ tsp	1 tsp	2 tsp
Ground allspice	¼ tsp	½ tsp	¾ tsp
Ground cinnamon	¼ tsp	½ tsp	¾ tsp
Grated nutmeg	¼ tsp	½ tsp	¾ tsp
Ground black pepper	¼ tsp	½ tsp	¾ tsp
Ripe medium plantains, peeled and cut into 2-inch pieces	1	2	4
Yellow onion, chopped	1 medium	1 large	1 large plus 1 medium
Medium shrimp (about 30 per pound), peeled and deveined	1½ pounds	2½ pounds	4 pounds

1 Place the scallions, chile, vinegar, apple juice, honey, ginger, coriander, thyme, garlic, allspice, cinnamon, nutmeg, and pepper in a large blender. Cover and blend until a thick paste forms, shutting off the machine occasionally to scrape down the inside of the canister with a rubber spatula.

2 Scrape the paste into the slow cooker. Stir in the plantain and onion. Cover and cook on high for 3 hours, or until the plantain bits are becoming meltingly tender.

3 Stir in the shrimp. Cover and continue cooking on high for 20 minutes, or until the shrimp are pink and firm.

TESTERS' NOTES

• This spice paste is lighter and more aromatic than that used for the Jerk Pork Shoulder (page 186), the better to pair with the shrimp.

• The plantains must be ripe; their skin should be deeply mottled, even black in places.

• Feel free to substitute scrubbed littleneck clams for the shrimp. Because of the clams' shell weight, use 25 more clams than shrimp. Or use a combination of shrimp and clams.

• For a kick in the sauce, substitute applejack brandy for the apple juice.

Serve It Up! Have a **Caribbean Slaw** on the side: Mix a bagged slaw mix with diced mango, pineapple, and cilantro leaves. Dress it with mayonnaise thinned with a little cider vinegar and spiked with a pinch of cayenne, as well as salt and pepper.

shrimp and black-eyed peas in coconut sauce

EFFORT: **A LITTLE** • PREP TIME: **15 MINUTES** • COOK TIME: **2 HOURS 50 MINUTES/5 HOURS 20 MINUTES** • KEEPS ON WARM: **2 HOURS THROUGH STEP 1** • SERVES: **3 TO 8**

INGREDIENTS	2- TO 3½-QT	4- TO 5½-QT	6- TO 8-QT
Drained and rinsed canned black-eyed peas	3½ cups	5½ cups	9 cups
Coconut milk	¾ cup	1¼ cups	2 cups
Ripe tomatoes, chopped	¼ pound	½ pound	¾ pound
Yellow onion, chopped	1 small	1 medium	1 large
Packed light brown sugar	2½ tsp	3½ tsp	2 tblsp
Minced peeled fresh ginger	2½ tsp	3½ tsp	2 tblsp
Ground coriander	1 tsp	2 tsp	1 tblsp
Ground cumin	½ tsp	1 tsp	½ tblsp
Finely grated lemon zest	¼ tsp	¾ tsp	1 tsp
Ground turmeric	¼ tsp	¼ tsp	½ tsp
Medium shrimp (about 30 per pound), peeled and deveined	¾ pound	1¼ pounds	2 pounds
Minced fresh cilantro leaves	¼ cup	⅓ cup	½ cup

1 Stir the black-eyed peas, coconut milk, tomatoes, onion, brown sugar, ginger, coriander, cumin, lemon zest, and turmeric in the slow cooker until the brown sugar dissolves. Cover and cook on high for 2½ hours or on low for 5 hours, or until the sauce is ridiculously aromatic.

2 Stir in the shrimp and cilantro. Cover, set the heat to high, and cook for 20 minutes, or until the shrimp are pink and firm.

TESTERS' NOTES
• This surprising mix of ingredients adds up to a big mélange of flavors. The many herbs enhance the coconut milk and the black-eyed peas give the whole thing a mild earthiness.
• There's no heat here. Feel free to add up to ½ teaspoon cayenne to a large slow cooker if you want some kick. However, increase the ginger by 1 or 2 teaspoons to compensate.

Serve It Up! Season cooked long-grain brown rice with toasted sesame oil, lime juice, and salt for a perky side dish.

lemon butter scallops

EFFORT: **NOT MUCH** • PREP TIME: **10 MINUTES** • COOK TIME: **2 HOURS 30 MINUTES (AT MOST)** • KEEPS ON WARM: **NO** • SERVES: **2 TO 6**

INGREDIENTS	2- TO 3½-QT	4- TO 5½-QT	6- TO 8-QT
Paper-thin, half-moon lemon slices	½ cup	1 cup	2 cups
Unsalted butter	2 tblsp, cut into small bits	4 tblsp (½ stick), cut into small bits	8 tblsp (1 stick), cut into small bits
Slivered peeled garlic	2 tsp	1½ tblsp	3 tblsp
Fresh thyme sprigs	1	2	4

Sea scallops	¾ pound	1½ pounds	3 pounds
Ground black pepper	½ tsp	1 tsp	2 tsp
Salt	¼ tsp	½ tsp	¾ tsp

1 Lay the lemon slices across the bottom of the slow cooker. Top with the butter, garlic, and thyme sprigs. Cover and cook on high for 2 hours, or until the lemon slices have softened considerably.

2 Add the scallops, toss well, and sprinkle with pepper and salt. Cover and continue cooking on high for 20 to 30 minutes, or until the scallops are firm and opaque.

TESTERS' NOTES

• Here's an easy supper from scallops—and economical, too, if you use frozen scallops you've thawed in the fridge for a day or two.

• Make sure you get every drop of the sauce. Even the softened lemon rings are lovely to eat with the scallops.

• We prefer a heavy dose of pepper in buttery sauces. You might want to cut back if you don't want your dinner to sting.

INGREDIENTS EXPLAINED In North America, we eat only the abductor muscle of scallops—that is, the muscle that opens and closes the shell, not the bright roe or other, smaller bits. At the seafood counter, look for dry-packed scallops, those shucked and shipped on ice (or just frozen), each with a slightly pink hue, rather than wet-packed, which have been doped with a whitening agent and preservatives (which can also give the meat a soapy flavor). Sea scallops are quite large, sometimes 2 or 3 ounces each; bay scallops, by contrast, are small, perhaps several to the ounce.

ALL-AMERICAN KNOW-HOW Scallops are done fast—and can also be overcooked in a matter of minutes. You'll need to watch the slow cooker closely, even more so than you do with shrimp. The scallops should be firm to the touch but not cracked, a little resistant but not

"springy." Cut one open to see if it is cooked through. We prefer ours a bit translucent at the center, about 20 minutes for medium sea scallops. If you like yours more done, cook them for 10 minutes longer.

scallops in buttery cream sauce

EFFORT: **A LITTLE** • PREP TIME: **20 MINUTES** • COOK TIME: **2 HOURS 30 MINUTES (AT MOST)** • KEEPS ON WARM: **1 HOUR THROUGH STEP 1** • SERVES: **2 TO 6**

INGREDIENTS	2- TO 3½-QT	4- TO 5½-QT	6- TO 8-QT
Low-sodium vegetable broth	1 cup	1¾ cups	3 cups
Medium celery ribs, chopped	2	3	4
Leeks (white and pale green part only), halved lengthwise, washed to remove internal sand, and thinly sliced	¼ pound (about ½ cup)	½ pound (about 1 cup)	¾ pound (about 1½ cups)
Dry vermouth	½ cup	¾ cup	1½ cups
Unsalted butter	2 tblsp	3½ tblsp	6 tblsp
Finely grated lemon zest	1 tsp	2 tsp	1 tblsp
Salt	½ tsp	1 tsp	½ tblsp
Ground black pepper	½ tsp	1 tsp	½ tblsp
Fresh tarragon sprigs	1	2	3
Sea scallops	1 pound	1¾ pounds	3 pounds
Heavy cream	3 tblsp	⅓ cup	½ cup

(continued)

1 Mix the broth, celery, leeks, vermouth, butter, lemon zest, salt, pepper, and tarragon sprigs in the slow cooker. Cover and cook on high for 2 hours, or until the vegetables have begun to get tender.

2 Add the scallops. Cover and continue cooking on high for 20 to 30 minutes, or until the scallops are firm and opaque.

3 Use tongs or a slotted spoon to remove the scallops from the slow cooker; set them on a large platter and tent with aluminum foil to keep warm.

4 Strain the sauce in the slow cooker through a fine-mesh sieve and into a saucepan. Stir in the cream. Bring to a boil over high heat, stirring occasionally. Boil to reduce until half its original volume, 2 to 5 minutes. Ladle the sauce over the scallops to serve.

TESTERS' NOTES

• In this simplified version of coquilles St. Jacques, you lose all the vegetables, but most of their flavor has dissolved into the sauce.
• Dry vermouth's herbal flavors will offer more punch here, rather than the sugary finish of white wine.
• If you don't have a fine-mesh sieve, line a colander with a coffee filter or cheesecloth. (The point is to catch even the small bits like the lemon zest.)
• Substitute peeled and deveined shrimp at will. Or even thawed frozen lobster tails, which will need 30 to 40 minutes in the slow cooker.

Serve It Up! For an **Herbed Salad** to stand up to this cream sauce: Mix chopped parsley leaves and stemmed thyme leaves with bagged salad greens, then dress it all with a lemon vinaigrette made from two parts oil to one part lemon juice, seasoned with salt and pepper.

scallop and shrimp couscous

EFFORT: **A LITTLE** • PREP TIME: **20 MINUTES** • COOK TIME: **3½ HOURS** • KEEPS ON WARM: **2 HOURS THROUGH STEP 1** • SERVES: **3 TO 8**

INGREDIENTS	2- TO 3½-QT	4- TO 5½-QT	6- TO 8-QT
Low-sodium vegetable broth	1 cup plus 1 tblsp	1⅔ cups	2½ cups
Drained no-salt-added canned diced tomatoes	⅔ cup	1 cup	1½ cups
Minced shallots	2 tblsp	3 tblsp	¼ cup
Minced garlic	1 tsp	½ tblsp	2 tsp
Dried oregano	½ tsp	¾ tsp	1 tsp
Ground cinnamon	Pinch	⅛ tsp	¼ tsp
Saffron	Pinch	Pinch	⅛ tsp
Bay leaf	½	1	1
Sea scallops, cut into quarters, or bay scallops, left whole	⅓ pound	⅔ pound	1 pound
Small shrimp, peeled and deveined (even salad or baby shrimp)	⅓ pound	⅔ pound	1 pound
Quick-cooking couscous	⅔ cup	1 cup	1½ cups

1 Stir the broth, tomatoes, shallots, garlic, oregano, cinnamon, saffron, and bay leaf in the slow cooker. Cover and cook on high for 3 hours, or until simmering and fragrant.

2 Remove the bay leaf. Stir in the scallops and shrimp. Cover and continue cooking on high for 20 minutes.

3 Stir in the couscous. Unplug the cooker and set aside, covered, for 10 minutes, or until almost all of the liquid has been absorbed.

TESTERS' NOTES
• Once again, the absence of good fish stock hampers a perfect dish. Vegetable broth does good service, but fish stock would be better if you can lay your hands on it.
• Quick-cooked couscous will soften and absorb most of the water as it sits. Unfortunately, it can dry the dish out if you leave it for more than the stated time, so be prepared to sit down at the table right away.

INGREDIENTS EXPLAINED Couscous is a North African and Middle Eastern staple, a pasta consisting of tiny balls of semolina wheat. Although traditional couscous is steamed for hours to get it tender, most North American supermarkets stock a parboiled dried product that is a pretty good stand-in. You can also find whole-grain quick-cooking couscous.

scallops and shrimp with coconut, carrots, and lime

EFFORT: **A LITTLE** • PREP TIME: **20 MINUTES** • COOK TIME: **3 HOURS (AT MOST)** • KEEPS ON WARM: **2 HOURS THROUGH STEP 1** • SERVES: **3 TO 8**

INGREDIENTS	2- TO 3½-QT	4- TO 5½-QT	6- TO 8-QT
Coconut milk	2 cups	3 cups	5 cups
Fresh lime juice	3 tblsp	5 tblsp	7 tblsp
Minced peeled fresh ginger	2 tblsp	3 tblsp	⅓ cup
Finely grated lime zest	1 tsp	½ tblsp	2½ tsp
Minced garlic	1 tsp	½ tblsp	2½ tsp
Red pepper flakes	¼ tsp	½ tsp	¾ tsp
Julienned peeled carrots	2 cups	3 cups	5 cups
Thinly sliced whole scallions	¼ cup	6 tblsp	⅔ cup
Sea scallops, cut into quarters, or bay scallops, left whole	¾ pound	1 pound 2 ounces	2 pounds
Medium shrimp (about 30 per pound), peeled and deveined	¾ pound	1 pound 2 ounces	2 pounds
Minced fresh basil leaves	3 tblsp	⅓ cup	½ cup

1 Mix the coconut milk, lime juice, ginger, lime zest, garlic, and red pepper flakes in the slow cooker; stir in the carrots and scallions. Cover and cook on high for 2½ hours, or until bubbling and fragrant.

2 Stir in the scallops and shrimp. Cover and continue cooking on high for 20 to 30 minutes, or until the shrimp are pink and firm. Stir in the basil before serving.

TESTERS' NOTES
• The basil is added after the shellfish has cooked so that it doesn't overpower the dish by leaching too many oils into the sauce.
• There's no salt in many of these shellfish dishes because shrimp, scallops, clams, and oysters leach so much briny water into the sauce as they cook.

Serve It Up! Serve this stew over cooked and drained rice noodles, cellophane noodles, or mung bean noodles.

clams with bacon and cream

EFFORT: **A LITTLE** • PREP TIME: **25 MINUTES** • COOK TIME: **3 HOURS 10 MINUTES (AT MOST)** • KEEPS ON WARM: **2 HOURS THROUGH STEP 2** • SERVES: **2 TO 6**

INGREDIENTS	2- TO 3½-QT	4- TO 5½-QT	6- TO 8-QT
Thin strips of bacon	2	3	5
Low-sodium vegetable broth	½ cup	1 cup	1½ cups
Leeks (white and pale green part only), halved lengthwise, washed to remove sand, and thinly sliced	¼ pound	½ pound	¾ pound
Medium celery ribs, diced	2	3	4
Medium yellow potatoes (such as Yukon Gold), diced	2	3	4
Dry vermouth	¼ cup	½ cup	¾ cup
Dried thyme	½ tsp	1 tsp	½ tblsp
Heavy cream	½ cup	½ cup	¾ cup
Small littleneck, mahogany, or manila clams, cleaned	2 pounds	4 pounds	6 pounds

1 Fry the bacon in a large skillet over medium-high heat until quite crisp, turning occasionally, 4 or 5 minutes. Transfer to a plate, pat dry with paper towels, and crumble into the slow cooker.

2 Stir in the broth, leeks, celery, potatoes, vermouth, and thyme. Cover and cook on high for 2½ hours, or until the sauce is simmering and the potatoes are tender.

3 Pour the cream into a small saucepan and bring to a simmer over medium-high heat.

4 Pour the cream into the slow cooker and stir in the clams, setting them in the sauce hinge side down as much as possible. Cover and continue cooking on high for 30 to 40 minutes, until the clams open.

TESTERS' NOTES

• If the bacon won't crumble into the slow cooker, you didn't fry it enough. Put it back in the skillet and cook until it's dark brown all over, then crumble it in.
• Boiling the cream before adding it to the cooker will keep it from breaking in the sauce.
• Substitute cockles for the clams. They'll need only about 15 minutes to cook on high. (Or you can substitute shell-on, deveined shrimp, and cook for about 20 minutes on high.)

INGREDIENTS EXPLAINED There are many varieties of edible clams:

• Littlenecks are the most common in North America, native to a long stretch of the Atlantic coast. They have gray shells and a pronounced, meaty flavor.
• Mahogany clams have brown shells and are harvested in the deep, cold waters off of Maine and the Canadian Maritimes. Their flavor is similar to littlenecks (if brinier).
• Manila clams, sometimes called Japanese littlenecks, are much smaller and sweeter than either of the previous clams. They're a Pacific specialty; they may well cook more quickly than littlenecks because of their size.

ALL-AMERICAN KNOW-HOW Hard-shelled clams need to be cleaned of surface sand that may adhere to the grooves on the shell and can turn your sauce into a gritty mess. Using a clean, new toothbrush or a soft potato brush, scrub gently but efficiently under running cool water to get the clams clean. Stiff wire brushes can nick the shells, leaving bits of grit in your food.

clams in spicy tomato sauce

EFFORT: **A LITTLE** • PREP TIME: **10 MINUTES** • COOK TIME: **3 HOURS 40 MINUTES (AT MOST)** • KEEPS ON WARM: **3 HOURS THROUGH STEP 1** • SERVES: **2 TO 6**

INGREDIENTS	2- TO 3½-QT	4- TO 5½-QT	6- TO 8-QT
No-salt-added canned diced tomatoes	1 cup	1¾ cups	3½ cups
Chopped yellow onion	2 tblsp	¼ cup	½ cup
Trimmed and chopped fennel bulb (see page 211)	2 tblsp	¼ cup	½ cup
No-salt-added tomato paste	½ tblsp	1 tblsp	2 tblsp
Minced garlic	½ tsp	1 tsp	2 tsp
Fennel seeds	¼ tsp	½ tsp	1 tsp
Red pepper flakes	¼ tsp	½ tsp	1 tsp
Small littleneck, mahogany, or manila clams, cleaned	2 pounds	4 pounds	6 pounds

1 Combine the tomatoes, onion, fennel, tomato paste, garlic, fennel seeds, and red pepper flakes in the slow cooker. Cover and cook on high for 3 hours, or until the vegetables have softened and the sauce is bubbling.

2 Add the clams, then stir so they're coated in the sauce. If possible, arrange most hinge side down. Cover and continue cooking on high for 30 to 40 minutes, until the clams have opened.

TESTERS' NOTES
• Yes, the sauce is spicy. You can still double the red pepper flakes at will.
• If desired, add thawed frozen artichoke quarters with the fennel, up to 1 cup of them for the largest slow cooker.
• For a sweeter sauce, drain the tomatoes, then add ⅓ cup white wine for a small slow cooker, ½ cup for a medium one, and 1 cup for a large slow cooker.

ALL-AMERICAN KNOW-HOW The timings for the clam recipes are a tad dependent on the size of the clams. Manila clams may open in 20 minutes; littlenecks, about 30 minutes. But in all cases, buy small clams for these recipes. Since they won't be sitting in a vigorously simmering sauce, they will open more slowly than on the stovetop, and larger clams will already be tough by the time they finally unhinge.

clams with chickpeas, peppers, and tomatoes

EFFORT: **A LITTLE** • PREP TIME: **15 MINUTES** • COOK TIME: **3 HOURS 40 MINUTES (AT MOST)** • KEEPS ON WARM: **3 HOURS THROUGH STEP 1** • SERVES: **2 TO 6**

INGREDIENTS	2- TO 3½-QT	4- TO 5½-QT	6- TO 8-QT
Drained and rinsed canned chickpeas	¾ cup	1⅔ cups	2½ cups
Grape tomatoes, halved	8	12	18
Dry sherry	½ cup	1 cup	1½ cups
Chopped jarred roasted red pepper (pimiento)	⅓ cup	⅔ cup	1 cup
Chopped yellow onion	3 tblsp	⅓ cup	½ cup
Minced fresh oregano leaves	½ tblsp	1 tblsp	1½ tblsp
Minced garlic	1 tsp	½ tblsp	2 tsp
Mild smoked paprika	1 tsp	½ tblsp	2 tsp
Small littleneck, mahogany, or manila clams, cleaned	2 pounds	4 pounds	6 pounds

(continued)

1 Stir the chickpeas, tomatoes, sherry, red pepper, onion, oregano, garlic, and paprika in the slow cooker. Cover and cook on high for 3 hours, or until the tomatoes have begun to break down into a bubbling sauce.

2 Stir in the clams, positioning most of them hinge side down in the sauce. Cover and continue cooking for 30 to 40 minutes, until clams have opened.

TESTERS' NOTES
• We modeled this dish on some pretty fine tapas we once had in New York City. The bar served two clams per plate; we wanted more.
• Small grape tomatoes will offer a sweeter, less acidic bite than more standard cherry tomatoes.

clams in a buttery tomato sauce

EFFORT: **NOT MUCH** • PREP TIME: **10 MINUTES** • COOK TIME: **3 HOURS 10 MINUTES (AT MOST)** • KEEPS ON WARM: **2 HOURS THROUGH STEP 1** • SERVES: **2 TO 6**

INGREDIENTS	2- TO 3½-QT	4- TO 5½-QT	6- TO 8-QT
Ripe tomatoes, chopped	¾ pound	1½ pounds	2¼ pounds
Unsalted butter	6 tblsp	12 tblsp (1½ sticks)	1¼ cups (2½ sticks)
Fresh lemon juice	2 tblsp	¼ cup	6 tblsp
Minced garlic	2 tsp	1 tblsp	2 tblsp
Finely minced lemon zest	1 tsp	2 tsp	1 tblsp
Ground black pepper	½ tsp	1 tsp	½ tblsp
Small littleneck, mahogany, or manila clams, cleaned	2 pounds	4 pounds	6 pounds
Minced fresh basil leaves	1 tblsp	2 tblsp	¼ cup

1 Stir the tomatoes, butter, lemon juice, garlic, lemon zest, and pepper in a small cooker. Cover and cook on high for 2½ hours, or until the tomatoes have begun to break down into a bubbling sauce.

2 Stir in the clams and basil, arranging as many of the clams hinge side down in the sauce as possible. Cover and continue cooking on high for 30 to 40 minutes, until all the clams open.

TESTERS' NOTES
• There's no point in going halfway with a butter sauce! Just make sure you have plenty of crunchy bread to sop up every drop.
• Clams open and release lots of brine into the sauce, making it quite salty.
• Substitute cleaned cockles for the clams; cook them until opened, only about 20 minutes.
• Substitute half as much stemmed thyme or minced oregano leaves for the basil.
• For heat, add up to 1 teaspoon red pepper flakes with the tomatoes.

INGREDIENTS EXPLAINED Clams are simple but hardy animals. Wild littlenecks can average about 400 years in the ocean; mahogany clams, up to 500 years. Although they don't last as long in the kitchen, they're one of the few live-food items you'll prepare and they need special attention. Buy clams only from a reputable market with a knowledgeable fishmonger. If they come sewn into a bag, ask that it be undone. Don't pay for any that are open and won't close when tapped. Also, don't pay for any with broken shells. Once cooked, toss out any that don't open. They are probably glued shut with muddy slime, something that you wouldn't want in your sauce anyway.

ALL-AMERICAN KNOW-HOW Since clams have to be alive when they're cooked, plan on eating them the same day you buy them. Get a bag of chipped ice from the supermarket for the ride home, then store them in a bowl in the refrigerator for no more than 6 hours. Some advocate immersing clams in cold water with a bit of cornmeal to help them open up and release any grit. Although you can do that, most clams sold today are farmed and don't have gunky bits inside the shell. However, no clam should be immersed in fresh water in the fridge for more than an hour or so because, as saltwater creatures, they will die.

shell-less clams casino

EFFORT: **A LOT** • PREP TIME: **35 MINUTES** • COOK TIME: **2 HOURS** • KEEPS ON WARM: **NO** • SERVES: **3 TO 8**

INGREDIENTS	2- TO 3½-QT	4- TO 5½-QT	6- TO 8-QT
Thinly sliced bacon	4 ounces	6 ounces	10 ounces
Chopped clams, any juices reserved	12 ounces	1½ pounds	2¼ pounds
Panko breadcrumbs	⅔ cup	1 cup	1¾ cups
Chopped yellow onion	½ cup	¾ cup (about 1 small)	1¼ cups
Parmigiano-Reggiano cheese, finely grated	1 ounce (about ¼ cup)	2 ounces (about ½ cup)	3 ounces (about ¾ cup)
Unsalted butter, melted	2 tblsp	3 tblsp	5 tblsp
Minced fresh parsley leaves	4 tsp	2 tblsp	3½ tblsp
Dried oregano	1¼ tsp	2 tsp	1 tblsp
Garlic powder	⅛ tsp	¼ tsp	½ tsp
Hot pepper sauce	⅛ tsp	¼ tsp	½ tsp
Fresh lemon juice	2 tsp	1 tblsp	5 tsp
Ground black pepper	¾ tsp	1 tsp	1¾ tsp
Mild smoked paprika	¼ tsp	½ tsp	¾ tsp

1 Fry the bacon in a large skillet set over medium heat, turning occasionally, until quite brown and crunchy, between 4 and 7 minutes. Transfer the bacon to a plate and blot dry with paper towels. Set the skillet aside to cool for 10 minutes.

2 Wipe up the warm grease in the skillet with a paper towel, then (huzzah!) use that paper towel to grease the inside of the slow cooker canister.

3 Crumble the bacon into a large bowl; stir in the clams, breadcrumbs, onion, cheese, butter, parsley, oregano, garlic powder, and hot sauce. Use just enough of the reserved clam juice to moisten the mixture without soaking it.

4 Spoon and layer the mixture into the slow cooker, gently smoothing it down without compacting it. Sprinkle the top with the lemon juice, pepper, and paprika.

5 Cover and cook on high for 2 hours, until hot at the center and bubbling at the edges. Serve by scooping up spoonfuls onto plates.

TESTERS' NOTES
• Truly a clam casserole, this dish would be welcome on the coffee table come game day.
• Although canned clams are probably the easiest way to get chopped clams, a better choice is to buy freshly shucked clams, available at the fish counter.
• If you don't have enough clam juice to moisten the casserole, use low-sodium vegetable broth.

mussels with white wine and fennel

EFFORT: **NOT MUCH** • PREP TIME: **15 MINUTES** • COOK TIME: **2 HOURS 40 MINUTES** • KEEPS ON WARM: **2 HOURS THROUGH STEP 1** • SERVES: **1 TO 4**

INGREDIENTS	2- TO 3½-QT	4- TO 5½-QT	6- TO 8-QT
Dry white wine, such as Chardonnay	6 tblsp	¾ cup	1½ cups
Low-sodium vegetable broth	¼ cup	½ cup	1 cup
Chopped yellow onion	¼ cup	½ cup	1 cup (about 1 medium)
Trimmed and chopped fennel bulb (see page 211)	¼ cup	½ cup	1 cup
Finely grated orange zest	½ tsp	1 tsp	2 tsp
Minced garlic	½ tsp	1 tsp	2 tsp
Fennel seeds	½ tsp	1 tsp	2 tsp
Stemmed fresh thyme leaves	¼ tsp	½ tsp	1 tsp
Small to medium mussels, cleaned and debearded	1 pound	2 pounds	4 pounds

1 Mix the wine, broth, onion, fennel, orange zest, garlic, fennel seeds, and thyme in the slow cooker. Cover and cook on high for 2 hours, or until the vegetables have begun to get tender.

2 Stir in the mussels. Cover and continue cooking on high for 40 minutes, or until the mussels have opened.

TESTERS' NOTES
• A pot of mussels makes about the best dinner we can imagine. If the insert will come out of your slow cooker, simply lift it up and bring it to the table to set on a trivet.
• Mussels can fill up a slow cooker in no time. The number of servings are thus a tad small—from 1 to 4 people. One pound of mussels, which makes one serving, fills a small slow cooker. However, we gauged these numbers as main-course fare. If you're serving mussels as a first course, the same amounts will yield double the number of servings.
• For the best consistency, chop the onion and fennel into similar size pieces, about ½ inch each, so you can get them together on spoonfuls of the sauce.

INGREDIENTS EXPLAINED Like clams, mussels are a live-food product: they should be cooked the day you buy them. Don't cook any that won't close when tapped and do store them in a clean bowl in the fridge until you're ready to drop them into the cooker.

ALL-AMERICAN KNOW-HOW Mussels need to be scrubbed to get rid of any sandy grit adhering to their shells. Use a potato brush or a clean toothbrush and work under running, cold water. They may also need to be debearded—that is, the hairy filaments that stick out of the shell should be removed. To do so, grasp these filaments and zip them along the shell's seam, pulling them free at the end. Many mussels today are farm-raised so they don't need to be debearded; however, all mussels should be cooked as soon as they are debearded.

mussels with butter and dill

EFFORT: **NOT MUCH** • PREP TIME: **5 MINUTES** • COOK TIME: **2 HOURS 40 MINUTES** • KEEPS ON WARM: **2 HOUR THROUGH STEP 1** • SERVES: **1 TO 4**

INGREDIENTS	2- TO 3½-QT	4- TO 5½-QT	6- TO 8-QT
Moderately dry, fruity white wine, such as Pinot Blanc	½ cup	¾ cup	1½ cups
Unsalted butter, cut into small bits	1½ tblsp	3 tblsp	6 tblsp

Minced shallot	1 tblsp	2 tblsp	¼ cup
Minced garlic	¼ tsp	½ tsp	1 tsp
Bay leaf	1	1	2
Small or medium mussels, cleaned and debearded	1 pound	2 pounds	4 pounds
Chopped fresh dill fronds	1 tblsp	2 tblsp	¼ cup

1 Stir the wine, butter bits, shallot, garlic, and bay leaf into the slow cooker. Cover and cook on high for 2 hours, or until bubbling and hot.

2 Stir in the mussels and dill. Cover and continue cooking for 40 minutes, or until the mussels have opened. Discard the bay leaf before serving.

TESTERS' NOTES
• Because mussels release so much briny liquid into the stew, a slightly sweeter white wine works better than dry vermouth—a less confusing set of flavors to set off the bivalve's natural sweetness.
• Truly mince the shallot, the better to melt into the sauce.

INGREDIENTS EXPLAINED Never eat mussels that don't open. While culinary types debate whether they're safe even if they don't open, they're often full of slimy gunk which is better off in the trash can.

Serve It Up! Although a pot of mussels doesn't need much else to make it dinner, a crunchy **Spinach Salad** on the side is often welcome: Toss baby spinach leaves with thinly sliced strawberries, very thinly sliced red onion, and toasted sliced almonds in a large bowl. Whisk one part red wine vinegar and four parts olive oil in a separate small bowl, season with salt and pepper, and dress the salad, tossing gently.

mussels with beer, chorizo, and chipotles

EFFORT: **NOT MUCH** • PREP TIME: **10 MINUTES** • COOK TIME: **3 HOURS 10 MINUTES** • KEEPS ON WARM: **2 HOURS THROUGH STEP 1** • SERVES: **1 TO 4**

INGREDIENTS	2- TO 3½-QT	4- TO 5½-QT	6- TO 8-QT
Dark beer, such as porter or brown ale	½ cup	¾ cup	1½ cups
Low-sodium vegetable broth	2 tblsp	¼ cup	½ cup
Dried Spanish chorizo, chopped (see page 40)	2 ounces	4 ounces	8 ounces
Chopped yellow onion	2 tblsp	¼ cup	½ cup
Stemmed and minced chipotles in adobo sauce	½ tblsp	1 tblsp	2 tblsp
Minced garlic	½ tsp	1 tsp	2 tsp
Ground cumin	⅛ tsp	¼ tsp	½ tsp
Small or medium mussels, cleaned and debearded	1 pound	2 pounds	4 pounds

1 Stir the beer, broth, chorizo, onion, chipotles, garlic, and cumin in the slow cooker. Cover and cook on high for 2½ hours, or until the sauce is bubbling and aromatic.

2 Stir in the mussels. Cover and continue cooking on high for 40 minutes, or until the mussels have opened.

TESTERS' NOTES
• Dark beer has the right heft and sweetness to stand up to the very deep-tasting ingredients in this simple stew. To keep it from foaming too much, pour the beer slowly down the inside wall of the slow cooker.

(continued)

• For a fresher, less complex taste, use fresh Mexican chorizo, cut into 1-inch sections. Brown it first in a skillet with a little vegetable oil set over medium heat.

mussels with pickled ginger and wasabi

EFFORT: **A LITTLE** • PREP TIME: **10 MINUTES** • COOK TIME: **2 HOURS 40 MINUTES** • KEEPS ON WARM: **NO** • SERVES: **1 TO 4**

INGREDIENTS	2- TO 3½-QT	4- TO 5½-QT	6- TO 8-QT
Low-sodium vegetable broth	¼ cup	½ cup	1 cup
Sake	¼ cup	½ cup	1 cup
Chopped pickled ginger (sushi ginger)	2 tblsp	¼ cup	½ cup
Thinly sliced whole scallions	1 tblsp	2 tblsp	¼ cup
Soy sauce	1 tblsp	2 tblsp	¼ cup
Wasabi paste	Up to 1 tsp	Up to ½ tblsp	Up to 1 tblsp
Small or medium mussels, cleaned and debearded	1 pound	2 pounds	4 pounds

1 Stir the broth, sake, pickled ginger, scallions, soy sauce, and wasabi paste in the slow cooker until the wasabi paste dissolves. Cover and cook on high for 2 hours, until delectably fragrant.

2 Stir in the mussels. Cover and continue cooking on high for 40 minutes, or until the mussels have opened.

TESTERS' NOTES
• This Japanese-inspired concoction is a fresh, summery way to prepare mussels.
• If you can only find wasabi powder in the Asian aisle at your supermarket, make an equivalent amount of paste with water, using the directions on the package.
• Look for pickled ginger in the Asian aisle. Buy it in glass jars so you can tell if it's fresh—no evidence of browning anywhere, no matter if you've got the pink or white type in hand. Don't substitute jarred minced ginger.

INGREDIENTS EXPLAINED Sake is Japanese rice wine. In Japanese, *sake* actually refers to any alcoholic beverage, not just the wine we so identify in English. For cooking, choose a somewhat sweet, fairly straightforward sake, not an aged or overly dry sake.

barbecued mussels

EFFORT: **A LITTLE** • PREP TIME: **15 MINUTES** • COOK TIME: **2 HOURS 40 MINUTES** • KEEPS ON WARM: **4 HOURS THROUGH STEP 1** • SERVES: **1 TO 4**

INGREDIENTS	2- TO 3½-QT	4- TO 5½-QT	6- TO 8-QT
No-salt-added canned crushed tomatoes	¼ cup	½ cup	1 cup
Low-sodium vegetable broth	¼ cup	½ cup	1 cup
Minced celery	2 tblsp	¼ cup	½ cup
Minced yellow onion	2 tblsp	¼ cup	½ cup
Chili powder	½ tblsp	1 tblsp	2 tblsp
Cider vinegar	½ tblsp	1 tblsp	2 tblsp
Worcestershire sauce	1 tsp	½ tblsp	1 tblsp
Mild paprika	1 tsp	½ tblsp	1 tblsp

Honey	1 tsp	½ tblsp	1 tblsp
Dry mustard (see page 392)	½ tsp	1 tsp	2 tsp
Liquid smoke	¼ tsp	½ tsp	1 tsp
Small or medium mussels, scrubbed and debearded	1 pound	2 pounds	4 pounds

1 Stir the tomatoes, broth, celery, onion, chili powder, vinegar, Worcestershire sauce, paprika, honey, mustard, and liquid smoke in the slow cooker. Cover and cook on high for 2 hours, or until the sauce is hot and bubbling.

2 Stir in the mussels. Cover and continue cooking on high for 40 minutes, or until the mussels have opened.

TESTERS' NOTES

• Mince the veggies so they make a sauce, not a stew.
• This one's best if you've cleaned the mussel shells enough that you can slurp the sauce right off them.
• Standard chili powder isn't really that hot. If you want a spicier dish, use a combination of chipotle chile powder and standard chili powder.
• This barbecue sauce is very savory, even a little sour. If you like barbecue sauce that's sweeter, add more honey in step one: 1 tablespoon in a small batch, 2 tablespoons in a medium one, or ¼ cup in a large batch.

Serve It Up! Make a bed for the mussels and their sauce by frying corn kernels and diced zucchini with unsalted butter in a large skillet over medium heat, just until warmed through but still crunchy.

red curry mussels

EFFORT: **NOT MUCH** • PREP TIME: **10 MINUTES** • COOK TIME: **2 HOURS 40 MINUTES** • KEEPS ON WARM: **4 HOURS THROUGH STEP 1** • SERVES: **1 TO 4**

INGREDIENTS	2- TO 3½-QT	4- TO 5½-QT	6- TO 8-QT
Coconut milk (see page 22)	½ cup	1 cup	2 cups
Sweet white wine, such as Spätlese	3 tblsp	⅓ cup	⅔ cup
Minced peeled fresh ginger	1 tblsp	2 tblsp	¼ cup
Red Thai curry paste (see page 331)	Up to 2 tsp	Up to 1½ tblsp	Up to 3 tblsp
Minced garlic	1 tsp	2 tsp	1½ tblsp
Fish sauce (see page 96)	1 tsp	2 tsp	1½ tblsp
Fresh lime juice	1 tsp	2 tsp	1½ tblsp
Honey	1 tsp	2 tsp	1½ tblsp
Small to medium mussels, scrubbed and debearded	1 pound	2 pounds	4 pounds
Minced fresh cilantro leaves	2 tblsp	¼ cup	½ cup

1 Mix the coconut milk, wine, ginger, curry paste, garlic, fish sauce, lime juice, and honey in the slow cooker until the honey dissolves. Cover and cook on high for 2 hours, or until the sauce is fragrant.

2 Stir in the mussels and cilantro. Cover and continue cooking on high for 40 minutes, or until the mussels pop open.

TESTERS' NOTES

• One last mussel stew, and this recipe is the spiciest of the lot.
• A Riesling or a Spätlese will work wonderfully here—and you'll love finishing the rest of the bottle as you relish this tongue-spanking meal.

(continued)

Serve It Up! Cook short-grain rice in coconut milk (instead of water) for a sweet, aromatic side dish.

oyster étouffée

EFFORT: **A LITTLE** • PREP TIME: **15 MINUTES** • COOK TIME: **2 HOURS 20 MINUTES** • KEEPS ON WARM: **NO** • SERVES: **3 TO 6**

INGREDIENTS	2- TO 3½-QT	4- TO 5½-QT	6- TO 8-QT
Yellow onion, chopped	1 small	1 medium	1 large
Medium celery ribs, chopped	1	2	4
Stemmed, seeded, and chopped green bell pepper	¼ cup	½ cup	1 cup (about 1 medium)
Minced garlic	1 tsp	2 tsp	1½ tblsp
Dried thyme	½ tsp	1 tsp	2 tsp
Cayenne	⅛ tsp	¼ tsp	½ tsp
Low-sodium vegetable broth	1¼ cups	2½ cups	5 cups
Dry vermouth	½ cup	1 cup	2 cups
Heavy cream	2 tblsp	¼ cup	½ cup
All-purpose flour	2 tblsp	¼ cup	½ cup
Shucked oysters, with their juices	1 pint	1½ pints	2 pints

1 Stir the onion, celery, bell pepper, garlic, thyme, and cayenne in the slow cooker.

2 Whisk the broth, vermouth, cream, and flour in a bowl until the flour has completely dissolved; pour over the vegetables and spices in the slow cooker. Cover and cook on high for 2 hours, stirring twice, until thickened and bubbling.

3 Stir in the oysters. Cover and continue cooking on high for 20 minutes, or until they are cooked through.

TESTERS' NOTES
• Shucked oysters make a satisfying stew, especially in this Louisiana favorite.
• Feel free to substitute peeled and deveined medium shrimp, crawfish tail meat, or shucked clams.

Serve It Up! You need white rice in the bowls to make a bed for this stew. Sprinkle each serving with chopped parsley leaves.

ALL-AMERICAN KNOW-HOW Shucked oysters are available in pasteurized, refrigerated tins at some fish counters—you can even find cartons of freshly shucked oysters in larger supermarkets. Use these oysters the day you buy them. In all cases, avoid canned unrefrigerated oysters, as they are too strong a taste for this dish.

calamari in sweet-and-sour chile sauce

EFFORT: **A LITTLE** • PREP TIME: **20 MINUTES** • COOK TIME: **2 HOURS** • KEEPS ON WARM: **NO** • SERVES: **3 TO 8**

INGREDIENTS	2- TO 3½-QT	4- TO 5½-QT	6- TO 8-QT
Peanut oil	1 tblsp	1½ tblsp	3 tblsp
Serrano chiles, stemmed and thinly sliced	2	4	8

Medium garlic cloves, slivered	1	2	4
No-salt-added canned crushed tomatoes	⅓ cup	⅔ cup	1⅓ cups
White wine vinegar	⅓ cup	½ cup	1 cup
Low-sodium chicken broth	¼ cup	⅓ cup	⅔ cup
Thinly sliced whole scallions	3 tblsp	⅓ cup	⅔ cup
Sugar	3 tblsp	⅓ cup	⅔ cup
Minced peeled fresh ginger	½ tblsp	1 tblsp	2 tblsp
Frozen calamari rings, thawed	1½ pounds	2½ pounds	4 pounds
Minced fresh basil leaves	1 tblsp	2 tblsp	¼ cup
Minced fresh cilantro leaves	1 tblsp	2 tblsp	¼ cup

1 Set a large skillet over medium heat for a few minutes, then swirl in the oil. Add the chiles and garlic; cook, stirring often, until blistered and even a little browned, about 3 minutes. Scrape the contents of the skillet into the slow cooker.

2 Stir in the tomatoes, vinegar, broth, scallions, sugar, and ginger until the sugar has dissolved. Stir in the calamari rings.

3 Cover and cook on high for 2 hours, or until the sauce is wonderfully perfumed. Stir in the basil and cilantro before serving.

TESTERS' NOTES
• By browning the garlic and chiles, you'll add piquant, slightly bitter notes to the sauce, the better to accent all that vinegar and sugar.
• Make sure you use plain calamari rings, neither breaded nor seasoned.

INGREDIENTS EXPLAINED
Calamari—squid—is available by the bagful in the freezer case, usually near the shrimp. Thaw them inside their bag in a bowl in the fridge for a day or two. Drain in a colander set in the sink before stirring them into the slow cooker.

cioppino

EFFORT: **A LITTLE** • PREP TIME: **25 MINUTES** • COOK TIME: **6 HOURS 45 MINUTES (AT MOST)** • KEEPS ON WARM: **3 HOURS THROUGH STEP 3** • SERVES: **3 TO 8**

INGREDIENTS	2- TO 3½-QT	4- TO 5½-QT	6- TO 8-QT
Olive oil	1½ tblsp	2½ tblsp	¼ cup
Red onion, chopped	1 small	1 medium	1 large
Minced garlic	1 tsp	2 tsp	1 tblsp
No-salt-added canned crushed tomatoes	1⅓ cups	3⅓ cups	5 cups
Drained no-salt-added canned diced tomatoes	⅔ cup	1⅓ cups	2 cups
Low-sodium vegetable broth	½ cup	1 cup	1½ cups
Rosé wine	⅓ cups	⅔ cup	1 cup
Minced fresh basil leaves	2 tblsp	3 tblsp	¼ cup
Minced fresh oregano leaves	2½ tsp	1½ tblsp	2 tblsp
Red pepper flakes	⅛ tsp	¼ tsp	½ tsp
Fennel seeds	¼ tsp	½ tsp	½ tsp
Bay leaf	1	1	2
Medium shrimp (about 30 per pound), peeled and deveined	⅓ pound	⅔ pound	1 pound
Lump crab meat, picked over for shell and cartilage	⅓ pound	⅔ pound	1 pound
Sea scallops, quartered, or bay scallops, left whole	⅓ pound	⅔ pound	1 pound
Frozen calamari rings, thawed	⅓ pound	⅔ pound	1 pound

1 Put a large skillet over low heat for a few minutes, then add the oil. Turn and tilt the skillet to slick the hot surface, then add the onion. Cook, stirring often, until softened and

(continued)

somewhat sweet, between 12 and 17 minutes. If the onion begins to brown at all, reduce the heat even further. Stir in the garlic, cook for 1 minute, then scrape everything into the slow cooker.

2 Stir in the crushed and diced tomatoes, broth, wine, basil, oregano, red pepper flakes, fennel seeds, and bay leaf.

3 Cover and cook on low for 6 hours, or until bubbling and aromatic.

4 Stir in the shrimp, crab meat, scallops, and calamari. Cover, turn the cooker to high, and cook for 35 to 45 minutes, until the shrimp are pink and firm. Discard the bay leaf before serving.

TESTERS' NOTES
• This is a shellfish riot based on the San Francisco stew, sometimes made with ketchup. Sweetening the onion over low heat does the trick much better.
• Most people make cioppino as a soup. We prefer it as a stew, thicker and with less broth. This one calls for a hefty amount of seafood. You can also make some substitutions, like small clams for the scallops, or double up on some seafood, adding twice the amount of shrimp and nixing the calamari rings, for example.

Serve It Up! Make a **Pepper Jelly Vinaigrette** for a tossed green salad: Stir ¼ cup pepper jelly and ¼ cup cider vinegar in a small saucepan over very low heat until the jelly dissolves. Set aside to cool to room temperature, then whisk in ½ cup olive oil and some salt and pepper. Use this as a dressing for a salad of chopped romaine, toasted walnut pieces, and crumbled Gorgonzola or blue cheese. Save any remaining dressing in a tightly sealed jar in the fridge for up to 2 weeks.

crab cake casserole

EFFORT: **NOT MUCH** • PREP TIME: **15 MINUTES** • COOK TIME: **2 HOURS** • KEEPS ON WARM: **NO** • SERVES: **3 TO 8**

INGREDIENTS	2- TO 3½-QT	4- TO 5½-QT	6- TO 8-QT
Fresh breadcrumbs	1 cup	2 cups	3 cups
Large eggs/whites, well beaten in a small bowl	1 whole plus 1 white	3 whole	4 whole plus 1 white
Minced yellow onion	¼ cup	½ cup	¾ cup
Minced celery	¼ cup	½ cup	¾ cup
Minced fresh parsley leaves	2 tblsp	¼ cup	6 tblsp
Sour cream (regular or low-fat)	¼ cup	½ cup	¾ cup
Dijon mustard	½ tblsp	1 tblsp	1½ tblsp
Worcestershire sauce	1 tsp	2 tsp	1 tblsp
Lump crab meat, picked over for shell and cartilage	1 pound	2 pounds	3 pounds
Mild paprika	½ tsp	1 tsp	½ tblsp
Ground black pepper	¼ tsp	½ tsp	¾ tsp

1 Smear unsalted butter around the inside of the crock, either by rubbing it around on a paper towel or simply running the unwrapped stick over all the exposed surfaces.

2 Stir the breadcrumbs, eggs, onion, celery, parsley, sour cream, mustard, and Worcestershire sauce in a large bowl, then pour into the slow cooker and spread into a fairly even but not terribly compact layer. Very gently stir in the crab meat so you preserve its lumpiness. Sprinkle with the paprika and pepper.

3 Cover and cook on high for 2 hours, or until hot and set.

• It's not exactly a fried crab cake, but this casserole mimics those flavors and textures—and like any good crab cake, has more crab than cake.
• There's no call for using jumbo lump crab meat. And although lump crab meat has a slightly less assertive flavor than the more economical backfin, claw, or special crab grades, you can also use those to good success.
• If your market doesn't sell fresh breadcrumbs in the bakery section, buy a loaf of Italian bread, cut it into small pieces, and whirl it in a food processor. One slice will yield between ⅓ and ½ cup fresh breadcrumbs. Store any extra in a sealed plastic bag in the freezer for up to 6 months.

INGREDIENTS EXPLAINED The best crab meat is available in pasteurized cartons or tins in the refrigerator case of the fish section. It is far less fishy than the canned stuff. However, you'll need to make sure it contains no shell or sharp cartilage. Spread it out on a cutting board and gently run your fingers through it to find any offending bits.

crab legs with butter, garlic, and dill

EFFORT: **NOT MUCH** • PREP TIME: **10 MINUTES** • COOK TIME: **1½ HOURS** • KEEPS ON WARM: **NO** • SERVES: **3 TO 9**

INGREDIENTS	2- TO 3½-QT	4- TO 5½-QT	6- TO 8-QT
Frozen king or snow crab legs, thawed	2 pounds	4 pounds	6 pounds
Lemon, cut into ¼-inch-thick wedges	1 small	1 medium	1 large
Minced garlic	1 tsp	2 tsp	1 tblsp
Fresh dill sprigs	2	4	6
Unsalted butter, melted	4 tblsp (½ stick)	8 tblsp (1 stick)	12 tblsp (1½ sticks)

1 Layer the crab legs, lemon wedges, garlic, and dill sprigs in the slow cooker, making as compact a set of layers as you can, snapping the legs to make them fit, but also taking advantage of the slow cooker's curving sides to accommodate shorter pieces of the legs. Drizzle the whole kit and caboodle with melted butter.

2 Cover and cook on high for 1½ hours, or until the crab legs are hot. Use tongs to transfer the legs to a serving platter. Serve with the decadent, herbaceous butter sauce from the crock.

TESTERS' NOTES
• King and snow crab legs make an elegant dinner, especially when piled high on a platter.
• Snapping the legs into sections can be a bit of a chore. Yes, there's the natural break at the joints, but these may not come as clean as you imagine. Use a heavy chef's knife or a sharp cleaver to cut the legs into the requisite pieces for your cooker.

Serve It Up! Although the butter sauce seems a natural, how about some **Spicy Cocktail Sauce**, too? Stir 1 cup ketchup, ¼ cup horseradish, 2 tablespoons lemon juice, 2 tablespoons minced dill fronds, 1 tablespoon Worcestershire sauce, and a few dashes of hot pepper sauce in a bowl.

crab and artichoke dip

EFFORT: **A LOT** • PREP TIME: **40 MINUTES** • COOK TIME: **2½ HOURS** • KEEPS ON WARM: **2 HOURS** • SERVES: **8 AS AN APPETIZER**

INGREDIENTS FOR A 1-QUART, ROUND, HIGH-SIDED BAKING DISH

1 tblsp unsalted butter

2 whole medium scallions, white and green parts, thinly sliced

1 tsp minced garlic

½ cup heavy cream

One 9-ounce package frozen artichoke heart quarters, thawed

12 ounces regular or low-fat cream cheese, at room temperature

¼ cup canned chopped mild green chiles

1 ounce Parmigiano-Reggiano cheese, finely grated (about ¼ cup)

1 tsp dried dill

1 tsp ground black pepper

12 ounces lump crab meat, picked over for shell and cartilage

1 ounce fontina cheese (see page 394), shredded (about ¼ cup)

1 Melt the butter in a large skillet set over medium heat. Add the scallions; cook, stirring often, until they begin to soften, about 2 minutes. Stir in the garlic, cook for a few seconds, then pour in the cream. Bring to a full simmer and continue boiling, stirring often, until reduced to half its original volume. Remove the skillet from the heat.

2 Squeeze the artichoke hearts by handfuls over the sink to remove most of their moisture. Chop and set aside.

3 Beat the cream cheese in a large bowl with an electric mixer at medium speed until soft. Beat in the chopped artichokes, green chiles, Parmigiano-Reggiano, dill, and pepper. Scrape down and remove the beaters.

4 Stir the contents of the skillet into the cream cheese mixture. Stir in the crab. Scrape and spread the mixture into a 1-quart, high-sided baking or soufflé dish. Top with the grated fontina.

5 Set the baking dish in the slow cooker. Cover and cook on high for 2½ hours, or until the fontina has melted and the dip is bubbling.

TESTERS' NOTES

• This luscious dip is baked in a baking dish that will fit inside almost all slow cookers except for the very smallest. The humid environment will keep the dip ridiculously moist.

• If you want some heat in the dip, skip the green chiles and instead add up to ½ teaspoon cayenne with the dill and pepper.

Serve It Up! Although crackers may seem like the best dip vehicle, try celery spears or even broccoli florets. And there's no question that this dip isn't rich enough to make dinner for 4. Just have a vinegary slaw on the side—or make dessert from sliced strawberries, macerated all afternoon in the fridge with a little sugar, balsamic vinegar, and ground black pepper, then spooned over vanilla ice cream.

crab risotto

EFFORT: **A LITTLE** • PREP TIME: **25 MINUTES** • COOK TIME: **1 HOUR 45 MINUTES** • KEEPS ON WARM: **NO** • SERVES: **3 TO 6**

INGREDIENTS	2- TO 3½-QT	4- TO 5½-QT	6- TO 8-QT
Unsalted butter	2½ tblsp	4 tblsp (½ stick)	6 tblsp
Yellow onion, chopped	1 small	1 medium	1 large
Dry white wine, such as Pinot Grigio	½ cup	¾ cup	1 cup plus 2 tblsp
Low-sodium vegetable broth	2⅔ cups	4 cups (1 quart)	6½ cups
Uncooked white Arborio rice	1 cup	1½ cups	2½ cups
Minced fresh tarragon leaves	2 tsp	1 tblsp	1½ tblsp
Lump crab meat, picked over for shell and cartilage	1 pound	1½ pounds	2¼ pounds
Parmigiano-Reggiano cheese, finely grated	½ ounce (about 2 tblsp)	1 ounce (about ¼ cup)	1½ ounces (about 6 tblsp)
Minced fresh parsley leaves	2½ tblsp	¼ cup	6 tblsp
Ground black pepper	½ tsp	¾ tsp	1 tsp

1 Melt the butter in a large skillet placed over low heat. Add the onion and cook, stirring often, until golden and fairly sweet, about 10 minutes.

2 Raise the heat to medium-high and pour in the wine. Stir until it comes to a full simmer, then bubble away until the liquid has reduced to a thick glaze, stirring occasionally, between 3 and 6 minutes. Scrape the contents of the skillet into the slow cooker.

3 Stir in the broth, rice, and tarragon. Cover and cook on high for 45 minutes. Stir well, then cover and continue cooking on high for another 45 minutes, or until almost all the liquid has been absorbed.

4 Very gently stir in the crab, cheese, parsley, and pepper. Cover and continue cooking on high for 15 minutes, or until hot and aromatic. Serve at once.

TESTERS' NOTES

• No, you won't make a perfectly creamy risotto without all that stirring at the stove. But you'll make a pretty fine imitation, one that can stand up on its own for dinner with a green salad on the side. Our serving sizes indicate main-course servings.

• Don't even think about using imitation crab meat; it won't have enough flavor to enhance the rice. However, stir in an equivalent amount of peeled, deveined, and chopped medium shrimp for a more economical meal.

vegetables & side dishes

VEGETABLES ARE THE SLOW COOKER'S FORGOTTEN STEPCHILDREN.
They get short shrift, partly because many are quick-cookers and are best
when they retain a bit of crunch. The slow cooker often deals harshly with
the likes of asparagus and sugar snap peas, morphing their prized textures
into something too similar to their canned kin.

But such abuse doesn't rule out the category. From Mushroom
Sloppy Joes to Spicy Scalloped Potatoes, from some pretty fine collard
greens to Chinese-Style Braised Eggplant, the slow cooker can help prepare a host of vegetable dishes without sacrificing either good taste or
crisp freshness. Plus, we can do all that without a chemical tsunami of
bottled sauces or canned cream-of-somethings.

Let's lay down three general rules for our vegetable recipes. First,
to play to the machine's strength, we'll use plenty of tubers and roots like
potatoes and carrots, or long-cookers like artichokes and cabbage, or

sturdy pantry staples like rice and lentils. Nothing caramelizes onions quite so well as a slow cooker; delicata squash is perfect in a simple braise at low heat. Even sliced asparagus can be a tasty addition to a pilaf. But the cost of cooking those whole spears in a slow cooker may be too high. Why force them into a place they don't fit?

Second, we'll vary our cooking temperatures between high and low—and watch the timings carefully. A chicken stew or beef braise is a forgiving thing—another hour or so is hardly a make-or-break situation. But just a little additional time can render cauliflower florets squishy and broccoli pabulum. Vigilance pays off.

Besides, we figure about two-thirds of these vegetable dishes are things to go alongside a meal off the grill or out of the oven. You're probably not intending to set up a cooker of Candied Sweet Potatoes to make an entire meal of it later on. You're probably around the kitchen while it's cooking, preparing the rest of the meal; so you can pay attention to when the veggies are at their best.

Finally, many of these recipes skew as a tad more traditional: Mac and Cheese as a main course, Kale in a Spicy Tomato Sauce for a side. Since you probably already have a repertoire of main-course classics, we felt free to mix it up a bit in other chapters. Vegetarian main courses and side dishes are a little less well known to most of us. Did you realize you can make some pretty fine plain brown rice in a slow cooker? Or make just about the creamiest mashed potatoes you've ever had? You will now! You can even poach broccoli rabe in olive oil or braise cauliflower florets in browned butter.

Sure enough, life's too short for overcooked sugar snap peas. But it's also exhausting enough to deserve some pretty fine carrots, sweet potatoes, or kale—side dishes for any meal—as well as a host of full-on vegetarian and vegan entrees. So pick a recipe and head to the produce aisle. You'll be surprised at what you can make.

vegetarian main courses

Both of us are omnivores. We often prove the worth of our bicuspids on pork shoulder roasts and braised birds. Nonetheless, we're also pretty partial to vegetables.

But our fondness often doesn't extend to vegetarian fare itself. Back in the day—we're old enough to be talking about the '70s—recipes for the patchouli set seemed to wage war against the produce that comprised them. What came to the table was pretty washed out: brown rice, maybe steamed broccoli, tofu slathered in some sticky, too-sweet sauce. You could make a meal of it. But another? And another?

So we set out to remedy that problem, trying to keep vegetarian meals satisfying, varying them across the wide range of flavors—even developing the umami savoriness often associated with meat. Over the years, we've learned to craft vegetarian and vegan main courses that rely on the full flavor spectrum. To do that, we need to rely heavily on the spice cabinet, maybe even more than in our meatish entrees. We also need to go with vegetable strengths: bright flavors, pronounced sweet notes, bitter undertones.

We start with Pulled Vegetables, Mac and Cheese, and other favorites, before getting to less well-known dishes like a tagine made with loads of roots as well as a potato dish modeled on the flavors of pizza, sure to please even the most finicky eaters.

Just remember: these dishes are slightly less forgiving than the sturdier braises and stews. You'll need to keep an eye on the slow cooker. Be patient and exacting and you, too, will create fabulous vegetarian fare. You might even prove the worth of your own bicuspids without a pork roast in sight.

pulled vegetables

EFFORT: **NOT MUCH** • PREP TIME: **15 MINUTES** • COOK TIME:
4½ HOURS • KEEPS ON WARM: **3 HOURS** • SERVES: **3 TO 8**

INGREDIENTS	2- TO 3½-QT	4- TO 5½-QT	6- TO 8-QT
Savoy cabbage, cored and very thinly shredded	1 pound	1¾ pounds	3 pounds
Yellow potatoes (such as Yukon Gold), shredded	10 ounces	1¼ pounds	2 pounds
Carrots, shredded	3 ounces	6 ounces	10 ounces
Ketchup	½ cup	¾ cup	1½ cups
Cider vinegar	6 tblsp	⅔ cup	1 cup
No-salt-added tomato paste	3 tblsp	⅓ cup	½ cup
Packed dark brown sugar	2 tblsp	3½ tblsp	6 tblsp
Mild paprika	2 tsp	1 tblsp	2 tblsp
Dry mustard (see page 392)	2 tsp	1 tblsp	2 tblsp
Celery seeds	½ tsp	¾ tsp	½ tblsp
Ground black pepper	½ tsp	¾ tsp	½ tblsp

1 Stir the cabbage, potatoes, carrots, ketchup, vinegar, tomato paste, brown sugar, paprika, mustard, celery seeds, and pepper into the slow cooker, until the vegetables are evenly coated in the sauce and spices.

2 Cover and cook on high for 3 hours. Uncover and continue cooking on high for 1½ hours, stirring occasionally, until the vegetables are quite tender and heavily sauced.

TESTERS' NOTES

• Here's the best way to get the great "pulled" barbecue taste without any meat in the mix.
• Cut the savoy cabbage head in half, remove the root stem at the base, and slice it crosswise into thin threads, well smaller than ¼ inch for each cut. Separate those threads from one another before you add them to the slow cooker.
• Grate the potatoes and carrots through the large holes of a box grater or with the grating blade in a food processor.
• If you want a smoky taste, substitute smoked paprika for the mild paprika.

Serve It Up! You'll need lots of toasted buns but little else in terms of condiments. However, there will be some liquid remaining in the cooker when the vegetables are ready. For less sloppy sandwiches, use tongs to lift the pulled vegetables from the crock.

mac and cheese

EFFORT: **A LITTLE** • PREP TIME: **15 MINUTES** • COOK TIME:
1½ HOURS • KEEPS ON WARM: **NO** • SERVES: **3 TO 8**

INGREDIENTS	2- TO 3½-QT	4- TO 5½-QT	6- TO 8-QT
Cheddar cheese, preferably mild, shredded	6 ounces (about 1½ cups)	10 ounces (about 2½ cups)	1 pound (about 4 cups)
Dried whole wheat elbow macaroni	6 ounces	10 ounces	1 pound
All-purpose flour	2 tblsp	3 tblsp	⅓ cup
Milk (regular or low-fat)	1½ cups	2½ cups	4 cups
Dry mustard	½ tsp	¾ tsp	1 tsp
Dried thyme	½ tsp	¾ tsp	1 tsp
Ground black pepper	½ tsp	¾ tsp	1 tsp
Onion powder	⅛ tsp	¼ tsp	½ tsp
Garlic powder	⅛ tsp	⅛ tsp	¼ tsp

(continued)

1 Smear a bit of unsalted butter around the inside of the slow cooker.

2 Mix the cheese, pasta, and flour in a bowl until the cheese and pasta are well coated in flour. Pour into the slow cooker.

3 Whisk the milk, mustard, thyme, pepper, onion powder, and garlic powder in that same bowl until the mustard has dissolved into the milk. Pour over the macaroni mixture.

4 Cover and cook on high for 45 minutes, stir well, and continue cooking on high for an additional 45 minutes, or until the cheese has fully melted and the top has firmed up. Scoop it out by the spoonful.

TESTERS' NOTES

• Mac and cheese from a slow cooker is so easy: the gentle heat allows you to make the classic casserole without having to first stir a milk-and-flour sauce over the heat.

• Substitute shredded Swiss cheese, a firm mozzarella, or Monterey Jack for the Cheddar—or use a combo of cheeses, such as half Cheddar and half Swiss.

• We prefer the slightly firmer texture of whole wheat pasta; the standard stuff gets too gummy.

Serve It Up! With this comfort-food classic, try this **Zesty Fruit-Stocked Salad**: Mix halved seedless red grapes, drained canned mandarin orange sections, and some walnuts with a bag of salad greens, then dress it with an orange vinaigrette made from three parts orange juice, two parts olive oil, one part white wine vinegar, and one part honey. Season with salt just before serving.

INGREDIENTS EXPLAINED Dry mustard, sometimes called powdered mustard, is made from finely ground mustard seeds—usually the spicy yellow seeds, although brown seeds may be in the mix. Some recipes claim you can substitute jarred (or prepared) mustard for dry—but not here or in any recipe that includes a healthy dose of dairy without some precooking. Jarred mustard often has vinegar or lemon juice in the mix and will curdle the milk, especially over the long duration in a slow cooker.

mac and brie with apples and peas

EFFORT: **A LITTLE** • PREP TIME: **15 MINUTES** • COOK TIME: **1½ HOURS** • KEEPS ON WARM: **NO** • SERVES: **3 TO 8**

INGREDIENTS	2- TO 3½-QT	4- TO 5½-QT	6- TO 8-QT
Brie cheese, rind removed, diced	6 ounces	10 ounces	1 pound
Dried ziti or fusilli pasta	6 ounces	10 ounces	1 pound
Chopped dried apples	½ cup	¾ cup	1¼ cups
Green peas, thawed frozen or shelled fresh	½ cup	¾ cup	1¼ cups
All-purpose flour	2 tblsp	3 tblsp	⅓ cup
Milk (whole or low-fat)	1¼ cups	2 cups	3 cups
Evaporated milk (regular or low-fat)	½ cup	1 cup	1¾ cups
Dried thyme	½ tsp	¾ tsp	1¼ tsp
Mild paprika	½ tsp	¾ tsp	1¼ tsp
Salt	½ tsp	¾ tsp	1 tsp
Ground black pepper	½ tsp	¾ tsp	1 tsp

1 Generously grease the inside of the slow cooker crock with unsalted butter.

2 Whisk the Brie, pasta, apples, peas, and flour in a large bowl until the ingredients are evenly coated in flour. Dump and scrape all this into the slow cooker, spreading it out into a fairly even layer.

3 Whisk the milk, evaporated milk, thyme, paprika, salt, and pepper in the same bowl; pour over the pasta mixture.

4 Cover and cook on high for 45 minutes, stir well, and continue cooking on high for 45 more minutes, or until the cheese has melted, the pasta is tender, and the sauce is creamy.

TESTERS' NOTES
• Why stand on tradition when you can pair Brie with apples and turn it into an elegant casserole even the kids might like?
• Check the Brie at the supermarket before you buy it. You don't want a very ripe piece—one that's running out from the rind. There should definitely be no ammonia smell (a sign the cheese is beyond its prime). Look for a firm, co-herent slice in the cheese case.
• We skipped the whole wheat pasta here because we wanted a cleaner set of flavors to let the Brie and apples shine through—taste over texture, in other words. But if you want to use whole wheat pasta, by all means do so.
• It's imperative that you stir the casserole halfway through its cooking. Doing so will reincorporate the milk with the cheese for a better texture and appearance in the final dish.

INGREDIENTS EXPLAINED Brie is a soft, somewhat runny cow's milk cheese with a thick white rind. Although made in wheels, it is often sold in slices. That said, a wheel may be the freshest choice—and you can freeze the remainder for another use for up to 3 months.

broccoli and cheese casserole

EFFORT: **NOT MUCH** • PREP TIME: **15 MINUTES** • COOK TIME: **2 HOURS/4 HOURS** • KEEPS ON WARM: **1 HOUR** • SERVES: **4 TO 10**

INGREDIENTS	2- TO 3½-QT	4- TO 5½-QT	6- TO 8-QT
Broccoli, cut into small bits	3 cups	5 cups	8 cups
Semi-soft fontina cheese, shredded	3 ounces (about ¾ cup)	4 ounces (about 1 cup)	6 ounces (about 1½ cups)
Low-sodium vegetable broth	⅔ cup	1 cup	1⅔ cups
Milk	⅔ cup	1 cup	1⅔ cups
All-purpose flour	¼ cup	⅓ cup	½ cup plus 1 tblsp
Dry mustard (see page 392)	¼ tsp	½ tsp	¾ tsp
Ground black pepper	¼ tsp	½ tsp	¾ tsp
Parmigiano-Reggiano cheese, finely grated	1 ounce (about ¼ cup)	2 ounces (about ½ cup)	3 ounces (about ¾ cup)

1 Use a little unsalted butter on a paper towel to grease the inside of the slow cooker. Gently mix the broccoli and fontina right in the crock to keep as much of the butter on the sides and bottom as possible.

2 Whisk the broth, milk, flour, mustard, and pepper in a bowl until the flour and mustard have dissolved. Pour over the broccoli and cheese. Top with an even layer of the Parmigiano-Reggiano.

3 Cover and cook on high for 2 hours or on low for 4 hours, or until the broccoli is tender

(continued)

and even beginning to brown, and the cheese sauce is bubbling a bit. Serve by big spoonfuls.

TESTERS' NOTES
• You can even use the tougher, thicker broccoli stems for this casserole, provided you cut them into small bits, no more than ¼-inch-thick rings or ½-inch cubes.
• Add up to 2 teaspoons minced garlic, 2 teaspoons minced chives, or 1 teaspoon red pepper flakes for various sorts of kick with the broccoli and fontina.

INGREDIENTS EXPLAINED Fontina (*fon-TEE-nah*) is an Italian cow's milk cheese prized for its moderately strong flavor. It can range from a somewhat pungent, sour, creamy semi-soft (or young) fontina (the best for melting and the choice here) to a firm, aged, musky, grating cheese. All that said, Danish fontina is the most common form found in the United States; it has a red wax coating and is milder than Italian fontina, so it might be a better choice if there will be kids at the table who might turn up their noses at the stinkier stuff.

ALL-AMERICAN KNOW-HOW Fontina can be gooey even to shred. For the easiest way to work with it, freeze it for up to 24 hours, then grate through the large holes of a box grater.

vegetable curry

EFFORT: **A LITTLE** • PREP TIME: **25 MINUTES** • COOK TIME: **8 HOURS** • KEEPS ON WARM: **2 HOURS THROUGH STEP 3** • SERVES: **4 TO 10**

INGREDIENTS	2- TO 3½-QT	4- TO 5½-QT	6- TO 8-QT
Unsalted butter	1½ tblsp	2½ tblsp	4 tblsp (½ stick)
Chopped yellow onion	⅓ cup	½ cup	¾ cup (about 1 small)
Minced peeled fresh ginger	½ tblsp	2½ tsp	1 tblsp
Minced garlic	1 tsp	½ tblsp	2 tsp
Curry powder	1 tblsp	1½ tblsp	2 tblsp
Salt	½ tsp	¾ tsp	1 tsp
Cauliflower, stemmed and cut into florets	6 ounces	¾ pound	1¼ pounds
Eggplant, diced	6 ounces	¾ pound	1¼ pounds
Zucchini, diced	6 ounces	¾ pound	1¼ pounds
Red bell peppers, stemmed, seeded, and chopped	1 small	1 medium	2 medium
Plain yogurt (regular or low-fat)	¼ cup	⅓ cup	½ cup
Fresh lime juice	1 tblsp	1½ tblsp	2 tblsp
No-salt-added tomato paste	1½ tblsp	2½ tblsp	¼ cup

1 Melt the butter in a large skillet set over medium heat. Add the onion and cook, stirring often, until translucent but golden, between 4 and 7 minutes, depending on the size of the batch. Dump in the ginger and garlic; stir until aromatic, about 1 minute. Stir in the curry powder and salt.

2 Scrape the contents of the skillet into the slow cooker. Add the cauliflower florets, eggplant, zucchini, bell pepper, yogurt, and lime juice. Stir well, until all the veggies are coated in the sauce.

3 Cover and cook on low for 8 hours, or until the vegetables are tender, even a little soft.

4 Stir in the tomato paste, cover, and let stand for 10 minutes to blend the flavors.

TESTERS' NOTES
• There's not much liquid added to this main course mélange; you don't want a soup or stew. Rather, this mix, moistened only with the yogurt, will slowly give up its essential moisture (and flavors) to create the sauce.
• Stirring in the tomato paste will also help bring the sauce back together at the end of cooking.

- This curry is not at all spicy and so is fit for both kids and grown-ups. If you want to knock its heat up, add a little cayenne—or pass bottled sambal oelek at the table.

ALL-AMERICAN KNOW-HOW Consider making your own **Aromatic Curry Powder:** Mix 2 tablespoons ground coriander, 1 tablespoon ground cinnamon, ½ tablespoon turmeric, ½ tablespoon ground cumin, ½ teaspoon ground cloves, and ½ teaspoon ground cardamom. Save what you don't use in a small glass bottle, sealed, in the spice drawer or pantry for up to 4 months.

root vegetable tagine with pistachios and dried cherries

EFFORT: **A LITTLE** • PREP TIME: **25 MINUTES** • COOK TIME: **8 HOURS** • KEEPS ON WARM: **2 HOURS** • SERVES: **3 TO 10**

INGREDIENTS	2- TO 3½-QT	4- TO 5½-QT	6- TO 8-QT
Parsnips, peeled and cut into ½-inch-thick slices	½ pound	1 pound	1½ pounds
Rutabaga, peeled and cubed	6 ounces	¾ pound	1 pound 6 ounces
Carrots, cut into ½-inch-thick slices	6 ounces	¾ pound	1 pound 6 ounces
Potatoes, peeled and cut into ½-inch cubes	5 ounces	10 ounces	1¼ pounds
Yellow onion, chopped	1 small	1 medium	1 large
Dried sweet cherries	6 tblsp	¾ cup	1¼ cups
Shelled unsalted pistachios	¼ cup	½ cup	¾ cup plus 2 tblsp
Minced peeled fresh ginger	Up to 1½ tblsp	Up to 3 tblsp	Up to ¼ cup
Ground cinnamon	½ tsp	1 tsp	1¾ tsp
Ground cumin	½ tsp	1 tsp	1¾ tsp
Ground coriander	¼ tsp	½ tsp	1 tsp
Salt	¼ tsp	½ tsp	¾ tsp
Cayenne	Up to ¼ tsp	Up to ½ tsp	Up to ¾ tsp
Low-sodium vegetable broth	1¼ cups	2½ cups	3 cups

1 Toss the parsnips, rutabaga, carrots, potatoes, onions, cherries, pistachios, ginger, cinnamon, cumin, coriander, salt, and cayenne in the slow cooker until the spices and vegetables are evenly distributed throughout. Pour the broth over the top.

2 Cover and cook on low for 8 hours, or until the vegetables are spoon-tender.

TESTERS' NOTES
- The big chore here is chopping all those vegetables. Perhaps there are some teenagers at home. What else did you have kids for? If you missed this golden opportunity for kitchen help, look for the vegetables peeled, seeded, and chopped in the produce section's refrigerator case.
- For a slightly better texture—and definitely more work—chop both the dried cherries and the pistachios so they blend more evenly throughout.

Serve It Up! Although we often advocate for brown rice because of its better nutritional values, medium-grain white rice would be the best thing for this aromatic braise.

vegetable pot pie

EFFORT: **A LOT** • PREP TIME: **30 MINUTES** • COOK TIME: **5 HOURS 20 MINUTES** • KEEPS ON WARM: **2 HOURS THROUGH STEP 3** • SERVES: **3 TO 10**

INGREDIENTS	2- TO 3½-QT	4- TO 5½-QT	6- TO 8-QT
Fennel bulbs, trimmed and chopped (see page 211)	¾ pound (about 2 cups)	1¼ pounds (about 3 cups)	2 pounds (about 5 cups)
Carrots, cut into ½-inch-thick rounds	10 ounces (about 2 cups)	1 pound (about 3 cups)	1 pound 10 ounces (about 5 cups)
Yellow potatoes (such as Yukon Gold), peeled and cut into ½-inch cubes	10 ounces (about 2 cups)	1 pound (about 3 cups)	1 pound 10 ounces (about 5 cups)
Yellow onion, chopped	1 small	1 medium	1 large
Medium celery ribs, thinly sliced	2	3	5
Dried dill	1 tsp	½ tblsp	1 tblsp
Dried thyme	1 tsp	½ tblsp	1 tblsp
Salt	½ tsp	¾ tsp	1 tsp
Ground black pepper	½ tsp	¾ tsp	1 tsp
Evaporated milk	1 cup	1½ cups	2½ cups
Dry white wine, such as Chardonnay	½ cup	¾ cup	1¼ cups
All-purpose flour	¼ cup	6 tblsp	⅔ cup
Green peas, thawed frozen or shelled fresh	½ cup	¾ cup	1¼ cups
4-inch frozen puff pastry squares, thawed	3	6	10

1 Mix the fennel, carrots, potatoes, onion, celery, dill, thyme, salt, and pepper in the slow cooker.

2 Whisk the evaporated milk, wine, and flour in a big bowl until the flour dissolves; pour over the vegetables.

3 Cover and cook on low for 5 hours, or until the potatoes are tender.

4 Position the rack in the center of the oven; heat the oven to 400°F. While the oven heats, stir the peas into the stew.

5 Lay the pastry squares on a large, rimmed baking sheet. Bake about 12 minutes, until browned and puffed. Cool on the baking sheet for 5 minutes; then ladle the stew into bowls, topping each with a puff pastry square.

TESTERS' NOTES

• An aromatic but simple stew morphs into a pot pie with those baked puff pastry squares in the bowls. Is that cheating? A bit. But the slow cooker would never brown them properly.

• Make sure the flour has truly dissolved in the milk and wine. There can be dry pockets lurking at the bottom of the bowl—use a whisk, not a wooden spoon. Stir the stew once or twice as it cooks to make sure no flour can burn—not a necessary step at all, just a safeguard if your machine runs a bit hot.

vegetable stew
with cheddar dumplings

EFFORT: **A LOT** • PREP TIME: **25 MINUTES** • COOK TIME: **6 HOURS** •
KEEPS ON WARM: **2 HOURS THROUGH STEP 2** • SERVES: **3 TO 8**

INGREDIENTS	2- TO 3½-QT	4- TO 5½-QT	6- TO 8-QT
FOR THE VEGETABLE STEW			
No-salt-added canned diced tomatoes	1¾ cups	2⅓ cups	4 cups
Cauliflower, trimmed and cut into small florets	¾ pound (about 1½ cups)	1¼ pounds (about 2½ cups)	2 pounds (about 3¾ cups)
Zucchini, diced	6 ounces (about 1½ cups)	¾ pound (about 2½ cups)	1¼ pounds (about 3¾ cups)
Green beans, chopped	¼ pound (about 1 cup)	6 ounces (about 1½ cups)	1 pound (about 3¼ cups)
Yellow onion, chopped	1 small	1 medium	1 large
Green peas, thawed frozen or shelled fresh	½ cup	¾ cup	1¼ cups
Low-sodium vegetable broth	½ cup	⅔ cup	1 cup plus 2 tblsp
Dried basil	2 tsp	1 tblsp	1½ tblsp
Dried marjoram	1 tsp	½ tblsp	2 tsp
Salt	¼ tsp	½ tsp	¾ tsp

	2- TO 3½-QT	4- TO 5½-QT	6- TO 8-QT
FOR THE CHEDDAR DUMPLINGS			
All-purpose flour	1 cup	1⅓ cups	2¼ cups
Baking powder	½ tsp	¾ tsp	1 tsp
Dry mustard (see page 392)	½ tsp	¾ tsp	1 tsp
Salt	¼ tsp	½ tsp	¾ tsp
Cold unsalted butter, cut into little bits	2 tblsp	3 tblsp	4½ tblsp
Cheddar cheese, preferably mild, shredded	1 ounce (about ¼ cup)	1½ ounces (about ⅓ cup)	2 ounces (about ½ cup)
Milk	⅓ cup	½ cup	¾ cup

1 Combine the tomatoes, cauliflower, zucchini, green beans, onion, peas, broth, basil, marjoram, and salt in the slow cooker.

2 Cover and cook on low for 5 hours, or until the stew is beginning to meld with lots of sauce around the vegetables.

3 Whisk the flour, baking powder, mustard, and salt in a large bowl. Cut in the butter with a pastry cutter or a fork, working the dough repeatedly through the tines until the mixture resembles coarse but dry sand.

4 Stir in the cheese and milk until a wet dough forms. Drop by rounded tablespoons all over the top of the stew.

5 Cover and cook on high for 1 hour, or until the dumplings are set and the sauce is bubbling around them.

TESTERS' NOTES
• The butter needs to be very cold, right out of the fridge, so that it can be cut into the dry ingredients without squishing or (heaven forfend!) liquefying.

(continued)

- Whisk the dry ingredients together as soon as the stew starts bubbling, then cut in the butter and add the wet ingredients just before you're ready to add the dumplings to the batch.
- Drop the dumplings into the stew so they're about half submerged in the liquid. They'll turn tender as the stew bubbles.
- There's no need for expensive aged white Cheddar here. Standard shredded American Cheddar works better. Or substitute Colby, if you like.

mushroom sloppy joes

EFFORT: **A LITTLE** • PREP TIME: **25 MINUTES** • COOK TIME: **8 HOURS** • KEEPS ON WARM: **2 HOURS** • SERVES: **4 TO 10 AS SANDWICHES**

INGREDIENTS	2- TO 3½-QT	4- TO 5½-QT	6- TO 8-QT
Cremini or brown button mushrooms, thinly sliced	13 ounces (about 4 cups)	1 pound 2 ounces (about 6 cups)	2 pounds (about 10 cups)
Fresh portobello mushroom caps, diced	7 ounces (about 2 cups)	10½ ounces (about 3 cups)	1 pound (about 5 cups)
Drained and rinsed canned kidney beans	1 cup	1½ cups	2½ cups
No-salt-added canned crushed tomatoes	¾ cup	1¼ cups	2 cups
Minced yellow onion	¾ cup	1 cup plus 2 tblsp	2 cups
Minced celery	½ cup	¾ cup	1¼ cups
Minced carrots	½ cup	¾ cup	1¼ cups
No-salt-added tomato paste	¼ cup	6 tblsp	⅔ cup
Packed dark brown sugar	2 tblsp	3 tblsp	⅓ cup
Chili powder	1 tblsp	1½ tblsp	2½ tblsp
Dry mustard (see page 392)	1 tsp	½ tblsp	2½ tsp
Salt	½ tsp	¾ tsp	1¼ tsp
Ground black pepper	½ tsp	¾ tsp	1 tsp

1 Working in batches as necessary to avoid crowding, put the cremini and portobello mushrooms in a large food processor and pulse, scraping down the inside of the container occasionally, until finely ground but not a paste. Scrape into the slow cooker.

2 Process the beans in the food processor as well, grinding until just shy of a paste. Scrape into the slow cooker as well.

3 Stir in the tomatoes, onion, celery, carrots, tomato paste, brown sugar, chili powder, mustard, salt, and pepper until the tomato paste has dissolved and the entire mixture looks pretty uniform.

4 Cover and cook on low for 7 hours. Uncover and continue cooking on low for 1 more hour, stirring occasionally, until thickened.

TESTERS' NOTES
- You need a food processor to make this vegetarian reinterpretation of the classic American sandwich filling. Otherwise, you'd have to mince every single mushroom to a fine grind and you'll have dinner on the table sometime next week.
- Process the mushrooms in batches; if you jam too many mushrooms into the food processor at once, some will turn to mush before others are ground.
- Grinding the beans allows them to become the thickening agent.

Serve It Up! Serve this vegetarian main course in whole wheat pita pockets with chopped iceberg lettuce and a sauce made from equal parts sour cream, yogurt, and tahini (sesame paste).

ALL-AMERICAN KNOW-HOW So long as carrots are washed to remove dirt and grime, you don't need to peel them for long braises. That exterior "skin" is really just the carrot itself, drying out after contact with the air. It's none too savory in fresh salads and slaws, but it'll soften just like the rest of the vegetable in a long-cooked dish.

barbecued portobello mushrooms

EFFORT: **A LITTLE** • PREP TIME: **15 MINUTES** • COOK TIME: **5½ HOURS** • KEEPS ON WARM: **1 HOUR** • SERVES: **2 TO 6**

INGREDIENTS	2- TO 3½-QT	4- TO 5½-QT	6- TO 8-QT
Fresh portobello mushrooms caps, sliced into ½-inch-thick strips	1 pound	1¾ pounds	3 pounds
Maple syrup	3 tblsp	⅓ cup	½ cup
Soy sauce	2 tblsp	3½ tblsp	⅓ cup
Minced peeled fresh ginger	1 tblsp	1½ tblsp	2½ tblsp
Pomegranate molasses	1 tblsp	1½ tblsp	2½ tblsp
Dijon mustard	2 tsp	1 tblsp	1½ tblsp
Minced garlic	2 tsp	1 tblsp	1½ tblsp
Water	2 tsp	1 tblsp	5 tsp
Cornstarch	1 tsp	2 tsp	1 tblsp

1 Arrange the mushrooms in the cooker so they make as compact and even a layer as possible.

2 Whisk the maple syrup, soy sauce, ginger, molasses, mustard, and garlic in a bowl until fairly smooth. Pour over the mushrooms, toss gently to coat, and rearrange into a compact layer.

3 Cover and cook on low for 5 hours, or until the mushrooms have become tender and are drenched in the sauce.

4 Turn the cooker to high. Whisk the water and cornstarch in a small bowl. Pour over the mushroom mixture and toss again.

5 Cover and cook on high for 30 minutes, or until the sauce has begun to thicken around the mushrooms.

TESTERS' NOTES
• Although portobello caps are often sold sliced, those strips can be unfortunately dry—in fact, darn near tough. Better to slice your own.
• Substitute sliced cremini mushrooms for a less firm texture but a much easier dish. (Cremini mushrooms are just baby portobellos anyway!)
• There's a lot of garlic here. If you're phobic, reduce the amount by half.

Serve It Up! Consider these the vegetarian alternative for fajitas or tacos—and serve them the same way: with diced avocado or even guacamole, grilled red onion rings, sliced roasted red peppers, and pico de gallo in soft flour tortillas or crisp corn shells.

INGREDIENTS EXPLAINED Pomegranate molasses is a Middle Eastern condiment, a thickened paste made from boiled-down pomegranate juice. It's a sour spark and so makes a tasty addition to barbecue sauces. Look for it near the couscous and other Middle Eastern foods in your supermarket.

creamy tofu and mushroom stroganoff

EFFORT: **A LITTLE** • PREP TIME: **20 MINUTES** • COOK TIME: **5 HOURS** • KEEPS ON WARM: **2 HOURS THROUGH STEP 2** • SERVES: **2 TO 6**

INGREDIENTS	2- TO 3½-QT	4- TO 5½-QT	6- TO 8-QT
Low-sodium vegetable broth	½ cup	1 cup	1½ cups
Soft silken tofu	6 tblsp (about 4 ounces)	¾ cup (about 8 ounces)	1¼ cups (about 12 ounces)
Cremini or brown button mushrooms, thinly sliced	10 ounces (about 3 cups)	1 pound 3 ounces (about 6 cups)	1¾ pounds (about 9 cups)
Chopped yellow onion	6 tblsp	¾ cup (about 1 small)	1¼ cups
Minced garlic	1 tsp	2 tsp	1 tblsp
Dried thyme	1 tsp	2 tsp	1 tblsp
Mild paprika	1 tsp	2 tsp	1 tblsp
Fennel seeds	½ tsp	1 tsp	½ tblsp
Swiss cheese, finely grated	1 ounce (about ¼ cup)	1½ ounces (about 6 tblsp)	2 ounces (about ½ cup)

1 Put the broth and tofu in a blender or a food processor; blend or process until a creamy sauce. Pour into the slow cooker. Stir in the mushrooms, onion, garlic, thyme, paprika, and fennel seeds.

2 Cover and cook on low for 5 hours, or until the mushrooms are tender.

3 Stir in the cheese. Cover and set aside, preferably on the *keep warm* setting, until the cheese melts, no more than 10 minutes.

TESTERS' NOTES
• Not all tofu dishes have to have an Asian bend. Here, a creamy vegetarian stroganoff is made with tofu standing in for the more common thickeners and cream, creating a protein-rich main course even without any meat in the mix.
• Make sure you use soft silken tofu, sometimes available in packages outside the refrigerator case and in the Asian aisle or near the canned goods.

Serve It Up! Serve the stew in bowls over wide egg noodles or more traditional pappardelle.

braised tofu with shiitake mushrooms

EFFORT: **A LITTLE** • PREP TIME: **20 MINUTES** • COOK TIME: **2 HOURS 20 MINUTES/5 HOURS 20 MINUTES** • KEEPS ON WARM: **2 HOURS THROUGH STEP 2** • SERVES: **2 TO 8**

INGREDIENTS	2- TO 3½-QT	4- TO 5½-QT	6- TO 8-QT
Low-sodium vegetable broth	¾ cup	1½ cups	3 cups
Soy sauce	3 tblsp	6 tblsp	¾ cup
Dry sherry	1½ tblsp	3 tblsp	6 tblsp
Asian red chile paste (see page 139)	1 tsp	2 tsp	1 tblsp
Sugar	1 tsp	2 tsp	1 tblsp

	3 ounces	6 ounces	12 ounces
Fresh shiitake mushrooms, stemmed, the caps thinly sliced	3 ounces	6 ounces	12 ounces
Carrots, thinly sliced	1 medium	2 medium	4 medium
Medium whole scallions, thinly sliced	1	2	4
Minced peeled fresh ginger	2 tsp	1½ tblsp	3 tblsp
Minced garlic	2 tsp	1½ tblsp	2 tblsp
Extra-firm tofu packed in water, cut into 1-inch cubes	8 ounces	1 pound	2 pounds
Cornstarch	1 tsp	2 tsp	1½ tblsp
Rice vinegar	1 tsp	2 tsp	1½ tblsp

1 Mix the broth, soy sauce, sherry, chile paste, and sugar in the slow cooker until the sugar dissolves. Stir in the shiitakes, carrot, scallions, ginger, and garlic. Nestle the tofu cubes among these ingredients.

2 Cover and cook on high for 2 hours or on low for 5 hours.

3 Whisk the cornstarch and vinegar in a small bowl. Gently stir into the casserole. Cover and cook on high for 20 minutes, or until slightly thickened.

TESTERS' NOTES
• This Asian-based stew cries out for cooked white rice—and not much more. It's spicy in only a middling way, thanks to the way the slow cooker eats through capsaicin. Plan on passing hot sauce at the table, particularly sambal oelek (see page 404).
• The real trick here is stirring in the cornstarch slurry without breaking up the tofu cubes. Use a rubber spatula to be safe.

INGREDIENTS EXPLAINED Tofu is pressed soybean curd, a staple in diets around the world at this point. It comes in several varieties, mostly divided somewhere on the line of extra-firm, firm, and soft. There are also regular, low-fat, and even fat-free varieties. We suggest avoiding the low-fat and fat-free versions; these can be downright insipid. So-called silken tofu is a variant and will not also work in a dish like this one.

spicy sweet potato stew

EFFORT: **A LITTLE** • PREP TIME: **20 MINUTES** • COOK TIME: **8 HOURS 10 MINUTES** • KEEPS ON WARM: **2 HOURS** • SERVES: **2 TO 6**

INGREDIENTS	2- TO 3½-QT	4- TO 5½-QT	6- TO 8-QT
Low-sodium vegetable broth	⅓ cup	⅔ cup	1 cup
Chunky natural-style peanut butter	¼ cup	6 tblsp	½ cup
Sweet potatoes, peeled and diced	¾ pound	1¼ pounds	2 pounds
No-salt-added canned diced tomatoes	1¼ cups	2¼ cups	3½ cups
Drained and rinsed canned chickpeas	½ cup	1 cup	1¾ cups
Minced peeled fresh ginger	2 tsp	4 tsp	2 tblsp
Minced garlic	1 tsp	1¼ tsp	2 tsp
Ground cumin	1 tsp	1¼ tsp	2 tsp
Ground cinnamon	¼ tsp	½ tsp	½ tsp
Cayenne	Up to ⅛ tsp	Up to ¼ tsp	Up to ½ tsp
Packed stemmed and chopped spinach leaves	1⅓ cups	2⅔ cups	4 cups (about ½ pound)

1 Whisk the broth and peanut butter in the slow cooker until the peanut butter dissolves.

(continued)

2 Add the sweet potatoes, tomatoes, chickpeas, ginger, garlic, cumin, cinnamon, and cayenne; stir well until the vegetables are coated in the sauce. Cover and cook on low for 8 hours, or until the vegetables are tender and sweet.

3 Stir in the spinach, cover, and cook on low for 10 more minutes to wilt the leaves.

TESTERS' NOTES
• The chunky peanut butter adds some peanuts to the mix, but you can add more—up to ¼ cup chopped roasted unsalted peanuts.
• Steer clear of gigantic spinach leaves, which can be pretty tough even after wilting. If you have no other choice, remove their tough, fibrous central stems before chopping the leaves. Make sure you also wash them for sand and grit.

Serve It Up! Top bowlfuls with sour cream or plain yogurt, as well as minced cilantro leaves and even some minced red onion.

pizza potatoes

EFFORT: **NOT MUCH** • PREP TIME: **15 MINUTES** • COOK TIME:
5 HOURS • KEEPS ON WARM: **1 HOUR** • SERVES: **2 TO 6**

INGREDIENTS	2- TO 3½-QT	4- TO 5½-QT	6- TO 8-QT
Yellow potatoes (such as Yukon Gold), cut into 1-inch pieces	1 pound	2 pounds	3 pounds
Drained no-salt-added canned diced tomatoes	¾ cup	1½ cups	2¼ cups
Red onion, chopped	1 small	1 medium	1 large
Olive oil	1 tblsp	2 tblsp	3 tblsp
Chopped pitted black olives	1 tblsp	2 tblsp	3 tblsp

Minced fresh oregano leaves	½ tblsp	1 tblsp	1½ tblsp
Red pepper flakes	¼ tsp	½ tsp	¾ tsp
Parmigiano-Reggiano cheese, finely grated	1 ounce (about ¼ cup)	2 ounces (about ½ cup)	3 ounces (about ¾ cup)

1 Mix the potatoes, tomatoes, onion, olive oil, olives, oregano, and red pepper flakes in the slow cooker until the potatoes are evenly coated in the spices. Top with an even layer of cheese.

2 Cover and cook on low for 5 hours, or until the potatoes are fork-tender. Scoop it up by the spoonful.

TESTERS' NOTES
• These potatoes pick up all the flavors of pizza to make this a great vegetarian meal for kids.
• For the best flavor, use only yellow potatoes. They have the right balance of starch to become creamy yet never turn waxy.
• Substitute grated Cheddar cheese, Monterey Jack, or Gruyère for the Parmigiano-Reggiano.
• If you're a pepperoni pizza fan, toss a handful of thinly sliced pepperoni into the slow cooker with the potatoes.

fried rice

EFFORT: **A LITTLE** • PREP TIME: **20 MINUTES** • COOK TIME: **2 HOURS**
• KEEPS ON WARM: **NO** • SERVES: **3 TO 8**

INGREDIENTS	2- TO 3½-QT	4- TO 5½-QT	6- TO 8-QT
Peanut oil	1½ tblsp	2 tblsp	3½ tblsp
Cooked long-grain white or brown rice	3 cups	5 cups	9 cups

Frozen mixed vegetables, thawed	1½ cups	2½ cups	4½ cups
Medium whole scallions, thinly sliced	1	2	4
Minced peeled fresh ginger	1 tblsp	1½ tblsp	3 tblsp
Minced garlic	1 tsp	½ tblsp	2½ tsp
Soy sauce	2 tblsp	3 tblsp	6 tblsp
Rice vinegar	2 tblsp	3 tblsp	6 tblsp
Five-spice powder (see page 122)	¼ tsp	½ tsp	¾ tsp

1 Pour the oil into the slow cooker; smear it around with a paper towel. Add the rice, vegetables, scallions, ginger, and garlic; stir well.

2 Cover the slow cooker and cook on high for 1 hour, tossing twice.

3 Stir in the soy sauce, vinegar, and five-spice powder. Cover and continue cooking on high for 1 additional hour, tossing two more times during the cooking.

TESTERS' NOTES
• Already-cooked rice makes a better version of fried rice in the slow cooker because the grains don't turn gummy as they cook.
• Use any mix of frozen vegetables you prefer, even an Asian blend for stir-fries (particularly a blend for broccoli stir-fry), provided said blend has no sauce or seasonings on it.
• Skip the frozen mixed vegetables and use cored, seeded, and minced red bell pepper; thinly sliced cremini or white button mushrooms; thinly sliced carrots; small broccoli or cauliflower florets; and/or shelled peas.

fresh tomato pasta sauce

EFFORT: **A LITTLE** • PREP TIME: **30 MINUTES** • COOK TIME: **4½ TO 6½ HOURS** • KEEPS ON WARM: **4 HOURS** • SERVES: **3 TO 8 (ON COOKED PASTA)**

INGREDIENTS	2- TO 3½-QT	4- TO 5½-QT	6- TO 8-QT
Chopped yellow onion	½ cup	⅔ cup	1 cup (about 1 medium)
Olive oil	2 tsp	1 tblsp	2 tblsp
Minced garlic	½ tblsp	2 tsp	1 tblsp
Red pepper flakes	⅛ tsp	¼ tsp	½ tsp
Ripe plum tomatoes, chopped	2 pounds	3¼ pound	5 pounds
Minced fresh parsley leaves	2 tblsp	3 tblsp	⅓ cup
Minced fresh basil leaves	2 tsp	1 tblsp	2 tblsp
Minced fresh oregano leaves	½ tblsp	2 tsp	2 tblsp
Salt	¼ tsp	½ tsp	1 tsp
Ground black pepper	¼ tsp	¼ tsp	½ tsp

1 Mix the onion, olive oil, garlic, and red pepper flakes in the slow cooker. Cook on high *uncovered* for 1 hour 30 minutes, stirring occasionally, until the onion has softened and smells sweet.

2 Stir in the tomatoes, parsley, basil, oregano, salt, and pepper. Continue cooking on high *uncovered,* stirring occasionally, for 3 more hours in a small slow cooker, 4 more hours in a medium one, and 5 more hours in a large cooker, or until the tomatoes have broken down and the sauce is somewhat thickened.

(continued)

TESTERS' NOTES

• Although this recipe doesn't employ a traditional slow cooker technique—as it's uncovered and stirred occasionally—it nonetheless yields a bright fresh tomato sauce, best on cooked fresh spinach pasta (and topped with finely grated Parmigiano-Reggiano).

• Because globe or large tomatoes are not flavorful year-round, plum tomatoes make an adequate substitute in the cold months. However, if you're able to make this sauce in the summer when all varieties of tomatoes are at their peak, do so without pause.

• For better texture (and none of those irritating squishy skins in the mix), peel the tomatoes. Drop them a few at a time into boiling water just until their skins crack, about 15 seconds; immediately ladle them into a bowl of ice water. The skins will slip right off once they're cold. (Keep replenishing the ice in the bowl as it melts with additional batches.)

• This sauce freezes exceptionally well; store it in sealed containers for up to 4 months. It also can be used in all sorts of baked pasta casseroles—ziti, eggplant parmesan, and the like.

• To morph this fresh tomato sauce into a pizza sauce, whisk 1 tablespoon no-salt-added tomato paste into every ½ cup sauce before smearing it on the pie.

chinese-style braised eggplant

EFFORT: **A LITTLE** • PREP TIME: **15 MINUTES** • COOK TIME: **5 HOURS** • KEEPS ON WARM: **2 HOURS** • SERVES: **2 TO 6**

INGREDIENTS	2- TO 3½-QT	4- TO 5½-QT	6- TO 8-QT
Italian eggplants, cut into 2-inch cubes	2 pounds	3 pounds	4½ pounds
Leeks (white and pale green part only), halved lengthwise, washed carefully to remove internal sand, and thinly sliced	½ pound	¾ pound	1¼ pounds
Chopped pitted dates	6 tblsp	⅔ cup	1 cup
Low-sodium vegetable broth	2 cups plus 2 tblsp	3 cups	5 cups
Soy sauce	¼ cup	6 tblsp	⅔ cup
Packed dark brown sugar	2 tblsp	3 tblsp	5 tblsp
Minced peeled fresh ginger	1½ tblsp	2 tblsp	3 tblsp
Dry sherry	2 tsp	2 tblsp	2½ tblsp
Sambal oelek	2 tsp	2 tblsp	2½ tblsp
Minced garlic	2 tsp	1 tblsp	1½ tblsp

1 Mix the eggplants, leeks, and dates in the slow cooker.

2 Whisk the broth, soy sauce, brown sugar, ginger, sherry, sambal oelek, and garlic in a large bowl until the brown sugar dissolves. Pour over the eggplant mixture.

3 Cover and cook on high for 5 hours, or until the eggplant pieces are meltingly tender.

TESTERS' NOTES

• Here's a Chinese restaurant classic without the need to heat up a wok! But we added dates, very nontraditional, because they gave the dish a delicate richness.

• There's no need to peel the eggplant. The skin will get soft during the long cooking.

• Pass extra sambal oelek at the table for those who want to spice up the dish.

Serve It Up! Although white rice seems the traditional choice, this braise can also be served over wilted chard or spinach leaves for a more complex set of flavors.

INGREDIENTS EXPLAINED Sambal oelek is one of a series of Filipino, Indonesian, and southwest Asian chile pastes, all grouped loosely under the name *sambal*. Sambal oelek is fiery, made from ground, red chiles, seeds and all, with salt and vinegar. By contrast, sambal barjak includes garlic and spices in the mix. Almost any sambal will do for any recipe in this book, but sambal oelek is the most common bottling found in our grocery stores and has the brightest, cleanest flavor that will not compete with other ingredients.

eggplant parmesan casserole

EFFORT: **A LOT** • PREP TIME: **45 MINUTES** • COOK TIME: **8 HOURS** • KEEPS ON WARM: **1 HOUR** • SERVES: **3 TO 8**

INGREDIENTS	2- TO 3½-QT	4- TO 5½-QT	6- TO 8-QT
Large eggplant, stemmed and cut into ½-inch-thick slices	1½ pounds	2½ pounds	3½ pounds
Salt	1 tsp	2 tsp	1 tblsp
No-salt-added canned diced tomatoes	1½ cups	2½ cups	3½ cups
No-salt-added canned tomato paste	6 tblsp	½ cup	⅔ cup
Dried basil	1 tblsp	1½ tblsp	2 tblsp
Olive oil	1 tblsp	1½ tblsp	2 tblsp
Dried oregano	1 tsp	2 tsp	1 tblsp
Fennel seeds	½ tsp	¾ tsp	1 tsp
Red pepper flakes	½ tsp	¾ tsp	1 tsp
Parmigiano-Reggiano cheese, shredded through the large holes of a box grater	3 ounces	5 ounces	8 ounces

1 Lay the eggplant slices on paper towels on a clean, dry work surface. Sprinkle half the salt over the slices, turn them over, and sprinkle with the remaining salt. Cover with a second layer of paper towels and leave them be to leach moisture for 30 minutes.

2 Meanwhile, dump the tomatoes, tomato paste, basil, olive oil, oregano, fennel seeds, and red pepper flakes into a large food processor. (For large amounts, you will need to work in batches.) Cover and process, scraping down the inside of the container once or twice, until a smooth puree. Pour into a bowl and continue processing as necessary.

3 Smear ¼ to ½ cup sauce over the bottom of the slow cooker. Build the layers of the casserole: eggplant slices, sauce, and cheese, working your way up layer by layer until you end with the last of the cheese on top. You'll want to cut eggplant slices so they make even, not-overlapping layers with only a few holes.

4 Cover and cook on low for 8 hours, or until the sauce is bubbling and the eggplant is tender. Let stand uncovered for 10 minutes before slicing into chunks with a nonstick-safe spatula or knife right in the cooker—or dishing it up by the big spoonful.

TESTERS' NOTES
• This is a no-fry eggplant parmesan, healthier but also fresher tasting.
• If you want to get really fancy, you can shave the Parmigiano-Reggiano with a cheese plane, layering the larger sheets in the casserole.
• Dried herbs give this casserole a comfort-food feel: less bright, more earthy.
• There's no real way to predict the number of layers you'll make based on the varying sizes and shapes of slow cookers. Just make sure you finish the dish with a layer of grated cheese.

ziti puttanesca

EFFORT: **NOT MUCH** • PREP TIME: **20 MINUTES** • COOK TIME:
2½ HOURS • KEEPS ON WARM: **NO** • SERVES: **2 TO 6**

INGREDIENTS	2- TO 3½-QT	4- TO 5½-QT	6- TO 8-QT
No-salt-added canned crushed tomatoes	1¾ cups	3½ cups	5¼ cups
Uncooked ziti pasta	4 ounces	8 ounces	12 ounces
Low-sodium vegetable broth	½ cup	1 cup	1½ cups
Chopped yellow onion	¼ cup	½ cup	¾ cup (about 1 small)
Chopped pitted black olives	2 tblsp	¼ cup	6 tblsp
Chopped pitted green olives	2 tblsp	¼ cup	6 tblsp
Minced fresh basil leaves	2 tblsp	¼ cup	6 tblsp
Minced garlic	½ tblsp	1 tblsp	1½ tblsp
Drained, rinsed, and minced capers	½ tblsp	1 tblsp	1½ tblsp
Minced canned anchovy fillets	½ tblsp	1 tblsp	1½ tblsp
Dried oregano	1 tsp	2 tsp	1 tblsp
Fennel seeds	½ tsp	1 tsp	½ tblsp
Red pepper flakes	¼ tsp	½ tsp	¾ tsp

1 Stir the tomatoes, ziti, broth, onion, both kinds of olives, basil, garlic, capers, anchovies, oregano, fennel seeds, and red pepper flakes in the slow cooker.

2 Cover and cook on low for 2½ hours, stirring once after 1½ hours, until the flavors have blended and the pasta is tender.

TESTERS' NOTES
• Puttanesca is a traditional Italian dish of olives, tomatoes, and other aromatics. Here, we've turned it into a "braising" medium for pasta, an exceptionally satisfying (and dairy-free!) vegetarian dinner.
• Mince the basil, garlic, capers, and anchovies—the strong flavors—so they become well blended in the sauce.

ALL-AMERICAN KNOW-HOW Why rinse capers after draining them in a little strainer over the sink? They're packed in a salty brine, so rinsing them helps cut down on the sodium content of the final dish.

spinach mushroom lasagna

EFFORT: **A LOT** • PREP TIME: **40 MINUTES** • COOK TIME: **4 HOURS** •
KEEPS ON WARM: **NO** • SERVES: **3 TO 6**

INGREDIENTS	2- TO 3½-QT	4- TO 5½-QT	6- TO 8-QT
Drained no-salt-added canned diced tomatoes	1⅔ cups	2¼ cups	2¾ cups
No-salt-added tomato paste	2½ tblsp	3 tblsp	¼ cup
Dried oregano	2 tsp	2½ tsp	1 tblsp
Dried basil	2 tsp	2½ tsp	1 tblsp
Minced garlic	2 tsp	2½ tsp	1 tblsp
Unsalted butter	1 tblsp	2 tblsp	3 tblsp
Cremini or brown button mushrooms, thinly sliced	6 ounces (about 2 cups)	8 ounces (about 2½ cups)	10 ounces (about 3 cups)

Frozen chopped spinach, thawed and squeezed dry of excess moisture	1 cup	1¼ cups	1½ cups
Mozzarella, shredded (regular or low-fat)	4 ounces (about 1 cup)	5 ounces (about 1¼ cups)	6 ounces (about 1½ cups)
Ricotta (regular or low-fat)	⅔ cup	¾ cup	1 cup
Grated nutmeg	½ tsp	¾ tsp	1 tsp
Ground black pepper	¼ tsp	½ tsp	½ tsp
Uncooked lasagna noodles	6	8	10
Parmigiano-Reggiano cheese, finely grated	2 ounces (about ½ cup)	2½ ounces (about 10 tblsp)	3 ounces (about ¾ cup)

1 Puree the tomatoes, tomato paste, oregano, basil, and garlic in a covered large blender, scraping down the inside of the container a few times, until smooth. (You may have to work in batches for the largest set of ingredients.)

2 Melt the butter in a large skillet set over medium heat. Add the mushrooms; cook, stirring often, until they release their moisture and it reduces to a glaze, about 5 minutes.

3 Mix the spinach, mozzarella, ricotta, nutmeg, and pepper in a large bowl until fairly creamy.

4 Layer the casserole in the slow cooker. Start by spreading a thin layer of tomato sauce on the bottom of the cooker. Lay about a third of the lasagna noodles across the cooker, breaking them into pieces to fit in as even a layer as possible. Dollop half the cheese mixture on the noodles and spread it out with a rubber spatula. Top with half the mushrooms and a third of the remaining tomato sauce. Now repeat with half of the remaining noodles, all the remaining cheese mixture, all the remaining

mushrooms, and half of the remaining tomato sauce. Finally, build the last layer with the remainder of the noodles, the remainder of the tomato sauce, and all the grated Parmigiano-Reggiano.

5 Cover and cook on low for 4 hours, or until the cheese has melted and the casserole is beginning to set. Uncover and let stand unplugged for 15 minutes before serving to firm up the casserole and bring the cheese down to mouth-safe temperatures.

TESTERS' NOTES

• Look no more—this is the lasagna that's creamy but light, satisfying but best for springtime.
• The work here is getting the ingredients prepped for building the casserole—which is truly the most difficult part of this meal. Make sure the layers are even and as compact as possible without pressing down.
• To spread the ricotta mixture evenly, dampen the spatula occasionally.

Serve It Up! Since the casserole is pretty creamy, you'll want a tame vinaigrette on a tossed salad. Here's an easy **Raspberry Vinaigrette**: Spoon a 10-ounce jar of seedless raspberry jam into a large microwave-safe bowl and microwave on low for about 1 minute, until melted. Whisk in ⅓ cup rice vinegar and ⅓ cup olive oil. Season with salt and lots (seriously, lots) of ground black pepper. This can be stored in a glass container in the fridge for up to 2 weeks.

pumpkin ricotta lasagna

EFFORT: **A LOT** · PREP TIME: **20 MINUTES** · COOK TIME: **4 HOURS** · KEEPS ON WARM: **NO** · SERVES: **3 TO 6**

INGREDIENTS	2- TO 3½-QT	4- TO 5½-QT	6- TO 8-QT
Ricotta (regular or low-fat)	1½ cups	2 cups	2½ cups
Canned pumpkin puree	¾ cup plus 2 tblsp	1 cup plus 2 tblsp	1½ cups
Heavy cream	7 tblsp	9 tblsp	¾ cup
Parmigiano-Reggiano cheese, finely grated	½ ounce (about 2 tblsp)	¾ ounce (about 3 tblsp)	1 ounce (about ¼ cup)
Minced fresh sage leaves	1 tblsp	1½ tblsp	2 tblsp
Grated nutmeg	¼ tsp	½ tsp	¾ tsp
Red pepper flakes	⅛ tsp	¼ tsp	½ tsp
Uncooked lasagna noodles	6	8	10
Drained and rinsed canned cannellini beans	1 cup	1⅓ cups	1¾ cup
Gruyère cheese, grated	5 ounces (about 1¼ cups)	6½ ounces (about 1⅔ cups)	8 ounces (about 2 cups)

1 Whisk the ricotta, pumpkin puree, cream, Parmigiano-Reggiano, sage, nutmeg, and red pepper flakes in a large bowl until fairly smooth.

2 Layer the casserole in the slow cooker: Start by spreading a thin but even smear of the ricotta mixture over the bottom of the canister. Top with a third of the noodles, broken as necessary to form as even a layer as possible. Top with a third of the remaining ricotta sauce, half the beans, and a third of the grated Gruyère, each in an even layer. Make a second set of layers with half the remaining noodles, half the remaining ricotta sauce, the rest of the beans, and half the remaining Gruyère. Finally, build a layer with all the remaining noodles, all the remaining ricotta sauce, and all the remaining Gruyère.

3 Cover and cook on low for 4 hours, or until the cheese has melted and the casserole is set. Scoop out spoonfuls—or let the casserole sit, covered, for 15 minutes to slice into wedges or squares with a nonstick-safe knife or spatula.

TESTERS' NOTES

• This gooey, cheesy lasagna is actually not as thick as the other lasagnas in our batch, the better to hold its shape without any tomato sauce or meat.
• The beans actually give the casserole a little bump in flavor, their earthy taste and firmer texture balancing the pumpkin puree.
• Make sure you use pure pumpkin puree for this lasagna rather than a spiced pumpkin puree or (horrors!) canned pumpkin pie filling.

Serve It Up! If you're serving this casserole at a dinner party, you'll want to start off with a vinegary dish to counter the richness to come. Offer oven-roasted tomatoes (page 295) and chickpeas, drizzled with lemon juice and aged balsamic vinegar. Sprinkle minced mint leaves over each serving.

vegetable lasagna

EFFORT: **A LOT** • PREP TIME: **20 MINUTES** • COOK TIME: **4 HOURS 15 MINUTES** • KEEPS ON WARM: **NO** • SERVES: **2 TO 6**

INGREDIENTS	2- TO 3½-QT	4- TO 5½-QT	6- TO 8-QT
Shredded zucchini	½ cup	1 cup	1½ cups
Ricotta (regular or low-fat)	1 cup	1½ cups	2 cups
Shredded carrots	⅔ cup	1 cup	1⅓ cups
Grated nutmeg	¼ tsp	½ tsp	¾ tsp
Large egg/yolk, beaten in a small bowl	1 whole	1 whole plus 1 yolk	2 whole
Drained no-salt-added canned diced tomatoes	1 cup	2¼ cups	3¼ cups
No-salt-added canned crushed tomatoes	1 cup	2¼ cups	3¼ cups
Dried oregano	½ tblsp	1 tblsp	1½ tblsp
Minced garlic	1 tsp	2 tsp	1 tblsp
Red pepper flakes	⅛ tsp	¼ tsp	½ tsp
Dried whole wheat lasagna noodles	5	8	12
Shredded mozzarella (regular or low-fat)	1 cup	2 cups	3 cups

1 Squeeze the zucchini by handfuls over the sink to get rid of its excess moisture, then separate the threads and set them in a large bowl. Mix in the ricotta, carrots, nutmeg, and egg until uniform. Set aside.

2 Combine both tomatoes, oregano, garlic, and red pepper flakes in a second bowl.

3 Pour some olive oil into the slow cooker and generously grease its bottom and sides by smearing the oil with a paper towel. Spread a quarter of the tomato sauce across the bottom of the cooker.

4 Build a layer as follows: a third of the noodles, broken to fit in as even a layer as possible; half of the ricotta mixture; a third of the remaining tomato sauce; and a third of the shredded mozzarella. Repeat with half the remaining noodles, again broken to fit; the remaining ricotta mixture; half the remaining tomato sauce; and half the remaining shredded mozzarella. Finally, make the last layer with the remaining lasagna noodles and the remaining sauce, spread evenly over the noodles. Set the rest of the mozzarella in the fridge.

5 Cover and cook on low for 4 hours, or until the casserole has set.

6 Turn off the slow cooker, sprinkle the remaining mozzarella over the casserole, and set aside, covered, for 15 minutes to melt the cheese and firm up the lasagna. Use a nonstick-safe spatula or knife to cut squares or wedges from the casserole to serve.

TESTERS' NOTES

• In this lasagna, the vegetables are mixed with the ricotta to make a creamy sauce—and to provide the cheese with essential moisture so that it doesn't firm up too much as it cooks.

• The first piece of lasagna out of the cooker is always the hardest. Look for an offset spatula, a spatula with a crook in the blade, the better to slip it under that first piece and pry it out.

savory mushroom bread pudding

EFFORT: **A LOT** • PREP TIME: **30 MINUTES** • COOK TIME: **2½ TO 3½ HOURS** • KEEPS ON WARM: **NO** • SERVES: **2 TO 6**

INGREDIENTS	2- TO 3½-QT	4- TO 5½-QT	6- TO 8-QT
Dried mushrooms, preferably porcini	¼ ounce	½ ounce	1 ounce
Boiling water, for soaking the mushrooms	1 cup	2 cups	3 cups
Unsalted butter	1 tblsp	2 tblsp	3 tblsp
Chopped yellow onion	⅓ cup	¾ cup (about 1 small)	1¼ cups
Cremini or brown button mushrooms, sliced	3 ounces (about 1 cup)	6 ounces (about 2 cups)	10 ounces (about 3 cups)
Fresh shiitake mushrooms, stems removed, the caps thinly sliced	1½ ounces (about ½ cup)	3 ounces (about 1 cup)	5 ounces (about 1½ cups)
Cubes of Italian bread, ½ inch, toasted	4 cups	8 cups	12 cups
Dried sage	½ tsp	1 tsp	½ tblsp
Dried thyme	½ tsp	1 tsp	½ tblsp
Salt	½ tsp	1 tsp	½ tblsp
Ground black pepper	½ tsp	1 tsp	½ tblsp
Low-sodium vegetable broth	Up to ¾ cup	Up to 1½ cups	Up to 2¼ cups
Large eggs	1	2	3

1 Souse the porcini with boiling water in a large bowl by about 2 inches. Set aside to soak for 20 minutes.

2 Drain the porcini in a colander set over a bowl in the sink (thereby saving the soaking liquid). Chop the porcini into small bits and dump them into the slow cooker.

3 Melt the butter in a large skillet set over medium heat. Add the onion and cook, stirring often, until translucent and somewhat soft, between 3 and 5 minutes. Add the fresh mushrooms; continue cooking, stirring often, until they release their moisture and it evaporates to a glaze, 7 to 10 minutes.

4 Scrape the contents of the skillet into the slow cooker. Add the bread cubes, sage, thyme, salt, and pepper. Toss well until the mushrooms are even throughout the mixture.

5 Measure the amount of mushroom soaking liquid you have saved, then add enough broth to it so that the total volume comes to 1 cup for a small slow cooker, 2 cups for a medium cooker, or 3 cups for a large one. Crack the eggs into the liquid and whisk until smooth. Pour over the contents of the slow cooker, then press down with the back of a wooden spoon to make sure all the bread cubes soak up the liquid.

6 Cover and cook on low for 2½ hours in a small slow cooker, 3 hours in a medium one, or 3½ hours in a large cooker, or until the casserole is set with little liquid rimming it in the canister. Scoop it up with a big spoon to serve.

TESTERS' NOTES
• A savory bread pudding is just what it seems: a chunky bread casserole, here laced with vegetables. Although you'll need to rehydrate dried mushrooms, there's not much more to making this hearty casserole.

- Although dried porcini are our choice, they are very expensive. A mixed batch makes a more economical casserole. Since there are fresh shiitakes in the casserole, use a blend that omits them.
- Some dried mushrooms are quite sandy. If you notice sediment in the bottom of the soaking liquid, strain the liquid through cheesecloth or a large coffee filter set over a 1-quart measuring cup.
- Toast the bread cubes on a large baking sheet set in a preheated 350°F oven for 10 minutes, tossing occasionally until lightly browned.

SHORTCUTS Use unseasoned croutons instead of the toasted bread cubes.

INGREDIENTS EXPLAINED Dried mushrooms should smell earthy and bright, not musky or acrid. (You can sniff them through the thin bags or through holes in the top of the bag.) They should be whole, not broken into tiny chips, and give no evidence of squishy spots.

spinach and feta pudding

EFFORT: **NOT MUCH** · PREP TIME: **15 MINUTES** · COOK TIME: **2 TO 3 HOURS** · KEEPS ON WARM: **NO** · SERVES: **2 TO 6**

INGREDIENTS	2- TO 3½-QT	4- TO 5½-QT	6- TO 8-QT
10-ounce boxes frozen chopped spinach, thawed and squeezed by handfuls over the sink to remove excess moisture	1	2	3
Ricotta (regular or low-fat)	2 cups	4 cups	6 cups
Crumbled feta cheese	½ cup	1 cup	1½ cups
Large eggs	3	6	9

	2- TO 3½-QT	4- TO 5½-QT	6- TO 8-QT
Finely chopped yellow onion	¼ cup	½ cup (1 small)	¾ cup
All-purpose flour	2 tblsp	¼ cup	6 tblsp
Minced fresh dill fronds	1 tblsp	2 tblsp	3 tblsp
Grated nutmeg	¼ tsp	½ tsp	¾ tsp
Aged Pecorino cheese, preferably Pecorino Romano (see page 356), finely grated	1 ounce (about ¼ cup)	2 ounces (about ½ cup)	3 ounces (about ¾ cup)

1 Use some olive oil dabbed on a paper towel to grease the bottom and sides of the inside of the slow cooker.

2 Whisk the spinach, ricotta, feta, eggs, onion, flour, dill, and nutmeg in a large bowl until the mixture is fairly uniform, the spinach and dill even throughout with no visible bits of egg white. Pour into the slow cooker; top with a thin layer of the grated cheese.

3 Cover and cook on low for 2 hours in a small slow cooker, 2½ hours in a medium model, or 3 hours in a large one, or until the casserole is set and a bit firm to the touch. Scoop up big spoonfuls to serve.

TESTERS' NOTES
- Savory puddings are a lost art. They are sort of like a quiche, sort of like a cheesy pudding, and utterly irresistible. This one is also great for brunch.
- The spinach must be squeezed in small bits so that you really can get rid of that excess moisture. Otherwise, it'll interfere with the eggs and cause the casserole to become boggy, rather than set.

INGREDIENTS EXPLAINED Feta is a dry, crumbly sheep's or sheep/goat's milk cheese, often sold in blocks held in a brine to preserve their freshness. It has a sharp, fairly sour flavor that pairs well with bitter notes, particularly those found in leafy greens.

corn and roasted red pepper pudding

EFFORT: **A LITTLE** • PREP TIME: **15 MINUTES** • COOK TIME: **1½ TO 2½ HOURS** • KEEPS ON WARM: **NO** • SERVES: **3 TO 8**

INGREDIENTS	2- TO 3½-QT	4- TO 5½-QT	6- TO 8-QT
Thinly sliced jarred roasted red peppers	2 cups	3 cups	5 cups
Corn kernels, thawed frozen, or fresh, sliced off the cob	1 cup	1½ cups	2½ cups
Gruyère cheese, grated	4 ounces (about 1 cup)	6 ounces (about 1½ cups)	10 ounces (about 2½ cups)
Stemmed fresh thyme leaves	1 tblsp	1½ tblsp	2 tblsp
Grated nutmeg	⅛ tsp	¼ tsp	½ tsp
Large eggs	6	9	15
Milk	1½ cups	2¼ cups	3¾ cups
Heavy cream	½ cup	¾ cup	1¼ cups
Salt	½ tsp	¾ tsp	1 tsp
Ground black pepper	½ tsp	¾ tsp	1 tsp
Parmigiano-Reggiano cheese, finely grated	3 ounces (about ¾ cup)	4 ounces (about 1 cup)	6 ounces (about 1½ cups)

1 Generously grease the inside of the slow cooker with unsalted butter.

2 Toss the red peppers, corn, Gruyère, thyme, and nutmeg in a large bowl; spread into an even layer in the cooker.

3 Whisk the eggs, milk, cream, salt, and pepper in that same bowl; pour over the corn mixture. Sprinkle the grated Parmigiano-Reggiano evenly over the top.

4 Cover and cook on high for 1½ hours in a small slow cooker, 2 hours in a medium one, or 2½ hours in a large model, or until the casserole is set and the cheese is bubbling.

TESTERS' NOTES
• Corn pudding is a holiday favorite; but with a little more cheese and some roasted red vegetables, it can easily morph into a hearty entree for almost any time of the year.
• You can either cut the corn kernels off the cob if it's summer and the corn is tasty, or you can use frozen corn kernels, provided you thaw them first.

Serve It Up! Offer sliced cucumbers, tomatoes, and red onions in this **Honey-Lemon Vinaigrette**: Whisk ¼ cup lemon juice, 3 tablespoons honey, 1 tablespoon stemmed thyme leaves, 2 teaspoons Dijon mustard, 1 teaspoon minced garlic, ½ teaspoon salt, and ½ teaspoon ground black pepper in a small bowl, then whisk in ⅓ cup olive oil until fairly creamy.

vegetable and rice side dishes

The real omnivore's dilemma is being an omnivore at all. Most of us get so fixated on the meat for a meal that we miss the side dishes. Or we just toss some vegetables into the main dish. Sure, a beef stew can have potatoes and onions; a fish braise, tomatoes and leeks. But those aren't legit sides. They're flavoring agents.

We humans are designed to eat a wide range of foods. In fact, we can't function properly without a healthy dose of vegetables because they provide both soluble and insoluble fiber, the very things meat lacks. In other words, your mother was right: if you want to eat a braised short rib, you need to eat your broccoli, too.

So here's a chapter full of side dishes from the slow cooker, none a full meal in itself. Instead, this is a compilation of plate-fillers like some pretty fine Smashed Potatoes (page 415), Cauliflower in Browned Butter (page 427), and Succotash (page 436).

Portions here are a little harder to negotiate, since we're not sure exactly how much real estate a side dish takes up on your plate. To be blunt, a side should be at least as large as the meat portion. That may sound like a pipe dream for most Americans, but your whole digestive track will thank you for the effort. You'll feel better both when you're at the table and when you get up from it. And sitting at the table is where you'll be with these dishes. Most of us don't make a side dish when we're going to plop down in front of our favorite movie.

That's too bad. We should always plan on side dishes, not only so we can be healthier but also so we can be the omnivores we're supposed to be. Maybe the slow cooker can help. And while you're enjoying every bite, make sure you savor the fact that most of life isn't solely about what's at the center of the plate. Life is actually more about what happens on the side.

hard-cooked eggs

EFFORT: **A LITTLE** • PREP TIME: **5 MINUTES** • COOK TIME: **1 HOUR 50 MINUTES TO 2 HOURS 50 MINUTES** • KEEPS ON WARM: **NO** • SERVES: **3 TO 10**

INGREDIENTS	2- TO 3½-QT	4- TO 5½-QT	6- TO 8-QT
Large eggs	Up to 4	Up to 8	Up to 12

1 Fill the slow cooker's canister halfway with water. Cover and cook on high for 1½ hours in a small slow cooker, 2 hours in a medium cooker, or 2½ hours in a large cooker. The water should be steaming hot when you lift the lid.

2 Slip the eggs into the water. Cover and continue cooking on high for 18 minutes. Use a slotted spoon to remove the eggs from the water; drop them in a bowl of cold tap water. Cool until easily handled, then peel.

TESTERS' NOTES
• Slow cookers make perfectly set hard-cooked eggs without chalkiness or that green-gunk ring.
• The eggs should be cold from the fridge, not at room temperature, so they slowly come up to the right temperature as they cook.
• Lower the eggs into the water with a slotted spoon. Don't drop them in or they might crack!

Serve It Up! Sure, you can salt and pepper them for a meal on the go. But you can also turn them into deviled eggs of all sorts. Slice the shelled eggs in half lengthwise, then scoop the yolks into a bowl and mash with the ingredients here for one of these five fillings, each enough to fill 12 hard-cooked egg halves. (You'll need to modify amounts if you have more or less than we suggest.)

Classic Deviled Eggs = 6 hard-cooked egg yolks, 2 tablespoons softened unsalted butter, 1 tablespoon mayonnaise, 1 teaspoon white wine vinegar, ¼ teaspoon dry mustard, ¼ teaspoon salt, and a few dashes of hot pepper sauce

Gingered Eggs = 6 hard-cooked egg yolks, 1 minced small shallot, 2 tablespoons mayonnaise, 1 tablespoon minced peeled fresh ginger, 1 teaspoon Asian red chile paste (see page 139), and ¼ teaspoon salt

Curried Eggs = 6 hard-cooked egg yolks, 2 tablespoons mayonnaise, 2 teaspoons dry mustard, 2 teaspoons curry powder, 2 teaspoons lemon juice, and ¼ teaspoon salt

French Onion-Dip Eggs = 6 hard-cooked egg yolks, 1½ tablespoons sour cream, 1 tablespoon mayonnaise, 1 tablespoon minced chives, ½ teaspoon onion powder, and ½ teaspoon salt

Cocktail Sauce Eggs = 6 hard-cooked egg yolks, 2 tablespoons ketchup, 1 to 2 teaspoons prepared horseradish, 1 teaspoon lemon juice, ¼ teaspoon salt, and a few dashes of hot pepper sauce

smashed potatoes

EFFORT: **NOT MUCH** • PREP TIME: **15 MINUTES** • COOK TIME: **5 HOURS** • KEEPS ON WARM: **3 HOURS THROUGH STEP 2** • SERVES: **3 TO 10**

INGREDIENTS	2- TO 3½-QT	4- TO 5½-QT	6- TO 8-QT
Skin-on yellow potatoes (such as Yukon Gold), cut into 1-inch chunks	1½ pounds	3 pounds	5 pounds
Low-sodium vegetable broth	½ cup	1 cup	1½ cups
Salt	½ tsp	¾ tsp	1 tsp
Ground black pepper	½ tsp	¾ tsp	1 tsp
Half-and-half	Up to ½ cup	Up to 1 cup	Up to 1¼ cups
Dijon mustard	2 tsp	1½ tblsp	2 tblsp

1 Stir the potatoes, broth, salt, and pepper in the slow cooker.

2 Cover and cook on low for 5 hours, or until the potato pieces are quite tender.

3 Warm the half-and-half in a small saucepan over very low heat.

4 Use a potato masher to begin to mash the potatoes with the mustard, then add the warmed half-and-half in small increments, mashing all the while, until you reach your desired consistency, thicker or creamier.

TESTERS' NOTES

• You'll need an old-fashioned potato masher to make great mashed potatoes in the slow cooker. Look for the tool in almost all housewares stores or online shops. If your slow cooker has a nonstick finish, use a tool designed for that coating; you can then work right in the canister without having to dirty another bowl. If you don't have this workaday tool in your arsenal, you'll need to scrape the contents of the cooker into a large bowl and mash the potatoes with an electric mixer at medium-low speed until you reach your preferred consistency.

• For more heft to the potatoes, substitute chicken broth for the vegetable broth.

• For garlicky mashed potatoes, add the following with the salt and pepper: ½ teaspoon minced garlic for a small slow cooker, 1 teaspoon minced garlic for a medium cooker, and ½ tablespoon minced garlic for a large one.

• Yep, you may warm a little more half-and-half than you need, but then you'll then have extra to drizzle over sliced strawberries for dessert.

herb-roasted potatoes

EFFORT: **NOT MUCH** • PREP TIME: **10 MINUTES** • COOK TIME: **3 HOURS** • KEEPS ON WARM: **3 HOURS** • SERVES: **3 TO 8**

INGREDIENTS	2- TO 3½-QT	4- TO 5½-QT	6- TO 8-QT
Tiny red-skinned potatoes or thin red fingerling potatoes	1 pound	2 pounds	3 pounds
Olive oil	2 tblsp	¼ cup	6 tblsp
Medium garlic cloves, peeled	3	6	10
Dried rosemary	½ tsp	1 tsp	1¼ tsp
Salt	½ tsp	1 tsp	½ tblsp
Ground black pepper	½ tsp	1 tsp	½ tblsp

1 Stir the potatoes, olive oil, garlic, rosemary, salt, and pepper in the slow cooker until the potatoes are greased and coated in the seasonings. Make as even a layer of the potatoes as you can.

(continued)

2 Lay paper towels over the top of the cooker, hanging down over the outside in long strips. Cover and cook on high for 3 hours, or until the potatoes are tender and the garlic has softened.

TESTERS' NOTES
• Search in the bin for the smallest potatoes you can find—or the thinnest fingerlings.
• The cooker should not be full. Rather, almost all the potatoes should touch the bottom or sides of the cooker so they get a roasted flavor from direct contact with the heat.
• The paper towels keep moisture from dripping down onto the potatoes, and so allows them to have more roasted texture, not nearly as soggy.
• Don't peel or cut the potatoes. Cooking them with their skins on preserves moisture inside, rather than letting it leach out to braise the spuds.

INGREDIENTS EXPLAINED Fingerling potatoes are thin, long potatoes, mostly heirloom varieties.

spicy scalloped potatoes

EFFORT: **A LITTLE** • PREP TIME: **20 MINUTES** • COOK TIME: **8 HOURS** • KEEPS ON WARM: **1 HOUR** • SERVES: **4 TO 10**

INGREDIENTS	2- TO 3½-QT	4- TO 5½-QT	6- TO 8-QT
Evaporated milk	1¾ cups	2⅔ cups	4½ cups
Roasted unsalted cashews	¾ cup	1 cup plus 2 tblsp	2 cups
Medium garlic cloves, peeled and quartered	1	2	3
Salt	½ tsp	¾ tsp	1¼ tsp
Grated nutmeg	⅛ tsp	¼ tsp	½ tsp
Cayenne	⅛ tsp	¼ tsp	½ tsp
Yellow potatoes (such as Yukon Gold), peeled and cut into ¼-inch-thick slices	2 pounds	3 pounds	5 pounds

1 Combine the evaporated milk, cashews, garlic, salt, nutmeg, and cayenne in a large blender. Cover and blend until a smooth puree, stopping the machine occasionally to scrape down the inside of the container.

2 Smear a small bit of this puree over the bottom of the slow cooker. Layer the potatoes and sauce in the cooker, working to create even, slightly overlapping layers and topping each one with ¼ to ½ cup of the sauce. Make sure you end with sauce on top, not exposed potatoes. Jiggle the cooker a bit to make sure the sauce gets down into the nooks and crannies.

3 Cover and cook on low for 8 hours, or until the casserole is somewhat set and the potatoes are tender. Let stand for 10 minutes before scooping out with a big spoon.

TESTERS' NOTES
• This rich, decadent side dish is best with roast beef or a grilled pork loin.
• Only yellow potatoes will work here; baking potatoes are too starchy and red-skinned potatoes, too dry.
• Raw cashews simply don't have enough flavor to offer the sauce anything but the ooze of their fat. Roasted cashews add flavor and heft.
• There's no real way to know how many layers you'll make in your cooker, so you'll need to eyeball it as you build them up. Just remember to save some sauce to cover the top of the casserole. And no matter how much sauce you have left over after building up the layers, pour it all evenly over the top.

mashed butternut squash and sweet potatoes

EFFORT: **A LITTLE** • PREP TIME: **10 MINUTES** • COOK TIME: **6 HOURS** • KEEPS ON WARM: **2 HOURS** • SERVES: **4 TO 10**

INGREDIENTS	2- TO 3½-QT	4- TO 5½-QT	6- TO 8-QT
Butternut squash, peeled, seeded, and cubed	1¼ pounds	2½ pounds	4 pounds
Sweet potatoes, peeled and cubed	10 ounces	1 pound	1½ pounds
No-sugar-added apple cider	½ cup	¾ cup	1¼ cups
Unsalted butter, at room temperature	Up to 4 tblsp (½ stick)	Up to 6 tblsp	Up to 10 tblsp (or 1 stick plus 2 tblsp)
Maple syrup	2 tblsp	3 tblsp	⅓ cup
Heavy cream	2 tblsp	3 tblsp	⅓ cup
Salt	½ tsp	¾ tsp	1¼ tsp

1 Stir the squash, sweet potatoes, and cider in the slow cooker.

2 Cover and cook on low for 6 hours, or until the vegetables are quite tender, enough to be mashed with the back of a flatware spoon.

3 Add the butter, maple syrup, cream, and salt. Use a potato masher to mash the ingredients into a smooth puree right in the cooker.

TESTERS' NOTES
• This creamy, wintry side dish would be perfect at the Thanksgiving table—or anytime you've got a bird, a hunk of pork, or a slab of beef in the oven.

• Although butternut squash is the most common type of winter squash in our supermarkets—and usually already cut into chunks somewhere in the produce section—you can substitute cubed acorn squash or just about any other winter squash, even pumpkin.
• If you want to forgo some of the richness here, substitute half-and-half or whole milk for the cream—or even use low-fat milk.

candied sweet potatoes

EFFORT: **NOT MUCH** • PREP TIME: **20 MINUTES** • COOK TIME: **2½ HOURS/5½ HOURS** • KEEPS ON WARM: **2 HOURS** • SERVES: **4 TO 12**

INGREDIENTS	2- TO 3½-QT	4- TO 5½-QT	6- TO 8-QT
Sweet potatoes, peeled and diced	1¼ pounds	2 pounds	3 pounds
Unsweetened pineapple juice	½ cup	¾ cup plus 2 tblsp	1½ cups
Packed dark brown sugar	⅓ cup	½ cup plus 1 tblsp	1 cup
Unsalted butter, cut into tiny bits	1 tblsp	1½ tblsp	2½ tblsp
Ground cinnamon	½ tsp	¾ tsp	1¼ tsp
Vanilla extract	½ tsp	¾ tsp	1¼ tsp
Salt	¼ tsp	½ tsp	¾ tsp

1 Stir the sweet potatoes, pineapple juice, brown sugar, butter, cinnamon, vanilla, and salt in the slow cooker.

(continued)

2 Cover and cook on high for 2½ hours or on low for 5½ hours, or until the sweet potatoes are very tender and glazed in the sauce.

TESTERS' NOTES
• The classic holiday side dish is so easy! Unsweetened pineapple juice will be slightly tarter than regular pineapple juice and so offers a better spike.
• Add up to ½ cup chopped pecans.
• If you miss the marshmallows, don't stir them into the slow cooker; they'll melt. Instead, spoon the finished dish into a broiler-safe baking dish. Top with marshmallows, then broil on an oven rack set 4 to 6 inches from a heated broiler for up to 4 minutes, until the marshmallows soften and begin to brown.

honey-glazed carrots and onions

EFFORT: **NOT MUCH** • PREP TIME: **10 MINUTES** • COOK TIME: **4 HOURS** • KEEPS ON WARM: **2 HOURS** • SERVES: **4 TO 10**

INGREDIENTS	2- TO 3½-QT	4- TO 5½-QT	6- TO 8-QT
Carrots, cut into 1-inch segments	1¼ pounds	2¼ pounds	3½ pounds
Red onions, halved and thinly sliced	2 medium	3 medium	3 large
Unsalted butter, melted	2 tblsp	3½ tblsp	5 tblsp
Honey	2 tblsp	3½ tblsp	⅓ cup
Salt	½ tsp	¾ tsp	1 tsp
Ground black pepper	½ tsp	¾ tsp	1 tsp

1 Stir the carrots, onions, and butter in the slow cooker until the vegetables are greased. Drizzle the honey over the vegetables. Sprinkle with salt and pepper.

2 Cover and cook on high for 4 hours, stirring twice during the cooking, until the carrots are tender when picked at with a fork.

TESTERS' NOTES
• This easy side dish would be best with anything grilled, particularly if it had a spicy, Cajun-style or Tex-Mex rub on it before it hit the heat.
• We suggest an herbal honey, such as one made from rosemary or thyme flowers.
• Spinkle in up to ¾ teaspoon ground cinnamon with the salt and pepper, or up to ½ teaspoon grated nutmeg, or up to ½ teaspoon red pepper flakes.

ALL-AMERICAN KNOW-HOW By cutting the onions in half, the resulting slices don't become unwieldy rings. To do so, slice the onion through the root, then place it cut side down on your cutting board and slice it into ½-inch-thick rings.

sweet and sour roots

EFFORT: **NOT MUCH** • PREP TIME: **15 MINUTES** • COOK TIME: **3½ HOURS/6 HOURS** • KEEPS ON WARM: **2 HOURS** • SERVES: **4 TO 10**

INGREDIENTS	2- TO 3½-QT	4- TO 5½-QT	6- TO 8-QT
Carrots, cut into 1-inch segments	¾ pound	1¼ pounds	1¾ pounds
Parsnips, peeled and cut into 1-inch segments	¾ pound	1¼ pounds	1¾ pounds

	¾ pound	1¼ pounds	1¾ pounds
Turnips, peeled and cut into 1-inch chunks	¾ pound	1¼ pounds	1¾ pounds
Chopped red onion	½ cup	¾ cup (about 1 small)	1¼ cups
Dry vermouth	2 tblsp	3½ tblsp	⅓ cup
Olive oil	2 tblsp	3½ tblsp	⅓ cup
Balsamic vinegar	2 tblsp	3½ tblsp	⅓ cup
Honey	1 tblsp	5 tsp	2½ tblsp
Salt	½ tsp	¾ tsp	1 tsp
Ground black pepper	½ tsp	¾ tsp	1 tsp

1 Toss the carrots, parsnips, turnips, and red onion in the slow cooker.

2 Whisk the vermouth, olive oil, vinegar, honey, salt, and pepper in a large bowl until it's like a vinaigrette. Pour over the vegetables.

3 Cover and cook on high for 3½ hours or on low for 6 hours, or until the vegetables are fork-tender.

TESTERS' NOTES
• The most important part of this recipe is your knife technique: the vegetables should be cut into similarly sized pieces so they cook evenly.
• Dry vermouth has a slightly herbaceous edge that will work better than white wine with these root vegetables. But if all you've got is white wine on hand, use it. Or substitute low-sodium vegetable broth if you don't want any alcohol.
• There's no call for an aged syrupy balsamic vinegar here. Use a good-quality but rather inexpensive bottling.
• Substitute peeled and chunked rutabaga or even white potatoes for the turnips.

braised beets

EFFORT: **NOT MUCH** • PREP TIME: **15 MINUTES** • COOK TIME: **8 HOURS** • KEEPS ON WARM: **2 HOURS** • SERVES. **4 TO 10**

INGREDIENTS	2- TO 3½-QT	4- TO 5½-QT	6- TO 8-QT
Beets, peeled and diced	2 pounds	3½ pounds	5 pounds
Finely grated orange zest	1 tblsp	2½ tblsp	3½ tblsp
Salt	½ tsp	1¼ tsp	1½ tsp
Fresh thyme sprigs	2	5	7
Water	½ cup	1¼ cups	1¾ cups
Olive oil	1 tblsp	2½ tblsp	¼ cup

1 Stir the beets, orange zest, and salt in the slow cooker. Tuck in the thyme sprigs. Pour the water over the beets, then drizzle with olive oil.

2 Cover and cook on low for 8 hours, or until the beets are tender but still somewhat firm to the touch. Discard the thyme sprigs before serving with a slotted spoon (so as to keep the plates from getting waterlogged).

TESTERS' NOTES
• These beets are best if they're still a little firm to the bite, although tender throughout.
• Beets can, of course, stain everything in sight. It's best not to serve this dish to young children who can easily wipe beet juice onto furniture or linens. You'll also want to dish them up with the bowl quite close to the slow cooker, to avoid drips from all that purple juice.

ALL-AMERICAN KNOW-HOW To avoid stains on your hands, wear rubber gloves when peeling beets. If your hands do get stained, remove all jewelry, then rub your hands with fresh lemon juice, working it

(continued)

around your fingers and palms, until you notice that some of the stain is lifting off. Rinse well, then pour a small amount of coarse or kosher salt into your hands and rub them together. As the salt dissolves, more beet stain should lift off. Rinse and repeat to get off even more. Use a hand moisturizer when done, since the salt will dry out your skin.

wild rice with almonds and cherries

EFFORT: **A LITTLE** • PREP TIME: **30 MINUTES** • COOK TIME: **6 HOURS** • KEEPS ON WARM: **2 HOURS** • SERVES: **3 TO 8**

INGREDIENTS	2- TO 3½-QT	4- TO 5½-QT	6- TO 8-QT
Low-sodium vegetable broth	2¾ cups	5 cups	8 cups (2 quarts)
Wild rice (see page 88)	1 cup plus 2 tblsp	2 cups	3¼ cups
Chopped yellow onion	½ cup	¾ cup (about 1 small)	1¼ cups
Chopped celery	½ cup	¾ cup	1¼ cups
Chopped roasted unsalted almonds	6 tblsp	⅔ cup	¾ cup
Dried sour cherries	6 tblsp	⅔ cup	¾ cup
Dried sage	½ tsp	1 tsp	½ tblsp
Dried thyme	½ tsp	1 tsp	½ tblsp
Ground black pepper	½ tsp	1 tsp	½ tblsp
Salt	¼ tsp	½ tsp	¾ tsp

1 Mix the broth, rice, onion, celery, almonds, cherries, sage, thyme, pepper, and salt in the slow cooker.

2 Cover and cook on low for 6 hours, or until the wild rice is tender and almost all the liquid has been absorbed. Turn off the appliance and let stand, covered, for 10 minutes before serving.

TESTERS' NOTES
• Since this simple side dish offers big flavors, like those in the dried sour cherries, it will work best when paired with sweet-and-savory dishes—anything with a sweet barbecue sauce, or a deep pot roast braise with dried fruit in the mix.
• Look for roasted unsalted almonds either in the specialty foods aisle of your supermarket or in the nut section near the produce. Chop the almonds into bits so they blend throughout the dish, no piece of almond greater than a grain of rice.

spicy green rice

EFFORT: **A LITTLE** • PREP TIME: **20 MINUTES** • COOK TIME: **2 HOURS** • KEEPS ON WARM: **NO** • SERVES: **4 TO 10**

INGREDIENTS	2- TO 3½-QT	4- TO 5½-QT	6- TO 8-QT
Mild canned chopped green chiles	½ cup	¾ cup	1 cup
Thinly sliced whole scallions	3 tblsp	¼ cup	6 tblsp
Stemmed, seeded, and minced fresh jalapeño chile	2 tsp	1 tblsp	1½ tblsp
Medium garlic cloves, quartered	½	1	2
Chopped fresh cilantro leaves	¾ cup	1 cup	1½ cups

Uncooked long-grain white rice	1¾ cups	2½ cups	3¾ cups
Low-sodium chicken broth	3¼ cups	4½ cups (1 quart plus ½ cup)	6¾ cups

1 Place the chiles, scallions, jalapeño, and garlic in a large blender. Pulse a few times to get everything going on the blades, then scrape down the sides, add the cilantro, and blend into a paste.

2 Scrape this paste into the slow cooker. Stir in the rice and broth. Cover and cook on high for 1 hour.

3 Stir well, then cover and continue cooking on high for 1 additional hour, or until the rice is tender and almost all the liquid has been absorbed. Turn off the appliance and let stand, covered, for 10 minutes before serving.

TESTERS' NOTES
• Here's a spicy, flavorful side dish that'll go great with your next Tex-Mex meal. If you've got a second slow cooker, make refried beans, too (page 442).
• The jalapeño will carry the slightly sour, spiky heat into the dish, rather than the duller heat that would come from canned hot green chiles. Once again, there's no added salt here because the green chiles are notoriously doped with the stuff. Pass extra salt at the table.
• There's a ton of cilantro here—it *is* green rice, after all. Use down to half that amount, if you fear the herb.

ALL-AMERICAN KNOW-HOW Cilantro leaves can be quite sandy and leave behind unwanted grit. To wash them, clean your sink, then fill it halfway with cool water. Add the leaves, submerge them, agitate a bit, and leave them be for 5 minutes. Any grit will now sink to the bottom. Fish out the leaves without draining the sink and dry them on layers of paper towels laid out on your work surface. Finally, drain the sink to wash away the grit.

basic brown rice

EFFORT: **NOT MUCH** • PREP TIME: **15 MINUTES** • COOK TIME: **2 HOURS** • KEEPS ON WARM: **NO** • SERVES: **4 TO 10**

INGREDIENTS	2- TO 3½-QT	4- TO 5½-QT	6- TO 8-QT
Uncooked long-grain brown rice, such as jasmine or basmati	2 cups	3 cups	5 cups
Unsalted butter, cut into small pieces	2 tblsp	3 tblsp	5 tblsp
Salt	½ tsp	¾ tsp	1¼ tsp
Boiling water	3½ cups	5¼ cups	8¾ cups

1 Mix the rice, butter, and salt in the slow cooker. Pour the boiling water over the rice.

2 Cover and cook for 2 hours on high, or until the rice is tender and the water has been absorbed.

TESTERS' NOTES
• We find that without other starches or culinary safeguards, white rice turns gummy in the slow cooker; but brown rice works perfectly.
• Measure just how much water you need into the saucepan, then bring it to a boil over high heat. Watch closely so you can pour it over the rice the moment it's at a boil (and so you don't lose too much water to evaporation). Cover the slow cooker quickly to preserve the heat.

Serve It Up! Add minced chives or any other fresh minced herbs to the batch, or substitute sesame oil for the butter.

ALL-AMERICAN KNOW-HOW Cooked rice should be left off the heat to steam a few minutes before serving. The temperature cools somewhat as the steam settles and the grains plump from the extra moisture at the end.

brown rice pilaf
with asparagus and cashews

EFFORT: **NOT MUCH** • PREP TIME: **15 MINUTES** • COOK TIME:
3 HOURS • KEEPS ON WARM: **NO** • SERVES: **3 TO 8**

INGREDIENTS	2- TO 3½-QT	4- TO 5½-QT	6- TO 8-QT
Low-sodium vegetable broth	3 cups	5 cups	8 cups (2 quarts)
Uncooked long-grain brown rice, such as brown basmati	1¼ cups	2 cups	3¼ cups
Thin asparagus spears, trimmed and cut into 1-inch pieces	¼ pound	½ pound	¾ pound
Chopped toasted unsalted cashews	⅓ cup	½ cup	¾ cup
Minced shallot	3 tblsp	¼ cup	7 tblsp
Minced garlic	2 tsp	1 tblsp	1½ tblsp
Stemmed fresh thyme leaves	½ tblsp	2 tsp	1 tblsp
Ground turmeric	¼ tsp	½ tsp	¾ tsp
Salt	¼ tsp	½ tsp	¾ tsp
Ground black pepper	¼ tsp	½ tsp	¾ tsp

1 Stir the broth, rice, asparagus, cashews, shallot, garlic, thyme, turmeric, salt, and pepper in the slow cooker.

2 Cover and cook on high for 3 hours, or until the rice is tender and almost all the liquid has been absorbed. Turn off the appliance and let stand for 10 minutes, covered, before serving.

TESTERS' NOTES
• This simple pilaf offers fairly big flavors as a payoff for a simple prep. You can't beat that!

• Brown jasmine rice is a tad aromatic for this dish. The rice should simply become the starchy background to the other ingredients.

• Asparagus stalks can be woody and tough, particularly if they're more than ½ inch in diameter. Shave the thicker ones down with a vegetable peeler to a more appropriate size; always remove and discard any woody or desiccated bottoms to the stalks.

brown rice and pumpkin risotto

EFFORT: **A LOT** • PREP TIME: **30 MINUTES** • COOK TIME: **2½ HOURS**
• KEEPS ON WARM: **NO** • SERVES: **2 TO 8**

INGREDIENTS	2- TO 3½-QT	4- TO 5½-QT	6- TO 8-QT
Unsalted butter	1½ tblsp	2 tblsp	3 tblsp
Chopped yellow onion	½ cup	¾ cup (about 1 small)	1 cup plus 2 tblsp
Minced garlic	1 tsp	2 tsp	1 tblsp
Cremini or brown button mushrooms, thinly sliced	4 ounces (about 1¼ cups)	6 ounces (about 2 cups)	10 ounces (about 3 cups)
Salt	¼ tsp	½ tsp	¾ tsp
Dry white wine, such as Pinot Grigio	3 tblsp	⅓ cup	½ cup
Peeled, seeded, and diced pumpkin	2½ cups	4 cups	6 cups
Low-sodium chicken broth	1½ cups	2½ cups	3¾ cups
Uncooked medium-grain brown rice, such as brown Arborio	½ cup plus 1 tblsp	1 cup	1½ cups

	½ tsp	1 tsp	½ tblsp
Dried thyme	½ tsp	1 tsp	½ tblsp
Ground black pepper	¼ tsp	½ tsp	¾ tsp
Parmigiano-Reggiano cheese, finely grated	¾ ounce (about 3 tblsp)	2 ounces (about ½ cup)	2½ ounces (about ⅔ cup)

1 Melt the butter in a large skillet set over medium-low heat. Add the onion and cook, stirring often, until it softens and begins to turn golden, between 5 and 8 minutes.

2 Add the garlic, stir over the heat for 10 seconds, then dump in the mushrooms and salt. Raise the heat to medium and cook, stirring often, until the mushrooms give off their liquid and that liquid reduces to a thick glaze, between 5 and 8 minutes.

3 Pour in the wine and bring to a boil, scraping up any browned bits in the skillet. Pour and scrape the contents of the skillet into the slow cooker. Stir in the pumpkin, broth, rice, thyme, and pepper.

4 Cover and cook on high for 2 hours 15 minutes, or until the liquid has been mostly absorbed and both the rice and pumpkin are tender.

5 Uncover and cook on low for 15 minutes, until the risotto is creamy and moist without much noticeable moisture. Stir in the cheese to serve.

TESTERS' NOTES
• This whole-grain side dish could also be a quick evening meal, perhaps started before you head out to the movies and then finished when you get home.
• It's important to dice the pumpkin—that is, prep it into bits no larger than ¼ inch. Otherwise, the rice will be done long before the vegetable.
• The chicken broth gives the dish a bit more heft. Use vegetable broth for a vegetarian side.

SHORTCUTS Omit the pumpkin and substitute diced peeled and seeded butternut squash.

ALL-AMERICAN KNOW-HOW Mushrooms are stocked full of moisture, sometimes near 90 percent of their total weight. All that water comes out when they are heated and turns a sauce soggy. Anyone who's baked raw mushrooms on a pizza knows the problem. It's important, then, to get rid of the moisture by cooking the mushrooms a bit. Don't crowd the skillet; rather, use one large enough so that the released liquid can boil away quickly and efficiently.

creamed corn

EFFORT: **NOT MUCH** • PREP TIME: **10 MINUTES** • COOK TIME: **2 HOURS** • KEEPS ON WARM: **2 HOURS** • SERVES: **3 TO 8**

INGREDIENTS	2- TO 3½-QT	4- TO 5½-QT	6- TO 8-QT
Corn kernels, fresh cut from cob, or thawed frozen	4 cups	6 cups	9 cups
Evaporated milk	¾ cup	1 cup plus 2 tblsp	1¾ cups
Heavy cream	¼ cup	6 tblsp	½ cup plus 1 tblsp
All-purpose flour	2 tblsp	3 tblsp	4½ tblsp
Sugar	1½ tblsp	2½ tblsp	¼ cup
Salt	½ tsp	¾ tsp	1 tsp
Ground black pepper	⅛ tsp	¼ tsp	½ tsp

1 Whisk the corn, evaporated milk, cream, flour, sugar, salt, and pepper in the slow cooker until the flour dissolves.

(continued)

2 Cover and cook on high for 1 hour. Stir well, mashing some of the kernels against the sides of the cooker before stirring them back into the mix. Cover and cook on high for 1 more hour, or until somewhat thickened.

TESTERS' NOTES
• Once you make creamed corn at home, you'll never go back to the can. You can use regular or low-fat evaporated milk, and light cream or half-and-half instead of the heavy cream.

• Use either frozen corn kernels, thawed, or fresh kernels cut off the ears. An ear of corn should yield about ½ cup of kernels.

INGREDIENTS EXPLAINED In the United States, there are marked differences among types of cream. Heavy cream, also called whipping cream, has a butterfat content of between 36 and 40 percent. Light cream is no diet product, but at about 20 percent butterfat it is indeed "lighter" than heavy cream. Half-and-half, despite its name, is a combination of cream and whole milk that leans toward the milk part of that equation, with about 12 percent butterfat.

loaded cornbread

EFFORT: **A LITTLE** • PREP TIME: **15 MINUTES** • COOK TIME: **1 HOUR 5 MINUTES TO 1 HOUR 15 MINUTES** • KEEPS ON WARM: **NO** • SERVES: **4 TO 8**

INGREDIENTS	2- TO 3½-QT	4- TO 5½-QT	6- TO 8-QT
Fine- or medium-ground cornmeal	¾ cup	1 cup plus 2 tblsp	1½ cups
All-purpose flour	¾ cup	1 cup plus 2 tblsp	1½ cups
Baking soda	½ tsp	¾ tsp	1 tsp
Large eggs, at room temperature	2	3	4
Buttermilk (regular or low-fat)	1 cup	1½ cups	2 cups
Drained and rinsed canned black beans	½ cup	¾ cup	1 cup
Cheddar cheese, shredded	2 ounces (about ½ cup)	3 ounces (about ¾ cup)	4 ounces (about 1 cup)
Canned chopped green chiles, hot or mild	3 tblsp	4½ tblsp	6 tblsp
Unsalted butter, melted	2 tblsp	3 tblsp	4 tblsp (½ stick)

1 Generously butter the inside of the slow cooker canister.

2 Whisk the cornmeal, flour, and baking soda in a bowl until combined.

3 Whisk the eggs in a second bowl until creamy, then whisk in the buttermilk, beans, cheese, chiles, and butter. Stir the cornmeal mixture into the buttermilk mixture for a smooth but fairly thick batter. Pour the batter into the slow cooker. Lay overlapping paper towels over the top of the cooker.

4 Cover and cook on high for 1 hour 5 minutes in a small slow cooker, 1 hour 10 minutes in a medium cooker, or 1 hour 15 minutes in a large model, or until the top of the cornbread is set when touched. Uncover and cool in the cooker for at least 1 hour—or remove the insert from the cooker and set it, uncovered, on a wire rack to cool for at least 30 minutes. Use a nonstick-safe spatula or knife to cut squares of the cornbread right out of the canister.

TESTERS' NOTES
- You could make a meal of this well-stocked side dish with a bowl of tomato soup on the side.
- Because of the cheese in the batter, the cornbread has a tendency to stick in the cooker, no matter how much you buttered it. Run a nonstick-safe spatula around the edge of the cornbread before you cut it.

buttery onions

EFFORT. **NOT MUCH** • PREP TIME: **10 MINUTES** • COOK TIME: **12 TO 16 HOURS** • KEEPS ON WARM: **3 HOURS** • SERVES: **4 TO 10**

INGREDIENTS	2- TO 3½-QT	4- TO 5½-QT	6- TO 8-QT
Yellow onions, cut in half through the root and then into very thin half-moons	5 medium	5 large	7 large
Unsalted butter, cut into small bits	4 tblsp (½ stick)	6 tblsp	8 tblsp (1 stick)
Salt	½ tsp	¾ tsp	1 tsp

1 Separate the onion half-moons into individual half-rings. Stir the onions, butter, and salt in the slow cooker.

2 Cover and cook on low for 12 hours in a small slow cooker, 14 hours in a medium cooker, or 16 hours in a large cooker, or until the onions are incredibly soft, sweet, and even mahogany brown.

TESTERS' NOTES
- If you want to make softened onions for just about any sauce or condiment, look no further for the ultimate recipe. Not only will the onions caramelize but the butter will also brown a bit, adding a nutty, earthy flavor to the sweetened onions.

- Set the onion halves cut side down on your cutting board and slice them as thin as possible. And make sure the individual strips have separated from the slices for even cooking.

Serve It Up! These are great on burgers or hot dogs, with grilled brats or kielbasa, in omelets or on eggs of all kinds, in baked potatoes, or alongside roasted just-about-anything. They're also a good sandwich spread. Mix them with sour cream and mayonnaise for a dip. Or pump up store-bought hummus by stirring some in. Or stuff them into trout or whole fish before grilling.

caramelized onions with cranberries and walnuts

EFFORT: **NOT MUCH** • PREP TIME: **15 MINUTES** • COOK TIME: **12 TO 14 HOURS** • KEEPS ON WARM: **3 HOURS** • SERVES: **3 TO 8**

INGREDIENTS	2- TO 3½-QT	4- TO 5½-QT	6- TO 8-QT
White onions, halved and thinly sliced	5 medium	6 large	9 large
Olive oil	¼ cup	⅓ cup	½ cup
Dried cranberries	¼ cup	⅓ cup	½ cup
Chopped walnuts	¼ cup	⅓ cup	½ cup
Salt	1 tsp	½ tblsp	2 tsp

1 Stir the onions, olive oil, cranberries, walnuts, and salt in the slow cooker.

(continued)

2 Cover and cook on low for 12 hours in a small slow cooker, 13 hours in a medium one, or 14 hours in a large cooker, or until the onions have become dark, thick, and rich.

TESTERS' NOTES

• This may well be the ultimate Thanksgiving side dish for the roast turkey. Or just ladle these onions onto a baked potato with some sour cream.

• For more flavor, toast the walnut pieces in a dry skillet over medium-low heat for about 5 minutes, stirring often, until very aromatic and lightly browned. Remove from the heat and cool for at least 15 minutes before chopping into small bits.

stuffed roasted onions

EFFORT: **A LITTLE** • PREP TIME: **30 MINUTES** • COOK TIME: **8 HOURS** • KEEPS ON WARM: **2 HOURS** • SERVES: **4 TO 8**

INGREDIENTS	2- TO 3½-QT	4- TO 5½-QT	6- TO 8-QT
Medium white onions	4	6	8
Cooked white rice	2 cups	3 cups	4 cups
Finely chopped cremini or brown button mushrooms	½ cup	¾ cup	1 cup
Stemmed, seeded, and minced red bell pepper	¼ cup	6 tblsp	½ cup
Parmigiano-Reggiano cheese, finely grated	½ ounce (about 2 tblsp)	¾ ounce (about 3 tblsp)	1 ounce (about ¼ cup)
Dried oregano	½ tsp	¾ tsp	1 tsp
Dried thyme	½ tsp	¾ tsp	1 tsp
Dried rosemary, crumbled	½ tsp	¾ tsp	1 tsp
Dried marjoram	½ tsp	¾ tsp	1 tsp
Salt	⅛ tsp	¼ tsp	½ tsp

1 Cut the top quarters of the onions off the root ends and discard the tops. Peel the papery skins off the onions, then slice a small bit off the root ends, just so the onions will stand up on a flat surface.

2 Use a melon baller or an apple corer to remove the cores of the onions, taking care to leave plenty of support (and layers) around their walls and making sure you don't break through the bottoms.

3 Dab some olive oil on a paper towel and grease the inside of the slow cooker. Brush the outside of each onion with olive oil.

4 Mix the rice, mushrooms, bell pepper, cheese, oregano, thyme, rosemary, marjoram, and salt in a small bowl. Stuff this mixture into the hollows of each onion; stand them up in the slow cooker.

5 Cover and cook on low for 8 hours, or until the onions are very soft and lightly golden. Remove them from the slow cooker with a large slotted spoon.

TESTERS' NOTES

• These stuffed onions can be a side dish to almost any meat—lamb to pork, beef to turkey.

• The mushrooms need to be very finely chopped. An easy way to do that is to drop them into a food processor and pulse until coarsely ground but not yet a paste. Likewise, the bell pepper should be minced, no single piece bigger than a grain of cooked rice.

SHORTCUTS Omit the oregano, thyme, rosemary, marjoram, and salt; instead, use a bottled Italian seasoning blend: 2 teaspoons for a small batch, 1 tablespoon for a medium batch, and 1½ tablespoons for a large batch. If the blend includes salt, omit the additional salt from the recipe.

cauliflower in browned butter

EFFORT: **A LITTLE** • PREP TIME: **15 MINUTES** • COOK TIME: **2½ HOURS** • KEEPS ON WARM: **NO** • SERVES: **3 TO 8**

INGREDIENTS	2- TO 3½-QT	4- TO 5½-QT	6- TO 8-QT
Whole cauliflower	1 pound	1¾ pounds	2½ pounds
Unsalted butter	3 tblsp	6 tblsp	8 tblsp
Sliced almonds	2 tblsp	3 tblsp	¼ cup
Salt	¼ tsp	½ tsp	1 tsp

1 Remove the leaves from the cauliflower, then slice the head in half stem to top. Cut out the stem as well as the hard core from each half. Chunk the cauliflower into large pieces, 2 inches each, and set these in the slow cooker.

2 Melt the butter in a large skillet over medium heat. Add the almonds and salt; cook until the nuts are golden, stirring often, between 2 and 4 minutes. Scrape the contents of the skillet over the cauliflower chunks.

3 Cover and cook on low for 2½ hours, or until the butter has browned and the cauliflower is tender. Transfer to plates by the spoonful, getting some buttery sauce with each serving.

TESTERS' NOTES
• As butter browns, it takes on a nutty, slightly bitter flavor, a perfect match for cauliflower.
• In order to make sure the cauliflower has some firmness after cooking, cut into larger chunks rather than florets.
• Check the cauliflower occasionally, sticking a toothpick or cake tester into a piece to make sure you still meet some resistance. It should be tender, not mushy.

vermouth-braised fennel

EFFORT: **NOT MUCH** • PREP TIME: **10 MINUTES** • COOK TIME: **3 HOURS** • KEEPS ON WARM: **1 HOUR** • SERVES: **4 TO 10**

INGREDIENTS	2- TO 3½-QT	4- TO 5½-QT	6- TO 8-QT
Fennel bulbs, trimmed and cut into 4-inch long chunks (see page 211)	4 medium	4 large	6 large
Dry vermouth	⅔ cup	1 cup	2 cups
Fresh oregano sprigs	2	3	5
Medium garlic cloves, peeled	2	3	5
Salt	½ tsp	¾ tsp	1 tsp
Ground black pepper	½ tsp	¾ tsp	1 tsp
Olive oil	1 tblsp	2 tblsp	3 tblsp

1 Place the fennel chunks in the slow cooker; pour the vermouth over them. Tuck the oregano sprigs and garlic cloves among the chunks. Sprinkle with salt and pepper, then drizzle with olive oil.

2 Cover and cook on high for 3 hours, or until the fennel is crisp-tender. Lift the fennel out of the slow cooker with a slotted spoon and discard the poaching liquid.

TESTERS' NOTES
• You can use large fennel bulbs cut into quarters, medium bulbs cut in halves, or small bulbs left whole.
• The liquid in the slow cooker isn't a good sauce—but don't miss those softened garlic cloves, especially if you can spread them on a slice of crunchy bread.
• For more fennel flavor in the poaching liquid, add some of the feathery fennel fronds to the mix. One warning: they may well glom onto the fennel chunks.

olive oil–poached broccoli rabe

EFFORT: **A LITTLE** • PREP TIME: **15 MINUTES** • COOK TIME: **2½ HOURS** • KEEPS ON WARM: **NO** • SERVES: **3 TO 10**

INGREDIENTS	2- TO 3½-QT	4- TO 5½-QT	6- TO 8-QT
Olive oil	⅔ cup	1 cup	2¼ cups
Thinly sliced garlic	3 tblsp	¼ cup	⅓ cup
Red pepper flakes	1 tsp	½ tblsp	2 tsp
Broccoli rabe, trimmed of tough ends and cut into 4-inch pieces	1 pound	2 pounds	3½ pounds
Salt	½ tsp	1 tsp	½ tblsp

1 Pour the olive oil into a skillet. Heat slowly for 3 or 4 minutes over low heat. Add the garlic and fry, stirring occasionally, until lightly browned around the edges and even a little blistered, about 4 minutes. Remove the garlic from the oil with a slotted spoon and set aside.

2 With the skillet still over low heat, add the red pepper flakes and cook until aromatic, 20 to 30 seconds. Scrape into the slow cooker. Add the broccoli rabe and salt; toss well.

3 Cover and cook on high, stirring twice, for 2½ hours, or until the broccoli rabe is tender. Remove the vegetables from the slow cooker with tongs, leaving the oil behind. Slice the browned garlic into small bits and serve with the rabe.

TESTERS' NOTES
• Look no further for the ultimate side dish for your next Italian-themed supper or dinner party. The olive oil here will give the broccoli rabe a velvety sheen and texture, a luxury indeed.

• Some broccoli rabe, particularly organic selections or those from farmers' markets, may have grit adhering to the heads. Wash them well and dry completely before adding to the oil. There should not be a drop of water anywhere.

INGREDIENTS EXPLAINED Broccoli rabe—also called *rapini* or *broccoletti*—is a prized vegetable in southern European and even Chinese cooking. A member of the mustard family, high in vitamins A and C as well as potassium and iron, broccoli rabe has a spiky, peppery flavor. Each stem has a number of curly leaves that surround a small head of buds that somewhat resemble broccoli.

wine-steamed artichokes

EFFORT: **A LITTLE** • PREP TIME: **25 MINUTES** • COOK TIME: **6 HOURS** • KEEPS ON WARM: **1 HOUR** • SERVES: **4 TO 10**

INGREDIENTS	2- TO 3½-QT	4- TO 5½-QT	6- TO 8-QT
Medium artichokes	4	6	10
Lemons, halved	2	3	5
4-inch rosemary sprigs	1	2	3
Moderately dry white wine, such as a French Chablis	½ cup	¾ cup	1¼ cups

1 Trim each artichoke by first removing the stem, then cutting off the top third, thereby removing many of the thorny leaf tips. Pull off the very fibrous outer leaves, then pry open the vegetable and scrape out the hairy, thistle bits that cover the heart. Rub the artichoke all over with a cut lemon, then set it in the slow cooker and continue trimming and preparing the remainder, placing them in one layer, preferably cut side down.

2 Tuck the lemon halves and rosemary sprigs among the artichokes. Pour in the wine, then add enough water to the slow cooker so that the liquid comes halfway up the artichokes.

3 Cover and cook on low for 6 hours, or until the stem ends of the artichokes are tender when pricked with a fork. Use tongs to remove them, draining them of excess water by turning them upside down before placing on plates.

TESTERS' NOTES
• Although it seems you lose a lot when you trim an artichoke, most of what disappears is too fibrous or thorny to make for good dining. That said, if the stems are not too thick, toss them into the slow cooker.
• If you add some purchased cooked shrimp and a tangy cocktail sauce, you've got dinner.

Serve It Up! Eat the artichoke by pulling off the leaves and drawing the inside curve against your upper teeth, thereby scraping off some of the edible bits. Once you get down to the heart, it becomes a fork-and-knife affair. Melted butter is the usual dipping medium for the leaves, but there's no reason to stand on ceremony. Try cocktail sauce, ketchup, mustard, Ranch dressing, Russian dressing, a creamy vinaigrette, or even salsa.

ALL-AMERICAN KNOW-HOW Artichokes are prone to discoloration, thanks to the way oxidizing compounds turn brown when exposed to the air. Rubbing the prepared vegetables well with lemon juice may take care of some of the problem. However, the artichokes may still turn brown during the long cooking. It may be unsightly but they are still perfectly edible.

roasted brussels sprouts and chestnuts

EFFORT: **NOT MUCH** • PREP TIME: **15 MINUTES** • COOK TIME: **3 HOURS** • KEEPS ON WARM: **1 HOUR** • SERVES: **3 TO 8**

INGREDIENTS	2- TO 3½-QT	4- TO 5½-QT	6- TO 8-QT
Small Brussels sprouts, trimmed	3 cups	5 cups	8 cups
Jarred roasted chestnuts	¾ cup	1¼ cups	2 cups
Leeks (white and pale green part only), halved lengthwise, the interior sections washed for sand, and thinly sliced	¼ pound	½ pound	¾ pound
Unsalted butter, melted	2 tblsp	3 tblsp	4 tblsp (½ stick)
Dried sage	½ tsp	1 tsp	½ tblsp
Salt	¼ tsp	¾ tsp	1 tsp
Grated nutmeg	⅛ tsp	¼ tsp	½ tsp

1 Put the Brussels sprouts, chestnuts, leeks, butter, sage, salt, and nutmeg in the slow cooker. Stir well.

2 Cover and cook on high for 3 hours, tossing after the first and second hours, until the Brussels sprouts are crisp-tender when poked with a fork.

TESTERS' NOTES
• The best Brussels sprouts are the smaller heads, sweeter and not quite so bitter. You may have to poke around in the bin to find the small ones.
• To trim Brussels sprouts, cut off the woody stem end and pull off any fibrous, yellowing, or loose outer leaves until you have a compact head. If you're lucky enough to find

(continued)

Brussels sprouts still on the stalk, slice them off one by one and trim them as well.
• For some heat, add up to 1 teaspoon red pepper flakes.

---

sesame beans

EFFORT: **NOT MUCH** • PREP TIME: **10 MINUTES** • COOK TIME: **2 HOURS** • KEEPS ON WARM: **NO** • SERVES: **3 TO 8**

INGREDIENTS	2- TO 3½-QT	4- TO 5½-QT	6- TO 8-QT
Green beans, trimmed and tipped	1 pound	1¾ pounds	2½ pounds
Medium whole scallions, minced	1	2	3
Ginger jam	2 tblsp	3½ tblsp	5 tblsp
Soy sauce	2 tblsp	3½ tblsp	5 tblsp
Toasted sesame oil (see page 196)	2 tblsp	3½ tblsp	5 tblsp
White sesame seeds	2 tsp	1 tblsp	1½ tblsp

1 Stir the green beans and scallions in the slow cooker. Whisk the ginger jam, soy sauce, sesame oil, and sesame seeds in a large bowl until the jam dissolves. Pour over the vegetables and toss well.

2 Cover and cook on high for 2 hours, or until the beans are crisp-tender.

TESTERS' NOTES
• These green beans would be a welcome treat alongside almost any Asian stir-fry, as well as most things off the grill—especially tuna steaks with a wasabi rub.
• We like some crunch to our green beans. If you want them softer, cook for 3 hours.

INGREDIENTS EXPLAINED Ginger jam is a salty, spicy condiment often found in the international foods aisle, usually near other British foods.

ALL-AMERICAN KNOW-HOW Most green beans have a small bit of their stem and blossom at one end; this should be removed. The other end has a small "tail," as it were, which can be excessively fibrous. While edible, it's considered culinarily unappealing and so is usually snapped or cut off—and thus, the green beans will have been *tipped*.

---

kale in a spicy tomato sauce

EFFORT: **A LITTLE** • PREP TIME: **20 MINUTES** • COOK TIME: **4½ HOURS** • KEEPS ON WARM: **1 HOUR** • SERVES: **3 TO 8**

INGREDIENTS	2- TO 3½-QT	4- TO 5½-QT	6- TO 8-QT
No-salt-added canned crushed tomatoes	1⅔ cups	2¼ cups	3½ cups
Drained no-salt-added canned diced tomatoes	½ cup	¾ cup	1¼ cups
Chopped yellow onion	½ cup	¾ cup (about 1 small)	1¼ cups
Minced garlic	2½ tsp	1½ tblsp	2 tblsp
Red pepper flakes	¼ tsp	½ tsp	1 tsp
Salt	¼ tsp	½ tsp	1 tsp
Ground black pepper	⅛ tsp	¼ tsp	½ tsp
Kale, washed, stemmed, and chopped	¾ pound	1 pound	1¼ pounds

1 Mix the tomatoes, onion, garlic, red pepper flakes, salt, and pepper in the slow cooker. Cover and cook on high for 3 hours.

2 Add the kale; stir well. Cover and cook on high for 45 minutes. Stir again, then continue cooking on high for another 45 minutes, or until the kale is wilted and tender.

TESTERS' NOTES
• Good enough to be a light, vegetarian entree on its own when served over whole wheat pasta, this tasty side dish would also be welcome alongside a steak, a veal chop, or roast chicken.
• Kale leaves often have a tough, fibrous center stem that should be removed from each leaf before chopping. However, some varieties of kale have a much smaller center stem that tenderizes quickly. Ask the person in the produce section of your supermarket for guidance—or the farmer, if you're lucky enough to buy the kale at a farmers' market.

collards and bacon

EFFORT: **A LITTLE** • PREP TIME: **15 MINUTES** • COOK TIME: **4 HOURS** • KEEPS ON WARM: **1 HOUR** • SERVES: **3 TO 8**

INGREDIENTS	2- TO 3½-QT	4- TO 5½-QT	6- TO 8-QT
Thin strips of bacon, chopped	3 ounces	4 ounces	8 ounces
Minced garlic	1½ tblsp	2 tblsp	3 tblsp
Red pepper flakes	¼ tsp	½ tsp	¾ tsp
Dry white wine, such as Chardonnay	⅔ cup	1 cup	1⅔ cups
White wine vinegar	2 tsp	1 tblsp	2 tblsp
Collard greens, washed, stemmed, and chopped	¾ pound	1 pound	1½ pounds

1 Fry the bacon in a large skillet set over medium heat until crisp, stirring occasionally, between 4 and 7 minutes. Add the garlic and red pepper flakes; cook until the garlic begins to brown at the edges, about 1 minute.

2 Scrape the contents of the skillet into the slow cooker, then set the skillet back over the heat and pour in the wine. Raise the heat to high and bring to a full boil, scraping up any browned bits in the skillet. Continue boiling until the wine has reduced by half its original volume, between 2 and 4 minutes. Pour the reduced wine sauce into the slow cooker.

3 Stir in the vinegar. Add the collard greens and toss well, getting the garlic and red pepper flakes distributed evenly throughout the greens.

4 Cover and cook on low for 4 hours, or until the greens are tender but not squishy.

TESTERS' NOTES
• If you're making fried chicken or a pan-fried slice of ham, you'll want to have this side dish going—and maybe have some cornbread baking in the oven as well.
• Collard greens can be quite sandy, particularly if you bought them at a farmers' market. Wash the leaves well, then dry them between sheets of paper towels before chopping.

spaghetti squash
with pine nuts and sage

EFFORT: **A LOT** • PREP TIME: **15 MINUTES** • COOK TIME: **6 HOURS 45 MINUTES** • KEEPS ON WARM: **2 HOURS** • SERVES: **3 TO 8**

INGREDIENTS	2- TO 3½-QT	4- TO 5½-QT	6- TO 8-QT
Small spaghetti squash (about 2½ pounds)	1	2	3
Unsalted butter, cut into small chunks	6 tblsp	8 tblsp (1 stick)	10 tblsp
Pine nuts	¼ cup	⅓ cup	½ cup
Chopped fresh sage leaves	2 tblsp	3 tblsp	¼ cup
Salt	½ tsp	¾ tsp	1 tsp

1 Use a metal skewer or a meat fork to poke holes all over the spaghetti squash. Set in the slow cooker. Pour water into the cooker to come 2 inches up the squash.

2 Cover and cook on low for 6 hours, or until the squash feels tender to the touch and is perhaps even collapsing at points.

3 Transfer the squash to a cutting board; drain the liquid from the cooker. Turn the cooker off and cool the squash for 30 minutes, or until easily handled.

4 Stir the butter, pine nuts, sage, and salt in the slow cooker; cover and cook on high while you complete the next step.

5 Slice the squash in half lengthwise. Scrape out the seeds, then use a fork to scrape the flesh into threads. Transfer the squash threads to the cooker and stir well.

6 Cover and cook on high for 15 minutes to heat everything through. Stir well again and scoop up by the spoonful.

TESTERS' NOTES
• Spaghetti squash cooks up into little threads, about like spaghetti only sweeter and a bit firmer. Mixed with butter, sage, and pine nuts, it's a wonderful side dish—or even a simple vegetarian dinner.
• Use the squash as a bed for pan-fried pork chops or chicken breasts. For a fancier presentation, mound the squash on a platter, and top with one or two whole grilled fish.
• If you can only find large spaghetti squash, say 5 to 7 pounds, you can make it in the large slow cooker; however, plan on cooking it on low for 8 hours to get tender.

Serve It Up! Toss the cooked squash with finely grated Parmigiano-Reggiano.

cider-braised delicata squash

EFFORT: **NOT MUCH** • PREP TIME: **15 MINUTES** • COOK TIME: **3 HOURS** • KEEPS ON WARM: **2 HOURS** • SERVES: **4 TO 10**

INGREDIENTS	2- TO 3½-QT	4- TO 5½-QT	6- TO 8-QT
Medium delicata squash, halved, seeded, and sliced into 2-inch-thick half-moons	3	5	8
Fresh cranberries, roughly chopped	¼ cup	⅓ cup	½ cup
No-sugar-added apple cider	½ cup	¾ cup	1¼ cups
Salt	¼ tsp	½ tsp	¾ tsp
Ground cinnamon	¼ tsp	¼ tsp	½ tsp
Honey	1 tblsp	2 tblsp	3 tblsp

1 Stir the squash and cranberries in the slow cooker. Pour the cider over them, sprinkle with the salt and cinnamon, then drizzle with the honey.

2 Cover and cook on high for 3 hours, or until the squash is tender when poked with a fork.

TESTERS' NOTES
• Since the skin of delicata squash is edible, there's no need to peel it before it goes into the cooker.
• For a richer dish, drizzle up to 2 tablespoons melted butter over the squash with the honey.
• The juices and cranberries make a great sauce for roast chicken, turkey, or ham.

ratatouille

EFFORT: **NOT MUCH** • PREP TIME: **20 MINUTES** • COOK TIME: **8 HOURS** • KEEPS ON WARM: **2 HOURS** • SERVES: **3 TO 10**

INGREDIENTS	2- TO 3½-QT	4- TO 5½-QT	6- TO 8-QT
Zucchini, cubed	½ pound	1¼ pounds	2 pounds
Eggplant, cubed	6 ounces	1 pound	1½ pounds
Medium green bell peppers, stemmed, seeded, and chopped	1	2	4
Ripe tomatoes, chopped	½ pound	1 pound	1½ pounds
Yellow onion, chopped	1 small	1 large	2 medium
Minced mixed leafy green herbs, such as marjoram and rosemary, or oregano, thyme, and parsley	1½ tblsp	2½ tblsp	¼ cup
Olive oil	1½ tblsp	2½ tblsp	¼ cup
Minced garlic	1 tsp	2 tsp	1 tblsp
Salt	¼ tsp	½ tsp	1 tsp
Ground black pepper	¼ tsp	½ tsp	1 tsp

1 Stir the zucchini, eggplant, bell pepper, tomatoes, onion, herbs, olive oil, garlic, salt, and pepper in the slow cooker.

2 Cover and cook on low for 8 hours, or until the tomatoes break down and the mixture has a stew-like consistency.

TESTERS' NOTES
• There's no need to peel the eggplant or tomatoes for this easy version of the side-dish favorite. Those skins will soften beautifully during the long cooking.
• Chop the zucchini and eggplant into 1-inch cubes so they retain some texture in the final dish.
• Add up to 1 teaspoon red pepper flakes with the other ingredients for some spiky heat.

Serve It Up! Our favorite way to enjoy ratatouille is to poach eggs and then set them in a bowl of the warm vegetable stew, letting the runny yolk mix with the tomatoes and vegetables.

caponata

EFFORT: **A LITTLE** • PREP TIME: **30 MINUTES** • COOK TIME: **5 HOURS** • KEEPS ON WARM: **3 HOURS** • SERVES: **4 TO 10**

INGREDIENTS	2- TO 3½-QT	4- TO 5½-QT	6- TO 8-QT
Eggplant, diced	1 pound	1½ pounds	3 pounds
Red onion, diced	1 small	1 medium	1 large
Medium celery ribs, diced	1	2	3
Minced pitted green olives	¾ cup	1 cup plus 2 tblsp	1¾ cups
Drained, rinsed, and minced capers	¼ cup	6 tblsp	½ cup
Olive oil	¼ cup	6 tblsp	½ cup
No-salt-added tomato paste	¼ cup	6 tblsp	½ cup
Red wine vinegar	¼ cup	6 tblsp	½ cup
Packed dark brown sugar	3 tblsp	⅓ cup	½ cup
Minced golden raisins	3 tblsp	⅓ cup	½ cup
Minced garlic	2 tsp	1 tblsp	1½ tblsp
Dried oregano	2 tsp	1 tblsp	1½ tblsp
Red pepper flakes	½ tsp	¾ tsp	1 tsp

1 Stir the eggplant, red onion, celery, green olives, capers, olive oil, tomato paste, vinegar, brown sugar, golden raisins, garlic, oregano, and red pepper flakes in the slow cooker.

2 Cover and cook on high for 5 hours, or until the eggplant breaks apart into an almost spreadable relish, the whole kit and caboodle thickened to a soft, sauce-like condiment.

TESTERS' NOTES
• This traditional Italian side dish is best served as a sauce on steamed or roasted vegetables—or with almost anything off the grill. It's also great as an appetizer, spread on toasted baguette slices.

• Dice the eggplant into small bits, about ½ inch each, so they melt into the sauce.

• This caponata freezes exceptionally well for up to 3 months. Thaw containers in the fridge overnight (rather than quickly in the microwave) for the best texture.

sweet and sour red cabbage

EFFORT: **NOT MUCH** • PREP TIME: **20 MINUTES** • COOK TIME: **8 HOURS** • KEEPS ON WARM: **2 HOURS** • SERVES: **3 TO 8**

INGREDIENTS	2- TO 3½-QT	4- TO 5½-QT	6- TO 8-QT
Red cabbage, cored and chopped	1 pound	2 pounds	3 pounds
Red onion, chopped	1 small	2 small	2 medium
Fresh orange juice	½ cup	1 cup	1½ cups
Red wine vinegar	½ cup	1 cup	1½ cups
Packed light brown sugar	¼ cup	½ cup	¾ cup
Red currant jelly	¼ cup	½ cup	¾ cup
Finely grated orange zest	2 tsp	1½ tblsp	2 tblsp
Salt	½ tsp	1 tsp	½ tblsp
Ground black pepper	½ tsp	1 tsp	½ tblsp
Fresh thyme sprigs	1	2	3
4-inch cinnamon sticks	1	1½	2

1 Dump the red cabbage, onion, orange juice, vinegar, brown sugar, red currant jelly, orange zest, salt, pepper, thyme sprigs, and cinnamon sticks into the slow cooker. Stir until the brown sugar and jelly dissolve.

2 Cover and cook on low for 8 hours, or until the cabbage is tender but with just a little firmness to the bite. Discard the thyme sprigs and cinnamon sticks before serving.

TESTERS' NOTES
• If you're assigned to bring the side dish to a potluck buffet, here's a great option. The blend of flavors will work with almost anything else others bring.
• Make sure you remove the tough core from the cabbage before chopping the leaves. And keep the pieces fairly small—thin strips of cabbage no more than ¼ inch wide.

rutabaga gratin

EFFORT: **A LOT** • PREP TIME: **20 MINUTES** • COOK TIME: **8 HOURS** • KEEPS ON WARM: **NO** • SERVES: **3 TO 8**

INGREDIENTS	2- TO 3½-QT	4- TO 5½-QT	6- TO 8-QT
Rutabaga	1 large (about 2¾ pounds)	2 medium (about 4 pounds)	2 large (about 5½ pounds)
Minced chives or scallion greens	2 tblsp	3 tblsp	¼ cup
Stemmed fresh thyme leaves	2 tsp	1 tblsp	1½ tblsp
Salt	½ tsp	¾ tsp	1 tsp
Ground black pepper	½ tsp	¾ tsp	1 tsp
Evaporated milk	1½ cups	2⅓ cups	3 cups
Unsalted butter	2 tblsp	3 tblsp	4 tblsp (½ stick)

1 Peel the rutabaga, then slice in half. Lay the halves cut side down on a cutting board and slice into half-moon sections no more than ¼ inch thick—and even thinner, if possible.

2 Lightly butter the inside of the slow cooker canister well, making sure you get into the seam between the wall and the bottom. Mix the chives, thyme, salt, and pepper in a small bowl.

3 Create a single, barely overlapping layer of rutabaga slices in the slow cooker, then top with a sprinkling of the herb mixture. Continue making more rutabaga layers, sprinkling each with the herb mixture. Then make a final layer of rutabaga slices and pour the condensed milk over the casserole. Dot with butter.

4 Cover and cook on low for 8 hours, or until the rutabagas are tender when pierced with a toothpick or cake tester. Spoon off any excess liquid sitting in the cooker before slicing the gratin with a nonstick-safe spatula and lifting out individual portions.

TESTERS' NOTES
• Rutabagas add a mustardy earthiness to the traditional gratin, a nice side dish to sausages off the grill or out of the frying pan.
• There's no moisture reduction in the slow cooker, of course, so there is still plenty of liquid around the gratin when it's done. Nonetheless, the rutabaga itself will have condensed into a tighter, more uniform casserole.
• You can remove the whole gratin from the slow cooker. Spoon off as much of the liquid as you can, then slip two large spatulas under the entire casserole to lift it out—or cut it in half widthwise and remove one half at a time.

succotash

EFFORT: **NOT MUCH** • PREP TIME: **15 MINUTES** • COOK TIME:
6 HOURS • KEEPS ON WARM: **2 HOURS THROUGH STEP 2** •
SERVES: **3 TO 8**

INGREDIENTS	2- TO 3½-QT	4- TO 5½-QT	6- TO 8-QT
Frozen lima beans, thawed	2 cups	4 cups	6 cups
Corn kernels, thawed frozen, or fresh, cut from the cob	1 cup	2 cups	3 cups
Chopped yellow onion	¼ cup	½ cup	¾ cup (about 1 small)
Minced celery	¼ cup	½ cup	¾ cup
Shredded carrots	¼ cup	½ cup	¾ cup
Drained no-salt-added canned diced tomatoes	¼ cup	½ cup	¾ cup
Unsalted butter	1 tblsp	2 tblsp	3 tblsp
Mild paprika	½ tblsp	1 tblsp	1½ tblsp
Minced garlic	1 tsp	2 tsp	1 tblsp
Dried marjoram	1 tsp	2 tsp	1 tblsp
Salt	½ tsp	1 tsp	½ tblsp
Ground black pepper	¼ tsp	½ tsp	¾ tsp
Heavy cream	2 tblsp	¼ cup	6 tblsp

1 Mix the lima beans, corn, onion, celery, carrots, tomatoes, butter, paprika, garlic, marjoram, salt, and pepper in the slow cooker.

2 Cover and cook on low for 6 hours, or until the mixture becomes stew-like.

3 Stir in the cream and cook on low to heat for 10 minutes before serving.

TESTERS' NOTES
• Make sure any frozen vegetables are fully thawed for use in this Southern favorite. (They must not chill the other ingredients.)
• Shred the carrots through the large holes of a box grater.
• Feel free to substitute light cream or half-and-half if you want a slightly less rich dish. However, never use so-called fat-free half-and-half, a mix of stabilizers and sweeteners that will sugar up the dish inexcusably.
• The cream should not be cold from the refrigerator. Leave it out on the counter for 20 minutes before adding it to the slow cooker.

savory blue cheese cake

EFFORT: **A LOT** • PREP TIME: **25 MINUTES** • COOK TIME: **2½ HOURS**
• KEEPS ON WARM: **NO** • SERVES: **6 TO 8**

INGREDIENTS FOR A 1-QUART, HIGH-SIDED, ROUND BAKING DISH

½ cup finely ground fresh breadcrumbs

1 tsp dried thyme

1 pound cream cheese (regular or low-fat)

½ cup crumbled blue cheese

½ cup sliced almonds

2 large eggs

¼ cup heavy cream

2 tblsp all-purpose flour

1 tsp ground black pepper

1 Set a 1-quart, high-sided, round soufflé or baking dish in a slow cooker of any size or shape. Pour water into the slow cooker to come a third of the way up the outside of the baking dish. Remove the dish, cover the slow cooker, and set to cook on high while you prepare the recipe.

2 Grease the inside of the baking dish with unsalted butter. Mix the breadcrumbs and thyme in a small bowl, then pour into the baking dish. Turn the dish this way and that to coat evenly the bottom and inside walls of the dish.

3 Put the cream cheese, blue cheese, and almonds in a large food processor; process until smooth, stopping the machine occasionally to scrape down the interior.

4 Add the eggs one at a time and continue processing until smooth each time. Pour in the cream and again process until smooth. Scrape down the interior, add the flour and pepper, and again process until smooth and somewhat thick.

5 Scrape and pour the mixture into the prepared baking dish; use a rubber spatula or an offset spatula to smooth the top of the batter. Set the filled baking dish in the slow cooker. Lay overlapping, long strips of paper towels across the top of the slow cooker before setting the lid in place.

6 Cook on high for 2½ hours, or until the cake is set to the touch. Use paper towels or silicone baking mitts to lift the baking dish out of the cooker. Cool on a wire rack for 1 hour before unmolding and flipping right side up onto a serving platter.

TESTERS' NOTES
• There are no sizes for the slow cookers here because you make the savory cake in a 1-quart round, high-sided baking dish set into a slow cooker. It should fit in all but the very smallest, oval slow cookers, ones actually smaller than the dimensions we've been working with.
• This savory cake can be cut into wedges to serve instead of potatoes or rice with almost any meal. Or better yet, slice it into wedges and offer as a nibble with cocktails or wine before dinner.
• The paper towels are to keep condensed water from dripping from the lid and onto the cake. Lay long swaths of them over the cooker before you set the lid in place so that the edges of the paper towels can't inadvertently fall onto the cake as it bakes.

SHORTCUTS Any sort of blue cheese will work here, although the packaged blue cheese crumbles may well be the best shortcut for this recipe.

beans, lentils, and grains

If vegetables are the neglected stepchildren of the slow cooker's story, beans and whole grains may be the tattered orphans. And that's a shame because the slow cooker's gentle heat renders this long-cooking fare easier than ever. Beans don't go mushy as they do in roiling water; whole grains maintain their essential crunchy exterior and creamy interior.

Although most of these dishes can function as sides to substantial meals, many can do double-duty as main courses; just pair them with a salad and a creamy vinaigrette.

There's one drawback we might as well address right off the bat: dried beans and whole grains don't last forever. They have a shelf life—a little over a year in most places, maybe a few months shy of that if you live in a humid locale. Store them in a sealed container in a cool, dry, dark place at the very back of your pantry. You'll be able to tell if they're good by both appearance and aroma: beans, lentils, and whole grains should have a smooth skin or exterior surface, not be shriveled or mottled. They should smell slightly earthy, without any bitter tang or acrid odor.

We don't buy these items in bulk. First off, we're not sure whose hands have been in the bin. Second, we're not sure how long those lentils or beans have sat in that bin— and how many have been crushed. We'd rather buy ones in a clear plastic bag so we can see what we're getting. Plus, many of those bags include a *packed-on* date as well as a *sell-by* date.

So let's get down to business: whipping up some pretty hearty fare in the slow cooker.

maple baked beans

EFFORT: **A LITTLE** • PREP TIME: **12 HOURS 20 MINUTES (INCLUDES SOAKING THE BEANS)** • COOK TIME: **10 HOURS** • KEEPS ON WARM: **4 HOURS** • SERVES: **2 TO 6**

INGREDIENTS	2- TO 3½-QT	4- TO 5½-QT	6- TO 8-QT
Dried pink beans	⅔ cup	1⅓ cups	2 cups
Low-sodium chicken broth	1⅓ cups	2⅔ cups	4 cups (1 quart)
Yellow bell pepper, stemmed, seeded, and chopped	1 small	1 medium	2 medium
Yellow onion, chopped	1 small	1 medium	1 large
Maple syrup	⅓ cup	⅔ cup	1 cup
Cider vinegar	1½ tblsp	2½ tblsp	¼ cup
Minced jarred pickled jalapeño rings	1 tblsp	2 tblsp	3 tblsp
Dry mustard (see page 392)	½ tblsp	1 tblsp	1½ tblsp
Worcestershire sauce	½ tblsp	1 tblsp	1½ tblsp
Liquid smoke	½ tsp	1 tsp	½ tblsp

1 Put the beans in a large bowl, fill it two-thirds with cool tap water, and set aside on the counter for at least 12 hours or up to 16 hours.

2 Drain the beans in a colander set in the sink. Stir them and add the broth, beans, bell pepper, onion, maple syrup, vinegar, jalapeño, mustard, Worcestershire sauce, and liquid smoke to the slow cooker.

3 Cover the slow cooker and cook on low for 10 hours, or until the beans are tender and the flavors have blended.

TESTERS' NOTES
• Nothing could be easier than this family favorite. Use real maple syrup, not pancake syrup with its artificial sweeteners and flavors.
• If you're concerned about stomach upset, bring the beans to a boil in a large pot of water set over high heat, and boil for 5 minutes, then drain them in a colander set in the sink, rinse, and cool to room temperature under running water before using in this recipe.
• Feel free to use frozen chopped vegetables; thaw them before adding.
• If you want to make this for a potluck crowd, double the ingredients in the medium slow cooker but prepare the dish in a large one.

INGREDIENTS EXPLAINED Sometimes called chili beans, pink beans are small, pinkish-brown, oval-shaped beans popular in the western United States and the Caribbean. The beans have a meaty, velvety texture with a semisweet but mild taste.

boston baked beans

EFFORT: **A LITTLE** • PREP TIME: **12 HOURS 15 MINUTES (INCLUDES SOAKING THE BEANS)** • COOK TIME: **12 HOURS** • KEEPS ON WARM: **2 HOURS** • SERVES: **3 TO 10**

INGREDIENTS	2- TO 3½-QT	4- TO 5½-QT	6- TO 8-QT
Dried navy beans	1 cup	2 cups	3 cups
Boiling water	1 cup plus 3 tblsp	2⅓ cups	3½ cups
Salt pork or salted fat back, diced	2 ounces	4 ounces	6 ounces
Molasses, preferably unsulfured	2 tblsp	¼ cup	½ cup
Packed dark brown sugar	2 tblsp	¼ cup	½ cup
Chopped yellow onion	2 tblsp	¼ cup	½ cup
Dry mustard (see page 392)	¾ tsp	1¼ tsp	2 tsp
Ground black pepper	¼ tsp	¾ tsp	1 tsp

1 Fill a large bowl two-thirds full with cool water, then add the beans and stir until they sink. Set aside to soak overnight—or 12 hours but no more than 16 hours.

2 Bring the water to a boil in a large saucepan over high heat.

3 Drain the beans in a colander set in the sink; clatter them into the slow cooker. Pour in the boiling water; stir in the pork, molasses, sugar, onion, mustard, and pepper.

4 Cover the slow cooker and cook on low for 12 hours, or until the beans are tender and the liquid has become thick, syrupy, and dark.

black beans and rice

EFFORT: **NOT MUCH** • PREP TIME: **15 MINUTES** • COOK TIME: **2 HOURS 15 MINUTES/5 HOURS** • KEEPS ON WARM: **NO** • SERVES: **3 TO 8**

INGREDIENTS	2- TO 3½-QT	4- TO 5½-QT	6- TO 8-QT
Water	2 cups	3 cups	5 cups
Drained and rinsed canned black beans	1¾ cups	3¼ cups	4¾ cups
Uncooked long-grain white rice	1 cup	1½ cups	2½ cups
Green bell peppers, seeded and chopped	1 medium	1 large	1 large and 1 medium
Red onion, chopped	1 small	1 medium	1 large
Chopped fresh cilantro leaves	½ cup	¾ cup	1¼ cups
Finely grated orange zest	2 tblsp	3 tblsp	⅓ cup
Stemmed, seeded, and minced fresh jalapeño chile	2 tblsp	3 tblsp	⅓ cup

Dried marjoram	1 tblsp	1½ tblsp	2½ tblsp
Ground cumin	½ tblsp	2 tsp	1 tblsp
Salt	½ tsp	¾ tsp	1 tsp
Bay leaves	2	3	5

1 Mix the water, beans, rice, bell pepper, onion, cilantro, orange zest, jalapeño, marjoram, cumin, salt, and bay leaves in the slow cooker.

2 Cover and cook on high for 2 hours 15 minutes or on low for 5 hours, or until the water has been absorbed and the rice is tender. Discard the bay leaves before serving.

TESTERS' NOTES

• Our version of this Caribbean specialty is a little more fragrant and complex, thanks to the orange zest and marjoram. With a green salad on the side, it's truly a main course.

• If you peel the zest off the orange with a vegetable peeler, make sure you mince those strips into tiny bits, the better to balance them throughout the dish.

• We crafted this as a quick-cooking dish, using canned black beans. You can, however, use dried black beans; you'll need to plug the various ingredients into the formula in the recipe for Red Beans and Rice (at right), plus make a few changes: boil the dried beans for 5 minutes, drain them, use the amount of liquid (water or broth) called for in the red beans recipe, cook the beans and everything else on low for 5 hours, add the rice, and cook an additional 4 hours on low.

Serve It Up! Top this dish with an easy picadillo: cooked ground beef, generously spiced with ground allspice and red pepper flakes, laced with dried currants, chopped onion, minced garlic, and minced ginger.

red beans and rice

EFFORT: **A LITTLE** • PREP TIME: **15 MINUTES** • COOK TIME: **9 HOURS** • KEEPS ON WARM: **NO** • SERVES: **4 TO 8**

INGREDIENTS	2- TO 3½-QT	4- TO 5½-QT	6- TO 8-QT
Dried red kidney beans	1 cup	1⅓ cups	2 cups
Low-sodium chicken broth	5 cups (1 quart plus 1 cup)	6⅔ cups	10 cups (2½ quarts)
Spicy turkey sausage or kielbasa, cut into ¼-inch rings	¼ pound	⅓ pound	½ pound
Chopped yellow onion	½ cup	⅔ cup	1 cup
Stemmed, seeded, and chopped green bell pepper	½ cup	⅔ cup	1 cup
Chopped celery	½ cup	⅔ cup	1 cup
Minced garlic	½ tblsp	2 tsp	1 tblsp
Dried thyme	½ tsp	¾ tsp	1 tsp
Dried sage	½ tsp	¾ tsp	1 tsp
Salt	½ tsp	¾ tsp	1 tsp
Celery seeds	¼ tsp	½ tsp	½ tsp
Cayenne	Up to ¼ tsp	Up to ¼ tsp	Up to ½ tsp
Uncooked long-grain white rice	1 cup	1⅓ cups	2 cups

1 Pour the beans into a large saucepan, cover with water to a depth of several inches, and bring to a boil over high heat. Boil for 10 minutes, then drain the beans in a colander set in the sink and rinse with cool water until room temperature.

2 Stir the beans with the broth, sausage, onion, bell pepper, celery, garlic, thyme, sage, salt, celery seeds, and cayenne in the slow

(continued)

cooker until the spices are evenly distributed throughout. Cover and cook on low for 5 hours.

3 Stir in the rice. Cover and continue cooking on low for 4 more hours, or until the rice is tender and the liquid has been absorbed.

TESTERS' NOTES
• A meal on its own, this Louisiana favorite would be even better with some bottled hot sauce on the side.
• The consistency here shouldn't be stewlike, nor should it be like fluffy, white rice. Rather, the rice should be moist but firm to the bite. If you find there's too much liquid in the cooker, let it go another 30 minutes on low—or if there's only a little, set it aside, unplugged but covered, for 15 or 20 minutes before serving.
• For a more authentic kick, substitute Cajun andouille for the turkey sausage or kielbasa.

SHORTCUTS Omit the thyme, sage, celery seeds, and cayenne; substitute ½ tablespoon Creole seasoning for a small slow cooker, 2 teaspoons for a medium cooker, or 1 tablespoon for a large one. If the seasoning blend includes salt, omit the salt as well.

Serve It Up! Boil some shell-on, deveined shrimp until pink and firm, drain well, and serve warm right on top.

INGREDIENTS EXPLAINED Red kidney beans have a high quantity of phytohemagglutinin, a sugar-binding protein that can yield toxic side effects in humans, particularly dire digestive distress. Boiling the beans will take care of the problem, unless you live at high altitudes where the boiling point of water is below 212°F. In that case, soak the dried beans in water for at least 5 hours, then boil them as directed and continue with the recipe.

refried beans

EFFORT: **A LOT** • PREP TIME: **25 MINUTES** • COOK TIME: **10 HOURS** • KEEPS ON WARM: **3 HOURS** • SERVES: **3 TO 6**

INGREDIENTS	2- TO 3½-QT	4- TO 5½-QT	6- TO 8-QT
Water	3 cups	4 cups	8 cups
Dried pink beans	¾ cup	1¼ cups	2½ cups
Salt	1 tsp	½ tblsp	1 tblsp
Red pepper flakes	¼ tsp	½ tsp	¾ tsp
Rendered bacon fat or lard	1½ tblsp	2 tblsp	¼ cup
Minced yellow onion	1½ tblsp	2 tblsp	¼ cup
Minced garlic	½ tsp	1 tsp	2 tsp

1 Mix the water, beans, salt, and red pepper flakes in the slow cooker.

2 Cover and cook on low for 10 hours, or until the beans are brilliant tender, almost mushy.

3 Melt the bacon fat or lard in a large Dutch oven set over medium heat. Add the onion and garlic; cook, stirring often, until softened and aromatic, 3 to 4 minutes.

4 Use a slotted spoon to transfer the beans from the cooker to the pot, about 2 cups at a time. Stir, mashing the beans against the walls of the pot with a potato masher or the back of a wooden spoon to form a paste, adding a little cooking liquid if the paste becomes dry.

5 Continue ladling beans into the pot with a slotted spoon, mashing them as before and also stirring in judicious amounts of cooking water to create a soft, fairly smooth paste, about like mashed potatoes, stirring all the while to prevent scorching.

	1 medium	1 large	2 large
Green bell peppers, stemmed, seeded, and chopped	1 medium	1 large	2 large
Shredded carrots	¾ cup	1½ cups	2½ cups
Yellow onion, chopped	1 small	1 medium	1 large
Chili powder	2½ tblsp	¼ cup	⅓ cup
Ground cumin	2 tsp	1 tblsp	5 tsp
Dried oregano	2 tsp	1 tblsp	5 tsp
Ground cinnamon	½ tsp	1 tsp	1¾ tsp
Salt	½ tsp	1 tsp	½ tblsp

1 Mix the tomatoes with chiles, beans, bell peppers, carrots, onion, chili powder, cumin, oregano, cinnamon, and salt in the slow cooker.

2 Cover and cook on low for 6 hours, or until the flavors have blended.

TESTERS' NOTES

• This bean chili is ridiculously easy, thanks to the canned beans and the flavorings already in those canned tomatoes. Since it keeps well on warm for so long, it's perfect to have ready for when you get home from work.

• If you're concerned that this chili is too hot, use canned tomatoes without any chiles. You can always spike servings with hot sauce at the table.

• Standard chili powder is used almost like a thickener in some Southwestern dishes, so we don't advocate buying it in small jars. Purchase the larger, more economical containers, because you'll go through it faster than, say, the more esoteric ancho chile powder.

• Shred the carrots through the large holes of a box grater. You can also use pre-chopped carrot matchsticks, available in the produce section or even on the salad bar. Dice these into small bits for even cooking.

TESTERS' NOTES

• Refried beans are not fried twice! Rather, the original name (*frijoles refritos*) means something like "beans fried very well." In lard or bacon fat, they are! Bacon fat will give the beans a smoky flavor; lard will allow them to have a cleaner and more velvety finish.

• Pinto beans are the usual culprits for refried beans, but we find that pink beans mush up better after being cooked in the slow cooker. If you can't find pink beans, substitute pinto beans for a somewhat grainier finish.

• We don't first soak the beans. Soaking them to improve their texture would actually be wasted energy since we're just going to mush them up.

• After turning the beans into a thick puree, you can scrape them back into the slow cooker and set it on *keep warm* for another 3 hours.

• If you want to make refried beans for a mob, triple the stated amounts for the medium cooker but cook this behemoth batch in a large cooker.

---

three-bean chili

EFFORT: **NOT MUCH** • PREP TIME: **20 MINUTES** • COOK TIME: **6 HOURS** • KEEPS ON WARM: **4 HOURS** • SERVES: **3 TO 8 AS A MAIN COURSE**

INGREDIENTS	2- TO 3½-QT	4- TO 5½-QT	6- TO 8-QT
Canned diced tomatoes with chiles, such as Rotel	2 cups	3½ cups	5½ cups
Drained and rinsed canned pink beans	1 cup	1¾ cups	2¾ cups
Drained and rinsed canned black beans	1 cup	1¾ cups	2¾ cups
Drained and rinsed canned kidney beans	1 cup	1¾ cups	2¾ cups

black bean and quinoa chili

EFFORT: **NOT MUCH** • PREP TIME: **15 MINUTES** • COOK TIME:
6 HOURS • KEEPS ON WARM: **2 HOURS THROUGH STEP 2** •
SERVES: **3 TO 6 AS A MAIN COURSE**

INGREDIENTS	2- TO 3½-QT	4- TO 5½-QT	6- TO 8-QT
Drained and rinsed canned black beans	1½ cups	2 cups	3 cups
Low-sodium vegetable broth	1½ cups	2 cups	3 cups
Quinoa, preferably black quinoa	¾ cup	1 cup	1½ cups
No-salt-added canned crushed tomatoes	½ cup	⅔ cup	1 cup
Chopped yellow onion	¼ cup	⅓ cup	½ cup
Stemmed, seeded, and chopped green bell pepper	¼ cup	⅓ cup	½ cup
Minced celery	2 tblsp	2½ tblsp	¼ cup
Stemmed, seeded, and minced fresh jalapeño chile	1 tblsp	4 tsp	2 tblsp
Chili powder	1 tblsp	4 tsp	2 tblsp
Molasses, preferably unsulfured	1 tblsp	4 tsp	2 tblsp
Ground cumin	½ tsp	¾ tsp	1 tsp
Ground coriander	½ tsp	¾ tsp	1 tsp
Dried oregano	½ tsp	¾ tsp	1 tsp
Salt	½ tsp	¾ tsp	1 tsp
Minced fresh cilantro leaves	¼ cup	⅓ cup	½ cup

1 Stir the beans, broth, quinoa, tomatoes, onion, bell pepper, celery, jalapeño, chili powder, molasses, cumin, coriander, oregano, and salt in the slow cooker.

2 Cover and cook on low for 6 hours, or until the flavors have melded and the quinoa is tender.

3 Stir in the cilantro before serving.

TESTERS' NOTES

• Quinoa adds a musky heft to this veggie-heavy chili. Although any quinoa will work, black quinoa would be the best choice, partly because of the aesthetics of black quinoa and black beans, and partly because black quinoa has a slightly more bitter bite that works better against the sweet beans.

• Some quinoa needs to be rinsed before using to get rid of a bitter chemical left on the grains. Read the package carefully for instructions.

• For an even larger batch, double the quantities for the medium slow cooker but cook them in a large model.

pasta with red beans and parmesan

EFFORT: **NOT MUCH** • PREP TIME: **15 MINUTES** • COOK TIME: **2½ HOURS** • KEEPS ON WARM: **NO** • SERVES: **2 TO 6 AS A MAIN COURSE**

INGREDIENTS	2- TO 3½-QT	4- TO 5½-QT	6- TO 8-QT
No-salt-added canned diced tomatoes	1⅓ cups	2¼ cups	3½ cups
Drained and rinsed canned red kidney beans	⅔ cup	1 cup	1¾ cups
Low-sodium vegetable broth	½ cup	¾ cup	1¼ cups
Dried ziti, farfalle, or fusilli pasta	3 ounces	5 ounces	8 ounces

Stemmed, seeded, and chopped green bell pepper	6 tblsp	⅔ cup	1 cup (about 1 medium)
Chopped yellow onion	3 tblsp	⅓ cup	½ cup
Parmigiano-Reggiano cheese, finely grated	¾ ounce (about 3 tblsp)	1¼ ounces (about 5 tblsp)	2 ounces (about ½ cup)
Dried oregano	¼ tsp	½ tsp	1 tsp
Dried rosemary	¼ tsp	½ tsp	1 tsp
Garlic powder	Pinch	⅛ tsp	¼ tsp

1 Stir the tomatoes, beans, broth, pasta, bell pepper, onion, cheese, oregano, rosemary, and garlic powder in the slow cooker. Make sure the pasta is submerged in the liquid.

2 Cover and cook on low for 1 hour 15 minutes. Stir well, then continue cooking on low for an additional 1 hour 15 minutes, until the pasta is tender.

TESTERS' NOTES
• This recipe is a slow cooker, main-course adaptation of *pasta e fagioli*, or pasta and beans, a popular comfort food among Italian immigrants in North America, but here with more vegetables. For the more traditional soup, see page 74.
• For a sweeter dish, substitute a dry white wine such as Chardonnay for the broth—or use half broth and half wine.

Serve It Up! This stew could also become the bed for grilled or pan-fried sausages. Drizzle some cold-pressed extra-virgin olive oil over each bowl.

smoky peachy beans

EFFORT: **NOT MUCH** • PREP TIME: **20 MINUTES** • COOK TIME: **10 HOURS** • KEEPS ON WARM: **3 HOURS** • SERVES: **3 TO 8**

INGREDIENTS	2- TO 3½-QT	4- TO 5½-QT	6- TO 8-QT
Slab bacon, diced	2 ounces	4 ounces	6 ounces
Low-sodium vegetable broth	1⅓ cups	2⅔ cups	4 cups (1 quart)
No-salt-added canned diced tomatoes	1 cup plus 2 tblsp	2¼ cups	3½ cups
Dried pinto beans	⅔ cup	1⅓ cups	2 cups
Minced whole scallions	⅓ cup	⅔ cup	1 cup
Ripe medium peaches, pitted and finely chopped	1	1½	2½
Packed dark brown sugar	2 tblsp	¼ cup	6 tblsp
Molasses, preferably unsulfured	2 tsp	4 tsp	2 tblsp
Dijon mustard	2 tsp	4 tsp	2 tblsp
Worcestershire sauce	2 tsp	4 tsp	2 tblsp
Minced garlic	1 tsp	2 tsp	1 tblsp
Dried oregano	¾ tsp	½ tblsp	2 tsp
Ground cumin	¾ tsp	½ tblsp	2 tsp
Chipotle chile powder (see page 147)	¼ tsp	½ tsp	1 tsp

1 Mix the bacon, broth, tomatoes, pinto beans, scallions, peaches, brown sugar, molasses, mustard, Worcestershire sauce, garlic, oregano, cumin, and chile powder in the slow cooker until the brown sugar dissolves and the beans are evenly distributed throughout.

(continued)

2 Cover and cook on low for 10 hours, or until the beans are tender and the sauce has thickened to a chili-like, but still somewhat soupy, consistency. Serve in bowls.

TESTERS' NOTES
• There's no need to brown the bacon or soak the beans. The whole mélange slowly melts into a wonderful side dish, hearty enough for a main course meal if you've got something like Loaded Cornbread on the side (page 424).
• Make sure the peaches and the bacon are in fairly small chunks, no larger than ½ inch.

SHORTCUTS Thaw frozen sliced peaches, then dice them into pieces no larger than ½ inch.

INGREDIENTS EXPLAINED Pinto beans are moderately sized, mottled brown beans the same color as a pinto horse. The beans have a long history in the Americas as a staple food; they're a favorite in chilis and soups, particularly in the American South.

black bean and cornbread casserole

EFFORT: **A LOT** • PREP TIME: **20 MINUTES** • COOK TIME: **3 HOURS** • KEEPS ON WARM: **NO** • SERVES: **4 TO 10**

INGREDIENTS	2- TO 3½-QT	4- TO 5½-QT	6- TO 8-QT
No-salt-added canned diced tomatoes	2¼ cups	3½ cups	6 cups
Drained and rinsed canned black beans	2¼ cups	3½ cups	6 cups
Canned chopped mild green chiles	⅔ cup	1 cup	1¾ cups
Green bell pepper, seeded and chopped	1 medium	1 large	2 large
Red onion, chopped	1 medium	1 large	2 large
Chili powder	2½ tblsp	¼ cup	7 tblsp
Ground cumin	½ tblsp	2 tsp	4 tsp
Milk	¼ cup	½ cup	¾ cup
Corn kernels, thawed frozen, or fresh cut from cobs	2 tblsp	¼ cup	6 tblsp
Large egg/yolk, at room temperature	1 yolk	1 white	1 whole
Canola oil	2½ tsp	1½ tblsp	⅓ cup
Fine- or medium-ground yellow cornmeal	¼ cup	½ cup	¾ cup
All-purpose flour	¼ cup	½ cup	¾ cup
Sugar	½ tblsp	1 tblsp	1½ tblsp
Baking powder	½ tsp	1 tsp	½ tblsp
Salt	¼ tsp	½ tsp	¾ tsp

1 Stir the tomatoes, beans, chiles, bell pepper, onion, chili powder, and cumin in the slow cooker. Cover and cook on low for 2 hours.

2 After 1 hour and 40 minutes have passed, start the cornbread. Puree the milk, corn kernels, egg, and oil in a large blender, scraping down the inside of the container once or twice, until smooth.

3 Mix the cornmeal, flour, sugar, baking powder, and salt in a large bowl. Pour the wet ingredients into the dry and stir until a loose batter forms. Let stand for 10 minutes.

4 Spoon the batter over the stew in tablespoon-size blobs. Use the back of a wooden spoon to connect those blobs into a single top layer as well as you can without submerging them.

5 Lay long, overlapping strips of paper towels over the top of the slow cooker, with excess hanging down over the sides. Cover and cook for 1 additional hour, or until the cornbread is set and somewhat firm to the touch. Serve by scooping up heaping spoonfuls of the cornbread with the stew underneath.

TESTERS' NOTES

• Not a straightforward casserole, but rather cornbread over a bean-rich stew, this slow cooker dinner needs nothing except a green salad on the side.

• Use either thawed frozen corn kernels or corn kernels cut right off the cob. Since you're pureeing them with the milk, their texture is not as important as in some other recipes.

• The batter is fairly loose with just enough stiffness to float. If you need help connecting those blobs of batter in the stew, wet the back of the wooden spoon occasionally.

gigantes beans
with tomatoes and dill

EFFORT: **A LITTLE** • PREP TIME: **20 MINUTES** • COOK TIME: **10 HOURS** • KEEPS ON WARM: **2 HOURS** • SERVES: **4 TO 10**

INGREDIENTS	2- TO 3½-QT	4- TO 5½-QT	6- TO 8-QT
Olive oil	3 tblsp	¼ cup	6 tblsp
Yellow onion, chopped	1 small	1 medium	2 medium
No-salt-added canned diced tomatoes	1¼ cups	2 cups	3½ cups
Dried gigantes beans (see page 167)	1¼ cups	2 cups	3½ cups
Dry vermouth	1 cup	1¾ cups	3 cups
Honey	3 tblsp	¼ cup	⅓ cup
No-salt-added tomato paste	2 tblsp	3 tblsp	¼ cup
Bay leaf	1	1	2
Chopped fresh dill fronds	¼ cup	⅓ cup	½ cup
White wine vinegar	2 tblsp	3 tblsp	¼ cup
Salt	½ tsp	1 tsp	½ tblsp
Ground black pepper	¼ tsp	½ tsp	½ tsp

1 Set a large skillet over medium heat for a few minutes, then swirl in the oil. Add the onion, reduce the heat to low, and cook until the onion is soft, golden, and sweet, about 10 minutes, stirring often.

2 Scrape the contents of the skillet into the slow cooker. Stir in the tomatoes, beans, vermouth, honey, tomato paste, and bay leaf until the tomato paste dissolves. Cover and cook on low for 5 hours.

3 Stir in the dill, vinegar, salt, and pepper. Cover and continue cooking on low for an additional 5 hours, or until the beans are tender but still slightly firm to the bite. Remove the bay leaf before serving.

TESTERS' NOTES

• Here's a side dish often served as part of a meal of small plates in Turkey or Greece. The beans become incredibly silky in the slightly sour tomato sauce.

• There's no heat here, partly because we feel any spiciness can obscure the tart dash of the sauce. If you would like a little fire, add up to ½ teaspoon red pepper flakes with the tomatoes.

• A sweet Vidalia onion would work even better in that tomato sauce.

Serve It Up! If you want to put together your own spread of small plates for dinner, serve this with hummus, baba ganoush, and tabbouleh, as well as pita bread wedges.

spicy black-eyed peas and rice

EFFORT: **A LITTLE** • PREP TIME: **12 HOURS 20 MINUTES (INCLUDES SOAKING THE PEAS)** • COOK TIME: **7 HOURS** • KEEPS ON WARM: **NO** • SERVES: **3 TO 8**

INGREDIENTS	2- TO 3½-QT	4- TO 5½-QT	6- TO 8-QT
Dried black-eyed peas	1 cup	1¾ cups	3 cups
Low-sodium chicken broth	1 cup	1¾ cups	3 cups
Canned diced tomatoes with chiles, such as Rotel	1 cup	1¾ cups	3 cups
Red bell pepper, seeded and chopped	1 small	1 medium	2 medium
Medium whole scallions, minced	3	4	5
Stemmed, seeded, and minced fresh jalapeño chile	1½ tblsp	2 tblsp	¼ cup
Minced garlic	2 tsp	1 tblsp	2 tblsp
Uncooked long-grain white rice	⅔ cup	¾ cup plus 2 tblsp	1¾ cups

1 Pour the black-eyed peas into a large bowl and fill it about two-thirds full with water. Set aside to soak overnight, for at least 12 hours, or up to 16 hours.

2 Drain the peas in a colander. Pour them into the cooker, then stir in the broth, tomatoes, bell pepper, scallions, jalapeño, and garlic. Cover and cook on low for 4 hours.

3 Stir in the rice, making sure the grains are submerged in the liquid. Cover and continue cooking on low for an additional 3 hours, or until the rice and peas are tender and quite a bit of the liquid has been absorbed (although the final consistency is more stew than pilaf).

TESTERS' NOTES
• This Southern dish of rice, black-eyed peas, and tomatoes may well stand in for a main course on its own.
• Since the rice can get a little gummy if the dish sits too long on *warm*, it's best to eat this side dish when it's ready.

lentil bolognese sauce *for pasta*

EFFORT: **A LITTLE** • PREP TIME: **25 MINUTES** • COOK TIME: **6 HOURS** • KEEPS ON WARM: **3 HOURS** • SERVES: **3 TO 8 OVER COOKED PASTA**

INGREDIENTS	2- TO 3½-QT	4- TO 5½-QT	6- TO 8-QT
Olive oil	1½ tblsp	2 tblsp	3 tblsp
Minced yellow onion	½ cup	¾ cup	1¼ cups
Drained and rinsed canned cannellini or white beans	⅓ cup	½ cup	¾ cup
Almond milk	2½ tblsp	¼ cup	7 tblsp
No-salt-added canned crushed tomatoes	2¼ cups	3½ cups	6 cups
Dry white wine, such as Chardonnay	¾ cup plus 2 tblsp	1½ cups	2⅓ cups
Brown lentils	⅔ cup	1 cup	1⅔ cups
Minced carrot	⅓ cup	½ cup	¾ cup
Minced celery	⅓ cup	½ cup	¾ cup
No-salt-added tomato paste	1½ tblsp	2 tblsp	3½ tblsp
Dried oregano	2 tsp	1 tblsp	1½ tblsp
Dried basil	2 tsp	1 tblsp	1½ tblsp
Minced garlic	½ tblsp	2 tsp	1 tblsp

1 Set a large skillet over low heat for a couple of minutes, then pour in the oil. Dump in the onion and cook, stirring often, until golden and softened, about 10 minutes. Set aside.

2 Plop the beans into the slow cooker; pour in the almond milk. Use a potato masher or the back of a wooden spoon to mash the beans into a smooth paste with the almond milk. Scrape the contents of the skillet into this paste and stir until fairly smooth.

3 Stir in the tomatoes, wine, lentils, carrot, celery, tomato paste, oregano, basil, and garlic. Leave no lumps of tomato paste in the mix.

4 Cover and cook on low for 6 hours, or until the lentils are tender and the sauce has thickened somewhat.

TESTERS' NOTES
• This is a creamy, vegan, Bolognese-style pasta sauce best served over wide noodles like papardelle.
• Some almond milk is sweetened; some is not. Choose which you like, based on whether you want a sweeter taste against the acidic tomatoes or a more savory finish to complement the lentils.

INGREDIENTS EXPLAINED Lentils are the edible seeds of various plants in the legume family, related to beans but with a muskier flavor. There's a wide variety of lentils, from the common brown to the more elegant French green lentils (sometimes called *le Puy lentils*), from the murky red lentils favored in East Indian cooking to the inky black lentils with their sweet, creamy texture.

red lentil stew
with tomatoes and spinach

EFFORT: **NOT MUCH** • PREP TIME: **20 MINUTES** • COOK TIME: **6 HOURS** • KEEPS ON WARM: **2 HOURS THROUGH STEP 2** • SERVES: **3 TO 8 AS A MAIN COURSE**

INGREDIENTS	2- TO 3½-QT	4- TO 5½-QT	6- TO 8-QT
Low-sodium chicken broth	2 cups	4 cups (1 quart)	6 cups (1½ quarts)
Red lentils	1 cup	2 cups	3 cups
Frozen chopped spinach, thawed and squeezed of excess moisture	1 cup	2 cups	3 cups
No-salt-added canned diced tomatoes	1 cup	1¾ cups	2⅔ cups
Chopped yellow onion	6 tblsp	¾ cup	1 cup (about 1 medium)
Minced peeled fresh ginger	½ tblsp	1 tblsp	1½ tblsp
Minced garlic	½ tblsp	1 tblsp	1½ tblsp
Curry powder	1 tblsp	2 tblsp	3 tblsp
Salt	1 tsp	2 tsp	1 tblsp
Minced cilantro leaves	¼ cup	½ cup	¾ cups
Honey	½ tblsp	1 tblsp	1½ tblsp
Lemon juice	½ tblsp	1 tblsp	1½ tblsp

1 Mix the broth, lentils, spinach, tomatoes, onion, ginger, garlic, curry powder, and salt in the slow cooker.

2 Cover the slow cooker and cook on low for 6 hours, until rich and creamy, the lentils broken into a paste.

(continued)

3 Stir in the cilantro, honey, and lemon juice. Cover and keep warm for 10 minutes to blend the flavors.

TESTERS' NOTES
• This luxurious stew is great for a chilly evening. Rather than bread, offer na'an, an East Indian flatbread, on the side. Or just flour tortillas.
• Squeeze the spinach in very small handfuls over the sink so excess moisture doesn't bog down the stew.

INGREDIENTS EXPLAINED Red lentils, which actually are more salmon colored, are the sweetest lentils. A favorite in East Indian cooking, they cook up in no time and turn soft, a natural thickener.

lentil meatloaf

EFFORT: **A LOT** • PREP TIME: **45 MINUTES** • COOK TIME: **4 TO 6 HOURS** • KEEPS ON WARM: **NO** • SERVES: **4 TO 10**

INGREDIENTS	2- TO 3½-QT	4- TO 5½-QT	6- TO 8-QT
Brown lentils	½ cup	1 cup	2 cups
Olive oil	1 tblsp	1½ tblsp	3 tblsp
Chopped yellow onion	¼ cup	½ cup	1 cup (about 1 medium)
Shredded carrot	¼ cup	½ cup	1 cup
Minced celery	2 tblsp	¼ cup	½ cup
Minced garlic	½ tsp	1 tsp	2 tsp
Cremini or brown button mushrooms, thinly sliced	2¼ ounces (about ½ cup)	3½ ounces (about 1 cup)	7 ounces (about 2 cups)
Plain dry breadcrumbs	¼ cup	½ cup	1 cup
Large eggs, well beaten in a small bowl	1	2	3
Parmigiano-Reggiano cheese, finely grated	½ ounce (about 2 tblsp)	1 ounce (about ¼ cup)	2 ounces (about ½ cup)
Chopped parsley leaves	2 tblsp	¼ cup	½ cup
Finely chopped walnuts	2 tblsp	¼ cup	½ cup
No-salt-added tomato paste	1 tblsp	1½ tblsp	3 tblsp
Italian seasoning	½ tsp	1 tsp	2 tsp

1 Pour the lentils into a large saucepan, then fill that saucepan about two-thirds full of water. Bring to a boil over high heat and continue boiling until the lentils are a tad beyond tender, in fact mushable, about 25 minutes. Drain in a colander set in the sink.

2 Put a large skillet over medium heat for a few minutes, then pour in the oil. Tilt the skillet to grease its interior, then add the onion, carrot, and celery. Cook, stirring often, until the onion softens, between 3 and 5 minutes.

3 Add the garlic, stir over the heat for 20 seconds, then dump in the mushrooms. Continue cooking, stirring occasionally, until the mushrooms give off their liquid and it evaporates to a thick glaze, 8 to 12 minutes. Scrape the contents of the skillet into a large food processor fitted with the chopping blade; cool for 5 minutes.

4 Pour the drained lentils into the food processor; add the breadcrumbs, eggs, cheese, parsley, walnuts, tomato paste, and seasoning. Cover and pulse to a coarse paste, about like wet sand, not smooth at all, scraping down the inside of the container occasionally. There is almost no way the ingredients for a large slow cooker will fit in even a very large food processor. Work in batches if you must, scraping each into a bowl before adding the next and using fairly proportionate ratios of the various ingredients in each batch to get the right consistency; mix all the batches well with a wooden spoon to make sure they're evenly blended.

5 Scrape down and remove the blade. Dab some olive oil on a paper towel and grease the inside of the slow cooker. Dump the lentil mixture into the cooker and use your clean, still-wet hands to form it into a lump with at least ½ inch space between the lump and the slow cooker's walls, smoothing the top to create a fairly flat surface.

6 Cover and cook on low for 4 hours in a small slow cooker, 5 hours in a medium cooker, or 6 hours in a large one, or until the meatloaf is firm and set to the touch, even in the middle. Remove the crock if possible and cool on a wire rack for 10 minutes—or unplug the machine and cool, uncovered, for 15 minutes. Use a nonstick-safe knife or spatula to cut the meatloaf into slices right in the crock.

TESTERS' NOTES

• Mince the vegetables before they go into the food processor so there's no chance of random bits of this or that in the final, rather smooth meatloaf.
• The loaf doesn't freeze well; it will fall apart when thawed.
• The amount of ingredients for a large slow cooker may well be too much for your food processor. If so, work in batches, making sure each batch contains proportioned amounts of the ingredients.

SHORTCUTS Omit the Italian seasoning and use Italian-seasoned dry breadcrumbs.

parmesan polenta

EFFORT: **NOT MUCH** • PREP TIME: **10 MINUTES** • COOK TIME: **1½ HOURS** • KEEPS ON WARM: **NO** • SERVES: **4 TO 10**

INGREDIENTS	2- TO 3½-QT	4- TO 5½-QT	6- TO 8-QT
Low-sodium vegetable broth	2 cups	3 cups	7½ cups
Coarse-ground polenta (not instant; see page 33)	⅔ cup	1 cup	2½ cups
Salt	¼ tsp	½ tsp	1¼ tsp
Ground black pepper	¼ tsp	½ tsp	1¼ tsp
Parmigiano-Reggiano cheese, finely grated	2 ounces (about ¼ cup)	2½ ounces (about 6 tblsp)	3 ounces (about ¾ cup)
Minced chives (optional)	1½ tblsp	2 tblsp	⅓ cup

1 Stir the broth, polenta, salt, and pepper in the slow cooker.

2 Cover and cook on high, stirring once, for 1½ hours, or until the broth has been absorbed and the polenta is creamy. Stir in the cheese and chives (if using) to serve.

TESTERS' NOTES

• You don't need to stir this polenta over a hot stove!
• Add herbs with the polenta: up to 1¼ teaspoons dried thyme, crumbled dried rosemary, or dried oregano.
• For a bolder flavor, substitute aged Asiago cheese for the Parmigiano-Reggiano. Or do a French twist by substituting half the amount of minced fresh tarragon for the chives and using aged Gruyère instead of Parmigiano-Reggiano.
• If you can't find coarse-grain polenta at your supermarket, substitute standard grits (not instant).

barley risotto
with peas and leeks

EFFORT: **A LITTLE** • PREP TIME: **15 MINUTES** • COOK TIME: **4½ HOURS** • KEEPS ON WARM: **NO** • SERVES: **3 TO 6 AS A MAIN COURSE**

INGREDIENTS	2- TO 3½-QT	4- TO 5½-QT	6- TO 8-QT
Low-sodium chicken broth	4 cups (1 quart)	5¼ cups	8 cups (2 quarts)
Leeks (white and pale green part only), halved lengthwise, washed for internal sand, and thinly sliced	½ pound	¾ pound	1 pound
Pearled barley (see page 24)	1 cup plus 2 tblsp	1½ cups	2¼ cups
Stemmed fresh thyme leaves	2 tsp	1 tblsp	1½ tblsp
Ground black pepper	½ tsp	1 tsp	½ tblsp
Saffron	Up to ⅛ tsp	Up to ¼ tsp	Up to ½ tsp
Green peas, thawed frozen or shelled fresh	⅔ cup	1 cup	1¾ cups
Parmigiano-Reggiano cheese, finely grated	3 ounces (about ¾ cup)	4 ounces (about 1 cup)	7 ounces (about 1¾ cups)
Unsalted butter, cut into small bits	1 tblsp	1½ tblsp	2 tblsp

1 Stir the broth, leeks, barley, thyme, pepper, and saffron in the slow cooker.

2 Cover and cook on low for 4½ hours, or until the liquid is mostly absorbed and the barley is tender.

3 Stir in the peas, cheese, and butter. Let stand, unplugged but covered, for 5 minutes before serving.

TESTERS' NOTES
• If you're looking for a side dish with a little more heft and a lot less sweetness than the more standard risotto made with rice, consider this grain risotto your answer. Or serve it as a vegetarian main course with a crunchy salad on the side.
• For a dish that's a little closer to whole-grain goodness, substitute semi-pearled (*semi-perlato*) barley for the pearled barley.
• Slice the leeks thin enough so that they almost melt into the sauce. If you like, substitute thinly sliced onions, softened in a skillet over low heat in a little butter, for the leeks. (If you're substituting onions, omit the unsalted butter at the end of the recipe.)

whole grains
from a slow cooker

EFFORT: **NOT MUCH** • PREP TIME: **12 HOURS (INCLUDES SOAKING THE GRAINS)** • COOK TIME: **5½ HOURS (AT MOST)** • KEEPS ON WARM: **2 HOURS** • SERVES: **2 TO 20**

INGREDIENTS	2- TO 3½-QT	4- TO 5½-QT	6- TO 8-QT
Water	6 cups	10 cups	16 cups
Wheatberries, spelt berries, Kamut, triticale berries, rye berries, whole-grain farro, sorghum, or oat groats	Up to 1½ cups	Up to 3 cups	Up to 5 cups

1 Mix the water and grain of choice in the slow cooker. Cover and soak overnight, at least 12 hours or up to 16 hours.

2 Keep covered and cook on high for 4½ to 5½ hours, until the grains are tender. Drain in a colander set in the sink, then rinse with cool tap water until room temperature. Drain thoroughly before using.

TESTERS' NOTES

• Whole grains are so easy in a slow cooker—especially since you can set them to soak, then turn the machine on the next day.

• Although the cooking time is set at 4½ hours, it may not tell the tale, given the way whole grains lose moisture as they sit on the shelf (and may then take longer to get tender). Check the grains after 4 hours—bite into one and see if it's tender. From there, you'll need to adjust the cooking time, checking about every 30 minutes until done.

• We've listed a range of whole grains, some of which will turn rather sticky (like oat groats) and some which will stay separate and firm (like hard red winter wheatberries). Choose any you like. However, it's best not to mix and match, since cooking times may vary.

Serve It Up! Once drained, store the whole grains, covered, in the fridge for up to 4 days. Toss them into salads with any number of chopped vegetables: fennel, tomatoes, celery, carrots, asparagus, or peas; add your favorite dressing to taste. Or add these grains to soups, stews, and braises for a savory pop among the other ingredients. (We particularly like them in marinara sauce with meatballs—and then hold the pasta.)

three-grain pilaf

EFFORT: **NOT MUCH** • PREP TIME: **15 MINUTES** • COOK TIME: **8 HOURS** • KEEPS ON WARM: **2 HOURS** • SERVES: **3 TO 8**

INGREDIENTS	2- TO 3½-QT	4- TO 5½-QT	6- TO 8-QT
Low-sodium vegetable broth	1¾ cups	3½ cups	5¼ cups
Shredded carrots	¾ cup	1½ cups	2¼ cups
Frozen shelled edamame (soy beans), thawed	½ cup	1 cup	1½ cups
Wheatberries, hard red winter or soft white spring	⅓ cup	⅔ cup	1 cup
Pearled barley (see page 24)	¼ cup	½ cup	¾ cup
Medium-grain brown rice, such as brown Arborio	¼ cup	½ cup	¾ cup
Minced yellow onion	¼ cup	½ cup	¾ cup
Minced celery	¼ cup	½ cup	¾ cup
Dried sage	½ tsp	1 tsp	½ tblsp
Salt	¼ tsp	½ tsp	¾ tsp
Ground black pepper	¼ tsp	½ tsp	¾ tsp

1 Stir the broth, carrots, edamame, wheatberries, barley, brown rice, onion, celery, sage, salt, and pepper in the slow cooker.

2 Cover and cook on low for 8 hours, or until the liquid has been absorbed and the grains are tender. Fluff with a fork, then cover and set aside for 10 minutes before serving.

TESTERS' NOTES

• The wheatberries will determine the final texture of this grainy side dish: hard winter wheatberries are firm and chewy; soft white ones, luxurious and silky.

• If you can't find edamame, substitute frozen peas, thawed.

barley, raisins, and cabbage

EFFORT: **NOT MUCH** • PREP TIME: **25 MINUTES** • COOK TIME: **8 HOURS** • KEEPS ON WARM: **2 HOURS** • SERVES: **3 TO 8**

INGREDIENTS	2- TO 3½-QT	4- TO 5½-QT	6- TO 8-QT
Green cabbage, cored and chopped	1 pound	1½ pounds	2½ pounds
Leeks (white and pale green part only), halved lengthwise, washed well for internal sand, and thinly sliced	¼ pound	½ pound	¾ pound
Pearled barley (see page 24)	⅓ cup	½ cup	¾ cup plus 2 tblsp
Chopped golden raisins	¼ cup	6 tblsp	⅔ cup
Dried dill	½ tsp	1 tsp	½ tblsp
Salt	¼ tsp	½ tsp	¾ tsp
Ground white pepper	¼ tsp	½ tsp	¾ tsp
Caraway seeds	¼ tsp	¼ tsp	½ tsp
Beer, preferably a pale ale or a lager	1 cup	1½ cups	2½ cups

1 Mix the cabbage, leeks, barley, raisins, dill, salt, pepper, and caraway seeds in the slow cooker. Pour the beer over everything.

2 Cover and cook on low for 4 hours. Stir well. Cover and continue cooking on low for 4 more hours, or until the cabbage is tender and the dish is stew-like.

TESTERS' NOTES
• This rib-sticker has flavors influenced by traditional German or Jewish cooking—and so might be best alongside roasted or grilled sausages, sauerbraten, or a stewed brisket.

• To keep the beer from foaming, pour it slowly down the inside wall of a large glass measuring cup, tilted to meet the bottle. Pour the beer very slowly over the ingredients in the slow cooker, a slow drizzle to keep the froth from building.

barley-and-apple stuffed cabbage

EFFORT: **A LOT** • PREP TIME: **1 HOUR** • COOK TIME: **6 HOURS** • KEEPS ON WARM: **2 HOURS** • SERVES: **3 TO 8 AS A MAIN COURSE**

INGREDIENTS	2- TO 3½-QT	4- TO 5½-QT	6- TO 8-QT
Large leaves from green cabbage	6	10	16
Boiling water	1¼ cups	2¼ cups	3½ cups
Quick-cooking barley (instant barley, not pearled)	¾ cup plus 2 tblsp	1½ cups	2⅓ cups
Chopped dried apple	⅓ cup	½ cup	¾ cup
Minced red onion	3 tblsp	¼ cup	½ cup
Dried thyme	½ tsp	1 tsp	½ tblsp
Ground cinnamon	¼ tsp	½ tsp	¾ tsp
Ground allspice	⅛ tsp	¼ tsp	½ tsp
Ground black pepper	⅛ tsp	¼ tsp	½ tsp
No-salt-added canned crushed tomatoes	1⅓ cups	2½ cups	2¾ cups
Unsweetened frozen apple juice concentrate, thawed	3 tblsp	¼ cup	½ cup
Dried dill	1½ tsp	2 tsp	1 tblsp
Salt	⅛ tsp	¼ tsp	½ tsp

1 Bring a large pot of water to a boil over medium heat. Drop the cabbage leaves in the water; submerge them by pressing down with the back of a wooden spoon. Cook until slightly softened, not quite tender, about 5 minutes. Use tongs to transfer them to a cutting board. Cool the leaves a few minutes and slice out the tough, thick stem at one end if necessary. Dump out the water.

2 Bring the precise amount of water for your size slow cooker to a boil in a second saucepan set over high heat. Stir in the barley, then cover, reduce the heat to low, and simmer slowly until the water has been absorbed and the barley is tender, about 10 minutes. Stir in the dried apple, onion, thyme, cinnamon, allspice, and pepper. Set aside to cool for 20 minutes.

3 Lay a prepared cabbage leaf on your work surface. Scoop up ⅓ cup of the barley filling and plop it near the bottom center of the leaf. Roll the leaf up, enclosing the filling, then fold the sides closed as well. Set the stuffed cabbage roll seam side down in the slow cooker and continue making more as required and stacking them neatly in layers as necessary.

4 Whisk the tomatoes, apple juice concentrate, dill, and salt in a large bowl. Pour over the stuffed leaves.

5 Cover and cook on low for 6 hours, or until the dish is aromatic and the leaves are quite tender. Lift the stuffed cabbage leaves gently out of the slow cooker into individual bowls, spooning the sauce over them.

TESTERS' NOTES
• Yep, this vegan main course is labor-intensive—which is why these sorts of recipes are probably a lost art, made by our grandmothers. But the results are also wholesome and hearty.
• Not every cabbage leaf needs its center vein removed. After they've all cooled a bit, see if the center vein will easily roll with the leaf. If so, there's no need to remove it. If not, cut it out in a triangular shape, leaving as much of the leaf intact as possible.

INGREDIENTS EXPLAINED Quick-cooking barley is not pearled barley; rather, it's rolled and steamed, about like rolled oats. It cooks in no time and is the preferred type of barley for a filling like this one.

desserts & party drinks

WE'LL ADMIT IT: WHEN WE STARTED WRITING THIS BOOK, WE HAD never once made any dessert in a slow cooker. Sure, we were schooled in the short rib curriculum, the chicken thigh program, even the shrimp seminar. But cakes? Or puddings?

We couldn't figure it out. For one thing, most of these treats are not set-it-and-walk-away affairs, the way soups and braises are. Most get done in around 2 hours, maybe more quickly. So what's the point? Why not make these things stovetop and in the oven?

Then we tested the first recipes: a buttery pudding, a steamed banana chocolate chip cake. Bingo: we knew what we'd been missing—ridiculously luxurious desserts that need a bit less fat than the old-fashioned recipes because of the way the moist environment under the lid protects them. The treat stays moist not because it's larded with butter; it doesn't dry out because of the way the appliance works.

We were hooked. We started taking slow cooker cakes just about everywhere we went: to book groups, to knitting classes, to social events. And our fare was always met with the same reaction: "From a slow cooker?" It seems we weren't the only ones who didn't know. So we invite you into the club. After an easy cobbler, a decadent lemon ricotta bread pudding, and an incredibly delicious dulce de leche, you'll wonder why you didn't join years ago.

 A note up front: the stated cooking time in these recipes does not include an often mandatory cooling period, sometimes 2 hours, sometimes more. You can't necessarily make a dessert and eat it the moment it comes out of the crock. Some cakes must condense to build structure; some puddings must continue to set. Read the recipe through completely before you begin, especially if you have easily disappointed little faces at the counter, already eager with forks or spoons in hand.

At the end of this chapter, we've got another great reason to break out the appliance: mulled cider, hot cocoa and mulled wine, and with some pretty potent libations. The slow cooker is actually the perfect tool for creating these winter warmers: they stay at just the right temperature, no boiling over, no cooling off. Better yet, they can sit out all night at a party, the drinks ready for your guests as the night goes on.

So welcome to the treats, the things you probably shouldn't make every day but just when you want them. Which may indeed be every day.

cakes and steamed puddings

No, we can't fashion a three-layer cake from a slow cooker. Or we shouldn't. For that matter, we can't make a proper sponge cake. But we can craft some pretty fine steamed puddings, more like ultra-moist cakes, all in the tradition of figgy pudding and other holiday desserts. And we can use that basic formula to bring back a slow cooker version of sticky date bread, popular when we were kids, almost always slathered in cream cheese and served at cocktail parties. Using the natural steaminess inside the canister, we can also turn out some pretty fudgy brownies as well as a very moist carrot cake. It's all about going with what works. We have to take the machine's capabilities and limitations in hand. Cheesecake? Great! Meringue layers for a dacquoise? Not so much.

Beyond that, we'll insist on only one fussy step: mixing the dry ingredients together first in their own bowl, rather than dumping them one by one into a wet batter and stirring away. We want the leavenings—baking soda, baking powder—distributed throughout the batter, rather clumped in one spot. The latter leads to uneven, tilted cakes—and in fact even more dramatic ones than emerge from the oven, since the moist heat can speed up the chemical reactions that give cakes loft. So yes, you have to dirty another bowl. Isn't cake worth it?

You'll also need one specific tool beyond the slow cooker: a 1-quart, high-sided, round ceramic soufflé or baking dish. Yes, some batters can be scraped right into the slow cooker; but many need to be formed in this specialty dish—or need to be kept away from direct contact with the (relatively) hot walls. Look for this sort of baking dish at almost any kitchenware store or some online outlets. Don't spend a fortune; get a sturdy baking dish to insulate the batter. The sides should also be about 3 inches tall so the batter can have some stability as it rises.

Cakes baked right in the slow cooker canister without this baking dish have a range of timings because of the varying shapes of cookers. A cake in a 4-quart narrow, round slow cooker will take a little longer than the same batter in a 5-quart wide, oval slow cooker. In all cases, the very center of the cake may not look set—however, if you touch it, you'll realize the batter has indeed firmed up, despite a sheen on the cake's surface. In oval cookers, the cake will not dome up but will be flat, even a little sunken at the center. Watch carefully: the sides will cook more quickly and so can dry out. As for all baking, even in a slow cooker, timings are mere suggestions. Your 6-quart is certainly different from our 8-quart. So pay attention to visual and physical cues more than stated timings. This chapter is the only one in the book where such detail matters—and it matters greatly.

You'll also need a few standard tools: a mixer, bowls, a rubber spatula, a wooden spoon. Nothing fancy is required for these recipes—no pastry bags or brushes. After all, these are slow cooker cakes and steamed puddings. We don't have to go crazy. We just have to make them.

hazelnut swirl pound cake

EFFORT: **A LITTLE** • PREP TIME: **20 MINUTES** • COOK TIME: **2½ TO 3½ HOURS** • KEEPS ON WARM: **NO** • SERVES: **6 TO 12**

INGREDIENTS	2- TO 3½-QT	4- TO 5½-QT	6- TO 8-QT
All-purpose flour, plus more for dusting the canister	2 cups	3 cups	4 cups
Baking powder	½ tsp	¾ tsp	1 tsp
Salt	¼ tsp	¼ tsp	½ tsp
Unsalted butter, plus more for greasing the canister	1 cup (2 sticks)	1½ cups (3 sticks)	2 cups (4 sticks)
Sugar	1 cup	1½ cups	2 cups
Large eggs, at room temperature	6	9	12
Vanilla extract	1 tblsp	1½ tblsp	2 tblsp
Nutella	¼ cup	6 tblsp	½ cup

1 Whisk the flour, baking powder, and salt in a bowl. Set aside.

2 Butter the inside of the slow cooker's canister, then dust it with flour to coat the surface finely but evenly. Tap out any excess flour.

3 Beat the butter and sugar in a large bowl with an electric mixer at medium speed until creamy and smooth, most of the sugar dissolved into the mix, 5 to 10 minutes. Beat in the eggs one at a time, making sure each is fully incorporated before adding the next. Finally, beat in the vanilla.

4 Scrape down and remove the beaters. Fold in the flour mixture with a rubber spatula, just until there are no bits of dry flour anywhere. Remove and save ¼ cup batter for a small slow cooker, 6 tablespoons for a medium one, and ½ cup for a large one; spread the rest evenly in the slow cooker.

5 Stir the Nutella into the reserved batter in a small bowl. Dollop this mixture by tablespoonfuls over the top of the batter in the canister. Use the blade of a flatware knife to run into, through, and out of these blobs, thus swirling them into the batter below.

6 Lay long, overlapping strips of paper towel across the top of the cooker, then set the lid in place. Bake on high for about 2½ hours in a small slow cooker, about 3 hours in a medium one, or about 3½ hours in a large one, or until the cake is puffed and set to the touch. Unplug, uncover, and cool for 1 hour before setting a cutting board over the cooker, inverting everything, and releasing the cake onto the board. Remove the slow cooker and turn the cake right side up onto a platter to serve.

TESTERS' NOTES
• You can skip buttering and flouring the canister if you've got baking spray on hand.
• Swirling in the Nutella mixture may well be the toughest part of this recipe. Insert the blade of the knife into the batter, then start moving it around, connecting the dots, as it were, moving back and forth among them as some of the chocolate mixture is dragged into the batter (and some of the batter is then dragged into the chocolate mixture).
• Inverting the cake is a tricky process, given all the upside down and right-side-up fandango. For large cakes in a large slow cooker, they may well split in half from their weight. Unless you're deft at these maneuvers, and quite strong to boot, you might be wise to cut your losses and use a nonstick-safe knife to slice wedges of the cake right out of the cooker. If your slow cooker doesn't have a removable insert, it may well be an impossible task anyway.
• This cake freezes exceptionally well. Wrap it tightly in plastic wrap, then a second layer of aluminum foil and store in the freezer for up to 4 months.

ALL-AMERICAN KNOW-HOW There's no need to soften butter before making most batters. In fact, cool butter, cut into little chunks right out of the fridge, will trap and hold air bubbles more effectively than the loosey-goosey stuff you spread on bread. That said, if you have an old-model hand mixer, it might not handle cold butter; you'll have to soften the butter for a few minutes before going at it.

INGREDIENTS EXPLAINED Nutella spread is a mixture of chocolate and ground hazelnuts with sugar, oil, and fat-free milk. It has been widely popular in Europe since the early '60s and can be found near the jams or the peanut butter in almost all North American supermarkets.

fudgy brownie cake

EFFORT: **A LOT** • PREP TIME: **25 MINUTES** • COOK TIME: **1 HOUR 20 MINUTES TO 2 HOURS** • KEEPS ON WARM: **NO** • SERVES: **6 TO 12**

INGREDIENTS	2- TO 3½-QT	4- TO 5½-QT	6- TO 8-QT
Unsalted butter, cut into small bits, plus more for greasing the canister	6 tblsp (¾ stick)	8 tblsp (1 stick)	12 tblsp (1½ sticks)
Dark chocolate, chopped	6½ ounces	9 ounces	13 ounces
Unsweetened chocolate, chopped	1½ ounces	2 ounces	3 ounces
Sugar	¾ cup	1 cup	1½ cups
Large eggs/yolk, at room temperature	1 whole plus 1 yolk	2 whole	3 whole
Vanilla extract	½ tblsp	2 tsp	1 tblsp
All-purpose flour, plus more for coating the canister	½ cup	⅔ cup	1 cup
Salt	¼ tsp	½ tsp	1 tsp

1 Generously grease the inside of the slow cooker canister by holding a small slice of butter with a paper towel and rubbing the butter all over the surfaces. Add some flour, then turn the crock this way and that to coat both the bottom and the walls with a fine, even dusting. Tap out any excess flour.

2 Set up a double boiler with about 1 inch of water in the bottom pan, simmering over medium heat—or place a large, heat-safe metal bowl over a medium saucepan with a similar amount of simmering water. Add the butter and both chocolates. Stir with a rubber spatula until about two-thirds of the chocolate has melted. Remove the top half of the double boiler or the bowl from the saucepan below, then continue stirring off the heat until all the chocolate has melted. Cool for 10 minutes.

3 Meanwhile, beat the sugar, eggs, and vanilla in a large bowl with an electric mixer at medium speed until quite thick and pale yellow, up to 10 minutes.

4 Beat in the cooled chocolate mixture until smooth, then scrape down and remove the beaters. Fold in the flour and salt with a rubber spatula, using wide, gentle arcs to make sure every speck of flour has been moistened. Pour and spread this mixture into the slow cooker.

5 Lay long strips of paper towels across the top of the slow cooker, overlapping each other and hanging down the sides for stability. Set the lid in place, then cook on high for about 1 hour 20 minutes in a small slow cooker, about 1 hour 40 minutes in a medium one, or about 2 hours in a large model, or until the cake is firm to the touch and the edges are dry while the middle is dark and moist. Unplug, uncover, and cool in the canister for 30 minutes before cutting out slices with a nonstick-safe knife or

(continued)

setting a cutting board over the cooker, inverting it, and turning the cake out.

TESTERS' NOTES

• Because of the way the slow cooker traps moisture inside, brownies come out fudgy, dense, and moist. The edges, however, will dry out a bit—and be a boon to those who like cakey brownies.

• When you're melting chocolate over a double boiler, control the heat so the water below barely simmers. Too much steam can condense into the chocolate, causing it to *seize*—that is, break into threads and a thin liquid. If the chocolate seizes, there may be no help for it. Try stirring in a little cream to see if the mixture will cohere. You may have to start over, even with the best of intentions.

• Room-temperature eggs stabilize batters, building structure in tiny air pockets that create that vaunted *crumb*, the hallmark of good baked fare. To bring eggs to room temperature, leave them on the counter (but still in their shells) for 20 minutes, or immerse them (again, still in their shells) in a bowl of warm (not hot) tap water for 3 to 4 minutes.

• We also like these with a little kick from up to ½ teaspoon cayenne added with the salt.

SHORTCUTS Omit greasing and flouring the slow cooker and instead use baking spray, a mix of oil and flour.

INGREDIENTS EXPLAINED Good-quality chocolate is most often sold with a percentage on the label—55 percent, 60 percent, 70 percent, and so on. The number refers to the percent of cocoa solids (the bitter chocolate stuff) as opposed to the sugar, cocoa butter, and certain stabilizers. As a general rule for this book, 40 to 55 percent is semisweet chocolate, 60 to 65 percent is bittersweet, and 70 to 85 percent is dark chocolate.

Milk chocolate is just that: chocolate with milk added to the mix. And unsweetened chocolate, sometimes called *baking chocolate*, has no (or in some brands, very little) sugar in the mix.

ALL-AMERICAN KNOW-HOW For the best baked goods, beat and beat and beat the sugar and eggs. The more air you add, the more loft you'll get. Yes, you can beat in so much air that the cake will not hold together when cut; but in general, beat until you think you've got a smooth, thick mixture—then beat it some more.

However, once you add the flour, stop beating altogether. *Fold* the flour mixture into most batters with a rubber spatula (yes, there are exceptions). Beating will elongate the flour's glutens, resulting in tough, chewy cakes. Folding will hold off said elongation. Don't overdo even the folding: work just until you see no more dry pockets. Some graininess from moistened but undissolved flour is expected—and encouraged.

sour cream brownie cake

EFFORT: **A LOT** • PREP TIME: **25 MINUTES** • COOK TIME: **1½ HOURS TO 2½ HOURS** • KEEPS ON WARM: **NO** • SERVES: **6 TO 12**

INGREDIENTS	2- TO 3½-QT	4- TO 5½-QT	6- TO 8-QT
All-purpose flour, plus more for dusting the crock	1 cup	1½ cups	2 cups
Baking soda	¾ tsp	1 tsp	½ tblsp
Salt	¼ tsp	½ tsp	¾ tsp
Dark chocolate, chopped into small bits	4 ounces	6 ounces	8 ounces
Unsalted butter, cut into small bits, plus more for greasing the canister	6½ tblsp	10 tblsp (1 stick plus 2 tblsp	13 tblsp (1 stick plus 5 tblsp
Unsweetened chocolate, cut into small bits	2½ ounces	3¾ ounces	5 ounces
Sugar	1 cup plus 2 tblsp	1⅔ cups	2¼ cups
Sour cream (regular or low-fat)	⅓ cup	½ cup	⅔ cup

Large eggs, at room temperature	2	3	4
Vanilla extract	2 tsp	1 tblsp	1½ tblsp

1 Whisk the flour, baking soda, and salt in a bowl; set aside.

2 Butter the inside of the canister, then toss in a little flour and tilt the canister this way and that to coat the interior with a fine dusting. Shake out any excess flour.

3 Set up a double boiler over about an inch of slowly simmering water—or set a heat-safe metal bowl over a medium saucepan with a similar amount of simmering water. Add the dark chocolate, butter, and unsweetened chocolate; stir until about two-thirds of the chocolate has melted. Remove the top half of the double boiler or the bowl from the heat; continue stirring until all the chocolate has melted. Cool for 5 minutes.

4 Beat the sugar into the chocolate mixture with an electric mixer at medium speed, until creamy but dense. Beat in the sour cream until smooth, then beat in the eggs one at a time, making sure each is fully incorporated before adding the next. Finally, beat in the vanilla before scraping down and removing the beaters.

5 Fold in the flour mixture with a rubber spatula just until there are no unmoistened bits of flour in the mix. Scrape and spread this batter into the slow cooker.

6 Lay long, overlapping strips of paper towels over the top of the slow cooker, hanging down over the sides. Set the lid in place and cook on high for about 1½ hours in a small slow cooker, about 2 hours in a medium slow cooker, or about 2½ hours in a large one, or until the cake begins to pull away from the sides of the cooker, the cake's edges are higher than the middle, and that middle is darker and fallen a bit from its wet density but still a bit soft when touched. Unplug, uncover, and cool for 30 minutes. Afterwards, set a cutting board over the crock, turn it upside down, and release the cake before inverting it right side up on a platter.

TESTERS' NOTES
• The tangy hit of sour cream will balance the chocolate perfectly in this fudgy cake. Once again, the edges will be slightly drier than the middle, so those who like the corners of the brownie pan will be in luck.
• If you're using a standard double boiler, the upper pan may well be large enough that you can beat and fold the whole batter right inside it. Otherwise, you'll need to scrape the melted chocolate mixture into a large bowl.
• If you jury-rig a bowl over a saucepan to create a double boiler, make sure (1) the bowl fits tightly so steam doesn't escape and (2) the bottom of the bowl in no wise touches the simmering water below. Also, watch out when you remove that bowl; escaping steam can burn your fingers. Wear oven mitts, turn off the heat under the simmering water, and tilt the bowl up before taking it off the saucepan to release steam.

ALL-AMERICAN KNOW-HOW Chopping the chocolate before melting it gives it a head start—and so less time over the heat with a smaller chance of scorching (and turning bitter) or seizing (and being rendered useless). The best chopping tool is a chocolate fork, its big tines designed to break through chocolate. However, you can also chop the chocolate on a cutting board with a heavy, sharp knife.

lemon buttermilk pudding cake

EFFORT: **A LITTLE** • PREP TIME: **20 MINUTES** • COOK TIME:
55 MINUTES TO 1 HOUR 10 MINUTES • KEEPS ON WARM: **NO** •
SERVES: **2 TO 6**

INGREDIENTS	2- TO 3½-QT	4- TO 5½-QT	6- TO 8-QT
Large eggs, at room temperature	2	3	5
Salt	½ tsp	¾ tsp	1 tsp
Sugar	½ cup	¾ cup	1¼ cups
Buttermilk (regular or low-fat)	⅔ cup	1 cup	1⅔ cups
Fresh lemon juice	3 tblsp	4½ tblsp	½ cup
Finely grated lemon zest	1 tblsp	1½ tblsp	2½ tblsp
All-purpose flour	¼ cup	6 tblsp	½ cup plus 2 tblsp

1 Generously grease the inside of the canister with unsalted butter, taking special care to get into the seam between the bottom and the wall.

2 Separate the eggs, putting the whites in one large bowl and the yolks in a second.

3 Add the salt to the egg whites and beat with an electric mixer at high speed until you can make soft, droopy peaks when you dip the turned-off beaters into the mixture. Set aside.

4 Clean and dry the beaters. Add the sugar to the egg yolks and beat at medium speed, scraping down the bowl occasionally, until the mixture is smooth and thick, about like a quick-bread batter, perhaps 4 minutes. Add the buttermilk, lemon juice, and lemon zest; continue beating at medium speed until smooth, about 1 minute. Scrape down the inside of the bowl and add the flour. Beat at low speed just until smooth.

5 Use a rubber spatula to fold the beaten egg whites into the buttermilk batter. Use long, slow, smooth arcs to get the egg whites incorporated; but do not leave any lumps of undissolved egg white in the batter. If necessary, stir more vigorously after folding and press the lumps against the side of the bowl to dissolve them.

6 Pour and scrape the batter into the prepared slow cooker. Lay long strips of paper towels over the top of the slow cooker to cover it completely, then set the lid in place. Cook on low for about 55 minutes in a small slow cooker, about 1 hour in a medium one, or about 1 hour 10 minutes in a large slow cooker, until the top of the cake is set, a bit spongy, and puffed slightly in the center. Serve immediately, scooping up bits of the cake with the warm pudding that has formed underneath.

TESTERS' NOTES

• This is a true pudding cake, a runny lemon curd underneath a spongy cake. If you underbake it slightly, as well you should, you won't be able to cut it into pieces. Serve it by the spoonful.

• Because slow cookers work at varying temperatures, and even go out of whack over time, it's important to watch this cake. A gooey mess is not called for—no underdone batter—but nonetheless a definite layer of pudding-ness underneath with a wet cake.

• Make sure the bowl with the egg whites is scrupulously clean and dry, without a whit of egg yolk in it. Otherwise, you'll get little to no loft out of the whites when beaten.

• Here, the flour is actually beaten into the batter because we need that bit of gluten to create a good sponge cake over the curd.

• The serving sizes here are low. Unfortunately, more batter in the crock will not get done quickly enough, resulting in set edges and uncooked middles.

Serve It Up! Make **Whipped Cream** for dolloping! Chill a large bowl and beaters in the fridge for 30 minutes, then pour in heavy cream—as much as you like. Beat with an electric mixer at high speed until slightly thickened, then start adding 1 tablespoon sugar for each ½ cup heavy cream you've used. Beat until just barely stiff, still saucy. Beat in a little vanilla extract and serve at once. (If you use confectioners' sugar rather than standard white sugar, the whipped cream will hold its shape in the fridge for a couple of hours.)

gluten-free chocolate almond pudding cake

EFFORT: **A LOT** • PREP TIME: **25 MINUTES** • COOK TIME: **1½ TO 2½ HOURS** • KEEPS ON WARM: **NO** • SERVES: **4 TO 12**

INGREDIENTS	2- TO 3½-QT	4- TO 5½-QT	6- TO 8-QT
FOR THE CAKE			
Almond flour, plus more for dusting the canister	1½ cups	3 cups	4½ cups
Gluten-free baking powder	2 tsp	4 tsp	1½ tblsp
Unsalted butter, cut into small bits, plus more for greasing the canister	6 tblsp	12 tblsp (1½ sticks)	18 tblsp (2 sticks plus 2 tblsp)
Dark chocolate, chopped (see page 463)	2 ounces	4 ounces	6 ounces
Granulated sugar	⅔ cup	1⅓ cups	2 cups
Milk	⅓ cup	⅔ cup	1 cup
Unsweetened cocoa powder	3 tblsp	6 tblsp	½ cup plus 1 tblsp
Large egg yolks	1	2	3
Vanilla extract	1 tblsp	1½ tblsp	2 tblsp
FOR THE TOPPING			
Packed dark brown sugar	¼ cup	½ cup	¾ cup
Unsweetened cocoa powder	3½ tblsp	7 tblsp	⅔ cup
Hot tap water	½ cup	1 cup	1½ cups

1 Grease the inside of the slow cooker canister with some butter, then add a bit of almond flour that will coat the canister as you tip and twist it. Tap out any excess.

2 Whisk the almond flour and baking powder in a bowl; set aside.

3 Set up a double boiler over about 1 inch of simmering water of medium heat in the bottom pan—or put a heat-safe metal bowl on a medium saucepan with a similar amount of simmering water in it. Add the butter and chocolate, reduce the heat so the water simmers slowly, and stir until about two-thirds of the chocolate has melted. Remove the top half of the double boiler or the bowl from the heat and continue stirring until all the chocolate has melted. Cool for 5 minutes.

4 Use an electric mixer at medium speed to beat the sugar into the chocolate mixture until smooth, then beat in the milk, cocoa powder, egg yolks, and vanilla.

5 Scrape down and remove the beaters. Add the almond flour mixture and fold with a

(continued)

rubber spatula until there are no dry pockets anywhere in the batter. Spoon and spread this mixture into the slow cooker.

6 To make the topping, place the brown sugar and cocoa powder in a small bowl; stir in the hot water until smooth. Pour this mixture over the batter in the cooker.

7 Cover and cook on high for about 1½ hours in a small slow cooker, about 2 hours in a medium one, or about 2½ hours in a large cooker, or until the cake has just begun to pull away from the sides of the cooker but is still very moist, even jiggly at the center. (It will look wet even when set.) If possible, remove the insert from the slow cooker. In any case, cool, uncovered, for 10 minutes; then scoop out by the large spoonful into bowls.

TESTERS' NOTES
• You don't even have to have a gluten allergy to enjoy this decadent dessert, somewhere halfway between a pudding and a cake.
• The cake won't keep well, so plan on eating it when it's still hot from the cooker.
• As with all cakes, remember that timings are a matter of suggestion, not a rule. They will differ slightly among shapes and sizes of slow cookers in each category.
• You might consider some whipped cream (page 465). Use granulated sugar to be sure it's gluten free.

INGREDIENTS EXPLAINED
Unsweetened cocoa powder comes in two forms: (1) *Dutch-processed*, with a darker color and an alkali in the mix to help it dissolve more readily and make the chocolate a tad lighter in taste (despite its darker color); and (2) *natural cocoa powder*, without said alkali in the mix, lighter in color but deeper in flavor, more bitter and sophisticated, like dark chocolate. Either type of cocoa powder will work for all these recipes; let your taste be your guide.

carrot cake

EFFORT: **A LITTLE** • PREP TIME: **25 MINUTES** • COOK TIME: **2 HOURS 10 MINUTES TO 2 HOURS 30 MINUTES** • KEEPS ON WARM: **NO** • SERVES: **3 TO 8**

INGREDIENTS	2- TO 3½-QT	4- TO 5½-QT	6- TO 8-QT
All-purpose flour, plus more for dusting the canister	1½ cups	2¼ cups	3¾ cups
Baking powder	1 tsp	½ tblsp	1 tblsp
Ground cinnamon	1 tsp	½ tblsp	1 tblsp
Baking soda	½ tsp	¾ tsp	1¼ tsp
Salt	¼ tsp	½ tsp	¾ tsp
Sugar	1 cup	1½ cups	2½ cups
Walnut oil, plus more for greasing the canister	6 tblsp	9 tblsp	1 cup
Large eggs	2	3	5
Unsweetened pineapple juice	¼ cup	6 tblsp	⅔ cup
Vanilla extract	1 tsp	½ tblsp	1 tblsp
Packed grated carrots	1 cup	1½ cups	2½ cups
Finely chopped walnuts	6 tblsp	9 tblsp	1 cup

1 Generously grease the inside of the slow cooker canister with some walnut oil dabbed onto a paper towel, then add some flour and tilt the canister to coat its sides and bottom. Knock out any excess flour.

2 Whisk the flour, baking powder, cinnamon, baking soda, and salt in a bowl until the cinnamon is even throughout. Set aside.

3 Use an electric mixer at medium speed to beat the sugar and oil in a large bowl until most of the sugar has dissolved and the mixture is fairly creamy. Beat in the eggs one at a time, then beat in the pineapple juice and vanilla until smooth.

4 Remove the beaters and fold in the flour mixture with a rubber spatula, using gentle, long arcs to get the flour fully moistened, no dry bits anywhere. Fold in the carrots and walnuts; spread this mixture into the canister.

5 Lay overlapping lengths of paper towels over the top of the slow cooker. Set the lid in place and cook on high for about 2 hours 10 minutes in a small slow cooker, about 2 hours 20 minutes in a medium cooker, or about 2 hours 30 minutes in a large cooker, or until the cake is firm to the touch and set in the middle. Unplug, uncover, and cool for 1 hour; then slice pieces right out of the canister with a nonstick-safe knife or invert the cooker over a cutting board to release the cake before righting it on a serving platter.

TESTERS' NOTES
• Walnut oil adds a mellow richness to this cake—although you can use the far more tasteless canola oil for a more economical dessert.
• The cake is lighter than the standard carrot cake, not quite as dense.
• The good thing about greasing and then flouring the canister is that you can tell if there are any spots without oil—there's no flour adhering to them. Grease the missing spots and add more flour (or just use a nonstick baking spray and be done with it).

Serve It Up! Since there's no frosting on this cake, make a **Cream Cheese Sauce:** Use an electric mixer at medium speed to beat 3 ounces room-temperature cream cheese with 5 tablespoons heavy cream in a bowl; beat in 1½ tablespoons confectioners' sugar and 1 teaspoon vanilla extract. Drizzle on each piece—or make a puddle of it in the plate and "float" a piece of cake in it.

apple cake

EFFORT: **A LOT** • PREP TIME: **30 MINUTES** • COOK TIME: **3 TO 4 HOURS** • KEEPS ON WARM: **NO** • SERVES: **4 TO 8**

INGREDIENTS	2- TO 3½-QT	4- TO 5½-QT	6- TO 8-QT
Moderately tart baking apples (such as Braeburn), cored, peeled, and chopped	1 large	3 medium	3 large
Granulated sugar	½ cup plus 1 tblsp	¾ cup	1 cup plus 2 tblsp
Almond oil or canola oil, plus more for greasing the canister	¼ cup	6 tblsp	½ cup
Large eggs	1 whole	1 whole plus 1 yolk	1 whole plus 1 white
All-purpose flour	1 cup plus 3 tblsp	1⅔ cups	2⅓ cups
Baking powder	¾ tsp	1 tsp	½ tblsp
Ground cinnamon	½ tsp	¾ tsp	1¼ tsp
Salt	⅛ tsp	¼ tsp	½ tsp
Sliced almonds	2½ tblsp	¼ cup	⅓ cup
Packed dark brown sugar	1½ tsp	2 tsp	1 tblsp

1 Dab some oil on a paper towel and thoroughly grease the inside of the slow cooker canister.

2 Whisk the apples, granulated sugar, oil, and eggs in a large bowl until the sugar dissolves. Set aside for 15 minutes to macerate.

3 Whisk the flour, baking powder, cinnamon, and salt in a second bowl. Stir the dry mixture

(continued)

into the apple mixture until there are no pockets of undissolved flour visible.

4 Spread the batter into the slow cooker canister; sprinkle the top with the sliced almonds and brown sugar.

5 Lay long, overlapping strips of paper towel over the top of the slow cooker; set the lid in place. Cook on high for about 3 hours in a small slow cooker, about 3½ hours in a medium one, or about 4 hours in a large cooker, or until a toothpick or cake tester inserted into the center of the cake comes out with a few moist crumbs attached. Unplug, uncover, and cool for 2 hours, until the top is dry and the cake is room temperature. Set a cutting board over the canister, invert the whole thing, and turn the cake out before setting it right side up on a serving platter.

TESTERS' NOTES
• By letting the apples sit with the sugar and oil, they begin to release their moisture, a necessary part of the cake's success.
• Crumble the brown sugar grains between your fingers so you get the best coverage over the cake's top.
• A nut oil tastes best in this cake; we chose almond oil to match the topping. Of course, if you don't want to spring for a nut oil, you can always use canola oil.
• Unfortunately, this cake doesn't freeze very well. Store it, sealed in plastic wrap, at room temperature for up to 2 days.

maple chocolate chip cake

EFFORT: **A LITTLE** • PREP TIME: **25 MINUTES** • COOK TIME: **1 HOUR TO 1 HOUR 40 MINUTES** • KEEPS ON WARM: **NO** • SERVES: **4 TO 12**

INGREDIENTS	2- TO 3½-QT	4- TO 5½-QT	6- TO 8-QT
All-purpose flour, plus more for dusting the canister	¾ cup plus 2 tblsp	1¾ cups	2⅔ cups
Baking powder	½ tsp	¾ tsp	1¼ tsp
Salt	¼ tsp	½ tsp	¾ tsp
Unsalted butter, plus more for greasing the canister	6 tblsp	12 tblsp (1½ sticks)	18 tblsp (2 sticks plus 2 tblsp)
Packed light brown sugar	6 tblsp	¾ cup	1 cup plus 2 tblsp
Maple syrup, preferably grade B	¼ cup	½ cup	¾ cup
Large eggs, at room temperature	1	2	3
Vanilla extract	¾ tsp	½ tblsp	2½ tsp
Semisweet or bittersweet chocolate chips	¼ cup	½ cup	¾ cup

1 Use some butter to grease the inside of the slow cooker. Add some flour, tilt the canister to coat it in a fine dusting, and tap out any excess flour.

2 Whisk the flour, baking powder, and salt in a bowl; set aside.

3 Use an electric mixer at medium speed to beat the butter and brown sugar in a large bowl until creamy and even a bit fluffy, almost no undissolved sugar in the mix. Beat in the maple syrup until smooth, then beat in the eggs one at a time. Finally, beat in the vanilla.

4 Scrape down and remove the beaters. Add the flour mixture and fold in with a rubber spatula just until all the flour has been moistened. Fold in the chocolate chips. Scrape and spread this batter evenly in the slow cooker.

5 Lay overlapping lengths of paper towels over the top of the slow cooker, with excess hanging over the sides. Set the lid in place, then cook on high for about 1 hour in a small slow cooker, about 1 hour 15 minutes in a medium cooker, or about 1 hour 40 minutes in a large model, or until the cake is puffed and set to the touch. Unplug, uncover, and cool for 1 hour. If desired, set a cutting board over the canister, invert everything, and shake gently to dislodge the cake; remove the canister, then set the cake right side up on a serving platter or another cutting board.

TESTERS' NOTES
• Dense and somewhat chewy, this cake gets most of its flavor from the maple syrup—which should be a very dark grade for the best punch.
• Use bittersweet chocolate chips for a more elegant flavor, a tad acidic against the sweet cake.
• This cake freezes well when wrapped tightly in plastic wrap and then aluminum foil. Unwrap and thaw on the counter for 3 or 4 hours before serving.

INGREDIENTS EXPLAINED In baking recipes, *sugar* can mean granulated white sugar or either light or dark brown sugar. In keeping with standard recipe practice, if we merely ask for *sugar*, then we're talking about granulated sugar. That said, if we use two types of sugar in a recipe, we name them both. And if we call for just brown sugar, we specify either light or dark.

peanut butter chocolate chip blondies

EFFORT: **A LITTLE** • PREP TIME: **20 MINUTES** • COOK TIME: **1½ TO 2 HOURS** • KEEPS ON WARM: **NO** • SERVES: **3 TO 8**

INGREDIENTS	2- TO 3½-QT	4- TO 5½-QT	6- TO 8-QT
All-purpose flour, plus more for dusting the canister	½ cup plus 1 tblsp	1 cup plus 2 tblsp	1½ cups plus 1 tblsp
Baking powder	¼ tsp	½ tsp	¾ tsp
Granulated sugar	¼ cup	½ cup	¾ cup
Packed light brown sugar	3 tblsp	6 tblsp	½ cup plus 1 tblsp
Unsalted butter, plus more for greasing the canister	2 tblsp	4 tblsp (½ stick)	6 tblsp
Smooth natural-style peanut butter	2 tblsp	¼ cup	6 tblsp
Large eggs, at room temperature	1	2	3
Vanilla extract	1 tsp	2 tsp	1 tblsp
Semisweet or bittersweet chocolate chips	⅔ cup	1⅓ cups	2 cups

1 Generously butter the inside of a canister, then add a little flour and tilt it all around to coat the sides and bottom. Dump out any excess flour inside.

2 Whisk the flour and baking powder in a bowl; set aside.

3 Beat both sugars, butter, and peanut butter in a large bowl with an electric mixer at

(continued)

medium speed until creamy and light, scraping down the inside of the bowl occasionally with a rubber spatula. Beat in the eggs one at a time, making sure each is fully incorporated before adding the next. Beat in the vanilla until smooth.

4 Scrape down and remove the beaters. Add the flour mixture and fold in with a rubber spatula just until fully moistened. Fold in the chocolate chips. Scrape and smooth this thick batter into the slow cooker.

5 Overlap long lengths of paper towels on top of the slow cooker, then set the lid in place. Cook on high for about 1½ hours in a small or medium cooker, or about 2 hours in a large cooker, or until the cake is firm throughout, a tad dry at the edges, and set to the touch in the middle. Remove the canister from the cooker, if possible, and cool on a wire rack for 30 minutes—or cool in the cooker, turned off, for 45 minutes. If desired, invert the canister or cooker on a cutting board, shake gently to release the blondies, then remove the canister or cooker and turn the blondies right side up before cutting into pieces.

TESTERS' NOTES
• This one is truly more like bar cookies than a cake. It won't rise up too much and so ends up very much like standard blondies. Again, the edges will get more done than the center.
• Make sure you beat the sugars, butter, and peanut butter well—certainly until they change consistency and get airy. This will lighten up the still-dense cake considerably.

chewy brown sugar chocolate chip oat cake

EFFORT: **A LITTLE** • PREP TIME: **20 MINUTES** • COOK TIME: **1 HOUR 20 MINUTES TO 2 HOURS** • KEEPS ON WARM: **NO** • SERVES: **3 TO 8**

INGREDIENTS	2- TO 3½-QT	4- TO 5½-QT	6- TO 8-QT
All-purpose flour, plus more for dusting the canister	¾ cup	1 cup plus 2 tblsp	1½ cups
Baking soda	½ tsp	¾ tsp	1 tsp
Ground cinnamon	½ tsp	¾ tsp	1 tsp
Salt	⅛ tsp	¼ tsp	½ tsp
Unsalted butter, plus more for greasing the canister	8 tblsp (1 stick)	12 tblsp (1½ sticks)	1 cup (2 sticks)
Granulated sugar	6 tblsp	½ cup plus 1 tblsp	¾ cup
Packed dark brown sugar	6 tblsp	½ cup plus 1 tblsp	¾ cup
Large eggs/white, at room temperature	1 whole	1 whole plus 1 white	2 whole
Vanilla extract	1 tsp	½ tblsp	2 tsp
Rolled oats (not quick-cooking or steel-cut)	1¼ cups	1¾ cups plus 2 tblsp	2½ cups
Semisweet or bittersweet chocolate chips	1¼ cups	1¾ cups	2½ cups

1 Generously butter the inside of the canister, then add some flour and tilt it until it's evenly coated. Tap out any excess flour.

2 Whisk the flour, baking soda, cinnamon, and salt in a bowl; set aside.

3 Use an electric mixer at medium speed to beat the butter and both sugars in a large bowl until fluffy and pale yellow, with only a few bits of undissolved sugar in the mix. Beat in the eggs one at a time, then beat in the vanilla until smooth.

4 Scrape down and remove the beaters. Stir in the flour mixture, followed by the oats and chocolate chips, just until there are no dry specks of ingredients in the batter. Spoon and spread into the slow cooker.

5 Overlap long lengths of paper towels across the top of the cooker, then set the lid in place. Cook on high for about 1 hour 20 minutes in a small slow cooker, about 1½ hours in a medium cooker, or about 2 hours in a large cooker, or until the cake is soft but set, puffed yet pulling back from the canister's sides. Unplug, uncover, and cool for 1 hour, then either cut pieces of the cake out of the cooker with a nonstick-safe knife or invert the cooker over a cutting board, shake the cake free, and set it right side up on a serving platter.

TESTERS' NOTES
• A dense, chewy cake, this one's best with a strong cup of coffee, even as an afternoon snack.
• The cake will pack well: wrap pieces in wax paper to send in lunches.

sour cream cheesecake

EFFORT: **A LOT** • PREP TIME: **25 MINUTES** • COOK TIME: **2 HOURS** • KEEPS ON WARM: **NO** • SERVES: **6**

INGREDIENTS FOR A 1-QUART, HIGH-SIDED, ROUND BAKING DISH

All-purpose flour, for dusting the baking dish

1¼ cups graham cracker crumbs

5 tblsp unsalted butter, melted and cooled for 5 minutes, plus more for greasing the baking dish

⅔ cup plus 1½ tblsp sugar

¼ tsp ground cinnamon

¼ tsp salt

12 ounces cream cheese (regular or low-fat), softened to room temperature

2 large eggs, at room temperature

1 cup sour cream (regular or low-fat)

2 tsp vanilla extract

1 Set a 1-quart, high-sided, round baking or soufflé dish in the slow cooker. Fill the canister with warm tap water around the dish until it comes halfway up the sides. Remove the dish, cover the cooker, and set to high while you prepare the batter.

2 Butter the inside of the baking dish. Mix the graham cracker crumbs, butter, 1½ tblsp sugar, the cinnamon, and salt in a small bowl; pour into the baking dish and press the crumb mixture against the sides and bottom to form a crust.

3 Use an electric mixer at medium speed to beat the cream cheese and remaining ⅔ cup sugar in a large bowl until the most of the

(continued)

sugar has dissolved, about 4 minutes, scraping down the inside of the bowl occasionally with a rubber spatula.

4 Beat in the eggs one at a time, making sure each is thoroughly incorporated before adding the next and continuing to scrape down the bowl after each addition. Finally, beat in the sour cream and vanilla.

5 Pour and scrape this batter into the prepared baking dish. Set it in the hot water in the slow cooker. Lay overlapping, long lengths of paper towels over the top of the slow cooker, hanging the excess down the sides.

6 Cover and cook on high for about 2 hours, or until puffed and set but still a bit jiggly in the center.

7 Unplug the cooker, remove the lid and paper towels, and let stand for 1 hour. Remove the baking dish, cover with plastic wrap, and chill in the fridge for at least 3 hours or up to 2 days before slicing into wedges to serve.

TESTERS' NOTES
• Here's the first of our steamed desserts, incredibly light and moist. In many ways, the slow cooker is functioning as a water bath, a bain-marie, providing a constant humidity to set this cheesecake (and subsequent steamed puddings).
• The baking dish used here—and in all the subsequent steamed puddings—will fit in almost any slow cooker except the very tiniest, oval ones. You may also use a high-sided, 6-inch cheesecake pan for these desserts. However, do not use a pan with removable sides and bottom; the water can leach in and ruin the dessert.

ALL-AMERICAN KNOW-HOW
It can be tough to get the hot baking dish out of a slow cooker, particularly a small model. To alleviate any difficulty, before you begin the recipe, lay a long strip of cheesecloth in the cooker, the excess hanging over the sides. Set the baking dish on top of it, add the water, and continue on with the recipe. At the end, this cheesecloth strip can be used to leverage the baking dish out of the cooker, lifting the baking dish up in its cradle, as it were. You'll still have to support it lest the cheesecloth break; but you'll be spared digging with your fingers into a still-warm cooker.

steamed gingerbread

EFFORT: **A LOT** • PREP TIME: **25 MINUTES** • COOK TIME: **2½ HOURS** • KEEPS ON WARM: **1 HOUR** • SERVES: **6**

INGREDIENTS FOR A 1-QUART, HIGH-SIDED, ROUND BAKING DISH

2 cups all-purpose flour, plus more for dusting the baking dish

1 tblsp ground ginger

2 tsp ground cinnamon

2 tsp baking soda

½ tsp ground cloves

¼ tsp salt

8 tblsp (1 stick) unsalted butter, cut into small bits, plus more for greasing the canister

1 cup packed dark brown sugar

1 large egg, at room temperature

¾ cup plain yogurt

1 tsp vanilla extract

1 Place a 1-quart, round, high-sided baking or soufflé dish in the slow cooker and fill the canister with warm tap water until it comes about 1 inch up the sides of the dish. Remove the dish, cover the cooker, and set on high while you prepare the batter.

2 Grease the inside of the baking dish with some butter, then add some flour and turn the dish to coat the sides and bottom thoroughly. Knock out any excess flour.

3 Whisk the flour, ginger, cinnamon, baking soda, cloves, and salt in a bowl; set aside.

4 Beat the butter and brown sugar in a large bowl with an electric mixer at medium speed, scraping down the inside of the bowl occasionally with a rubber spatula, until there are almost no undissolved sugar grains in the mix. Beat in the egg until smooth, scrape down the bowl again, then beat in the yogurt and vanilla. Scrape down and remove the beaters.

4 Add the flour mixture and fold in with a rubber spatula just until there are no bits of dry flour left in the batter. Pour and scrape the batter into the prepared baking dish.

5 Set it in the cooker, then lay long lengths of overlapping paper towels over the top of the cooker. Cover and cook on high for about 2½ hours, or until the cake is puffed and set in the middle but still quite moist.

6 Remove the baking dish from the cooker and set it on a wire rack to cool for 30 minutes. Either cut slices right out of the dish or invert the baking dish onto a cutting board, shake it gently to release the cake, remove the baking dish, and set it right side up on a serving plate to cut into wedges.

TESTERS' NOTES

• Steaming a cake like this is an old-fashioned technique, mostly gone out of style although deserving a comeback with the slow cooker. Once, these desserts were all called puddings, not because they were soft but because they set through steam rather than dry heat. We've put them among the cakes because they are certainly not custards and most Americans will find their texture more in keeping with other cakes, if decidedly moister.

• If you want a bit of a sour pop to balance the ginger, add up to 1 teaspoon finely grated fresh lemon zest or finely grated orange zest for a less assertive flavor.

Serve It Up! A steamed gingerbread calls for a dollop of crème fraîche—a cultured cream sort of like sour cream, but with a higher butterfat content. Look for it in the refrigerator case near the butter and sour cream, then doctor it at home with a little confectioners' sugar and some vanilla extract.

steamed marmalade pecan cake

EFFORT: **A LOT** • PREP TIME: **20 MINUTES** • COOK TIME: **3 HOURS** • KEEPS ON WARM: **1 HOUR** • SERVES: **6**

INGREDIENTS FOR A 1-QUART, HIGH-SIDED, ROUND BAKING DISH

1 cup all-purpose flour, plus more for dusting the baking dish

3½ ounces pecans, finely ground (1 scant cup)

½ tsp baking powder

½ tsp salt

4 tblsp (½ stick) unsalted butter, cut into small bits, plus more for greasing

½ cup granulated sugar

¼ cup packed light brown sugar

⅓ cup orange marmalade

2 large eggs, at room temperature

1 tsp vanilla extract

(continued)

1 Set a 1-quart, round, high-sided baking dish in the slow cooker and fill the canister with warm tap water until it comes about 1½ inches up the outside of the dish. Remove the baking dish, then cover the cooker and set on high while you prepare the batter.

2 Generously butter the inside of the baking dish, getting down into the seam between the wall and the bottom. Add some flour, turn the dish every which way to coat the interior, then tap out the excess flour over the sink so there's just a fine film remaining inside.

3 Whisk the flour, pecans, baking powder, and salt in a bowl; set aside.

4 Use an electric mixer at medium speed to beat the butter and both sugars in a large bowl until light and fluffy, even pale yellow in color, scraping down the inside of the bowl occasionally, about 5 minutes. Beat in the orange marmalade, eggs, and vanilla. Scrape down and remove the beaters.

5 Pour in the flour mixture, then fold with a rubber spatula just until there are no dry specks of flour anywhere. Scrape the batter into the prepared baking dish.

6 Butter one side of a 10-inch piece of aluminum foil, then set it buttered side down over the baking dish. Crimp and seal the foil against the baking dish, then set it all in the hot water.

7 Cover and cook on high for about 3 hours, until the cake is firm and set but still quite moist. Remove the baking dish from the hot water, peel off the foil, and cool on a wire rack for 30 minutes before cutting slices out of the dish or setting a cutting board over the baking dish, inverting it all, releasing the cake, removing the dish, and setting the cake back right side up on a serving platter.

steamed banana chocolate chip cake

EFFORT: **A LOT** • PREP TIME: **25 MINUTES** • COOK TIME: **2 HOURS** • KEEPS ON WARM: **1 HOUR** • SERVES: **6**

INGREDIENTS FOR A 1-QUART, HIGH-SIDED, ROUND BAKING DISH

1¼ cups all-purpose flour, plus more for dusting the baking dish

½ tsp baking powder

¼ tsp salt

6 tblsp unsalted butter, plus more for greasing

6 tblsp sugar

1 large egg, at room temperature

2 ripe medium bananas, peeled and mashed

2 tblsp milk (whole or low-fat)

¼ cup semisweet or bittersweet chocolate chips

1 Set a 1-quart, high-sided soufflé or baking dish in the slow cooker, then fill the slow cooker with warm tap water to come about 1½ inches up the outside of the baking dish. Remove the baking dish, cover the cooker, and set on high while you prepare the batter.

2 Generously butter the inside of the baking dish, then add some flour and turn the dish to get a fine film of flour over its insides. Tap out any excess.

3 Whisk the flour, baking powder, and salt in a bowl. Set aside.

4 Beat the butter and sugar in a large bowl with an electric mixer at medium speed until light and fluffy, scraping down the inside of the bowl occasionally with a rubber spatula, about 5 minutes. Beat in the egg, then the mashed banana and milk. Scrape down and remove the beaters.

5 Fold in the flour mixture with a rubber spatula just until there's no unmoistened flour anywhere to be seen. Fold in the chocolate chips, then pour and scrape the batter into the prepared bowl.

6 Butter one side of a 10-inch piece of aluminum foil, then set it over the baking dish, buttered side down, and crimp the edges to seal tightly. Set the baking dish in the hot water in the cooker.

7 Cover and cook on high for about 2 hours, until the cake is firm and set but still quite moist, even a tad spongy. Remove the baking dish from the cooker, remove the foil, and cool on a wire rack for 30 minutes before slicing out wedges or setting a cutting board over the baking dish, inverting it all, releasing the cake, removing the dish, and setting the cake back right side up on a serving platter.

TESTERS' NOTES

• A very moist cake, almost sticky when first cut, this one will be a big hit with a cup of hot tea.

• Because steamed cakes are so moist, they don't pack well in lunches. That said, they'll be waiting for you when you get home.

• For the best flavor, make sure the bananas are quite ripe, even a tad soft, with lots of brown spots mottled over their skins. The best ones for this recipe are, frankly, probably on the discount produce rack at your supermarket.

• The batter may appear broken—that is, with soggy threads throughout—after the addition of the banana. The flour will take care of the problem.

• The sheet of foil used for the cover should be only a tad larger than the baking dish. Otherwise, it can hang down into the water; steam can then get under it and onto the cake.

Serve It Up! Serve slices with this **Easy Chocolate Sauce**: Bring ¼ cup water and ¼ cup sugar to a boil in a small saucepan set over medium-high heat, stirring often. Boil for 1 minute, then remove from the heat and stir in 6 ounces chopped, semisweet or bittersweet chocolate until smooth. Whisk in 2 tablespoons unsalted butter and 1 tablespoon brandy, cognac, or Armagnac.

steamed sticky date-nut bread

EFFORT: **A LOT** • PREP TIME: **25 MINUTES** • COOK TIME: **3 HOURS** • KEEPS ON WARM: **1 HOUR** • SERVES: **8**

INGREDIENTS FOR A 1-QUART, HIGH-SIDED, ROUND BAKING DISH

1 cup plus 2 tblsp all-purpose flour, plus more for dusting the baking dish

3¾ tsp baking soda

½ tsp salt

1⅓ cups chopped pitted dates

⅔ cup packed dark brown sugar

3 tblsp toasted walnut oil, plus more for greasing

2 large eggs, at room temperature

½ tblsp vanilla extract

⅔ cup finely chopped walnuts

1 Set a 1-quart high-sided, round soufflé or baking dish in the slow cooker, then add enough warm tap water to come halfway up the outside of the dish. Remove the baking dish, cover the cooker, and set on high while you prepare the batter.

2 Generously grease the inside of the baking dish with some walnut oil dabbed on a paper towel, then add some flour and give it a fine coating by twisting and turning it before knocking out any excess flour over the sink.

3 Whisk the flour, baking soda, and salt in a bowl until well combined, and set aside.

4 Use an electric mixer at medium speed to beat the dates, brown sugar, and oil in a large bowl until thick and pasty. Beat in the eggs one at a time, then scrape down the inside of the bowl. Beat in the vanilla until smooth. Scrape down and remove the beaters.

5 Pour in the flour mixture, then use a rubber spatula to fold it in just until there are no dry pockets of flour in the bowl. Fold in the walnuts.

6 Pour and scrape the batter into the prepared baking dish. Oil one side of a 16-inch piece of aluminum foil with some walnut oil dabbed on a paper towel, then set the foil, oil side down, over the baking dish and seal tightly to the edges. Set the baking dish in the hot water.

7 Cover and cook on high for about 3 hours, or until the cake is sticky but set, moist but still firm to the touch even under the foil. Remove the baking dish from the slow cooker, take off the foil, and cool on a wire rack for 30 minutes. Either cut wedges right out of the baking dish or set a cutting board over the baking dish, invert the whole contraption, jiggle the cake free, remove the baking dish, and right the cake onto a serving platter.

TESTERS' NOTES

• If you're as old as we are, you may remember date-nut bread baked in a clean coffee can, a staple sweet at '70s parties. This recipe replicates that classic without the metallic aftertaste.

• Don't use desiccated baking dates for this recipe. You'll need moist, sticky, juicy, pitted dates, such as Medjools. You must be able to mash the dates between your fingers.

• You really can't overbeat the mixture in step 4. Keep going to make the dates as sticky as possible.

Serve It Up! Smear every slice with cream cheese.

custards and puddings

These desserts often haunt us professional food writers—or their success does. On the stovetop, they're temperamental, no doubt about it. A vanilla pudding or a creamy custard won't set without first coming to the right temperature—and holding there without nudging much above it, a razor's edge of success without copious amounts of thickeners like flour or cornstarch.

The slow cooker takes care of those problems. Puddings and custards come out creamy every time. With this important caveat: you'll get what's considered among the mavens as the perfect set, never hard. After years of eating the instant stuff from chemical-laced packets, some of us have gotten the idea that you should be able to cut a pudding almost like a cake. But puddings should have a rich and creamy texture, velvety and smooth. They should also ride the line between a sauce and whipped cream—wet and moist, yet dense. When you scoop a bit out of a bowl, the rest should slowly flow in place to fill the void.

But don't just think vanilla and chocolate puddings. We've also got Chocolate Fondue, a range of rice and tapioca puddings, and even three bread puddings. Why are these last not in the cake section? Because puddings and custards rely more heavily on eggs for their setting, not thickeners. And there's no leavening in the mix, so they don't rise well. Sure, a bread pudding may puff a bit, but that's mostly about the hot air that gets trapped between the bread cubes. Once the thing cools, it settles. Although you won't—because puddings are about the best desserts around. They make everyone happy. You should have seen us during recipe testing, giddy over pots and pots of custards!

chocolate pudding

EFFORT: **A LITTLE** • PREP TIME: **25 MINUTES** • COOK TIME: **1 HOUR 10 MINUTES TO 1 HOUR 20 MINUTES** • KEEPS ON WARM: **NO** • SERVES: **4 TO 8**

INGREDIENTS	2- TO 3½-QT	4- TO 5½-QT	6- TO 8-QT
Unsweetened chocolate (see page 462)	3 ounces	4½ ounces	6 ounces
Milk	3½ cups	5¼ cups	7 cups
Sugar	¾ cup	1 cup plus 2 tblsp	1½ cups
All-purpose flour	¼ cup	6 tblsp	½ cup
Vanilla extract	1 tblsp	1½ tblsp	2 tblsp
Salt	½ tsp	¾ tsp	1 tsp
Large eggs/yolks, at room temperature	3 yolks	1 whole plus 3 yolks	6 yolks

1 Grate the chocolate into the slow cooker with a microplane or the small holes of a box grater. Whisk in the milk, sugar, flour, vanilla, and salt until the flour has dissolved.

2 Cover and cook on high for 30 minutes, then whisk well. Cover and continue cooking on high for 30 to 40 minutes, whisking every 15 minutes, or until thickened and bubbling.

3 Whisk the eggs in a medium bowl, then whisk in about 1 cup of the hot pudding until smooth. Whisk the combined mixture back into the slow cooker until smooth. Set the temperature to low and cook, uncovered, for 10 minutes, stirring twice.

4 If possible, remove the canister from the slow cooker and refrigerate, uncovered, for at least 4 hours before serving. Or spoon the pudding into a bowl and refrigerate for up to 2 hours. Afterwards, cover the canister with its lid or the bowl with plastic wrap and store in the fridge for up to 3 days.

TESTERS' NOTES
• Although the chocolate will firm up in the fridge, this pudding is still a little thicker than the Buttery Brown Sugar Pudding (below). That said, it's soft and rich rather than chewy or stiff.
• Make sure you tap any bits of chocolate stuck in the box grater or on the microplane into the slow cooker.

buttery brown sugar pudding

EFFORT: **A LITTLE** • PREP TIME: **15 MINUTES** • COOK TIME: **1 HOUR 10 MINUTES TO 1 HOUR 20 MINUTES** • KEEPS ON WARM: **NO** • SERVES: **4 TO 8**

INGREDIENTS	2- TO 3½-QT	4- TO 5½-QT	6- TO 8-QT
Milk	3 cups	4¾ cups	6 cups
Packed dark brown sugar	½ cup	⅔ cup	1 cup
All-purpose flour	⅓ cup	½ cup plus 1 tblsp	⅔ cup
Vanilla extract	1 tblsp	1½ tblsp	2 tblsp
Salt	¼ tsp	½ tsp	½ tsp
Cold unsalted butter, cut into small pieces	3 tblsp	5 tblsp	6 tblsp
Large egg yolks, at room temperature	5	8	10

1 Whisk the milk, brown sugar, flour, vanilla, and salt in the slow cooker until no bits of undissolved flour or sugar remain in the mix. Stir in the butter bits.

2 Cover and cook on high for 30 minutes. Whisk well, then continue cooking on high for 30 to 40 minutes, whisking every 15 minutes, until thickened and bubbling.

3 Whisk the egg yolks in a medium bowl, then whisk a cup or two of the hot pudding into them until smooth. Whisk the combined mixture back into the pudding in the cooker.

4 Set the temperature on low and cook, uncovered, for 10 minutes, whisking twice, until again somewhat thickened.

5 Remove the canister from the cooker if possible and chill the canister in the fridge for at least 4 hours. Or spoon the pudding into a large bowl and refrigerate for at least 2 hours. Cover and store in the fridge for up to 3 days.

TESTERS' NOTES
• Puddings from a slow cooker will never get solidly thick unless there's so much flour or cornstarch in the mix that they become almost gelatinous. But that's the good news! You'll end up with a more traditional set, certainly nothing akin to what comes out of instant pudding boxes.
• Be fairly aggressive with your whisking, both in steps 1 and 4. You need to make sure you break the pudding up so it stays soft and velvety.
• Use a nonstick-safe whisk if your cooker has a nonstick finish.

ALL-AMERICAN KNOW-HOW The pudding will definitely form a skin as it cools, the result of a large milk protein coming to the surface and drying out as it meets the air. If you're a skin-o-phobe, seal plastic wrap right against the pudding's surface when it goes into the fridge. The lack of air contact will keep a skin from forming.

raspberry cream cheese puddings

EFFORT: **A LITTLE** • PREP TIME: **25 MINUTES** • COOK TIME: **1½ TO 2 HOURS** • KEEPS ON WARM: **NO** • SERVES: **2 TO 4**

INGREDIENTS	2- TO 3½-QT	4- TO 5½-QT	6- TO 8-QT
Cream cheese (regular or low-fat), at room temperature	8 ounces	12 ounces	1 pound (16 ounces)
Packed light brown sugar	2 tblsp	3 tblsp	¼ cup
Large eggs/white, at room temperature	1 whole	1 whole plus 1 white	2 whole
Raspberry jam	3 tblsp	4½ tblsp	6 tblsp
Chambord or other raspberry liqueur	2 tsp	1 tblsp	4 tsp
Graham cracker crumbs	2 tblsp	3 tblsp	¼ cup

1 Place two 1-cup, high-sided ramekins in a small slow cooker, or three in a medium model, or four in a large one. Pour enough warm tap water into the slow cooker to come 1 inch up the sides of the ramekins. Remove them from the cooker, then cover it and cook on high while you prepare the batter.

2 Beat the cream cheese and brown sugar in a large bowl with an electric mixer at medium speed until light and fluffy, about 5 minutes. Beat in the egg, scrape down the inside of the bowl, and beat in the jam and liqueur. Divide this mixture among the ramekins; set them in the cooker.

3 Cover and cook on high for 1½ to 2 hours, or until the pudding is set but still wiggles in its center when the ramekin is tapped. Remove

(continued)

the ramekins to a wire rack and cool for 1 hour. Cover with plastic wrap and refrigerate for at least 4 hours or up to 2 days. Serve by sprinkling each pudding with graham cracker crumbs.

TESTERS' NOTES
• These are really a cross between a pudding and a cheesecake. They can be kept in the fridge for several days—dessert ready when you are.
• Four ramekins may not fit in some large cooker models. Check before you begin: if you can't get four ramekins in your model without crowding, use only three—and thus the ingredients listed for the medium cooker.
• Substitute any jam and liqueur combination for the raspberry—apricot jam and apricot schnapps, cherry jam and Cheery Herring, and so forth.

dark chocolate pot de crème

EFFORT: **A LOT** • PREP TIME: **30 MINUTES** • COOK TIME: **1 HOUR 45 MINUTES** • KEEPS ON WARM: **NO** • SERVES: **6**

INGREDIENTS FOR A 1-QUART, HIGH-SIDED, ROUND BAKING DISH

2 cups heavy cream

2 tsp vanilla extract

5 ounces bittersweet chocolate (see page 462), chopped

5 large egg yolks, at room temperature

2 tblsp sugar

½ tsp salt

1 Set a 1-quart, high-sided, round soufflé dish or baking dish in the slow cooker. Fill the canister (not the baking dish) with warm tap water until it comes about halfway up the dish. Remove it, then cover the cooker and cook on high while you prepare the chocolate mixture.

2 Warm the cream and vanilla in a small saucepan set over medium-low heat just until bubbles fizz around the outer edge of the pan.

3 Place the chopped chocolate in a large bowl; pour in the warmed cream. Stir with a rubber spatula until the chocolate melts. Set aside to cool at room temperature for 10 minutes.

4 Use an electric mixer to beat the egg yolks and sugar at medium speed in a second bowl until thick and pale yellow, even fluffy, about 5 minutes. Beat in the chocolate mixture and salt until smooth, then pour into the prepared baking dish.

5 Cover the baking dish with plastic wrap and set it all in the slow cooker. Cover and cook on high for 1 hour 45 minutes, or until the custard barely jiggles when the baking dish is tapped. Remove the baking dish from the slow cooker, peel off the plastic wrap, and cool on a wire rack for 1 hour before refrigerating for at least 4 hours or up to 2 days, all before serving. After 4 hours in the fridge, cover the baking dish again with new plastic wrap.

TESTERS' NOTES
• Pot de crème (*poh-duh-CREM*) is like a dense chocolate pudding but with no thickeners in the mix—no flour, no cornstarch. It's as elemental a dessert as you can imagine—and made wondrously silky by moist heat.
• Bittersweet chocolate offers a more pleasing, acidic bite than semisweet chocolate would.
• For an easy way to get a hot baking dish out of the slow cooker using cheesecloth, see page 472.
• Spoonfuls of this dessert in bowls call out for whipped cream (page 465).

chocolate fondue

EFFORT: **NOT MUCH** • PREP TIME: **10 MINUTES** • COOK TIME: **2 HOURS** • KEEPS ON WARM: **2 HOURS AFTER WHISKING** • SERVES: **8**

INGREDIENTS FOR A 1-QUART, HIGH-SIDED, ROUND BAKING DISH

16 ounces (1 pound) semisweet chocolate
(see page 462), chopped

1 cup heavy cream

4 tblsp (½ stick) unsalted butter, cut into small pieces

1 tblsp vanilla extract

¼ tsp salt

1 Mix the chocolate, cream, butter, vanilla, and salt in a round, high-sided, 1-quart soufflé or baking dish. Set that dish in the slow cooker.

2 Cover and cook on low for 2 hours, or until the chocolate has melted and the fondue is hot. Whisk until smooth.

TESTERS' NOTES

• You've never had fondue as the slow cooker can make it. There's no chance of the chocolate turning bitter.

• Some recipes call for melting the chocolate mixture right in the slow cooker, no baking dish needed. However, we feel it's too difficult to spear bits of strawberries or pound cake cubes, dunk them into the deep cooker, and get them somewhere near your plate. Instead, we prefer to be able to bring the smaller, shallower baking dish to the table. (We even set it on a stand over a candle to keep it warm.)

• You needn't make this great quantity. You can halve the ingredients and use a 2-cup ramekin. The cooking time will be reduced to 1½ hours.

Serve It Up! You'll need bamboo skewers and various things to dip: strawberries, sliced bananas, cubed pound cake, or marshmallows. Or skip the spears and go simple: use graham crackers and some peanut butter to smear on them before they take a dunk.

dulce de leche

EFFORT: **A LITTLE** • PREP TIME: **10 MINUTES** • COOK TIME: **4 TO 7 HOURS** • KEEPS ON WARM: **NO** • SERVES: **6 TO 12 AS A SAUCE**

INGREDIENTS	2- TO 3½-QT	4- TO 5½-QT	6- TO 8-QT
Evaporated whole milk	3 cups	4½ cups	6 cups
Sweetened condensed milk (regular or low-fat)	2½ cups	3¾ cups	5 cups
Light corn syrup	1 tblsp	1½ tblsp	2 tblsp
Baking soda	1 tsp	½ tblsp	2 tsp
Vanilla extract	1 tsp	½ tblsp	2 tsp
Salt	½ tsp	¾ tsp	1 tsp
4-inch cinnamon sticks	1	1½	2

1 Stir the evaporated milk, condensed milk, corn syrup, baking soda, vanilla, and salt in the slow cooker until the corn syrup dissolves. Add the cinnamon sticks.

2 Cover and cook on high for 1 hour.

3 Uncover, then continue cooking on high, stirring every 30 minutes, for 3 to 4 hours in a small slow cooker, 4 to 5 hours in a medium cooker, or 5 to 6 hours in a large cooker until the mixture is thick, brown, and sticky. Spoon into glass jars, seal, and refrigerate for up to 2 weeks.

TESTERS' NOTES

• This is the iconic caramel sauce, usually made just from sweetened condensed milk, but here it is morphed to fit the slow cooker's unique heat, with some vanilla and cinnamon added for even more flavor. Do not use fat-free sweetened condensed milk for this treat.

• No, you won't get away from all that stirring, but you won't have to do as much as you would stovetop. Once the

(continued)

lid comes off, you need to do so every 30 minutes to keep the mixture from scorching as it reduces and caramelizes.
• The timings here are given in a range since this technique is essentially candy-making, and thus dependent on the day's weather, humidity, and even temperature.

Serve It Up! Spoon it onto ice cream, stir it into coffee, drizzle it on shortbread, or simply lick it off the spoon.

INGREDIENTS EXPLAINED *Light* corn syrup refers only to its color, as opposed to dark corn syrup. Do not use reduced-calorie corn syrup, since it won't provide the right ratio of sugars to make the sauce gooey.

lemon ricotta bread pudding

EFFORT: **A LOT** • PREP TIME: **25 MINUTES** • COOK TIME: **2 HOURS** • KEEPS ON WARM: **NO** • SERVES: **6**

INGREDIENTS FOR A 1-QUART, HIGH-SIDED, ROUND BAKING DISH

2 large eggs, at room temperature

1 cup ricotta (regular or low-fat)

⅔ cup milk

½ cup sour cream (regular or low-fat)

⅓ cup sugar

2 tsp finely grated lemon zest

1 tsp vanilla extract

¼ tsp salt

3 cups cubed rustic or hearty white bread cubes

⅓ cup golden raisins

¼ tsp ground cinnamon

1 Set a round, high-sided, 1-quart baking or soufflé dish in the slow cooker, then fill the surrounding canister with warm tap water until it comes about halfway up the side of the baking dish. Remove the dish, cover the cooker, and cook on high while you prepare the bread pudding.

2 Whisk the eggs, ricotta, milk, sour cream, sugar, lemon zest, vanilla, and salt in a large bowl until creamy and light. Add the bread cubes and raisins; stir until well moistened. Pack everything into the prepared baking dish, pouring any excess liquid in the bowl over the top of the bread cubes. Sprinkle the top with cinnamon.

3 Set the baking dish in the slow cooker. Overlap long strips of paper towels over the top of the cooker, hanging down the sides for stability. Cover and cook on high for 2 hours, or until set and firm. Transfer the baking dish to a wire rack and cool for 10 minutes before scooping out servings.

TESTERS' NOTES
• This bread pudding is denser than most, partly because it's steamed and partly because of the nature of the cheese-laced custard. When cold, cut it into wedges.
• Fat-free ricotta and fat-free sour cream are loaded with stabilizers that will cease to work in the hot, steamy cooker—and lead the sauce to break. A little extra fat, even in the low-fat versions, safeguards the pudding.
• If you've removed the zest from the lemon with a citrus zester, mince those strips into fine bits so there are no lemony threads in the mix.

peanut butter and jam bread pudding

EFFORT: **A LITTLE** • PREP TIME: **15 MINUTES** • COOK TIME: **1 HOUR 45 MINUTES TO 2½ HOURS** • KEEPS ON WARM: **NO** • SERVES: **4 TO 12**

INGREDIENTS	2- TO 3½-QT	4- TO 5½-QT	6- TO 8-QT
Cubes of French or Italian bread (1-inch cubes)	4 cups	8 cups	12 cups
Strawberry jam	7 tblsp	¾ cup	1¼ cups
Milk	1 cup	2 cups	3¼ cups
Creamy natural-style peanut butter	7 tblsp	¾ cup	1¼ cups
Large eggs, at room temperature	2	4	6
Sugar	¼ cup	½ cup	¾ cup plus 2 tblsp
Vanilla extract	1 tsp	2 tsp	1 tblsp
Salt	Pinch	⅛ tsp	¼ tsp

1 Generously grease the inside of the canister with unsalted butter, taking care to get into the seam between the wall and the bottom.

2 Lay the bread cubes out on a clean, dry work surface; then spread one side of as many as you can with the strawberry jam. Toss them into the slow cooker.

3 Blend the milk, peanut butter, eggs, sugar, vanilla, and salt in a large covered blender until smooth, scraping down the inside of the container once or twice. Pour this puree over the bread cubes, then press down with the back of a wooden spoon until they are submerged and have soaked up a good deal of the liquid.

4 Cover and cook on high for 1 hour 45 minutes in a small slow cooker, 2 hours in a medium model, or 2½ hours in a large cooker, or until the pudding is set with little trace of moisture anywhere in the cooker. Scoop up warm servings without delay.

TESTERS' NOTES
• There are already bread puddings in the Breakfast chapter, but these are sweeter, more in keeping with dessert (or an afternoon treat).
• Spreading the bread with the jam is the hardest part of this recipe. The best tool is a small spreader for soft cheeses or creamy dips, rather than a flatware knife.
• By getting the bread to absorb much of the liquid before you begin to cook the bread pudding, you'll reduce the risk of having the eggs scramble and adhere to the sides of the cooker.
• Unfortunately, none of these bread puddings makes a good leftover for dessert the next day. The bread turns to mush.

chocolate cinnamon bread pudding

EFFORT: **A LOT** • PREP TIME: **35 MINUTES** • COOK TIME: **1½ TO 2½ HOURS** • KEEPS ON WARM: **NO** • SERVES: **4 TO 8**

INGREDIENTS	2- TO 3½-QT	4- TO 5½-QT	6- TO 8-QT
Cubes of cinnamon-swirl bread or cinnamon babka (1-inch cubes)	4 cups	6 cups	8 cups
Chopped walnuts	½ cup	¾ cup	1 cup
Salt	⅛ tsp	¼ tsp	½ tsp
Milk	1 cup	1½ cups	2 cups
Bittersweet or dark chocolate (see page 462), chopped	2 ounces	3 ounces	4 ounces
Unsweetened cocoa powder	¼ cup	½ cup	¾ cup
Sugar	¼ cup	½ cup	¾ cup
Large eggs, at room temperature	2	3	4

1 Heat the oven to 350°F. In the meantime, generously butter the inside of the canister.

2 Spread the bread cubes on a large, lipped baking sheet and toast in the oven until golden brown, stirring occasionally, about 10 minutes. Cool on a wire rack for 10 minutes. Toss the bread cubes, walnuts, and salt in the slow cooker.

3 Heat the milk in a large saucepan set over medium-low heat until it begins to fizz and bubble at the edges of the pan. Whisk in the chocolate, cocoa powder, and sugar, until the chocolate has fully dissolved and the mixture is uniform in color. Cool for 15 minutes.

4 Whisk the eggs into the chocolate mixture, then pour over the bread cubes and nuts. Press down with the back of a wooden spoon so that the bread is thoroughly moistened, even soaking up most of the liquid.

5 Cover and cook on high for 1½ hours in a small slow cooker, 1 hour 45 minutes to 2 hours in a medium cooker, or 2 to 2½ hours in a large cooker, or until the pudding is puffed and set without any evidence of liquid in the cooker. Scoop out big spoonfuls to serve.

TESTERS' NOTES

• We prefer dark chocolate here, maybe even 75 or 80 percent dark, to work against the already sweet cinnamon bread. We'd keep any cinnamon-*raisin* bread away from this recipe, but that's just our preference.

• Make sure you cool the chocolate for at least 15 minutes in step 2 to avoid scrambling the eggs.

• For these bread puddings, cut the bread into small cubes. Larger ones won't soften as they would in the oven.

cherry-almond rice pudding

EFFORT: **NOT MUCH** • PREP TIME: **10 MINUTES** • COOK TIME: **4 HOURS** • KEEPS ON WARM: **NO** • SERVES: **4 TO 8**

INGREDIENTS	2- TO 3½-QT	4- TO 5½-QT	6- TO 8-QT
Milk (regular or low-fat)	3⅔ cups	6 cups (1½ quarts)	8 cups (2 quarts)
White Arborio rice	1 cup	1⅔ cups	2¼ cups
Roughly chopped dried sweet or tart cherries	1 cup	1½ cups	2¼ cups
Sugar	1 cup	1½ cups	2 cups
Unsalted butter, cut into little bits	3 tblsp	5 tblsp	8 tblsp (1 stick)
Vanilla extract	1 tsp	2 tsp	1 tblsp
Ground cinnamon	½ tsp	¾ tsp	1 tsp
Salt	⅛ tsp	¼ tsp	½ tsp
Almond extract	⅛ tsp	¼ tsp	½ tsp
Large egg yolks, at room temperature	1	2	3

1 Stir the milk, rice, cherries, sugar, butter, vanilla, cinnamon, salt, and almond extract in the slow cooker until the sugar has dissolved.

2 Cover and cook on high, stirring twice, for 4 hours, or until thick and rich.

3 Whisk the egg yolks in a medium bowl until creamy, about 1 minute. Whisk in a cup or two of the hot rice pudding until smooth. Whisk the mixture back into the pudding in the cooker until evenly distributed. Serve warm.

TESTERS' NOTES

• Arborio rice, the same kind used to make risotto, gives this pudding a thick, sticky texture.
• Use sweet or tart cherries, depending on preference.
• The egg yolks here are not really thickeners; instead, they're enrichers, designed to take this pudding over the top. Thus, they don't need extra cooking time for setting the pudding. And in terms of food safety, they'll pop right up to a hot temperature, given the volume of the pudding.

mango-coconut tapioca pudding

EFFORT: **A LITTLE** • PREP TIME: **15 MINUTES** • COOK TIME: **2 HOURS 10 MINUTES** • KEEPS ON WARM: **NO** • SERVES: **4 TO 8**

INGREDIENTS	2- TO 3½-QT	4- TO 5½-QT	6- TO 8-QT
Coconut milk	1 cup	1½ cups	2¼ cups
Milk	1 cup	1½ cups	2¼ cups
Sugar	7 tblsp	¾ cup	1 cup plus 2 tblsp
Small pearl tapioca	⅓ cup	½ cup	¾ cup
Unsweetened shredded coconut	⅓ cup	½ cup	¾ cup
Salt	⅛ tsp	¼ tsp	½ tsp
Large eggs/yolk	1 yolk	1 whole	1 whole plus 1 yolk
Diced, peeled, and pitted mango	⅓ cup	½ cup	¾ cup

(continued)

1 Stir the coconut milk, milk, sugar, tapioca, coconut, and salt in the slow cooker until the sugar dissolves.

2 Cover and cook on high for 2 hours, or until the tapioca is transparent and soft.

3 Whisk the egg in a medium bowl, then whisk in a cup or two of the hot pudding. Whisk the mixture back into the pudding in the cooker until uniform throughout.

4 Set the temperature on low and cook, uncovered, for 10 minutes, or until thickened a bit. Stir in the mango to serve.

TESTERS' NOTES
• Tapioca puddings are an old-fashioned dessert, rich and comforting.
• Don't use instant tapioca, sometimes found in the baking aisle; and don't use the large tapioca pearls found in bubble teas at Asian restaurants. Instead, use the standard small tapioca pearls.

INGREDIENTS EXPLAINED Tapioca is a starch from the cassava root, used as a thickener or additive in custards and sauces. By the way, in Great Britain, tapioca is a pudding thickened with arrowroot—not at all this American dessert.

ALL-AMERICAN KNOW-HOW To peel and pit a mango, balance it on one long, thin side on your cutting board, then slice down on either side of the large pit inside, leaving about 1 inch in the center of the fruit. With the cut side facing you slice the flesh in each half into small squares while still in the peel without cutting through, like cutting brownies in a pan. Invert the peels, turning them inside out like knitted caps, and slice off these small squares. Finally, cut the remaining peel away from the flesh around the pit and slice off as much flesh as possible, dicing or chopping it as the recipe requires.

fruit desserts

Given our druthers, we'd always have fruit for dessert. Or better yet, fruit *in* dessert. We're partial to crisps, cobblers, and clafoutis. Unfortunately, fruit isn't a year-round thing, despite the illusion induced by international trade. Apples in May are a tad squishy; plums in January, unforgivable.

The slow cooker is more forgiving. Many of these desserts will work well with frozen peaches, raspberries, or sour cherries. In fact, much of that frozen fruit is picked closer to perfection than the stuff that ends up in the supermarket bins. After all, the fruit in the freezer case has had no time to ripen further in transport and storage. It has to be picked fairly ripe before it hits the deep freeze.

But in most cases, frozen fruit has to be thawed before it can go into the slow cooker. And here's the problem: you put it in a bowl in the fridge overnight and the next day, you're left with lots of water as well as thawed fruit. Drain off that water; it can bog down these desserts.

Beyond the crisps and such, we've got some desserts that are elemental: Stuffed Apples (page 491), Wine-Poached Pears (page 492), and Bananas Foster (page 493). And we round it out with some fruit-based dessert sauces, perfect for drizzling onto pound cake slices, spooning over ice cream, or layering in a trifle or parfait. No wonder we like fruit for dessert.

peach raspberry granola crisp

EFFORT: **A LITTLE** • PREP TIME: **15 MINUTES** • COOK TIME: **6 HOURS**
• KEEPS ON WARM: **2 HOURS THROUGH STEP 1** • SERVES: **4 TO 12**

INGREDIENTS	2- TO 3½-QT	4- TO 5½-QT	6- TO 8-QT
Peeled, pitted, and sliced peaches	4 cups	8 cups	12 cups
Fresh raspberries	1 cup	2 cups	3 cups
Granulated sugar	¼ cup	½ cup	¾ cup
Instant tapioca (see page 491)	2 tblsp	¼ cup	6 tblsp
All-purpose flour	1 tblsp	2 tblsp	3 tblsp
Fresh lemon juice	1 tblsp	2 tblsp	2½ tblsp
Salt	⅛ tsp	⅛ tsp	¼ tsp
Unsalted butter	2 tblsp	4 tblsp (½ stick)	6 tblsp (¾ stick)
No-fruit-added plain granola	1 cup	2 cups	3 cups

1 Stir the sliced peaches, raspberries, sugar, tapioca, flour, lemon juice, and salt in the slow cooker until the sugar dissolves. Cover and cook on low for 6 hours, or until thick and bubbling.

2 Melt the butter in a skillet set over medium heat. Stir in the granola; cook, tossing often, until buttery, warm, and aromatic, about 3 minutes.

3 Dish up the peach filling into bowls and sprinkle the granola topping over each serving.

TESTERS' NOTES
• Feel free to substitute frozen peach slices and frozen raspberries for the fresh fruit here. Thaw in a big bowl, then pour off the excess liquid.

• Vary the size of the skillet, depending on how much granola you need. You might even want to prepare the topping for a large slow cooker in batches—or simply enough for the number of servings you'll be dishing up right then. If so, reduce the butter to compensate.

sour cherry and almond cobbler

EFFORT: **A LITTLE** • PREP TIME: **20 MINUTES** • COOK TIME: **1½ TO 2 HOURS** • KEEPS ON WARM: **NO** • SERVES: **4 TO 8**

INGREDIENTS	2- TO 3½-QT	4- TO 5½-QT	6- TO 8-QT
FOR THE FILLING			
Pitted sour cherries	4 cups	6 cups	8 cups
Granulated sugar	⅔ cup	1 cup	1⅓ cups
Instant tapioca (see page 491)	1½ tblsp	2 tblsp	3 tblsp
All-purpose flour	1 tblsp	5 tsp	2 tblsp
FOR THE TOPPING			
All-purpose flour	1 cup	1½ cups	2 cups
Packed light brown sugar	3 tblsp	5 tblsp	6 tblsp
Ground almonds	3 tblsp	5 tblsp	6 tblsp
Baking powder	1 tsp	½ tblsp	2 tsp
Salt	¼ tsp	¼ tsp	½ tsp
Milk	6 tblsp	½ cup plus 1 tblsp	¾ cup
Unsalted butter, melted and cooled for 5 minutes	4 tblsp (½ stick)	6 tblsp (¾ stick)	8 tblsp (1 stick)
Almond extract	½ tsp	¾ tsp	1 tsp

1 To make the filling, mix the cherries, sugar, tapioca, and flour in the slow cooker until the sugar has begun to dissolve on the cherries.

2 To make the topping, whisk the flour, brown sugar, almonds, baking powder, and salt in a large bowl. Whisk the milk, butter, and almond extract in a second bowl until creamy. Then use a wooden spoon to stir these wet ingredients into the flour mixture.

3 Use a tablespoon to dollop the batter over the top of the filling. Overlap long strips of paper towels over the top of the cooker.

4 Cover and cook on high for 1½ hours in a small slow cooker, 1 hour 45 minutes in a medium cooker, or 2 hours in a large one, or until the filling is bubbling and the topping is firm if still a tad spongy to the touch.

TESTERS' NOTES
• Use fresh sour cherries or thawed frozen ones. Or use drained canned pitted sour cherries packed in water. Because some of the tartness is missing from canned cherries, add up to ½ tablespoon lemon juice to the filling ingredients.
• As you well know, things don't brown in the slow cooker. If pale biscuits as a cobbler topping bother you, sprinkle each with a light dusting of ground cinnamon before cooking.

apricot clafouti

EFFORT: **A LITTLE** • PREP TIME: **15 MINUTES** • COOK TIME: **1 HOUR 15 MINUTES TO 1 HOUR 45 MINUTES** • KEEPS ON WARM: **1 HOUR** • SERVES: **3 TO 8**

INGREDIENTS	2- TO 3½-QT	4- TO 5½-QT	6- TO 8-QT
Small fresh apricots, halved and pitted	6	10	16
Large egg yolks, at room temperature	4	6	10
Sour cream (regular or low-fat)	¾ cup	1 cup plus 2 tblsp	2 cups
Packed light brown sugar	⅓ cup	½ cup	¾ cup plus 1 tblsp
Milk	¼ cup	6 tblsp	½ cup plus 2 tblsp
Vanilla extract	½ tblsp	2½ tsp	1 tblsp
Salt	⅛ tsp	¼ tsp	½ tsp
All-purpose flour	½ cup	¾ cup	1¼ cups

1 Generously grease the inside of the slow cooker canister with unsalted butter. Set the apricots cut side down in the canister.

2 Whisk the yolks, sour cream, brown sugar, milk, vanilla, and salt in a large bowl until creamy. Whisk in the flour until smooth. Pour over the apricot halves.

3 Cover and cook on high for 1 hour 15 minutes in a small slow cooker, 1 hour 30 minutes in a medium cooker, or 1 hour 45 minutes in a large cooker, or until the batter is set and firm to the touch. Scoop out by the spoonfuls to serve.

(continued)

• A clafouti (*clah-foo-TEE*) is an Old World dessert, a custard baked over fruit. The slow cooker makes it even creamier than the standard oven variety!

• Substitute an equivalent amount of whole sweet cherries, such as Bing. Add up to ½ teaspoon almond extract along with the vanilla.

Serve It Up! Rather than serving with whipped cream, sweeten additional sour cream with confectioners' sugar and whisk in some vanilla extract to use as a dolloped topping.

apple walnut crisp

EFFORT: **A LITTLE** • PREP TIME: **20 MINUTES** • COOK TIME: **2 TO 2½ HOURS** • KEEPS ON WARM: **NO** • SERVES: **3 TO 8**

INGREDIENTS	2- TO 3½-QT	4- TO 5½-QT	6- TO 8-QT
FOR THE FILLING			
Moderately tart medium baking apples (such as Gala or Braeburn), peeled, cored, and chopped	3	6	9
Granulated sugar	3 tblsp	⅓ cup	½ cup
All-purpose flour	½ tblsp	1 tblsp	1½ tblsp
Instant tapioca	½ tblsp	1 tblsp	1½ tblsp
Fresh lemon juice	1 tsp	½ tblsp	2 tsp
FOR THE TOPPING			
Chopped walnuts	6 tblsp	¾ cup	1 cup plus 2 tblsp
Packed light brown sugar	6 tblsp	¾ cup	1 cup plus 2 tblsp
All-purpose flour	6 tblsp	¾ cup	1 cup plus 2 tblsp
Unsalted butter, melted and cooled	4 tblsp (½ stick)	8 tblsp (1 stick)	12 tblsp (1½ sticks)
Ground cinnamon	¼ tsp	½ tsp	¾ tsp
Salt	⅛ tsp	¼ tsp	½ tsp

1 To make the filling, stir the apples, granulated sugar, flour, tapioca, and lemon juice in the slow cooker until the sugar dissolves.

2 To make the topping, mix the walnut pieces, brown sugar, flour, butter, cinnamon, and salt in a large bowl until the mixture is uniform, everything sliced with butter and sugar. Sprinkle over the top of the apple filling, making an even, full layer.

3 Lay overlapping lengths of paper towels over the top of the cooker. Cover and cook on high for 2 hours in a small or medium slow cooker, or 2½ hours in a large slow cooker, or until the apple filling is bubbling around the bits of topping. Uncover and let stand unplugged for 5 minutes before serving.

TESTERS' NOTES

• A crisp is a fabled American dessert: a pie filling underneath a crunchy, nut-laced crust.

• For more flavor, before chopping them toast the walnut pieces on a large baking sheet in a 350°F oven until lightly browned and aromatic, tossing occasionally, perhaps as much as 10 minutes.

• Substitute peeled and pitted peaches or nectarines for the apples, and increase by 50 percent the amounts of the flour and tapioca for the filling.

INGREDIENTS EXPLAINED Instant tapioca, which is the consistency of coarse cornmeal, was your grandmother's secret thickener for making perfect pies. It creates a rich, thick filling without the incipient gumminess of flour or the stiffness of cornstarch.

stuffed apples

EFFORT: **A LITTLE** • PREP TIME: **20 MINUTES** • COOK TIME: **2½ HOURS/5 HOURS** • KEEPS ON WARM: **3 HOURS** • SERVES: **2 TO 6**

INGREDIENTS	2- TO 3½-QT	4- TO 5½-QT	6- TO 8-QT
Large baking apples, such as Cortland, Rome, or Northern Spy	2	4	6
Chopped pecans	2 tblsp	¼ cup	6 tblsp
Finely chopped stemmed dried figs	2 tblsp	¼ cup	6 tblsp
Packed dark brown sugar	2 tblsp	¼ cup	6 tblsp
Ground cinnamon	¼ tsp	½ tsp	¾ tsp
Salt	Pinch	⅛ tsp	¼ tsp
Unsalted butter	1 tblsp	2 tblsp	3 tblsp
Unsweetened apple juice or apple cider	¼ cup	½ cup	¾ cup

1 Use a melon baller to core the apples, working down through the stem end into the flesh, turning the baller in tight circles as you work down, until you have removed all the seeds and core without breaking through the sides or bottom and leaving as much flesh as possible.

2 Mix the pecans, figs, brown sugar, cinnamon, and salt in a bowl; pack this into the core of each apple. Top the stuffing with ½ tablespoon butter on each apple. Set them stuffing side up in the slow cooker and pour the apple juice around them.

3 Cover and cook on high for 2½ hours or on low for 5 hours, or until the apples are soft—until you could cut them with a spoon. Use a large slotted spoon to transfer to serving bowls and cool a few minutes before you dig in.

TESTERS' NOTES
• Since you can cook these on low for so long, and they'll stay warm for a while, you might also consider stuffed apples for breakfast, setting up the slow cooker before you're off to bed.
• Using a melon baller to core an apple is pretty easy once you get the hang of it. If this is your first time, you might buy one extra apple, just in case you slip and break through the flesh of the apple.

wine-poached pears

EFFORT: **A LITTLE** • PREP TIME: **10 MINUTES** • COOK TIME: **2 TO 5 HOURS** • KEEPS ON WARM: **3 HOURS** • SERVES: **4 TO 8**

INGREDIENTS	2- TO 3½-QT	4- TO 5½-QT	6- TO 8-QT
Small, firm pears	4	6	8
Moderately dry, fruity red wine, such as a Pinot Noir	At least 3 cups	At least 5 cups	At least 6 cups
Sugar	1½ cups	2½ cups	3 cups
4-inch cinnamon sticks	1	1½	2
Whole cloves	4	6	8

1 Peel the pears, then slice off about ¼ inch of their wide bottoms. Core them by circling a melon baller or a serrated grapefruit spoon up from their wide bottoms and into the flesh, pulling out the seeds and tough core without breaking through the sides.

2 Set the pears cut side down in the slow cooker. Pour in the wine—and perhaps more—until the pears are submerged, then remove the pears to a plate. (This is to determine how much poaching liquid you need.)

3 Whisk the sugar into the poaching liquid until it dissolves. Return the pears to the slow cooker, cut side down. Drop in the cinnamon sticks and cloves.

4 Cover and cook on high for 2 to 3 hours in a small slow cooker, 3 to 4 hours in a medium cooker, or 4 to 5 hours in a large one, or until the pears are still firm but easily cut with a spoon. Use a slotted spoon to transfer them from the poaching liquid to serving bowls. If desired, spoon some of the poaching liquid around them, after having discarded the cinnamon sticks and cloves.

TESTERS' NOTES

• Bosc or Forelle pears work best for this dessert because they're firm but still very sweet. Some Forelle pears are exceptionally small; choose the largest ones you can find. However, the timings are stated in a range because firmer pears will take longer than softer ones.

• Skip the deep red wines for this dish and go for a lighter Pinot Noir, Gamay, or even Lambrusco.

• If a thick syrup is desired, remove the herbs from the poaching liquid, pour the liquid into a large saucepan, and boil it down until reduced by three-quarters.

Serve It Up! Chill a large bowl and the beaters for an electric mixer in the fridge for at least 1 hour. Then beat heavy cream with an electric mixer at high speed in that bowl until soft and luscious, not yet stiff. Beat in 1 or 2 tablespoons of the poaching liquid to sweeten the cream, turning it back into a rather loose sauce to serve with the pears.

brandy-poached plums

EFFORT: **A LOT** • PREP TIME: **20 MINUTES** • COOK TIME: **2 HOURS** • KEEPS ON WARM: **1 HOUR** • SERVES: **3 TO 6**

INGREDIENTS	2- TO 3½-QT	4- TO 5½-QT	6- TO 8-QT
Sugar	1 cup	1½ cups	2 cups
Water	⅓ cup	½ cup	⅔ cup
Red plums, halved and pitted	6	10	12
Brandy	½ cup	⅔ cup	1 cup
Ground cinammon	⅛ tsp	¼ tsp	½ tsp

1 Pour the sugar into a large, high-sided skillet. Set it over medium-low heat and melt the sugar, stirring occasionally, until golden brown.

2 Pour in the water, but watch out: it will splatter like mad. Stir constantly until the sugar dissolves into a caramel sauce. Pour and scrape the sauce into the slow cooker.

3 Place the plums cut side down in the cooker. Drizzle the brandy over them, then sprinkle with cinnamon.

4 Cover and cook on low for 2 hours, or until the plums are tender and the sauce is bubbling. Use a thin spatula to transfer the plums to serving bowls, then spoon the sauce over them.

TESTERS' NOTES
• The sugar will seize into a ball the moment the water hits the pan. Put any children and pets out of the kitchen. Work carefully; keep stirring until that sugar melts again.
• For a richer dessert, dot up to 2 tablespoons unsalted butter, cut into little bits, among the plums before cooking.

bananas foster

EFFORT: **NOT MUCH** • PREP TIME: **10 MINUTES** • COOK TIME: **1½ TO 2½ HOURS** • KEEPS ON WARM: **NO** • SERVES: **3 TO 8**

INGREDIENTS	2- TO 3½-QT	4- TO 5½-QT	6- TO 8-QT
Ripe firm bananas, peeled and cut into 1-inch segments	3	5	8
Packed light brown sugar	¼ cup	6 tblsp	⅔ cup
Ground cinnamon	½ tsp	¾ tsp	1¼ tsp
Apricot jam	¼ cup	6 tblsp	⅔ cup
Unsalted butter, cut into ¼-inch pieces, plus more for greasing the canister	2 tblsp	3½ tblsp	6 tblsp

1 Butter the inside of the canister. Toss the banana slices, brown sugar, and cinnamon in the cooker until the sugar coats the bananas evenly.

2 Dollop the jam in teaspoonfuls evenly over everything. Sprinkle the butter bits over everything.

3 Cover and cook on low for 1½ hours in a small slow cooker, 2 hours in a medium cooker, or 2½ hours in a large one, or until the bananas are soft and the sauce is bubbling around them.

TESTERS' NOTES
• You can hardly flambé bananas foster in a slow cooker! Still and all, this slow cooker riff will be welcome over vanilla ice cream, frozen yogurt, or (especially) gelato.
• We used apricot jam here because many recipes for bananas foster call for the dish to be flamed with apricot brandy.

spiced cranberry cassis sauce

EFFORT: **NOT MUCH** • PREP TIME: **10 MINUTES** • COOK TIME: **4 HOURS** • KEEPS ON WARM: **4 HOURS** • SERVES: **6 TO 12 AS A SAUCE**

INGREDIENTS	2- TO 3½-QT	4- TO 5½-QT	6- TO 8-QT
Fresh cranberries	4 cups	6 cups	8 cups
Sugar	1 cup	1½ cups	2 cups
Cored, peeled, and chopped fresh pears, such as Comice	⅔ cup	1 cup	1⅓ cups
Water	⅓ cup	½ cup	⅔ cup
Cassis or other black currant liqueur	3 tblsp	¼ cup	6 tblsp
Ground allspice	¼ tsp	½ tsp	¾ tsp
Ground cinnamon	¼ tsp	½ tsp	¾ tsp
Ground cloves	⅛ tsp	¼ tsp	½ tsp
Salt	⅛ tsp	¼ tsp	½ tsp

1 Stir the cranberries, sugar, pears, water, liqueur, allspice, cinnamon, cloves, and salt in the slow cooker until the sugar dissolves.

2 Cover and cook on low for 3 hours, or until the cranberries are soft.

3 Use a potato masher to smash the cranberries into a puree right in the slow cooker. Stir well, cover, and continue cooking on high for 1 hour, or until bubbling and aromatic.

TESTERS' NOTES

• Although we think of this as an ice cream sauce, it could just as well be ladled over plain yogurt, particularly Greek yogurt.
• Cranberries are not available year round. Stock up when you see them and toss the bags in your freezer.
• This sauce will freeze well in a sealed glass jar or plastic container for up to 4 months.

mixed berry dessert sauce

EFFORT: **NOT MUCH** • PREP TIME: **10 MINUTES** • COOK TIME: **2½ HOURS** • KEEPS ON WARM: **2 HOURS** • SERVES: **4 TO 12 AS A SAUCE**

INGREDIENTS	2- TO 3½-QT	4- TO 5½-QT	6- TO 8-QT
Fresh blueberries	1 cup	2 cups	3 cups
Fresh blackberries	1 cup	2 cups	3 cups
Fresh raspberries	1 cup	2 cups	3 cups
Unsweetened pineapple juice	½ cup	1 cup	1½ cups
Sugar	¼ cup	½ cup	¾ cup
Water	2 tblsp	¼ cup	6 tblsp
Cornstarch	1 tblsp	2 tblsp	3 tblsp

1 Stir the blueberries, blackberries, raspberries, pineapple juice, and sugar in the slow cooker until the sugar dissolves.

2 Cover and cook on high for 2 hours, or until the berries begin to break down into a sauce.

3 Whisk the water and cornstarch in a small bowl until smooth, then stir this mixture into the berry sauce until dissolved. Cover and continue cooking on high for 30 minutes, or until thickened.

TESTERS' NOTES

• We don't recommend using frozen berries for this easy sauce. They will have broken down a bit in thawing and may well be too wet.
• Add up to ¼ cup brandy or rum with the juice for a boozy version.

Serve It Up! Although great over ice cream and in sundaes, drizzle this sauce over pieces of pound cake—or ladle a bit onto plates and set a piece of sponge cake afloat on top. Or layer it into trifles and parfaits.

party drinks

When we told an editor at a rather chic food magazine over dinner one night that we were writing a mammoth slow cooker book, she said, as she poured herself another glass of wine, "Are there going to be drinks in that thing?"

Frankly, we hadn't thought about it. But there have to be drinks! It's hard to imagine a better tool for mulling wine or creating some pretty wicked hot libations for a midwinter night. We even did a slow cooker morph on that retro drink favored in the Upper Midwest during the holidays: the Tom and Jerry (page 499), sort of a stiff eggnog.

But it's not all about alcohol here. The slow cooker can keep a pretty fine hot cocoa warm for hours as well as mull a decidedly delicious cider. Better yet, you can mix these drinks, then set the slow cooker on a buffet or near the bar, letting your guests serve themselves (so long as you make sure the lid goes back in place to keep the punch warm). And you don't have to worry about alcohol igniting around an open flame, as it might on the stovetop. In fact, that may be the best reason to make a punch in our favorite appliance.

When you come to think about it, it's hard to imagine why we hadn't thought of drinks right off the bat when we started working on this enormous book. After all, when we thought about testing and writing over 500 recipes, we sure could have used one of these.

malted hot cocoa

EFFORT: **NOT MUCH** • PREP TIME: **5 MINUTES** • COOK TIME: **3 HOURS** • KEEPS ON WARM: **3 HOURS** • SERVES: **4 TO 12**

INGREDIENTS	2- TO 3½-QT	4- TO 5½-QT	6- TO 8-QT
Milk	4 cups (1 quart)	8 cups (½ gallon)	12 cups (3 quarts)
Sugar	½ cup	1 cup	1½ cups
Unsweetened cocoa powder (see page 466)	¼ cup	½ cup	¾ cup
Malted milk powder	¼ cup	½ cup	¾ cup
Vanilla extract	1 tsp	2 tsp	1 tblsp
Salt	¼ tsp	½ tsp	¾ tsp

1 Whisk the milk, sugar, cocoa powder, malted milk powder, vanilla, and salt in the slow cooker until smooth, no bits of undissolved cocoa powder or sugar anywhere.

2 Cover and cook on low for 3 hours, or until the mixture is hot and well blended. Ladle into mugs to serve.

TESTERS' NOTES

• The only real trick here is to whisk the ingredients smooth in the canister. Dutch-processed cocoa powder will blend more quickly, although it will also offer a less-chocolaty flavor.
• For quicker blending, use superfine sugar, sometimes called *bar sugar*, often available near the drink mixings and club soda in the supermarket, or in the baking goods aisle.
• If you want to go over the top, substitute half-and-half for part of the milk.
• If your crock has a nonstick finish, you need to use a whisk specifically designed for nonstick surfaces.

very adult white chocolate cocoa

EFFORT: **NOT MUCH** • PREP TIME: **10 MINUTES** • COOK TIME: **3 HOURS** • KEEPS ON WARM: **3 HOURS** • SERVES: **5 TO 10**

INGREDIENTS	2- TO 3½-QT	4- TO 5½-QT	6- TO 8-QT
Milk	3 cups	4½ cups (1 quart plus ½ cup)	6½ cups (1 quart plus 2½ cups)
Coconut milk	2 cups	3 cups	4⅓ cups
Packed light brown sugar	⅓ cup	½ cup	¾ cup
White chocolate, chopped	2 ounces	3 ounces	4½ ounces
Vanilla extract	1 tsp	½ tblsp	2 tsp
Bourbon	½ cup	¾ cup	1 cup plus 2 tblsp

1 Whisk the milk, coconut milk, brown sugar, white chocolate, and vanilla in the slow cooker until the brown sugar dissolves.

2 Cover and cook on low for 30 minutes. Stir well, then cover and continue cooking on low for 2½ hours, or until smooth and mellow.

3 Stir in the bourbon before serving.

TESTERS' NOTES

• Bourbon gives hot cocoa a smooth, aromatic hit—in our books, more in keeping with its spirit than whiskey or rum. If you want a much cleaner taste, substitute vodka.
• If you want to forgo the alcohol, stir in a similar amount of unsweetened pineapple juice before serving.

ALL-AMERICAN KNOW-HOW White chocolate is not all created equal. The best white chocolate is simply cocoa butter with a stabilizer or two, rather than with hydrogenated shortening and artificial flavorings. In fact, even white chocolate made only from cocoa butter varies in quality. Look for brands that are not "deodorized." They retain more of the dark chocolate taste, something removed from some varieties for a milder flavor in baking.

cranberry ginger mulled cider

EFFORT: **NOT MUCH** • PREP TIME: **10 MINUTES** • COOK TIME: **3 HOURS/5 HOURS** • KEEPS ON WARM: **5 HOURS** • SERVES: **4 TO 12**

INGREDIENTS	2- TO 3½-QT	4- TO 5½-QT	6- TO 8-QT
Unsweetened apple cider	2 cups	4 cups (1 quart)	7 cups
Cranberry juice	⅔ cup	1⅓ cups	3 cups
Orange juice	⅔ cup	1⅓ cups	3 cups
Fresh lemon juice	⅓ cup	⅔ cup	1¼ cups
Honey	Up to ¼ cup	Up to ½ cup	Up to ¾ cup
Very thinly sliced peeled fresh ginger	2 tblsp	¼ cup	½ cup
4-inch cinnamon sticks	1	2	3

1 Stir the cider, juices, honey, ginger, and cinnamon sticks in the slow cooker.

2 Cover and cook on low for 3 hours on high or 5 hours on low, or until deeply aromatic. Fish out the ginger slices and cinnamon sticks with a slotted spoon before ladling into mugs.

TESTERS' NOTES
• Substitute unsweetened apple juice for the cider, but the resulting punch will have less body.
• If desired, add up to 4 whole cloves and 3 allspice berries along with the other ingredients. For a very sophisticated finish, toss in a green cardamom pod as well. Remove all of these before serving.

ALL-AMERICAN KNOW-HOW To slice the ginger properly, first cut a piece of the root a couple of inches long, then peel this piece with a vegetable peeler, taking care to remove only the papery skin. Slice into paper-thin coins. If needed, cut another piece, peel, and make more coins, as the recipe requires.

mulled wine

EFFORT: **NOT MUCH** • PREP TIME: **10 MINUTES** • COOK TIME: **2 HOURS/4 HOURS** • KEEPS ON WARM: **3 HOURS** • SERVES: **4 TO 8**

INGREDIENTS	2- TO 3½-QT	4- TO 5½-QT	6- TO 8-QT
Unsweetened apple cider	3 cups	4½ cups	6½ cups
Dry, fruit-forward red wine, such as American Zinfandel	3 cups	4½ cups	6½ cups
Honey	¼ cup	6 tblsp	⅔ cup
Orange juice	¼ cup	6 tblsp	⅔ cup
4-inch cinnamon sticks	1	1½	2
Star anise	2	3	4

1 Mix the cider, wine, honey, orange juice, cinnamon sticks, and star anise in the slow cooker until the honey dissolves.

2 Cover and cook on high for 2 hours or on low for 4 hours, or until gorgeously aromatic.

(continued)

Remove the cinnamon sticks and star anise with a slotted spoon before serving.

TESTERS' NOTES

• Not a true mulled wine, and also not a Scandinavian *glögg*, this hot punch is a hybrid, with apple cider added for body and a silky finish.

• A vanilla bean, split lengthwise, would enhance this drink as well.

• Never pour mulled wine into a standard wine glass—the punch can shatter it. Instead, ladle this into mugs.

• For a boozy finish, top the mugfuls with a splash of aquavit or *eau-de-vie*.

almond irish coffee

EFFORT: **NOT MUCH** • PREP TIME: **10 MINUTES** • COOK TIME: **3 HOURS** • KEEPS ON WARM: **2 HOURS** • SERVES: **4 TO 10**

INGREDIENTS	2- TO 3½-QT	4- TO 5½-QT	6- TO 8-QT
Strong brewed coffee	4 cups (1 quart)	6 cups (1½ quarts)	10 cups (2½ quarts)
Blended whiskey	⅔ cup	1 cup	1⅔ cups
Amaretto or other almond-flavored liqueur	¼ cup	½ cup	¾ cup
Bailey's Irish Cream or other Irish cream whiskey liqueur	¼ cup	½ cup	¾ cup

1 Mix the coffee, whiskey, amaretto, and liqueur in the slow cooker.

2 Cover and cook on low for 3 hours. Ladle into mugs and top each with a dollop of whipped cream, if desired.

TESTERS' NOTES

• The stronger the coffee, the better. That said, espresso may be too assertive. When you prepare drip coffee, use an extra scoop or two of ground coffee.

• Don't waste a single malt on this. Instead, use a sturdy but mellow whiskey made from a blend of various years.

• Substitute rum for the whiskey for a more tropical flare.

hot buttered cider

EFFORT: **A LITTLE** • PREP TIME: **20 MINUTES** • COOK TIME: **2 HOURS/4 HOURS** • KEEPS ON WARM: **3 HOURS THROUGH STEP 2** • SERVES: **4 TO 10**

INGREDIENTS	2- TO 3½-QT	4- TO 5½-QT	6- TO 8-QT
Packed light brown sugar	¾ cup	1½ cups	2¼ cups
Unsalted butter, at room temperature	4 tblsp (½ stick)	8 tblsp (1 stick)	12 tblsp (1½ sticks)
Ground cinnamon	½ tsp	1 tsp	½ tblsp
Grated nutmeg	¼ tsp	½ tsp	1 tsp
Ground cloves	¼ tsp	½ tsp	¾ tsp
Salt	⅛ tsp	¼ tsp	½ tsp
Unsweetened apple cider	3 cups	6 cups	9 cups
Water	1½ cups	3 cups	4½ cups
Gold rum	1 cup	2 cups	3 cups
Dark rum, such as Myers's	½ cup	1 cup	1½ cups

1 Mash the brown sugar, butter, cinnamon, nutmeg, cloves, and salt in a large bowl with a pastry cutter or a table fork until a smooth paste forms. Set aside at room temperature.

2 Stir the cider, water, and both rums in the slow cooker. Cover and cook on high for 2 hours or on low for 4 hours.

3 To serve, put 2 tablespoons of the butter mixture in a large mug, then ladle the hot cider-and-rum concoction on top.

TESTERS' NOTES
• Skiing, anyone? A mug of this will make the day right.
• The butter mixture can be saved for more go-rounds in the future. Cover tightly with plastic wrap, pressing the wrap right down on top of the butter mixture in the bowl, then refrigerate for up to 1 month.

tom and jerry

EFFORT: **A LOT** • PREP TIME: **20 MINUTES** • KEEPS ON WARM: **6 HOURS** • SERVES: **4 TO 12**

INGREDIENTS	2- TO 3½-QT	4- TO 5½-QT	6- TO 8-QT
Milk (whole or low-fat)	4 cups (1 quart)	8 cups (½ gallon)	12 cups (3 quarts)
Large eggs, at room temperature	3	6	9
Sugar	½ cup	1 cup	1½ cups
Vanilla extract	2 tsp	1½ tblsp	2 tblsp
Ground cinnamon	⅛ tsp	¼ tsp	½ tsp
Ground allspice	⅛ tsp	¼ tsp	½ tsp
Ground cloves	⅛ tsp	¼ tsp	½ tsp
Grated nutmeg	⅛ tsp	¼ tsp	½ tsp
Salt	⅛ tsp	¼ tsp	½ tsp
Gold rum	Up to 1½ cups	Up to 3 cups	Up to 4½ cups

1 Turn the slow cooker to the *keep warm* setting and cover.

2 Heat the milk in a large saucepan set over medium-low heat until bubbles begin to fizz around the interior edge.

3 Beat the eggs and sugar in a large bowl with an electric mixer at medium speed until thick and pale, almost fluffy. Beat in the vanilla, cinnamon, allspice, cloves, nutmeg, and salt.

4 With the mixer at medium speed, beat about a third of the hot milk into the egg mixture. Continue beating until smooth, scraping down the inside of the bowl at least once. Beat the mixture into the milk in the pan, again using an electric mixer at medium speed.

5 Cook over low heat, stirring constantly, just until the mixture is thick enough to coat the back of a wooden spoon.

6 Pour the mixture into the slow cooker. Cover and keep warm for up to 6 hours.

7 To serve, pour about 2 ounces (1 tablespoon) rum in a mug and top with the milk custard. Garnish with whipped cream, if desired.

TESTERS' NOTES
• This cocktail has been long a tradition at Upper Midwestern holiday parties and certain Wisconsin restaurants. It's ridiculously retro and indulgent.
• No, the slow cooker doesn't really "make" the drink. Instead, the slow cooker is the perfect tool for keeping it warm during the whole party. What a perfect way to end our book!

index